Professional
SQL Server™ 2005 Administration

Professional
SQL Server™ 2005 Administration

Brian Knight, Ketan Patel, Wayne Snyder,
Jean-Claude Armand, Ross LoForte, Brad McGehee,
Steven Wort, Joe Salvatore, Haidong Ji

Wiley Publishing, Inc.

Professional SQL Server™ 2005 Administration

Published by
Wiley Publishing, Inc.
10475 Crosspoint Boulevard
Indianapolis, IN 46256
www.wiley.com

Copyright © 2007 by Wiley Publishing, Inc., Indianapolis, Indiana

Published by Wiley Publishing, Inc., Indianapolis, Indiana

Published simultaneously in Canada

ISBN-13: 978-0-470-05520-5
ISBN-10: 0-470-05520-0

Manufactured in the United States of America

10 9 8 7 6 5 4 3 2 1

1B/RW/RR/QW/IN

For general information on our other products and services or to obtain technical support, please contact our Customer Care Department within the U.S. at (800) 762-2974, outside the U.S. at (317) 572-3993 or fax (317) 572-4002.

Library of Congress Cataloging-in-Publication Data:
Professional SQL server 2005 administration / Brian Knight . . . [et al.].
    p. cm.
  Includes index.
  ISBN-13: 978-0-470-05520-5 (paper/website)
  ISBN-10: 0-470-05520-0 (paper/website)
 1. SQL server. 2. Database management. 3. Client/server computing. I. Knight, Brian, 1976–
  QA76.9.D3P7667 2007
  005.75'85—dc22

                                         2006032940

For my two boys, Colton and Liam, who constantly reset my priorities.

About the Authors

Brian Knight, SQL Server MVP, MCSE, MCDBA, is the co-founder of SQLServerCentral.com and JumpstartTV.com. He runs the local SQL Server users group in Jacksonville (JSSUG) and was recently on the Board of Directors of the Professional Association for SQL Server (PASS). Brian is a contributing columnist for SQL Server Standard, maintains a regular column for the database Web site SQLServerCentral.com, and does regular Web casts at Jumpstart TV. He is the author of *Admin911: SQL Server* (Osborne/McGraw-Hill Publishing) and coauthor of *Professional SQL Server DTS* and *Professional SQL Server 2005 Integration Services* (Wrox Press). Brian has spoken at conferences like PASS, SQL Connections and TechEd and many Code Camps. His blog can be found at `http://www.whiteknighttechnology.com`. Brian is an independent consultant at White Knight Technology.

Ketan Patel, B.E. Electronics Engineering, MCSE, MCDBA, is a Development Manager for the Business Intelligence Center of Excellence group at Microsoft. He has worked with SQL Server and other Microsoft technologies for nearly eight years. Ketan has also spoken at TechEd. He spends his spare time with his family and playing cricket, especially in the summer.

Wayne Snyder is recognized worldwide as a SQL Server expert and Microsoft Most Valued Professional (MVP), with over 25 year of experience in project management, database administration, software design, performance measurement, and capacity planning. He is a sought-out consultant, trainer, writer, and speaker and produces a series of web-based seminars on SQL Server 2005. Wayne has edited many SQL Server books, has SQL Training CDs with Learnkey, is on the Board of Directors for PASS (Professional Association for SQL Server), plays keyboard for a cover band named SoundBarrier (`www.soundbarrier band.com`), and is a managing consultant for Mariner, a Business Intelligence Company.

Jean-Claude Armand is a Senior SQL Server technology specialist with Microsoft Corporation. Jean-Claude has been working with SQL Server since version 4.21a at Dun & Bradstreet. He also worked as a senior consultant for MicroAge and CompuCom Systems prior to coming to Microsoft where he has been working for the past seven years. Jean-Claude has spoken at events such as TechEd, SQL Connection, VSLive, SQL Server Magazine Connections, numerous other partner forums, and various Pass chapters.

Ross LoForte is a SQL technology architect at the Microsoft Technology Center Chicago who specializes in Microsoft SQL Server solutions. Ross has more than 16 years of business development, project management, and architecting SQL solutions on large and mission-critical database platforms. For the past six years, Ross has been working with the Microsoft Technology Centers and has led architecture design and proof-of-concept sessions for Microsoft's largest and most strategic customers to design enterprise, mission-critical SQL Server solutions. Additionally, Ross presents at TechEd, SQL PASS, Gartner, TDWI, and other conferences as well as delivering Microsoft customer presentations around SQL Server. Ross has been active with the Professional Association for SQL Server, with the Chicago SQL Server Users Group, and with the SQL Server community for many years.

Brad McGehee, SQL Server MVP, MCSE, MCSD, is the founder of SQL-Server-Performance.Com. He is a well-known SQL Server industry expert, focusing on writing, speaking, and teaching about SQL Server. He specializes in SQL Server performance tuning and clustering. His personal Web site is at `www.sqlHawaii.com`.

Steven Wort has been working with SQL Server for the past 12 years. He spent much of that time working as a freelance application developer and database architect building VB and web applications on SQL Server for many of London's largest financial institutions. He moved to the United States seven years ago, joining Microsoft over five years ago as a SQL Expert in PSS on the SIE team. He spent three years traveling the world working on many very interesting customer issues. Two years ago, he moved over to the SQL Server Product group spending a year working on SQL Server Scalability and took a brief diversion into the SQL Server Best Practices Team before moving onto the SQL Playback team. Earlier this year, Steven moved to the Windows Reliability team and now spends his time writing nasty SQL queries, building SSIS packages, designing SSRS reports, and analyzing Crash and Hang dumps. When he is not involved with technology, Steven is a member of the Pacific Northwest Adventure Racing community and a passionate kayaker, cyclist, runner, inline skater, and downhill and cross-country skier.

Joe Salvatore is a Microsoft Solutions Technical Lead for Idea Integration. He is presently focused on architecting Business Intelligence and Reporting solutions using SQL Server 2005. He has had more than 10 years of programming experience, focused on getting meaningful information out of systems using Crystal Reports, Crystal Enterprise, Visual Basic.NET, T-SQL, Integration Services, Analysis Services, and Reporting Services. Joe has spoken at the Jacksonville SQL Server Users Group (JSSUG), the Jacksonville Developer's User Group (JAXDUG) and at many Microsoft Code Camps in the Southeastern United States.

Haidong Ji, 季海东**,** MCSD and MCDBA, is a developer and senior database administrator. He manages enterprise SQL Server systems, along with Oracle and MySql systems on Unix and Linux. Haidong enjoys sharing his expertise through technical writing, consulting, training, and mentoring. He has coauthored *Professional SQL Server 2005 Integration Services* (Wrox Press). He maintains his own blog at http://www.HaidongJi.com. He can be reached at Haidong.Ji@gmail.com.

Credits

Executive Editor
Robert Elliott

Development Editor
Brian MacDonald

Technical Editor
G. T. Woody

Production Editor
William A. Barton

Copy Editor
C.M. Jones

Editorial Manager
Mary Beth Wakefield

Production Manager
Tim Tate

Vice President and Executive Group Publisher
Richard Swadley

Vice President and Executive Publisher
Joseph B. Wikert

Project Coordinator
Ryan Steffen
Jennifer Theriot

Graphics and Production Specialists
Carrie A. Foster
Brooke Graczyk
Barbara Moore
Barry Offringa
Alicia B. South

Quality Control Technicians
John Greenough
Jessica Kramer

Media Development Specialists
Angela Denny
Kit Malone
Travis Silvers

Proofreading and Indexing
Techbooks

Contents

Contents

Contents

Contents

Contents

Contents

Contents

Contents

Contents

Contents

Acknowledgments

Once again, I must give my eternal gratitude to my wife, Jennifer. Without her, my career of late nights and early mornings would never have been possible. I owe so much to her, I could never possibly start to repay it all. Likewise, my children have had many nights without a "daddy jungle gym" for a few hours while I had to write. —*Brian Knight*

I would like to thank my parents, Thakorbhai and Induben, for their unwavering and selfless support and inspiration in my life. Whatever I am today is because of them. The word "thanks" cannot express the feeling I have for them. I also would like to thank my sister-in-law and my best friend, Pramakshi, for her altruistic support, encouragement, and belief in me and in everything I do. I would like to thank my wife, Sweety, for her invaluable support when I go into writing mode all those weekends. I would like to acknowledge Brian Knight and JC, coauthors of this book, for providing me with a great opportunity to coauthor this book. Last but not the least, I would like to acknowledge my reviewers, Stefano Stefani, Roger Wolter, Remus Rusanu, Mark Wistrom, and Jakub Kulesza, all from SQL Server team, Brian MacDonald, the editor for this book, and Jennifer Coughlan, my colleague, because without them this book would not exist or contain the level of depth that it has. Finally, I want to say thank you to B.J. Moore and Mark Mincin, both General Managers at Microsoft, for their support. —*Ketan Patel*

Thank you to my loving wife, Vickie, whose generosity and support make my life better each day. —*Wayne Snyder*

First and foremost, I would like to thank my wife, Jacqui, who supported me by taking on our son Jacob while she was mourning the loss of her mother. I would also thank my son Jake, who was stuck shopping with his Mom as Daddy was busy with this book. I would also like to thank the good folks with the Microsoft SQL Server Customer Assistance Team (CAT), and Slava Oks who provided guidance and feedback during this process. —*Jean-Claude Armand*

I'd like to thank my wife Anna and my daughter Jennifer for their support while writing this book. Additionally, I'd like to thank Adam Hecktman and Tony Surma for their support and for making the Microsoft Technology Center Chicago a great facility to learn and experience. —*Ross LoForte*

I have to start by thanking my wife, Tracy, and two daughters, Eleanor and Caitlin, for putting up with me over the past few months of writing. They have been infinitely patient and understanding while I have spent many long hours working. Thanks to Sanjay Mishra for hooking me up with the rest of the team on this book and getting me started on my first attempt at writing. Thanks to my many former colleagues in SQL Release Services, the SQL Server Scalability team, and the SQL Playback Performance team. —*Steven Wort*

Acknowledgments

I would like to give thanks to my Lord, Jesus Christ, with whom all things are possible and whose guidance and inspiration are always a blessing. The loving support, sacrifice, and understanding provided by my loving wife, Linda, and son, Andrew, due this November were so very important and rightfully deserve a very big thank you. Professionally, I'd like to thank Brian Knight for his continued friendship, inspiration, and encouragement. My mother, Kathy, father, Richard, and sister, Maria, must also be acknowledged for supporting me during this and all my other adventures. Lastly, I would like to thank all my extended family members, friends, and co-workers for their interest and excitement. —*Joe Salvatore*

Once again, I'd like to thank Brian Knight for the opportunity to coauthor this book. I also want to express my gratitude to Michael and Susan Merrick and their extended family: thanks so much for your hospitality, friendship, and help over the years. It meant a lot to me. Finally, I'd like to thank Maria and Benjamin for their love and support. —*Haidong Ji*

Introduction

SQL Server 2005 is easily the largest leap forward for SQL Server since its inception. Because of this rapid evolution, the learning curve in using some of the newest features can be challenging. It is no longer unheard of to have 20-terabyte databases running on a SQL Server. SQL Server administration used to just be the job of a database administrator (DBA), but now, as SQL Server proliferates through-out smaller companies, many developers have begun to act as administrators as well. Additionally, some of the new features in SQL Server are more developer-centric, and poor configuration of these features can result in poor performance. We've provided a comprehensive, tutorial-based book to get you over the learning curve of how to configure and administrate SQL Server 2005.

Who This Book Is For

Whether you're an administrator or developer using SQL Server, you can't avoid wearing a DBA hat at some point. Developers often have SQL Server on their own workstations and must provide guidance to the administrator on how they'd like the production configured. Often, they're responsible for creating the database tables and indexes. Administrators or DBAs support the production servers and often inherit the database from the developer.

This book is intended for developers, DBAs, and casual users who hope to administer or may already be administering a SQL Server 2005 system and its business intelligence features such as Integration Services. This is a *professional* book, meaning that the authors assume that you know the basics on how to query a SQL Server and have some rudimentary concepts of SQL Server already. For example, the authors of this book will not show you how to create a database or walk you through the installation of SQL Server through the wizard. Instead, the author of the installation chapter may provide insight to how to use some of the more advanced concepts of the installation. This book will not cover how to query a SQL Server database, but it will cover how to tune the queries you've already written.

How This Book Is Structured

The first ten chapters of the book are about administering the various areas of SQL Server, including the developer and business intelligence features. Chapter 1 briefly covers the architecture of SQL Server and the changing role of the DBA. Chapters 2 and 3 dive into best practices on installing and upgrading to SQL Server 2005. Managing your SQL Server database instance is talked about in Chapter 4. This chapter also goes over some of the hidden tools you may not even know you have.

Once you know how to manage your SQL Server, you can learn in Chapter 5 how to automate many of the redundant monitoring and maintenance tasks. This chapter also discusses best practices on configuring SQL Server Agent. Chapters 6 and 7 cover how to properly administer and automate many tasks inside of the Microsoft business intelligence products such as Integration Services and Analysis Services. Developers will find that Chapter 8 is very useful, as it covers how to administer the development features like SQL

CLR. Chapter 9 talks about how to secure your SQL Server from many common threats and how to create logins and users. Chapter 10 covers how to create a SQL Server project and do proper change management in promoting your scripts through the various environments.

Chapters 11 through 15 make up the performance-tuning part of the book. Chapter 11 discusses how to choose the right hardware configuration for your SQL Server to perform optimally. After the hardware and operating system is configured, Chapter 12 shows you how to optimize your SQL Server instance for the best performance. Chapter 13 shows you how to monitor your SQL Server instance for problematic issues like blocking and locking. Chapters 14 and 15 discuss how to optimize the T-SQL that accesses your tables and then how to index your tables appropriately.

Chapters 16 through 20 consist of the high-availability chapters of the book. Chapter 16 covers how to use the various forms of replication, while database mirroring is covered in Chapter 17. Classic issues and best practices for backing up and recovering your database are discussed in Chapter 18. Chapter 19 dives deeply into what the role of log shipping is in your high-availability strategy, and Chapter 20 presents a step-by-step guide to clustering your SQL Server.

What You Need to Use This Book

To follow this book, you will only need to have SQL Server 2005 installed. If you wish to learn how to administer the business intelligence features, you will need to have Analysis Services and the Integration Services component installed. You'll need a machine that can support the minimum hardware requirements to run SQL Server 2005. You'll also want to have the AdventureWorks and AdventureWorksDW databases installed. Some features in this book (especially in the high-availability part) require Enterprise or Developer Edition of SQL Server. If you do not have this edition, you will still be able to follow through some of the examples in the chapter with Standard Edition.

Conventions

To help you get the most from the text and keep track of what's happening, we've used a number of conventions throughout the book.

> **Boxes like this one hold important, not-to-be forgotten information that is directly relevant to the surrounding text.**

Tips, hints, tricks, and asides to the current discussion are offset and placed in italics like this.

As for styles in the text:

❑   We *highlight* new terms and important words when we introduce them.

❑   We show keyboard strokes like this: Ctrl+A.

❑   We show filenames, URLs, and code within the text like so: `persistence.properties`.

❑   We present code in two different ways:

```
In code examples we highlight new and important code with a gray background.
The gray highlighting is not used for code that's less important in the present
context, or has been shown before.
```

Source Code

As you work through the examples in this book, you may choose either to type all the code manually or to use the source code files that accompany the book. All of the source code used in this book is available for download at `http://www.wrox.com`. Once at the site, simply locate the book's title (either by using the Search box or by using one of the title lists) and click the Download Code link on the book's detail page to obtain all the source code for the book.

> *Because many books have similar titles, you may find it easiest to search by ISBN; this book's ISBN is 0-470-05520-0 (changing to 978-0-470-05520-5 as the new industry-wide 13-digit ISBN numbering system is phased in by January 2007).*

Once you download the code, just decompress it with your favorite compression tool. Alternately, you can go to the main Wrox code download page at `http://www.wrox.com/dynamic/books/download.aspx` to see the code available for this book and all other Wrox books.

Errata

We make every effort to ensure that there are no errors in the text or in the code. However, no one is perfect, and mistakes do occur. If you find an error in one of our books, like a spelling mistake or faulty piece of code, we would be very grateful for your feedback. By sending in errata, you may save another reader hours of frustration, and at the same time you will be helping us provide even higher-quality information.

To find the errata page for this book, go to `http://www.wrox.com` and locate the title using the Search box or one of the title lists. Then, on the book details page, click the Book Errata link. On this page you can view all errata that has been submitted for this book and posted by Wrox editors. A complete book list, including links to each book's errata, is also available at `www.wrox.com/misc-pages/booklist.shtml`.

If you don't spot "your" error on the Book Errata page, go to `www.wrox.com/contact/techsupport.shtml` and complete the form there to send us the error you have found. We'll check the information and, if appropriate, post a message to the book's errata page and fix the problem in subsequent editions of the book.

p2p.wrox.com

For author and peer discussion, join the P2P forums at p2p.wrox.com. The forums are a Web-based system for you to post messages relating to Wrox books and related technologies and interact with other readers and technology users. The forums offer a subscription feature to e-mail you topics of interest of your choosing when new posts are made to the forums. Wrox authors, editors, other industry experts and your fellow readers are present on these forums.

At http://p2p.wrox.com you will find a number of different forums that will help you not only as you read this book but also as you develop your own applications. To join the forums, just follow these steps:

1. Go to p2p.wrox.com and click the Register link.

2. Read the terms of use and click Agree.

3. Complete the required information to join as well as any optional information you wish to provide and click Submit.

4. You will receive an e-mail with information describing how to verify your account and complete the joining process.

You can read messages in the forums without joining P2P, but in order to post your own messages, you must join.

Once you join, you can post new messages and respond to messages other users post. You can read messages at any time on the Web. If you would like to have new messages from a particular forum e-mailed to you, click the Subscribe to this Forum icon by the forum name in the forum listing.

For more information about how to use the Wrox P2P, be sure to read the P2P FAQs for answers to questions about how the forum software works, as well as many common questions specific to P2P and Wrox books. To read the FAQs, click the FAQ link on any P2P page.

SQL Server 2005 Architecture

The days of SQL Server being a departmental database are long gone, and SQL Server can now easily scale to databases dozens of terabytes in size. In this chapter, we lay some of the groundwork that will be used throughout the book. We first discuss how the role of the DBA has changed since some of the earlier releases of SQL Server and then quickly jump into architecture and tools available to you as an administrator. This chapter is not a deep dive into the architecture but provides enough information to give you an understanding of how SQL Server operates.

Growing Role of a DBA

The role of the database administrator (DBA) has been changing slowly over the past few versions of the SQL Server product. In SQL Server 2005, this slow transition of the DBA role has been accelerated immensely. Traditionally, a DBA would fit into one of two roles: development or administration. It's much tougher to draw a line now between DBA roles in SQL Server 2005. As lines blur and morph, DBAs have to quickly prepare themselves to take on different roles. If you don't position yourself to be more versatile, you may be destined for a career of watching SQL Server alerts and backups.

Production DBA

Production DBAs fall into the traditional role of a DBA. They are a company's insurance policy that the production database won't go down. If the database does go down, the company cashes in its insurance policy in exchange for a recovered database. The Production DBA also ensures the server is performing optimally and promotes database changes from development to QA to production.

Since SQL Server 2000, there has been a trend away from full-time Production DBAs, and the role has merged with that of the Development DBA. The trend may have slowed, though, with laws such as Sarbanes-Oxley, where you need a separation of power between the person developing the change and the person implementing the change. Other tasks that a Production DBA does are:

❑ Install SQL Server instances and service packs

❑ Monitor performance problems

❑ Install scripts from development

❑ Create baselines of performance metrics

❑ Configure the SQL Server optimally

❑ Create disaster recovery and scalability plans

❑ Ensure that backups have been run

In a large organization, a Production DBA may fall into the operations department, which would consist of the network and Windows-support administrators. Placing a Production DBA in a development group removes the separation of power that may be needed for some regulatory reasons. It may create an environment where "rush" changes are immediately put into production, without proper inspection and auditing.

Development DBA

Development DBAs also play a very traditional role in an organization. They wear more of a developer's hat and are the development staff's database experts and representatives. This administrator ensures that all stored procedures are optimally written and that the database is modeled correctly, both physically and logically. He or she also may be the person who writes the migration processes to migrate the database from one release to the next. The Development DBA typically does not receive calls at two in the morning, unless the Production DBA needs to escalate. Other Development DBA roles may be:

❑ Model an application database

❑ Create stored procedures

❑ Develop the change scripts that go to the Production DBA

❑ Performance-tune queries and stored procedures

❑ Possibly create any data migration

❑ Serve as an escalation point for the Production DBA

The Development DBA typically would report to the development group. He or she would receive requests from a business analyst or another developer. In a traditional sense, Development DBAs should never have modification access to a production database. They should, however, have read-only access to the production database to debug in a time of escalation.

Business Intelligence DBA

The Business Intelligence (BI) DBA is a new role that has grown due to the increased surface area of SQL Server. In SQL Server 2005, BI has grown to be an incredibly important feature set that many businesses cannot live without. The BI DBA is an expert at these features. He or she is the one who creates your SSIS packages to perform Extract Transform and Load (ETL) processes or reports for users. In many organizations, the role is so large that the BI DBA functions may be broken into smaller subsets, and you may have specialized DBAs to perform tasks such as SSIS or reports. In the world of SQL Server, a BI DBA is responsible for the following types of functions:

- ❑ Develop data-migration packages
- ❑ Model Analysis Services cubes and solutions
- ❑ Work with the analyst to develop KPI measures for Business Scorecard Manager
- ❑ Create reports using Reporting Services
- ❑ Develop a Notification Services solution
- ❑ Create ETL using Integration Services
- ❑ Develop deployment packages that will be sent to the Production DBA

Organizationally, the BI DBA most often reports to the development group. In some cases with Analysis Services experts, you may see them report to the analyst group or the project management office. In some small organizations, the BI DBA may report directly to an executive such as a CFO.

Hybrid DBA

The most exciting role for a DBA is a hybrid of all the roles we just mentioned. This Hybrid DBA is very typical with smaller organizations but is becoming popular with larger organizations as well. An organization with high turnover may want to spread their investment over many Hybrid DBAs instead of specialized roles.

Organizationally, you may see these DBAs reporting directly to the product organization or to a specialized DBA group. No matter where these DBAs report, each typically has a slate of products that he or she supports and performs every DBA function for that product. Such DBAs should also have adequate backup personnel to reduce the organization's risk if the Hybrid DBA leaves the company. Also, this DBA should never install his or her own changes into production. Ideally, for regulatory reasons and for stability, the DBA's backup DBA should install the change into production. That way, you can ensure that the DBA who installed the script didn't make ad-hoc changes in order to make the change work. We cover much more about this change-management process in Chapter 10.

The only role of a Hybrid DBA that's questionable is development of stored procedures. In most organizations where we see this role, the Hybrid DBA does not develop stored procedures. Instead, he or she creates difficult stored procedures or tunes the ones causing issues. The developer working on the application develops his or her own stored procedures and then provides them to the Hybrid DBA to package and proof. The main reason for this is that the DBA is too taxed for time, working on other functions of the database.

Industry Trends

We'll get into the SQL Server 2005 features momentarily, but you'll notice a trend as you begin to see the list. Feature after feature will require that a DBA become acclimated to a .NET programming language such as C# or VB.NET to remain effective. For example, if you are a DBA trying to debug a performance problem with a CLR stored procedure, you're going to need to know the language the stored procedure is written in to understand the performance problem. Features like Integration Services and Reporting Services are very much tied to expressions, which are variants of VB.NET.

Each new release of SQL Server since 7.0 has required DBAs to know more things that were traditional concerns of developers only, such as XML. With SQL Server 2005, though, there is a leap forward in the knowledge a DBA must have to be effective. Essentially, if you don't know a .NET programming language, you may be stuck as a Production DBA indefinitely. There are still roles for Production DBAs, but even in such roles, you may be less effective.

SQL Server Architecture

In older editions of SQL Server, you had to use many different tools depending on the function you were trying to perform. In SQL Server 2005, the challenge for Microsoft was to avoid increasing the number of management tools while increasing the features and products that ship with SQL Server. They accomplished this by creating one tool for business-intelligence development and another for management of the entire platform, including business intelligence and the database engine. Both of these tools are based on a lightweight version of Visual Studio 2005.

SQL Server envelops a large surface now. It can act as a reporting tool and store your OLAP cubes. It can also perform your ETL services through SQL Server Integration Services. Most people just use SQL Server for its classic use to just store data. SQL Server 2005 can run on Windows XP, 2000, Vista, and Windows Server 2000 and 2003. Tools such as SharePoint and Office quickly integrate on top of SQL Server and can provide an easy user interface (UI) for SQL Server data. This book covers administration on each of these tiers.

Transaction Log and Database Files

The relational database has experienced a number of enhancements in SQL Server 2005 to make it more robust and scalable. As you make changes to a database in SQL Server, the record is first written to the transaction log. Then, at given checkpoints, it is quickly transferred to the data file. This may be why you see your transaction log grow significantly in the middle of a long-running transaction even if your recovery model is set to simple. (We cover this in much more detail in Chapter 18.)

When you first start SQL Server after a stop, it performs a recovery process on each database. This process reads the transaction log for any transaction written to the transaction log but never sent to the data file and rolls it forward onto the data file. Also, any transaction that has not completed will be rolled back. In SQL Server 2005 Enterprise Edition, this process can be done in parallel across all the databases on your instance. Additionally, a fast recovery feature in Enterprise Edition makes databases available after the roll-forward process is complete.

The transaction log's most important purpose is to serve as an exact point in time in case you need to recover your database. Each data-modifying transaction is logged into the transaction log (although this behavior can be minimized if you turn on certain features). If the database becomes corrupt for whatever reason, you could take a transaction log backup and overlay it on top of your full backup, specifying that you wish to recover to the point in time right before the corruption. Corruption is extremely rare since SQL Server 7.0, but protecting against the remote chance of corruption is the DBA's primary job.

A database can consist of multiple file groups that logically group one or multiple database files. Those data files are written into in 8K data pages. You can specify how much free space you wish to be available in each data page with the fill factor of each index. (We go much more into this in Chapter 14.) In SQL Server 2005, you have the ability to bring your database partially online if a single file is corrupt. In this instance, the DBA can bring the remaining files online for reading and writing, and the user receives an error if he or she tries to access the other parts of the database that are offline. (We cover that much more in Chapter 18.)

The most that you can write into a single row is 8K. You are allowed to create a table larger in width than 8K only if there is a chance that it may not hold 8K of data, such as a table that has all varchar columns. If you attempt to write more than 8K to the row, you will receive an error. Also, if you create a table that writes more than 8K of data, you will receive an error.

SQL Native Client

The SQL Native Client is a data-access method that ships with SQL Server 2005 and is used by both OLE DB and ODBC for accessing SQL Server. The SQL Native Client simplifies access to SQL Server by combining the OLE DB and ODBC libraries into a single access method. The access type exposes some of the new features in SQL Server:

- ❑ Database mirroring
- ❑ Multiple Active Recordsets (MARS)
- ❑ Snapshot isolation
- ❑ Query notification
- ❑ XML data type support
- ❑ User defined data types (UDTs)
- ❑ Encryption
- ❑ Password expiration

In some of these features, you can make the feature work in other data layers such as Microsoft Data Access Components (MDAC), but it will take more work. MDAC still does exist, and you can still use it if you don't need some of the new functionality of SQL Server 2005. If you are developing a COM-based application, you should use SQL Native Client, and if you are developing a managed code application like in C#, you should consider using the .NET Framework Data Provider for SQL Server, which is very robust and includes the SQL Server 2005 features as well.

System Databases

The system databases in SQL Server are crucial, and you should leave them alone most of the time. The only exception to that rule is the model database, which allows you to deploy a change like a stored procedure to any new database created. If a system database is tampered with or corrupted, you risk your SQL Server not starting. They contain all the stored procedures and tables needed for SQL Server to remain online.

The Resource Database

New to SQL Server 2005 is the Resource database. This database contains all the read-only critical system tables, metadata, and stored procedures that SQL Server needs to run. It does not contain any information about your instance or your databases, because it is only written to during an installation of a new service pack. The Resource database contains all the physical tables and stored procedures referenced logically by other databases. The database can be found by default in C:\Program Files\ Microsoft SQL Server\MSSQL.1\MSSQL\Data\mssqlsystemresource.mdf, and there is only one Resource database per instance.

In SQL Server 2000, when you upgraded to a new service pack, you would need to run many long scripts to drop and recreate system scripts. This process took a long time to run and created an environment that couldn't be rolled back to the previous release after the service pack. In SQL Server 2005, when you upgrade to a new service pack or quick fix, a copy of the Resource database overwrites the old database. This allows you to quickly upgrade your SQL Server catalog and allows you to roll back a release.

The Resource database cannot be seen through Management Studio and should never be altered unless you're under instruction to do so by Microsoft Product Support Services (PSS). You can connect to the database under certain single-user mode conditions by typing the command USE MSSQLSystemResource. The majority of what a DBA does is run simple queries against it while connected to any database. For example, if you were to run this query while connected to any database, it would return your Resource database's version and the last time it was upgraded:

```
SELECT serverproperty('resourceversion') ResourceDBVersion,
serverproperty('resourcelastupdatedatetime') LastUpdateDate
```

Do not place the Resource database on an encrypted or compressed drive. Doing this may cause upgrade or performance issues.

The Master Database

The master database contains the metadata about your databases (database configuration and file location), logins, and configuration information about the instance. If this important database is lost, your SQL Server may not be able to start. For example, by running the following query, you will see what databases are installed on the server:

```
SELECT * FROM sys.databases
```

The master database's role has been slightly diminished in SQL Server 2005 with the addition of the Resource database, but it is no less important. The main difference between the Resource and master databases is that the master database holds data specific to your instance, while the Resource database just holds the schema and stored procedures needed to run your instance. You should always back up the `master` database after creating a new database, adding a login, or changing the configuration of the server.

You should never create objects in the `master` *database. If you create objects here, it may cause you to have to make more frequent backups.*

Tempdb Database

The `tempdb` database is like your database's swap file. It's used to hold temporary objects for all logins, and the server may use the database to hold row-version information or system temporary objects. The `tempdb` database is created each time you restart SQL Server. The database will be recreated to be its original database size when the SQL Server is stopped. Since the database is recreated each time, there is no reason to back it up. When you create a temporary object in the `tempdb` database, it writes minimal information into the log file. It is important to have enough space allocated to your `tempdb` database, because many operations that you will use in your database applications use the `tempdb`. Generally speaking, you should set `tempdb` to autogrow as it needs space. If there is not enough space, the user may receive one of the following errors:

❑ 1101 or 1105: The session connecting to SQL Server must allocate space in `tempdb`.

❑ 3959: The version store is full.

❑ 3967: The version store must shrink because `tempdb` is full.

Model Database

`model` is a system database that serves as a template when SQL Server creates a new database. As each database is created, the first step is to copy the objects out of the `model` database and into the empty shell of the new database. The only time this does not apply is when you restore or attach a database from a different server.

You can add objects or adjust the settings of the `model` *database so that any subsequent databases will have those properties set or contain those objects.*

msdb Database

`msdb` is a system database that contains information used by SQL Server agent, log shipping, SSIS, and the backup and restore system for the relational database engine. The database stores all the information about jobs, operators, alerts, and job history. Because it contains this important system-level data, you should back up this database regularly.

Schemas

Schemas enable you to compartmentalize database objects into groups based on their purpose. For example, you may create a schema called `HumanResource` and place all your employee tables and stored procedures into that schema. You could then protect that schema to prevent users from seeing data from within the schema. Think of a schema as a logical grouping of objects within a database.

When you call an object from within a schema, you use a two-part name at a minimum. You may be familiar with the `dbo` schema, which is the default schema for a given database. An `Employee` table in the default dbo schema is called dbo.Employee. This table would be different from HumanResource.Employee, if you had that table in the database. It is a best practice always to refer to a database object by its two-part name, like this from the AdventureWorks database:

```
SELECT EmployeeID, Salary
FROM HumanResource.Employee
```

Schemas have been around since earlier releases of SQL Server but were not used in the same manner. Previously, schemas were tied to your user name. If a DBA were to leave the company, you could not remove that DBA's account from SQL Server until you ensured that all the objects inside the DBA's schema were also moved. That typically created additional development, as you were now pointing all your application to new stored procedure names. This is no longer a problem in SQL Server 2005.

Synonyms

A *synonym* creates an abstraction layer between the database object and the client. It essentially creates a secondary logical name for a database object. This abstraction comes in handy when you use linked servers; with linked servers, you have to refer to the four-part qualifier, like the following code:

```
SELECT Column1, Column2
FROM LinkedServerName.DatabaseName.SchemaName.TableName
```

This long a name creates a usability issue for developers, who at a minimum will receive a massive hand cramp after typing that long an object name all day long. With synonyms, you can create what equates to a redirector so that anytime someone types SchemaName.SynonymName, they're redirected to LinkedServerName.DatabaeName.SchemaName.Tablename.

As an abstraction layer, synonyms are also useful also if you think you may want to redirect that query to a new table or server some day. For example, you may have a table named Sales2004, and your synonym name could be Sales. When 2005 arrives, you can point the synonym to the new Sales2005 table.

A synonym cannot reference another synonym.

Dynamic Management Views

Dynamic management views (DMVs) and functions return information about your SQL Server instance and the operating system. Much of the information you would use very elaborate scripts for in SQL Server 2000 to view operational data is now available through simple queries in SQL Server 2005 using DMVs. In most cases, you could not see the type of operational data available in DMVs at all in SQL Server 2000. DMVs can provide you with various types of information, from data about the I/O subsystem and RAM to information about Service Broker.

Whenever you start an instance, SQL Server begins saving server-state and diagnostic information into DMVs. When you stop and start the instance, the information is flushed from the views and fresh data begins to be loaded. You can query the views just like any other table in SQL Server with the two-part qualifier. For example, the following query uses the sys.dm_exec_sessions DMV to retrieve the number of sessions connected to the instance, grouped by login name.

```
SELECT login_name, COUNT(session_id) as NumberSessions
FROM sys.dm_exec_sessions GROUP BY login_name
```

In fact, DMVs are also sometimes functions and accept parameters. For example, the following code uses the sys.dm_io_virtual_file_stats dynamic management function (we use the term *DMV* for simplicity throughout this book) to retrieve the I/O statistics for the AdventureWorks data file.

```
SELECT * FROM
sys.dm_io_virtual_file_stats(DB_ID('AdventureWorks'),
FILE_ID('AdventureWorks_Data'))
```

We cover much more about DMVs throughout this book, starting in Chapter 4.

SQL Server 2005 Data Types

As you create a table, you must assign a data type for each column. In this section, we cover some of the more commonly used data types in SQL Server. Even if you create a custom data type, it must comply with the standard SQL Server data types in some way. For example, you may have created a custom data type (Address) by using the following syntax, but notice that it still has to fit inside the varchar data type.

```
CREATE TYPE Address
FROM varchar(35) NOT NULL
```

If you are changing the data type of a column in a very large table in SQL Server Management Studio's table designer interface, the operation may take a very long time. The reason for this can be observed by scripting the change from the Management Studio interface. Management Studio creates a secondary temporary table that has a name like tmpTableName and then copies the data into the table. Finally, the interface deletes the old table and renames the new table with the new data type. There are other steps along the way, of course, to handle indexes and any relationships in the table.

If you have a very large table with millions of records, this process can take more than ten minutes and in some cases more than hour. To avoid this, you can use a simple one-line T-SQL statement in the query window to change the column's data type. For example, to change the data type of the Title column in the Employees table to a varchar(70), you could use the following syntax.

```
ALTER TABLE HumanResources.Employee ALTER COLUMN Title Varchar(70)
```

When you convert to a data type that may be incompatible with your data, you may lose important data. For example, if you convert from a numeric data type that has data such as 15.415 to an integer, the number 15.415 would be rounded to a whole number.

Oftentimes, you may wish to write a report against your SQL Server tables to output the data type of each column inside the table. There are dozens of ways to do this, but one method we often see is to join the sys.objects table with the sys.columns table. There are two functions that you may not be familiar with in the following code. The type_name() function translates the data type id into its proper name. To go the opposite direction, you could use the type_id() function. The other function of note is schema_id(), which is used to return the identity value for the schema. This is mainly useful when you wish to write reports against the SQL Server metadata.

```
SELECT  o.name AS ObjectName,
        c.name AS ColumnName,
        TYPE_NAME(c.user_type_id) as DataType
FROM    sys.objects o JOIN sys.columns c
ON      o.object_id = c.object_id
WHERE   o.name = 'Department'
and o.Schema_ID = schema_id('HumanResources')
```

This code returns the following results (note that the Name data type is a user-defined type):

```
ObjectName          ColumnName      DataType
-------------------------------------------------
Department          DepartmentID    smallint
Department          Name            Name
Department          GroupName       Name
Department          ModifiedDate    datetime
```

Character Data Types

Character data types include varchar, char, nvarchar and nchar, text, and ntext. This set of data types store character data. The primary difference between the varchar and char types is data padding. If you have a column called FirstName that is a varchar(20) data type and you store the value of "Brian" in the column, only five bytes will be physically stored. If you store the same value in a char(20) data type, all 20 bytes would be used.

If you're trying to conserve space, why would you ever use a char data type? There is a slight overhead to using a varchar data type. If you are going to store a two-letter state abbreviation, you're better off using a char(2) column. In some DBAs' eyes, this may be a religious conversation, but generally speaking, it's good to find a threshold in your organization and set a small mental standard that anything below this size will become a char versus a varchar. Our guideline is that, in general, any column that is less than or equal to eight bytes should be stored as a char data type instead of a varchar data type. Beyond that point, the benefit of using a varchar begins to outweigh the cost of the overhead.

The nvarchar and nchar data types operate the same way as their varchar and char sister data types, but these data types can handle international Unicode characters. This comes at a cost though. If you were to store the value of "Brian" in an nvarchar column, it would use ten bytes, and storing it as an nchar(20) would use 40 bytes. Because of this overhead and added space, do not use Unicode columns unless you have a business or language need for them.

The last data types to mention are text and ntext. The text data type stores very large character data on and off the data page. You should use these sparingly, as they may affect your performance. They can store up to 2GB of data in a single row's column. Instead of using the text data type, the varchar(max) type is a much better alternative because the performance is better.

Numeric Data Types

Numeric data types consist of bit, tinyint, smallint, int, bigint, numeric, decimal, money, float, and real. All of these data types store different types of numeric values. The first data type, bit, stores only a 0 or 1, which in most applications translates into true or false. Using the bit data type is perfect for on and off flags, and it occupies only a single byte of space. Other common numeric data types are shown in the following table.

Data Type	Stores	Storage Space
Bit	0 or 1	1 byte
Tinyint	Whole numbers from 0 to 255	1 bytes
Smallint	Whole numbers from –32,768 to 32,767	2 bytes
Int	Whole numbers from –2,147,483,648 to 2,147,483,647	4 bytes
Bigint	Whole numbers from –9,223,372,036,854,775,808 to 9,223,372,036,854,775,807	8 bytes
Numeric	Numbers from -10^{38} +1 through $10^{38} - 1$	Up to 17 bytes
Decimal	Numbers from -10^{38} +1 through $10^{38} - 1$	Up to 17 bytes
Money	–922,337,203,685,477.5808 to 922,337,203,685,477.5807	8 bytes
Smallmoney	–214,748.3648 to 214,748.3647	4 bytes

Numeric data types, such as decimal and numeric, can store a variable amount of numbers to the right and left of the decimal place. *Scale* refers to the amount of numbers to the right of the decimal. *Precision* defines the total size of the number, including the digits to the right of the decimal place. So 14.88531 would be a numeric(7,5) or decimal(7,5). If you were to insert 14.25 into a numeric(5,1) column, it would be rounded to 14.3.

Binary Data Types

Binary data types such as varbinary, binary, varbinary(max), or image store binary data such as graphic files, Word documents, or MP3 files. The image data type stores up to 2GB files outside the data page. The alternative to an image data type is the varbinary(max), which can hold more than 8K of binary data and generally performs slightly better than an image data type.

XML

When XML first came out, developers began to store this hierarchical data into a text or varchar column. You would typically store data in XML in a database when the columns in the application would be variable, such as a survey application. This wasn't optimal, as you can imagine, because you can't index this type of data inside a text column. In SQL Server 2005, you have the option to store XML data into a proper XML data type that can be indexed, and schema can now be enforced. (We cover much more about these in Chapter 15.)

DateTime

The datetime and smalldatetime types both store the date and time data for a value. The smalldatetime is 4 bytes and stores from January 1, 1900 through June 6, 2079 and is accurate to the nearest minute. The datetime data type is 8 bytes and stores from January 1, 1753 through December 31, 9999 to the nearest 3.33 millisecond.

Unfortunately, there is no date or time data type. If you wish to store just the date, the time of midnight will be time-stamped on each record. If you wish to insert just the time, today's date is implicitly inserted. To get only the date out of a `datetime` data type, you must essentially "fool" the data type by converting it:

```
SELECT CONVERT(varchar, GetDate(), 101)
```

CLR Integration

In SQL Server 2005, you can also create your own data types and stored procedures using CLR (Common Language Runtime). This allows you to write more complex data types to meet your business needs in Visual Basic or C#, for example. (We cover the administration aspect of these much more in Chapter 8.)

Editions of SQL Server

With SQL Server 2005, there are numerous editions of the SQL Server product. The features available to you in each edition vary widely. The editions you can install on your workstation or server also vary based on the operating system. The editions of SQL Server range from SQL Express on the lowest end to Enterprise Edition on the highest. The prices of these also vary widely, from free to more than $20,000 per processor.

SQL Express

SQL Express is the free version of SQL Server meant for installation to laptops or desktops to support distributed applications such as a remote sales force application. You can use this edition to store sales or inventory data for your disconnected sales force and replicate updated data to them when they become connected again. SQL Express was called Microsoft Desktop Edition (MSDE) in SQL Server 2000. It is extremely lightweight and does not occupy much hard drive space. Vendors are free to distribute SQL Express, and it can be wrapped into your application's installation as just another component.

SQL Express is not meant to scale past a few users. Key features missing from SQL Express are SQL Agent and some of the robust management tools. It does ship with a very lightweight tool for managing the database, but scheduling of backups will have to be done in the Windows scheduler, not SQL Server.

Workgroup and Standard Editions

The Workgroup Edition of SQL Server is the lowest-cost edition of SQL Server editions that you pay for. It scales minimally up to two processors and 3GB of RAM, but it's adequate for small and medium-sized businesses. This edition of SQL Server was initially introduced to compete with lower-end vendors such as MySQL.

The Standard Edition of SQL Server has been beefed up in SQL Server 2005. It now has high-availability options that were exclusive to the Enterprise Edition in SQL Server 2000. For example, you can now cluster SQL Server 2005 Standard Edition instances.

Enterprise, Evaluation, and Developer Editions

Enterprise Edition is the best option for SQL Server if you need to use some of the more advanced business intelligence features or if the uptime of your database is very important. Although the Standard

Edition of SQL Server allows you to have high-availability options, Enterprise Edition far outdoes its sister edition with higher-end clustering as well as more advance mirroring and log-shipping options. The counter to this, of course, is the price. This edition of SQL Server will cost you more than $20,000 per processor if you choose that licensing model. (We discuss licensing later in this chapter.)

The Evaluation Edition of SQL Server is a variant of SQL Server Enterprise Edition that expires after a given time. After the allotted evaluation period, SQL Server will no longer start. The Developer Edition of SQL Server allows you to run all the Enterprise Edition features in a development environment. Neither of these editions is licensed for production use.

Operating System

The edition of SQL Server that you can install varies widely based on the operating system on your server or workstation, as summarized in the following table.

Operating System	SQL Express	Workgroup	Standard	Developer	Enterprise
Windows 2000 Professional (with SP4+)	✓	✓	✓	✓	
Windows 2000 Server (with SP4 +)	✓	✓	✓	✓	✓
Windows 2003 Server (SP1+)	✓	✓	✓	✓	✓
Windows XP Home Edition (with SP2+)	✓			✓	
Windows XP Professional Edition (with SP2+)	✓	✓	✓	✓	✓

Maximum Capacity of SQL Server

Memory and the number of processors is a huge contributing factor when you're scaling SQL Server. As you can imagine, the amount of memory you can scale and the number of processors will vary based on the edition of SQL Server you purchase. In some cases, your scalability is restricted only to the operating system's maximum memory or number of processors. This is where 64 bit becomes really useful. (We cover 64-bit scalability much more in Chapter 15.)

Capacity	SQL Express	Workgroup	Standard	Enterprise
Memory Supported 32 bit	1GB	3GB	OS Maximum	OS Maximum
Memory Supported 64 bit	N/A	N/A	OS Maximum	OS Maximum
Maximum Database Size	4 GB	No Limit	No Limit	No Limit
Number Processors	1	2	4	Non Limit

Database Features by Edition

The main benefit from one edition of SQL Server to the next are the features enabled. In the following set of grids, you can see how the features line up to each other across the various editions. These grids do not capture all the features of SQL Server but instead focus on areas that we receive common questions about and areas that help distinguish the editions.

Developer Features by Edition

SQL Server 2005 really tries to appeal to the developer. It has many features that will improve the efficiency of the developer's day-to-day job or make his or her code more reliable. In most cases, you can see that the developer slate of features works across all the various editions.

Feature	SQL Express	Workgroup	Standard	Enterprise
CLR Integration	✓	✓	✓	✓
XML Data Type	✓	✓	✓	✓
Try...Catch Exception Handling	✓	✓	✓	✓
Service Broker	Client Only	✓	✓	✓

Business Intelligence Features by Edition

The fastest-growth area for SQL Server revolves around business intelligence. Business intelligence allows you to bring the large amounts of data you have in your systems to the mass of users that would normally not touch this data.

Feature	SQL Express	Workgroup	Standard	Enterprise
Analysis Services (SSAS)			Up to 16 instances	Yesup to 50 instances
SSAS Clustering			2 nodes	✓
Parallelism for Data Mining Model Processing				✓
SSAS Data Mining			✓	✓
SSAS Perspectives				✓
SSAS Translations				✓
SSAS Proactive Caching				✓
Partitioned Cubes				✓
Reporting Services	✓	✓	✓	✓
Report Caching			✓	✓
Report Scheduling			✓	✓

Feature	SQL Express	Workgroup	Standard	Enterprise
Report Subscriptions			✓	✓
Data-Drive Subscriptions				✓
Report Builder		✓	✓	✓
Report Manager		✓	✓	✓
Infinite Drill-down				✓
Notification Services			✓	✓
SQL Server Integration Services (SSIS)		✓	✓	✓

DBA Features by Edition

The DBA features have the largest disparity among editions. You can see in the following table that most of the disparity revolves around high availability. If it's of the utmost importance that your system remain available all the time, use Enterprise Edition.

Feature	SQL Express	Workgroup	Standard	Enterprise
Indexed Views	✓	✓	✓	✓
Indexing of XML Data Type		✓	✓	✓
Failover Clustering			2-node	✓
Number of Instances Supported	16	16	16	50
Log Shipping		✓	✓	✓
Database Snapshots				✓
Database Mirroring Primary or Secondary			Safety Full Mode Only	✓
Dedicated Administrator Connection		✓	✓	✓
Dynamic AWE				✓
Fast Start of the Instance				✓
Hot Memory Addition				✓
Online Indexing Operations				✓
Online Page and File Restoration				✓
Replication	Subscriber Only	✓	✓	✓
Table partitioning				✓
Updatable Partitioned Views				✓

Licensing

Every DBA has probably received a dreaded licensing question or two, and we hope to answer some of those common questions in this section. There are several ways to license SQL Server, and we can't address this ever-changing landscape completely in this book. Instead, we've tried to answer common questions that are not as likely to change from year to year. If you were to purchase any of the licenses we refer to in this section, they are compatible with previous releases of SQL Server as well as SQL Server 2005.

The Server plus User Client Access License (CAL) licensing model works well if you can trace each connection to a user and if you have a low number of connections to your SQL Server services. This license licenses the server and each named user connecting to SQL Server.

The Server plus Device CAL licensing model works well if you expect that a moderate number of named devices will connect to your instance. In this model, you license the server and then each device (a kiosk or desktop, for example) connecting to the services of SQL Server. If you have multiple users using a single desktop, you need only a single device CAL.

The Processor licensing model works well if you expect to have a high number of connections on your SQL Server or if you can't identify connections, such as an Internet application exposed to others outside your company. This model licenses each physical or virtual processor available to the server. If you were to disable a processor to the operating system and in turn SQL Server, this processor would not have to be licensed. Once the available processors are licensed, you can have unlimited connections to the server.

Modern Processor Issues

In 2005, Microsoft clarified its licensing stance on multiprocessor systems. Hyperthreading allows a single processor to simulate multiple processors. If you had a four-processor server, you would actually see eight processors in Task Manager. With SQL Server, if you were licensing per processor, you would only have to license the physical chip connected to the mainframe and would not be charged for the hyper-threaded processors. This also applies in a multicore server. In a multicore machine, you would have one physical chip connected to the mainframe that had multiple processors sitting on it. It's essentially a processor hub. You are charged only for a single chip versus each processor on the chip.

Scaling and High Availability Licensing Issues

As we mentioned earlier, you are only charged for the physical chips on the machine if you choose the per-processor model. If you have 10 instances of SQL Server on a single server, you're not charged for each instance in a per-processor model. Another common question is with clusters. In an active-passive cluster, you are only charged for the active server, and the passive server is at no charge. In an active-active cluster, you are charged for each active node, so you might be charged for each node.

Oftentimes, DBAs decide to scale out SSRS, SSIS, or SSAS to avoid slowing down the relational engine. If you were to scale one of the SQL Server BI products off of the SQL Server machine, you would need to license the other server even though SQL Server may not be installed on it.

Summary

In this chapter, we covered the basic architecture for how SQL Server stores its data and how it communicates. We also addressed the various data types and when to use one over another data type. Last, we answered some of the many dreaded SQL Server edition and licensing questions that we often hear from users. Now that we have the groundwork down, we're ready to jump into installing SQL Server and some of the common issues that you may experience.

2

SQL Server 2005 Installation Best Practices

SQL Server is relatively easy to install. You can put the CD or DVD into the drive, in most cases click straight though, and you'll get a running, useful install. Several decisions are made by default as you click through, however. In this chapter, you learn about those decisions and discover the related gotchas and how to avoid them.

The installation process should be something like this:

- ❏ Plan the system.
- ❏ Get the hardware and software.
- ❏ Install the operating system and service packs.
- ❏ Setup the IO subsystem.
- ❏ Install SQL Server and service packs.
- ❏ Burn in the system.
- ❏ Do post-install configurations if necessary.
- ❏ Clean up for deployment and go!

We will focus our attention on the plan and the actual install.

Planning the System

Preinstallation planning will pay off with happier users and time-savings for you. Because it is so easy to pop in the CD and click through to install the product, it is equally easy to forego the planning process — but resist the temptation!

You will involve several functions in your planning, including the funding source, network group, and infrastructure (hardware/operating systems group). The funding source or business group will need to tell you something about the dollars available and the planning period that this configuration should support. Are you building something to last for four months or two years? The business people will also have some requirements around up-time and scalability. Incremental up-time and scalability is always more expensive as your tolerance for problems decreases. The infrastructure group will be able to advise you as to your company's configuration rules, hardware-vendor recommendations, and approved levels of software. Don't forget about support as well.

Let's drill into some of the details.

Hardware Choices

If you are in a growing organization, you should probably buy bigger and more than you think you need. More memory and faster or more processors are almost always good. At the very least, ensure that you have room to grow. For instance, if you have four memory slots and plan on buying 2GB of memory, do not buy four 512MB sticks of memory, because you will have used up all of the slots. Instead, consider buying two 1GB sticks, leaving two slots available for expansion.

Microsoft recommends some minimum configurations, and you'd better believe they mean *minimum*. Even for a small test machine, the minimum will not be enough. You should take this to heart. The minimum configuration means the product will most likely not run with fewer resources. It also means that you will need more hardware for any significant usage.

You are going to have to do some homework here. How many concurrent connections do you expect? How many of them will actually be doing work at any given point in time? How will that translate into disk I/Os? If you have an existing system, measure it. If you are using some purchased software (such as SAP, PeopleSoft, or any of a host of others), talk with the software vendor about hardware requirements. Many vendors have people who specialize in configuration of their application; use them.

Although we are primarily discussing SQL Server Engine in this section, you may be working with other parts of SQL Server.

Processors

For SQL Server installs where you expect many connections, more processors are better. This means that two 1.6Ghz processors will likely be better than a single 3Ghz processor. Although SQL multithreads, having two processors instead of one (or four instead of two), help prevent a situation where a single connection ties up the system, it's just a safer bet. The new multicore processors are great also. While dual-core processors are not quite as fast as two separate processors, they are certainly cheaper to purchase and license for software. Intel has also announced plans to develop chips with tens to hundreds of cores on a single processor chip. Most serious production systems should be 64 bit, especially Analysis Services and Reporting Services Report Manager.

Disk Configuration

When you plan your disk drives, consider availability, reliability, space requirements, and throughput. You will need to design the disk I/O subsystem to meet your needs. You will need to decide how to implement availability and reliability, which usually transfers into Redundant Array of Inexpensive Disks (RAID) and Storage Area Network (SAN) decisions.

- ❑ How will master and model databases be protected? (Probably mirrored)
- ❑ How will the data files for the database be configured? (Probably Raid 5 or Raid 10)
- ❑ How will the log files be configured? (Mirrored)
- ❑ Where will tempdb be placed and configured? (Away from other files and probably mirrored)

We suggest three rules for data-disk configuration to get maximum recoverability. Although these are used mostly when creating user databases, the system databases need to be on a different drive from the one you expect to use for your user databases. The rules are:

- ❑ Keep the log away from data. Keep a database's log files on a different physical drive from the data.
- ❑ Keep the data away from the master. Keep the user database files on a different physical drive from `master/model/tempdb`.
- ❑ Mirror the log.

SQL Server will not know anything about your decisions regarding RAID levels and SAN or Network Attached Storage (NAS) storage. It uses only the drive letters that have been exposed to the operating system. Therefore, you need to make and implement all of these decisions before you install SQL Server.

Disk Throughput

Disk throughput is the most common mistake people make when configuring SQL Server. Suppose you've been told by an administrator, "I need to have 300GB of storage for my production database." You buy a couple of 1500GB hard drives, and off you go. If this database is expected to get 300 IOs per second of requests, though, you are going to be in trouble. Imagine an Ultra-320 Scsi with the following specifications:

- ❑ Capacity: 147GB
- ❑ Spindle Speed: 10K RPM
- ❑ Average Seek: 4.5 msec
- ❑ Average Latency: 3.0 msec
- ❑ Track-to-Track Seek Time: 0.3 ms
- ❑ Max External Transfer Rate: 320 Mbits/sec

This is a commonly available, high-performance drive. Now consider how this performance should play into your thinking about SQL Server install and configuration.

With no data transfer, the theoretical max random IOs/second would be 1,000 Mbits/second / (4.5 seek + 3.0 latency) = 133 IOs/second. The theoretical max Serial IOs/second would be 1,000 Mbits/second / (3.0 latency) = 333 IOs/second.

For your calculations, however, you should use a more conservative capability estimate of 100 random IOs and 200 Sequential IOs per second for this configuration. It is much more likely that you will be constrained by the IO transfers per second than the 32Mbytes/second the hard drive can yield (320 Mbits/second / 10 bits/byte including parity bits = 32 Mbytes/second). Now, you'll find that 100 random IOs/second * 8K per transfer = 0.8 Mbytes/second.

This calculation is for random reads and writes to a single drive. SQL Server's lazy writer, worker threads, and other processes do 8K random IOs. Notice that this is well under the maximum advertised throughput of 32 Mbytes per second.

Even if we are doing sequential IOs, 1.6 Mbytes/second is still way under the max throughput of 32 Mbytes/second: 100 Sequential IOs/second × 8K = 1.6 Mbytes/second.

Read-ahead Manager does 64K IOs. Read-ahead manager also tries to order the IOs so that they become sequential IOs, which provide much better throughput. The results are 100 Random IOs/second × 64K = 6.4 Mbytes/second and 300 Sequential IOs/second × 64K = 12.8 Mbytes/second.

Even at the fastest throughput one might reasonably expect from this hard drive, the limitation will be the IO transfer rate, not the 32 Mbytes advertised maximum throughput.

If you use RAID 5, each logical write is physically two reads and two writes. This IO will be spread across two drives, so the throughput of each drive is divided in half. That would bring your IO transfer rate for write operations down from 100 to 50.

In this example, you need 300 logical writes per second against a RAID 5 array, so you must have 300/50 or six drives). Even though you need only about 300GB of disk storage, your configured RAID 5 array will contain about 600 GB of usable storage (five usable drives of the six, each 150GB/drive). The bottom line is this: Do not configure only for storage; you must think about transfer-rate needs as well.

Note that the actual time to transfer the data is a small part of the overall IO time. Transferring an 8K chunk of data would take about 1/4 of a millisecond (32,000,000 Bytes/second/8,000 bytes). Transferring 64K bytes of data would take about 2 milliseconds. This is small when compared to the average seek and average latency time of 7.5 milliseconds for this drive (4.5 + 3.0).

Some disk drives are faster than the one we used as an example here, and disk capabilities change over time, so you must do your own research and come up with your own numbers.

Best Practices

In general, to get higher throughput, you should spread the IOs across multiple physical drives. Hardware-based arrays are faster (and more expensive) than software arrays. Consider the transfer rates necessary to support the concurrent users you expect on your system. Also note that even though you may have 500 users connected, most of them will likely be waiting rather than active. You will have to do some research to better understand your users to get an idea of what percentage of connected users will actually be *active* at any given time. If most of your users are heads-down, data-entry folks, you may have nearly 90 to 100 percent of them active most of the time. If your users are a mix of inquirers and updaters who keep the application running all day but only use it occasionally, you may have as few as 10 percent of your users active. This knowledge should be part of your research and part of your plan.

Because most large IOs in SQL Server are 64K bytes, that would be a good stripe size to choose when you are configuring your RAID arrays.

SQL does not officially support data files on NAS or network file shares but will run if you enable Trace flag 1807. Do not expect to get good performance from NAS or network file shares. Better advice would simply be to always use direct-connected hard drives or SAN for your SQL files. Finally, you should always use NTFS for your data files. NTFS provides better security and more fault tolerance via soft sector sparing.

Disk Controllers

Disk controllers have a throughput limit as well. Take the maximum throughput expected from your earlier drive calculations to determine the maximum number of drives you should attach to a controller.

You need to be careful about the caching on these controllers. Disk caching can bring wonderful performance improvements to your system, but you can easily get into trouble by using it. The issue is that you must be able to guarantee that transaction-log writes will be completed under all circumstances. Controller caching works like this: When SQL Server sends a write command to the controller, the controller can save the data in cache and immediately send an IO Complete message back to SQL Server. One of the things the hardware controller can do is attempt to batch up multiple smaller IOs into what might become a single larger sequential IO, instead of many smaller random IOs. SQL Server continues to work, even though the IO has not actually been committed to disk. As long as the IO eventually makes it to disk, life is good. But if the IO gets lost, for any reason, SQL recovery will not work, because part of the log is missing. Then you are in big trouble.

The way to avoid this problem is to ensure that you are using a disk controller designed for use in a data-critical transactional DBMS environment. You should be able to turn off write caching and take advantage of read-only caching. Not all controllers allow this. You should be covered by a UPS, but this is not enough to ensure that the IO will be completed. UPSs cannot cover everything, such as operating system traps, memory parity errors, or operating system errors that cause a system reset.

Another problem that can circumvent proper write caching is an operations issue. A normal server shutdown (from the operating system) will wait until all of the IOs are complete. Operators should generally wait until disk activity is complete before rebooting a system. When Ctrl+Alt+Delete is used to shut down or the system reset button is pressed, cached writes can be discarded, corrupting the databases.

There are disk controllers that avoid all of these problems. They can intercept the RST (reset) bus signals to bypass resets that would discard cached writes. They also include ECC (error checking and correcting) memory, as well as onboard battery backup.

Although many controllers have a cache, most of the cache is protected by capacitors, not onboard battery backup. Capacitor-based caching cannot protect data from power failures and only ensures that the current sector is written. Onboard battery backup can protect a cached write for several days. As long as power is restored within these time limits, the controller will prevent new access, complete the pending IOs, and then allow new access.

Some controllers also allow selective write-through, allowing transaction-log IOs to bypass caching, while other writes are cached to improve performance.

Software and Install Choices

The next step in the plan is making choices about the software and installation options, such as choosing where the files will be located, setting security options, and configuring your disks.

Collation

When you choose a collation, you choose a character set, called a code page. The code page contains the mapping between the hex digits stored in the database and the characters they represent. For instance, x20 (hex 20) is a space character. The thing that makes it a space character is the code page you are using. You look up the hex 20 in the character-set map (code page), and you can see that it represents a space in the language (or character set) that is part of your collation.

Collation affects two other things: case sensitivity and sort order. You will see more details about these two items in a moment.

In versions of SQL Server before SQL Server 2000, choosing the correct collation was a big deal. The collation you chose during the install was the collation used for everything on the entire server. If you needed a different collation, you had to install another server. SQL Server 2005 allows you to make collation choices at the server, database, column, and expression levels.

The collation you choose during install is the collation for the system databases, including tempdb, and the default collation for everything else. Those who add new objects to this instance of SQL Server may choose other collations for their objects.

There are two general types of collations: SQL Server collations and Windows collations.

SQL Server Collations

SQL Server collations affect the code page used to store data in char, varchar, and text columns. They also affect how comparisons and sorting is done on these data types. They do not, however, affect Unicode data types. Unicode data types may compare and sort differently. This is the primary shortcoming of using SQL collations. You can set up an environment where single-byte and double-byte character sets use different collations. You should use SQL collations for backward compatibility. All of the SQL collation names begin with SQL_. Any other collation name is a Windows collation.

Windows Collations

Windows collations use rules based on the chosen windows locale for the operating system. The default behavior is that comparisons and sorting follow the rules used for a dictionary in the associated language. You may specify binary, case, accent, Kana, and width sensitivity. The key point is that Windows collations ensure that single-byte and double-byte characters sets behave the same way in sorts and comparisons.

Case Sensitivity

Your collation is either case sensitive or not. Case sensitive means that U is different from u. This will be true for everything in the region to which the collation applies (in this case, master, model, resource, tempdb, and msdb). This is true for all of the data in those databases. Here is the gotcha: Think about what the data in those databases actually is. The *data* includes the data in all of the system tables, which means object names are also case sensitive. The function to list the collations supported by SQL 2005 is `fn_helpcollations()`. On a case-sensitive server, this command would give you an "invalid object name" error:

```
Select * from FN_HELPCOLLATIONS()
```

This command, however, would work correctly:

```
Select * from fn_helpcollations()
```

If you have a case-sensitive database where all of the objects are also case sensitive, you have a table name `Emp`, with a single column named `Firstname`, with four rows with values Tom, Mary, tom, and mary.

The following command finds no rows, because the objects are case sensitive:

```
SELECT * FROM  Emp WHERE Firstname = 'TOM'
```

The following command files only one row, Tom:

```
SELECT * FROM  Emp WHERE Firstname = 'Tom'
```

To find all the rows regardless of case, you would have to write something like:

```
SELECT * FROM Emp WHERE Upper(Firstname) LIKE 'TOM'
```

Binary collations are case sensitive. If you choose a dictionary collation, you may choose the case sensitivity you need. However, as you can see, collation affects comparisons.

Sort Order

The collation you choose also affects sorting. Binary orders (`Latin1_General_BIN`, for instance) sort based on the bit value of character; they are case sensitive. Using the example table from earlier and a binary order, consider the following statement:

```
SELECT * FROM Emp ORDER BY Firstname
```

The result set would be:

```
Mary
Tom
mary
tom
```

If you choose a dictionary sort order (Latin1_General_CS_AI, for instance), the previous statement would yield the following result set:

```
mary
Mary
tom
Tom
```

Most business applications that contain character data types generally need a dictionary sort. Microsoft Books Online for SQL Server will provide you with a list of the extensions (_CI, _CS, and so on) and their meanings. Here you need only to understand the conceptual differences.

Collation Best Practices and Warnings

The big deal here is compatibility. If you try to compare two text fields that have different collations, which collation should be used for the comparison? You must provide the collation name in your code. This is a pain to do. Some collations are not comparable, which is even worse. Think about your use of linked servers in an environment of mixed collations. If you are using SQL replication between this instance and some other server, particularly SQL Server 2000 and SQL Server 7, you'd better make sure the data being shared also shares the same collation.

Try to standardize a collation across the enterprise.

Ensure compatibility with other servers where necessary. Change the default only if you need to do it for compatibility with other servers. The caveat here is that if you have an earlier version of SQL Server installed on this server, it will automatically choose a SQL collation. In this case, you must decide whether you need compatibility with that earlier version. If you do not need compatibility, choose a Windows collation.

SQL collations cannot be used with SQL 2005 Analysis Services. If you choose a SQL collation and are also installing Analysis Services, the install will choose a Windows collation that most closely matches your SQL collation choice. Your results, however, may be inconsistent. To guarantee consistent results between your database engine and Analysis Services, use a Windows collation.

If you have servers that have regional settings for both English (UK) and English (United States), you might be in for a surprise. The default collation for English (UK) is Latin1_General_CI_AS, whereas the default collation for English (United States) is SQL_Latin1_General_CP1_CI_AS. You will have to choose the proper collation for one of these to ensure consistency. They both use code page 1252, however.

In general, when you do not have to ensure compatibility with multiple servers, use the default Windows collation, and choose the case-sensitivity options to suit your needs.

If you are upgrading an earlier version in place, use the default SQL collation chosen by install.

If you are trying to replicate with another SQL Server 2005 instance, you can discover its collation with the following statement on the existing system:

```
SELECT SERVERPROPERTY(N'Collation')
```

If you are trying to replicate with SQL Server 7.0 or SQL Server 2000, for instance, use the following command on the existing instance to get the collation information:

```
EXEC sp_helpsort
```

Microsoft recommends that if you are trying to match the Windows locale of another computer (without changing your server's Windows locale), you must obtain the locale name from the other server. For Windows 2000 or Windows 2003, this can be found in Control Panel ➪ Regional Options. On Windows XP, this is under Control Panel ➪ Regional and Language Options. Once you have the region name, search MSDN for the topic "Collation Settings in Setup." This topic provides a mapping between locale name and default collation.

Microsoft's recommendation here does not take into account the possibility that the other server might not use the default collation. I would prefer to use `serverproperty` and `sp_helpsort` to get the collation directly. I provide Microsoft's recommendation only for completeness.

System Files Location

For most servers where higher availability is a requirement, we recommend that you mirror the C: drive where the operating system lives. You should place the SQL Server install in the default Program Files folder on the C: drive as well. This means that the master, model, resource, msdb, and tempdb will also be on the C: drive by default.

Tempdb might need some extra consideration, because it performs more duties in SQL Server 2005 than it did in SQL Server 2000. It will contain more information related to certain locking schemes, and it supports several other new features. As a post-install item, you may wish to either move tempdb using the Alter database command or have it grow to another disk drive. To do this, turn off autogrow for the existing file, and add new files in some new location. The preferred method is simply to move it to an otherwise not busy disk drive, since tempdb could see lots of IO.

Disk Setup

Without getting into the doldrums of discussing each of the RAID types, we'll offer some simple advice: Mirror the OS, SQL exe files, the system databases, and all transaction logs. Data files for other databases where high availability is necessary should be protected via RAID, with duplicate disk controllers. The more disk spindles you use, the better your IO throughput will be. If you have the money, RAID 10 or SAN will give the best performance. A less expensive option that does not provide as good performance is Raid 5. Whatever you do, use hardware RAID. For SQL Server, 64K is a good RAID stripe size.

Security Considerations

Do not install SQL Server Engine on a domain controller or on the same box as IIS. Reporting Services, of course, must be installed on an IIS box, since it depends on IIS. Use the concept of least security, only allowing the minimum security to get the job done.

While you can get the details about service accounts on MSDN (look for Setting Up Windows Service Accounts), we will give you only the reminders that you need to know. Up to 10 services are part of SQL Server 2005, depending on what you install. If you install more than one instance, that is up to 10 per instance. For maximum security, use a different local Windows login for each account, instead of sharing a single account locally. Local Windows logins are safer than domain logins, but they are more trouble because you have to keep up with more logins.

Although Microsoft's suggestion is to use separate local accounts for each service, most companies use a single domain login account for all services, using the minimum security settings. Some things can only be done when the service is running under a domain account, for example:

- Remote procedure calls
- Replication
- Backing up to network drives
- Heterogeneous joins that involve remote data sources
- SQL Server Agent mail features and SQL Mail

As we said, most companies use a single domain account for all services on all production servers. This makes maintenance easier; for instance, you have to set up only a single file share with permissions for backing up to a network drive. There are several kinds of service accounts you can choose from:

❑ **Domain Account:** This is an active directory domain account that you create and is the preferred account type for SQL Server services needing network access.

❑ **Local System Account:** This is a highly privileged account you should not use for services.

❑ **Local Service Account:** This is a special, preconfigured account that has the same permissions as members of the Users Group. Network access is done as a null session with no credentials.

❑ **Network Service Account:** This account is the same as the Local Service Account, except that network access is allowed, credentialed as the computer account. Do not use this account for SQL Server or SQL Agent Service accounts.

❑ **Local Server Account:** This is a local windows account that you create. This is the most secure method you can use for services that do not need network access.

If you are making any changes to properties related to a SQL Service, do not use Windows Services dialog boxes. As an example, suppose the password for a domain windows account for your SQL Service has been changed. You need to change the stored password for the SQL Service. Although this can be done via Windows Administrative Tools, you should always use SQL Server Configuration Manager to manage the services associated with SQL Server.

Installing SQL Server

In this section you learn about the different types of installations: side by side, upgrade, and new install. Details about upgrades are covered in Chapter 3. You can also create a script that installs SQL Server for you. This can be very useful when you need to complete many similar installations.

> *Each install works with a single instance. If you wish to install a named instance of the database engine and a default instance of Analysis Services, you must go through two separate install processes.*

Side by Side, Upgrade, and New Install

A new install occurs when no other SQL Server components are on the server and you have a clean slate to work with. Be careful that there are no remnants of previous SQL installs. Check the directories and registry to ensure that you have a clean system.

If SQL Server components exist on the box, you can upgrade the existing instance. In this case you install SQL Server on top of the existing instance. SQL Server also supports side-by-side install. A side-by-side install occurs when you are adding another instance of SQL Server. SQL Server 2005 supports multiple instances of the Database Engine, Reporting Services, and Analysis Services on the same box. SQL Server 2005 will also run side-by-side with previous versions of SQL Server. If the existing instance is a default instance, of course, your new install must be a named instance. The following table indicates which versions can run side by side with SQL 2005. This table was obtained from SQL Server Books Online.

Side-by-side support	SQL Server 2000 (32-bit)	SQL Server 2000 (64-bit)	SQL Server 2005 (32-bit)	SQL Server 2005 (64-bit) IA64	SQL Server 2005 (64-bit) X64
SQL Server 7	Yes	No	Yes	No	No
SQL Server 2000 (32-bit)	Yes	No	Yes	No	Yes
SQL Server 2000 (64-bit)	No	Yes	No	Yes	No
SQL Server 2005 (32-bit)	Yes	No	Yes	No	Yes
SQL Server 2005 (64-bit) IA64	No	Yes	No	Yes	No
SQL Server 2005 (64-bit) X64	Yes	No	Yes	No	Yes

The biggest issue with side-by-side installs is memory contention. Make sure you set up your memory so that each instance is not trying to acquire the entire physical memory.

Some companies who need many instances of low-usage SQL Servers are placing a single instance of SQL Server in a virtual machine and placing several virtual machines on a single server. VMWare and Microsoft's Virtual Server software support this architecture. Using Microsoft's Virtual Server and Virtual PC, you can create an image using Virtual PC and quickly load as a virtual machine to Virtual Server. This is more often found in the development environment than production but is dependent on the load placed on the servers and the size of the physical box. This does allow you to move the instances around transparently and to provision new instances quickly.

Scripted Installation

You can install SQL Server via command prompt calls to Setup.exe. In our experience, this was used in the past more frequently than today. You could create a small setup script, with all of your options selected, send it to a remote site, and have someone run the script to do the installation. We include a couple of the command-line syntax examples in this section. If you wish to do a very small number of installations, you can connect to the server via a remote desktop connection and do the install as if you were local. You can also use scripting to upgrade or uninstall SQL Server.

If you are installing SQL from a remote share, you must have read and execute permissions on the share. Expect all commands to be case sensitive. Also, make sure you notice the direction of the slashes in the commands; it matters.

First, ensure that the SQL Install CD/DVD is in the disk drive. Use the following command-line prompt to install all components:

```
Start /wait <CD or DVD Drive> \setup.exe /qb INSTANCENAME=<InstanceName>
ADDLOCAL=All PIDKEY=<pidkey> SAPWD=<StrongPassword>
```

The Database Engine, SQL Server Agent, Reporting Server, and Analysis Services are all instance aware. To install any or all of these components without installing everything, use the following syntax:

```
Start /wait <CD or DVD Drive> \setup.exe /qb INSTANCENAME=<InstanceName>
ADDLOCAL=SQL_Engine, SQL_Replication
```

Either the /qn or /qb flag is required. Using /qn suppresses the user interface, and all setup messages and errors are placed in the setup log. Using /qb shows the user interface during install and displays messages in dialog boxes. You can think of /qn as the unattended install and /qb as an attended install.

The other components, which are not instance aware, do note require the INSTANCENAME token. If you are installing to the default instance, use INSTANCENAME=MSSQLSERVER.

The ADDLOCAL option describes the software you wish to install. You can get the complete list of option values in Books Online. The thing you need to know here is that there is a two-level hierarchy of software pieces. As an example, the SQL_Engine parent has three children: SQL_Data_Files, SQL_Replication, and SQL_FullText. If you include only the parent, only the parent, none of its children, is installed. Installing a child feature automatically installs the parent, however. Removing a parent automatically removes all of the child features. These features are all case sensitive and must be included in a comma-delimited list with no spaces.

PIDKEY is the software key that comes with your software. Do not include spaces or the - character in the key.

The SAPWD option is used to specify the SA password. Always use a strong password. A strong password contains at least eight characters and includes characters from at least three of the following groups: uppercase characters, lowercase characters, digits, other special characters. (More details regarding securing your SQL Server install are covered in Chapter 9.)

There are many other parameters you can use in the command prompt, many of which are login passwords for service accounts, virtual names, and IP addresses for cluster installs. Check out Books Online to get the complete list.

You can also take all of the options, format them in an .ini style, and place them in a text file. Then reference the ini file as follows:

```
Start /wait <CD or DVD Drive> \setup.exe /settings C:\sqlinstall.ini /qn
```

An ini file is an "initialization" file formatted in an ini style. Microsoft provides an ini file that you can modify to meet your needs. The filename is Template.ini, and it is located in the root directory of your install CD or DVD.

Remote Installation

Remote installations are not supported; you need to use Remote Desktop Connections instead. In previous editions of SQL Server, you could sit at one machine and do an install directly to another machine. This is called a remote install. This is beneficial if you are in one city and need to install SQL Server on a machine in another city. However, since the operating system now allows Remote Desktop Connections, there is no need for the SQL product to include this capability. You can make a Remote Desktop Connection by selecting Start ⇨ All Programs ⇨ Accessories ⇨ Communications ⇨ Remote Desktop Connection. You will be prompted for a server name to connect to and login credentials. Once logged in, you install SQL as if you were sitting at the Server Console.

We are not going to go through each of the dialog boxes for the install, but I will take you through the more critical ones.

Our test installs were from the MSDN Universal DVD. Microsoft Developer Network (MSDN) subscriptions allow developers to purchase much of Microsoft's Operating System, Servers, Office Products, and more at a very attractive price and use them for development purposes. My installations were done from this software source.

To get started, put in the CD or DVD. You may get an automatically started dialog box and have to navigate to the correct version of SQL you wish to install. If you have to navigate on your own, you will eventually see 'Setup.exe' in the Servers Directory of the version that you need. Run it.

You must agree to the license terms and the process may install some prerequisites. Then it will run a system configuration check, as shown in Figure 2-1. Do not ignore anything that does not pass. Even warnings should be addressed now, not after you have completed what may be a partially successful install. IIS is only required for Reporting Services installations, even though the warning occurs.

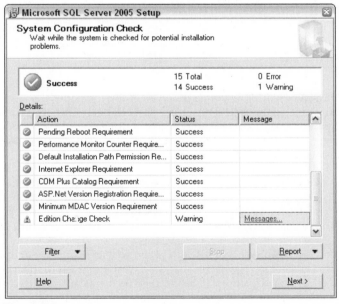

Figure 2-1

Next, choose the components you wish to install, as shown in Figure 2-2.

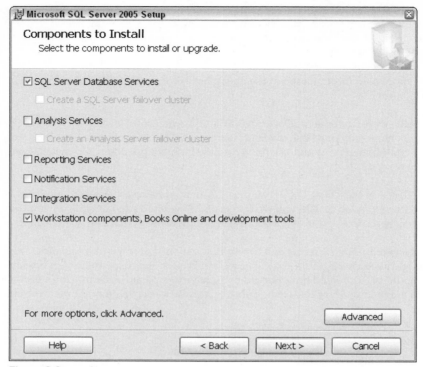

Figure 2-2

Your license for SQL Server will allow you to install all of the components on a single box. However, if you decide you wish to install the SQL Server engine on one box, SQL Server Reporting Services on another box, and Analysis Services on a third box, that is three licenses, not one. Licensing for Microsoft products changes over time and can become very complicated. You should contact your vendor or Microsoft representative to ensure you are in compliance.

SQL Server includes two demonstration databases with SQL 2005. AdventureWorks is a transactional sample, and AdventureWorksDW is a data warehouse sample. These demo databases are not installed by default. If you want to install them now, and you probably do, click the Advanced button on the Components to Install dialog box. You will be taken to the Feature Selection dialog box, shown in Figure 2-3.

In this dialog box you can customize which features you wish to install. Open up Documentation, Samples, and Sample Databases. You will see that they are not selected for install. Open up Sample Databases and select the "Entire feature will be installed on the local hard drive" option. This will install the sample databases. You can install them later, but doing so now will save you a little time. Click Next.

Five dialog boxes later, you will eventually get to the Collation Settings dialog box, as shown in Figure 2-4. Make your collation-setting choice here. You should have a good reason for your choice; think about it and make a good decision.

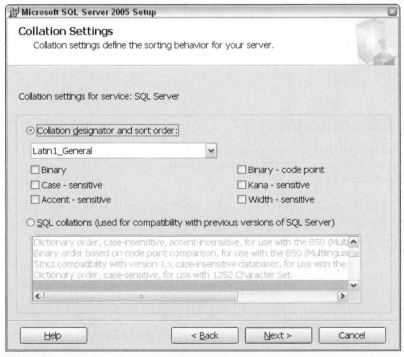

Figure 2-3

Figure 2-4

Continue through the install. You will get a Setup Progress dialog box, as shown in Figure 2-5.

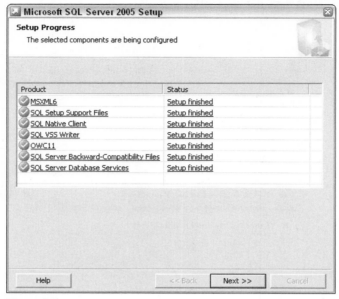

Figure 2-5

This gives you status information about the install. If you click any row, it will open up the log file for that item. This log file contains a huge amount of detail regarding the specifics of the install. If you encounter any problems during your install, you should go here to get those details. This information is stored in the `<SQL Install Directory>\90\Setup Bootstrap\LOG\Files` directory. If you get into trouble and have to call Product Support Services (PSS), you will need to have these files ready.

Once your install is complete, make sure you check out your new server. Make sure you can log in, and do some work.

Where is AdventureWorks?

Installing the sample databases is a little strange. On some systems, there was no additional effort required to install, other than the installation steps outlined in the previous section. On other systems, more work was required.

Nothing we did in the initial install allowed us to get the sample databases installed. You must go to Control Panel ➪ Add or Remove Programs to get this done.

Select Microsoft SQL Server 2005 and choose Change, and you will be presented with the Component Selection dialog box, as shown in Figure 2-6. Choose Workstation Components.

Click Next until you get to the Change or Remove Instance dialog box, and choose Change Installed Components. You will then see the Feature Selection Dialog Box, as you did during the initial install, as shown in Figure 2-7. Select "Entire Feature will be installed on the local hard drive" for the sample databases. You might want to do this for the sample applications as well.

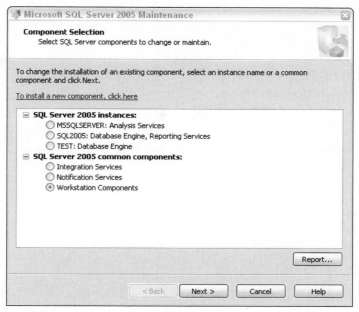

Figure 2-6

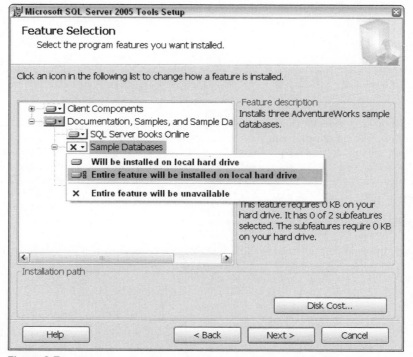

Figure 2-7

You'll then see the Sample Databases Setup dialog box shown in Figure 2-8. Choose "Install and Attach Sample Databases," choosing the instance where you wish them to be installed. Then click through, and you should now be able to use the sample databases.

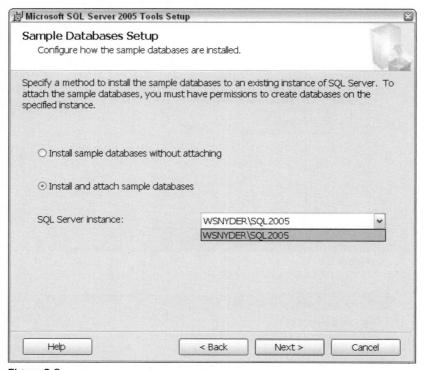

Figure 2-8

When you install AdventureWorks via attach, it will use the SQL_Latin1_General_CP1_CI_AS collation, not the default server collation. If you wish to use a different collation, you must drop the database and recreate it from the installation script. The script is named `C:\Program Files\Microsoft SQL Server\90\Tools\Samples\AdventureWorks OLTP\instawdb.sql`. You can also use this script to revert AdventureWorks to its original state, but first you need to change the script as follows. Search for the following string:

```
SET @data_path = @sql_path + 'AWDB\';
```

Directly below this line you will find the following instructions for reverting the database.

```
SET @data_path = @sql_path + 'AWDB\';

--
-- To reinstall AdventureWorks from this script change the SELECT statement
above
to the following.
```

```
--
-- SET @data_path = 'C:\Program Files\Microsoft SQL
Server\90\Tools\Samples\AdventureWorks OLTP\';
--
```

Where Are Pubs/Northwind?

The familiar and comfortable Pubs and Northwind databases are not included on the SQL Server CD. Although AdventureWorks is a much more complete sample, you may wish to continue using the Pubs and Northwind databases on SQL Server 2005. You can download them from Microsoft's Web site. The file name is `SQL2000SampleDB.msi`. Download and extract this file. By default it will go into the C:\SQL Server 2000 Sample Databases directory. There will be instructions that explain the install process, which is very simple.

Installing Analysis Services

You need to know a few things about installing Analysis Services. We are not going to go through the screens, because they're pretty much self-explanatory.

Suppose you want to install a default instance of SQL Server 2005 Analysis Services on a box that already has an instance of SQL Server 2000 Analysis Services. SQL Server 2000 Analysis Services does not support named instances. So if you have SQL Server 2000 Analysis Services on your install box, you must upgrade the SQL Server 2000 Analysis Services install to a SQL 2005 Named Instance. Then you can install another instance of SQL Server 2005 as the default instance.

Remember that SQL Server 2005 Analysis Services does not support SQL Collations. You can get weird behavior if your Database Engine Collation is a SQL collation and Analysis Services is a Windows collation.

Installing Reporting Services

Reporting Services (SSRS) installation can be easy as well, if you install everything on a single local server. There is also a new way to install Reporting Services, which is required to do a scale-out type of deployment. While you're going through the install dialog boxes, you select the "Install but do not configure" option in the Report Server Installation Options Page. This is called a *files-only install*. It copies the files, but you must configure the install in a separate step. Run the Reporting Services Configuration tool to configure and deploy this instance. You may choose the Report Server and Report Manager virtual directories. You can also create the Reporting Services database or connect to an existing Reporting Services database.

Be careful: Reporting Services uses server-specific encryption keys. During install or immediately after, you must create a backup copy of these keys using the Reporting Services Configuration tool, as shown in Figure 2-9. They will be required for you to restore your Reporting Services instance to another server. Do not put this off.

Figure 2-9

Reporting Services 2005 supports multiple instances, but Reporting Services 2000 does not. Reporting Services 2000 would have to be the default instance. A named instance of Reporting Services called MyTest would have a URL of http://myserver/reportserver$MyTest. Default configurations of multiple instances go to the same IIS IP address; however, you can configure different addresses if you wish.

If you're using a side-by-side install of Reporting Services 2000 and Reporting Services 2005, you must have two versions of the development tool. RS 2000 Report Designer runs in Visual Studio 2003, not Visual Studio 2005. Also, an SSRS 2005 install can use a SQL 2000 database as the Reporting Services metadata database.

RDLs created with SQL 2005 are not backward compatible with RS 2000. If you open an RS 2000 report in the SQL 2005 Report Designer, you will be asked if you wish to upgrade. When you upgrade the report, it will no longer be deployable to an RS 2000 Report Server. The SSRS Report Server Configuration tool cannot configure SQL 2000 RS.

Burning in the System

Before you move a system into common use, you should "burn it in." This means that you should stress the server. It is not unusual for a server to work in production for months or years with a hardware problem that existed at the time of the deployment of the server. Many of these failures will not show up when the server is under a light load but will become immediately evident when the server is pushed hard.

Several years ago, using SQL Server 6.5, I would get a 605 corruption error. This would cause me to have to restore the database that had the error. When the restore was complete, I'd run my DBCCs and get a clean result. Within a week I'd get another 605 error and have to stay up late in the evening restoring the same server. After getting really upset at this recurring problem, I discovered that I had a disk controller failing only near 100-percent utilization. This is exactly the kind of problem that burning in your system is intended to expose prior to production. It's much easier to fix hardware before it goes live.

A second use of some of these tools is to compare the IO throughput of your new system to your requirements or to the performance of an older system. While many tools are available, you can get two of them from Microsoft. One tool is called SQLIO, which is a disk subsystem benchmark tool. Microsoft provides this with no warranty and no support, but it is still a good tool to use. It is available from www.microsoft.com/downloads; search for SQLIO.

The second tool is SQLIOStress. You can download it from http://support.microsoft.com/default .aspx?scid=kb;en-us;231619 or search for SQLIOStress in Microsoft downloads. This tool simulates the IO patterns of SQL Server, although it does so directly, without using your SQL install. It simulates write-ahead logging, page inserts and splits, checkpoints, read-ahead, sorts, hashes, backup scans, and many other scenarios. In addition, it does over 150 verification and validation checks. I would not put a server into use without using this tool. When you use this tool, you must identify a data and log file. Be sure you use the same data and log file locations you will be using when you create your databases, so you will be testing the right areas of your I/O subsystem.

Neither of these tools depends on SQL Server being installed, so you can do this burn-in either before or after the SQL install.

Post-Install Configuration

Now that you have your SQL Server components installed, you will probably need to do some additional configuration. Beginning with SQL Server 2005, Microsoft and the world have taken a more serious approach to security. In the past, almost everything was enabled by default. We have learned that it is better to leave most things turned off, so you must make a decision to implement the features and capabilities you need. Microsoft is calling this "Secure by Default." You should run the Surface Area Configuration tool to turn on any features you will need.

Surface Area Configuration

Run the SQL Server Surface Area Configuration program. There are two pieces to the application: Surface Area Configuration for Services and Connections and Surface Area Configuration for Features. Click the Surface Area Configuration for Services and Connections, as shown in Figure 2-10.

If you are installing SQL Express and Evaluation Edition or Developer Edition, only local connections can be made. You can test this by going to another computer and trying to connect to this server. You will get an error indicating that remote connections are not allowed.

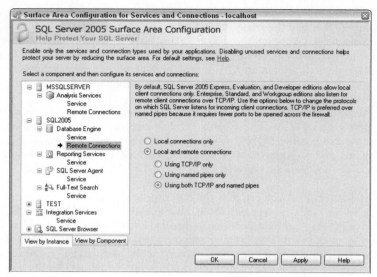

Figure 2-10

To enable remote connections, select the Database Engine; then select Remote Connections. Enable Local and Remote Connections using the protocols you need, as shown in Figure 2-10. In addition, go through each of the items available and ensure you have the proper capabilities enabled. This is also one of the places you can specify which SQL Services you want started automatically and manually. For a production server, you will wish to start SQL Server, SQL Agent, and the Browser. If this is an Analysis Server, it should autostart also.

Also open the Surface Area Configuration for Features, shown in Figure 2-11. You will find that features you need may be turned off. Items such as Remote Dedicated Administrator Connections, OLE Automation, CLR Integration, and Ad Hoc Remote Queries are turned off by default. Turn on only those items you know you need and leave the others off. This will give you a safer install.

You will have to restart SQL Server for changes to take effect.

SQL Server Configuration Manager

The SQL Server Configuration Manager tool allows you to specify SQL Server Services options and whether the service starts automatically or manually. You can also stop and start services here, since the Service Manager in the toolbar has gone away in this release. This program also includes a couple of very helpful features. Although I have not mentioned it before, I am sure you already know that SQL 2005 installs place items in strangely named directories: MSSQL.1, MSSQL.2, MSSQL.3, and so on. Each one might be an instance of Analysis Services, Reporting Services, or the SQL Engine. If you have many side-by-side installs of SQL Server, you could have MSSQL.1 through MSSQL.x. How can you find out which of these directories belongs to a particular instance? You can find this in the registry, of course, but this is one of the things you can use the SQL Server Configuration Manager for. It will tell you many of the properties of the service. Double-click on one of the services and go to the Advanced tab, as shown in Figure 2-12. There you will find lots of good information, including version information.

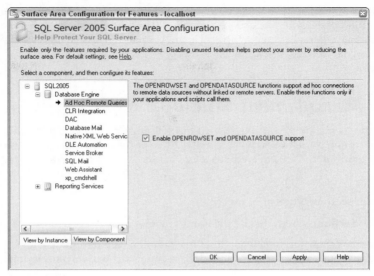

Figure 2-11

Figure 2-12

As with the Surface Area Configuration tool, you may set up the services, change service accounts, and auto start services. You can choose which network protocols SQL Server will listen on. This can be found in the SQL Server 2005 Network Configuration node. This node also allows you to import certificates for Secure Sockets Layer (SSL) encrypted communication.

The replacement for the Client Connectivity setup in SQL 2000 is located here as well, in the SQL Native Client Configuration node. You may choose which protocols the client uses and the order in which they will be used. You may also set up server aliases here. A server may listen on named pipes and TCP/IP. If you wish to force your client to use a specific protocol when communicating with a specific server, you may set up an alias for this.

SQL Server Management Studio

Once your instance is installed, you should visit the SQL Server Management Studio and complete any configuration or tuning changes you wish to make. Most of the items you change will be based on performance considerations and are covered in a later chapter. Among the items you may wish to consider changing are:

❑   **Processor section:** Number of processors

❑   **Memory Section:** Minimum and maximum memory

❑   **Database Section:** You may wish to set the default location for new data and log files. This is used when someone issues a create-database command without specifying file locations.

❑   **Permissions Section:** Some sites require that only database admins have admin access, which means that operating system administrators should not have SQL admin capability. The default install adds a login for the administrators group on the local server. This login has SQL Server sysadmin permissions. Practically speaking, this means you cannot prevent any local administrator from having sysadmin permission for SQL. All they have to do is add themselves to the local administrator group, which is set by default. This is true for any login in SQL Server that has sysadmin privileges. Local server admins merely have to add themselves to the group, and they will have sysadmin privileges again. In some shops, usually smaller ones, this is not a problem. However, if you wish to exclude local server admins from having SQL privileges, delete the Builtin/Administrators login. Then add only specific logins for your SQL Administrators, adding them to the sysadmin group.

Tempdb

Tempdb has taken on more responsibility than it had in the past. Tempdb historically is used for internal processes such as some index builds and table variable storage, as well as temporary storage space by programmers. The following is a partial list of some of the uses for tempdb:

❑   Bulk load with triggers

❑   Common table expressions

❑   DBCC operations

❑   Event notifications

❑   Indexes, including (SORT_IN_TEMPDB, partitioned index sorts, and online index operations)

❑   Large object type variables and parameters

❑   Multiple active result set operations

❑   Query notifications

❑   Row versioning

❑   Service broker

The location and attributes of tempdb have always been important. This is even truer now. Therefore, you should always ensure it is using Simple Recovery Mode.

Ensure enough space has been preallocated to handle most operations. You do this by setting the file size to an appropriate size. Even though autogrowth should be enabled, autogrow operations are expensive and time consuming. Think of autogrow as an emergency growth operation. When you enable auto-grow, choose a file-growth increment sufficiently large so that autogrow operations do not have to occur frequently. Microsoft recommends a file-growth increment of 10 percent of the tempdb data file size, with a maximum of 6GB. File-growth operations can be slow, causing latch timeouts. The length of file-growth operations should be less than two minutes.

Use instant database file initialization if possible. Normally, SQL Server will write zeros into a datafile to overwrite any data left on the disk from a preexisting file. This operation occurs under the following conditions:

❑   Creating a database

❑   Adding log files or data files to an existing database

❑   Increasing the size of a file (including autogrowth)

❑   Restoring a database or filegroup

Instant file initialization claims disk space without overwriting with zeros. This allows initialization, and in this case tempdb autogrowth, to occur much faster. Log files must still be initialized with zeros, so they cannot be initialized instantly.

Instant file initialization applies globally on all instances that use the same service account. This setting applies to all databases on the instance, not just to tempdb. It occurs automatically on Windows XP Professional and Windows Server 2003 or later, when the SQL Server Service account has been granted the SE_MANAGE_VOLUME_NAME privilege. Windows administrators can set this feature by adding the SQL Server Service Account to the Perform Volume Maintenance Tasks local security policy, as shown in Figure 2-13. You can get there from Control Panel ➪ Administrative Tools ➪ Local Security Policy.

There is a security issue related to using instant initialization. If files are not initialized to zeros, old data will be visible on reused areas of disk, which may be a security risk. You could drop a filegroup for one database and add a filegroup and files on the same drive to another database. If these newly added files are not initialized, they will still contain the information from their previous use. Of course, an intruder would have to open the files directly and get the information, but it is doable. You can prevent this by ensuring that the physical files have the appropriate discretionary access control list (DACL) or are simply not using instant initialization.

If you use instant file initialization and later turn it off, the existing files are not affected. They still contain the original data. Only newly created or expanded files will be initialized with zeros.

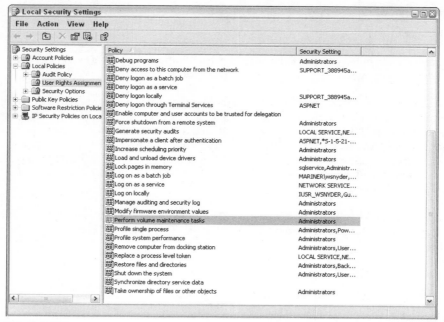

Figure 2-13

You should use multiple files in tempdb to ensure that tempdb operations can take advantage of all of the IO bandwidth available. Create about one file per processor but not more than two files per processor. Too many files simply increase the overhead and cannot be used simultaneously. (Dual-core CPUs count as two processors.) Ensure that each file is the same size. SQL Server 2005 continues to use the proportional fill algorithm from prior releases. This helps ensure the round-robin use of all files.

Finally, you should place tempdb on a fast IO subsystem, using striping if multiple disks are available, and place tempdb on a different drive from your user databases.

Back it up

After you have made all of your configuration changes, now would be a good time to do your initial backups, create your disaster-recovery plans, and get things going. Backups are discussed more thoroughly in Chapter 18.

Uninstalling SQL Server

To uninstall SQL Server 2005, use the Add/Remove Programs feature of Control Panel. If you wish to remove the entire instance, select Remove. If you wish to drop some of the services for the instance, but not all of them, select Change.

> You can also use the Add/Remove Programs feature of Control Panel to add or drop SQL Server Components from an existing instance.

Uninstalling Reporting Services

When you uninstall Reporting Services, you'll need to do manual cleanup on some items, which we discuss in this section. Before the uninstall, though, you'll need to gather some information. Make sure you know which databases are being used by this instance of Reporting Services. You can obtain this from the Reporting Services Configuration tool. Discover which directory this instance of Reporting Services is installed in by running SQL Server Configuration Manager. You also need to discover which directory the Reporting Services usage and log files are using. To do this, run the Error and Usage Report Program, in the All Programs ⇨ Microsoft SQL Server 2005 ⇨ Configuration Tools section, as shown in Figure 2-14.

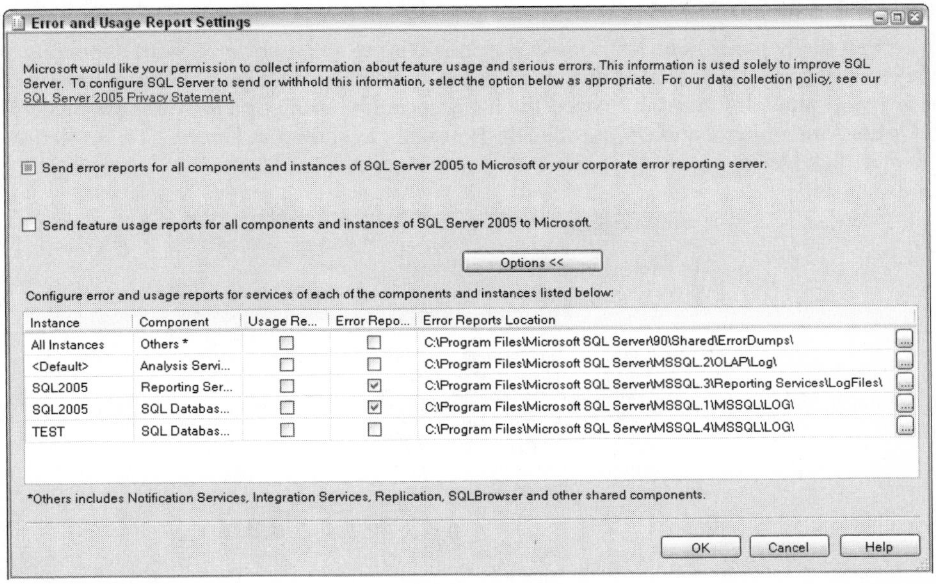

Figure 2-14

Delete the ReportServer Application Pool

The Reporting Services uninstallation process cleans up the virtual directories but does not remove the application pool named ReportServer. This may be because other instances of Reporting Services are using this pool, and the single instance would be unaware of these other uses. Although an additional application pool in IIS does not use significant resources, if you are sure there are no other users of this pool and you wish to clean up completely, remove it. Do so by running IIS Manager from the Administrative Tools Section of Control Panel. If you select the application pool in the left window, a list of all of the users of this pool will appear in the right detail window. If there are no users, simply right-click the ReportServer Application Pool and choose Delete.

Drop the ReportServer and ReportServerTempDB Databases

The Reporting Services uninstallation leaves the ReportServer and ReportServerTempDB databases so that you can reinstall another instance of Reporting Services and reuse the data. Note that these are the default database names, so you should ensure that you are dropping the appropriate databases. You should also make sure that no other instance of Reporting Services is using these databases. A Report Services Server Farm deployment would have many instances of Reporting Services sharing the same database. These instances would likely be on different servers as well. Once you are sure, just drop the databases.

Drop the Remaining Directories

The normal uninstall also leaves all of the Reporting Services log files. The default location is the RS install directory or the alternate location you discovered earlier. To delete them, simply delete the appropriate directories.

Drop the File Association

We are getting really picky here, but some file extensions are still associated with Reporting Services. RDL file extension is still associated with the Reporting Services development environment. RDLC may also be left associated. If you wish to drop the file association, bring up File Manager, Select the Tools ⇨ Folder Options menu item, and choose the File Types tab, as shown in Figure 2-15. Scroll down to RDL, select it, and click Delete.

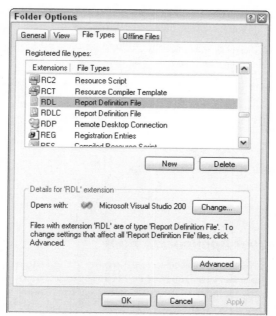

Figure 2-15

Uninstalling Analysis Services

Uninstalling Analysis Services is much like uninstalling Reporting Services, in that you need to do some manual cleanup. Once again, you should gather some information prior to the uninstall. Discover which directory this instance of Analysis Services is installed in by running SQL Server Configuration Manager. Also discover which directory the Analysis Services usage and log files are using by running the Error and Usage Report Program in the All Programs ⇨ Microsoft SQL Server 2005 ⇨ Configuration Tools section.

Although the normal uninstall does not leave any databases behind, it does leave all of the Analysis Services log files. The default location is the Analysis Services install directory or the alternate location you discovered previously. To delete them, simply delete the appropriate directories.

Uninstalling SQL Server Engine

As with the other service, log files are not deleted when you uninstall the SQL Server Engine. To delete them, simply delete the appropriate directories.

You may have to remove the MS SQL Server Native Client separately. You may find that the 90 directory remains and must be removed manually as well. If you have no other instances of SQL Server on your machine, instead of deleting only the 90 directory, you can delete the entire MS SQL Server directory under Program Files.

The .Net Framework 2.0 is also left on the machine. If you wish to remove it, do so from the Add/Remove Programs feature of Control Panel, but be sure no other apps are using it.

The PSS group is currently working with the development group to define a manual uninstall process. This would be used when you have problems in the middle of a normal uninstall. You might find yourself stuck (you can't install and you can't uninstall). If you find yourself in a situation where SQL is installed, you wish to uninstall, and there is no SQL 2005 entry in Add/Remove Programs, run the following program from the command line and see if it brings up the Add/Remove Program GUI:

```
"C:\Program Files\Microsoft SQL Server\90\Setup Bootstrap\ARPWrapper.exe"
Remove
```

For all other issues where you are only partially installed and can't successfully uninstall or install, call PSS. Microsoft PSS warns against trying to manually hack the instance out of the registry.

Although we've covered this in great detail previously, PSS comments are included here for completeness.

For instance-level collation settings, unless there is specific reason to pick a particular nondefault collation, you should go with the default. Some valid reasons might be application requirements, compatibility requirements, or company policy. The most important thing is to have a consistent collation on all servers in a particular environment or you'll run into collation-conflict issues when consolidating, moving databases around between QA and production, and so on. One caveat is that on a U.S. English server, SQL will default to SQL_Latin1_General_CP1_CI_AS, while on a U.K. or other non-U.S. English server, it will install with Latin1_General_CI_AS. In an environment that could have both, it would be best to pick one of the two collations and stick with it.

Help from Microsoft Product Support Services

In writing this chapter we contacted Ken Henderson, who is responsible for the Dallas, Texas, Product Support Services (PSS) group. Ken is a longtime SQL guy who knows his stuff. Ken connected us with some of his PSS guys, who told us about some of the common SQL 2005 install issues that people encounter and how to solve them. We got some information, presented here, from two generous guys: Eric Burgess and Bart Duncan. Both were enthusiastic, frank, and helpful.

Installing Client Tools from a Network Share

There is a common problem many folks run into when they try to install the SQL Client tools from a file-share copied from the install CD. They get the following error:

```
There was an unexpected failure during the setup wizard. You may review
the setup logs and/or click the help button for more information.
SQL Server Setup failed. For more information, review the Setup log file in
%ProgramFiles%\Microsoft SQL Server\90\Setup Bootstrap\LOG\Summary.txt.
```

When you go to the CORE(local).Log, you find the following information:

```
Running: InstallToolsAction.10 at: 2006/0/18 11:35:13
Error: Action "InstallToolsAction.10" threw an exception during execution.  Error
information reported during run:
Target collection includes the local machine.
Fatal Exception caught while installing package: "10"
        Error Code: 0x80070002 (2)
Windows Error Text: The system cannot find the file specified.   Source File Name:
sqlchaining\sqlprereqpackagemutator.cpp
Compiler Timestamp: Tue Aug  9 01:14:20 2005
     Function Name: sqls::SqlPreReqPackageMutator::modifyRequest
Source Line Number: 196

---- Context -----------------------------------------------
sqls::InstallPackageAction::perform

WinException caught while installing package. : 1603
        Error Code: 0x80070643 (1603)
Windows Error Text: Fatal error during installation.   Source File Name:
packageengine\installpackageaction.cpp
Compiler Timestamp: Fri Jul  1 01:28:25 2005
     Function Name: sqls::InstallPackageAction::perform
Source Line Number: 167

---- Context -----------------------------------------------
sqls::InstallPackageAction::perform
```

When you install from a networkshare, you must copy the contents of the two SQL install CDs to file-shares. There should be a share named *Servers*, which contains CD#1, and a share called *TOOLS*, which contains the contents for CD#2. These CDs are not marked clearly, and you may not copy CD#2 to the Tools share. The error we just showed you occurs as a result of this failure. Both of these fileshares should be under the same parent. Once you have copied CD#2 to the Tools folder, start setup again.

Admin Tools Not Installed by Default on Remote Cluster Nodes

To fix this, you must rerun setup on each of the secondary nodes to get the admin tool installed everywhere. Cluster installation is covered in Chapter 20.

Minimum Configuration Warning

SQL can install and run with the advertised 512MB RAM minimum, but it needs approximately 768MB of virtual memory. In other words, setup will fail spectacularly on a machine with just 512MB memory and no swap file. You'll need to temporarily create a swap file of at least 256MB (or add RAM).

Troubleshooting a Failed Install

SETUP.EXE compresses all the log files for each execution of setup into a single CAB file.

> *It is possible for setup to fail prior to creating the CAB file. If this is the case, the files will still exist singly.*

The CAB files will be in the following directory:

```
"%ProgramFiles%\Microsoft SQL Server\90\Setup Bootstrap\LOG\Files
```

The format of the CAB file name is:

```
SQLSetup[XXXX]_[Machine]_logs.CAB
```

The XXXX in the filename is a number incremented each time setup is run. You will be looking for the most recent CAB file. If setup fails, here are the initial troubleshooting steps PSS recommends:

1. The first and best place to get information is via the Web. Google for the error number. Also, go specifically to the Microsoft Knowledge Base and search for the error number there as well.

2. Setup installs components, each in its own MSI. The status of each of these installations is included in the Summary.txt file. Get it from the most recent SQLSetup[XXXX]_[Machine]_logs.cab. Each of the component installs should have a summary that looks like this one:

```
-----------------------------------------------------------------
Machine          : AMDF2002
Product          : Microsoft SQL Server 2005 Data Transformation Services
Product Version  : 9.00.1399
Install          : Successful
Log File         : D:\Program Files\Microsoft SQL Server\90\Setup
Bootstrap\LOG\Files\SQLSetup0003_AMDF2002_DTS.log
-----------------------------------------------------------------
```

3. You are looking for the first MSI install that failed. Search for "Install: Failed." The error number and message here may be sufficient to identify the cause of the failure. Use the error number and message you find to search for a resolution. If you need additional details, use the log file named in the summary. Look in this file for the component that failed. For the preceding summary, the log file is SQLSetup0003_AMDF2002_DTS.log. Search for "Return Value 3" in the Windows Installer log. The message you are looking for is usually just above this message, the first time it occurs.

4. If the `Summary.txt` file does not exist or does not have a failed component, check the datastore dump file (`SQLSetup[XXXX]_[Machine]_Datastore.XML`). It may have more error details. You are looking for "SetupStateScope." The error information, identified as "Watson*" properties, should be in this node.

5. The next place to check is the Core(Local) and Core(Patched) log. The filenames for these are `SQLSetup0001_<srvr>_Core(Local).log`. Search it for errors. You are in the neighborhood where PSS will likely need to assist with the interpretation.

6. Is this a cluster install? If so, search the Task Scheduler log on the failing node. The filename is `%WINDIR%\Tasks\SchedLgU.TXT`. Look for "TaskScheduler" error references. In a clustered SQL 2005 setup, the Task Scheduler service is used to launch setup on the remote nodes. To help you find this log, go to Control Panel ⇨ Scheduled Tasks, and then select View Log under the Advanced drop-down menu. This will open the log in Notepad, and you can File ⇨ Save As to keep a copy. Look for "Access Denied" errors in the log. These indicate a known Windows bug. As a workaround the "Access Denied" bug, log off any active sessions on the remote node before running setup again.

7. Of course, search the Knowledge Base for any errors you discover in these logs.

If you call PSS with a setup issue, they'll want that CAB file (plus other system logs).

Summary

Installation of SQL Server is generally quite easy. Ensure that you are using an enterprise compatible collation and that you have chosen appropriate service accounts. Remember that SQL is secure by default. This means that you will have to use the Surface Area Configuration tool to enable many of the things you will need for your server, such as database mail and remote connections. If you will be upgrading, there is some good advice coming up in Chapter 3.

3

Upgrading SQL Server 2005 Best Practices

Chapter 2 covers performing a new installation of SQL Server 2005. In this chapter, we discuss upgrading SQL Server from a previous edition. First, we cover reasons for upgrading to SQL Server 2005. We then discuss the pros and cons of various upgrade strategies. You learn about the various tools available to help mitigate risk during the upgrade process. We then explain how to use the new configuration tool. To wrap up, we discuss SQL Server 2005 behavior changes and discontinued features that you need to know about before upgrading. By the end of the chapter, you will have everything you need to perform a successful upgrade to SQL Server 2005.

Why Upgrade to SQL Server 2005

With the release of SQL Server 2005, Microsoft introduced numerous advancements in the areas of scalability, reliability, availability, and security.

As you'll see throughout this book, significant enhancements have been introduced throughout the product. During the development cycle, there were four pillars of focus for the product: developer productivity, security, business intelligence, and enterprise data management. The enterprise data management pillar had the following goals:

❑ Availability and security advancements. New and enhanced high-availability options include database mirroring, server clustering, peer-to-peer replication, fine-grained online repairs, dynamic management views, backup and restore, and many other improvements in the areas of online operations. These features ensure that SQL Server 2005 is available for your enterprise. Also, the SQL Server 2005 security initiative brought about security enhancements such as support for data encryption, password-policy enforcement, fine-grain security control, user-schema separation, and improved auditing capabilities.

❏ Continued focus on manageability. SQL Server Management Studio is the new integrated management toolset for relational and business intelligence technologies. This tool set is based on Visual Studio 2005 Integrated Development Environment (IDE), which brings about enhanced collaboration capabilities through the use of projects for storing code such as stored procedures. SQL Server 2005 also enhanced its ability to self-optimize and to load balance its workload across processors. The introduction of dynamic management view (DMV) along with support for dedicated admin connection (DAC) will ensure that administrators can get the information that they need to manage their environment under any conditions.

❏ Performance and scalability. Performance and scalability enhancements have been introduced through technologies such as data partitioning, snapshot isolation, and support for dynamic AWE memory. Enhancements in the area of buffer-pool management will also ensure that the right data is in the data cache. SQLOS is the improved abstraction layer that provides SQL Server 2005 the ability to scale on any technology platform. This capability empowers you with the technical and business flexibility to solve unique problems in a way that will best meet your needs.

In Appendix A, you'll find the lab report from Raymond James Financial, a client of Jean-Claude Armand, and their experiences with upgrading to SQL Server 2005. Raymond James Financial maintains a 3TB SQL 2000 Data Warehouse deployed on HP Itanium 2-based Superdome running on Windows Server 2003 Datacenter. During the fall of 2005, Raymond James wanted to evaluate what benefits SQL Server 2005 could bring to their enterprise.

Risk Mitigation — The Microsoft Contribution

As with all previous versions of SQL Server, the SQL team took extraordinary steps to ensure that the quality of SQL Server 2005 was as high grade as possible. The specific steps of the software engineering cycle are beyond the scope of this book, but we will highlight a few points considered public knowledge about the daily build process. We will also touch on a few points about how Trustworthy Computing improves this process. Ever since the January 2002 memo from Bill Gates on Trustworthy Computing, security procedures have been incorporated into every software development process.

Today, a daily process produces a 32-bit, X64, and Itanium versions of SQL Server 2005 code (called a build) that have gone through a battery of tests. This process is utilized for both the development of new releases and the development of service packs for SQL Server 2005. These tests are a convergence of in-house built tests, customer-captured workloads, and Trustworthy Computing processes. Microsoft Research is a group of 700 computer-science researchers who work on bringing innovations to Microsoft's products. For example, on the SQL Server 2005 release, these innovations were in the areas of data-mining algorithms and indexed-views performance enhancements. In the areas of software development, the MS Research team is an essential contributor to the software engineering and testing processes. They improve the test harness with enhancements in several areas, including threat modeling, testing efficiencies, and penetration analysis.

In addition, there are approximately 275 customer-captured workloads that are also part of the software testing harness. These workloads are acquired through an assortment of programs such as the Customer Playback program and various lab engagements including Yukon-compatibility labs.

The daily builds are tested against this gathered information, and out of this process come performance metrics, security metrics, and bugs. Bugs are subsequently filed, assigned, prioritized, and tracked until resolution. Once a bug has been fixed, its code goes through security testing as part of the software-engineering process. This happens before the code gets checked back into the software tree for the next testing cycle.

Independent Software Vendors (ISV) & SQL Community Contributions

Starting with SQL Server 2005, the concept of community technology preview (CTP) was adopted. The December 2004 CTP (2004) was the first of seven such releases. The decision to adopt this snapshot in time of code (or build) resulted in over 326,000 CTP downloads, providing unprecedented access to updated code to both ISV and SQL community testing. This type of access to beta code was leveraged as a means of identifying additional bugs, conducting additional testing of software fixes, and driving additional improvements based on community feedback. Paul Flessner was quoted by *Microsoft Watch* as saying that this will be his process of choice as part of his SQL Server Reengineering Initiative. This initiative is aiming for a 24 to 36 month release cycle going forward, putting the next release of SQL Server in the 2008 timeframe.

In addition, Microsoft migrated over 90 internal systems, including their own financial SAP (July 15, 2004), and 1000 customer databases were also upgraded to SQL Server 2005.

Upgrading to SQL Server 2005

The installation guidelines are covered in Chapter 2, so we focus this section mainly on upgrade strategies and considerations for the SQL Server 2005 database component. The upgrade of individual components outside of the database is covered in individual chapters.

A smooth upgrade requires a good plan. When you devise an upgrade plan, you need to break down the upgrade process into individual tasks. This plan should have sections for preupgrade tasks, upgrade tasks, and post-upgrade tasks.

Your preupgrade tasks should take into consideration SQL Server 2005 minimum hardware and software requirements. You should have an inventory of your applications that access the server, database-collation requirements, server dependencies, and legacy-systems requirements such as data-access methods. Plans should be in place for testing the upgrade process and applications. You should have a thorough understanding of backward-compatibility issues and have workarounds or fixes identified. You should also use the upgrade tool to assist in identifying and resolving issues.

The upgrade execution process should be a smooth execution of your well-documented and rehearsed plan.

Post-upgrade tasks should consist of reviewing the upgrade process, bringing the systems back online, monitoring, and testing the system. Specific database maintenance will also need to be performed before releasing the system to the user community. (These and other recommended steps are outlined later in the chapter.) We recommend that you run your database in backward-compatibility mode after the upgrade to minimize the amount of change to your environment. The database-compatibility mode should be updated as part of a follow-up upgrade process along with enabling new SQL Server 2005 features.

As part of deciding your upgrade strategy, we will discuss both the in-place (upgrade) and side-by-side migration methods for upgrading.

Upgrade in Place

The in-place server upgrade is the easier of the two options. This is an all-or-nothing approach to upgrading, meaning that once the upgrade is initiated, there is no simple recovery procedure. This type of upgrade has the added requirement of greater upfront testing to avoid using a complex back-out plan. The benefit of this approach is not having to worry about users and logins remaining in-sync, and database connectivity changes will not be required for applications. In addition, SQL Agent jobs will be upgraded during the upgrade process.

Here's a high-level scenario of an upgrade in place based on Figure 3-1. First, install the prerequisite files on your system. Before upgrading to SQL Server 2005, your server needs, at a minimum, .NET Framework 2.0, SQL Server 2000 with Service Pack 3 or 3a (or greater), or SQL Server 7.0 with Service Pack 4. The next step is to run the system configuration checker (SCC) without affecting the user environment. The SCC examines the destination computer for conditions that would prevent an upgrade from completing, such as not meeting the minimum hardware or software requirements. If such a condition is found, setup will be aborted and the SQL Server 2005 components will be uninstalled. Once verified, the SQL Server setup program is able to lay the 2005 bits and backward-compatibility support files on disk while SQL Server 2000 (or 7.0) is still available to users. However, planning to upgrade a server while users are online is not recommended. The setup program takes the server offline by stopping the existing SQL Server services. The 2005-based services assume control of the master database and the server identity. At this point, SQL Server service takes over the databases and begins to update them while allowing users back into the environment. When a request for data occurs in a database that has only been partially updated, the data associated with this request is updated, processed, and then returned to the user. The next step is to kick off the uninstall procedure for the old binaries. This step occurs only if no remaining SQL Server 2000 or 7.0 instances are on the server. Finally, SQL Server agent jobs get upgraded.

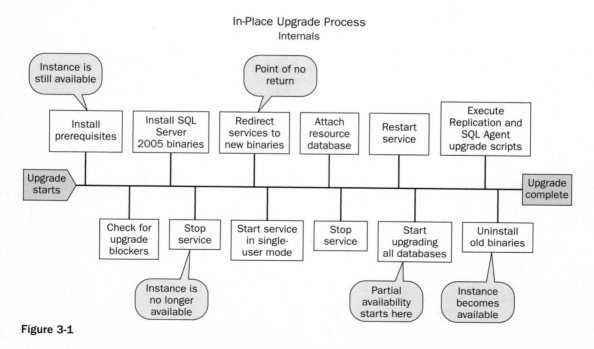

Figure 3-1

If you would like to change editions as a part of your upgrade, there are some limitations that you must be aware of. SQL Server 2000 Enterprise, Developer, Standard, and Workgroup editions can be upgraded to different editions of SQL Server 2005. SQL Server 2000 Desktop Editions can only be upgraded to either the Express or Workgroup editions of SQL Server 2005. If this is of interest to you, we suggest reading Books Online (BOL) for additional details.

If you are using SQL Server 7.0, there are a few additional items to keep in mind regarding your upgrade. First, SQL Server 7 is not supported on Windows Server 2003. SQL Server 2005 is not supported on NT 4.0. If you are trying to perform a Windows 2000-based in-place upgrade, Microsoft Data Access Components (MDAC) 2.8 SP1, IIS 5.0 or greater, Internet Explorer 6.1, and Windows Installer 3.1 will all have to be installed. If you are stuck in the 1960s and still have a SQL Server 7.0 cluster, side-by-side upgrade is the only option because SQL 7.0 clusters do not support MDAC greater than 2.6. Finally, SQL Server 7.0 based MSX/TSX jobs cannot be upgraded to SQL Server 2005.

Side-by-Side Upgrade

In a side-by-side upgrade, SQL Server 2005 is either installed along with SQL Server 2000 (or 7.0) as a separate instance or on a different server. You may want to select this option as part of a hardware refresh or migration to a new platform such as Itanium or X64. Because of the back-up and restore times involved in a back-out scenario, if you have a sizable database, this is definitely the option to go with.

As part of this method, you can simply back up the databases from the original server and then restore them to the SQL Server 2005 instance. Another option is to manually detach your database from the old instance and reattach it to the new instance. You can also leverage the copy database wizard to migrate your databases to the new server. Although this approach provides for the best recovery scenario, it has additional requirements beyond those of the in-place upgrade, such as maintaining the original server name, caring for application connectivity, and keeping users and their logins in synch. If traces are part of your testing, maintaining the database IDs will also be a concern.

Upgrade in Place versus Side-By-Side Upgrade Considerations

There are numerous factors you should consider before selecting an upgrade strategy. Your strategy should include the need for component-level upgrade, the ability to roll back in case of failure, the size of your databases, and the need for partial upgrade. For many of you, top priorities will be whether you will be able to upgrade to new hardware, to facilitate a change of strategy such as a server consolidation, or to manage a small server outage window for the upgrade.

The arguments in favor of a side-by-side upgrade are:

❑ More granular control over upgrade component-level process (database, Analysis Services, and others)

❑ Ability to run systems side-by-side for testing and verification

❑ Ability to gather real matrix for upgrade (outage window)

❑ Rollback strategy as original server is intact

❑ Ability to upgrade platforms from a 32-bit to 64-bit server

❑ Best for very large databases, as restore time could be sizable

The arguments against a side-by-side upgrade are:

❑ Additional hardware may be required for instance upgrade or additional physical server for physical server upgrade.

❑ Does not preserve SQL Server 2000 functionality

❑ Issue of instance name for connecting applications

❑ Space requirement on SAN, especially for very large databases

The advantages of an in-place upgrade are:

❑ Fast, easy, and automated (best for small systems)

❑ No additional hardware required

❑ Applications retain same instance name

❑ Preserves SQL Server 2000 "functionality" automatically

The disadvantages of an in-place upgrade are:

❑ Downtime incurred because the entire server is offline during upgrade

❑ No support for component-level upgrades

❑ Complex rollback strategy

❑ Very large databases require substantial rollback time

Pre-Upgrade Checks

To ensure that you have a successful upgrade to SQL Server 2005, here are a few housekeeping tips. Ensure that all system databases are configured to autogrow, and ensure that they have adequate hard-disk space. Make certain that all startup stored procedures are disabled, as the upgrade process will stop and start services on the SQL Server instance being upgraded. Now that we have covered the strategies for upgrading to SQL Server 2005, we can discuss the upgrade tools available to assist in this process.

SQL Server Upgrade Advisor

If you don't like to be first to adopt a technology, the SQL Server 2005 Upgrade Advisor is the tool for you. This tool is based on early adopters' feedback and internal lab-testing feedback. The SQL Server 2005 Upgrade Advisor is a free download available at www.microsoft.com/sql and is also available as part of the SQL Server 2005 installs media for all editions. The purpose of this utility is to identify known upgrade issues and provide guidance for workarounds or fixes for the identified issues on a per-server components basis. Microsoft worked hard on this tool as a risk-mitigation effort to empower SQL Server 7.0 (SP4) and SQL Server 2000 (SP3 or higher) users to upgrade to SQL Server 2005. So, whether you are running Analysis Services, DTS packages, Notification Services, Reporting Services components, or a combination of components, the Upgrade Advisor tool can help.

Installing the SQL Server 2005 Upgrade Advisor

The Upgrade Advisor is a relatively simple tool to use. The tool can be found in the "Prepare" section of the default screen of the install CD/DVD. It can also be found at www.microsoft.com/sql. Select the download section on the left side of the page, and then select SQL Server 2005. As shown in Figure 3-2, be sure to select "check for updates," as upgraded versions of the tool are available online.

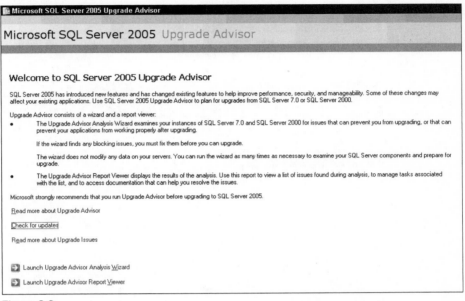

Figure 3-2

The tool is constantly being updated to reflect the lessons learned by the DBAs who updated before you. Although the SQLUASetup.msi file itself is a little over 4 MB; it will require the installation of the .NET Framework 2.0, which can be downloaded through Windows Update service or from MSDN. There are also X64 and Itanium versions of the tool and .Net framework that you can choose to install. Or you can choose to install a single instance and version of the tool to test servers across your enterprise. This option supports a zero-footprint interrogation with read-only access to servers.

This tool is read-intensive and should be tested on a test server to evaluate the potential impact on your systems.

The installation process is straightforward; the only option is to select the location where you would like to install the tool. The default install path is C:\Program Files\Microsoft SQL Server 2005 Upgrade Advisor. At the time of this writing, there are four incremental releases of this Upgrade Advisor with a total of 20 additional rules from the original release, for a grand total of 103 rules. These rules represent conditions, situations, or known errors that could affect your upgrade to SQL Server 2005. I also recommend checking "readme file" and q-article 905693 for the latest updates.

Using the Upgrade Advisor

Once installed, the Upgrade Advisor presents you with two choices: Launch the Upgrade Advisor Analysis Wizard or Upgrade Advisor Report Viewer. Launch the Upgrade Advisor Analysis Wizard to run the tool. As shown in Figure 3-3, you simply select a server and the component to analyze for upgrade, or you can click the Detect button, which kicks off an inspection process that selects the components installed on your system.

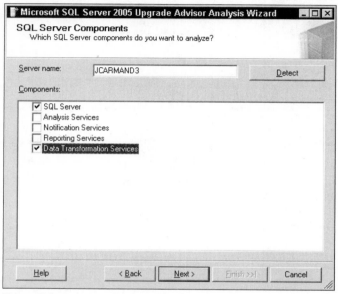

Figure 3-3

After you select the components for testing, the next decision is to select the databases that you would like to have evaluated for upgrade, as shown in Figure 3-4. The best part of this process is that you have the option to analyze trace and batch files to help make this a comprehensive analysis. That is, by adding these files to the evaluation process, Upgrade Advisor is not only evaluating the database but its workload and job scripts as well. All you have to do is to select the path to the directory where your trace file(s) or your batch file(s) are located.

After you have completed the configuration of the components that you want to evaluate, you will be prompted to begin the analysis. If you have any questions during the configuration steps, the Help button brings up an Upgrade Advisor-specific book online (UABOL) that is rich in information and guides you through the options. As the component-level analysis completes, a green, yellow, or red dialog box will indicate the outcome of the test.

Once completed, you can view the discovered issues via the Upgrade Advisor Report Viewer. The reports themselves, as shown in Figure 3-5, are presented in an interface similar to a Web browser. The information can be analyzed by filtering the report presented by Server, Instance, component, or issue type. How to interpret the results of this report is discussed later in this chapter.

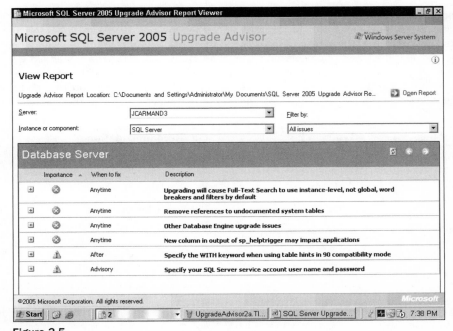

Figure 3-4

Figure 3-5

Scripting the Upgrade Advisor

If you have a server farm or if you just prefer scripting, a command-line utility is also available. With the `UpgradeAdvisorWizardCmd` utility, you can configure the tool via an XML configuration file and receive results as XML files. The following arguments can be passed to the `UpgradeAdvisorWizardCmd` utility:

- ❏   `ConfigFile` (config file path)
- ❏   `SQLUser`
- ❏   `SqlPassword`
- ❏   `Servername` and/or `InstanceName`
- ❏   CSV (where to deliver the XML results doc)

All capabilities and parameters discussed in the wizard section are exposed through the configuration file. The results from a command-style interrogation can still be viewed in the report viewer, via XML documents or Excel if you used the CSV option.

You can also install or remove the Upgrade Advisor application via the command prompt. From there you can control the install process with or without the UI. You can also configure the install path and process-logging options.

Resolving Upgrade Issues

The Upgrade Advisor's report contains a wealth of information. The key is to understand how this information is presented, what needs to be resolved, and when. As you see in Figure 3-5, the first column shows the importance of a finding or a recommendation, the second column tells you when it needs to be addressed, and the Description column tells you about the issue. The recommended way to approach this is to first categorize the information by "importance" and "when to fix" the items. Specifically, the sum of the indicators should dictate whether issues should be addressed before or after the upgrade process. The following table provides our recommendations of when to address these issues.

Importance	When to Fix	Our Recommendation
Red	Before	Resolve Before Upgrade
Red	Anytime	Resolve Before Upgrade
Red	After	Resolve After Upgrade
Yellow	Anytime	Resolve After Upgrade
Yellow	After	Resolve After Upgrade
Yellow	Advisory	Resolve After Upgrade

Issues that have been flagged with an "Importance" of red and "When to Fix" of "Before" or "Anytime" should be addressed before an upgrade process. Typically, these issues require remediation because of SQL Server 2005 functionality changes. The remaining issues can usually be resolved after the upgrade process, because they either have a workaround within the upgrade process or will not affect it at all.

If you expand the error in question, additional information appears, as shown in Figure 3-6.

The "Show affected object" link shows the exact objects flagged by the Upgrade Advisor process as affected, while the "Tell me more about this issue and how to resolve it" link takes you to the corresponding section of the Upgrade Advisor BOL. The UABOL describes the conditions and provides guidance regarding corrective action to address the issue. The Upgrade Advisor BOL is a true gem, as it provides guidance for problem resolution in areas beyond the scope of the tools (such as replication, SQL Server Agent, and Full-Text search).

The "This issue has been resolved" checkmark is for your personal tracking of the issues that have been resolved. This metadata checkmark is in place to support remediation processes by allowing the report to be viewed by filtered status of resolved issues or preupgrade (unresolved) issues.

If you that prefer scripting, the viewer is nothing more than a XSLT transformation applied to the XML result file located in your "My Documents\SQL Server 2005 Upgrade Advisor Reports\" directory. Individual component results and configuration files can be found in each server name-based directories. You can even export viewer-based reports to other output formats such as CSV or text.

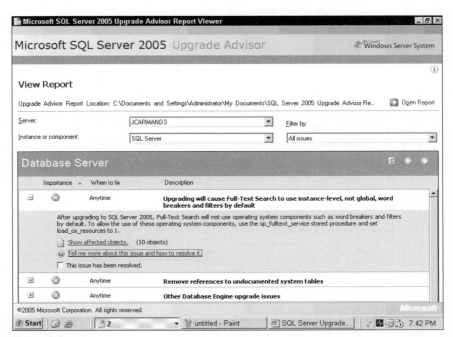

Figure 3-6

SQL Server Upgrade Assistant

If you feel comfortable with the content we have covered to date, feel free to skip to the post-upgrade checks and best-practice section of this chapter. In this section, we discuss a tool for the overachievers and Type-A personalities: the SQL Server Upgrade Assistant (SQL UA).

SQL UA was developed for use in the SQL Server 2005 application-compatibility lab engagements run as part of the Microsoft Ascend (Yukon customer training) and Touchdown (Yukon partner training) programs. The purpose of these labs was to help customers analyze their SQL Server 2000 applications to understand the impact of upgrading to SQL Server 2005 and to provide guidance on any changes that may be necessary to successfully migrate both their database and their application. The labs helped improve the quality of SQL Server 2005 by running upgrades and performing impact analysis on real customer workloads against SQL Server 2005. The labs themselves were run by Microsoft personnel and staffed by partners such as Scalability Experts. Nearly 50 labs were run worldwide, and hundreds of SQL Server 2000 applications were tested. Scalability Experts will continue to offer their expertise and the tools used to conduct the application-compatibility labs to interested parties at no charge. For more information, see the www.scalabilityexperts.com.

From a conceptual standpoint, the difference between this tool and Upgrade Advisor is that SQL UA naturally encompasses the essence of a true upgrade and testing process. By reviewing the results of a SQL Server 2000 workload against the results of the same workload being run against SQL Server 2005, you can identify upgrade blockers and application-coding changes that may be required.

We will walk you through an overview of this process and then provide details of the steps contained in the wizard-driven toolkit, which you can see in Figure 3-7. By using the wizard, you will back up all databases and the users and capture a subset of production workload. You will then restore the databases and users you just backed up and process the workload you captured. The goal of this is to develop a new output file, also known as a baseline. You will then upgrade the test server to SQL Server 2005 and rerun the workload to capture a SQL 2005 reference output for comparison.

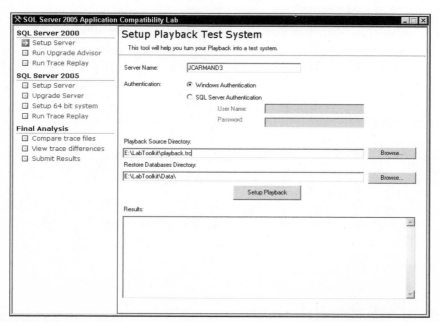

Figure 3-7

At the time of this writing, the tool is still in development, so we will not be able to provide screenshots beyond this one.

Capturing the Environment

You should establish your baseline by running DBCC CheckDB on each database and by backing up all SQL Server 2000 systems and user databases from your server. Following this step, you need to start capturing your trace file to avoid gaps in the process. When you capture a trace file, it needs to be a good representation of the workloads that characterize your environment. To do this, it might be necessary to create an artificial workload that better represents the workloads of the application over time. While capturing the trace file, it's a good idea to avoid multiserver operations such as linked server calls or bulk-copy operation. It is also equally important to know that there is a performance cost of six to ten percent while tracing. The sum of the trace files and database backups represent a repeatable and reusable workload called a playback.

Setting up the Baseline Server

Now that you have captured the playback, you can set up the baseline system that will be used for the remainder of the test. This server should be loaded with SQL Server 2000 with SP3a, which is the minimum requirement for upgrading to 2005. In reality, it should be identical to the source system in collation and patching level. The tool will then check your server for this matching. If necessary, you will be prompted to patch or rebuild the master database. It will then restore your databases in the correct order so that your DB IDs are matched to production (this will also include padding the DB creation process to accomplish this). Finally SQL UA will recreate your logins and ensure that the IDs match production as all of this is necessary to run the trace file. The next step in the process is to run the Upgrade Advisor as described earlier in this chapter. Once the environment has been remediated, you can then proceed to the next step of replaying the trace.

Running the Trace

When you run the trace, first the statistics will be updated on all databases. The replay tool will then use the API and run all of the queries within the trace file in order. The thing to keep in mind with this tool is that it is single-threaded, so it's possible that blocking can occur because we captured a multithreaded workload. To compensate for this, the tool has a blocking-detection process that runs every minute (this value is configurable). This is accomplished by monitoring and killing queries that have been running longer than two minutes. The output from this step will generate a trace-output file for comparison in the final analysis.

Upgrading to SQL Server 2005

At this point, you have two choices. You can use the tool to restore the state of the server to its baseline and then upgrade to SQL Server 2005, or you can do the old "cooking show switch" by restoring the baseline to an existing SQL Server 2005 or instance. The thing to remember here is that you are not measuring performance metrics, so these servers don't have to be identical. You are measuring workload behavior between two versions of SQL Server. After restoring the baseline on a SQL Server 2005 platform, you will go through the "Running the Trace" step again.

Final Analysis

After completing all of these processes, you can get to the final steps of comparing the output files by filtering and comparing all batches in both trace files for discrepancies. The output file generated from this comparative process is actually an XML document that can be exported or read by the trace viewer application. The viewer shows one error condition at a time by showing the last correct step, the error step, and the next correct sequences of the batch files. Once a condition has been identified, it can be filtered from the error-reviewing process to allow the DBA to focus on identifying new error conditions.

Backward Compatibility

This section of the chapter covers major changes in the product that are classified in one of three categories. These behavior changes are categorized as unsupported, discontinued, or affecting the way SQL Server 2000 behaves today. Although, the Upgrade Advisor tool will highlight these conditions if they are relevant to your environment, you should read this section to familiarize yourself with these changes.

Unsupported and Discontinued Features

From time to time, to move a technology forward, choices have to be made. For this release of SQL Server 2005, the following features are no longer available.

- ❑ English Query is no longer included, so don't look for it on your setup CD.
- ❑ `isql.exe` and `rbuildm.exe` are no longer present. You will have to use sqlcmd.exe and setup.exe instead if you need to rebuild the master database or rebuild the registry.
- ❑ The Northwind and Pubs databases have been replaced by the AdventureWorks and AdventureWorksDW databases. These new sample databases are intended to be more like real-life databases. If you really want to get your hands on Northwind or Pubs databases, they are available on the Microsoft download site.
- ❑ Allow updates option of `sp_configure` is still present but not functional.
- ❑ Metadata component of SQL Server 2000 DTS repository is deprecated as a feature. As part of the upgrade, the DTS packages will be migrated to the filesystem, and the specific tables will be present in `msdb` after upgrade.

SQL Server 2005 Deprecated Database Features

These features are no longer available as of the SQL Server 2005 release or the next scheduled release of the product. The following are some of the features scheduled for deprecation; it is recommended that you try to change these features over time with the recommended items:

Use Backup Database and Restore Database instead of the Dump Database or Dump Transaction and LOAD Database or Load Transaction (Load Headeronly) statements. These statements are available today for backward compatibility only.

In the area of security, use "Execute As" instead of SETUSER in statements. SETUSER statements are available today for backward compatibility. The following stored procedures are also scheduled for deprecation: `sp_addalias`, `sp_dropalias`, `sp_addgroup`, `sp_changegroup`, `sp_dropgroup`, `sp_helpgroup`. It is recommended that you familiarize yourself with the new security model and leverage role-based security.

For a very long time, Microsoft has told us not to use system tables, as they are subject to change. With this release, most known (documented or undocumented) system tables have been omitted. References to a few popular system tables have been preserved through the use of views such as sysusers (sys.sysusers). The remainder of them, including syslocks, have been discontinued. Therefore, this instruction:

```
Select * from syslocks
```

Will return the following results:

```
Msg 208, Level16, Stat 1, Line 1
Invalid object name 'syslocks'.
Refer to books online section "Mapping SQL Server 2000 System Tables to SQL Server
2005 system views" for list of discontinued system table and mapping to system
views.
```

Other SQL 2005 impacting Behavior Changes

The behavior changes in these features could adversely affect SQL Server migration to SQL Server 2005.

❑   Ensure that you have set AUTO_UPDATE_STATISTICS ON before you upgrade any databases. If not, the database statistics will not be updated as part of the upgrade to SQL Server 2005. This will most likely cause suboptimal query plans.

❑   Unlike the SQL Server 2000 behavior, the max server memory option in SQL Server 2005 will not take advantage of the available memory beyond its limit. If your setting is set too low, you will simply get an "insufficient system memory" error. This will happen despite memory availability beyond max server memory setting.

❑   In SQL Server 2005, the query governor cost limits option works. In SQL Server 2005, setting it to a value other than "0" means that you have enabled a server-wide query timeout value measured in seconds.

❑   SQL Server 2005 no longer supports Banyan VINES, Multiprotocol, AppleTalk, or NWLink IPX/SPX. MDAC versions 2.6 or earlier are not supported, because they do not support named instances.

❑   SQL Server 2005 does not support the creation or upgrade of databases on compressed drives. Once updated, read-only databases or filegroups can be placed on NTFS compressed drives. They must, however, be set to READ_WRITE permission prior to going through the upgrade process.

With the exception of the Model database, after the upgrade process, all databases remain in 8.0 backward-compatibility mode.

❑ Additional space will be required for data and log files. Extra space is required to maintain user objects and permissions. Additional space is required for metadata information for LOB objects on a column basis. If your database also contains full-text catalog, additional space is needed for the full-text document ID map to be stored in the data file.

Set database log and data files to autogrow during the upgrade process.

❑ Before upgrading to SQL Server 2005, use the `sp_dropextendedproc` and `sp_addextended-proc` stored procedures to reregister any extended stored procedure that was not registered with full pathname.

❑ It is a good idea to allocate additional space or to have plenty of space for tempdb to grow during the upgrade process. Overall guidance for tempdb is covered in greater detail in Chapter 14.

tempdb is responsible for managing temporary objects, row versioning, and online index rebuilds.

❑ You should disable all trace flags before upgrading to SQL Server 2005. The possibility exists that either the trace-flag functionality will be different in SQL server 2005 or will not exist. After the upgrade process, you should work with PSS to determine which (if any) of your trace flags are still required.

In SQL Server 2005, trace flags are now deterministic and can be set at the local or global level based on additional arguments (default behavior is local).

❑ Migrate to database mail. If you happen to like SQL mail, the good news is that as long as you have Outlook 2002 (or greater) as a mail client, you will be able to upgrade to SQL Server 2005.

SQL Server 2005 database mail does not have a requirement for Outlook mail client.

SQL Server Component Considerations

In this section, we discuss individual components along with their respective considerations that should be evaluated during an upgrade process. Components not covered here are covered in their individual chapters.

Upgrading Full-Text Catalog to SQL Server 2005

During the upgrade process, all databases with full-text catalog are marked full-text disabled. This is because of the potential time involved in rebuilding the catalog. Before you upgrade your Full-Text Search environment, you should familiarize yourself with some of the enhancements. In the area of manageability, there is now a Full-Text Search (MSFTSSQL) service for each SQL Server 2005 instance. Full-Text Search now supports XML data types, XML indexes, and XML queries. Full-text catalogs are now a fully integrated part of the database back-up and restore process. This functionality is also supported in the database attach and detach processes. I also recommend reading BOL to learn about additional behavior changes (for example, running the full-text actions against master and tempdb is no longer supported).

Upgrading DTS to SQL Server 2005 Integration Services (SSIS)

First, understand that SSIS is a new application. Other than in a few areas for the purpose of backward compatibility, most DTS codes never made it over to SSIS. As part of an upgrade scenario, DTS will continue to run as is. SQL Server 2000 runtime and backward-compatibility tools are installed automatically to facilitate this as a part of an upgrade process. If you are doing an install on new hardware, you can get the DTS Designer Components (2000 runtime) or backward-compatibility components from the SQL Server 2005 download site (feature pack). The DTS Designer Components will enable developers and DBAs to manage and edit DTS packages and components in a SQL Server 2005 environment. The SQL Server Backward Compatibility package includes all of the DTS Designer Components and additional support for SQL-DMO, DSO, and SQL VDI technologies. These components emulate SQL Server 2004 SP4 functionality.

The DTS 2000 packages will continue to run in a mixed environment. For example, packages can call each other via DTS API from one version to the other. In our experience, most DTS 2000 packages continue to run at plus or minus 10 percent of their original performance level. To achieve the promise of SQL Server Integration Services, you will most likely need to redesign your existing packages. Microsoft provides the means of migrating your existing packages from the command line via DTSMigrationWizard.exe or from applications like Business Intelligence (BI) Studio and SQL Server Workbench. These wizards are only available in the Standard, Enterprise, and Developer editions of the product.

These wizards provide a "best attempt style" migration; that is, the wizard will do a task-for-task migration. Complex tasks that cannot be converted get encapsulated in a 2000 construct as part of the package migration. To avoid errors with the migration of your DTS packages, you should test them with the Upgrade Advisor tool, covered later in this chapter. Neither Upgrade Advisor nor the DTS Migration Wizard can process SQL Server 7.0 packages that have not been saved to disk. To make things worse, SQL Server 7.0 packages must be upgraded to SSIS completely, because they cannot be maintained with the 2000 runtime after upgrade.

Figure 3-8 shows a SQL Server 2000 managed by Management Studio. As you can see, the "Northwind Orders Schema" package is stored locally and can be found nested in the DTS folder, which is in the legacy folder that can be found under the management folder.

As an example, we'll walk through migrating this simple DTS 2000 package. This package builds four dimensions and a fact table from Northwind database. With the exception of the "Time Dimension," which relies on a Visual Basic script to parse out levels of a time dimension, this package is simple in nature.

From the Management Studio environment, right-click the Northwind Orders Schema package and select the Migrate option. The first step of the migration wizard asks for the source of the package or packages, specifically, which SQL Server or directory they reside in. In this example, the file resides on a SQL 2000 Server. The wizard then asks you to select a destination location for the migrated package. As you can see in Figure 3-9, the options are for a SQL Server destination or a DTSX file repository.

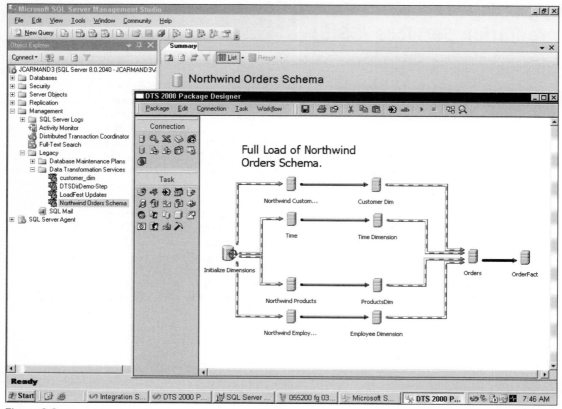

Figure 3-8

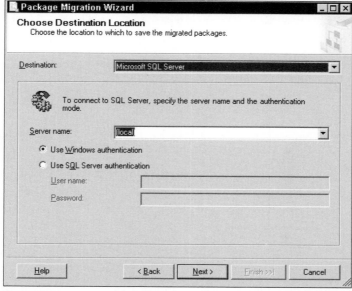

Figure 3-9

Select a local SQL Server 2005 instance as the destination. The next step presents you with a listing of packages that reside on the source server, as shown in Figure 3-10. After selecting the lone package, enter the location of the error log to be captured for the migration process. Note that only copies of the original packages actually get migrated. The original packages are left functional and intact.

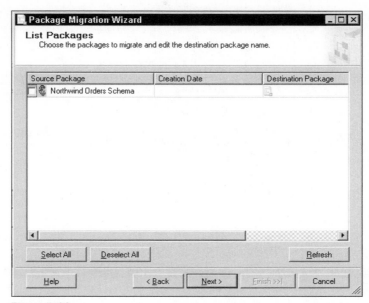

Figure 3-10

Other than maintenance packages and simple import/export wizard-based packages, authoring of packages is no longer supported on the server side. All packages (SSIS or DTS) must be authored in the BI workbench and imported to production server from development.

Finally, you'll see a summary screen of all your previous choices, allowing you to do a final check of everything. With the next click, the process of migrating a copy of the actual package is kicked off. Figure 3-11 identifies the migrated package shown in the SQL Server 2005 Integration Services instance. Meanwhile, the original package remains intact as part of the SQL Server 2000 "SharePointPortal" named instance.

We opted to do the migration from the SQL Server Workbench to make a point: The packages are independent of each other and fully functional. The ideal place to perform this migration would have been in the BI Workbench. To accomplish this, you would have started a new SSIS project and selected a migration option. The steps for the migration would have been identical from that point on. What makes the BI Workbench the ideal location for the migration is that it provides the ability to edit the package after migration.

Although we will not introduce SSIS to you here, we will briefly discuss the concepts for ease of conversation. SSIS will be presented in greater detail in the BI chapters of the book: 6, 7, and 8. An SSIS package is made up of one control-flow construct (or container) and one or many data-flow constructs (or containers). The control flow is more of a process construct made up of tasks such as FTP, e-mail, Sequence Containers, and Data Flow Tasks. The Data Flow Task is a pipeline-transformation construct optimized to transform the data from process to process (or task to task) all in-flight. Tasks that perform actions such as sorting, aggregation, data-type conversions, and conditional splits make up the data-flow pipeline. Figure 3-12 shows a control-flow view of the migrated package.

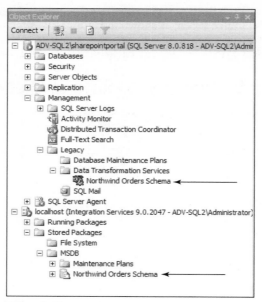

Figure 3-11

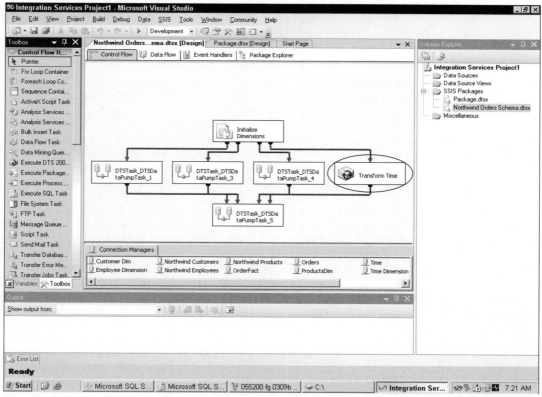

Figure 3-12

As part of the migration, each of the DTS pipeline tasks is transformed into distinct tasks. This creates a total of six tasks: one Execute SQL task for the truncate tables statements, a data-flow task for each of the pipeline tasks (one per dimension), and one to load the fact table. The highlighted component called "transform time" is the "Time Dimension" that we mentioned as not being migrateable, because of the use of Visual Basic. If you edit this task, you'll be presented with properties about this task. The cool thing to remember here is that this task now has the capabilities of a SQL Server 2005 environment, meaning that you can take advantage of feature-like expressions by wrapping this task as part of a looping transform or a sequence container. To see the actual task, all you have to do is to edit it again, and it will be presented in a DTS 2000 environment, as shown in Figure 3-13.

Remember that although the SSIS team tried to preserve the look and feel of DTS, the tool has been completely redesigned from the ground up. SSIS is not included as a feature of Express; all existing packages will now have to be managed by another edition. If you try to save a DTS package in the Meta Data repository after applying SP4, you'll find that this feature is no longer supported. So, it's now official — SQL server 2000 Meta Data Services is a deprecated feature. To learn more about SSIS, read Books Online, or see *Professional SQL Server 2005 Integration Services,* by Brian Knight, et al (Wrox, 2006).

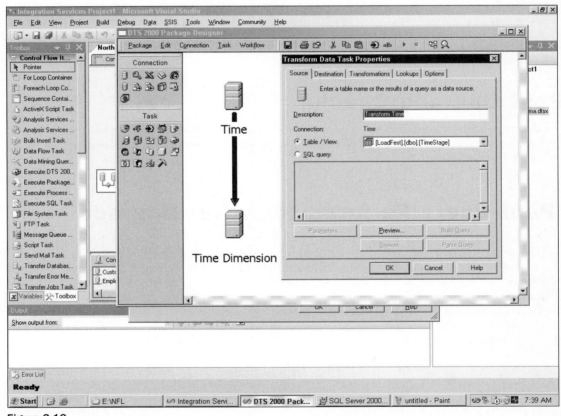

Figure 3-13

Log Shipping

SQL Server 7.0 and 2000 log-shipping sessions cannot be directly upgraded. SQL Server 2000 implemented log shipping through `xp_sqlmaint`, which is no longer available in SQL Server 2005. Because of this, you will have to reconfigure these sessions after upgrading to SQL Server 2005 or evaluate a different option. Refer to Chapter 19 for available upgrade options and details.

Failover Clustering

Failover clustering has undergone a few modifications that make the upgrade process a bit more complex. You will not be able to downgrade your cluster from SQL Server 2000 Enterprise Edition to SQL Server 2005 Standard Edition. Upgrading your existing cluster is discussed in detail in Chapter 20.

Upgrading to 64-bit

Upgrading from a SQL Server 7.0 or 2000 32-bit to SQL Server 2005 64-bit platform is not supported. Although running SQL Server 2000 with Service Pack 4 32-bit on a Windows on Windows 64-bit (WOW) subsystem is supported, upgrading this configuration to SQL Server 2005 64-bit environment is not supported. Side-by-side migration is the only supported upgrade path for migrating databases from 32-bit to 64-bit platform.

Post Upgrade Checks

The information being shared with you in the following sections is really about product behaviors that have surprised a lot of people. Paying attention to this information will ensure that you do not place a call to Premier Support.

Poor Query Performance After Upgrade

A possible reason for poor query performance after upgrading to SQL 2005 is that the old statistics are considered outdated and cannot be used by the query optimizer. For most situations, this should not be an issue as long as you have enabled the autoupdate statistics and autocreate statistics options. This will allow for statistics to be automatically updated by default when needed for query compilation. It is important to keep in mind that the statistics built from these features are only built from sampled data. Therefore, they are less accurate than statistics built from sampling the entire column. In databases with large tables, or in tables where previous statistics were created with fullscan, the difference in quality would cause the SQL Server 2005 query optimizer to produce a suboptimal query plan.

Anytime an index gets created, the statistics that are part of that dataset are based on fullscan. In SQL Server 2005, they are created at index-creation time, which is a new feature.

To mitigate this issue, you should update the statistics immediately after upgrading to SQL Server 2005. Using `sp_updatestats` with the `resample` argument will rebuild statistics based on inherited sampling ratio for all existing statistics. Typically, that ends up being a full sample for index-based statistics and sampled statistics for the rest of the columns. An additional benefit that could be gained from this process is that if the data is less than 8MB, (new minimum sampling size), the statistics will also be built with fullscan.

Since we are already discussing statistics, I will take the opportunity to go over a few improvements in this area. There have been numerous additions to the statistics that SQL Server 2005 collects. This allows for the optimizer to better evaluate the resources needed and the cost of different methods for getting information from tables or indexes. Although this process is a bit more expensive in SQL Server 2005, the benefits far outweigh the costs. Multicolumn statistics are now possible. You can use the following sample code to have a quick look at this cool feature.

```
use adventureWorksDW
go
sp_helpstats 'dbo.DimCustomer', 'ALL'
GO

-- Create a multi-column statistics object on DimCustomer.
CREATE STATISTICS FirstLast ON dbo.DimCustomer(FirstName,LastName)
GO

-- Validate that multi-column statistics created on DimCustomer.
sp_helpstats 'dbo.DimCustomer', 'ALL'
GO

Drop Statistics dbo.DimCustomer.FirstLast
GO

-- Create a multi-column index and a multi-column statistic is also created on
table
-- DimCustomer
CREATE INDEX demo_firstlast
    ON dbo.DimCustomer (FirstName,LastName);
GO

-- Drop a multi-column index and a multi-colum statistic will also be dropped from
-- table DimCustomer
Drop Index demo_firstlast  on dbo.DimCustomer
go
```

Autocreate statistics can only create single-column statistics.

Statistics have been added for large-object support, such as images, text, and the new-max data types. Improvements have also been introduced in the area of computed columns. Statistics can now be manually or automatically created. In addition, autocreate statistics can generate statistics on computed columns if they are needed. Along with support for date correlation across multiple tables, string-summary statistics have also been added, specifically string-summary statistics to assist with 'Like' operators by maintaining frequency-distribution information. The date-correlation optimization feature supports faster join queries across tables when correlated between date-time columns. Statistics on partitioned tables are maintained at the table level, not at the partition level. There have also been improvements in the compilation and recompilation logic. Minimal sample size has been increased to 8MB. Improvements in optimizer resulted in better selectivity of the statistics to be evaluated for a particular operation and in the evaluation process as part of these operations.

There are numerous additional statistical enhancements that the optimizer has to take into consideration beyond the ones that I mentioned. The reason that I am discussing this is twofold.

The default sampling for creating statistics on a table is one percent, and there are times when that will not be enough. Therefore, we recommend that you either update the sample to 10 to 20 percent or, if time allows, go for a full sampling (with fullscan) for tables that approach 100 million rows. Second, the behavior change associated with this enhancement is a longer compilation time, which ultimately results in a more efficient execution plan. Although the cost of compilation is higher, it is well justified, as the resulting complied plan is leveraged by the subsequent queries in delivering much faster query results.

For these reasons, if your application uses mostly dynamic SQL, it could see overall performance degradation. But don't worry; the SQL Server team implemented features such as simple and forced parameterization to assist in these scenarios. The role of these features is to parameterize dynamic queries by creating execution plans that could be leveraged by similar queries. The goals of these features are to minimize the parse and compilation times. The benefits will vary from workload to workload. Understanding these features and selecting and applying the correct feature (simple or forced parameterization) will help you mitigate the incremental cost.

Surface Area Configuration Tool

At the server level, there are behavioral changes between SQL Server 2000 and 2005. First, we recommend familiarizing yourself with the Surface Area Configuration tool (SAC). It is one of the five menu choices you have when you choose Configuration Tools under the Microsoft SQL Server 2005 directory. As Figure 3-14 shows, you have two choices: the Surface Area Configuration for Services and Connections tool and the Surface Area Configuration for Features tool.

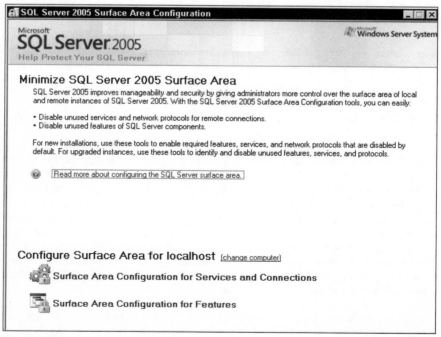

Figure 3-14

Surface Area Configuration for Services and Connections tool

This interface allows you to configure all of the SQL Server component services installed. From there you can also select the availability for local and remote connections to both SQL Server instances and Analysis Services instances. It is also possible to choose whether the protocols allowed will be only TCP/IP, only Named Pipes, or both.

Banyan VINES, Multiprotocol, AppleTalk, and NWLink IPX/SPX protocol are no longer supported.

Surface Area Configuration Features tool

From this interface, you can configure features, and again, you can view them by instance or by component.

These SQL Servers Database features are off by default:

- ❑ Ad-Hoc Remote Queries
- ❑ CLR Integration
- ❑ Dedicated Administrator Connection (DAC)
- ❑ Database Mail
- ❑ Native XML Web Services
- ❑ OLE Automation
- ❑ Service Broker
- ❑ SQL Mail
- ❑ Web Assistant
- ❑ xp_cmdshell

These SQL Analysis Services features are off by default:

- ❑ Ad-Hoc Data Mining Queries
- ❑ Anonymous Connections
- ❑ Linked Objects
- ❑ User Defined Functions

These Reporting Services features are off by default:

- ❑ Scheduled Events and Reports Delivery
- ❑ Web Services and HTTP Access
- ❑ Windows Integrated Security

Additional information on these features is available from the Surface Area Configuration tool itself or from Books Online.

Features enabled as part of an upgrade will still be enabled after the upgrade. Only new features will be disabled.

As part of upgrading to SQL Server 2005, it is a great time to evaluate and reflect whether features that you have installed should be turned off. This will help reduce your area of exposure to external and potentially internal treats brought on by your developers.

Update Usage Counters

In previous versions of SQL Server, the values for the table and index row counts and page counts could become incorrect. To correct invalid row or page counts, it's recommended that you run DBCC UPDATEUSAGE on all databases following the upgrade. These inaccuracies may cause incorrect space-usage reports returned by the sp_spaceused system stored procedure. This issue has been resolved in SQL Server 2005. Databases created on SQL Server 2005 should never experience incorrect counts; however, databases upgraded to SQL Server 2005 may contain invalid counts.

Summary

In this chapter, we covered the compelling proof point of why to upgrade. We reviewed strategies and tools that can be leveraged to ensure a successful upgrade. Several deprecated features were identified, along with features whose behavior change could also affect your upgrade. Now that we have done the groundwork for a successful upgrade, let's jump into familiarizing you with the new management environment.

4

Managing and Troubleshooting the Database Engine

With the server now installed or upgraded, the first thing you need to do is configure it for your environment. In this chapter, we discuss how to configure your SQL Server instance. After configuring the instance, we show you how to manage the instance with Management Studio and a number of stored procedures or DMVs. The chapter also covers how to monitor connections on your SQL Server and how to troubleshoot problems.

This chapter assumes you already know the basics of Management Studio navigation and focuses on what you'll need to know as a DBA. Many other chapters in this book spend much of their time driving into certain areas of Management Studio, and those points have been left out of this chapter (backing up your database, for example, is covered in Chapter 18).

Configuration Tools

Now that you have SQL Server installed, or have upgraded to SQL Server 2005, it will probably not be configured specifically for you out of the box. In SQL Server 2005, Microsoft has chosen to reduce the feature set of SQL Server dramatically out of the box by turning off features after installation. The features turned off may vary based on the edition of SQL Server. For example, TCP/IP is disabled in Developer edition by default, and every edition has CLR integration turned off. This makes the environment more usable for you as an administrator by not having features you don't care about crowding your administration screen. It also reduces the options that a hacker can use to penetrate your system.

SQL Server Configuration Manager

The SQL Server Configuration Manager configures the SQL Server services much like the Services applet in the control panel, but it has much more functionality than the applet. For example, the program can also change what ports SQL Server listens on and what protocols each instance uses. You can open the program (Figure 4-1) from Start ⇨ SQL Server 2005 ⇨ Configuration Tools.

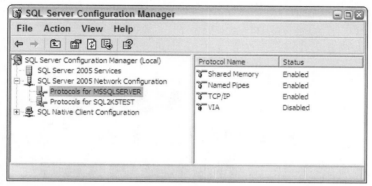

Figure 4-1

You can select the SQL Server 2005 Services tree to configure the various SQL Server services. To configure an individual service such as SQL Server, double-click the service name to open the service Properties page. In the Log On tab, you can configure which account starts SQL Server. We recommend that you start SQL Server with a regular domain user account with minimal rights. The account should not have the privilege to Log on Locally, for example. There is no reason for the account to be a local or domain administrator in SQL Server 2005. Additionally, you should create a nonexpiring password so your SQL Server doesn't immediately cease to start. If you don't see the SQL Server services communicating outside the instance's machine, you could start the service with the Local System account, but the account may have more local rights than you wish. (We talk more about this in Chapter 9.)

In the Service tab, you can specify whether you'd like the service to start automatically, manually, or be disabled. If you go to the Advanced tab (shown in Figure 4-2) for each service, you can configure the more interesting options. For example, here you can turn off Customer Feedback Reporting. This feature enables Microsoft to receive utilization reports from your SQL Server. Even if you wanted to do this, in most production environments your SQL Server may not be able to send the report, due to a lack of Internet access from production servers.

The Error Reporting option in the Advanced tab will e-mail Microsoft whenever a critical error has occurred. The minimal information is sent over a secure HTTPS protocol. Alternatively, you may also wish to send these errors to your own internal Corporate Error Reporting (CER) system, which is a product that you can download from Microsoft.

In the SQL Server 2005 Network Configuration page in Configuration Manager, you can see a list of network protocols that SQL Server is listening on by instance. If you wish to turn a protocol on or off, you can do so by right-clicking the protocol and selecting Enable or Disable. By enabling only the Shared Memory protocol, you turn off all communication to the instance outside your single server.

Figure 4-2

SQL Server Surface Area Configuration

When SQL Server 2005 shipped, it added a large number of new features that some DBAs considered controversial. For example, many DBAs were frightened (to put the term lightly) by the CLR integration feature and did not want it turned on by default. To keep the system secure and more usable, Microsoft decided to turn off many features by default. The SQL Server Surface Area Configuration tool (also called SQL SAC) is the tool you can use to turn on many of the features turned off in SQL Server by default and its ancillary products. When you open the tool, you can choose whether you want to configure the Services and Connections or Features. The Services and Connections page allows you to configure the SQL Server services and networks much like the SQL Server Configuration Manager we covered earlier. The Features page allows you to turn on given features such as SQL CLR Integration.

You can click Change Computer to point the tool at a remote server for configuration, if you have permission to do so. If you click Services and Connections, you can see a part of the tool that in many ways looks like the SQL Server Configuration Manager. For example, a good portion of the tool gives you an interface to configure how the SQL Server services will start (automatic, manual, or disabled).

The most important area to configure in this part of the configuration tool is under the Database Engine tree, under Remote Connections (Figure 4-3). In this section, you can specify whether you wish SQL Server to allow remote connections or only be limited to connections from within your workstation or server. This setting is set to Local Connections Only in the Developer, Evaluation, and SQL Express editions of SQL Server. This is because in usability studies, most used these editions for local development or applications and never required external connections. If you set this setting to Local and Remote Connections, you can specify what protocols you want SQL Server to listen on, and the setting will also be mirrored in the SQL Server Configuration Manager. A similar setting is also available for the Analysis Services service, but the service must be running to enable it.

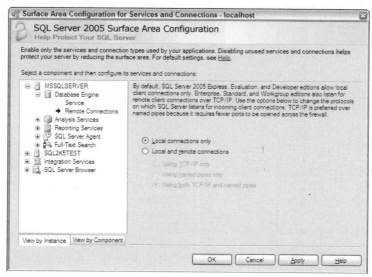

Figure 4-3

Changing this setting will require that you stop and start SQL Server at some point.

The biggest part of the product is under the Configuration for Features area of the application, which you can get to from the main page by clicking Surface Area Configuration for Features. The SQL Server services must be started in order to configure the services using this application, and you can only use the tool to manage SQL Server 2005 instances. You can click View by Instance or View by Component to sort the features in different methods.

The Ad-Hoc Remote Queries page allows you to turn on the OpenRowSet and OpenDataSource functions. The functions allow you to connect to a SQL Server and then use that server to connect to other servers and run queries. These two functions are disabled by default because if the functions are not protected, they can be exploited by a hacker. For example, a hacker can use SQL injection to connect to your SQL Server through your Web server and then attack other servers from the valid connection. You should keep this setting off unless you have a strong need to use the feature.

On the CLR Integration page, you can enable one of the most controversial features for an administrator: CLR integration. With this disabled, developers will not be able to use one of the most developer-centric features in SQL Server 2005. If the developer tries to use CLR, he or she will receive an error.

In the DAC page, you can turn on the Dedicated Administrator Connection. Essentially, it allows an administrator to gain access to your SQL Server when the CPU is at full utilization and normal users can't do anything. This connection is given extra priority, and Microsoft was worried that administrators would use the connection for day-to-day work and so disabled it.

You should only use a DAC in special circumstances. For example, in some cases, you may find that a user is running a query that has utilized all of your system's resources. The user may be using so much of the system's resources that no other users, including yourself, can log in to the system to kill the user's connection. This would be a great use for the DAC. Under this situation before, you would have to stop and start the SQL Server if some time had passed. With the DAC enabled, as a DBA you can log in if you have sysadmin rights by qualifying the server with ADMIN:. For example, if you wanted to log in to the localhost machine, you would use ADMIN:localhost. You will receive an error if the feature is disabled.

In the Database Mail page, you can enable the new Database Mail feature. This feature allows you to send e-mail from your database server using SMTP. The stored procedures that this feature uses are not turned on by default and must be enabled here. (We talk more about this feature in Chapter 5.)

In the Native XML Web Services page, you can quickly see in one console which Web services are enabled. Then you can disable services that you do not wish to be listening. The Services Broker page operates much the same way with Service Broker queues.

Two of the most dangerous extended stored procedures in SQL Server are the OLE Automation stored procedures (ones that begin with SP_OA and xp_cmdshell). The OLE Automation extended stored procedures allow a T-SQL programmer to instantiate objects inside a T-SQL script, like objects for e-mail or a third-party component. All of that functionality can be replaced with CLR integration, but the feature was left in, although turned off, for backward compatibility. The xp_cmdshell stored procedure is used by hackers and DBAs to shell out to DOS and run executables. The problem is that hackers can do this to run dangerous commands against your machine.

Two other legacy features are also disabled by default. The SQL Mail feature is what SQL Server 2000 used to send mail through MAPI and has been replaced by Database Mail. The Web Assistant stored procedures allow you to create a Web page from a SQL query and are not generally used by DBAs.

Most of the options that you set here will require that you stop and start the SQL Server instance that you're configuring in order to make the setting active.

Startup Parameters

SQL Server has an array of switches you can use to troubleshoot or enable advanced settings for the database engine. You can do this by setting the switches for the service or by running SQL Server from a command prompt. One way you can change the SQL Server service's startup parameters so it uses the switch every time is in SQL Server Configuration Manager. In the SQL Server 2005 Services page, double-click SQL Server (MSSQLServer by default but may vary based on your instance name) and go to the Advanced tab. Add any switches you wish in the Startup Parameters option, separated by semicolons. You can see in Figure 4-4 that one additional switch is enabled: -f. We'll discuss this switch momentarily.

The second way to start SQL Server is by running sqlservr.exe from the command prompt. The file is located by default in the C:\Program Files\Microsoft SQL Server\MSSQL.1\MSSQL\Binn directory. You can then turn on any nondefault parameters you wish by adding the switch after sqlservr.exe, as shown in Figure 4-5. This is generally the preferred way to start your SQL Server in a one-off debug mode, since you won't leave any settings intact that you may not want to. You can stop the SQL Server by using the Ctrl+C combination or by closing the command prompt window. Never start SQL Server this way on an ongoing basis; after you log off the machine, your command prompt will close, stopping SQL Server.

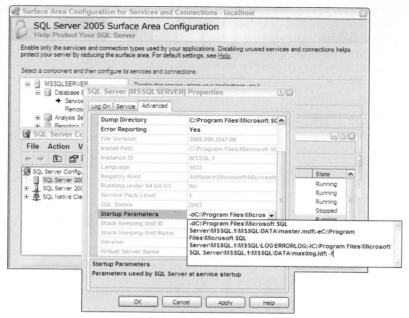

Figure 4-4

Figure 4-5

The startup options are really useful in troubleshooting a problem or for solving quick, one-off problems. We won't cover all the switches in this section but instead want to give you the ones you may find yourself using on a periodic basis. You can obtain the rest of the switches by using the -? switch. For example, you can change which master database the SQL Server is using, by using the –d and –l switches:

```
SQLServr.exe -d C:\temp\TempMasterDB.mdf -lC:\temp\TempMasterLog.ldf
```

The –d switch specifies the database file, and the –l switch specifies the log file. This may be useful if you want to use a temporary configuration of the master database that may not be corrupt. Another useful switch is the –T, which enables you to start given trace flags for all the connections for a SQL Server instance. This can be used, for example, to turn on a trace flag to monitor deadlocks in your SQL Server instance (note that it is uppercase):

```
SQLServr.exe -T1204
```

We discuss much more about trace flags later in this chapter. The –g switch is used to reserve additional memory outside SQL Server's main memory pool for use by extended stored procedures, mainly. This should never be turned on unless you see the following error messages in your SQL Server error log:

```
WARNING: Failed to reserve < n > bytes of contiguous memory.
WARNING: Failed to reserve contiguous memory of Size= 65536.
WARNING: Due to low virtual memory, special reserved memory
used < X > times since startup. Increase virtual memory on server.
```

The –m switch puts SQL Server in single-user mode and suspends the CHECKPOINT process, which writes data from disk to the database device. This switch is useful when you wish to recover the master database from a backup. The –f switch places SQL Server in minimal mode and only allows a single connection. By placing SQL Server in minimal mode, SQL Server suspends the CHECKPOINT process, and remote connections are not allowed. Probably the most important options disabled in minimal mode are user-defined startup stored procedures. An administrator may have defined a startup stored procedure that is causing problems and not allowing SQL Server to fully start. You can place SQL Server in minimal mode, remove or correct the startup stored procedure, and then start SQL Server again without the switch to repair the problem.

Make sure you stop SQL Server Agent before placing SQL Server in single-user mode. Otherwise, SQL Server Agent will take the only available connection.

Startup Stored Procedures

Startup stored procedures execute T-SQL whenever the SQL Server instance is started. For example, you may have a startup stored procedure that e-mails you when the instance starts. You can also use startup stored procedures to create objects in the tempdb when SQL Server starts. These stored procedures run under the sysadmin server role, and only a sysadmin can create a startup stored procedure. Errors written out from the stored procedure will be written to the SQL Server error log. Make sure that you only do the examples in this section against a development server until you're certain you want to do this in production.

By default, SQL Server does not scan for startup stored procedures. To enable it to do so, you must use sp_configure, as follows:

```
sp_configure 'scan for startup procs', 1
RECONFIGURE
```

After you run this, you must restart the SQL Server instance to commit the setting. Try a simple example. First, create a table called SQLStartupLog in the master database that will log any time the SQL Server instance is started.

```
CREATE TABLE master.dbo.SQLStartupLog
(StartTime datetime)
GO
```

Next, create a stored procedure to log in to the table. The following stored procedure will do the trick, logging the current date to the table.

```
CREATE PROC master.dbo.InsertSQLStartupLog
as
INSERT INTO master.dbo.SQLStartupLog
SELECT GETDATE()
```

Last, you need to use the sp_procoption stored procedure to make the stored procedure a startup stored procedure. The sp_procoption stored procedure sets only one parameter. First, you must specify the stored procedure you wish to set; the only available option name is startup with a value of 1 (on) or 0 (off). Before running the following stored procedure, ensure that your SQL Server will scan for startup stored procedures.

```
sp_procoption @ProcName = 'master.dbo.InsertSQLStartupLog',
  @OptionName= 'startup',
  @OptionValue = 1
```

Next, stop and start your SQL Server instance and query the master.dbo.SQLStartupLog to see if the record was written. Before you leave this section, make sure that you disable the setting by running the following query:

```
sp_procoption @ProcName = 'master.dbo.InsertSQLStartupLog',
  @OptionName= 'startup',
  OptionValue = 0

USE MASTER
GO
DROP TABLE master.dbo.SQLStartupLog
DROP PROC dbo.InsertSQLStartupLog
```

Rebuilding the System Databases

If one of your system databases becomes corrupt and your backups cannot be found, it may be time to rebuild the system databases. This will essentially reinstall the system databases and rid your system of anything that may be causing it to act unpredictably. The repercussion of this is that you must reinstall any service packs, and all your user-defined databases, including the Reporting Services support database, will disappear. Additionally, any logins or server configurations will have to be redone.

Rebuilding your system databases should not be taken lightly. It is a high-impact technical decision when all else fails. When you rebuild the system databases, the databases may appear to have disappeared, but their files are still in the operating system and can be reattached or restored. Reattaching the databases is generally the lowest-impact action.

To rebuild your system databases, locate your SQL Server installation media and go to a command prompt. From the command prompt, run `setup.exe` as if you were installing SQL Server, but you'll need to pass in a few new switches:

```
start /wait setup.exe /qn INSTANCENAME=<InstanceName> REINSTALL=SQL_Engine
REBUILDDATABASE=1 SAPWD=<NewStrongPassword>
```

The `/qn` switch will suppress any error or information messages and send them to the error log. You will essentially see a blank screen for a few minutes before the database is finally rebuilt. You can append the `/qb` switch to see some of the messages. If you are reinstalling the system databases for the default instance, use `MSSQLSERVER` for your instance name.

After the databases are rebuilt, you are returned to your default configuration and databases. You will need to restore the master database (more on this in Chapter 18) or reattach each user-defined database and recreate the logins. The preferable option, of course, is to recover the master database. Then your logins and databases will automatically appear.

Management Studio

As you probably know by now, SQL Server Management Studio is where a DBA spends most of his or her time. In the tool, you can perform most of your management tasks and run queries. It's a major evolution of Enterprise Manager (SQL Server 2000's management interface) and uses a light version of Visual Studio 2005. Since this is a professional-level book, we won't go into every aspect of Management Studio, but we will cover some of the more common and advanced features that you might like to use for administration.

Reports

One of the most impressive enhancements to the SQL Server management environment is the integrated reports that help a DBA in each area of administration. There are two levels of reports (server level and database level) and each runs as a Reporting Services report inside of SQL Server Management Studio. Server-level reports give you information about the instance of SQL Server and the operating system. Database-level reports drill into information about each database. You must have access to each database you wish to report on, or your login must have enough rights to run the server-level report.

Server Reports

You can access server-level reports from the Summary tab in Management Studio, by left-clicking the instance of SQL Server you wish to retrieve information on and then selecting the report from the Report drop-down box in the Summary Window. If the Summary Window is not active, select Summary under the View menu.

A report favorite at the server level is the Server Dashboard, which is shown in Figure 4-6. The Server Dashboard report gives you a wealth of information about your SQL Server 2005 instance:

❑ What edition and version you're running of SQL Server

❑ Anything for that instance that is not configured to the default SQL Server settings

❑ The IO and CPU statistics by type of activity (ad-hoc queries, Reporting Services, and so on)

❑ High-level configuration information such as whether the instance is clustered or using AWE

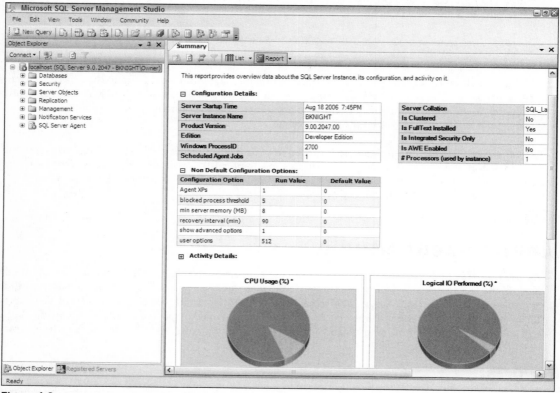

Figure 4-6

Keep in mind that the server and database reports that you see in Management Studio pull from Dynamic Management Views (DMVs) in some cases. Because of that, the data may only be as current as the last time you started SQL Server. For example, the Server Dashboard has a few graphs that show the CPU usage by type of query. This graph is not historical and instead is only showing you the CPU usage for the period of time that SQL Server has been online.

Database Reports

Database reports operate much like server-level reports but are executed when you have the database selected in Management Studio. With these reports, you can see information that pertains to the database that you have selected. For example, you can see all the transactions currently running against a database, users being blocked, or disk utilization for a given database, as shown in Figure 4-7.

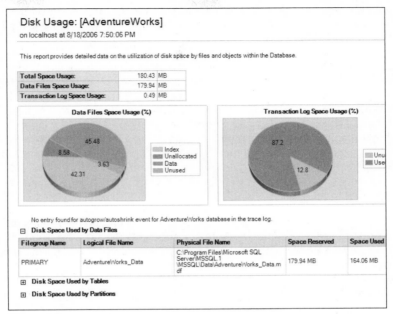

Figure 4-7

Configuring SQL Server

There are a few ways to configure your SQL Server. One mechanism covered earlier is to use SQL Configuration Manager or Surface Area Configuration. These two features will help you turn on various features and services. They do not, however, help you configure the individual instances. For the database engine, you have two main methods to configure the instance: the sp_configure stored procedure or the Server Properties screen. To access the Server Properties screen, you can right-click the database engine you wish to configure in Management Studio and select Properties. Be careful before altering the configuration of your instance. If you adjust some of these settings, you could affect your instance's performance or security. We'll talk about a few of the more important settings in this section, but we'll cover more throughout the entire book.

Using the Server Properties screen is much more user friendly, but it doesn't provide all the options available to you through sp_configure. The General tab in the Server Properties screen shows you information about your SQL Server instance that cannot be altered, such as the version of SQL Server you currently have installed and whether your instance is clustered. It also provides server information, such as the number of processors and amount of memory on the machine. Keep in mind that just because your server has 2GB of RAM available doesn't mean that all of that RAM is available to SQL Server.

In the Memory page of the Server Properties screen, you can see how much memory SQL Server is configured to use. By default, SQL Server is configured to use as much memory as the OS and the edition of SQL Server will allow it to consume. Typically, it is a good idea in your environment to set a floor of the minimum amount of memory that your instances will start to use. You can also turn on AWE from this screen. AWE enabled SQL Server 32 bit machines to utilize more memory once you pass 4 GB of RAM. (We talk much more about this feature in Chapter 11.)

In the Processors page, you can confine SQL Server to use given processors for I/O or threading operations. This is useful typically if you have eight or more CPUs and more than one instance of SQL Server. You may have one instance use four processors and the other instance use the other four processors. In some cases, when you have a large number of concurrent connections to your SQL Server, you may wish to set the Maximum Worker Threads option. Configuring this to 0 (default) allows SQL Server to automatically and dynamically find the best number of threads to allow on the processor. These threads are used for managing connections and other system functions such as performing CHECKPOINTs. Generally, leaving this setting alone will give you optimal performance. You can also select the SQL Server Priority option to force Windows to assign a higher priority to the SQL Server process. This setting may be tempting to set, but you should only adjust it after thorough testing.

In the Security page, you can adjust whether your SQL Server accepts connections through SQL Server and Windows Authentication or Windows Authentication only. This same question is asked during the setup of the instance, and this screen gives you another opportunity to change the setting. Under the Login Auditing section, you should always have at least Failed Logins Only selected. This will allow SQL Server to audit anytime someone mistypes a password or is trying to force their way into the instance. (We talk much more about the other security settings on this page in Chapter 9.)

In the Connections page (shown in Figure 4-8), you can adjust the default connection properties. One of the handy settings here that is sometimes set is the Query Governor. This setting may be a bit misleading to the DBA. The setting will tell SQL Server that if any SQL Server query is estimated to take more than the specified number of seconds, it will be terminated prior to execution. You can adjust this setting without having to restart your instance, and it can be overridden at a connection level if the connection uses the following syntax and is a sysadmin:

```
SET QUERY_GOVERNOR_COST_LIMIT 120
```

This query specifies that SQL Server will allow queries to execute estimated to use less than 120 seconds. If any query is sent to SQL Server that is estimated to take longer than this (200 seconds, in my case), the user's query will be cancelled, and he or she will receive the following error:

```
Msg 8649, Level 17, State 1, Line 4
The query has been canceled because the estimated cost of this query (200) exceeds
the configured threshold of 120. Contact the system administrator.
```

Because this setting is using the estimated cost of the query, it may not be perfect. The Query Optimizer may estimate that a query will take two seconds to run, but in actuality it takes 45 seconds sometimes, based on the system conditions. In this screen, you can also set default connection options if someone has not explicitly defined connection settings. A good one to set here would be SET NOCOUNT. This setting will stop the "8 Rows Affected" message from being sent to the client if they do not request it. There is a small performance enhancement by doing this, since this message is an additional recordset sent from SQL Server and may be unneeded traffic.

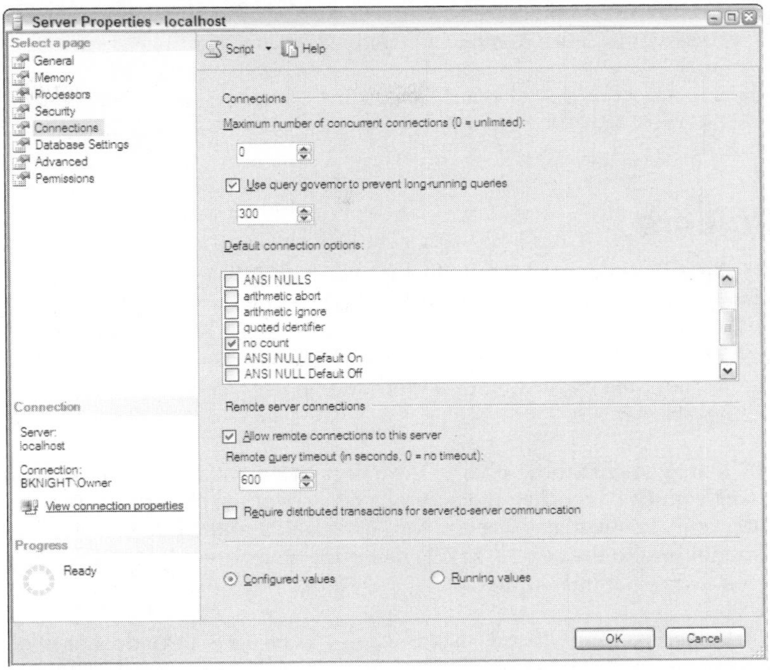

Figure 4-8

In the Database Settings page, a potentially great setting to set is the database and log default locations. A best practice is to separate data and log onto different drives. This allows you to get the most out of your RAID system, which we discuss in Chapter 11. The default setting, though, is to place the log and data files on the same drive under the `%System Drive%\Program Files\Microsoft SQL Server\MSSQL.1\Data` and `Log` directories.

If you want to configure the instance by using `sp_configure`, you can start by running the command without any parameters to see the current configuration. When you do this, you will by default only see the basic settings (about 14 as of Service Pack 1). Many settings that you'll want to configure are considered advanced. To see these options, you'll need to configure the instance to display advanced options. You can do this by running `sp_configure` as shown here:

```
sp_configure 'show advanced options', 1
RECONFIGURE
```

The setting is not moved from configured value to a running value until the RECONFIGURE command is issued. In some cases, you may have to issue a RECONFIGURE WITH OVERRIDE for some settings that will need a restart of the SQL Server instance. If you need to set one of these settings, you will be notified with a message, as shown here:

```
Msg 5807, Level 16, State 1, Line 1
Recovery intervals above 60 minutes not recommended. Use the RECONFIGURE WITH
OVERRIDE statement to force this configuration.
```

The following code shows you how to issue the override for the setting. After you set this, you will need to restart your SQL Server instance to make it effective.

```
EXEC sp_configure 'recovery interval', 90
RECONFIGURE WITH OVERRIDE
GO
```

Filtering Objects

SQL Server 2000 used an object model called DMO and SQL-NS to retrieve the list of objects for Enterprise Manager. When you had dozens or hundreds of objects to display, it would sometimes take minutes to display the list in Enterprise Manager because the old object models weren't built for showing that many objects. This became a problem when SQL Server implementations began to really scale and SQL Server was adopted by hosting providers and large enterprises that may have hundreds of databases on a single server.

SQL Server 2005 Management Studio uses a new object model called SQL Server Management Objects (SMO), which scales much better than the previous releases of the object model. For example, if you are in Management Studio, you can now expand the list of tables, and while you're waiting for the tree to expand, you can move on to the next task. Whenever the tables are fully ready to display, the menu expands and your task is not interrupted.

You can also filter objects easily, which is useful when you begin to have dozens of objects. To filter the objects in Management Studio, select the node of the tree that you wish to filter and click the Filter icon in the Object Explorer. The Object Explorer Filter Settings dialog box (shown in Figure 4-9) will open, which lets you filter by name, schema, or when the object was created. The operator drop-down box allows you to select how you wish to filter, and then you can type the name in the Value column.

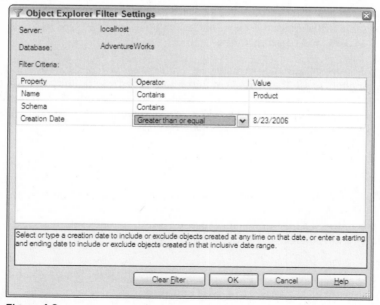

Figure 4-9

Error Logs

As you probably have already experienced, when something goes wrong with an application, the first thing to get blamed is typically the database. This leaves a DBA to disprove that it's his or her fault. The first thing the DBA does is typically connect to the server and look at the SQL Server instance error logs and then the Windows event logs.

In SQL Server 2005, you can now quickly look through the logs in a consolidated manner using Management Studio. To view the logs, right-click SQL Server Logs under the Management tree and select View ⇨ SQL Server and Windows Log. This will open the Log File Viewer screen. From this screen, you can check and uncheck log files that you wish to bring into the view. You can consolidate in logs from SQL Server, Agent, Database Mail, and the Windows Event Viewer, shown in Figure 4-10.

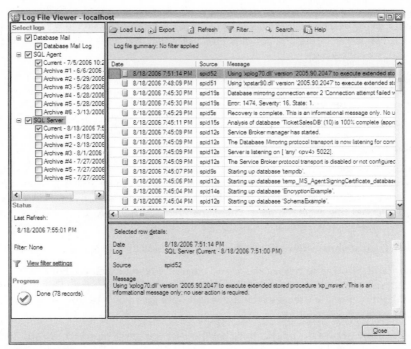

Figure 4-10

In some situations, you may want to merge the logs from several machines into a single view to determine what's causing an application problem. To do this, you can click the Load Log button and browse to your .LOG file. That file could be a Windows error log that's been output to .LOG format or a SQL log from a different instance. For example, you can use this to consolidate all the SQL logs from every instance on a single server to give you a holistic view of all the physical machine's problems.

Activity Monitor

The Activity Monitor gives you a view of connections that are currently active on an instance. The monitor can be used to determine if you have any processes blocking other processes. To open the Activity Monitor in Management Studio, double-click Activity Monitor under the Management tree in the tool.

The tool is a fantastic comprehensive way to view who is connecting to your machine and what they're doing. In the Process Info page (shown in Figure 4-11), you can see each login connecting to your machine (also called a SPID). It's easy to miss how much information is in this window. You can slide left to right to see loads of important data about each connection. It would take way too long to explain each column, but you'll find that most of the columns are very useful to you when debugging is a problem:

❑ **Process ID:** The unique number assigned to a process connected to SQL Server. This is also called a SPID. There will be an icon next to the number that represents what is happening in the connection. If you see an hourglass, you can tell quickly that that process is waiting on or is being blocked by another connection.

❑ **System Process:** Shows you whether processes that are internal SQL Server processes are connected. By default, these processes are filtered out by clicking Filter and must be added back in if you want to see the SQL Server internals.

❑ **User:** The user name in the database that the process is tied to

❑ **Database:** The database the user is connected to

❑ **Status:** Whether the user is active or sleeping. No, this doesn't mean the user is sleeping at his keyboard but instead means that SQL Server keeps the connection active even though there is no activity coming from the login until the user disconnects. Active means the user is performing a query at this exact moment. There are other statuses also, but we'll cover those later in this chapter and when we talk about performance tuning.

❑ **Open Transactions:** Shows the number of transactions the user has open at a given point

❑ **Command:** Shows the type of command currently being executed. For example you may see SELECT, DBCC, INSERT or AWAITING COMMAND here, to name a few. This won't show you the actual query that the user is executing, but it does give you a highlight of what type of activity is being run on your server.

❑ **Application:** Shows the application that the user is using to connect to your instance. This can be set by the developer in the connection string that the application uses.

❑ **Wait Time:** If the process is being blocked or waiting for another process to complete, it will show you how long the process has been waiting. Wait Type shows you what type of event you're awaiting.

❑ **CPU:** The number of processor resources that have been spent on the process since login

❑ **Login Time:** When the process first logged in

❑ **Last Batch:** When the process performed its last query

❑ **Physical I/O:** The amount of disk IO spent on the process since login

- ❑ **Memory Usage:** The amount of memory that spent on the process since login

- ❑ **Host:** The login's workstation or server name. This is a really useful item, but in some cases you have a Web server connecting to your SQL Server, which makes this sometimes less important.

- ❑ **Blocked By:** Shows which user's Process ID (SPID) is blocking this connection

- ❑ **Blocking:** Shows the quantity of processes blocked by this connection

You can click Refresh to manually refresh the data grid. You can also click View Refresh Settings to set the Activity Monitor to refresh automatically every 60 seconds (or whatever you define). Don't set the refresh to anything too frequent, like every two seconds, as it can cause latency, constantly running queries against active systems. You can also apply filters to show only certain hosts, logins, or connections using greater than a given number of resources. Last, you can sort by a given column by clicking it.

By double-clicking any process, you can see the last query run with the connection. You can also click the Kill Process button from this screen to disconnect the user. Processes can also be disconnected by right-clicking the user and clicking Kill Process from the main Activity Monitor page. The user logged in running a query would then see the following message:

```
Msg 0, Level 11, State 0, Line 0
A severe error occurred on the current command.  The results, if any, should be
discarded.
```

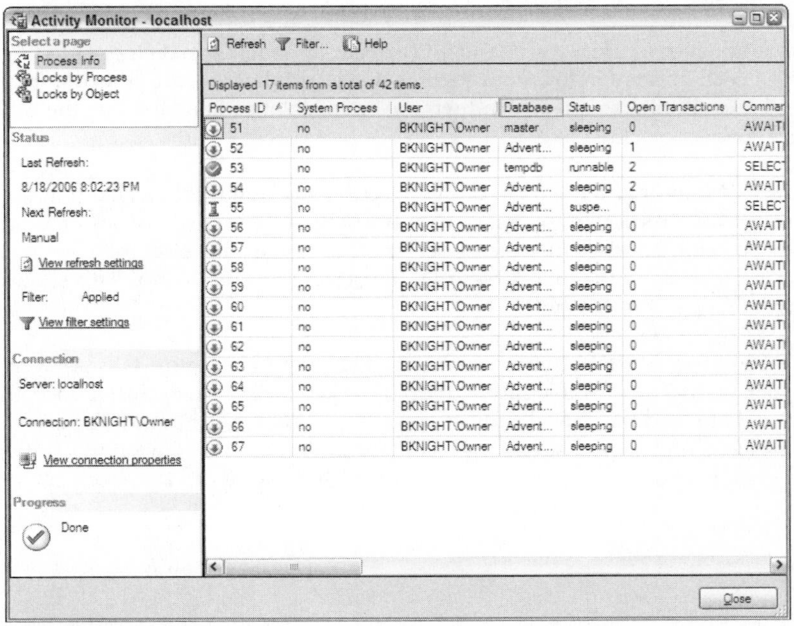

Figure 4-11

The Locks by Process and Locks by Object pages allow you to see what tables currently have locks on them, grouped by either the SPID or the object name. The window allows you to select a locked table, and it will then show you each lock on that object. You can then go back to the original screen to kill the connection causing the lock.

To learn how this screen works, you can try to create a lock problem by running the following query in one query window while connected to the AdventureWorks database (make sure you back up the AdventureWorks database before performing these steps):

```
BEGIN TRAN
DELETE from Production.ProductCostHistory
```

This query will return the number of records affected. Note that the query was not intentionally committed. In other words, there is a BEGIN TRAN but no ROLLBACK or COMMIT command. Without that, your table is currently locked. Typically, you may have run queries without a BEGIN TRAN. In these situations, you actually have an implicit transaction, and the transaction is committed as soon as the batch is complete.

Next, without closing the first window, open a new query window and run the following query in the AdventureWorks database:

```
SELECT *
FROM Production.ProductCostHistory
```

This query should never return a result and will appear to hang. Do not close either window. Note that at the bottom of each query window your login is displayed that you are signed in as, and your process ID is in parentheses. While the query windows are open, go ahead and explore the Activity Monitor to see what these connections look like.

Open the Activity Monitor and note that one connection has an hourglass next to it. Right-click that connection and select Kill Process. In the query window behind the Activity Monitor, you will now see the earlier mentioned error. Next, go into the Locks by Object page and select the Production.ProductCostHistory table from the object drop-down box. This shows you each of the key locks currently open for this table.

Note that in the Request Mode column, you see an X, as shown in Figure 4-12. An X means that there is an exclusive lock on that key (in this case, hundreds of key locks). An exclusive lock also means that no one else is allowed to read the data cleanly. If you see a request mode of S, SQL Server has granted a shared lock, which is under most situations harmless and others are allowed to see the same data. A user can request a dirty read of the uncommitted data by adding a hint of WITH (NOLOCK) clause:

```
SELECT *
FROM Production.ProductCostHistory
WITH (NOLOCK)
```

The Process ID column lets you know which Process ID is causing the problem. You can capture that ID and then go back to the Process Info page to kill the connection. The Type column lets you know what is currently locked. SQL Server starts at the lowest level of locking, which is a KEY lock, then moves to an EXTENT, TABLE, and lastly DATABASE as the most extensive lock.

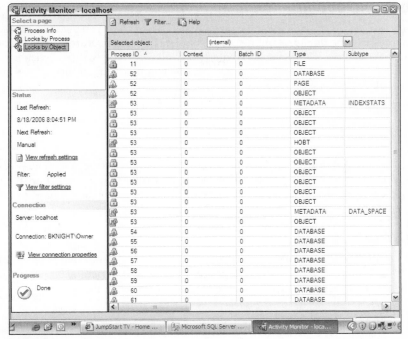

Figure 4-12

Monitoring Processes in T-SQL

You can also monitor the activity of your server via T-SQL. Generally, DBAs prefer this as a quick way to troubleshoot long-running queries or users that complain about slow performance. The reason DBAs typically prefer T-SQL is that the information you can retrieve is much more flexible than the Activity Monitor.

sp_who and sp_who2

The sp_who stored procedure also will return who is connecting to your instance, much like the Activity Monitor. You'll probably find yourself preferring the undocumented sp_who2 stored procedure, though, which gives you much more verbose information about each process. Whichever stored procedure you use, they both accept the same input parameters. For the purpose of this discussion, we'll go into more detail about sp_who2 and know that sp_who shows a subset of the information.

To see all the connections connected to your server, run sp_who2 without any parameters. This displays the same type of information in the Activity Monitor. You can also pass in the parameter of 'active' to see only the active connections to your server:

```
sp_who2 'active'
```

Lastly, you can pass in the process ID as shown here to see the details about an individual process:

```
sp_who2 55
```

sys.dm_exec_connections

The `sys.dm_exec_connections` dynamic management view gives you yet even more information to help you troubleshoot the database engine of SQL Server. This DMV returns a row per session in SQL Server. Because it's a DMV, it's displayed tabularly and allows you to write sophisticated queries against the view to filter out what you don't care about, as shown in this query, which shows only user connections that have performed a write operation:

```
SELECT * FROM
sys.dm_exec_sessions WHERE is_user_process = 1
AND writes > 0
```

In addition to the information you're shown in the earlier mentioned ways to view processes, you see in this DMV how many rows the user has retrieved since they opened the connection, the number of reads, writes, and logical reads. You can also see in this view the settings for each connection and what the last error was, if any.

DBCC INPUTBUFFER

`DBCC INPUT BUFFER` is a great DBCC command that allows you to see what SQL command an individual process ID is running. The command accepts only a single input parameter, which is the process id for the connection that you'd like to diagnose, as shown in the following query:

```
DBCC INPUTBUFFER (53)
```

This most important column the command returns is the event SQL command run in the EventInfo column. If you're running a particular batch that's large, you would only see the first 256 characters by default in the query window.

```
EventType       Parameters EventInfo
--------------  ---------- --------------------------------------------------------
Language Event 0           begin tran delete from production.productcosthistory

(1 row(s) affected)
```

Sys.dm_exec_sql_text

Sometimes you need the results of `DBCC INPUTBUFFER` in a tabular format. You can use the `sys.dm_exec_sql_text` dynamic management function to retrieve the text of a particular query. This can be used in conjunction with the `sys.dm_exec_query_stats` dynamic management view to retrieve the most poorly performing queries across all databases. The query below (the query can be downloaded from this book's page at www.wrox.com) retrieves the number of times a query has executed, the average runtime by CPU and duration, and the text for the query:

```
SELECT TOP 10 execution_count [Number of Executions],
total_worker_time/execution_count AS [Average CPU Time],
Total_Elapsed_Time/execution_count as [Average Elapsed Time],
(SELECT SUBSTRING(text,statement_start_offset/2,
(CASE WHEN statement_end_offset = -1 then
LEN(CONVERT(nvarchar(max), text)) * 2
ELSE statement_end_offset
end -statement_start_offset)/2)
```

```
FROM sys.dm_exec_sql_text(sql_handle)) AS query_text
FROM sys.dm_exec_query_stats
ORDER BY  [Average CPU Time] DESC
```

The `sys.dm_exec_query_stats` DMV also shows loads of other information that can be used. It shows you a line for each query plan that has been run. You can take the `sql_handle` column from this DMV and use it in the `sys.dm_exec_sql_text` function. Because this view is at a plan level, when someone changes some of the query's text, it shows the new query as a new line.

Trace Flags

Trace flags give you advanced mechanisms to tap into hidden SQL Server features and troubleshooting tactics. In some cases, they allow you to override the recommended behavior of SQL Server to turn on features like network-drive support for database files. In other cases, trace flags can be used to turn on additional monitoring as some flags that help diagnose deadlocks. To turn on a trace flag, use the DBCC TRACEON command, followed by the trace you'd like to turn on, as shown below:

```
DBCC TRACEON (1807)
```

To turn off the trace, use the DBCC TRACEOFF command. This command is followed by which traces you'd like to turn off (multiple traces can be separated by commas) as shown here:

```
DBCC TRACEOFF (1807, 3604)
```

When you turn on a trace, you are turning it on for a single connection by default. For example, if you turn on trace flag 1807, which helps diagnose deadlocks, you will only be able to diagnose deadlocks in the scope of the connection that issued the DBCC TRACEON command. You can also turn on the trace at a server level by issuing the command followed by the –1 switch:

```
DBCC TRACEON (1807, -1)
```

Once you've turned on the traces, the next thing you're probably going to want to do is determine whether the trace is actually running. To do this, you can issue the DBCC TRACESTATUS command. One method to issue the command is to interrogate if a given trace is running:

```
DBCC TRACESTATUS (3604)
```

This command would return the following results if the trace is not turned on:

```
TraceFlag Status Global Session
--------- ------ ------ -------
3604      0      0      0

(1 row(s) affected)
```

If you wish to see all traces that apply to the connection, run the command with the –1 parameter, as shown below:

```
DBCC TRACESTATUS (-1)
```

As you can see in the following results of this query, two traces are turned on. Trace flag 1807 is turned on globally for every connection into the SQL Server, and trace flag 3604 is turned on for this session:

```
TraceFlag Status Global Session
--------- ------ ------ -------
1807      1      1      0
3604      1      0      1

(2 row(s) affected)
```

If no traces are turned on, you would receive the following message:

```
DBCC execution completed. If DBCC printed error messages, contact your system
administrator.
```

Your instance of SQL Server should not have trace flags turned on indefinitely, unless you have support from Microsoft to do so. Trace flags may cause your instance to behave abnormally when left to run all the time. The flag you use today may also not be available in a future release or service pack of SQL Server. If you are in debug mode, you can turn on a trace flag from the command prompt when starting SQL Server. As mentioned earlier in this chapter, you can also start a trace when SQL Server starts up at the command prompt by calling the sqlservr.exe program and passing the –T switch after it.

To date, we've mentioned a few trace flags in passing but nothing in much more detail. As you proceed through this book, you'll see a number of other trace flags in practice. A favorite trace flag in your DBA toolbox, though, is certainly going to be the deadlock traces.

A deadlock is encountered when one or more resources try to access an item being permanently locked by another resource. The requesting connection would then be terminated, and a deadlock error would appear to the client. We cover much more about what deadlocks are and how they can affect your instance's performance in Chapters 6 and 7, but for the time being, note that if you turn on trace flag 1204, anytime a deadlock is encountered, a message the resembles the following message will be sent to the SQL Server error log:

```
Deadlock encountered .... Printing deadlock information
Wait-for graph
      Node:1
      RID: 8:1:140:0                  CleanCnt:3 Mode:X Flags: 0x2
        Grant List 1:
          Owner:0x03364B20 Mode: X        Flg:0x0 Ref:0 Life:02000000 SPID:59 ECID:0
XactLockInfo: 0x059D67D4
          SPID: 59 ECID: 0 Statement Type: UPDATE Line #: 10
          Input Buf: Language Event: exec p2
        Requested By:
          ResType:LockOwner Stype:'OR'Xdes:0x059D6248 Mode: U SPID:57 BatchID:0
ECID:0 TaskProxy:(0x04AEE33C) Value:0x335cfe0 Cost:(0/216)
      Node:2
      RID: 8:1:138:0                  CleanCnt:2 Mode:X Flags: 0x2
        Grant List 1:
          Owner:0x03364620 Mode: X        Flg:0x0 Ref:0 Life:02000000 SPID:57 ECID:0
XactLockInfo: 0x059D626C
          SPID: 57 ECID: 0 Statement Type: UPDATE Line #: 10
          Input Buf: Language Event: exec p1
```

```
        Requested By:
             ResType:LockOwner Stype:'OR'Xdes:0x059D67B0 Mode: U SPID:59 BatchID:0
ECID:0 TaskProxy:(0x05FD433C) Value:0x33645e0 Cost:(0/116)
        Victim Resource Owner:
             ResType:LockOwner Stype:'OR'Xdes:0x059D67B0 Mode: U SPID:59 BatchID:0 ECID:0
TaskProxy:(0x05FD433C) Value:0x33645e0 Cost:(0/116)
```

This should tell you that you have a serious problem with a query or series of queries. It outputs the SPID (also referred to as process ID from earlier sections) that blocked the other process (called the victim). In this case, the victim was SPID 59, the results of that query were lost, and you'd have to rerun the query.

Trace flag 1222 returns much more information than the 1204 trace flag to the error log, and it resembles an XML document (although it does not comply with an XSD). The results are very verbose, and that is why you typically only see this enabled as a secondary step if the 1204 results were inadequate for you to solve the problem. The results of the trace flag's output would give you the queries that were the victim and blocking queries and would resemble something like the following output from an error log:

```
        deadlock-list
        deadlock victim=process279b098
         process-list
          process id=process279b098 priority=0 logused=116 waitresource=RID:
7:1:141:0 waittime=10000 ownerId=22637 transactionname=user_transaction
lasttranstarted=2005-01-25T16:39:22.050 XDES=0x529e7e0 lockMode=U schedulerid=2
kpid=2120 status=suspended spid=55 sbid=0 ecid=0 transcount=2
lastbatchstarted=2005-01-25T16:39:35.357 lastbatchcompleted=2005-01-25T16:36:55.217
clientapp=SQL Server Management Studio - Query hostname=USER13 hostpid=2852
loginname=DOMAIN\user1 isolationlevel=read committed (2) xactid=236223201313
currentdb=7 lockTimeout=4294967295 clientoption1=671090784 clientoption2=390200
             executionStack
              frame procname=general.dbo.p2 line=10 stmtstart=186 stmtend=228
sqlhandle=0x03000700e8ea0d065c0a1101e7950000010000000000000
        UPDATE table1 SET column1=5
              frame procname=adhoc line=1
sqlhandle=0x0100070068747519405a6003000000000000000000000000
        exec p2
             inputbuf
        exec p2
          process id=process279b168 priority=0 logused=216 waitresource=RID:
7:1:144:0 waittime=2453 ownerId=22635 transactionname=user_transaction
lasttranstarted=2005-01-25T16:39:19.190 XDES=0x529e258 lockMode=U schedulerid=2
kpid=164 status=suspended spid=53 sbid=0 ecid=0 transcount=2 lastbatchstarted=2005-
01-25T16:39:32.503 lastbatchcompleted=2005-01-25T16:39:08.627 clientapp=SQL Server
Management Studio - Query hostname=USER13 hostpid=3192 loginname=DOMAIN\user1
isolationlevel=read committed (2) xactid=227633266690 currentdb=7
lockTimeout=4294967295 clientoption1=671090784 clientoption2=390200
             executionStack
              frame procname=general.dbo.p1 line=10 stmtstart=182 stmtend=224
sqlhandle=0x03000700afc619055c0a1101e795000001000000000000000
        UPDATE table1 SET column1=2
              frame procname=adhoc line=2 stmtstart=6
sqlhandle=0x01000700d6e53430205b6003000000000000000000000000
        exec p1
```

```
        inputbuf
    exec p1
      resource-list
       ridlock fileid=1 pageid=144 dbid=7 objectname=general.dbo.t2 id=lock368ab80
 mode=X associatedObjectId=72057594038517760
          owner-list
           owner id=process279b098 mode=X
          waiter-list
           waiter id=process279b168 mode=U requestType=wait
        ridlock fileid=1 pageid=141 dbid=7 objectname=general.dbo.t1 id=lock368ac80
 mode=X associatedObjectId=72057594038452224
          owner-list
           owner id=process279b168 mode=X
          waiter-list
           waiter id=process279b098 mode=U requestType=wait
```

The output will also give you other verbose information that can be used to debug your instance, such as the user name of the victim or deadlocking process and other connection information.

Getting Help from Support

Whenever you get stuck on a SQL Server issue, generally you'll call the next layer of support. Whether that next layer is Microsoft or a vendor, there are a number of new tools that you have available to communicate with that next layer of support. The SQLDumper.exe and SQLDiag.exe programs can be used to help you better communicate with support to give them an excellent picture of your environment and problem while you reproduce the error.

SQLDumper.exe

Beginning in SQL Server 2000 SP3, SQLDumper.exe was included to help your SQL Server perform a dump of its environment after an exception occurs. A support organization like Microsoft's Product Support Services (PSS) may also request that you execute the program on demand while you have a problem like a hung server.

If you wish to create a dump file on demand, you'll need the Windows process ID for the SQL Server instance. There are a few ways you can obtain this ID. You can go to Task Manager, look in the SQL Server log, or go to SQL Server Configuration Manager, explained earlier in this chapter. On the SQL Server 2005 Services page of Configuration Manager, you can see each of the SQL Server services and the process ID.

By default, SQLDumper.exe can be found in the C:\Program Files\Microsoft SQL Server\90\ Shared directory, as it's shared across all the SQL Server instances installed on a server. This directory may change, though, based on where you installed the SQL Server tools. To create a dump file for support, go to a command prompt and go to the C:\Program Files\Microsoft SQL Server\90\Shared directory. Once there, you can create a full or a minidump. A full dump is much larger than a minidump. If a minidump is less than a megabyte, a full dump may run 110MB on your system. To create a full dump, use the following command:

```
Sqldumper.exe <ProcessID> 0 0x01100
```

This will output the full dump to the same directory that you're in. The filename will be called `SQLDmpr0001.mdmp` if this is the first time you've run the `SQLDumper.exe` program. The filename would be sequentially named after each execution. You won't be able to open the dump file in a text editor like Notepad. Instead, you'll need advanced troubleshooting tools like Visual Studio or one of the PSS tools. A more practical dump would be a minidump, which contains most of the essential information the support will need. To create a minidump, use the following command:

```
Sqldumper.exe <ProcessID> 0 0x0120
```

You can view the `SQLDUMPER_ERRORLOG.log` file to determine if there were any errors when you created the dump file or if a dump has occurred. You will need to be a local Windows administrator to run `SQLDumper.exe` or be logged in with the same account that starts the SQL Server service.

SQLDiag.exe

A tool that's slightly less of a black box than `SQLDumper.exe` is `SQLDiag.exe`. If you're experienced with SQL Server 2000, you may be familiar with a tool called `PSSDiag.exe`, which produced SQL and Windows trace files as well as system configuration logs. `SQLDiag.exe` has replaced this tool and has added many new features to the old PSS tool. The tool consolidates and collects information about your system from:

❑ Windows System Monitor (sysmon)

❑ Windows Event Logs

❑ SQL Server Profile traces

❑ SQL Server error logs

❑ Information about SQL Server blocking

❑ SQL Server configuration information

Because `SQLDiag.exe` gathers so much diagnostic information, you should only run it when you're requested to or when you're trying to prepare for a call with support. The SQL Server Profiler trace files alone can grow large quickly, so prepare to output these files to a drive that has lots of space. The process also uses a sizable amount of processing power as it runs. You can execute the tool from a command prompt or as a service. You can use the `/?` switch to be shown what switches are available to you.

As you can see from the preceding switches, `SQLDiag.exe` can take a configuration file as input. By default, this file is called `SQLDiag.Xml` if one is not specified. If a configuration XML file does not exist, one will be created called `##SQLDiag.XML`. This file can be altered to your liking and then later distributed as `SQLDiag.XML`.

Now that you know what `SQLDiag.exe` can do, follow this example to use the tool against a local development server. If you cannot get in front of the server, you will have to use a support tool like Terminal Services to remote into a server, since you can't point `SQLDiag.exe` at a remote instance. To run the tool, go to a command prompt. Because the tool is referenced in the environment variables, you won't have to go to the individual directory where the file is located. Instead, for the purpose of this example, go to the `C:\Temp` directory or something similar to that on a drive that has more than 100MB available.

The default location for the files is `C:\Program Files\microsoft sql server\90\tools\Binn\ SQLDIAG`, but you can alter that to a new location with the `/O` switch. In this example, type the following command (note the lack of spaces after the + sign):

```
sqldiag /B +00:03:00 /E +00:02:00 /OC:\temp /C1
```

This command will instruct `SQLDiag.exe` to begin capturing trace information in three minutes from when you start and run for two minutes. This is done with the `/B` and `/E` switches. These two switches can also be used to start and stop the diagnostic at a given 24-hour clock time. The command also tells `SQLDiag.exe` to output the results of the traces and logs to the `C:\temp` directory, and the `/C` switch instructs the tool to compress the files using Windows compression. If you were running this in your environment, you would wait until you were instructed by `SQLDiag.exe` (in green text on your console) to attempt to reproduce the problem. The results will look something like Figure 4-13.

Figure 4-13

With the `SQLDiag.exe` now complete, you can go to the `C:\temp` directory to zip the contents up and send them to Microsoft. In the directory, you'll find a treasure chest of information for a support individual. Some of the items you'll find there will include:

❑   `##files.txt` — A list of files in the `C:\Program Files\Microsoft SQL Server\90\ Tools\binn` directory with their creation date. This can be used to see if you're not running a patch that support has asked to be installed.

- ❏ `##envvars.txt` — A list of all the environment variables for the server

- ❏ `SERVERNAME__sp_sqldiag_Shutdown.OUT` — A consolidation of the instance's SQL logs and the results from a number of queries

- ❏ `log_XX.trc` — A series of Profiler trace files of very granular SQL Server activities being performed

- ❏ `SERVERNAME_MSINFO32.TXT` — A myriad of details about the server system and hardware

These files may not only be useful for support individuals. You may want to consider running this on a regular basis to establish a baseline of your server during key times (before patches, monthly, or whatever your metric is). If you'd like to do this, you wouldn't want the Profiler part of `SQLDiag.exe` to run for more than a few seconds. You can gather useful baseline information if the tool is run in snapshot mode periodically. This mode performs the same functions as before but will exit immediately after it gathers the necessary information. The following command uses the `/X` switch to run `SQLDiag.exe` in snapshot mode and the `/N` switch (with 2 as the option) to create a new directory for each run of `SQLDiag.exe`:

```
sqldiag /OC:\temp\baseline /X /N 2
```

Each directory will be called `baseline_0000` and then named sequentially from there. Many corporations choose to run this through SQL Agent or Task Manager on the first of the month or before key changes to have an automatic baseline of their server and instance.

Summary

In this chapter, you learned some of the key concepts for managing and troubleshooting your SQL Server. You learned how to configure your server using SQL Server Configuration Manager, SQL Server Surface Area Configuration, and lastly Management Studio. We also covered how to monitor the connections in your server using Activity Monitor and some of the key stored procedures and DMVs. Last, we focused on how to use some troubleshooting tools like `SQLDumper.exe` and `SQLDiag.exe` to send valuable support information to your next tier in support or to create a baseline. With the key concepts out of the way, we can now drill into more specific areas to manage, such as security. In Chapter 5, you learn much more about automating your SQL Server processes.

5

Automating SQL Server

Much of the work that a DBA does is repetitive: backing up databases, rebuilding indexes, and checking for file sizes and disk-space availability. Responding to events such as the transaction log being full or being out of disk space may also be part of daily life for some DBAs. The problem grows rapidly with the number of servers you must administer. Automating this work is more than a convenience; it is a requirement for enterprise systems.

SQL Server Agent comes to the rescue, allowing you to automate routinely scheduled tasks, respond to predefined events, and notify you of status.

Automation Components

There are four basic components for SQL Server Agent, each of which we discuss in the following sections:

- ❑   **Jobs:** Defines the work to be done
- ❑   **Schedules:** Defines when the job will be executed
- ❑   **Alerts:** Allows you to set up an automatic response or notification when an event occurs
- ❑   **Operators:** The people who can be notified regarding job status and alerts

By default, the SQL Server Agent Service is not running, and the service is set to manual after the install of SQL Server. If you are going to be using this in production, be sure to use SQL Server Configuration Manager to set the Start Mode of this service to Automatic.

Jobs

A basic reason to use SQL Agent is to schedule work to be done automatically, like backing up a database. A SQL Agent job contains the definition of work to be done. A job has a name, description, owner, and category. A job can be enabled or disabled. Jobs can be run in several ways:

❑ By attaching it to one or more schedules

❑ In response to one or more alerts

❑ By executing `sp_start_job`

❑ Manually via SQL Server Management Studio

A job usually consists of many steps, but it can have as few as one. Each step has a name and a type. Be sure to give your jobs and steps good descriptive names that will be useful when they appear in error and logging messages. The job-step types that you might create are:

❑ ActiveX Script

❑ Operating System commands (CmdExec)

❑ SQL Server Analysis Services Command

❑ SQL Server Analysis Services Query

❑ SQL Server SSIS Package Execution

❑ Transact-SQL Script (T-SQL)

There are other job-step types that you do not usually create yourself. These jobs, with their associated steps, are usually created by setting up replication. The process of setting up replication defines jobs that use these step types, although there is nothing to prevent you from using these step types if you have need to:

❑ Replication Distributor

❑ Replication Merge

❑ Replication Queue Reader

❑ Replication Snapshot

❑ Replication Transaction Log Reader

The ActiveX job step allows you to execute VBScript, Jscript, or any other installable scripting language. The CMDExec job step allows you to execute command prompt items. You can execute `bat` files or any of the commands that would be contained in a `bat` or `cmd` file.

The SQL Server Analysis Services Command, SQL Server Analysis Services Query, and SQL Server SSIS Package Execution are new job steps for SQL Server 2005.

The SQL Server Analysis Services Command allows you to execute an XML for Analysis (XMLA) command. This must use the `Execute` method, which allows you to select data as well as administer and process Analysis Services objects.

The SQL Server Analysis Services Query step allows you to execute a Multidimensional Expression (MDX) against a cube. MDX queries allow you to select data from a cube.

While you could run DTS packages using SQL Agent in SQL Server 2000, you had to come up with a DTSRun CMDExec script or use stored procedures. There was a utility to assist your preparation of the DTSRun command line, but it was an extra step. The SQLServer SSIS Package Execution step allows you to do everything you need to do without going outside the environment. You can assign variable values, configurations, and anything else you need to execute the package. This is a nice improvement and certainly a time saver.

The T-SQL job step allows you to execute TSQL scripts. TSQL scripts do not use SQL Server Agent Proxy accounts described later in this chapter. If you are not a member of the sysadm fixed-server role, the TSQL step will run using your user credentials within the database. When members of the sysadm fixed-server role create T-SQL job steps, they may specify that the job step run under the security context of a specific database user. If they specify a database user, the step executes as the specified user; otherwise, the step will execute under the security context of the SQL Server Agent Service Account.

> *The GUI for T-SQL security can be confusing. Although there is a Run As: drop-down on the first page of the Job Step Properties page where you set up job steps, this is not the place you set the security for T-SQL steps. The Run As: drop-down here is used to specify security contexts for other types of steps. To set security for your T-SQL step, click the Advanced tab. At the bottom of the dialog is a Run as User drop-down. Set the T-SQL user security context here.*

Each job step runs under a *security context*. The security contexts for other type of job steps are described later in this chapter.

There is some control of flow related to job steps as well. You may specify an action for when the step succeeds and when the step fails. These actions can be "quit the job, indicating success," "quit the job with failure," or "go to another job step." You may also require that the job step be retried before it is failed. You may specify the number of retry attempts and the retry interval in minutes. A job step will be retried the number of times you specify in the Retry Attempts field before it executes the On Failure control of flow. If the Retry Interval in Minutes field has been set, the step will wait for the specified time period before retrying. This can be useful when there are dependencies between jobs. You may have a job step that does a bulk insert from a text file. The text file is placed into the proper directory by some other process, which may run late. You could create a VBScript job step that checks for the presence of the input file. To test for the file every 10 minutes for 30 minutes, you would set the retry attempts to 3 and the Retry Interval to 10.

When you create a job, you can place it into a job category. There are several predefined job categories such as [Uncategorized (Local)] and Database Engine Tuning Advisor. You can also create your own job categories. Each job can be in only one category. You can get to the Manage Categories Dialog Box from the Object Explorer Window of SQL Server Management Studio. Open the SQL Server Agent item in the tree view and right-click Jobs; then select Manage Job Categories. You will get the dialog box shown in Figure 5-1.

As trivial as it might seem, give some thought about organizing your jobs. Then create the categories now. You may be surprised how quickly the number of jobs on your server may grow. Sometimes finding the correct job is difficult when there are many.

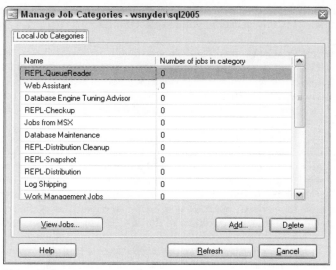

Figure 5-1

Job Step Logging

Each time a job is run, job history is created. Job history will tell you when the job started, when it completed, and if it was successful. Each job step may be configured for logging and history as well. All of the logging setup for a job step is on the Advanced Tab of the Job Step Properties. To append the job step history to the job history, select the "Include the step output in history" checkbox.

You may also choose to have the information logged to `dbo.sysjobstepslogs` in `msdb`. To log to this table, check the "Log to table" checkbox. To include step history from multiple job runs, also check the "Append output to existing entry in table." Otherwise, you will only have the most recent history.

Job steps executed by sysadm role members may also have the job step history written to a file. Enter the filename in the "Output file" textbox. Also, check the "Append output to existing file" checkbox, if you do not wish to overwrite the file. Job steps executed by others can only log to the `dbo.sysjobstepslogs` in `msdb`.

> *Anytime you refer to network resources such as operating system files, ensure that the appropriate proxy account has the correct permissions. Also, always use the UNC name for files, so the job or its steps are not dependent on directory maps. This is an easy place to get into trouble between the test and production environments if you are not very careful.*

In addition to the logging capabilities described so far, output from T-SQL, Analysis Services Steps, and CMDExec steps can be written to a separate output file.

Job Notifications

SQL Server Automation includes the ability for jobs to notify you when they complete, succeed, or fail. In the Job Properties Dialog, choose Notifications, and you will see the dialog box shown in Figure 5-2.

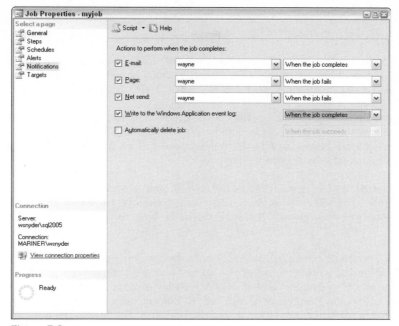

Figure 5-2

A job can send a notification via e-mail, pager, and Net Send.

> *Windows Messenger Service must be running on the server where SQL Agent is running to send notifications via Net Send. You can send a message to any workstation or user that can be seen from the SQL Agent server.*

As Figure 5-2 shows, there is a line in the dialog box for each of the delivery methods. Place a check beside the delivery method you wish; you may choose multiple methods. Each option has a drop-down menu that allows you to choose an operator to notify. An operator allows you to define the e-mail address for the delivery. (Operator setup is described later in this chapter.) Then choose the event that should trigger the notification. It can be when the job completes, when the job fails, or when the job succeeds.

You may not wish to be notified at all for some jobs. However, for mission-critical jobs, you might wish to be e-mailed always when the job completes and perhaps paged and notified through Net Send if the job fails, so you will know immediately.

Schedules

One of the big benefits of SQL Agent is that you can have your jobs scheduled. You can schedule a job to run at any of these times:

❑   When SQL Agent starts

❑   Once, at a specified date and time

- ❑   On a recurring basis
- ❑   When the CPU utilization of your server is idle

You can define when the CPU is idle by setting up the Idle CPU Condition in SQL Agent Properties⇨ Advanced. You can define a minimum CPU utilization and a duration. When the CPU utilization is less than your definition for the duration you specify, CPU idle schedules are triggered.

Once your schedule is created, you can associate it with one or more jobs. A job can also have multiple schedules. You may wish to create a schedule for nightly batching and another for end-of-month processing. A single job can be associated with both schedules. If a scheduled job is triggered, and the job is already running, that schedule is simply skipped.

To create a schedule in Management Studio, select SQL Server Agent, right-click Jobs, and choose Manage Schedules. The scheduler is particularly easy to use. You can easily create a schedule that runs on the last weekday of every month. It is very nice not to have to figure out which day is the last day of the month.

The naming of a schedule can be a problem. Should the schedule name have to do with *when* the schedule runs or *what* kind of work it includes? We suggest you use both; name regularly recurring jobs "minutely," "hourly," "midnight," and so on. For business-related schedules, you should create a schedule named "Accounts Payable End of Month" or "Bi Weekly Payroll Cycle." The reason for including business names is a matter of convenience. You can disable a schedule; when you do so, that schedule no longer causes jobs to run. If you name many schedules based on business processes and someone instructs you not to run the payroll cycle yet, you can simply disable the associated schedule.

I have never had occasion to create a schedule to run when SQL Agent starts, but there might be some clean up you wish to do. You might wish to be notified when the system restarts; this would be the place to do so.

There are times when CPU idle jobs are worthwhile. If the CPU is not otherwise busy, you can get some batch-related work done. Be careful, however; if you have many jobs scheduled for CPU idle, they will begin to run quickly, and you can overpower your system. Be prudent with the number of jobs of this type that you schedule.

One item that is sorely lacking in SQL Server Agent's arsenal is the ability to link jobs together so that one begins as the other ends. You can make this happen by adding a final step in one job that executes the second job, but that puts all of this navigation inside job steps. It shouldn't be there. It should be outside at the job level. Some third-party tools do a good job of this. However, if you wish to do it on your own, it is likely to be difficult to maintain.

Operators

An operator is a SQL Agent object that contains a friendly name and some contact information. Operators can be notified on completion of SQL Agent jobs and when alerts occur. (Alerts are covered in the next section.) You may wish to notify operators who will fix problems related to jobs and alerts, so they may go about their business of supporting the business. You may also wish to automatically notify management when mission-critical events occur, such as failure of the payroll cycle.

You should define operators before you begin defining alerts. This allows you to choose the operators you wish to notify as you are defining the alert, saving you some time. The Operator Properties Dialog box is shown in Figure 5-3.

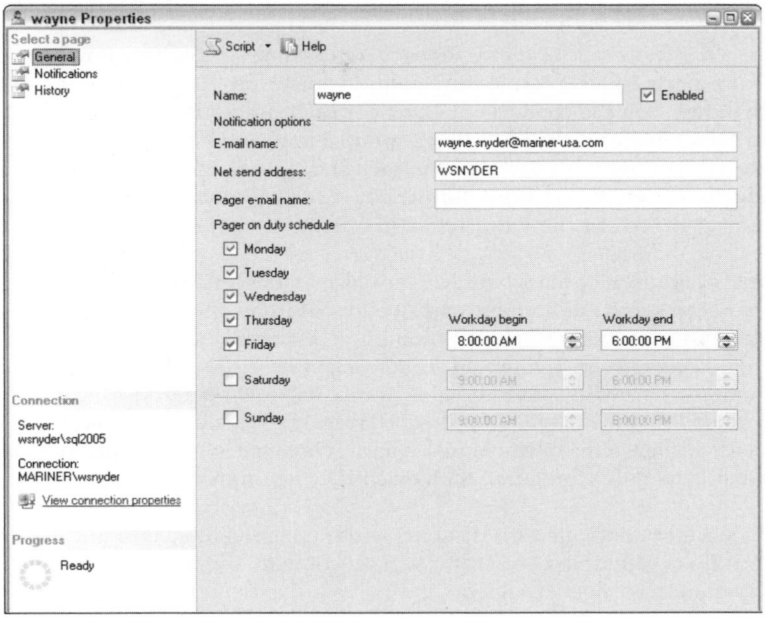

Figure 5-3

The operator name must be unique and fewer than 128 characters.

For e-mail notifications, you can provide an e-mail address. You may provide multiple e-mail addresses separated by semicolons. This could also be an e-mail group defined within your e-mail system. If you wish to notify many people, it is better to define an e-mail group in your e-mail system. This will allow you to change the list of people notified without having to change every job. One undocumented capability is that you can specify multiple e-mail addresses for an operator, but they must be separated by semicolons.

For pager notifications, you also provide an e-mail address. SQL Agent does not know anything about paging. You must have purchased paging via e-mail capabilities from a third-party provider. SQL Agent merely sends the e-mail to the pager address. Your pager software does the rest. Some pager systems require additional configuration characters to be sent around the Subject, CC, or To line. This can be set up in SQL Agent Configuration, covered at the end of this chapter.

Notice that there is a Pager on Duty Schedule associated with the Pager E-mail Name. This applies only to pagers. You can set up an on-duty schedule for paging this operator and then set this operator to be notified from an alert or job completion. When the job completes or the alert occurs, the operator will only be paged during his or her pager on-duty schedule.

You can also use Net Send to notify an operator. When Net Send is used, you must provide the name of the workstation for this operator, and a Message Dialog box will pop up on his or her workstation. This is the least-safe way of notifying, because the operator may not be at his or her desk.

Scheduling Notifications

Jobs allow you to notify a single operator for each of the three send types: e-mail, pager, and Net Send. Notifications from alerts allow you to notify multiple operators. This allows you the capability to do some very nice things. You can create an operator for each shift (First Shift Operators, Second Shift Operators, and Third Shift Operators), set up a group e-mail and a group page address for each of the shifts, set up the pager-duty schedule to match each shift's work schedule, and add all three operators to each alert. If an alert set up like this occurs at 2:00 A.M., only the third-shift operators will be paged. If the alert occurs at 10:00 A.M., only the first-shift operators will be paged.

There are several limitations of the schedule. Notice that the weekday schedule must be the same every day, although you can specify a different schedule for Saturday and Sunday. There is a big opportunity here for an enterprising individual. There is nothing to indicate company holidays or vacations. It would be really nice to be able to specify company holidays and let the schedule use the weekend schedule instead of the weekday schedule. It would also be nice to allow operators to specify vacation days that would be integrated into the system. You can disable an operator, perhaps because they are on vacation, but you cannot schedule the disablement in advance. There are lots of opportunities for an add-in. Microsoft has maintained this limitation with essentially no improvements since SQL 7.0.

You can tell if a job, alert, or operator is disabled without having to go into the properties of the object. Management Studio tags disabled objects for SQL Agent with a small red down arrow. In Figure 5-4, one alert and one operator have been disabled.

Figure 5-4

To use e-mail or pager notifications, Database Mail must be set up and enabled, and SQL Agent must be configured to use it. For pager notifications, you must have a third-party pager notification system. To use Net Send, Windows Messaging Service must be running on the same server as SQL Agent.

Failsafe Operator

What happens if an alert occurs and no operator is on duty, according to their pager on-duty schedule? Unless you specify a failsafe operator, no one would be notified. The failsafe operator is a security measure that allows an alert notification (not job notification) to be delivered for pager notifications (not e-mail or Net Send) that could not be sent.

Failures to send pager notifications include:

- ❑ None of the specified operators are on duty.
- ❑ SQL Server Agent cannot access the appropriate tables in `msdb`.

  SQL Server Books Online says that bad pager e-mail addresses will also cause the failsafe operator to be used, but in testing using SQL 2005 SP1, this was not the case.

The failsafe operator is only used when *none* of the specified pager notifications could be made or `msdb` is not available. An example of this is the following: You have a long job that begins. The `msdb` database then fails for some reason, although SQL Server is still running, as is SQL Agent. The job needs to do a pager notification, but the `sysoperators` and `sysnotifications` tables in `msdb` are not available. SQL Agent will read the registry and obtain the failsafe operator information and send the page.

If you have three pager operators associated with a specific alert, and one of them is notified, but two of them failed, the failsafe operator will *not* be notified.

You can indicate whether the failsafe operator will be notified using any or all of the three notification methods. Don't get confused here. A failsafe operator will only be notified if a pager notification cannot be successfully delivered. However, the failsafe operator in this case can be notified via e-mail, pager, Net Send, or a combination of these methods. Since the failsafe operator is a security mechanism, you may not delete an operator identified as failsafe. First, you must either disable the failsafe setup for SQL Agent, or choose a different failsafe operator. Then you can delete the operator.

You can disable an operator defined as failsafe. Disabling this operator will prevent any normal alter or job notifications from being sent but will not restrict this operator's failsafe notifications.

Alerts

An alert is a predefined response to an event. An event can be any of the following:

- ❑ SQL Server event
- ❑ SQL Server performance condition
- ❑ WMI event

An alert can be created as a response to any of the events of these types. The responses that can be triggered as the result of an event alert are:

- ❑ Start a SQL agent job
- ❑ Notify one or more operators

  You may only notify one operator for each notification type for job completion, but you may notify a list of operators for alerts.

When you create an alert, you give it a name. Ensure that this name tells you something about what is going on; it will be included in all messages. Names like "Log Full Alert" or "Severity 18 Alert on Production" might be useful.

Alert Event Types

You then choose the event type on which the alert is based, as shown in Figure 5-5. Three event types are covered in this section.

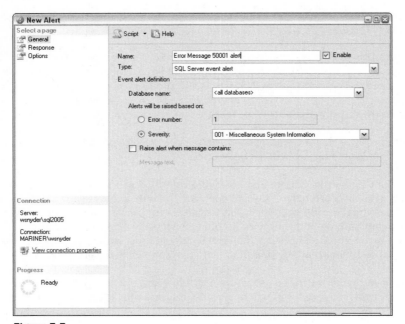

Figure 5-5

SQL Server Event

The SQL Server event alerts are based mainly on error messages. You can create an alert on a specific error message number or on an error severity. You might create an alert on error message number 9002 (log file full) or 1105 (out of disk space) message. An alert can be fired for any particular database or all databases. You may only care to get this alert when the Production database transaction log is full, not when the other test and development databases run out of log space. In this case, choose the Production database in the Database name drop-down list. I wish this dropdown was a multiselect, but it is not. If you wish to alert on two databases, but not all of them, you will have to create two separate alerts.

> *It is very common to set up 9002 alerts for your important databases to notify you if the database is out of log space. By the time your users call on the phone, you can tell them you are already aware of the problem and are working on it.*

You can also choose to create an alert on a specific error-severity level. Each error message has an error-severity level. Severity 19 and above are fatal server errors. You may wish to create an alert for each of the severity levels between 19 and 25, so you can be notified of fatal SQL errors in any database.

What happens if you create an error on a message that has a severity level of 16, then create another alert of all severity 16 messages? When both the message number and message severity are covered in two separate alerts, only the message alert will fire. You can think of the severity-level alert as a backup. Alerts defined on specific message numbers will fire when the message occurs. For all other error messages for that severity, the severity-level alert will fire. This is a nice implementation.

You cannot create two message-level or severity-level alerts with the same message or severity level and the same database. You can create an alert on message number 50001 for AdventureWorks and another alert on message number 50001 for <all databases>. In this case, when the error message occurs in AdventureWorks, the alert for AdventureWorks will fire, not the <all databases> alert. The <all databases> alert will fire for a message number 50001 that occurs in any other database other than AdventureWorks. The lesson here is that the most local handling of an event is the one that fires.

You may also create an alert that has an additional restriction on the text of the message. You can create an alert as before, but check the box "Raise alert when message contains:" and enter a text string in the textbox. The alert will then fire only on messages that include the specified text. You can create an alert on user messages severity (Severity 16) for all databases, which fires when the text 'Page Bob' is included in the error message. Then applications could raise user errors that cause the alert to occur, paging Bob. This is a great way to amuse your friends and annoy Bob. The same principle as before applies: If a message with matching text is sent, the associated alert fires. The more general alert will fire if there is no text match.

SQL Server alerts work by watching the operating system application event log. If the event is not logged, the alert will not fire. The application log might be full, or the error might not be logged. You can create error messages with the sp_addmessage stored procedure. You may specify whether the message is logged or not. For example, you can create a simple message using the following SQL:

```
sp_addmessage 50001,16 ,'MESSAGE', @with_log =  'TRUE'
```

This message has a message number of 50001 and a severity level of 16. You can then create alerts to test your system. Set these alerts to use e-mail as the response. To test the alert, use the following code:

```
Raiserror(50001,16,1)with log
Select * from msdb.dbo.sysmail_allitems
```

Raiserror sends the error message. Notice the included text with log. This is not necessary, because this message is always logged. You can cause an error message to be logged using the Raiserror command, if you have the appropriate permissions.

The second statement displays all of the mail items. Scroll to the bottom of the list to check for the mail notification that has been attached as a response to the alert.

SQL Server Performance Condition

When you install SQL Server, a collection of Windows Performance Monitor counters are also installed. The Windows Performance Monitor tool allows the operations staff to monitor the performance of the server. You may monitor CPU utilization, memory utilization, and much more. When SQL Server is installed, an additional collection of monitor counters is added to allow DBAs to monitor the performance and status of SQL Server instances. You can create an alert on a condition based on any of these SQL Server counters.

You cannot create SQL Server alerts on counters that are not specifically for SQL Server, like CPU utilization. However, the Performance Monitor tool gives you the capability to set alerts for these other non-SQL Server counters.

A SQL Server Performance Condition alert is shown in Figure 5-6.

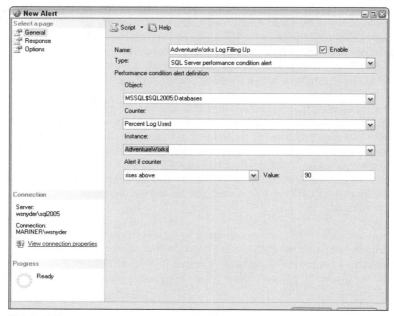

Figure 5-6

Performance counters are grouped according to their objects. For instance, the `Databases` object contains the counters associated with a specific database, like Percent Log Used and Transactions/sec. The `Buffer Manager` object includes counters specific to buffer management. You choose the object, then the counter for which you wish to create an alert.

You cannot create multicounter alerts. You cannot create an alert that fires when Percent Log Used is greater than 80 and Transactions/sec is greater than 100. You must choose to alert on a single counter.

The next choice you make is in the instance box. When you choose `Databases` objects, the instance box will contain the list of databases. You select the database on which to create the alert.

Next is the "Alert if counter" box. You can alert if the counter falls below, becomes equal to, or rises above a value you specify. You specify the value in the Value textbox.

You have seen how you can create an alert to notify you when the transaction log becomes full. That is really a little too late, although better than no alerts at all. It would be much better to know when it looks like the log may become full but before it actually does. To do this, create a Performance Condition alert on the `Databases` object, Percent Log Used counter for the database you are interested in. Choose when the counter rises above some safe limit, probably 80 to 95 percent. You will then be notified before the log is full. You will need to adjust this actual value so that you do not get notified too quickly. If you have set up your log to be what you believe is large enough, you might instead wish to notify on autogrowths.

Alert Responses

As you already know by now, you can respond to an alert by starting a SQL Agent job or notifying one or more operators. You set this up on the Response tab of the create Alert Dialog box. To execute a job, all you must do is check the checkbox and choose an existing job or create a new job. To notify an operator, check the appropriate box, and select the operators you wish to notify by choosing one or more of the notification methods. For alerts, it is really nice to have an operator for each shift you must cover, with the pager on duty set up appropriately, as discussed in the "Operators" section earlier in the chapter.

As you think about how you might best use this in your enterprise, imagine a scenario like the transaction log getting full. You could set up a performance alert to notify operators when the log is actually full and run a job that grows the log. You could set up an alert that backs up the log when it becomes 70-percent full and create another that backs up the log again when it is 80-percent full.

The scenario might play out like this. You are having lunch. Your pager goes off, notifying you that the log is 70-percent full. A job is run automatically that tries to back up the log to free space. In a couple of minutes you get a page telling you that the job completed successfully. After a couple more potato chips, your pager goes off yet again — the log is now 80-percent full. The prior log backup did not free up any space. There must be a long-running transaction. The log backup job is run again, and you are notified on its completion. You finish your lunch with no other pages. This means the last log backup freed up some space and you are now in good shape. Your pager may have gone off again, telling you that the log is completely full and the job that automatically increases the log size has run. It's probably time for you to get back to work, but the automation you have brought to the system has already been fighting this problem while you ate your lunch, notifying you of each step. With some thoughtful consideration, you might be able to account for many planned responses such as this, making your life easier and operations tighter.

The Alert Options page in the Create Alert dialog box allows you to do several things:

❑ Specify when to include more detailed information in the notification

❑ Add information to the notification

❑ Delay the time between responses

Sometimes the error text of the message might be long. Additionally, you may have a limit on the amount of data that can be presented on your devices. Some pagers limit you to as few as 32 characters. You should not include the error text for those message types that cannot handle the extra text, which are most commonly pagers.

There is a large textbox labeled "Additional notification message to send." You can type any text here, and it will be included in the notification message. Perhaps something like "Get up, come in, and fix this problem immediately" might be appropriate. Perhaps "Remember when you come in on the weekend or at night to fix a problem, you receive a $300 bonus, so don't feel bad" might even be better.

At the bottom of the page, you can set a delay between responses. The default value for this is 0. Imagine a scenario where an alert goes off many times during a very short period. Perhaps a program is executing `raiserror` over and over or a performance condition alert is going wild. The performance condition alerts that run because of limited resources are especially vulnerable to this problem. You run low on memory, which causes an alert or job to run, which uses memory. This causes the alert to fire again, using more memory, over and over. You get paged over and over as well. Knowing that the transaction log is getting full 20 times a second is no more useful than hearing about it every five minutes. To remedy this problem, set the delay you wish in minutes and seconds. When the alert occurs, it will be disabled for your delay time. Then it will be automatically enabled again. If the condition occurs again, the process starts all over again. This is a setting that you might find very useful from time to time.

You can right click any of the SQL Agent objects and create a script that can drop or create the object. If you wish the same object to exist on many servers, you can script it out, change the server name, and load it onto a different server. This would mean you would have to keep operators, jobs, alerts, and proxies in sync between multiple servers, which could be painful and error prone. We cover how to do multiserver jobs in a later section titled "Multiserver Administration."

Event forwarding can also simplify your life when you administer many servers. Event forwarding is covered in the "Advanced" section later in the chapter.

SQL Agent Security

SQL Agent security is more fine-grained than ever. In this section, we cover not only the service account but new security around who can create, see, and run SQL Agent jobs. What security do job steps run under? In SQL 2000, there was only the SQL Agent Service account and a single proxy account. SQL Server 2005 expands this to allow multiple, separate proxy accounts to be affiliated with each job step. These proxy accounts are associated with SQL logins. This provides excellent control for each type of job step.

Service Account

The SQL Server Agent service account should be a domain account if you plan on taking advantage of Database Mail or require any network connectivity. The account should map to a login that is also a member of the sysadm fixed server role.

Access to SQL Agent

After the installation, only members of the sysadm fixed server role have access to SQL Server Agent objects. Others will not even see the SQL Agent object in the Object Explorer of Management Studio. To allow other users access to SQL Agent, you must add them to one of three fixed database roles in `msdb` database:

❑   `SQLAgentUserRole`

❑   `SQLAgentReaderRole`

❑   `SQLAgentOperatorRole`

These are listed in order of increased capability. Each higher role includes the permissions associated with the lower roles. Therefore, it does not make sense to assign a user to more than one role.

Members of the sysadm fixed server role have access to all of the capabilities of SQL Agent and do not have to be added to any of these roles.

SQLAgentUserRole

Members of the user role have the most restricted access to SQL Agent. They can only see the Jobs node under SQL Agent and can only have access to local jobs and schedules that they own. They cannot use multiserver jobs, which are discussed later in this chapter. They can create, alter, delete, execute, start, and stop their own jobs and job schedules. They can view but not delete the job history for their own jobs. They can see and select operators to be notified on completion of their jobs and choose from the available proxies for their job steps.

SQLAgentReaderRole

The reader role includes all of the permissions of the user role. It can create and run the same things as a user, but this role can see the list of multiserver jobs, their properties, and history. They can also see all of the jobs and schedules on the local server, not just the ones they own. They can only see the Jobs node under SQL Agent as well.

SQLAgentOperatorRole

The operator role is the least restricted role and includes all of the permissions of the reader role and the user role. This role has additional read capabilities as well as execute capabilities. Members of this role can view the properties of proxies and operators. They can list the available proxies and alerts on the server as well.

Members of this role can also execute, start, or stop local jobs. They can enable or disable any job or operator, although they must use the `sp_update_job` and `sp_update_schedule` procedures to do so. They can delete job history for any job. Jobs, Alerts, Operators, and Proxies nodes under SQL Agent are visible to this role. Only the Error Log node is hidden.

Proxy Accounts

Job-step security has been completely redone in SQL Server 2005 to be much more granular. In SQL Server 2000, sysadm role members executed job steps under the context of the SQL Agent Service Account. SQL 2000 allowed you to set up one other proxy account, whose permission applied to all other users.

SQL Agent Subsystems

In SQL Server 2000, all job steps that accessed non-SQL resources (Active Script and Command Exec steps) operated under a single permission structure for everyone. The first step to making security finer grained is to break up the objects on which security can be defined. In SQL 2005, security can be placed on each SQL Agent subsystem. There are 11. In the order they appear when you are adding a job step, they are:

❑   ActiveX Script

❑   Operating System (CmdExec)

❑   Replication Distributor

❑ Replication Merge

❑ Replication Queue Reader

❑ Replication Snapshot

❑ Replication Transaction Log Reader

❑ Analysis Services Command

❑ Analysis Services Query

❑ SSIS Package Execution

❑ Transact SQL

The permissions for Transact SQL are not governed by proxy. Each user executes T-SQL under his own account. If you are a member of the sysadm group, you can choose any SQL login as the Run As Account.

All of the other subsystems use one or more proxies to determine permissions for the subsystem.

Proxies

Figure 5-7 shows the basic relationship among the parts.

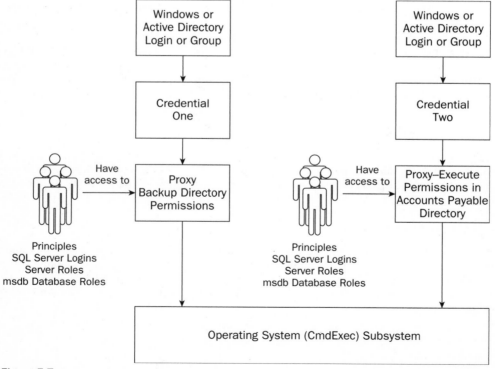

Figure 5-7

Each subsystem has its own permissions. Our example shows the setup for permissions for the operating system (CmdExec) subsystem. The issue is, what operating-system permissions are used when someone executes a CmdExec job step? How can we allow multiple levels of permissions for different groups of users?

The proxy combines the permissions for the CmdExec step, as well as the users who may run under this proxy.

Credentials

The first thing you must do is create a credential. The easiest way to create a credential is in Management Studio: Expand Security, right-click on Credentials, and choose New Credential. You will be presented with a dialog box like the one shown in Figure 5-8.

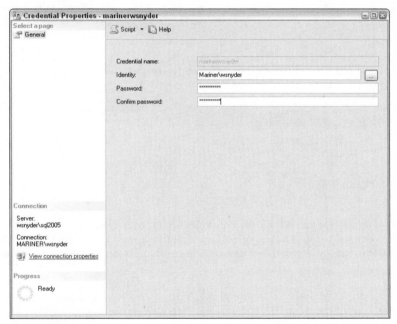

Figure 5-8

Give the credential a friendly name, and associate it with a Windows login or group. You must also provide the password to complete the creation. The permissions associated with this login or group will be the permissions applied to the CmdExec job step.

If your passwords time out on a regular basis, your job steps will begin to fail. You will have to reset the passwords for each credential or increase or drop the password expiration for the special accounts. These accounts should be created specifically for this and have the minimum security necessary for the job step to complete successfully.

Create Proxy

Now you can create your proxy. In Management Studio, expand SQL Agent, right-click Proxy, and choose New Proxy. You will get a New Proxy Account dialog box, shown in Figure 5-9.

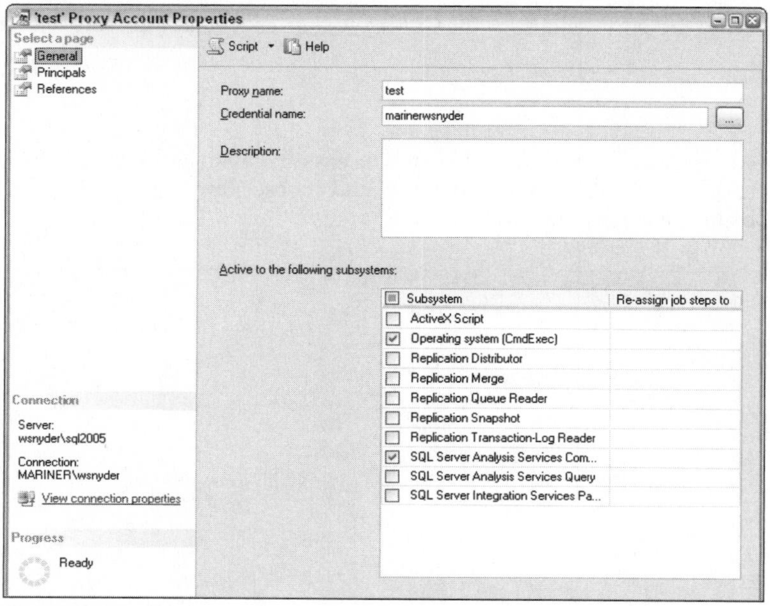

Figure 5-9

Give the Proxy a name that provides information about its security level or its intended use. Then associate a credential with the proxy. The proxy will provide the permissions associated with its credential when it is used. Provide a more detailed description of what the proxy allows and how it should be used and when.

Then select the subsystems that can use the proxy. A proxy can be associated with many subsystems. Then you create a list of users (principles) who may use this proxy. This is done on the Principles page. A principle can be a Server Role, a SQL Login, or an msdb role.

> If you upgraded from SQL 2000, the proxy information from SQL Agent was placed in a SQL 2005 proxy named UpgradedProxyAccount. Although this account should be temporary, your jobs will continue to run as they did in SQL 2000. This proxy account is only associated with the subsystems actually used in the SQL 2000 jobs, not all subsystems. You should create SQL 2005 proxies and replace this proxy.

Using Proxies

Now assume we have created the two proxies for the CmdExec subsystem as Figure 5-7 describes. Your SQL login is associated with both proxies. You wish to create a job that contains a CmdExec job step. When you add the job step, open the drop-down labeled Run as: This contains a list of all of the proxies you are allowed to use for your job step. Each proxy has its own permissions. Choose the proxy that contains the permissions you need for your job step, and you should be ready to go.

Configuring SQL Server Agent

Now that you have learned how things work in SQL Agent, you can take on the configuration task. You already know about many of the configurables, so now we will simply go through the dialogs with a brief description.

To start configuration, right-click SQL Agent node with Management Studio and choose properties. You will be shown the General page, as shown in Figure 5-10.

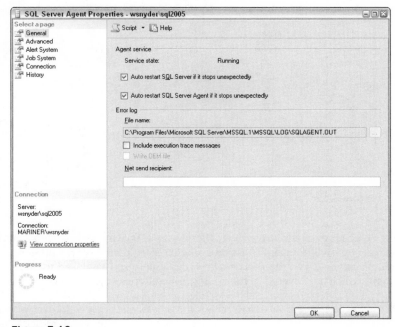

Figure 5-10

You should make sure to check the two top checkboxes: "Auto restart SQL Server if it stops unexpectedly" and "Auto restart SQL Server Agent if it stops unexpectedly." Processes will watch both of these services and bring them back up if possible.

We usually leave the error-log location to the default, but you can change it if you wish. If you need some additional logging, you can check "Include execution trace messages."

To get a Net Send when errors are logged, enter a workstation name in the Net Send recipient textbox. Of course, Windows Messaging Service must be running on the server for Net Sends to occur.

Now choose the Advanced Page on the top left, and you see the dialog box shown in Figure 5-11.

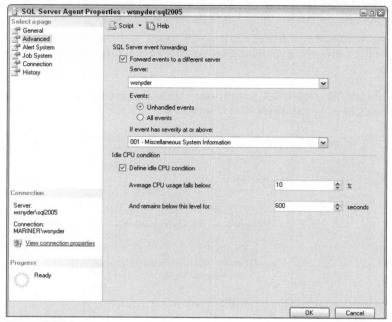

Figure 5-11

The top section, SQL Server event forwarding, allows you to forward your events from one server to another. You can set up operators and alerts on a single server, then have the other servers forward their events to the single server. If you plan on using this capability, you also need to understand how to use SQL Agent tokens, which are covered in the "Using Token Replacement" section.

If you wish this server to forward its events, check the box labeled "Forward events to a different server." Then select the server name. You can forward all events or only unhandled events. An unhandled event is one that does not have an alert defined for it. You also select how severe the error must be before it will be forwarded. You may not wish anything less than a severity 16 (Miscellaneous User Error) to be forwarded. Whether or not you forward 16s depends on whether you have application-defined errors that expect to do notifications.

The second section is "Idle CPU condition." Recall that you can create a schedule that runs when the CPU becomes idle. This is the place where you define what idle means. The default is CPU utilization at less than 10 percent for 10 minutes.

The next page is for the Alert System, as shown in Figure 5-12.

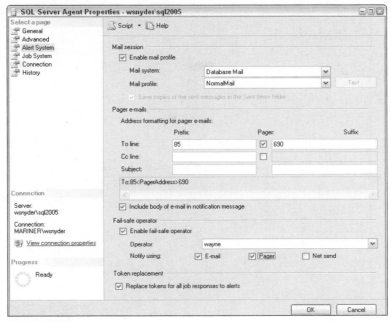

Figure 5-12

If you plan to use Database Mail or the older SQL Mail, you do the setup here. Although you may have many mail profiles in Database Mail, SQL Agent will use only one profile. Choose the mail system and profile.

The second section is for pager e-mails. If your pager system requires special control characters in the To:, CC:, or Subject line, you may add those characters here. You may add these control characters in front of the item (prefix) or after the item (suffix). As you make changes, you can see the effect in the small box below your data-entry section. You may also choose to include or exclude the body of the e-mail for pagers by indicating your selection in the appropriate checkbox.

The third section allows you to provide failsafe operator information. Please use this if you are doing any notifications. It is too easy to change a schedule in such a way that results in no one getting notified, so don't get caught. Enable this section, choose an operator, and indicate how the failsafe messages should be delivered (by e-mail, pager, Net Send, or some combination of these).

The last checkbox allows you to specify whether or not you wish to have tokens replaced in jobs run from alerts. Details of token replacement are covered in the Advanced section.

The Job System page is next, as shown in Figure 5-13.

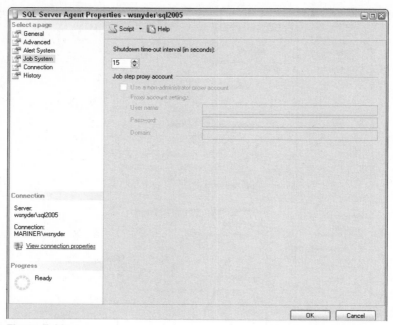

Figure 5-13

You are trying to shut down SQL Agent, and jobs are running. How long should SQL Agent wait for jobs to complete before killing them and shutting down? You specify that period in the Shutdown time-out interval (in seconds) list.

The second section is only available if you are administering a SQL Server 2000 Agent. This allows you to set the backward-compatible nonadministrator proxy. SQL 2000 only allowed one proxy. SQL 2005 allows many, so this is not necessary when administering SQL Server 2005 Agents.

The Connection Page is one that most users will not need. SQL Agent connects to SQL Server, by default, using the server name, default port, the SQL Agent Service account, and the highest-matching protocol between the client configuration and the protocols enabled for SQL Server. There are several circumstances where you may wish to alter these defaults:

❑ Your server has multiple network cards and you wish to specify a particular IP or port.

❑ You wish to connect using a specific protocol (IP, for instance).

❑ You wish SQL Agent to connect to the server using a login different from the service account login.

To accomplish this, you create an alias for the SQL Server, using Configuration Manager. Expand the SQL Native Client Configuration, right-click Aliases, and choose New Alias. Then set up the alias to suit your connectivity needs. Then on the SQL Agent connection page, enter the alias name and the connection information you wish for SQL Agent to use. Although SQL Server authentication is allowed, it is not recommended.

The last page is the History Page. You need to think about these settings. You can limit the size of the job-history log to a fixed number of rows. That's easy and fine to do. The Maximum job history rows per job is really a life saver, however. Imagine a job that runs over and over. It could be a job scheduled by a user to run every second, or it could be a job that runs from an alert that occurs over and over. In any case, the log entries from this job could fill up your entire job history, and you would have no history information for any other jobs. That could leave you in a tough spot if any other job needed debugging. This is exactly the situation that Maximum job history rows per job is intended to prevent. The default is 100 rows, but you can change it based on your needs.

New to SQL 2005 is the ability to remove older history rows, even if you have not reached your upper limit. Simply check the box, and set the age.

Database Mail

Database Mail is new to SQL Server 2005 and is a welcome relief from SQLMail, although you may still use SQLMail if you wish. Database Mail and SQLMail allow you to notify operators via e-mail and to send e-mails via stored procedures.

SQL Mail required Extended Messaging Application Programming Interface (MAPI) support, which could be problematic. Installing a new version of Office could cause SQLMail to fail, by installing a version of the MAPI driver that would be incompatible with SQLMail.

Database Mail is more secure, more reliable, and does not rely on MAPI. It uses Simple Mail Transfer Protocol (SMTP). It is cluster-aware, and allows automatic retry of failed e-mail messages as well as failover to another SMTP server, should the first become unavailable. Database Mail also allows you to set up multiple accounts and provide secured or public access to the accounts.

Database Mail is not available in SQL Server 2005 Express Edition.

Architecture

Database Mail is loosely coupled to SQL Server and is based on queuing, as shown in Figure 5-14. When an e-mail is sent, either by calling `sp_send_dbmail` or from SQL Agent notifications, security is checked. The email is stored in a table in `msdb`, and a message is placed in the Service Broker message queue in `msdb`. This activates an external program: `DatabaseMail90.exe`, located in the `MSSQL\Binn` directory. `DatabaseMail90.exe` reads the message and sends the e-mail with any attachments to one or more SMTP mail servers. It then places a message in the status queue, containing the results of the send process. The status queue insert activates a stored procedure in `msdb` to update the status of the e-mail in `msdb`.

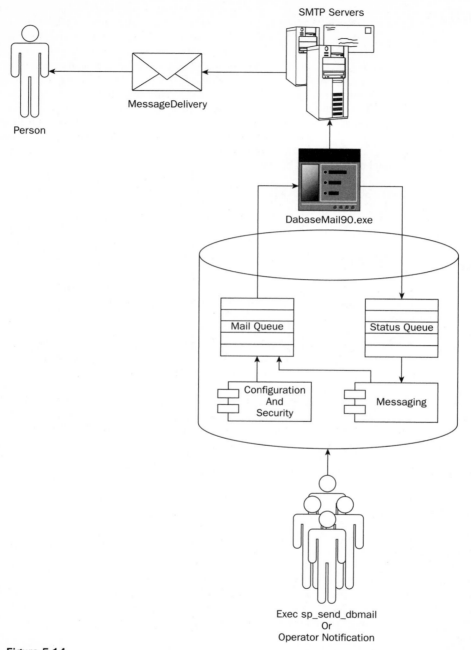

SMTP Servers

MessageDelivery

Person

DabaseMail90.exe

Mail Queue

Status Queue

Configuration
And
Security

Messaging

Exec sp_send_dbmail
Or
Operator Notification

Figure 5-14

Security

For security reasons, Database Mail is disabled by default. You can enable and configure it using the SQL Server Surface Area Configuration Tool, as shown in Figure 5-15, or the Database Mail Configuration Wizard.

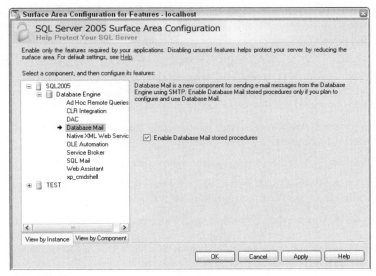

Figure 5-15

Additionally, to send notifications via Database Mail from SQL Agent, SQL Agent must be configured to use Database Mail. This is covered in the "SQL Agent Configuration" section of this chapter.

The external program, DatabaseMail90.exe, must have network access to the SMTP servers. It runs using the security credentials for the SQL Server Service account. Therefore, the SQL Server Service account must have network access, and the SMTP servers must allow connections from the SQL Server computer. Database Mail supports Secure Sockets Layer (SSL) if it is required by the SMTP server.

> *Local system and Local Service do not have network access, and cannot be used as service accounts for SQL Server if you use Database Mail. Database Mail would not be able to connect to another computer (the SMTP server).*

To send database mail, you must either be a member of the sysadm fixed server role or a member of the DatabaseMailUserRole in msdb. You can place a size limit on mail attachments and prohibit attachments with certain file extensions.

Configuration

To use database mail, you'll need to do some configuration. You'll need to set up the database mail account, configure the mail procedure itself, and set up archiving.

Database Mail Account

A Database Mail Account is a basic unit of configuration for Database Mail. An account contains the following configuration information:

❑ "From" information for the e-mail messages. All outgoing e-mail messages will say they are from the account you provide here. This does not have to be a real e-mail account.

❑ "Reply to" e-mail address. If the recipient of one of these e-mails tries to reply, the reply will be sent to the e-mail address provided for this account.

❑ SMTP connection information. The SMTP Server name and port number are included in the account configuration. Database Mail supports encrypted and unencrypted messages. Encryption is done via Secure Sockets Layer (SSL). Whether you wish the messages from this account to be encrypted is included in the account configuration.

❑ E-mail retry configuration. You may specify how many times to retry sending an e-mail and a wait period between retries.

❑ E-mail size limits. You may set a maximum size limit allowed for e-mails from this account.

❑ Excluded attachment extension list. You may provide a list of file extensions. Any attachment that has a file extension in the prohibited list will not be allowed.

❑ Logging level. You may specify how much logging should be done for this account.

If your SMTP Server requires a log in, you may wish to set up a specific local account, with minimum permissions, specifically for sending SMTP mail. The purpose of this account is to follow the principle of least privileges and should be used for no other purpose.

You may set up many accounts, but you should plan your implementation. You may wish to have accounts for several different SMTP servers. This will allow you to automatically fail over from one to another. This is done via profiles, which will be covered next. You may also wish to set up a special account that allows dangerous extensions or large attachments to be sent and restrict that account to special users.

Another reason to set up multiple accounts is to provide different From and Reply-to addresses. You may wish to do this for several departments in your company. For instance, you might set up an account named Accounts Payable, which has a from address of `AccountsPayable@mycompany.com` and a reply address of `IncomingAPEmail@mycompany.com`. This reply address could be an e-mail group that sends to the accounts payable service reps at your company.

Setup

In this section, you will set up Database Mail. Use the wizard by expanding Management in SQL Server Management Studio. Right-click Database Mail and choose Configure Database Mail.

Click through the introduction dialog box. The next box is the Select Configuration dialog box. Check the top radio button; we are setting up Database Mail for the first time. Click Next.

You will then receive a message box, asking if you wish to enable the Database Mail feature. Choose yes and continue.

This brings you to the New Database Mail Account dialog box, shown in Figure 5-16. This is where you provide the information needed to communicate with an SMTP server. Choose a name and description for this account.

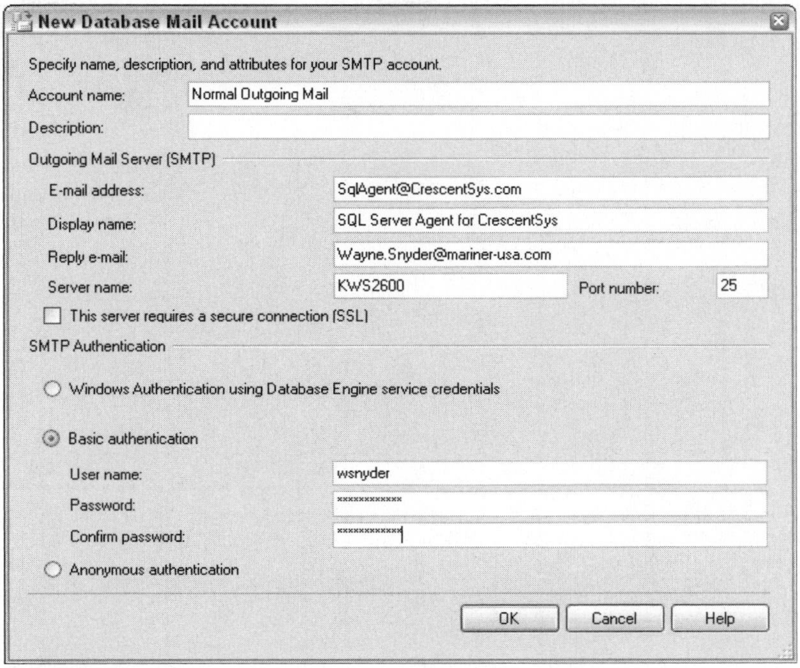

Figure 5-16

The next section is the Outgoing Mail Server (SMTP). The e-mails sent from this account will be tagged from the e-mail address and display name that you set in this section. If the recipients reply to the e-mail, the reply will be sent to the address you supply in the Reply e-mail textbox. In the Server Name textbox, you provide the name of the SMTP server. This is usually in the form of `smtp.myserver.com`. You do not provide the complete URL, such as `http://smtp.myserver.com`. Database Mail does this for you. If you check the box labeled "This server requires a secure connection (SSL)", the URL created will be `https://smtp.myserver.com`. The default port number of 25 will do, unless you have changed the SMTP port number.

You provide the SMTP login information in the SMTP authentication section. Not all SMTP servers require authentication; some require only a known sender e-mail, and others require nothing. Then click OK.

You will be taken to the Manage Profile Security dialog box, as shown in Figure 5-17.

Here you set up public and private profiles. Check the Public checkbox to make this a public profile. You may also wish to set this as a default profile. Click Next.

You should now be at the System Configuration Parameters dialog box, as shown in Figure 5-18.

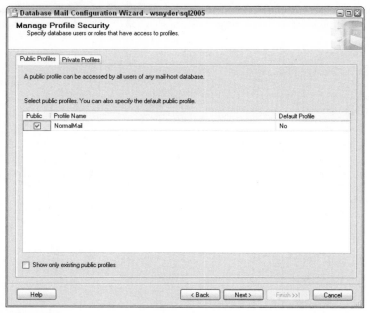

Figure 5-17

Figure 5-18

Set up the parameters as we discussed earlier to meet your needs. Click Next.

Then the setup will begin, and in the final dialog box you will see lots of green. Click Close.

To ensure things are working properly, you should send a test e-mail. In SQL Server Management Studio, expand Management, right-click Database Mail, and choose Send Test E-Mail. You will be prompted to enter an e-mail address. Send the mail and wait for receipt.

Archiving

You can access mail information in the `sysmail_allitems` view. Attachments can be accessed via `sysmail_mailattachments`, and the mail log is in `sysmail_eventlog`. The tables under these views are not automatically maintained. They will just get larger and larger. As a DBA, you will probably wish to do some maintenance. Microsoft provides stored procedures to delete items from these tables: `msdb.dbo.sysmail_delete_mailitems_sp` and `msdb.dbo.sysmail_delete_log_sp`. Both of these have two parameters: `@sent_before` and `@sent_status`.

`@sent_before` takes a `datetime` value and will delete all log or mail items with a time before the parameter time. When you do not specify a `sent_status`, all mail items that have a `send_request_date` prior to the parameter will be deleted, whether or not they have been sent. So be careful.

`@sent_status` can have values of `unsent`, `sent`, `failed`, or `retrying`. When you specify a `sent_status`, only the mail items that have a `sent_status` equal to the parameter will be deleted.

You may wish to archive this information prior to its deletion. Books Online will get you started with a small example that runs monthly and archives the month's mail, attachments, and logs into tables called `DBMailArchive_<year>_<month>`, `DBMail_Attachments_<year>_<month>`, and `DBMail_Log_<year>_<month>`.

Multiserver Administration

There are several tactics within SQL Server 2005 that enable you to administer multiple servers more easily. The focus of these tactics is to centralize your administration. This can be done by forwarding events to a central event management server. This allows you to centralize alert handling. Another optimization is to use master and target servers to create jobs on a single master server and have the jobs run on multiple target servers.

Using Token Replacement

SQL 2005 has some really nice new capabilities around SQL Agent job tokens. A token is a string literal that you use in your job steps (T-SQL scripts, CMDExec job steps, or Active Script). Before the job runs, SQL Agent does a string replacement of the token with its value. Tokens are usable only in SQL Agent jobs.

One of the tokens is (STRTDT). You might add the following in a T-SQL job step.

```
PRINT 'Job Start Date(YYYYMMDD):' + $ESCAPE_SQUOTE(STRTDT))
```

If you capture the output, it should look like this:

```
Job Start Date(YYYYMMDD):20060707
```

Tokens are case sensitive.

The following is a list of tokens that can be used in any job.

❑ (DATE): Current Date (YYYYMMDD)

❑ (INST): Instance name of the SQL Server. This token is empty for the default instance.

❑ (JOBID): SQL Agent job ID

❑ (MACH): Computer name where the job is run

❑ (MSSA): Master SQLServerAgent service name

❑ (OSCMD): Prefix for the program used to run CmdExec job steps

❑ (SQLDIR): SQL Server's install directory. The default install directory is C:\Program Files\Microsoft SQL Server\MSSQL.

❑ (STEPCT): The number of times this step has executed. You could use this in looping code to terminate the step after a specific number of iterations. This count does not include retries on failure. This is updated on each step run during the job, like a real-time counter.

❑ (STEPID): The job step ID

❑ (SVR): The server name of the computer running SQL Server, including the instance name

❑ (TIME): Current time (HHMMSS)

❑ (STRTTM): The job's start time (HHMMSS)

❑ (STRTDT): The job's start date (YYYYMMDD)

The following is a list of tokens that can *only* be used in a job that has been started from an alert. If these tokens are included in a job started any other way, the job will throw an error.

❑ (A-DBN): Database name where the alert occurred

❑ (A-SVR): The server name where the alert occurred

❑ (A-ERR): The error number associated with the alert

❑ (A-SEV): The error severity associated with the alert

❑ (A-MSG): The message text associated with the alert

The following token is available for use only on jobs run as the result of a WMI alert.

❑ (WMI(property)): This provides the value for the WMI property named *property*. $(WMI(DatabaseName)) returns the value of the DatabaseName property for the WMI alert that caused the job to run.

Beginning with SQL Server 2005 Service Pack 1 (SP1), you must use all of the tokens with escape macros. The purpose of this change is to increase the security around the use of tokens from unknown sources. Consider the following token, which you might have included in a T-SQL job step:

```
Print 'Error message: $(A-MSG)'
```

The T-SQL job step runs as the result of a user error (`raiserror`). A malicious user could raise an error like this one:

```
Raiserror(''';Delete from dbo.Employee',16,1)
```

The error returned would be:

```
';Delete from dbo.Employee
```

The print message would be:

```
Print 'Error message:';Delete from dbo.Employee
```

You have just been attacked with a SQL injection attack. The delete statement will run if the T-SQL job step has permission.

Beginning with SP1, you must add an escape macro. Since the `print` statement uses single quotes, a SQL injection attack would close out the single quote and then insert its own SQL. To prevent this attack, you could double-quote any quote that comes in via the token. The escape macro `ESCAPE_SQUOTE` does this very thing. It is used like this:

```
Print 'Error message: $(ESCAPE_SQUOTE(A-MSG))'
```

Continuing the example, you would end up with:

```
Print 'Error message:'';Delete from dbo.Employee
```

You would get an error due to the unmatched quote, and the step would fail; you would be safe.

The following is a list of escape macros:

❑   `$(ESCAPE_SQUOTE(token))`: Doubles single quotes (') in the replacement string

❑   `$(ESCAPE_DQUOTE(token))`: Doubles double quotes (") in the replacement string

❑   `$(ESCAPE_RBRACKET(token))`: Doubles right brackets (]) in the replacement string

❑   `$(ESCAPE_NONE(token))`: The token replacement is made without changes. This is used for backward compatibility only.

You can also use these values directly if you ensure proper data types. The SQL script-looping job with tokens contains the following code that terminates a job step after it has executed five times. The top line converts the STEPCT token to an integer so it can be used in a comparison. Then the JOBID token for this job is converted to a binary 16 and passed to the `sp_stop_job` stored procedure, which can take the job ID of the job you wish to stop.

```
IF Convert(int,$(ESCAPE_NONE(STEPCT))) >5
  BEGIN
  DECLARE @jobid binary(16)
  SELECT @jobid =Convert(Uniqueidentifier,$(ESCAPE_NONE(JOBID)))
  EXEC msdb.dbo.sp_stop_job @job_id = @jobid
  END
```

Imagine how you might use the alert-based tokens. You could create a SQL performance alert that fires when the `<any database>` transaction log gets greater than 80-percent full. Create a job with a T-SQL step like this:

```
DECLARE @a varchar(100)
SELECT @a = 'BACKUP LOG $(ESCAPE_SQUOTE(A-DBN))
  TO DISK = ''\\UNCName\Share\$(ESCAPE_SQUOTE(A-DBN))\log.bak'' '
SELECT @a
BACKUP LOG $(ESCAPE_SQUOTE(A-DBN))
  TO DISK = '\\UNCName\Share\\$(ESCAPE_SQUOTE(A-DBN))\log.bak'
```

Where UNCName is the name of the server where you wish the backup to be stored and Share is the share on the server. Make sure the job runs when the alert occurs. If the alert fires for AdventureWorks, the backup command will look like this:

```
BACKUP LOG AdventureWorks TO DISK = \\UNCName\Share\\AdventureWorks\log.bak
```

You would have to create the directory first and grant appropriate permissions to the proxy you use. You could create a CMDExec step, which creates the directory on the fly. Now a single log backup job can back up any transaction log. You might improve this by adding the date and time to the filename.

Event Forwarding

Where events and alerts are concerned, you can create operators and alerts on a single system and then have the other systems forward their events to your central alert handling SQL Server, who will respond to those alerts as necessary. The "Configuring SQL Server Agent" section of this chapter covers forwarding events.

You can set up operators on your master event management system. Create the jobs that will respond to the alerts. Then create alerts on the single master event management system to handle the event. The jobs you create can take advantage of SQL Agent tokens and can know what server and database the original event occurred on.

Using WMI

Windows Management Instrumentation (WMI) is a set of functions embedded into the kernel of Microsoft Operating Systems and Servers, including SQL Server. The purpose of WMI is to allow local and remote monitoring and management of servers. It is a standards-based implementation based on the Distributed Management Task Force's (DMTF) Web-Based Enterprise Management (WBEM) and Common Information Model (CIM) specifications.

WMI is a big initiative and could probably be an entire book all by itself. What you need to know is that WMI has many events for SQL Server. Search for WMI to get you started in Books Online, and you will discover the many, many events. You can create alerts on these events. There are Data Definition Language (DDL) events that occur when databases are created or dropped and when tables are created or dropped as an example.

WMI has a language to query these events called Windows Management Instrumentation Query Language (WQL). It is very much like T-SQL, and you will get comfortable with it immediately.

Browse Books Online for the kind of event you wish to monitor. Each event will have a list of attributes, just like a table has a list of columns. Using WMI, you can select the attributes from the event in an alert.

To create an alert, use SQL Serve Management Studio. In Object Explorer, open SQL Agent tree node, right-click Alerts, and choose New Alert. In the alert-type drop-down box, choose WMI Event Alert.

The namespace will be populated based on the server you are connected to and should look like this:

```
\\.\root\Microsoft\SqlServer\ServerEvents\SQL2005
```

The . represents the server name, which you can change, such as \\MYSQLSERVER\. The last node should be MSSQLSERVER for a default instance and the *instance name* for named instances. The instance I was running is called SQL2005.

In the textbox, you enter your WQL query, as shown here:

```
SELECT * FROM DDL_DATABASE_LEVEL_EVENTS
```

Or you could use this query:

```
Select TSQLCommand from DDL_DATABASE_LEVEL_EVENTS
```

To select only the TSQLCommand Attribute. There will be a parse when you click OK. If your namespace is incorrect, or the syntax or event/attribute names are incorrect, you will get a message immediately.

Then in your job you may use the WMI(attribute) event token, in this case:

```
Print '$(ESCAPE_SQUOTE(WMI(TSQLCommand)))'
```

To get events from a database, service broker notifications must be turned on for that database. To turn on service broker notifications for AdventureWorks, use the following syntax:

```
ALTER DATABASE AdventureWorks SET ENABLE_BROKER;
```

If your alerts are occurring but the text replacement for the WMI token is not being done, you probably need to turn on the service broker for your database.

> *The service account that SQL Server Agent uses must have permission on the namespace and ALTER ANY EVENT NOTIFICATION permissions. This will be done automatically if you use SQL Server Configuration Manager to set up accounts. However, to adjust these settings manually, from the Run prompt, type **wmimgmt.msc**. An administrative dialog will return, allowing you set up permissions.*

There is a test program for WMI on your server. To run it from the command line, type **WBEMTest**. It is installed in the WBEM directory of your Windows system directory.

Microsoft has an entire subsection of its Web site devoted to WMI. Just search for WMI on www.microsoft.com.

You might also create an alert for database mirroring. You need to know when a mirrored database's mirror status changes. This is exactly the kind of thing you would create a WMI alert for. This particular example and its implementation can be found at http://www.microsoft.com/technet/prod technol/sql/2005/mirroringevents.mspx.

Multiserver Administration — Using Master and Target Servers

SQL Server allows you to set up a master server (MSX). The master server can send jobs to be run on one or more target servers (TSX). The master server may not also be a target server, receiving jobs from another master server. The target servers receive and run jobs from a single master server, in addition to their own local jobs. You may have multiple master servers in your environment, but a target server is associated with a single master server. This is a very simple two-level hierarchy; a server is a master server, a target server, or neither. The language used to describe the process is military in character: You *enlist* target servers to add them, and they *defect* to go away.

Setting up servers is easy. In SSMS, right click the SQL Server Agent node, select Multiserver Administration, and choose Make this a Master. After the initial dialog box, you will see a box where you can provide the e-mail address, pager address, and Net Send location to set up a Master Server Operator. This operator will be set up on the master server and all target servers. This is the *only* operator who can be notified from multiserver jobs.

The next dialog box allows you to choose all of the target servers. The list includes the servers that you have registered in SSMS. You may add additional registrations by clicking the Add Connection button. Choose the servers that you want to be targets of this master, and Click next. SQL will check to ensure that the SQL versions of the master and targets are compatible. Close this dialog box. If the versions are not compatible, drop the target from the list; then continue. Later you can upgrade the target or master, so the versions are the same.

Target servers must connect to the master server to share job status information. The next dialog box allows you to have the wizard create a login on the target, if necessary, and grant it login rights to the master server. Once you have completed the setup, you can refresh your SQL Agent nodes and see the change. There is a note on the master server (MSX). There is also a note on the target server, as shown in Figure 5-19.

Now you can create jobs to be used at multiple target servers. Notice on the MSX that the jobs node is divided into two sections: local jobs and multiserver jobs. Right-click multiserver jobs, and select New job to create a simple job. You can see the new dialog box (Targets) in the New Job dialog, shown in Figure 5-20.

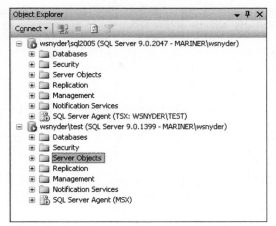

Figure 5-19

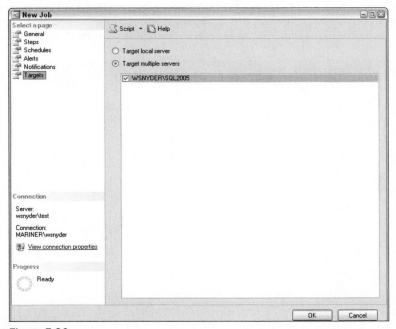

Figure 5-20

Now you can create jobs on the MSX server and have them run at one or many TSX servers. You should create a simple job right now. While doing this, be sure to go to the notifications page. The only operator you can notify is MSXOperator.

Creating multiserver jobs is a really nice way to manage a larger implementation without having to buy additional third-party products. No one on the TSX box can mess up your jobs, either. Use SSMS to connect to the target server as an administrator and look at the job properties for the job you just created and downloaded from the MSX. You can see the job, you can see the job history, and you can even run the job. You cannot delete the job, change the schedule, change the steps, or anything else. This job does not belong to you; it belongs to the MSX.

As you begin to think about how you might use this, be sure you consider the implications of a single job running on multiple servers. Any reference to directories, databases, and so on must be valid for all of the TSXs where this job runs. You can create a single backup share that all of the backups can use, for instance.

Since a job can start another job, you could also create a master job that has a single step that starts another job. This other job is created on each TSX and is specific to each TSX. This will allow you some customization, if necessary.

Back in SSMS, right-click the SQL Agent node on the master server, choose Multi Server Administration, and you can add target servers and manage target servers. Choose Manage Target Servers. In this dialog box, shown in Figure 5-21, you can monitor the status of everything. When you create a job for a target server, the job is automatically downloaded to the target server. If the unread instructions count does not go down to 0, as in this figure, poll the target server. This will wake it up to accept the instructions.

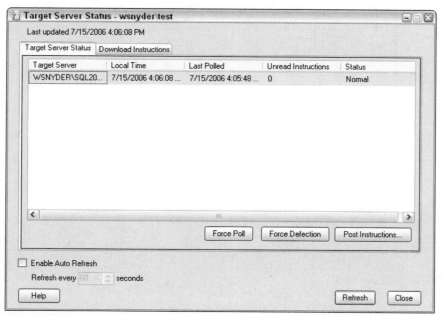

Figure 5-21

You can also see the details of downloaded instructions. This will show you details of when jobs are downloaded and updated, as in Figure 5-22.

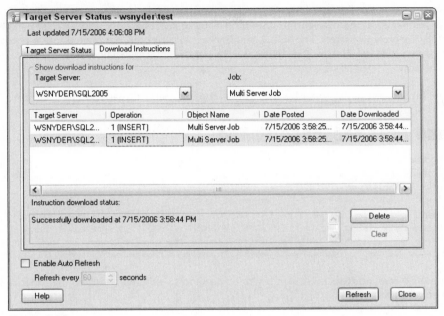

Figure 5-22

Using the Post Instructions button in the Target Server Status dialog, you can synchronize clocks between the servers, defect target servers, set polling intervals, and start jobs. You can also start the job directly from the jobs node on the MSX or the TSX.

Job histories can be seen on the MSX for the job, just like any other job, except you cannot see the job-step details. To get the step details, view the job history from the TSX.

You can defect TSXs from the TSX SQL Agent node or from the Manage Target Servers dialog on the MSX. Once all of the TSXs have been defected, the MSX is no longer an MSX.

Problem Resolution

While using SQL Agent with SQL Server 2005, we have encountered some problems. These problems are fixable, but it took some research to get to the solutions. We include these problems here, with the hope that this information will save you some time.

Job Failure Error 3621

When running a job, the following error occurs and the job terminates immediately.

```
The job failed.  Unable to determine if the owner (MARINER\wsnyder) of job myjob
has server access (reason: Could not obtain information about Windows NT group/user
'MARINER\wsnyder', error code 0x5. [SQLSTATE 42000] (Error 15404)  The statement
has been terminated. [SQLSTATE 01000] (Error 3621)).
```

In this case, the SQL Server Agent Service Account was local (WSNYDER\sqlserver), not a domain account. I created a job that was running under a domain account (MARINER\wsnyder). When I tried to run this job, the error occurred. The SQL Agent Service Account did not have domain permissions to check the domain active directory to determine the permissions associated with the Mariner\wsnyder domain account.

Use a domain account with proper permissions as the SQL Server Agent Service Account.

Database Mail Message Failed

You are trying to use Database Mail to send to an operator. Notifications work with some operators, but not with others, using the same mail profile in Database Mail. You check the Database Mail error log and see the following message:

```
The mail could not be sent to the recipients because of the mail server failure.
(Sending Mail using Account 1 (2006-07-08T10:46:20). Exception Message: Cannot send
mails to mail server. (Mailbox unavailable. The server response was: You must SMTP
authenticate before sending to wayne.snyder@someplace.com).)
```

Make sure the e-mail address is correct. If you try to send to an e-mail address that does not exist, you will also get an error.

Some ISPs block Email from Unknown SMTP Servers

Some Internet Service Providers (ISPs) block e-mail from unknown SMTP servers to prevent spam. To send to those e-mail addresses, you would have to create another account that uses the ISP's SMTP server and then add the new account to the existing profile.

One way to ensure this is the case is to send a test-message from the Database Mail item in Management Studio for a good e-mail address, and the e-mail is sent. Then send another test e-mail with the second e-mail address (associated with the ISP which may block SMTP messages), and the send fails. Yet you can send an e-mail to the address via your normal e-mail system. This is likely your problem.

SQL Agent Jobs Fail after Installing Service Pack 1

You have installed SP1, and now some of your SQL Agent jobs are failing. The ones that fail are called as the response to an alert. You are receiving the following error message:

```
Unable to start execution of step 1 (reason: The job step contains one or more
tokens. For SQL Server 2005 Service Pack 1 or later, all job steps with tokens must
be updated with a macro before the job can run.).  The step failed.
```

Before SQL Server 2005 SP1, you could use any of the tokens by simply including the token in a string ($(A-DBN)). SQL Server 2000 also allowed some bracketed tokens ([Date]). Beginning with SP1, you *must* use one of the escape macros, or your tokenized jobs will fail.

In a knowledge-base article (#915845), SQL Server Agent jobs fail when the jobs contain job steps that use tokens after you install SQL Server 2005 Service Pack 1 (http://support.microsoft.com/kb/915845)

Microsoft provides a function that will update all jobs, all jobs for an owner, or a specific job, adding the ESCAPE_NONE macro wherever tokens are used. This will allow your jobs to run. However, you should analyze and replace the escapes with one of the SQL injection-resistant escapes.

If you are using Master/Target Servers, you should run the function on the master and all targets.

Summary

SQL Server Agent brings many opportunities for you to make your life easier. Just creating a few simple backup jobs that notify operators will automate many normal tasks. If you wish to get fancy, go ahead, but do some planning first, especially when considering multiserver jobs.

The pager notifications and the related on-duty schedules can be used for regular e-mail or pagers. This is a good way to make sure the correct people are getting notified. If you are going to have many operators for alert notifications, consider creating e-mail groups, and off-load some of the notification work to your e-mail server.

Start small, and take your time. As you get more comfortable with SQL Agent, you can spread your wings and fly.

Integration Services Administration and Performance Tuning

In keeping with the theme of focusing on how SQL Server 2005 changes the role of the DBA, we now look at how you can be better equipped as a DBA to maintain the SQL Server's Business Intelligence components. The SQL Server 2005 Business Intelligence stack includes Integration Services (SSIS), Analysis Services (SSAS), and Reporting Services (SSRS). We focus our attention on Integration Services and Analysis Services in this book, because these components require considerable understanding in order to manage successfully. In this chapter, we look at the many and varied administrative tasks required for managing Integration Services. First, an overview of Integration Services is provided so that you can be more comfortable with and have a better understanding of the moveable parts that require the attention of an administrator. After getting comfortable with the architecture of Integration Services, we focus on the administration of the Integration Services service including configuration, event logs and monitoring activity. Next, you gain an understanding of the various administrative tasks required of Integration Services packages, the functional component within SSIS, including creation, management, execution, and deployment. Last, we review how to secure all of the Integration Services components.

> *For more in-depth information about Integration Services, see Professional SQL Server 2005 Integration Services, by Brian Knight et al. (Wrox, 2006).*

Tour of Integration Services

Certainly the most important Business Intelligence change from SQL Server 2000 to 2005 is found in the component responsible for the movement and manipulation of data. The 2000 platform used Data Transformation Services (DTS), while the 2005 platform uses Integration Services. The change in capabilities goes far beyond what a simple name change may imply, as Integration Services was a complete ground-up rewrite of DTS. In fact, not a single code line from DTS remains within Integration Services.

Integration Services is a solution that provides enterprise-level data integration and workflow solutions that have as their goal the extraction, transformation, and loading (ETL) of data from various sources to various destinations. Included in SSIS are a wide range of tools and wizards to assist in the creation of the workflow and dataflow activities that you need to manage in these complex data-movement solutions.

Integration Services Uses

Before discussing the detailed components within Integration Services, you need to understand some of the more common business uses that involve creating SSIS solutions.

One of the first scenarios involves combining data from different sources stored in different storage systems. In this scenario, SSIS would be responsible for connecting to each data source, extracting the data, and merging it into a single dataset. In today's information systems topology, this is becoming a very common scenario, as businesses' archive information is not needed for regular operations but is invaluable to analyze business trends or meet compliance requirements. Also, this scenario is found when different parts of a business use different storage technologies or different schemas to represent the same data. In these cases, SSIS is used to perform the homogenization of the information. SSIS seamlessly handles multiple divergent data sources and the transformations that can alter data types, split or merge columns, and look up descriptive information that becomes powerful assets for these situations.

Another common scenario is the population and maintenance of data warehouses and data marts. In these business uses, the data volumes tend to be exceptionally large and the window of time in which to perform the extraction, transformation, and loading of the data tends to be rather short. SSIS includes the ability to bulk load data directly from flat files in SQL Server and also has a destination component that can perform a bulk load into SQL Server. A key feature for large data volume and complex enrichment and transformation situations such as these is restartability. SSIS includes checkpoints to handle rerunning a package from a task or container within the controlflow so that you can elegantly handle various types of errors that may occur during these complex data loading scenarios. Often important in data warehouse loads is the ability to source a particular destination from many different tables or files. Often in the database world, we refer to this as *denormalization,* and SSIS packages can easily merge data into a single dataset and load the destination table in a single process without the need to stage or land the data at each step of the process. Lastly, we often require the management or partitioning of history within our data warehouses in order to review the state of activity as of a certain point in time. This history management creates complex updating scenarios, and SSIS handles this with the assistance of the Slowly Changing Dimension Wizard. This wizard dynamically creates and configures a set of data transformation tasks used to manage the insert and update of records, updating of related records, and adding new columns to tables to support this history management.

Often, businesses receive data from outside of their systems and need to perform data-quality routines to standardize and clean the data before loading it into their systems. This is commonly the case when different areas of the business use different standards and formats for the information or when the data is being purchased, as in the common case with address data. Sometimes the data formats are different because the platforms that they originate from differ from the intended destination. In these cases, SSIS includes a rich set of data-transformation tasks to perform a wide range of data-cleaning, converting, and enriching functions. You can replace values or get descriptions from code values by using exact or fuzzy lookups within SSIS. Identifying records that may be duplicates by using SSIS grouping transformations helps to successfully remove them before loading the destination.

The ability to dynamically adjust the data transformations being performed is a common scenario within businesses. Often, data needs to be handled differently based on certain values it may contain or even based upon the summary or count of values in a given set of records. SSIS includes a rich set of transformations that are useful for splitting or merging data based upon data values, applying different aggregations or calculations based on different parts of a dataset, and loading different parts of the data into different locations. SSIS containers specifically support evaluating expressions, enumerating across a set of information, and performing workflow tasks based on results of the data values.

Lastly, you commonly have operational administrative functions that require automation. SSIS includes a whole set of tasks devoted to these administrative functions. You can use tasks specifically designed to copy SQL Server objects or facilitate the bulk loading of data. Also, you have access in SSIS to a SQL Management Objects (SMO) enumerator to perform looping across our servers to perform administrative operations on each server in our environment. Additionally, you have the ability to schedule all of your SSIS packages and solutions using SQL Server Agent jobs.

Four Main Parts of Integration Services

Integration Services consists of four main parts, which are shown in Figure 6-1:

- ❑   The SSIS Service
- ❑   The SSIS runtime engine and the runtime components
- ❑   The SSIS object model
- ❑   The SSIS dataflow engine and the dataflow components

Integration Services Service

The component of architecture within Integration Services responsible for monitoring packages as they execute and managing the storage of packages is the SSIS Service.

Integration Services Runtime Engine and Runtime Components

The SSIS runtime engine is responsible for saving the layout and design of the packages, running the packages, and providing support for all additional package functionality such as transactions, breakpoints, configuration, connections, event handling, and logging. The specific executables that make up this engine include packages, containers, tasks, and event handlers.

Within the SSIS runtime engine, the basic organizational unit is the *package*, which subdivides into the functional units of *controlflow* and *dataflow*. Dataflow is specifically implemented within the controlflow through the use of the dataflow task. Additionally, your SSIS packages can be called from other packages to make use of previously developed functionality, which may yield very interesting and complex dependencies that will require your attention as an administrator.

Controlflow in SSIS is created using three types of objects: containers, tasks, and constraints. The *containers* structure package elements by grouping tasks. Often, these containers may be used to iterate through a dataset and perform operations on each element within an iteration (such as "For each"). The *tasks* enable you to develop sophisticated workflow actions such as executing SQL statements, sending mail, transferring files via FTP, or executing another package. Lastly, the *constraints* connect the package containers and tasks and enable you to specify conditions upon which the next steps of the workflow may be executed. Three default constraints are found within SSIS: success, completion, and failure.

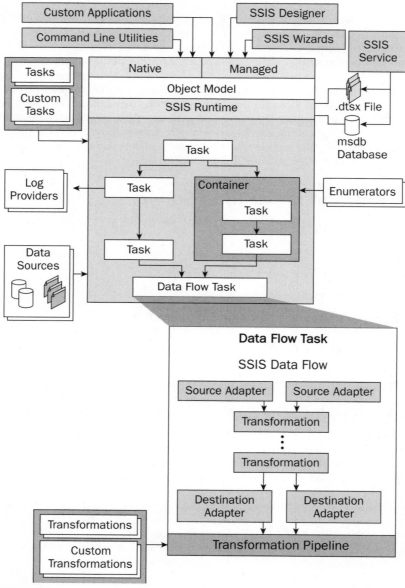

Figure 6-1

Integration Services Object Model

The managed application programming interface (API) used to access SSIS tools, command-line utilities, and custom applications is the SSIS object model. While we will not go into much detail about this object model, it is very important to acknowledge it as a major component of Integration Services.

Integration Services Dataflow Engine and Dataflow Components

Within an SSIS package's controlflow, a dataflow task creates instances of the dataflow engine. This engine is responsible for providing the in-memory data movement from sources to destinations. Additionally, this engine performs the requested transformations to enrich the data for the purposes you specify. Three primary components that make up the dataflow engine include sources, transformations, and destinations. The *sources* provide connectivity to and extract data from a wide range of sources such as database tables or views, files, spreadsheets, and even XML files. The *destinations* permit the insert, update, and deletion of information on a similar wide range of destinations. Lastly, the *transformations* enable you to modify the source data before loading into a destination using capabilities such as lookups, merging, pivoting, splitting, converting, and deriving information.

Project Management and Change Control

Clearly one of the areas needing an entirely different mindset than the previous version of SQL Server involves how DBAs interact with the development team. The shared view of development by administrators and developers alike is enacted through the Business Intelligence Developer Studio (BIDS). With regard to Integration Services, the BIDS environment is how solutions and projects are created. Generally, the configuration of the BIDS solutions and projects will be handled by the developers; however; the administrators will be called upon to help configure various aspects of these solutions. The administration and management of Integration Services is primarily performed within SQL Server Management Studio. Often, moving the Integration Services solutions from environment to environment will mean changing dynamic information within the package and also setting up any information reference by the packages. Examples of these elements include Package Configuration settings, referenced XML or configuration files, and solution data sources.

Administration of the Integration Services Service

Now that you have a better understanding of the parts of Integration Services, we'll look at the various administrative aspects of Integration Services and discuss the details needed to feel comfortable working with the components. We will start with a review of the Integration Services service and then look at various configuration elements of the service. Next, you'll look at how you can adjust properties of the SSIS service using either the Windows Services Snap-in or the SQL Server Configuration manager. Understanding how you can modify the Windows Firewall follows, and then you'll look at the management and configuration of event logs.

Last, we will look at performance monitoring.

Overview

The Integration Services service is a Windows service used to manage SSIS packages and is accessed through SQL Server Management Studio. The following summarizes the management capabilities provided by this service:

❑ Starting and stopping local and remote packages

❑ Monitoring local and remote packages

❑ Importing and exporting packages from different sources

❑ Managing the package store

❑ Customizing storage folders

❑ Stopping running packages when service is stopped

❑ Viewing the Windows Event Log

❑ Connecting to multiple SSIS server instances

To be very clear, you don't need this service for designing or executing packages. The primary purpose of this service is to manage packages within Management Studio. One side benefit to having the service running is that the SSIS Designer in Business Intelligence Developer Studio can use the service to cache the objects used in the designer, thus enhancing the performance of the designer.

Configuration

The configuration of the Integration Services service includes viewing and possibly modifying the XML file responsible for the runtime configuration of the service, setting service properties using either the Windows Services Snap-in or using SQL Server Configuration Manager and, potentially, configuring the Windows Firewall to permit access by Integration Services.

XML Configuration File

The `MsDtsSrvr.ini.xml` file responsible for the configuration of the Integration Services service is located in `C:\Program Files\Microsoft SQL Server\90\DTS\Binn` by default. This file includes settings for determining whether or not running packages are stopped when the service is stopped, a listing of root folders to display in the Object Explorer of Management Studio, and settings for specifying the folders in the filesystem that are managed by the service.

The configuration filename and location can be changed. This information is obtained by Management Studio from the Windows registry key `HKEY_LOCAL_MACHINE\SOFTWARE\Microsoft\MSDTS\ServiceConfigFile`. As with most registry key changes, you should back up the registry before making any changes, and you will need to restart the service after making changes in order for them to take effect.

One example of a configuration change that must be made is when you connect to a named instance of SQL Server. The following example shows the modification for handling a named instance:

```xml
<?xml version="1.0" encoding="utf-8"?>
<DtsServiceConfiguration xmlns:xsd="http://www.w3.org/2001/XMLSchema"
xmlns:xsi="http://www.w3.org/2001/XMLSchema-instance">
  <StopExecutingPackagesOnShutdown>true</StopExecutingPackagesOnShutdown>
  <TopLevelFolders>
    <Folder xsi:type="SqlServerFolder">
      <Name>MSDB</Name>
      <ServerName>MyServerName\MyInstanceName</ServerName>
    </Folder>
    <Folder xsi:type="FileSystemFolder">
      <Name>File System</Name>
      <StorePath>..\Packages</StorePath>
    </Folder>
  </TopLevelFolders>
</DtsServiceConfiguration>
```

Other common configuration file change scenarios include adding additional paths from which to display packages other than the default SSIS package store path of `C:\Program Files\SQL Server\ 90\Packages` and creating a centralized folder structure for multiple servers by storing the service configuration file in a central fileshare.

Now that you have seen how to configure the `MsDtsSrvr.ini.xml` file responsible for the configuration of the Integration Services service, you'll next need to get an understanding of how to set the service's properties.

Setting Service Properties Using the Windows Services Snap-in

As with any other Windows service, the Integration Services service has properties that dictate how it is to be started. Specifically, you can manage the following from the Windows Services Snap-in:

❑   Configure the startup type as Manual, Automatic, or Disabled.

❑   Request that the service is started, stopped, or restarted.

❑   Establish how the computer reacts to service failures.

❑   View or modify a listing of dependant services (none set up by default).

To view and modify SSIS Services properties using the Windows Services Snap-in, follow these steps:

1.   Open the Services Snap-in from Control Panel⇨Administrative Tools (or using the Category view from Performance and Maintenance⇨Administrative Tools).

2.   Locate and right-click SQL Server Integration Service in the list of services.

3.   Select Properties to view the settings currently applied to the service.

4.   On the General tab, you can view or change the Startup type (Automatic, Manual, or Disabled). When set to either Manual or Automatic, you can change the Service status to Start, Stop, or Resume (see Figure 6-2).

5.   On the Log On tab, you can view or alter the account used to start up and run the service. By default, this runs under the `NT AUTHORITY\NetworkService` account.

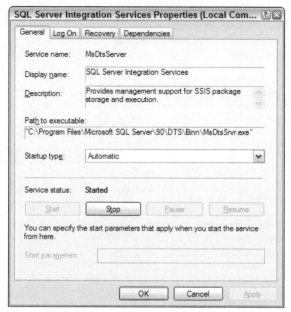

Figure 6-2

6. On the Recovery tab, you can configure how the server will respond to failures of the service by setting the First, Second, and Subsequent failures options to either Take No Action (the default), Restart the Service, Run a Program, or Restart the Computer (see Figure 6-3). Additionally, you can instruct the service to reset the failure count after a certain number of days.

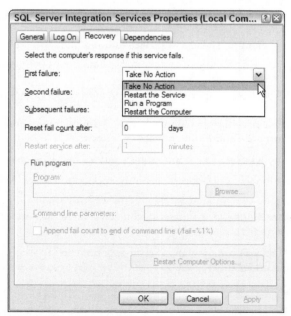

Figure 6-3

7. Last, you can modify the list of services that the SSIS service depends on (none by default) and view the list of services dependent on the SSIS service (none by default) on the Dependencies tab.

You have just learned how to configure the Integration Services service using the Windows Services Snap-in. Now we'll describe how you can perform some of this configuration using SQL Server Configuration Manger.

Setting Service Properties Using SQL Server Configuration Manager

As with using the Windows Services Snap-in, you can also configure a limited set of Integration Services service properties using SQL Server Configuration Manager. Specifically, you can both configure the logon information used by the service and establish the startup mode of the service.

Here's how to view and modify SSIS Services properties using the SQL Server Configuration Manager.

1. Open the SQL Server Configuration Manager from All Programs⇨Microsoft SQL Server 2005⇨Configuration Tools.

2. On the list of services on the right side, right-click SQL Server Integration Services and select Properties.

3. On the Log On tab, you can view or alter the account used to startup and run the service. By default, this runs under the NT AUTHORITY\NetworkService account.

4. On the Service tab, you can view or change the Startup type (Automatic, Manual, or Disabled).

Now that you are comfortable setting up the service properties for the Integration Services service using either the Windows Services Snap-in or using SQL Server Configuration Manger, you'll next see how you may need to modify Windows Firewall to permit accessing Integration Services.

Configuring Windows Firewall for Access

You'll probably find that your service requires modifications to be made to the Windows Firewall system in order to provide consistent access to Integration Services. The Windows Firewall system controls access to specific computer resources primarily by limiting access to preconfigured ports. We have no ability to modify the port number used by Integration Services, as it only works using port 135.

Here's how to configure the Windows Firewall to permit Integration Services access:

1. Open the Windows Firewall from Control Panel.

2. Select the Exceptions tab and click Add Program.

3. In the Add Program dialog, click Browse and select C:\Program Files\Microsoft SQL Server\90\DTS\Binn\MsDtsSrvr.exe. You should also, of course, use the Change Scope option in order to detail the computers that have access to the program by specifying a custom list of IP addresses, subnets, or both. The resulting exception is shown in the Windows Firewall dialog (see Figure 6-4).

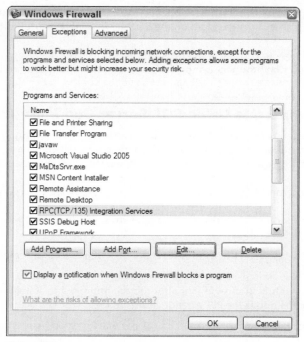

Figure 6-4

4. Click Add Port.

5. In the Add Port dialog, type a meaningful description like **RPC(TCP/135) Integration Services**, type **135** in the Port Number box, and select TCP as the protocol. You should also, of course, use the Change Scope option in order to detail the computers that have access to the port by specifying a custom list of IP addresses, subnets, or both. The resulting exception is shown in the Windows Firewall dialog in Figure 6-4.

Administrators often prefer to rely on commands and scripts rather than dialog boxes to configure various features and properties. Rather than using the dialog to configure the Windows Firewall, you can run the following commands at the command prompt.

```
netsh firewall add portopenint protocol=TCP port=135 name="RPC(TCP/135) Integration
Services" mode=ENABLE scope=SUBNET
netsh firewall add allowedprogram program="%ProgramFiles%\Microsoft SQL
Server\90\DTS\Binn\MsDtsSrvr.exe" name="SSIS Service" scope=SUBNET
```

You should use the scope argument of both commands to detail the computers that have access to the program and/or port by specifying a custom list of IP addresses, subnets, or both.

We have covered a substantial amount of the configuration required for the Integration Services service. Our next focus for understanding the Integration Services service is to understand event logging.

Event Logs

Integration Services records events raised by packages during their execution in logs. The SSIS log providers can write log entries to text files, SQL Server Profiler, SQL Server, Windows Event Log, or XML files. In order to perform logging, SSIS packages and tasks must have logging enabled. Logging can occur at the package, the container, and the task level, and you can specify different logs for packages, containers, and tasks. Additionally, to record the events raised, a log provider must be selected and a log added for the package. These logs can be created only at the package level, and a task or container must use one of the logs created for the package. Once you've configured the logs within packages, you can view them using the Windows Event Viewer or within SQL Server Management Studio.

Here's how to view SSIS event logs using the Windows Event Viewer:

1. Open the Event Viewer from Control Panel⇨Administrative Tools (or using Category view from Performance and Maintenance⇨Administrative Tools).

2. Within the Event Viewer dialog, click Application.

3. After the Application snap-in is displayed, locate an entry in the Source column valued as `SQLISService`.

4. Right-click the entry and select Properties to display descriptive information about the entry (see Figure 6-5).

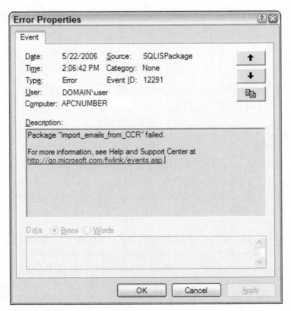

Figure 6-5

Here's how to view these events in SQL Server Management Studio:

1. Open Management Studio and connect to the target Integration Services server.

2. In Object Explorer, right-click Integration Services (topmost node) and click View Logs.

3. Select SQL Server Integration Services option from the Select Logs section.

4. You can see the details for an event displayed in the lower pane by clicking an event in the upper pane (see Figure 6-6).

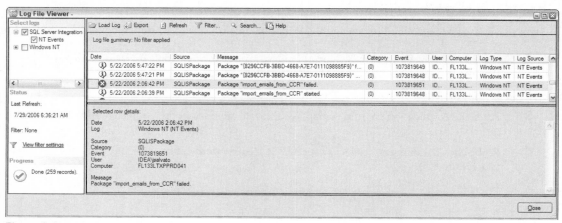

Figure 6-6

Now that you've learned about the event logs and seen how to view them, you're ready to monitor the activity of your service.

Monitoring Activity

Part of the performance monitoring of the Integration Services service includes configuring the logging of performance counters. These counters allow you to view and understand the use of resources consumed during the execution of SSIS packages. More specifically, the logging encompasses event-resource usage, while packages perform the dataflow tasks.

We'll begin by focusing on some of the more insightful counters, including Rows read, Buffers in use, and Buffers spooled. The Rows read counter provides us with the number of rows read from all data sources during package execution. The Buffers in use counter details the number of pipeline buffers (memory pools) in use throughout the package pipeline. Lastly, the Buffers spooled counter specifies the number of buffers used to handle the dataflow processes. The buffers spooled counter is specifically important because it is a good indicator of when your machine is running out of physical memory or is running out of virtual memory during dataflow processing. The importance of using buffers rather than disk cannot be understated, as SSIS has been tuned to effectively use memory rather than disk to provide a fast and efficient dataflow processing capability. Whenever SSIS has to use disk files rather than memory, performance of the data operations will degrade, and this will show up in the Buffers spooled counter.

Here's how to set up resource counters in order to monitor dataflow performance:

1. Open Performance (also referred to or known as PerfMon or Performance Monitor) from Control Panel⟹Administrative Tools (or using Category view from Performance and Maintenance⟹Administrative Tools).

2. Within Performance Monitor, expand Performance Logs and Alerts.

3. Add a new log by right-clicking Counter Logs, and select New Log Settings.

4. On the New Log Settings dialog, give your log a meaningful name such as `SSISDataFlowPerfLog`.

5. On the `SSISDataFlowPerfLog` (or whatever you named the log) dialog box, click Add Counters.

6. On the Add Counters dialog, either select the local computer or a computer from the list to specify a remote computer you wish to monitor. Also, select SQL Server: SSIS Pipeline in the Performance object list and select individual counters you wish to include in the log from the list of counters supplied. Your log configuration should now resemble Figure 6-7.

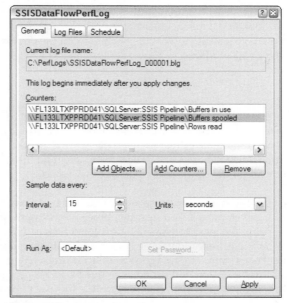

Figure 6-7

Now that you've added dataflow performance counters to Performance Monitor, you can monitor how critical resources are used by our Integration Services dataflows during package execution. One example of how these performance counters can be used includes ensuring that your server running the SSIS packages has enough memory. One of the bottlenecks in any transformation process includes input/output operations, whereby data is staged to disk during the transformations. Integration Services was designed to optimize system resources when transforming data between a source and destination including attempting to perform these transformations in memory rather than having to stage data to disk and incur I/O performance penalties. You should expect to see the value of the Buffers spooled counter remain at zero (0) when only memory is being used during the transformation processes being performed by the SSIS packages. When you observe that the Buffers spooled counter is normally valued higher than zero (0), you have a good indication that more memory is needed on the server processing the SSIS packages.

You can use SQL Server Profiler to analyze the data operations and query plans generated for various dataflow pipeline activities. You can use this information to refine indexes or apply other optimization techniques to the data sources your SSIS solution is using. The SQL Server Profiler is covered in more detail in Chapter 13.

Administration of Integration Services Packages

Now that you've learned about the various aspects of Integration Services service administration, we'll now detail the main elements involved with the administration of SSIS packages. We will start with an overview of SSIS package elements and administration and then look at various ways in which packages can be created. Next, we'll look at the management of the developed SSIS packages. Once you understand how to create and manage packages, we will conclude with the deployment, execution, and scheduling of SSIS packages and solutions.

Overview

A package represents the main organizational and executable component of Integration Services. Packages include a collection of controlflow tasks connected by precedence constraints used to manage the order of task execution, dataflow tasks that manage the complexities of moving data from sources to destinations with many transformation tasks in between and event handlers responsible for communicating various information about the status of the package and its tasks.

In order to better understand the various package administrative functions, we'll start by discussing the flow of package creation or development. You start this process by designing a package using either the import/export wizard or using Business Intelligence Developer Studio. Next, you store these packages in either the filesystem or in a SQL Server database in order to facilitate reuse or later execution. Often, you will need to move packages from one storage location to another with the aid of tools such as the DTUtil command line utility. Next, you will need to run our packages using either the DTExec or DTExecUI utilities. Commonly, you will also need to schedule the execution of packages using the SQL Agent job scheduler. Lastly, you need to monitor the performance and status of packages using Management Studio.

Creating Packages

You can create Integration Services packages using the Import and Export Wizard or by creating a Business Intelligence Developer Studio Integration Services solution. We will focus on the use of the Import and Export Wizard as creation and development of packages within BIDS is more likely to be done by developers. Furthermore, many resources are available to assist in understanding how to create and develop packages within BIDS. As an administrator, you should understand how you can configure package templates for use by your team members.

Using the Import and Export Wizard to Create Packages

In your day-to-day management of data, you often have to move or copy data to and from various data sources. Many times, these data management tasks are not in need of complex transformations or detailed workflow. These types of data management tasks are well suited for the Import and Export Wizard.

The key consideration for using the Import and Export Wizard revolves around the data transformation capabilities you need before loading the destination or target. The Wizard only permits modifications such as setting the names, data types, and data type properties of the columns as they will be defined at the destination. Absolutely no column-level transformations are supported when using the Import and Export Wizard.

Mapping of data types from sources to destinations is managed by mapping files located by default in C:\Program Files\Microsoft SQL Server\90\DTS\MappingFiles. An example of one of these mapping files is the OracleClientToMSSql.xml mapping file, used to map Oracle data types to SQL Server data types. The following is a sample of the XML used to map the Oracle DATE data type to SQL Server's datetime data type:

```
<!-- DATE -->
<dtm:DataTypeMapping >
   <dtm:SourceDataType>
      <dtm:DataTypeName>DATE</dtm:DataTypeName>
   </dtm:SourceDataType>
   <dtm:DestinationDataType>
       <dtm:SimpleType>
           <dtm:DataTypeName>datetime</dtm:DataTypeName>
       </dtm:SimpleType>
   </dtm:DestinationDataType>
</dtm:DataTypeMapping>
```

You can add mapping files to this directory to include new combinations of mappings that may not presently exist; you can alter existing mapping files if they don't meet your needs. You should note that after adding new or altering existing mapping files, you must restart the Import and Export Wizard or Business Intelligence Developer Studio in order to recognize these additions or modifications.

You can start using this Import and Export Wizard from the Business Intelligence Development Studio, from SQL Server Management Studio, or from a command prompt using the DTSWizard (C:\Program Files\Microsoft SQL Server\90\DTS\Binn). The only difference in starting this wizard from BIDS is that the wizard cannot run the resulting package as the very last step; instead the resulting package is saved as part of the solution in which the wizard was started.

You can start the Import and Export Wizard in a number of ways:

❑ In Management Studio, connect to a database server, and within the database node, right-click a database, select Tasks, and then select either Import Data or Export Data.

❑ In BIDS, open an SSIS solution, right-click the SSIS Packages Folder, and select SSIS Import and Export Wizard.

❑ Also in BIDS, click the Project⇨SSIS Import and Export Wizard.

❑ From a command prompt, run DTSWizard.exe (C:\Program Files\Microsoft SQL Server\90\DTS\Binn).

159

Here's how to run the Import and Export Wizard in order to move data:

1. Launch the Import and Export Wizard from Management Studio, BIDS, or the command prompt.

2. On the Choose a Data Source page, select the location to copy the data from by setting up the data source (such as SQL Native Client, Excel, or Flat File) and the required information for that data source (such as Server Name, Authentication, and Database for a SQL Native Client). Or if we selected to Export Data (within Management Studio), the source information is already pre-configured to include the server and database from which the wizard was launched.

3. On the Choose a Destination page, select the location to copy the data to by setting up the data source and the required information for that data source. If we selected to Import Data (with Management Studio), the destination information is preconfigured to include the server and database from which the wizard was launched.

4. On the Specify Table Copy or Query page, either copy the entire data source by selecting the option to Copy data from one or more tables, or you can specify that only a portion of the data source is copied by selecting the option to Write a query to specify the data to transfer. If you choose to write a query, on the Provide a Query Source page, you can either compose a SQL Statement or browse for a SQL file to load and use to limit the data source records.

5. On the Select Source Tables and Views page, specify all the tables and views to be included unless you previously selected the option to write a query to specify the data, in which case only one table (the query) is available to select.

6. Optionally, also on the Select Source Tables and Views page, you can configure various features that will indicate such things as whether to optimize for many tables or run in a transaction.

7. Optionally, from the Select Source Tables and Views page, when copying tables or views that already exist in the destination, you may select Edit Mappings in order to configure things such as whether or not to delete or append data to an existing table or whether or not to enable identity inserts (see Figure 6-8).

8. Optionally, from the Select Source Tables and Views page, when creating new tables or views that do not exist in the destination, you can select Edit Mappings to configure things such as whether to create destination tables or drop and recreate destination tables. Additionally, you can alter the destination mapping information for each column including the name, data type, nullability, size, precision, and scale (see Figure 6-9).

9. Lastly, if launched from Management Studio, on the Save and Execute Package page, you can choose to execute immediately and may optionally choose to save the SSIS package. When saving the package, you can save to SQL Server or to the filesystem, and you can configure the package-protection level to be applied to the saved package (see Figure 6-10).

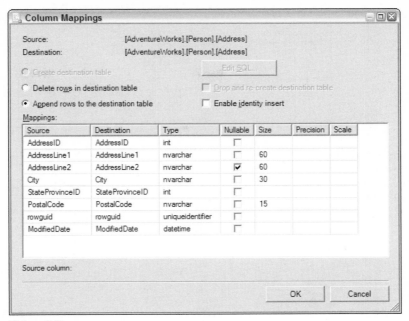

Figure 6-8

Figure 6-9

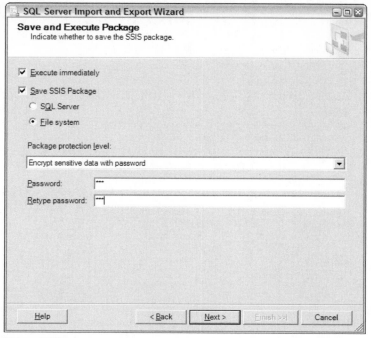

Figure 6-10

Creating and Using Package Templates

When you start a new Integration Services solution, the first thing you'll notice is that a package has already been included in the solution for your use. Although you cannot replace the default template that SSIS uses to generate this initial package (and any subsequent packages created by using the New SSIS Package command), you can design your own customized package or packages to be used as templates.

The primary benefits for creating these package templates include:

- ❑ Encapsulation of common package-design elements added to each package (such as logging or error handling)
- ❑ Productivity gained from inclusion of common package variables or package configurations
- ❑ Enforcement of package-design standards such as annotations
- ❑ Override SSIS package default protection level of EncryptSensitiveWithUserKey, which can be troublesome in multideveloper and deployment scenarios

A common scenario in which you may decide to implement a custom package template is when your team decides that the default package-protection level should be EncryptSensitiveWithPassword in order to enable sharing development tasks among multiple DBAs or developers. By customizing and using a custom package template, rather than the default package that SSIS would create, you can ensure that this desired package-protection level is automatically selected. Another scenario may involve the need for you to enforce common logging and error handling within your packages. The default SISS package does not contain any tasks to handle this functionality; however, you can build this type of functionality into your custom package template, and then, when used, each package would automatically have this functionality built into the design.

Here's how you can designate an SSIS package as a template.

1. Create and save an SSIS package.

2. Copy the package file (.dtsx) you wish to use as a template to the DataTransformationItems folder. This folder is commonly located in C:\Program Files\Microsoft Visual Studio.8\ Common7\IDE\PrivateAssemblies\ProjectItems\DataTransformationProject\ DataTransformationItems.

Once you have designated an SSIS package as a template, you can use it in Business Intelligence Developer Studio. Here's how you can use these templates to assist in SSIS package development.

1. Open an Integration Services project with Business Intelligence Developer Studio.

2. In Solution Explorer, right-click the solution or project (topmost node) and select Add.

3. From the options displayed on the Add submenu, select New Item.

4. Within the Add New Item – Project Name dialog, select the package you would like to use as a template and click Add.

5. By default, packages created using templates other than the default template shipped with SSIS have the same name and GUID as the template used for their creation. You should now change both of these package properties using the properties Page for the newly added package.

Management

Once you have started to create packages and solutions containing packages, you'll next need to focus on how these packages are managed. We will start by reviewing how the Integration Services service can assist in managing packages. Next, we will look at ways that you can configure Management Studio to meet our specific needs for managing packages. A brief tour of the DTUtil Package Management Utility will be provided next, along with some details to assist with the importing and exporting of packages. We will end with a review of package features that can be used in the package design and development stages to assist with the lifecycle management of packages and solutions.

Using Management Studio for Package Management

As discussed earlier in the "Integration Services Service" section, packages are managed primarily via Management Studio and its connection to the Integration Services service. Upon connecting to the service, you'll see two main folders: Running Packages and Stored Packages. The packages displayed are either stored in either the msdb database sysdtspackages90 table or the filesystem folders that are specified in the Integration Services service configuration file.

The main uses of Management Studio include monitoring running packages and managing the packages stored within the Integration Services environment. We'll now drill into some details surrounding these particular processes.

First, you can see information regarding currently executing packages within the Running Packages Folder. Information about these packages is displayed on the Summary page, while information about a particular executing package can be obtained by clicking the package under the Running Packages Folder and viewing the Summary page. You can stop the execution of a package listed within this folder by right-clicking the package and selecting Stop.

Secondly, we can make changes to the storage of packages by adding custom folders and by copying packages from one type of storage to another using the Import and Export utilities. You can configure the logical folders displayed within the MSDB folder in Management Studio by altering the sysdts packagefolders90 table within the msdb database. The root folders in this table are those in which the parentfolderid column contains null values. You can add values to this table in order to add logical folders, bearing in mind that the folderid and parentfolderid columns are the keys values used to specify the folder hierarchy. Additionally, you can configure the default folders in the filesystem that Management Studio displays. This is discussed at length in the "XML Configuration File" section of this chapter. Importing and exporting packages will be discussed in another section of this chapter.

The main management tasks you can perform on packages within Management Studio include:

❑ Creating new Object Explorer folders to display packages saved in either the file system or SQL Server (msdb database sysdtspackages90 table)

❑ Importing packages

❑ Exporting packages

❑ Running packages

❑ Deleting packages

❑ Renaming packages

Using DTUtil Package Management Utility

Other than using Management Studio to manage packages, you also have the assistance of a command prompt utility named DTUtil. The primary reason it is important to understand the DTUtil is that this utility permits you to manage packages using schedulers or batch files. As with using Management Studio, the DTUtil enables you to copy, delete, move, sign, and even verify if the server contains specified packages.

Using this utility, you include either the /SQL, /FILE, or /DTS options to specify where the packages that you want to manage are located. You use options (parameters) to specify particular behavior you want to use when running the utility. The options start with either a slash (/) or a minus sign (-) and can be added to the command line in any sequence.

Additionally, you will receive exit codes that let you know when you have things wrong with your syntax or arguments or simply have an invalid combination of options. When everything is correct, DTUtil returns exit code 0 and displays the message "The operation completed successfully." The following other exit codes may be returned:

❑ 1 — Failed

❑ 4 — Cannot locate package

❑   5 — Cannot load package

❑   6 — Cannot resolve the command

The following additional syntactical rules must be followed when you create these commands:

❑   Values for options must be strings and must be enclosed in quotation marks or contain no whitespace.

❑   Escaping single quotation marks in strings is done by enclosing the double-quoted string inside single quotation marks.

❑   Other than passwords, there is no case sensitivity.

One way you can use DTUtil is to regenerate package IDs for packages copied from other packages. Recall that when a copy of an existing package is made, the name and ID of the new package matches that of the copied package. Here's how you can use the DTUtil along with the /I [D Regenerate] switch to regenerate the package IDs. Of course, to update multiple packages with just a single execution of the DTUtil, you can create a batch file that could iterate through a given folder looking for all .dtsx (package) files and have the DTUtil regenerate the package IDs. At the command prompt, use the following syntax:

```
for %f in (<FilePath>\*.dtsx) do dtutil.exe /i /File %f
```

If you wish to execute this command from within a script, use the following syntax:

```
for %%f in (<FilePath>\*.dtsx) do dtutil.exe /i /File %%f
```

By understanding the DTExec utility, you have a very powerful weapon to add to your package management arsenals. We'll now take a look at how you can facilitate the movement of packages using import and export features.

Importing and Exporting Packages

Another common activity you need to understand as an administrator involves the ways in which you can move packages among the various storage locations and formats. The import and export functionality allows you to add or copy packages from one storage location and format to another storage location and format. Thus, not only can you add or copy the packages; you can also change storage formats (for example, from filesystem folders to the SQL Server msdb database).

Here's how you can import a package using the Integration Services Service from within Management Studio.

1.   Open Management Studio and connect to an Integration Services server.

2.   In Object Explorer, expand the Stored Packages folder and any subfolders to locate the folder into which you want to import a package.

3.   Right-click the target folder and select Import Package.

4.   On the Import Package dialog, select the package location from SQL Server, File System, or SSIS Package Store.

5. On the Import Package dialog, when the package location is SQL Server, you need to specify the server, authentication type, user name, and password.

6. On the Import Package dialog, when the package location is SSIS Package Store, you need to specify the server.

7. Also on the Import Package dialog, click the Browse button next to Package path and select the package to import.

8. Still on the Import Package dialog, you can change the package name as it will appear in the new location and also specify the protection level of the package (see Figure 6-11).

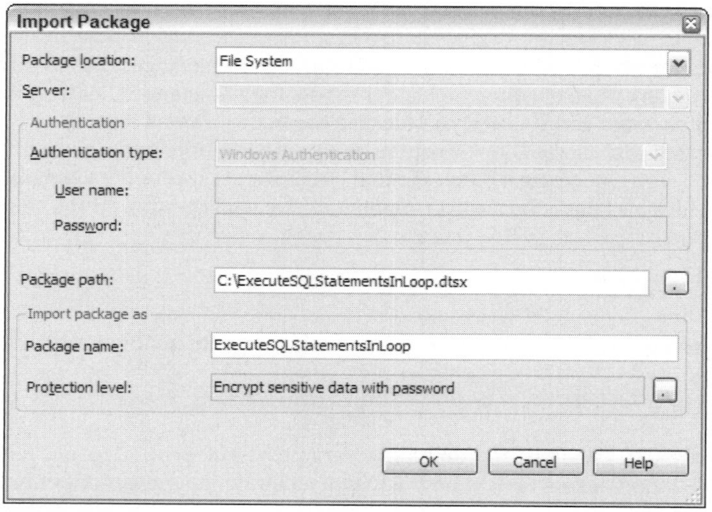

Figure 6-11

You can also export packages using similar steps as detailed for importing packages. The one notable difference is that you right-click the package to be exported and select Export rather than right-clicking the target folder and selecting Import. Additionally, recall that you can also perform these import and export operations using the DTUtil command-line utility.

Deployment

Once Integration Services packages and solutions have been developed either on local computers or on development servers, they need to be deployed to test on production servers. Usually, you start the deployment process once you have ensured that the packages run successfully within Business Intelligence Development Studio.

You deploy your packages or solutions by:

❑   Creating a Package Deployment Utility and using the Package Installer Wizard

❑   Using import or export package utilities in Management Studio

- ❑ Saving or moving copies of packages in the filesystem
- ❑ Executing the DTUtil Package Management Utility

Often, the modifications made to your Integration Service solution will dictate which deployment method and tools to use. For example, if you modify only a single package out of a 30-package solution, using the import package utility within Management Studio or saving or moving copies of packages in the filesystem might be simpler than deploying the entire solution using the Package Deployment Utility and Package Installer Wizard.

You can really further categorize these four options for deployment into automated and manual. Using the Package Deployment Utility in conjunction with the Package Installer Wizard would be best categorized as an automated deployment method, while the other options represent manual deployment methods. We'll take a look at the details for each of these deployment methods, starting with the automated method.

Creating a Package Deployment Utility

A very common way to deploy packages involves using the Package Deployment Utility. This utility builds your SSIS packages, package configurations, and any supporting files into a special deployment folder located within the bin directory for the Integration Services project. Additionally, this utility creates a special executable file named DTSDeploymentManifest.xml and places it within this deployment folder. After the creation of the Deployment Utility, you then execute the manifest file to install the packages.

This deployment method relies upon two separate steps. First, you create a deployment utility that contains all the files needed for deployment. Second, you use the Package Installer Wizard to perform the deployment of these files to a target deployment server.

The following are the steps necessary to use this Package Deployment Utility in order to deploy our Integration Services solution.

1. Open Business Intelligence Development Studio and open an Integration Services solution.

2. Right-click your solution or project (topmost node) in the Solution Explorer and select Properties.

3. On the [Solution/Project Name] Property Pages dialog, select the Deployment Utility section.

4. Within the Deployment Utility section of the Property Pages dialog, set the value of the CreateDeploymentUtility to true (see Figure 6-12).

5. Optionally, you can configure the deployment to enable configuration changes by setting the AllowConfigurationChanges value to true. This option provides the ability to update the configuration of key elements of your packages that would be machine or environment dependent, such as server names or database initial catalogs that are both properties of database connection managers.

6. Next, build your project as normal. The build process creates the DTSDeploymentManifest.xml file and copies the packages to the bin/Deployment folder or whatever folder was specified for the DeploymentOutputPath on the project property page in the Deployment Utility section.

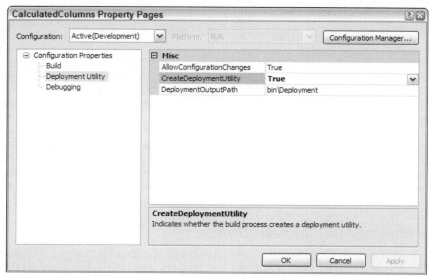

Figure 6-12

Because this utility copies all solution files as part of the process, you can deploy additional files such as a `Readme` file with the project by simply placing these files in the Miscellaneous folder of the Integration Services project.

Using the Package Installer Wizard

Once you have created a `DTSDeploymentManifest.xml` file using the Package Deployment Utility, you can install the packages by using the Package Installer Wizard. This wizard runs the `DTSInstall.exe` program and copies the packages and any configuration to a designated location.

Using the Package Installer Wizard, you get some really useful functionality that you can't find or is hard to achieve using the manual deployment methods. One example is that you may choose either a file-based or SQL-based deployment. You should note that your file-based dependencies will always be installed to the file system. Another important, as well as useful, capability of this deployment process includes the ability to modify configurations for use on the target deployment server. This gives you the ability to update the values of the configuration properties, such as a server name, as part of the wizard.

These are the steps you need to take to ensure a successful deployment of your packages using the Package Installer Wizard.

1. Use Windows Explorer to browse to the file path location in which the `DTSDeployment Manifest.xml` file was created (usually the solution or project location `/bin/Deployment`).

2. After creating the files within the `Deployment` folder, copy the `Deployment` folder and all its files to a target deployment server.

3. On the target deployment server, open the `Deployment` folder and double-click the `DTSDeploymentManifest.xml` file in order to launch the Package Installer Wizard (`DTSInstall.exe`).

4. On the Deploy SSIS Packages page, select whether you want to deploy your packages to the filesystem or to SQL Server (see Figure 6-13). Optionally, you can also have the packages validated after they have been installed.

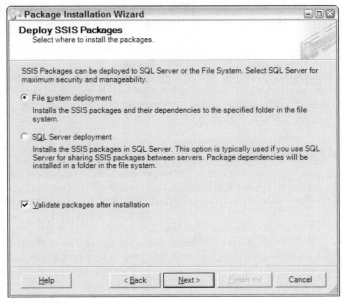

Figure 6-13

5. On the Select Installation Folder page, either provide a folder path for a filesystem deployment or provide a server name and the appropriate server credentials for a SQL Server deployment.

6. For a SQL Server deployment, on the Select Installation Folder page, provide a folder path for the package dependencies that will require storing within the filesystem.

7. Optionally, if the package includes configurations and you set the AllowConfigurationChanges value to true when the deployment manifest was created, the Configure Packages page will be displayed so that you can update the values for the configurations.

8. Optionally, if you requested validation of the packages, the Packages Validation page will be displayed so that you can review the validation results.

Now that you've seen how to deploy your packages using the Package Deployment Utility for preparing the files to copy and deploy on the target server using the Package Installation Wizard, we'll discuss how to perform various types of manual package deployments.

Manual Package Deployment

We referred to using the import or export package utilities, saving or moving copies of packages in the filesystem, and executing the DTUtil Package Management Utility as manual deployment methods. The primary contrast among these deployment methods and using both the Package Deployment Utility and the Package Installer Wizard is that the manual methods require a better understanding of exactly what files need to be moved and where the files need to be located on the deployment target machine, and they offer no automated way to reconfigure some of the dynamic elements within the packages that often require modification when deploying to another machine (such as connection string server and initial catalog values).

Despite the lack of sophistication available when using these deployment methods, there are situations in which they are rather useful, if not better than the automated methods. One example of a situation in which they may prove to be a better fit is when you modify a single package in a solution containing 20 or more packages. Under the automated deployment method, the entire solution would be redeployed, while the manual methods could simply import, export, save, or move the single effected package. This really has benefits with some levels of testing, as you can isolate the impacts of changing the one package and not have to recertify all the untouched packages just because they were redeployed over the older packages.

Import or Export Packages Deployment

Earlier in this chapter, we reviewed the use of the import and export functionality, which allows you to add or copy packages from one storage location and format to another storage location and format. One obvious use of this functionality is to deploy packages after the development and testing have been completed.

One interesting benefit this approach may yield involves the capability of the import or export to change storage formats (for example, from filesystem folders to the SQL server msdb database). This alteration of storage formats may be useful for disaster recovery, as a further safeguard for your Integration Services solutions by saving them in various storage formats and locations.

File Save/Move Package Deployment

Probably the simplest ways to get packages deployed involves copying them out of the Visual Studio project bin directory and placing them on the target server. This method does not have any of the more useful capabilities but can work quite well for smaller-scale Integration Services solutions. One distinct capability missing from this deployment method is the ability to deploy to SQL server.

DTUtil Package Deployment

As with using Management Studio, the DTUtil enables you to copy or move packages. As previously stressed in this chapter, the benefit surrounding the usage of DTUtil is that the commands created can be scheduled or run at a later time. So, using these capabilities, you could schedule the deployment of your packages to another server simply by using DTUtil copy or move commands to move the modified packages to a target server.

The following example demonstrates how a DTUtil copy command can be used for deployment.

```
dtutil /DTS srcPackage.dtsx /COPY SQL;destPackage
```

Now that you have packages deployed to an Integration Services server, we will discuss how to execute and schedule packages.

Execution and Scheduling

Thus far, we have looked at ways to create, manage, and deploy Integration Services solutions. Now we will focus our attention on the ways in which you can execute and schedule execution of these solutions. As you have seen with other package and solution administrative tasks, execution of packages can be performed using different tools. Specifically, you can execute packages from:

❑   Business Intelligence Development Studio

❑   SQL Server Import and Export Wizard (when run from Management Studio)

❑   DTExec package execution command line utility

❑   DTExecUI package execution utility

❑   SQL Server Agent jobs

The choice of which tool to use often depends on factors such as which stage of the package lifecycle we are presently working. As an example, the SSIS Designer within BIDS will be a logical choice for package execution during development due to the features designed to assist in development (such as visually displaying package execution progress by changing the background color of tasks).

Now that we know what options we have for executing or scheduling packages, we'll review how each one may be used.

Running Packages in Business Intelligence Development Studio

Probably the first executions of packages will occur within BIDS, as this is the development environment used to create our Integration Services solutions. Within BIDS, you simply either right-click the package and then select Execute Package or press the F5 function key (or the Start button on the menu bar).

Running Packages with SQL Server Import and Export Wizard

When you use the Import and Export Wizard from Management Studio, you are given an option to execute the package immediately. This provides an opportunity to both relocate and execute packages in one administrative step.

Running Packages with DTExec

The primary use of DTExec is to enable us to be able to run packages from the command line, from a script, or using a scheduling utility. All configuration and execution features are available using this command. Additionally, you can load and run packages from SQL Server, the SSIS Service, and the filesystem.

The following additional syntactical rules must be followed when you create these commands:

❑   Command options all start with a slash (/) or a minus sign (-).

❑   Arguments are enclosed in quotation marks when they contain any whitespace.

❑   Values that contain single quotation marks are escaped by using double quotation marks within quoted strings.

The general syntax for the DTExec commands is:

```
Dtexec /option value
```

Here's an example, where you are running the `CaptureDataLineage.dtsx` package:

```
Dtexec /FILE "C:\Program Files\Microsoft SQL Server\90\Samples\Integration
Services\Package Samples\CaptureDataLineage
Sample\CaptureDataLineage\CaptureDataLineage.dtsx" /CONNECTION
"(local).AdventureWorks";"\"Data Source=(local);Initial
Catalog=AdventureWorks;Provider=SQLNCLI.1;Integrated Security=SSPI;Auto
Translate=False;\""  /MAXCONCURRENT " -1 " /CHECKPOINTING OFF  /REPORTING
EWCDI
```

Whenever you execute a package using DTExec, an exit code may be returned. These values include:

- ❑   0 — Successful execution
- ❑   1 — Failed
- ❑   3 — Canceled by User
- ❑   4 — Unable to Find Package
- ❑   5 — Unable to Load Package
- ❑   6 — Syntax Not Correct

There are numerous options you can use to alter how the package execution gets run. Some examples include /Decrypt, which sets the package password used to secure information within the package, or /Set, which you use to assign SSIS variables values at runtime. The options are processed in the order in which they are specified. When using the /Set and /ConfigFile commands, the values are also processed in the order in which they are specified. Also, note that neither options nor arguments (except passwords) are case sensitive.

Running Packages with DTExecUI

You can configure the various options you need to run packages using the graphical equivalent to the DTExec utility: the DTExecUI utility. With the wizard that this utility uses to gather details regarding the package execution, you can better understand many of the options and see the syntax required to run the package execution.

You launch the DTExecUI utility by double-clicking a file with a .dtsx extension. You then select the types of options that we need to run the package along the left side of the utility pages and then configure the options in the main part of the page (see Figure 6-14). When you are done, you can view the last page, which shows us the command line needed to execute the package with the options we selected.

Once you have completed the various pages and reviewed the command line that will be submitted, click the Execute button. This will submit the command line to the Integration Services engine by using the DTExecUI utility. You need to be careful when you use this utility in a 64-bit environment, because this utility will run in Windows on Win32, not on Win64. Thus, for 64-bit environments, you should use the 64-bit version of the DTExec utility at the command prompt or use SQL Server Agent.

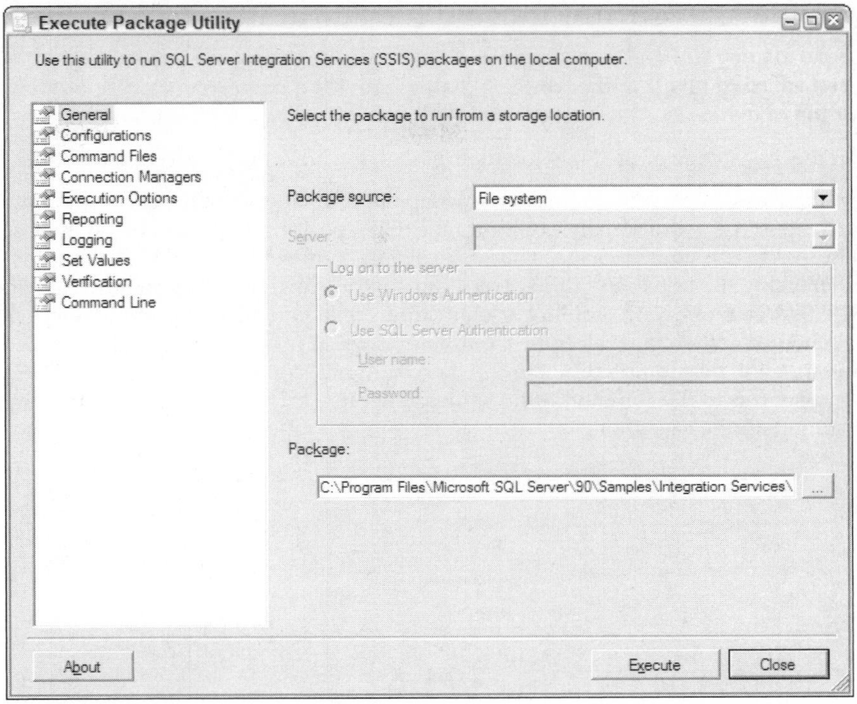

Figure 6-14

The main reason for us to become more familiar with both the DTExec and DTExecUI utilities is that they are very useful for testing your packages and ultimately validating the proper command line that we may schedule using the SQL Server Agent. We now will review how the SQL Server Agent can perform scheduled execution of our Integration Services packages.

Scheduling Execution with SQL Server Agent

Without a doubt, you will need the ability to automate the execution of your Integration Services packages. While you may use many popular scheduling tools to accomplish this automation, we will be looking at how SQL Server Agent can assist in automating execution.

You start by creating a job and then including at least one step of the SQL Server Integration Services Packages type. You can also configure other job options. One option we may configure includes job notifications to send e-mail messages when the job completes, succeeds, or fails. Another job option you may configure includes job alerts to send notifications for SQL Server event alerts, performance condition alerts, or WMI event alerts.

Here's how to set up SQL Server Agent to execute a package.

1. Open Management Studio and connect to a SQL Server.
2. In Object Explorer, expand the SQL Server Agent.

3. Within the SQL Server Agent section of Object Explorer, right-click the Jobs folder and select New Job.

4. On the General Page of the New Job dialog, provide a name, owner, category, and description for the job.

5. On the Steps Page of the New Job dialog, click the New button along the bottom.

6. On the New Job Step dialog, provide a step name and select SQL Server Integration Services Packages type. Additionally, configure the SSIS-specific tabbed sections with the information required to run your package. This SSIS section is almost identical to the options we provided when using the DTExecUI utility (see Figure 6-15). You have a package source that you set to SQL Server, filesystem, or SSIS Package Store. Next, you have to provide the package you wish to schedule. When you select the Command Line tab, you can review the detailed command line that will be submitted by the SQL Server Agent to execute the package. You may wish to compare this to the command-line values generated by the DTExecUI utility while you were testing package execution.

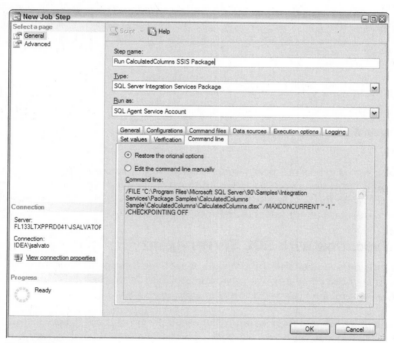

Figure 6-15

7. On the Advanced page of the New Job Step dialog, you can specify actions to perform when the step completes successfully, the number of retry attempts, the retry interval, and actions to perform should the step fail. After accepting the step configuration by pressing OK, the Step page of the New Job dialog will show your new step (see Figure 6-16). After adding multiple steps, you can reorder the steps on this page.

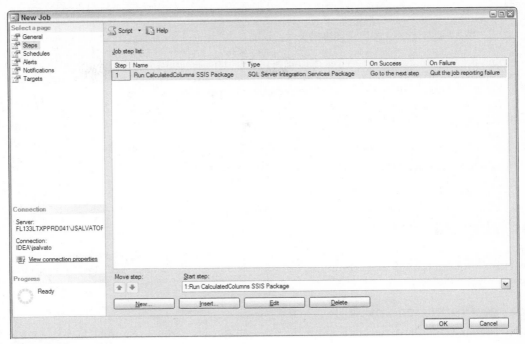

Figure 6-16

8. After accepting the step configuration, on the New Job dialog, you can optionally configure execution schedules, alerts, notifications, and target servers.

Applying Security to Integration Services

We have now looked at most of the important package administrative tasks including creating, managing, deploying, and executing Integration Services solutions. Additionally, we have reviewed the major Integration Services service administrative tasks. Now you will learn the detailed security options available within Integration Services.

Overview

Integration Services, like all of SQL Server, uses layers of security that rely upon different mechanisms to ensure the integrity of the design of packages as well as the administration and execution of packages. SSIS security is found on both the client and the server, implemented with features such as:

❑ Package-protection levels to encrypt or remove sensitive information from the package

❑ Package-protection levels with passwords to protect all or just sensitive information

❑ Restricting access to packages with roles

Chapter 6

❑   Locking down file locations where packages may be stored

❑   Signing packages with certificates

Within packages, Integration Services defines sensitive data generally as information such as passwords and connection strings. You are not able to define what should and should not be considered sensitive by SSIS unless you wish to do so within a custom-developed task.

Integration Services defines sensitive information as:

❑   Connection string password (Sensitive) or Whole connection string (All)

❑   Task-generated XML nodes tagged as sensitive by SSIS

❑   Variables marked as sensitive by SSIS

Securing Packages

The two primary ways in which you secure packages within Integration Services includes setting package-protection levels and configuring appropriate database SSIS roles. Let's look at these two security implementations.

Package Protection Levels

Many organizations have sensitive information in addition to wanting to control where that information resides within the organization. This implies that your packages, which are responsible for handling that information and must also include information that directs the packages to know the location of that information, must have means to protect against unauthorized access.

These security concerns are addressed in Integration Services through the use of package-protection levels. First, you can ensure that sensitive information that would provide details of where your information resides, like connection strings, can be controlled by using `EncryptSensitive` package-protection levels. Second, you can control who can open or execute a package by using `EncryptAll` package passwords.

We have the following package-protection levels available at our disposal within Integration Services:

❑   Do not save sensitive

❑   Encrypt (all/sensitive) with User Key

❑   Encrypt (all/sensitive) with Password

❑   Rely on server storage for encryption (SQL storage only)

The package-protection levels are first assigned using Business Intelligence Development Studio. You can update these package-protection levels after deployment or during import or export of the package using Management Studio. Also, you can alter the package-protection levels when packages are copied from BIDS to any other location in which packages are stored. This makes for a nice compromise between development and administration, as developers can configure these levels to suit their rapid development requirements and administrators can follow up and revise these levels to meet production security standards.

Database Integration Services Roles

If you deploy your packages to SQL Server (msdb database), you need to protect these packages within the database. Like traditional databases, this security is handled by using database roles. There are three fixed database-level roles to apply to the msdb database in order to control access to packages. These roles include db_dtsadmin, db_dtsltduser, and db_dtsoperator.

You apply these roles to packages within Management Studio, and these assignments are saved within the msdb database, sysdtspackages90 table within the readerrole, writerrole, and ownersid columns. As the column names imply, you can view the roles that have read access to a particular package by looking at the value of the readerrole column, the roles that have write access to a particular package by looking at the value of the writterrole column, and the role that created the package by looking at the value of the ownersid column.

Here's how we can assign a reader and writer role to packages

1. Open Management Studio and connect to an Integration Services server.

2. In Object Explorer, expand the Stored Packages folder and also expand the subfolder to assign roles.

3. Right-click the subfolder to assign roles.

4. On the Packages Roles dialog, select a reader role in the Reader Role list and a writer role in the Writer Role list.

You may also create user-defined roles if the default read and write actions for existing roles do not meet your security needs. In order to define these roles, you connect to a SQL Server instance and open the roles node within the msdb database. In the roles node, you right-click the database roles and select New Database Role. Once a new role has been added to the msdb database, we must restart the MSSQLSERVER service before you can use the role.

These database integration services roles help to configure your msdb database sysdtspackages90 table with package security options for reading and writing to specific packages. By applying this level of security, you provide security at the server, database, and table levels. Again, the security discussed within this section only applies when you save your packages within SQL Server (msdb database). Next, we will explore the options for securing packages stored outside of SQL Server.

Saving Packages

When you develop packages, they are stored to the filesystem as XML files with a .dtsx file extension. In the deployment section, you saw how you could move these files to our Integration Services server using import and export utilities, the DTUtil utility, or the package deployment wizard.

Without saving the packages and any related files (such as configuration files) within SQL Server (msdb database), you must apply the appropriate NTFS file permissions to secure these packages.

Next we will consider how you should restrict access to computers running the SQL Server service because they can enumerate stored packages on local and remote locations.

Running Packages

Once packages have been secured by using package protection and either database roles or filesystem security, you must limit access to currently running packages on your servers. Specifically, you need to manage who will have the rights to view the running packages and who can stop your executing packages.

The SQL Server service is used by Management Studio to determine and list currently executing packages. Only members of the Windows Administrators group are able to perform these actions. The service can also be used to enumerate folders and possibly even remote folders. These folders are where you store your packages, and therefore it is important that you control access to computers running this service and also that you apply NTFS folder and file permissions to locations where you store your packages.

Next, we will review the various package resources that also merit security planning.

Package Resources

Having addressed the security needs of packages stored within SQL Server and stored within the filesystem, as well as managing the access to running packages, we next turn our attention to the various resources used by our packages.

The package resources we will need to consider include:

❑   Configuration files

❑   Checkpoint files

❑   Log files

You must consider security for these resources, as they may contain sensitive information. For example, the configuration files often will contain login and password information for data sources used by your packages. Even if they do not contain sensitive information, you need to ensure that your packages can find and use them when they are executed. Another example would be the checkpoint files used for restartability of packages. These checkpoint files save the current state information from the execution of packages, including the current values of any variables defined within the packages. Often, we use the variables to store information that may be deemed sensitive, and, as a result, you should also ensure that only appropriate staff is able to access these files. In any case, you can store these various files in SQL Server and use the database Integration Services roles for security, or you need to apply appropriate NTFS permissions.

Digital Signatures

As a last line of defense for ensuring successful usage of valid packages during execution, you can sign packages with certificates. After signing the packages, when you execute a package using a utility or program, the package signature is checked, and a warning may be issued or the package may be prevented from executing should an invalid signature be determined. In order to ensure this validation takes place, we set the `CheckSignatureOnLoad` property for packages to true.

Summary

We have discovered many of the various administrative functions related to Integration Services. After getting a general introduction to Integration Services, we reviewed important Integration Services administration tasks such as managing the Integration Services service, including configuration, event logs, and monitoring activity. Next, we provided some insights into various administrative tasks required of Integration Services packages, including creation, management, execution, and deployment. Last, we reviewed how to implement security for all of the various Integration Services components. In Chapter 7 we discuss similar administrative functions related to Analysis Services.

7

Analysis Services Administration and Performance Tuning

We continue our discussion of business intelligence administration and performance tuning by looking at how the DBA can perform Analysis Services administrative and performance tuning tasks. Our focus will be on the regular activities that a DBA may be called upon to perform rather than discussing the various details that may be performed by developers. First, we will take a quick tour of Analysis Services so that you will have some common frame of reference for both the administrative and optimization aspects that will be covered. Next, we'll look at the administration of the Analysis Server itself, including reviewing server settings and required services. We will also address how to script various administrative activities such as moving an Analysis Services database from development to production and backing up an Analysis Services database. With that covered, we will review the management of the Analysis Services Databases, including deployment, backup, restore, and synchronization, and then look at how you can monitor the performance of Analysis Services. Next, we will look at administration of storage, including storage modes and configuring partitions, as well as discussing the design of aggregations. With storage concepts in mind, we will turn next to administration of processing tasks used to connect our designs with the data. Last, of course, we will discuss how to configure security for Analysis Services.

A discussion of how to use Analysis Services from a developer's prospective is beyond the scope of this book, so we will not examine that issue here. If you're interested in learning more, see Professional SQL Server Analysis Services with MDX, by Sivakumar Harinath and Stephen R. Quinn (Wrox, 2006).

Tour of Analysis Services

To better understand the various touch points that you must manage as a DBA, we will start with a quick tour of Analysis Services. The primary value that Analysis Services brings to businesses is useful, important, and timely information that can be difficult or impossible to obtain from other sources of information (enterprise resource planning systems, accounting systems, customer relationship management systems, supply chain management systems and so on). Analysis Services provides two distinct services that assist in supplying these business needs; Online Analytical Processing (OLAP) and data mining. With these services, Analysis Services differs from the more traditional Online Transaction Processing (OLTP) systems in that it is optimized for fast access to vast quantities of data often spanning many years. Our focus will be on the OLAP services provided.

The OLAP engine has to be optimized for lightning-quick data retrieval but also offers the following strategic benefits:

❑   Shared data access that includes security at the most granular level and the ability to write back data

❑   Rapid, unencumbered storage and aggregation of vast amounts of data

❑   Multidimensional views of data that go beyond the traditional row and column two-dimensional views

❑   Advanced calculations that offer better support and performance than RDBMS engine capabilities

Where SSAS differs from traditional OLAP servers is that the 2005 release offers a Unified Dimensional Model (UDM) focused on unifying the dimensional and relational models. The relational model represents the standard model used by transaction processing systems. This relational model is generally optimized for data validity and storage optimization rather than query performance. The dimensional model was developed specifically to address query performance primarily by the denormalization of relational model schemas into a simpler model characterized as having fewer joins and more user-friendly model elements (table and column names). Denormalization, as you might recall, is the process of optimizing the performance of a database by adding redundant data into a database table that would normally have been normalized or removed to additional tables.

Unified Dimensional Model Components

First you need to understand that in the 2005 release of Analysis Services, the Unified Dimensional Model (UDM) is the cube. Let's begin looking at the composition of the UDM.

Data Source View

At the heart of the UDM is the logical data schema that represents the data from the source in a familiar and standard manner. This schema is known as the data source view (DSV), and it isolates the cube from changes made to the underlying sources of data.

Dimensional Model

This model provides the framework from which the cube is designed. Included are the measures (facts) that users need to gain measurable insight into their business and the dimensions that users use to constrain or limit the measurements to useful combinations of factors.

Calculations (Expressions)

Often, a cube needs to be enhanced with additional calculations in order to add the necessary business value that it is expected to achieve. The calculations within the UDM are implemented by writing MDX expressions. MDX is a multidimensional expressions language that is to the cube as SQL is to the database. In other words, MDX is what you use to get information from a cube to respond to various user requests.

Familiar and Abstracted Model

Many additional features enhance the end-user analysis experience by making their reporting and navigation through the cube more natural. Again, like calculations, the model is often enhanced to include features not found in the data sources from which the cube was sourced. Features such as language translations, aliasing of database names, perspectives to reduce information overload, or Key Performance Indicators (KPIs) to quickly summarize data into meaningful measurements are all part of the UDM.

Administrative Configuration

With the cube designed and developed, the administrative aspects of the UDM come to the forefront. Often, administrative tasks such as configuring the security to be applied to the cube or devising a partitioning scheme to enhance both query and processing performance are applied to the UDM.

Analysis Services Architectural Components

Now that you understand the basics about the Unified Dimensional Model (UDM), we'll now discuss the various components that make up Analysis Services.

The Analysis Services server (msmdsvr.exe application) is implemented as a Microsoft Windows service and consists of security components, an XMLA listener, and a query processor (for MDX queries and DMX data-mining queries).

Query Processor

The query processor parses and processes statements similarly to the query processing engine within SQL Server. This processor is also responsible for the caching of objects, storage of UDM objects and their data, processing calculations, handling server resources, and managing transactions.

XMLA Listener

This listener component facilitates and manages communications between various clients and the Analysis Services server. The port configuration for this listener is located in the msmdsrv.ini file. A value of 0 in this file simply indicates that SSAS is configured to listen on the default port of 2725 for Analysis Services 2000 instances, 2383 for the default instance of SSAS 2005, and 2382 for other instances of SSAS 2005.

SSAS 2005 named instances can use a variety of ports. The SQL Server Browser keeps track of the ports on which each named instance listens and performs any redirection required when a client does not specify the port number along with the named instance. We highly recommend that you use a firewall to restrict user access to Analysis Services ports from the Internet.

XML for Analysis

XML for Analysis (XML/A) is a SOAP-based protocol used as the native protocol for communicating with SSAS. All client application interactions use XML/A to communicate with SSAS. This protocol is significant in that clients who need to communicate with SSAS do not need to install a client component as past versions of Analysis Services required (such as Pivot Table Services). As a SOAP-based protocol, XML/A is optimized for disconnected and stateless environments that require time- and resource-efficient access. In addition to the defined protocol, Analysis Services also added extensions to support metadata management, session management, and locking capabilities. You have two different methods to send XML/A messages to Analysis Services: The default method uses TCP/IP, and an alternative is HTTP.

Administering Analysis Services Server

In this section, we will look at some of the important administrative activities for the server instance of SSAS. We will start with a review of the configuration settings for the server, followed by detailing the services needed for SSAS to run, and end with an introduction to the Analysis Services Scripting Language (ASSL) and its use in performing administrative tasks.

Server Configuration Settings

These settings are important for configuring the behavior of the SSAS server instance. We will only highlight ones that may be useful in regular administrative duties.

Review and Adjust Server Properties

To review and adjust the server properties, perform the following steps:

1. Open SQL Server Management Studio.
2. Connect to the Analysis Services server using the Object Explorer.
3. Right-click the server (topmost node) and choose Properties. The results are shown in Figure 7-1.

Lock Manager Properties

The lock manager properties are used to resolve deadlocking issues as they pertain to server behaviors in handling locking and timeouts. Of the three properties, only DefaultLockTimeoutMS should be altered without the guidance of Microsoft support. The DefaultLockTimeoutMS property defines the lock-request timeouts in milliseconds and defaults to none (-1).

Log Properties

These log properties control how and where logging takes place. Details related to the error logging, exception logging, flight recorder, query logging, and tracing are included in this property group. Some examples include the QueryLog\QueryLogConnectionString and QueryLog\QueryLogTableName properties, which are used to direct the server as to where the query logging will get persisted (database and table).

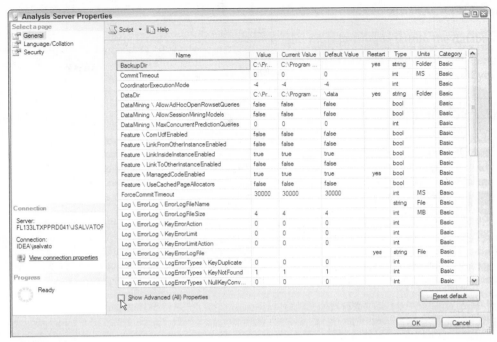

Figure 7-1

Memory Properties

The memory properties dictate how the server will utilize system memory resources. Only the `LowMemoryLimit` and the `TotalMemoryLimit` properties should be altered without the guidance of Microsoft support. The `LowMemoryLimit` represents a threshold percentage of total physical memory, at which point the server will attempt to perform garbage collection for unused resources to free more resources. The default value is configured at 75 percent of total physical memory. The `TotalMemoryLimit` is used to tell the server how much of the total physical memory of the server hardware should be made available for use by Analysis Services. This limit is configured to 80 percent of all server memory by default.

Network Properties

The network properties are used to control the network communication resources used by the server. Most notable are the settings that dictate whether the listener uses IPv4 or IPv6 protocols and whether the server will permit the use of Binary XML for requests or responses.

OLAP Properties

The OLAP properties control how the server will perform processing of the server objects (cubes, dimensions, and aggregations). Along with the processing properties, this section includes configuration properties for the way the server will process queries. Some of these query-processing properties are useful for simulating many testing scenarios. As an example, you could adjust the `IndexUseEnabled`, `UseDataSlice`, `AggregationUseEnabled` properties to benchmark different query-handling scenarios to determine if some of these optimizations are providing the desired performance enhancement.

Security Properties

These security properties are responsible for controlling how the server will handle permissions. Examples of these properties include RequireClientAuthentication, which is used to configure whether clients connecting to the server require authentication, and DisableClientImpersonation, which directs the server on how it should manage client use of impersonation.

Required Services

The core Windows services required by Analysis Services include SQL Server Analysis Services, SQL Server, SQL Server Agent, and SQL Server Browser. Most of theses services are obvious as to the role they play in supporting Analysis Services, but the SQL Server Browser service needs a bit of explanation. The SQL Server Browser service supports the Analysis Services redirector used when clients connect to named instances of Analysis Services.

All of these services are configured at the operating system level via Administrative Tools⇨Services (see Figure 7-2). As you would expect with configuring other services, the focus is on the logon account used by the service as the context in which to operate, the startup type used to detail if the service starts when the operating system starts, the recovery that indicates the actions taken by the service in the event of failure, and the dependencies that specify which other services are required for the service to function properly.

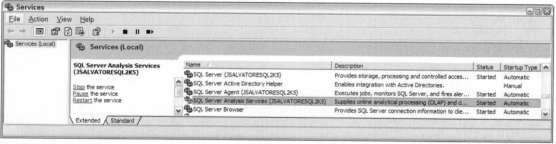

Figure 7-2

Commonly, the logon account used by any service should be one that has the least number of privileges required to function properly. More often than not, an account that has network rights will be required, and this account would need to be granted access rights on the remote resources in addition to configuring the account to be used by the service.

Analysis Services Scripting Language

We'll now direct your attention to how many of your administrative tasks can be automated by using the built-in scripting language, Analysis Services Scripting Language, or ASSL. This language is based on XML and is what client applications use to get information from Analysis Services.

This scripting language has two distinct parts. The first part is used to define the objects that are part of the server, including the objects used to develop solutions (measures and dimensions). The other part is used to request the server to perform actions, such as processing objects or performing batch operations.

We will focus on the scripting language components that help you manage the Analysis Services server. We'll start by looking at some examples of how you can use the language to process objects. Processing enables you to fill objects with data so they may be used by end users for business analysis. Some of the objects you can process include cubes, databases, dimensions, and partitions. To perform this processing using the scripting language, you will use the language's `Process` command.

An example of a script that would process the AdventureWorks employee dimension follows:

```
<Batch xmlns="http://schemas.microsoft.com/analysisservices/2003/engine">
  <Parallel>
    <Process xmlns:xsd="http://www.w3.org/2001/XMLSchema"
xmlns:xsi="http://www.w3.org/2001/XMLSchema-instance">
      <Object>
        <DatabaseID>Analysis Services Tutorial</DatabaseID>
        <DimensionID>Employee</DimensionID>
      </Object>
      <Type>ProcessUpdate</Type>
      <WriteBackTableCreation>UseExisting</WriteBackTableCreation>
    </Process>
  </Parallel>
</Batch>
```

Note that you can script many of the actions that you can configure in SQL Management Studio. For example, you can generate the example script shown here by right-clicking the AdventureWorks cube and selecting the Process Menu option. This will display the Process Cube dialog (see Figure 7-3). On this dialog, you click the Script button located along the top under the title bar and then select the location in which you want to generate the script.

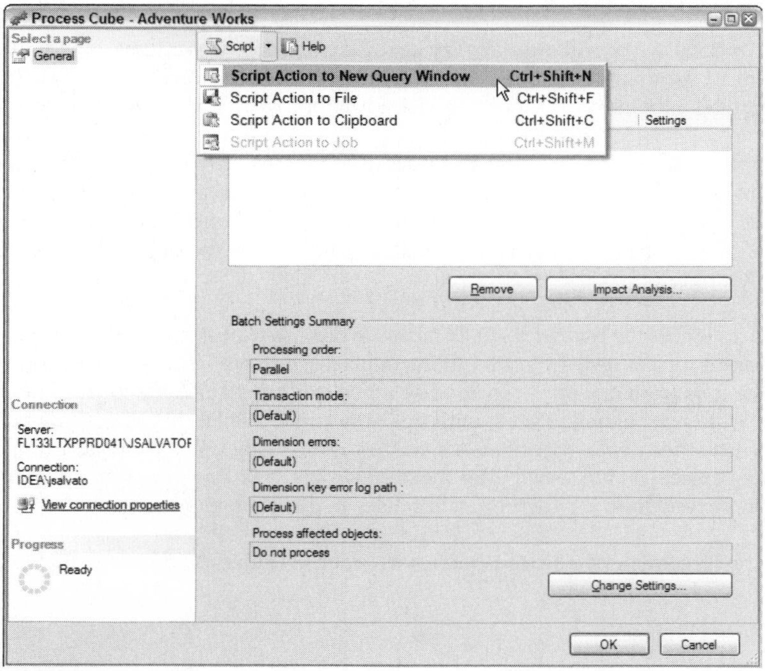

Figure 7-3

Administering Analysis Services Databases

Now that you understand more about the Analysis Services server, we will look at the administration tasks needed for the databases that will ultimately be deployed and run on the Analysis Services server. The primary tasks involved with managing the Analysis Services databases include deployment to the server, performing disaster recovery activities such as backup and restore operations, and synchronizing databases to copy entire databases.

Deploying Analysis Services Databases

Obviously, without deployment there really, is no value to running an Analysis Services server. Through deployment of Analysis Services databases to the server, original and changed designs are applied to the server.

When performing administrative tasks, you can either use Management Studio to affect changes directly in a database in what is commonly referred to as *online mode*, or you can work within the Business Intelligence Developer Studio to affect changes via a Build and Deploy process commonly referred to as *offline mode*.

More specific to database deployment, you have the following options:

❑   Deploy changes directly from Business Intelligence Developer Studio.

❑   Script changes and deploy from within Management Studio.

❑   Make incremental deployments using the Deployment Wizard.

❑   Process changes using the Synchronize Database Wizard.

Many of these options are useful only in very specific circumstances and as such will not be given much attention. The most useful and complete method of deploying the databases is to use the Deployment Wizard. Alternatively, the next best tool to assist with deployment is the Synchronize Database Wizard.

The main advantage of the Deployment Wizard is that it is the only deployment method that will apply the database project definition to production and allow you to keep many of the production database configuration settings, such as security and partitioning. This is important because neither direct deployment from BIDS nor scripting from Management Studio permits the deployment to maintain existing configuration settings.

The main scenario where the Synchronize Database Wizard is useful is when you are deploying changes from a quality-assurance or test environment into a production environment. This process copies the database and the data from one server to another while leaving it available for user queries. The advantage of this option should not be understated; with this option, the availability of your database is maintained. This contrasts with other deployment options, as they most likely will require additional processing of Analysis Services objects on the server after the deployment, and this process may require taking the database offline. We will look at synchronization later in this chapter.

Let's see how the Deployment Wizard operates in order to understand how valuable it is for handling deployment.

1. Launch the Deployment Wizard from the Start Menu under SQL Server 2005➪Analysis Services.

2. On the Specify Source Analysis Services Database page, enter a full path to an Analysis Services database (see Figure 7-4).

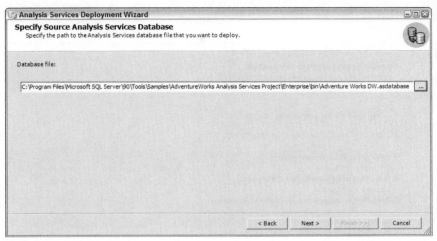

Figure 7-4

3. In the Installation Target page, indicate the Server to which the database should be deployed, along with the desired database name (defaults to the file name of the database).

4. In the Specify Options for Partitions and Roles page, indicate which configuration options (Partitions and Security) should be maintained on the deployment target database and thus not overwritten by this deployment (see Figure 7-5).

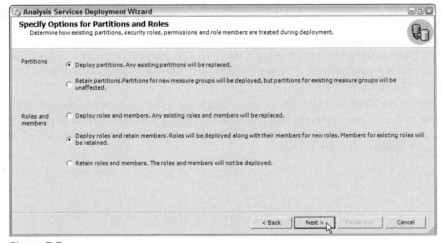

Figure 7-5

5. In the Specify Configuration Properties page, select which configuration settings from the current configuration file (.configsettings) should be applied to the target database. These settings provide a very useful way to redirect things such as data source connection strings to point to production sources rather than those used for development and testing. Also important to note is that the Retain checkboxes at the top provide an elegant way to manage updates of previous deployments, as they disable overwriting of both the configuration and optimization setting (see Figure 7-6).

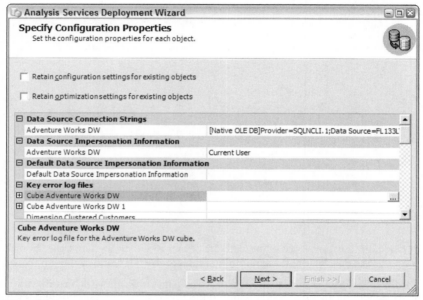

Figure 7-6

6. On the Select Processing Options page, enter the desired processing method and any writeback table options. To support a robust deployment, you may also select the option to include all processing in a single transaction that will roll back all changes should any part of the deployment fail. Note also the Default processing method. This method is used to let Analysis Services review the modifications to be applied and determine the optimal processing needed to be performed (see Figure 7-7).

7. Last, on the Confirm Deployment page, you have an option to script the entire deployment. This option is useful when either the person running the Deployment Wizard is not authorized to perform the actual deployment or the deployment will need to be scheduled so as not to interfere with other activities.

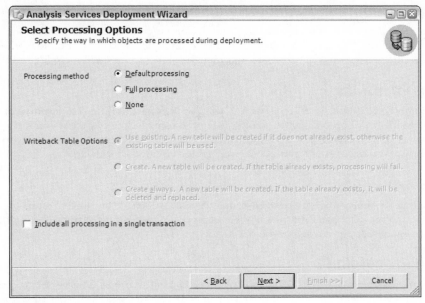

Figure 7-7

Processing Analysis Services Objects

Now that you understand how to deploy Analysis Services databases, you must add data to these objects by processing them. Additionally, if the cubes need to be updated to reflect development changes made after the initial deployment, you'll need to reprocess them. Last, when data sources have changes made to their information, you will need to perform, minimally, an incremental reprocessing of the cube to ensure that you have up-to-date data within the Analysis Services solution. It's also worthwhile to note that often developers will build and test designs locally. These local cubes must first be deployed to the server before performing any processing.

The Analysis Services objects that require processing include measure groups, partitions, dimensions, cubes, mining models, mining structures, and databases. The processing is hierarchical, in that processing an object that contains any other objects will also process those objects. For example, a database includes one or more cubes, and cubes contain one or more dimensions, so processing the database would also process all the cubes contained within that database and also will process all the dimensions contained in or referenced by each of the cubes.

Processing Dimensions

Analysis Services processes dimensions by simply running queries that will return data from the data source tables for the dimensions. This data is then organized into the hierarchies and ultimately into map files that list all of the unique hierarchical paths for each dimension.

Processing Cubes

The cube contains both measure groups and partitions and is combined with dimensions to give the cube a data definition. Processing a cube is done by issuing queries to get fact-table members and the related measure values such that each path of dimensional hierarchies will include a value.

Processing Partitions

Just as in database partitioning, the goal of Analysis Services partitioning is to improve query response times and administrator processing durations. This processing is special in that you must evaluate your hardware space and Analysis Services data structure constraints. Partitioning is the key to ensuring that your query response times are fast and your processing activities are efficient.

Reprocessing

After deploying an Analysis Services database, many events will create the need to reprocess some or all of the objects within the database. Examples of when reprocessing is required include object structural/schema changes, aggregation design changes, or refreshing object data.

Performing Processing

To perform processing of Analysis Services object, you can either use SQL Server Management Studio or Business Intelligence Development Studio or run an XML for Analysis (XMLA) script. An alternative approach may use Analysis Management Objects (AMO) to start processing jobs via programming tools.

When processing, it is important to note that as Analysis Services objects are being committed, the database will not be available to process user requests. The reason for this is that the processing commit phase requires an exclusive lock on the Analysis Services objects being committed. User requests are not denied during this commit process but rather are queued until the commit is successfully completed.

Let's look at how to perform processing for an Analysis Services database from within SQL Server Management Studio.

1. Open Management Studio and connect to an Analysis Services server.

2. Right-click an Analysis Services database and select Process. The Process Database dialog is now displayed to allow you to configure the details of the processing (see Figure 7-8).

3. You can request some understanding of the impact on related objects by performing the desired processing by clicking the Impact Analysis button.

4. You can configure processing options such as the processing order by clicking Change Settings. Available options for the order include processing in parallel within a single transaction or processing sequentially within one or separate transactions. A very important option is "Process affected objects." This option controls whether all of the other objects that have dependencies on the database will also be processed (see Figure 7-9). A common architectural design employed in data warehousing involves the use of shared dimensions. These dimensions are able to be shared across the organization and allow for low maintenance and uniformity. The "Process affected objects" setting can therefore have a profound impact when you're using an architecture involving shared dimensions, as the option may force reprocessing of many other databases in which the shared dimensions are used.

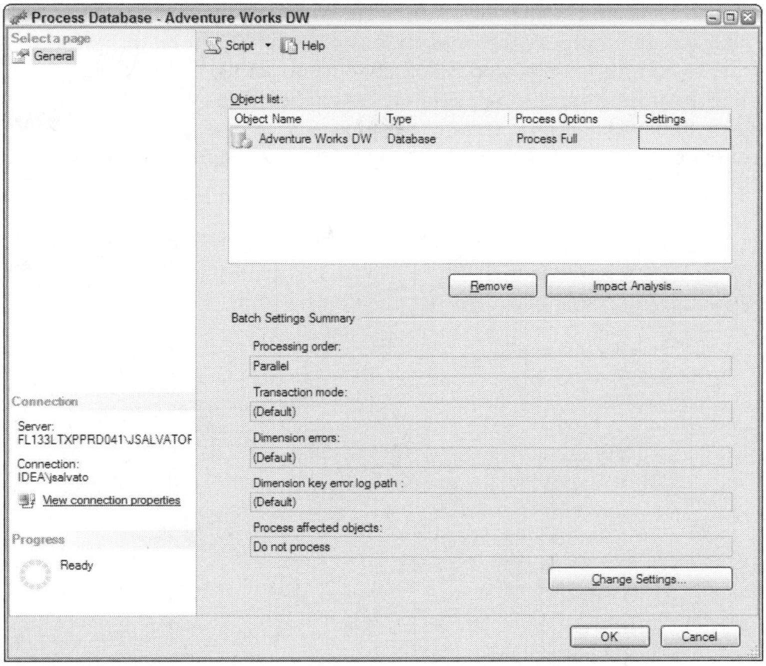

Figure 7-8

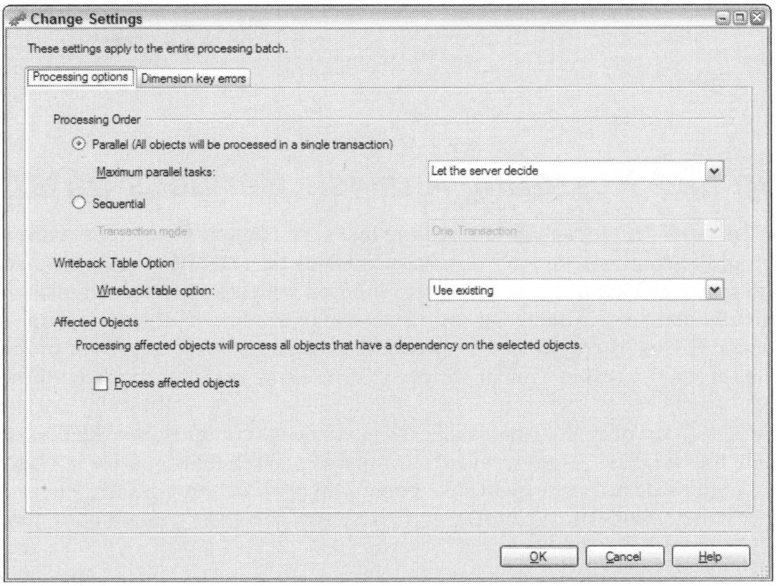

Figure 7-9

5. You can also configure very sophisticated dimension key error handling (see Figure 7-10). As an example, you can configure the options to use a custom error configuration, which will convert key errors to an unknown record rather than terminating the processing. Additionally, you can determine error limits and what action to take when those limits have been exceeded. Last, you can choose to handle specific error conditions such as "key not found" or duplicate keys by reporting and continuing to process, by ignoring the error and continuing to process, and by reporting and stopping the processing.

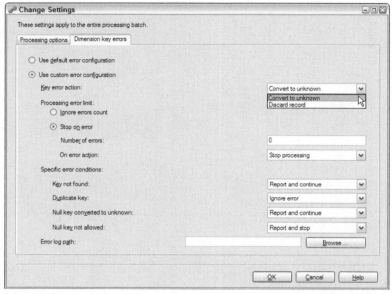

Figure 7-10

Backing Up and Restoring Analysis Services Databases

Without question, performing backup and restore tasks are common functions within the domain of any DBA. A backup of the Analysis Services database captures the state of the database and its objects at a particular point in time to a file on the filesystem (named with an .abf file extension), while recovery restores a particular state of the database and its objects to the server from a backup file on the filesystem. Backup and recovery, therefore, are very useful for data recovery in case of problems with the database on the server at a future time or simply to provide an audit of the state of the database.

The backups will back up only the Analysis Services database contents, not the underlying data sources used to populate the database. Therefore, we strongly suggest that you perform a backup of the data sources using a regular database or filesystem backup in conjunction with the Analysis Services backup to capture a true state of both the Analysis Services objects and their sources at or about the same point in time.

The information that the backup will include varies depending upon the storage type configured for the database. A detailed message displayed at the bottom of the backup database dialog clearly communicates the various objects included in a backup based on the type of storage. Although we'll cover storage options a bit later, you need to know that available options to be included in the backup are the metadata that defines all the objects, the aggregations calculated, and the source data used to populate the objects.

> *In the 2005 release of Analysis Service, you are no longer limited to a backup size limit of 3GB as was the case in the 2000 release.*

We'll now review what is involved with performing these functions for Analysis Services databases. Again, you can use Management Studio to assist with the setup and configuration of these tasks and script the results to permit scheduling.

1. Open Management Studio and connect to an Analysis Services server.

2. Right-click an Analysis Services database and select Backup. The Backup Database dialog is now displayed to permit configuring the details of the backup, such as applying compression, where the backup file should be located, or whether the file should be encrypted (see Figure 7-11). While we will cover storage types later, you get a very clear statement of what information is part of the backup at the bottom of this Backup Database dialog. Basically, the backup is only backing up the Analysis Services information (partitions, metadata, source data, and aggregations) available to a database based on the storage type.

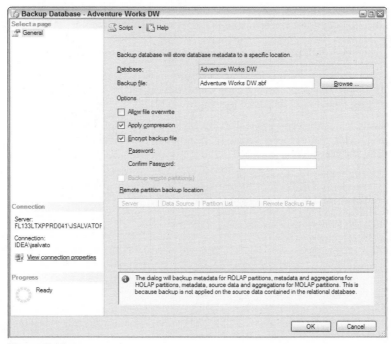

Figure 7-11

3. Optionally, you can script the backup by pressing the Script button along the top the dialog. The resulting script would look like the following example (including, of course, a poor practice of including the password).

```
<Backup xmlns="http://schemas.microsoft.com/analysisservices/2003/engine">
  <Object>
    <DatabaseID>Adventure Works DW</DatabaseID>
  </Object>
  <File>Adventure Works DW.abf</File>
  <Password>aw</Password>
</Backup>
```

Now that you have a backup of an Analysis Services database, it's time to turn your attention to recovery of Analysis Services databases. Recovery will take a previously created backup file (named with an .abf file extension) and restore it to an Analysis Services database. Several options are made available during this process:

❑   Using the original database name (or specifying a new database name)

❑   Overwriting an existing database

❑   Including existing security information (or skipping security)

❑   Changing the restoration folder for each partition (except that remote partitions cannot become local)

Following are the steps needed to perform a recovery of the database:

1. Open Management Studio and connect to an Analysis Services server.

2. Right-click an Analysis Services database and select Restore. The Restore Database dialog is now displayed to permit configuring the details of the restoration, such as including security or overwriting an existing database (see Figure 7-12).

3. Optionally, you can script the restore by clicking the Script button along the top the dialog. The resulting script would look like the following example (including, of course, a poor practice of including the password):

```
<Restore xmlns="http://schemas.microsoft.com/analysisservices/2003/engine">
  <File>C:\Program Files\Microsoft SQL Server\MSSQL.2\OLAP\Backup\
      Adventure Works DW.abf</File>
  <DatabaseName>Adventure Works DW</DatabaseName>
  <AllowOverwrite>true</AllowOverwrite>
  <Password>aw</Password>
</Restore>
```

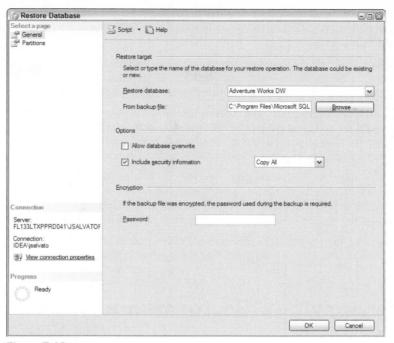

Figure 7-12

Synchronizing Analysis Services Databases

Another very important activity to perform involves synchronizing Analysis Services databases from one server to another. This is usually done as a mechanism for deploying from a test or quality-assurance server to a production server. The reason this feature is attractive for this purpose is that users can continue to browse the production cubes while the synchronization is taking place. When the synchronization completes, the user will automatically be redirected to the newly synchronized copy of the database, and the older version is removed from the server. This differs greatly from what happens when you perform a deployment, as part of the deployment usually involves processing of dimensions and or cubes. As you may recall, certain types of processing of Analysis Services objects require that the cube be taken offline and will, therefore, not be available for the user to browse until the processing completes.

As with many other database tasks, the synchronization can be run immediately from the wizard, or the results of the selections can be saved to a script file for later execution or scheduling.

The following are the steps to perform to synchronize an Analysis Services database between servers.

1. Open Management Studio and connect to the target Analysis Services server.

2. On this target server, right-click the databases folder and select Synchronize.

3. On the Select Databases to Synchronize page, specify the source server and database, and note that the destination server is hardcoded to the server from which you launched the synchronization.

4. If applicable, on the Specify Locations for Local Partitions page, the source folder displays the folder name on the server that contains the local partition while the destination folder can be changed to reflect the folder into which you want the database to be synchronized.

5. If applicable, on the Specify Locations for Remote Partitions page, you can modify both the destination folder and server to reflect where you want the database to be synchronized. Additionally, if the location has remote partitions contained in that location that need to be included in the synchronization, you must place a check beside the Sync option.

6. On the Specify Query Criteria page, you specify a value for the security definitions to include and also indicate whether or not compression should be used. The security options include copying all definitions and membership information, skipping membership information but including the security definitions, and ignoring all security and membership details.

7. On the Select Synchronization Method page, you can either run the synchronization now or script to a file for later use in scheduling the synchronization.

Analysis Services Performance Monitoring and Tuning

Successful use of Analysis Services requires continual monitoring of how user queries and other processes are performing and making the required adjustments to improve their performance. The main tools for performing these tasks include the SQL Profiler, Performance Counters, and the Flight Recorder.

Monitoring Analysis Services Events Using SQL Profiler

Chapters 13 and 14 provide detailed coverage of how to use SQL Profiler, so we'll focus on what is important about using this tool for monitoring your Analysis Services events. The capabilities of using SQL Profiler for Analysis Services have been vastly improved in the 2005 release and are now quite useful for this purpose. With SQL Server Profiler, you can review what the server is doing during processing and query resolution. Especially important is the ability to record the data generated by profiling to either a database table or file to review or replay it later to get a better understanding of what happened. Furthermore, you can also now either step through the events that were recorded or replay them as they originally occurred. Last, you can place the events side by side with the performance counters to spot trends impacting performance.

Our main focus will be tracing the Analysis Services server activity and investigating the performance of the MDX queries submitted to the server in order to process user requests for information.

The event categories that will be useful include:

❑ Command events provide insight into the actual types of statements issued to perform actions.

❑ Discovery events detail requests for metadata about server objects including the Discovery Server State events (such as open connections).

- ❑   Error and Warnings events

- ❑   Notification events

- ❑   Query events

Because of all the detail that a trace returns, you should use the Column Filter button to display only the activities sent to a specific Analysis Services database.

Creating Traces for Replay

Traces are important in that they allow you to determine various elements of status information for Analysis Services through certain counters. You start Performance Monitor by either selecting Administrative Tools from the Control Panel or by typing **PerfMon** at the command prompt. Two types of counters are used within Performance Monitor. The predefined counters measure statistics for our server and process performance, while user-defined counters are used to analyze events that may occur.

Just as in the monitoring of other SQL services, the CPU usage, memory usage, and disk IO rate are important counters to review in order to evaluate how Analysis Services is performing.

We'll now give you a better idea of how to configure these traces for replaying queries submitted to our Analysis Services server. Start the trace by opening SQL Profiler and selecting File⇨New trace. When prompted, specify the Analysis Services server to connect to and configure trace properties.

To profile user queries, you have to ensure that the SQL Profiler is capturing the Audit Login event class, the Query Begin event class, and the Query End event class (see Figure 7-13). The information detailing who was running the query and other session-specific information will be able to be determined because you are including the Audit Login event class. The Query Begin and End event classes simply permit understanding of what queries were submitted by reviewing the text of the query along with any parameters that would have been used during query processing.

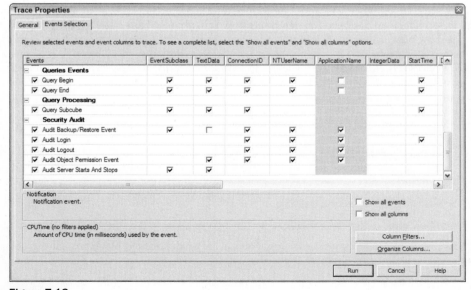

Figure 7-13

After you've set up the trace, you can start the selected trace. Now you can browse a cube within Management Studio to generate user activity involving the submission of queries to Analysis Services. The result in Profiler is a detailing of Events along with the Text Data recording the activities. As an example, in Management Studio, you can add the Customer and Date dimensions while also requesting that Order Count and Average Sales Amount be displayed. This activity all gets recorded with the Profiler, then showing the Query Begin as the EventClass and a Select statement recorded in the TextData (see Figure 7-14).

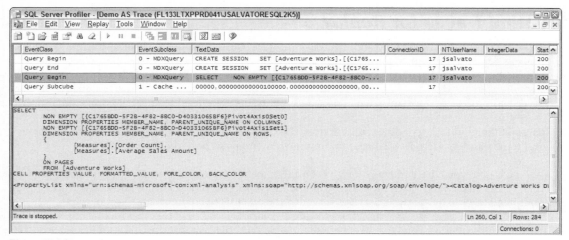

Figure 7-14

Using Flight Recorder for After the Fact Analysis

Often, administrators are disappointed when we cannot seem to find the cause of a particular problem. Mostly, we are stymied when we cannot reproduce reported problems. These situations arise as we attempt to recreate what happened to determine how things could have been handled differently to avoid the reported problem. Using the Flight Recorder, you may be able to replay the problem conditions that led to the reported problems. This Flight Recorder operates similar to a tape recorder; it captures the Analysis Services server activity during runtime without requiring a trace. In fact, each time the server is restarted, a new trace file is automatically started. Additionally, the recorder is automatically enabled and can be configured using the Analysis Services Server Properties.

Here's how you can use the trace file created by the Flight Recorder to replay server activity:

1. Open SQL Server profiler and open the trace file created by the Flight Recorder, by default located at `C:\Program Files\Microsoft SQL Server\MSSQL.2\OLAP\Log` and named `FlightRecorderCurrent.trc`.

2. Select Start Replay on the toolbar.

3. On the Connect To Server dialog, enter the server name and authentication information.

4. On the Replay Configuration dialog, you can set up the desired playback features such as replaying only statements issued to the server within a given timeframe (see Figures 7-15 and 7-16).

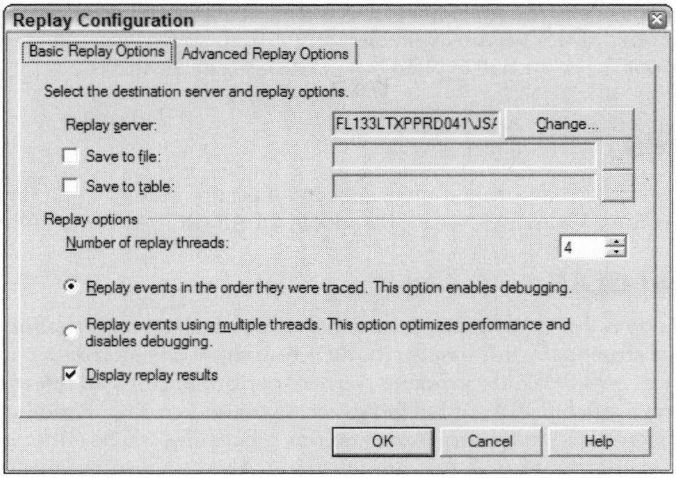

Figure 7-15

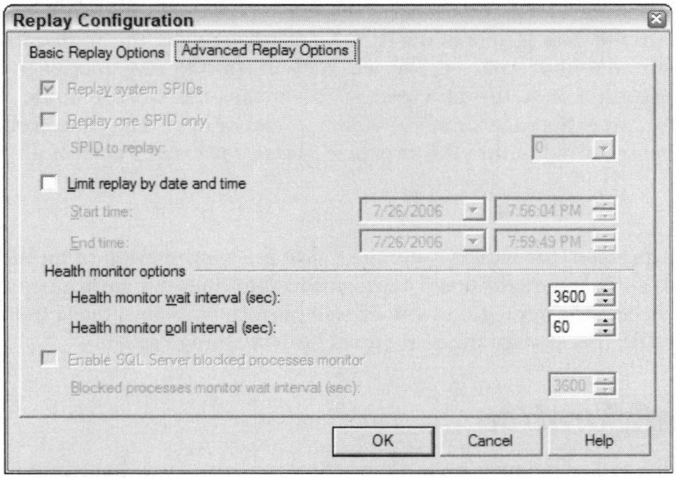

Figure 7-16

This replay is rather useful, as Analysis Services will begin to run the statements captured in the trace. As we all agree, factors such as number of open connections and even the number of sessions that existed at the time of the original problem are important to consider when troubleshooting problems. When you replay the traces made by Flight Recorder, these factors are simulated on your behalf.

Management of Analysis Services Storage

One of the main reasons for using Analysis Services centers on performance with complex data retrieval. The design of the storage within Analysis Services, therefore, becomes very important when trying to achieve the query and processing performance expected. In order to understand storage design, we'll first review what modes of storage are available within Analysis Services. Next, we will look at the configuration of partitions. Last, we will explain how to design aggregations.

Storage Modes

Analysis Services permits configuring dimensions and measure groups using the following storage modes: Multidimensional OLAP (MOLAP), Relational OLAP (ROLAP), and Hybrid OLAP (HOLAP).

Multidimensional OLAP

MOLAP storage mode is the most aggressive because it stores all the aggregations and a copy of the source data with the structure. Additionally, the structure stores the metadata required to understand the structure. The real benefit of this structure is query performance, as all information needed to respond to queries is available without having to access the source data. Periodic processing is required to update the data stored within the structure, and this processing can be either incremental or full. As a result, data latency is introduced with this storage mode. Also as a result of this structure, storage requirements become much more important due to the volume of information that the system requires.

Relational OLAP

Indexed views within the data source of the ROLAP structure store the aggregations, while a copy of the source data is not stored within Analysis Service. With this mode, any queries that the query cache cannot answer must be passed on to the data source. This makes this storage mode slower than MOLAP or HOLAP. The real benefit is that users can view data in real or near-real time, and because a copy of the source data is not being stored within the structure, the storage requirements are lower.

Hybrid OLAP

As you might have guessed, the HOLAP storage mode is a combination of multidimensional OLAP and relational OLAP. This storage mode stores aggregations but does not store a copy of the source data. As a result, queries that access the aggregated values will perform well, but those that do not will perform slower. Also as a result, this storage mode requires far less storage space.

Partition Configuration

When you are tasked with configuring partitions for your cubes, you have two primary activities. First, you have the configuration of the storage of the partition, and second you have the optimization of the partition by configuring aggregations. The storage options, which were previously discussed, include MOLAP, HOLAP, or ROLAP. Aggregations are precalculated summaries of data primarily employed so that query response time is made faster because the cube partition has prepared and saved the data in advance of its use.

You should understand that the configuration of storage in Analysis Services is configured separately for each partition of each measure group in a cube. This enables you to optimize your cube query strategies for each partition. An example would be to keep the current year's data in one partition optimized for more detailed and narrow queries, while keeping older data in another partition optimized for broader aggregated queries.

You configure your cube storage using either Business Intelligence Developer Studio or, after deployment, using Management Studio. Often, it is not necessary for developers to be involved with partitioning or configuration of storage, so this is a better fit for being done using Management Studio. The downside is that the Visual Studio project will not be updated to reflect the current storage settings, and you must be very careful during deployment that your selections made in Management Studio are not overwritten. Specifically, you will want to ensure that during deployment, when the Specify Options for Partitions and Roles page is displayed, you indicate that Partitions and Security should be maintained on the deployment target database and thus not overwritten by this deployment (see Figure 7-5).

When you deploy a cube for the first time, a measure group is set up to be entirely contained within a single partition, spanning the entire fact table used for the measures. With the Enterprise Edition, you can change that to define multiple partitions by setting the StorageMode property for each partition.

Here's how you can set the storage options in SQL Server Management Studio:

1. Open Management Studio and connect to the target Analysis Services server.

2. In Object Explorer, open the cube that contains the partition for which you want to set storage options. If you have more than one partition, right-click a partition and click Properties; otherwise, right-click a cube, and then click Properties.

3. In the Partition Properties (or Cube Properties) dialog box, select the Proactive Caching page.

4. On the Proactive Caching page, select the Standard setting radio button to accept the default storage settings for the storage type specified by the slider bar. Now you may move the slider bar to change the storage type from MOLAP to HOLAP and to ROLAP (see Figure 7-17).

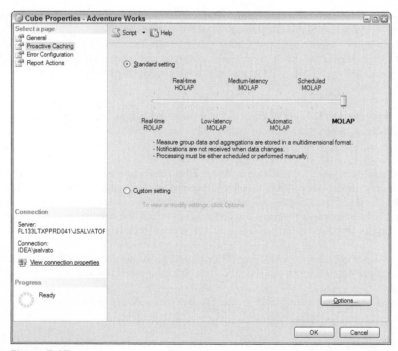

Figure 7-17

5. Optionally, you may select the Custom setting checkbox, and then click Options to set advanced storage options.

Designing Aggregations

Again, the primary role of aggregations is to precalculate summaries of the cube data so that user queries may be answered very fast. When a query is unable to use an aggregation, Analysis Services must query the lowest level of details it has stored and sum the values. Aggregations are stored in a cube in cells at the intersection of the selected dimensions.

Designing aggregations is all about tradeoffs between space and user performance. Additionally, optimizing query performance via aggregations also increases the time it takes to process the cube. When you have few aggregations, the time required to process the cube and the storage space occupied by the cube is rather small, but the query response time may be slow because the query cannot leverage a precomputed summary (aggregate) and must instead rely upon having to retrieve data from the lowest levels within the cube and summarize at query time.

You design aggregations by determining which combination of attributes are often used by queries and could benefit from precalculation. You can begin this process by using either the Aggregation Design Wizard, or after deployment you can use query usage statistics in conjunction with the Usage-Based Optimization Wizard. These methods obviously lend themselves to specific lifecycle usage. Developers would likely use the Aggregation Design Wizard to initially configure the aggregations prior to deployment, while administrators would opt for using the query statistics and the Usage-Based Optimization Wizard.

A good rule of thumb to start with is to optimize at a level of 20/80 and 80/20. When using the Aggregation Design Wizard, you are really not sure what the usage patterns will be, so optimizing to higher than a 20-percent performance increase would not be valuable. On the other hand, when you have actual query statistics that clearly represent production usage patterns, you should optimize at about an 80-percent performance increase level. This in effect states that you want 80 percent of user queries to be answered directly from aggregations.

Details of the Aggregation Design Wizard will not be reviewed, as we assume that most administration of the aggregations will be performed in either Management Studio or BIDS using Usage-Based Optimization.

Before using the Usage-Based Optimization Wizard, you need to ensure that the query log is enabled and that it has been populated. You enable this log in Management Studio via the Analysis Services Server properties. The CreateQueryLogTable setting enables logging to a database table when true, while the QueryLogConnectionString specifies the database in which the logging will be stored. Also, you need to note the setting of the QueryLogSampling, as this determines which queries will get logged.

Once the Query Log has been enabled and is populated with query statistics, you can run the Usage-Based Optimization Wizard. Here are the steps needed to use this wizard:

1. Open Management Studio and connect to the target Analysis Services server.

2. Select the desired database, cube, and measure group.

3. Right-click the partitions folder and select Usage Based Optimization.

4. On the Select Partitions to Modify dialog, specify any partitions that are to be evaluated. You can either select all partitions for the measure group or you can select combinations of individual partitions.

5. On the Specify Query Criteria dialog, you can view query statistics for the selected measure group partition, including the total number of queries and the average response time for processing the queries. Optionally, you can set some limits to filter the queries that you would like the optimization to consider (see Figure 7-18) including an interesting option for filtering the queries by Users. Presumably, one notable use of this option could be to enable you to make sure your executives' queries are delivering the best response time.

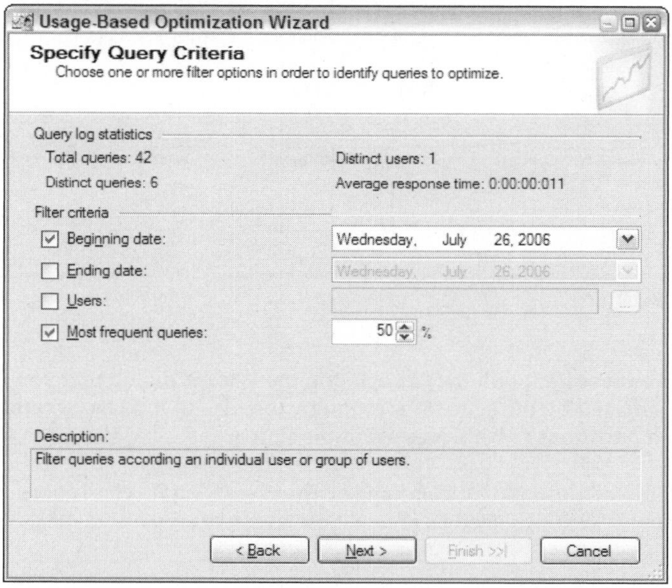

Figure 7-18

6. On the Review the Queries that will be Optimized dialog, you can view the specific dimension member combinations under the client request column, the occurrences of those combinations, and the average duration of those combinations. At this point, you also have a column of checkboxes beside each row that allows you to indicate that you do not want some of the suggested queries optimized.

7. On the Specify Storage and Cashing Options dialog, you can use the slider to change form MOLAP to HOLAP and to ROLAP.

8. Next, you specify the counts of various cube objects on the Specify Object Counts dialog.

9. Next, on the Set Aggregations Options dialog, you specify how long the aggregations should be designed. Options to consider include designing aggregations until a specified amount of storage has been used, until a specified percentage of performance gain has been reached or until you decide to stop the optimization process (see Figure 7-19). Because you are basing this optimization on real query statistics, you should consider optimizing until a performance gain of about 80 percent has been attained. This translates loosely to optimizing 80 percent of the queries to use the aggregations.

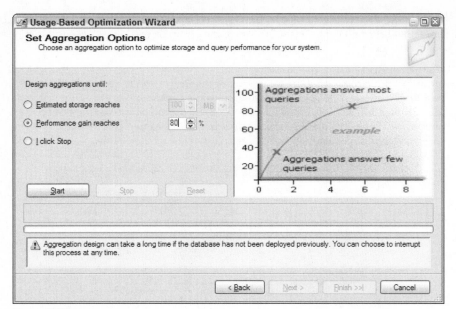

Figure 7-19

10. Last, we are presented with the Completing the Wizard dialog that you may use to review the partitions affected by the aggregation design and also to indicate whether or not you would like the effected partitions to be processed immediately.

You now have completed designing the storage of your Analysis Services cubes, set up partitions, and designed aggregations. Next, we need to review how to apply security to Analysis Services.

Applying Security to Analysis Services

Security within Analysis Services involves designing user permissions to selected cubes, dimensions, cells, mining models, and data sources. Analysis Services relies on Microsoft Windows to authenticate users, and only authenticated users who have rights within Analysis Services can establish a connection to Analysis Services.

Server and Database Roles

After a user connects to Analysis Services, the permissions that user has within Analysis Services are determined by the rights assigned to the Analysis Services roles to which that user belongs, either directly or through membership in a Windows role. The two roles available in Analysis Services are server and database roles.

Server Role

The server role permits unrestricted access to the server and all the objects contained on the server. This role also allows its members to administer security by assigning permissions to other users. By default, all members of the Administrators local group are members of the server role in Analysis Services and have server-wide permissions to perform any task. You configure this access by using Management Studio, Business Intelligence Development Studio, or an XMLA script.

Here's how you add additional Windows users or groups to this Server role.

1. Open Management Studio and connect to an Analysis Services server.

2. Right-click the server node in the Object Explorer and choose Properties.

3. On the Analysis Server Properties dialog, select the Security page. Note again how no users or groups are included automatically. Although not shown in the dialog, only members of the local Windows Administrators group are automatically assigned this server role.

4. Click the Add button and add users and groups with the standard Windows Select Users and Groups dialog.

5. After adding the users and groups, we can remove the local Administrators from the server role by selecting the General page and clicking on the Show Advanced (ALL) Properties checkbox. Then modify the `Security\BuiltinAdminsAreServerAdmins` property to false.

Database Role

Within Analysis Services, you can set up multiple database roles. Only the members of the server role are permitted to create these database roles within each database, grant administrative or user permissions to these database roles, and add Windows users and groups to these database roles.

These database roles have no administrative capabilities unless they are granted Full Control, otherwise known as Administrator rights, or a more limited set of administrator rights (such as Process the database, Process one or more Dimensions, and Read database metadata).

In summary, reading Analysis Services data is only available to members of the server role and members of a database role that have Full Control. Other users can only get this access if their database role expressly grants permissions to the objects in Analysis Services (dimensions, cubes, and cells).

You set up database roles using either Business Intelligence Developer Studio or Management Studio. In BIDS, you use the Role Designer, while in Management Studio you use the Create Role dialog. When Management Studio is used for setting up these roles, the changes do not require that you deploy the database, as these changes are made in online mode.

Here's how to add a database role to an Analysis Services database.

1. Open Management Studio and connect to an Analysis Services server.

2. Right-click the Roles folder located in one of the databases and select New Role.

3. On the Create or Edit Role dialog (see Figure 7-20), enter Data Admin as the role name and check the Full control (Administrator) checkbox.

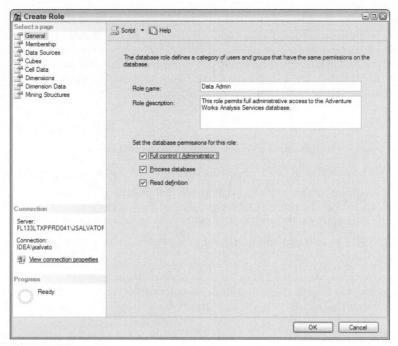

Figure 7-20

4. Select the Membership page and add a Windows user account.

Database Role Permissions

The easiest way to understand the granularity of permissions within Analysis Services is by reviewing the Create Or Edit Role dialog's pages. Previously, when you added a new role, you assigned the Full control (Administrator) database permissions. If you did not check that Full control checkbox, you would have the ability to assign very granular permissions by using the various pages of the Create Role dialog.

The permissions form a sort of hierarchy in which the topmost permissions need to be assigned before any of the next-level permissions. This hierarchy includes Cubes, Dimensions, Dimension Data, and Cell Data. Analysis Services permits a database to include more than one cube, and that is why you have that as a permission set for our roles. Within the cube, you have dimensions and measures. The measures are constrained by the various dimensions. Let's now look at some examples of assigning these permissions.

While reviewing the role permissions available, you'll note two in particular that will be regularly used to limit access to information: Dimensions and Dimension Data. These permit you to define what the user can see when browsing the cube. For example, you can configure security such that only staff in the Marketing department can use the Promotions dimension. Access permissions to an entire dimension are configured on the Dimensions page of the Create or Edit Role dialog (see Figure 7-21). You should understand that certain permissions require that other permissions be granted. In this example, you would have to ensure that the role for the Marketing department staff has been granted permissions to access the AdventureWorks cube.

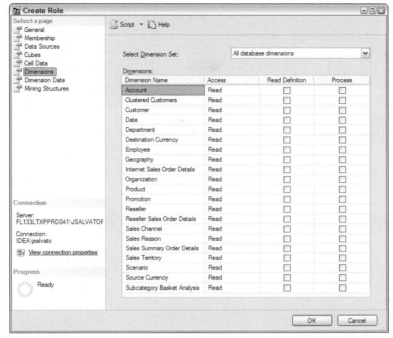

Figure 7-21

Once access has been modified for the dimensions, you have to define the specific attribute hierarchies and members within the dimension to which role members are allowed access. If you forget to do this, the role will not have permission to view any attribute hierarchies within the dimension, nor any of their members. For example, you can permit a regional sales manager access to the sales territories in which he manages by selecting the Dimension Data page and selecting the AdventureWorks DW.Sales Territory from the Dimension combo box (see Figure 7-22).

You may also encounter a security configuration that requires even more sophistication, and for that you have the Advanced tab on the Dimension Data page of the Create Role dialog (see Figure 7-23). This tab permits the creation of very complex combinations of allowed and denied listings of dimension members, along with configuration of default members for our role. Here is where administrators may need to work with developers to understand the multidimensional expression language (MDX) syntax that would be required to configure these advanced security options.

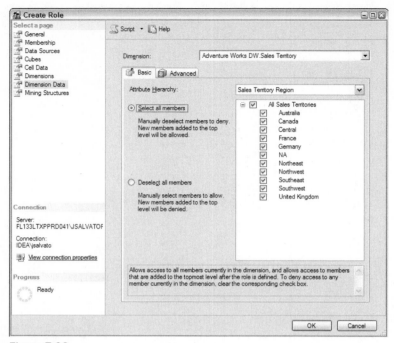

Figure 7-22

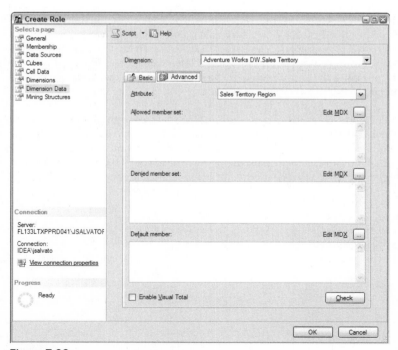

Figure 7-23

Summary

We have covered a lot of ground in understanding the various administrative functions related to Analysis Services. After getting a general introduction to the elements that compose the Unified Dimensional Model (UDM) and looking at the high-level architecture of Analysis Services, we reviewed important Server and Database administration tasks such as setting server configuration settings and deploying our databases. Next, we got some insight into performance monitoring and tuning. Then we turned our attention to storage administrative tasks such as configuring partitions or designing aggregations. Last, we reviewed the various security administration tasks such as creating database roles and assigning granular permissions to the roles. Now that you've learned about administering the Business Integration services, we'll move on in Chapter 8 to discussing how to administer the developer tools that SQL Server 2005 provides.

Administering the Development Features

SQL Server 2005 comes with a set of technologies capable of enlarging the horizon for database applications. One of the most remarkable technologies is the Service Broker, which makes it possible to build database-intensive distributed applications. The Service Broker implements a set of distributed communication patterns to add messaging capabilities to SQL Server applications. The other remarkable feature is the integration of the Common Language Runtime (CLR) component of the .NET Framework for Microsoft Windows with the SQL Server database engine. This integration enables developers to write procedures, triggers, and functions in any of the CLR languages, particularly Microsoft Visual C# .NET, Microsoft Visual Basic .NET, and Microsoft Visual C++. It also enables developers to extend the database with new types and aggregates.

In this chapter, we first explain how these new features work, and then you will learn how to administer them. We begin with the Service Broker, and then move on to CLR integration.

The Service Broker

The Service Broker may be the best feature added to this SQL Server release. This feature enables you to build secure, reliable, scalable, distributed, asynchronous functionality to database applications. You can use the Service Broker to build distributed applications, delegating all the system-level messaging details to the Service Broker and concentrating your efforts in the problem domain. You may find that implementing Service Broker application is tedious at first, but once you understand it, we think you will love it.

Service Broker Architecture

The Service Broker is designed around the basic functions of sending and receiving messages. It helps developers build asynchronous, loosely coupled applications, in which independent components work together to accomplish a task. The Service Broker is a framework and extension to T-SQL, and can create and use the components for building reliable and scalable message-based applications. The core of the Service Broker architecture is the concept of a *dialog*, which is a reliable, persistent, bidirectional, ordered exchange of messages between two *endpoints*. You will learn more about endpoints later. Figure 8-1 shows the basic architecture of the Service Broker (it includes a lot of terminology that is explained in the following sections).

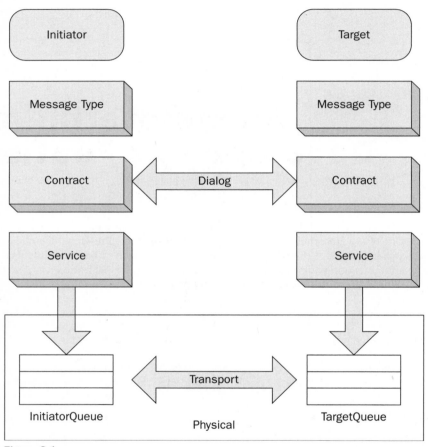

Figure 8-1

Message Type

A *message type* is a definition of the format of a message. The message type is an object in a database. *Messages* are the information exchanged between applications that use the Service Broker. The message type object defines the name of the message and the type of data it contains. The following code shows the syntax for creating a message type:

```
CREATE MESSAGE TYPE message_type_name
    [ AUTHORIZATION owner_name ]
    [ VALIDATION = {  NONE
```

```
                    |  EMPTY
                    |  WELL_FORMED_XML
                    |  VALID_XML WITH SCHEMA COLLECTION schema_collection_name
                 }
          ]
```

Permission for creating a message type defaults to members of the ddl_admin or db_owner fixed database roles and the sysadmin fixed server role. The REFERENCES permission for a message type defaults to the owner of the message type, members of the db_owner fixed database role, and members of the sysadmin fixed server role. When the CREATE MESSAGE TYPE statement specifies a schema collection, the user executing the statement must have REFERENCES permission on the schema collection specified.

Following are the arguments and their definitions for the CREATE MESSAGE TYPE statement:

❑ message_type_name: The name of the message type is just a SQL Server identifier. The convention is to use a URL for the name, but any valid name will suffice. By convention, the name has the form //hostname/pathname/name—for example, //www.wrox.com/bookorder/purchaseorder. Although using a URL format is not required, it's generally easier to ensure uniqueness if you use a URL, especially when conversations span distributed systems. The message_type_name may be up to 128 characters.

❑ AUTHORIZATION owner_name: This argument defines the owner of the message type. The owner can be any valid database user or role. When this clause is omitted, the message type belongs to the user who executed the statement. If you execute the CREATE MESSAGE TYPE statement as either dbo or sa, owner_name may be the name of any valid user or role. Otherwise, owner_name must be the name of the current user, the name of a user for whom the current user has impersonate permissions, or the name of a role to which the current user belongs.

❑ VALIDATION: This specifies how the Service Broker validates the message body for messages of this type. When this clause is not specified, validation defaults to NONE. The possible values are as follows:

   ❑ NONE: The message is not validated at all. The message body may contain any data, including NULL.

   ❑ Empty: The message body must be NULL.

   ❑ WELL_FORMED_XML: When this clause is specified, the receiving endpoint will load the XML into an XML parser to ensure that it can be parsed. If the message fails the validation, it is discarded and an error message is sent back to the sender.

   ❑ VALID_XML WITH SCHEMA COLLECTION schema_collection_name: This clause validates the message against the schema_collection_name specified. The schema collection must be created in SQL Server before you use it here. A schema collection is a new object in SQL Server 2005 that contains one or more XML schemas. Refer to the CREATE XML SCHEMA COLLECTION command in Books Online for more information. If WITH SCHEMA COLLECTION schema_collection_name is not specified, the message will not be validated; however, the XML will still have to be well formed because anytime you specify WELL_FORMED_XML or VALID_XML, the message of that type is loaded into the XML parser when it is received.

The following is an example of creating a message type:

```
CREATE MESSAGE TYPE [//www.wrox.com/order/orderentry]
VALIDATE = WELL_FORMED_XML
```

The two XML validations load every message of that type into an XML parser when each message is received. If you have thousands of messages coming per second, each message passing through the XML parser will have an effect on performance. Therefore, if your message volume is low, validation may make sense. If your application loads the message into a parser, it will be more efficient to handle parsing or validation in the application, rather than parse the message twice.

You can run the following query to view message types in the database in which you have created them:

```
SELECT * FROM sys.service_message_types
```

When you run this query, you will see some default message types. Later in the chapter, you will see some examples of using these default message types. These message types are an implicit part of every contract, which we'll discuss shortly, so any endpoint can receive instances of these message types.

You can ALTER or DROP a message type by using the following T-SQL command syntax:

```
ALTER MESSAGE TYPE message_type_name
    VALIDATION =
    {   NONE
      | EMPTY
      | WELL_FORMED_XML
      | VALID_XML WITH SCHEMA COLLECTION schema_collection_name
    }
```

Changing the validation of a message type does not affect messages that have already been delivered to a queue, which we'll discuss shortly. Permission to alter a message type defaults to the owner of the message type, members of the ddl_admin or db_owner fixed database roles, and members of the sysadmin fixed server role. When the ALTER MESSAGE TYPE statement specifies a schema collection, the user executing the statement must have REFERENCES permission on the schema collection specified.

The following example shows the syntax to drop a message type:

```
DROP MESSAGE TYPE message_type_name [,......n]
```

Permission for dropping a message type defaults to the owner of the message type, members of the ddl_admin or db_owner fixed database roles, and members of the sysadmin fixed server role. Note that you can drop multiple message types. If you try to drop a message type and a contract is referencing the message type, you will get an error.

Contracts

As described earlier, the Service Broker *contracts* define which message type can be used in a conversation. The contract is a database object. The following is the syntax for creating a contract:

```
CREATE CONTRACT contract_name
    [ AUTHORIZATION owner_name ]
```

```
(   {   message_type_name SENT BY { INITIATOR | TARGET | ANY } | [ DEFAULT ] }
    [ ,...n]
)
```

Permission for creating a contract defaults to members of the ddl_admin or db_owner fixed database roles and the sysadmin fixed server role. The REFERENCES permission for a contract defaults to the owner of the message type, members of the db_owner fixed database role, and members of the sysadmin fixed server role. The user executing the CREATE CONTRACT statement must have REFERENCES permission on all the message types specified unless the user executing the CREATE CONTRACT statement is a member of ddl_admin or db_owner, or the sysadmin role, because members of these roles have REFERENCES permission on all the message types by default.

The following list describes the arguments for the CREATE CONTRACT statement:

❑   contract_name: The name of the contract is just a SQL Server identifier. The convention is to use a URL, but any valid name will suffice. By convention, it has the form of //hostname/ pathname/name. So //www.wrox.com/bookorder/ordercontract is an example of a valid contract name. Although using a URL format is not required, it's generally easier to ensure uniqueness if you use a URL, especially when conversations span distributed systems. The contract_name may be up to 128 characters.

❑   AUTHORIZATION owner_name: This argument is the same as it is in the message type.

❑   message_type_name: The name of the message type that this contract uses. You can have multiple message types per contract, as you'll see later in the example.

❑   SENT BY: This clause defines whether the message type can be sent by the initiator of the conversation, sent by the target of the conversation, or either.

   ❑   INITIATOR: The initiator of the conversation can send the defined message type.

   ❑   TARGET: The target of the conversation can send the defined message type.

   ❑   ANY: The defined message type can be sent by either INITIATOR or TARGET.

❑   [DEFAULT]: If you query the sys.service_message_types catalog view, you will see a DEFAULT message type there.

The following code shows an example of creating a contract:

```
CREATE CONTRACT [//www.wrox.com/bookorder/ordercontract]
(
[//www.wrox.com/order/orderentry] SENT BY INITIATOR
[//www.wrox.com/order/orderentryack] SENT BY TARGET
)
```

When a contract is created, at least one message type needs to be marked as SENT BY INITIATOR or SENT BY ANY. Obviously, a message type must exist before you create the contract. In addition, the message type and direction cannot be changed once the contract is defined, so you cannot alter the contract once you create it. You can only change the authorization using the ALTER AUTHORIZATION statement.

Queue

We mentioned earlier that the Service Broker performs asynchronous operations. In asynchronous processing, you send a request to do something and then you start doing something else; the system processes the request you made later. Between the time you make the request and the time the system process acts on it, the request must be stored somewhere. The place where these requests are stored is called the *queue*.

The Service Broker implements queues with a new feature in SQL Server 2005 called a *hidden table*. You cannot use normal T-SQL commands to manipulate the data in the queue, and you cannot use INSERT, DELETE, or UPDATE commands on queues. In addition, you cannot change the structure of the queue or create triggers on them. A read-only view is associated with every queue, so you can use a SELECT statement to see what messages are in the queue. We will talk about T-SQL commands that work on queues later. The sender puts the message in the queue, using T-SQL commands that you will look at later. The transport layer moves that message reliably to the destination queue. The receiver application can then pull that message off the queue when it desires. The message from the initiator (first) queue is not deleted until that message has been successfully stored in a destination (second) queue, so there is no chance that the message will be lost in transit. Figure 8-2 shows how this works.

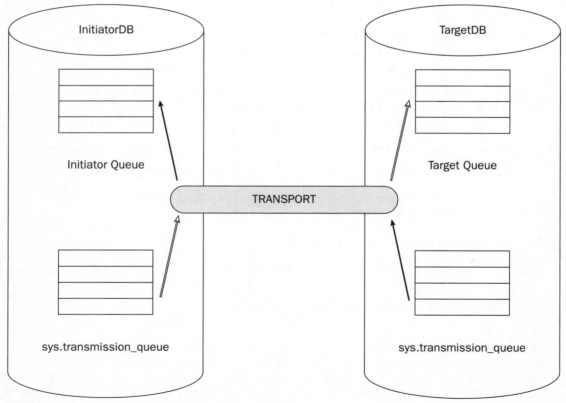

Figure 8-2

Assume that in Figure 8-2, the Service Broker is delivering a message from the database `InitiatorDB` on `InitiatorServer` to `TargetDB` on `TargerServer`, which means a network is involved in delivering this message. The Service Broker puts the messages that are to be sent over the network in a temporary queue called the `transmission_queue` on the server where the message is initiated. You can query this `transmission_queue` with the following `select` statement:

```
SELECT * FROM sys.transmission_queue
```

There is one such `transmission_queue` for each SQL Server instance. After a message is put into the `transmission_queue`, the Service Broker sends the message over the network and marks that message as waiting for acknowledgement in the `transmission_queue`. When the Service Broker receives the message from the `TargetServer` in the `TargetDB` queue, it sends an acknowledgment back to the `InitiatorServer`. When the `InitiatorServer` receives the acknowledgement message, it deletes the message from the `transmission_queue`. This process is called the *dialog*. We discuss the dialog and conversation later in this chapter. For now, just keep these terms in mind.

The following is the syntax to create a queue:

```
CREATE QUEUE queue_name
  [ WITH
    [ STATUS = { ON | OFF }  [ , ] ]
    [ RETENTION = { ON | OFF } [ , ] ]
    [ ACTIVATION
      (
        [ STATUS = { ON | OFF } , ]
          PROCEDURE_NAME = <procedure> ,
          MAX_QUEUE_READERS = max_readers ,
          EXECUTE AS { SELF | 'user_name' | OWNER }
      )
    ]
  ]
    [ ON { filegroup | [ DEFAULT ] } ]
```

The arguments to this statement are as follows:

❑   `queue_name`: The name of the queue that is created. This must be a SQL Server identifier. Because the queue is never referenced outside the database in which it is created, the URL-like syntax used for other Service Broker object names is not necessary for queue names.

❑   `STATUS`: When you create the queue, the `STATUS` parameter determines whether the queue is available (`ON`) or unavailable (`OFF`). If you don't specify the `STATUS`, the default value is `ON`. When the queue status is `OFF`, the queue is unavailable for adding or removing messages. When you deploy the application, it is a good idea to set the queue status to `OFF` so the application cannot submit the messages to the queue. Once the setup is done correctly, you can change this status to `ON` with the `ALTER QUEUE` statement, as you'll see shortly.

❑   `RETENTION`: When this parameter is `OFF` (the default setting), the message from the queue is deleted as soon as the transaction that receives the message commits. If `RETENTION` is `ON`, the queue saves all the incoming and outgoing messages until the conversation that owns the messages ends. This will increase the size of the queue, and it may affect the application's performance. You have to decide for your application requirements whether you need to retain the messages in the queue for a longer time or not. Later in the chapter you will look at an example that shows exactly what happens when RETENTION is either ON or OFF and when messages are deleted from the queue.

❑ ACTIVATION: We will talk about activation in detail later but for now it suffices to understand that this option specifies some information about a stored procedure to be executed when a message arrives in the queue:

❑ STATUS: If this parameter is ON, the Service Broker will activate (run) the stored procedure specified in the PROCEDURE_NAME argument. If this parameter is OFF, the queue does not activate the stored procedure. You can use this argument to temporarily stop activation of the stored procedure to troubleshoot a problem with an activation stored procedure. In addition, if you have made some changes to the activated stored procedure, it is good idea to change the STATUS to OFF before you deploy that stored procedure so that the next message in the queue will be processed by the modified stored procedure.

❑ PROCEDURE_NAME: This is the name of a stored procedure that is activated when a message arrives in the queue. The procedure has to be in the same database as the queue or be fully qualified. You will learn more about this later.

❑ MAX_QUEUE_READERS: This numeric value specifies the maximum number of instances of the stored procedure that the queue starts at the same time. The value of MAX_QUEUE_READERS must be a number between 0 and 32,767. Later you will learn about the effect of setting this value too high or too low.

❑ EXECUTE AS: This specifies the database user account under which the activation stored procedure runs. If you specify a domain account, your SQL Server must be connected to the domain because at the time of activation, SQL Server checks for permission for that user. If this is a SQL Server user, SQL Server can check permission locally. If the value is SELF, the activation stored procedure will run under the context of the user who is creating this queue. If the value is 'user_name', the activation stored procedure will run under the context of the user specified here. The user_name parameter must be a valid SQL Server user. In addition, if the user creating the queue is not in the dbo or sysadmin role, that user needs the IMPERSONATE permission for the user_name specified. See Chapter 9 for more details on impersonation. If the value is OWNER, the stored procedure executes as the owner of the queue. Keep in mind that the owners of the queue can be different users than the one who is running the CREATE QUEUE command.

❑ ON { filegroup | [DEFAULT]: This specifies the SQL Server filegroup on which you want to create the queue. If your application is going to have a high volume of messages coming in, you may want to put your queue on a filegroup with a lot of disk space. If you don't specify this option, the queue will be created on the default filegroup of the database in which you are creating the queue.

You can use the ALTER QUEUE command to change any of theses parameters. One additional parameter you can specify in ALTER QUEUE is to DROP the activation. That will delete all of the activation information associated with the queue. Of course, it will not drop the stored procedure specified in the PROCE-DURE_NAME clause.

Permission for altering a queue defaults to the owner of the queue, members of the ddl_admin or db_owner fixed database roles, and members of the sysadmin fixed server role.

The following code shows the creation of a queue. When you execute this statement, it will fail because the CREATE QUEUE statement requires that the activation procedure dbo.ProcessOrder exists in the database before you run this statement:

```
CREATE QUEUE dbo.acceptorder
WITH STATUS = ON
    ,RETENTION = OFF
    ,ACTIVATION (
                STATUS = ON
               ,PROCEDURE_NAME = dbo.ProcessOrder
               ,MAX_QUEUE_READERS = 5
               ,EXECUTE AS SELF
                )
```

Here's the code to alter the queue status:

```
ALTER QUEUE dbo.acceptorder WITH  STATUS = OFF, ACTIVATION (STATUS = OFF)
```

When you create a queue, you create an object of the type *SERVICE_QUEUE*. To view what queues exist in a database (keep in mind that the queue is for each database object, while sys.transmission_queue is for each SQL Server instance), you can use a SELECT statement as follows:

```
SELECT * FROM sys.service_queues
```

If you want to view the contents of the queue, you can issue the following statement:

```
SELECT * FROM dbo.acceptorder
```

Services

To understand how services work, consider the postal service. When you want to send a letter to your friend, you write his or her address on the envelope before mailing it. In the Service Broker world, that address on the envelope is called a *service*. A Service Broker service identifies an endpoint of a conversation. That endpoint is a queue in a database. A service is associated with a list of contracts that is accepted by the service. Note that mapping a service to a contract is an optional step on the initiator. On the target, if you do not specify any contract, you won't be able to send any messages to the target.

Here is the syntax to create the service:

```
CREATE SERVICE service_name
   [ AUTHORIZATION owner_name ]
   ON QUEUE [ schema_name. ]queue_name
   [ ( contract_name | [DEFAULT] [ ,...n ] ) ]
```

The following list describes the arguments for the CREATE SERVICE statement:

- ❑ service_name: This is the name of the service to create.

- ❑ Authorization: This is the same as discussed earlier in the message type section.

- ❑ Queue_name: This is the name of the queue that receives the messages from this service.

- ❑ Contract_name: This argument specifies a contract for which this service may be a target. If no contract is specified, the service may only initiate conversation.

The following code demonstrates how you create a service:

```
CREATE SERVICE orderentryservice
ON QUEUE acceptorder ([//www.wrox.com/bookorder/ordercontract])
```

You can query the catalog view SELECT * FROM sys.services to view the service defined in a database.

Now that you have an understanding of all the pieces of the architecture, Figure 8-3 shows the relationship among the metadata objects used by the Service Broker.

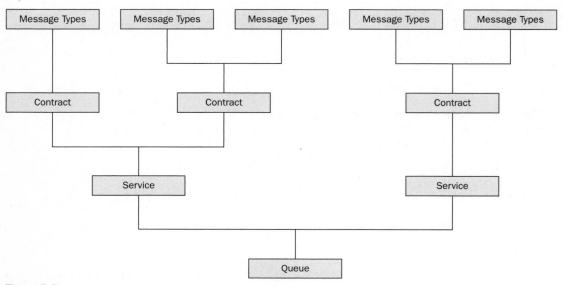

Figure 8-3

Service Broker Examples

Now you have enough information to write a small application. Although we have not covered some of the terms such as *activation* or *conversation,* we will do so as you go through the code.

> *Service Broker metadata names that are sent across the wire (message type, contract, service) are always case-sensitive.*

You'll start with a very simple example that involves Service Broker communication on the same server between two databases. You will look at three examples; this first example illustrates how messaging and activation work in the Service Broker. Don't worry about security in the first example. The second example features a Service Broker application that communicates between two instances of SQL Server, and the third involves communication between two SQL Server instances with certificates and message encryption. Security is a major part of these examples.

The first example assumes that you are the system administrator (sa) on the SQL Server. For now, our focus is on how the Service Broker works, and not on which tricks you can do with it yet. Download the code for this chapter from this book's Web site at www.wrox.com. Open the Chapter 8 folder, followed by the Sample1 folder, and double-click the Sample1 solution file. It is assumed that you have SQL Server Management Studio (SSMS) installed where you open this file.

In this example, you will send a message from the Initiator database asking for the customer and product count, and receive that message on the Target database on the same SQL Server instance. The Target database will respond to that message with the customer and product count. The initiator database will store that count in a table and call it good.

You will see the SetupInitiator.sql script in the Queries folder in the Sample1 solution. Open the file and connect to your SQL Server instance. Let's go through the code in that file. First you will set up the InitiatorDB and then the TargetDB. Do not run the script until after you have finished reading the explanation.

```
USE Master
GO

IF EXISTS(SELECT 1 FROM sys.databases WHERE name = 'InitiatorDB')
DROP DATABASE InitiatorDB
GO

CREATE DATABASE InitiatorDB;
GO

ALTER DATABASE InitiatorDB SET TRUSTWORTHY ON
GO

USE InitiatorDB
GO

SELECT Service_Broker_Guid, is_broker_enabled, is_trustworthy_on
FROM sys.databases
WHERE database_id = DB_ID()
GO
```

Create a brand-new database called InitiatorDB so that you don't interfere with other databases on your system. Notice that after creating the InitiatorDB, the next statement sets the TRUSTWORTHY bit to 1 for that database. If you are using certificate security with dialog encryption ON (explained later in the chapter), then setting the TRUSTWORTHY bit to ON is not necessary. The SELECT statement from the sys.databases catalog view will give you the Service_Broker_Guid, which is a unique Service Broker identifier for that database. The is_broker_enabled bit is set to 1 when you create a new database (not when you restore or attach from an existing database file). If this bit is 0, then message delivery in this database is not possible because the Service Broker is not enabled in this database.

```
-------------------------------------------------------------------------------
--Create table to log what's happened.
-------------------------------------------------------------------------------
CREATE  TABLE dbo.ProcessHistory
```

```
(
 RowID int IDENTITY(1,1) NOT NULL
,Process varchar(60)  NOT NULL
,StatusDate datetime NOT NULL
,Status varchar(50) NULL
,MessageText xml NULL
,SPID int NULL
,UserName varchar(60) NULL
 CONSTRAINT PK_ProcessHistory PRIMARY KEY CLUSTERED(RowID)
)
```

This table was created to log information so you can view what's happened by looking at the rows in the table.

Now the interesting part starts here. As discussed earlier, the first thing you have to do when you create Service Broker objects is to create message types, which is what happens here:

```
-------------------------------------------------------------------------------
--First we have to create Message Types on InitiatorDB
-------------------------------------------------------------------------------
CREATE MESSAGE TYPE [//www.wrox.com/MTCustomerInfo/RequstCustomersCount]
VALIDATION = WELL_FORMED_XML
GO

CREATE MESSAGE TYPE [//www.wrox.com/MTCustomerInfo/ResponseTotalCustomers]
VALIDATION = WELL_FORMED_XML
GO

CREATE MESSAGE TYPE [//www.wrox.com/MTProductInfo/RequestProductsCount]
VALIDATION = WELL_FORMED_XML
GO

CREATE MESSAGE TYPE [//www.wrox.com/MTProductInfo/ResponseTotalProducts]
VALIDATION = WELL_FORMED_XML
GO
```

This code created four message types. Notice that we have used WELL_FORMED_XML as the validation for the message body for all message types. When the message is received, it will go through an XML parser for validation.

The message type [//www.wrox.com/MTCustomerInfo/RequstCustomersCount] is used when the initiator sends the message to the target to request the number of customers. Similarly, when the target replies with the number of customers, it uses the [//www.wrox.com/MTCustomerInfo/Response TotalCustomers] message type.

The message type [//www.wrox.com/MTProductInfo/RequestProductsCount] is used when the initiator sends the message to the target to request the number of products. Similarly, when the target replies with the number of products, it uses the [//www.wrox.com/MTProductInfo/ResponseTotal Products] message type.

We have not used the AUTHORIZATION clause in the CREATE MESSAGE TYPE statement, so the owner of these message types will be dbo, assuming you are sa on the SQL Server instance. Don't get confused about the message type. It tells the Service Broker what to expect in the message body, including whether or not that message should be validated and how to validate it. In addition, based on the name of the message type, you can take some action.

The next bit of code creates a contract and binds the message types you created earlier to this contract. Later you will see how the contract is used.

```
CREATE CONTRACT [//www.wrox.com/CTGeneralInfo/ProductCustomer]
(
    [//www.wrox.com/MTCustomerInfo/RequstCustomersCount] SENT BY INITIATOR
  , [//www.wrox.com/MTProductInfo/RequestProductsCount] SENT BY INITIATOR
  , [//www.wrox.com/MTCustomerInfo/ResponseTotalCustomers] SENT BY TARGET
  , [//www.wrox.com/MTProductInfo/ResponseTotalProducts] SENT BY TARGET
)
```

Notice the SENT BY clause. When SENT BY is set to INITIATOR, it means that only the initiator of the message can send the message of that type. When SENT BY is set to TARGET, only the target can send the message of that type.

You still need to create the stored procedure CheckResponseFromTarget, but we'll ignore that here. For now, focus on the queue:

```
-------------------------------------------------------------------------------
--Create queue to receive the message from target.
-------------------------------------------------------------------------------
CREATE QUEUE dbo.ReceiveAckError
WITH STATUS = ON
    ,RETENTION = OFF
    ,ACTIVATION (
                STATUS = OFF
              ,PROCEDURE_NAME = dbo.CheckResponseFromTarget
              ,MAX_QUEUE_READERS = 5
              ,EXECUTE AS SELF
                )
```

The queue ReceiveAckError will be used to receive the response from the target. When the target sends the reply to the original request from the initiator, that message will go in here. Notice that the queue STATUS is ON. When the status is OFF, the queue is unavailable for adding or removing messages. Also notice that the stored procedure CheckResponseFromTarget will be executed when any message arrives in the queue ReceiveAckError. However, because the status of the ACTIVATION is set to OFF, the stored procedure will not be activated. The code specifies that a maximum of five instances of this stored procedure can be activated if necessary with the MAX_QUEUE_READER option. When you specify a stored procedure for activation, that stored procedure must exist before you create the queue; otherwise, the queue will not be created.

Now you need a service to which you can send or receive the messages. Each service is bound to one and only one queue. When you send the message, you send the message to a service and not to the queue. The service will put the message into the queue:

```
CREATE SERVICE InitiatorService
ON QUEUE dbo.ReceiveAckError ([//www.wrox.com/CTGeneralInfo/ProductCustomer])
```

Notice that you specify the contract [//www.wrox.com/CTGeneralInfo/ProductCustomer] in the CREATE SERVICE statement. That means that only message types defined by this contract can be sent to this queue. This queue will not receive any other message types. Now run the SetupInitiator.sql script.

Open the SetupTarget.sql script. You will notice that it looks similar to the SetupInitiator.sql script. You have created the same message types and the contract on TargetDB. The queue name is RequestQueue in the TargetDB, and the stored procedure activated when the message arrives is CheckRequestFromInitiator. You will understand the stored procedures CheckRequestFrom Initiator and CheckResponseFromTarget very soon.

Next, run the SetupTarget.sql script on the same SQL Server where you have run the SetupInitiator.sql script.

Your infrastructure is now ready to send your first message. At this point you may have some questions: How do you send the message? What happens when the message is sent? How will it be received?

Open the script SendMessageFromInitiator.sql and connect to the database InitiatorDB, which you created using the script SetupInitiator.sql. The following is the T-SQL code in the SendMessageFromInitiator.sql script:

```
USE InitiatorDB
GO

DECLARE @Conversation_Handle UNIQUEIDENTIFIER
      ,@SendMessage xml
      ,@MessageText varchar(255)

SET @MessageText =  'Request From Server: \\' + @@SERVERNAME
              + ', DATABASE: ' + DB_NAME()
              + ': ** Please send the total number of customers.'

SET @SendMessage = N'<message>'+ N'<![CDATA[' + @MessageText + N']]>' +
N'</message>'

BEGIN TRY
    BEGIN DIALOG CONVERSATION @Conversation_Handle
    FROM SERVICE [InitiatorService]
    TO SERVICE 'TargetService'
    ON CONTRACT [//www.wrox.com/CTGeneralInfo/ProductCustomer]
    WITH ENCRYPTION = OFF

    SELECT * FROM sys.conversation_endpoints
    WHERE conversation_handle = @Conversation_Handle;
    ------------------------------------------------------------
    SEND ON CONVERSATION @Conversation_Handle
    MESSAGE TYPE [//www.wrox.com/MTCustomerInfo/RequstCustomersCount]
    (@SendMessage);
    ------------------------------------------------------------
END TRY
```

```
BEGIN CATCH
    SELECT ERROR_NUMBER() AS ErrorNumber
          ,ERROR_MESSAGE() AS ErrorMessage
          ,ERROR_SEVERITY() AS ErrorSeverity
          ,ERROR_LINE() AS ErrorLine
END CATCH
```

Before you can understand the preceding code, you need to know what a conversation is. The core concept of the Service Broker is the conversation. A conversation is a reliable, ordered exchange of messages. Two kinds of conversations are defined in the Service Broker architecture:

❑ **Dialog**: This is a two-way conversation between exactly two endpoints. An *endpoint* is a source or destination for messages associated with a queue; it may receive and send messages. A dialog is established between an initiator and target endpoint (refer to Figure 8-1). The initiator is just an endpoint that issues the BEGIN DIALOG command to start the dialog. After that, the initiator and the target are peers. The first message always goes from the initiator to the target. Once the target receives the first message, any number of messages can be sent in either direction.

❑ **Monolog**: This is a one-way conversation between a single publisher endpoint and any number of subscriber endpoints. Monologs are not available in SQL Server 2005, though they will be included in future versions.

Now you can begin to understand the T-SQL code. Before sending a message, you must create a dialog conversation. The command to do that is BEGIN DIALOG CONVERSATION. The arguments of this statement are as follows:

❑ @Conversation_Handle: When you run the BEGIN DIALOG statement, it returns the value of the type uniqueidentifier. The conversation handle is stored in the @Conversation_ Handle variable. It is just a variable, so you can name it anything you like as long as the type of this variable is uniqueidentifier.

❑ Service: Because a dialog connects exactly two endpoints, you must specify both endpoints in the BEGIN DIALOG command. These endpoints are specified using service names. If a service is analogous to a postal address, then you need a "from" address and a "to" address. That's what you need in BEGIN DIALOG. In this case, the "from" service is [InitiatorService] and the "to" service is 'TargetService'. Note the syntax: The "from" service name is in sqaure brackets, and the "to" service is specified in quotes. The [InitiatorService] service is defined as the database InitiatorDB you created earlier, and the 'TargetService' is defined as the TargetDB you created earlier. In this case, the message will go from database InitiatorDB to TargetDB.

❑ Contract: The contract defines the content of a dialog. In the CREATE CONTRACT statement, we have defined four message types.

❑ Encryption: We discuss this clause later in the section "Security Considerations for the Service Broker." For now, set this to OFF.

Right after the BEGIN DIALOG statement is a SQL statement to select from the catalog view sys .conversation_endpoints. The effect of this statement is that every time you run the BEGIN DIALOG statement, you will see a row added to the sys.conversation_endpoints catalog view.

There are other clauses to the BEGIN DIALOG statement, but they are not covered here in order to keep the example simple. The only clause we need to discuss here is LIFETIME. The LIFETIME clause specifies the number of seconds that this dialog is allowed to live. If you don't specify this clause, the dialog lifetime is the maximum value of the int data type. We haven't specified the LIFETIME here because we are looking at how messaging works and we want the dialog to live longer while you examine the system view and the flow of the message. When you specify the LIFETIME to be 600 seconds, for example, if the dialog still exists after the lifetime expires (five minutes in this case), then an error will be returned to any statements that attempt to access it, and error messages are also sent to both endpoints of the dialog. Note that the dialog doesn't go away when its lifetime expires. It remains in the sys .conversation_endpoints table in an error state until it is ended with the END CONVERSATION statement, which we will look at later.

Now take a look at the SEND statement. As described earlier, before sending a message, you must obtain a conversation handle. If you are the initiator of a conversation, you obtain a conversation handle by executing a BEGIN DIALOG command. The target of a conversation obtains a conversation handle from a RECEIVE statement. SEND has three parameters:

❑   A conversation handle associated with an open conversation

❑   A message type that describe the contents of the message

❑   The message body

The message body in this case is contained in the variable @SendMessage. The message body of the Service Broker queue is a varbinary(max) column, so a message body can contain up to two gigabytes of binary data. That means when you send the message using the SEND command, it converts the message body to the varbinary(max) type. In this case, the variable @SendMessage, which is defined as an XML data type, is converted to varbinary(max) before SEND completes. Most SQL Server data types can be cast to or from varbinary(max), so you can send almost anything you want as a Service Broker message. If 2GB of data isn't enough, you can split large messages into 2GB pieces and reassemble then at the destination because the Service Broker ensures that the message arrives in order. You can use the XML data type that converts implicitly to and from varbinary(max), so using the Service Broker with the XML data types is simple and straightforward.

You need to know one last thing before you run the script. The BEGIN DIALOG and SEND statements are inside a while loop to show you how multiple threads of the activation stored procedure start when you have several messages in a queue and one instance of the activation procedure cannot handle all those messages. For now, you will send only one message, so the variable @NumberOfMessages is set to 1.

You are now ready to run the script SendMessageFromInitiator.sql. Press Execute. That will send the message from InitiatorDB database to TargetDB database. Where did it go? You saw earlier that when you send the message it goes to sys.transmission_queue first and then to the target queue, as shown in Figure 8-2. That is true when the message is going over the network, but if you are sending the message on the same instance of the SQL Server, then the message will be directly put into the target queue, which is RequestQueue in this case. If any error happens in that message transmission from initiator to target, you will see a row in the catalog view sys.transmission_queue, even if you are sending the message on the same instance of the SQL Server. So how did the message arrive at Request Queue on the TargetDB? When you sent the message from the InitiatorDB, the BEGIN DIALOG statement specified the "to" service as 'TargetService', and when you created the 'TargetService', you specified the queue (or endpoint) as RequestQueue.

Now take a look at the message in the target queue. Open the script `ViewInfoOnTarget.sql` and run the following code from the script:

```
USE TargetDB
GO

SELECT Conversation_Handle, CAST(message_body as xml) AS message_body, *
FROM dbo.RequestQueue

SELECT * FROM sys.conversation_endpoints
```

The output from this script is shown in Figure 8-4.

Figure 8-4

Notice that the messages in the queue are of the `varbinary` data type. The script converts the message into XML so you can read the content. You can also now see a row in the `sys.conversation_endpoints` catalog view. A `SELECT` statement is used to view the data in a queue.

Now you can retrieve the message from the `RequestQueue`. Open the script `ReceiveMessageOnTarget.sql`, which is shown here:

```
USE TargetDB
GO

DECLARE
    @message_type_name   nvarchar(256)
    ,@xmlmessage_body     xml
    ,@MessageFromTarget   varchar(255)
    ,@MessageText varchar(255)
    ,@conversation_handle UNIQUEIDENTIFIER

    ,@ErrorNumber int
    ,@ErrorMessage nvarchar(4000)
    ,@ErrSeverity int
    ,@ErrorLine int
    ,@comment nvarchar(4000)

    ,@ProcedureName varchar (60)
    ,@ResponseMessage xml
    ,@CustomerCount int
    ,@ProductCount int

    SET @ProcedureName = 'ManualMessageReceiveOnTarget'

BEGIN TRY
```

```
BEGIN TRANSACTION
-- Receive the next available message
WAITFOR
(
    RECEIVE TOP(1)
        @xmlmessage_body =  CASE WHEN validation = 'X'
                                 THEN CAST(message_body AS XML)
                                 ELSE CAST(N'<none/>' AS XML)
                            END
        ,@message_type_name = message_type_name
        ,@conversation_handle = conversation_handle
    FROM dbo.RequestQueue
), TIMEOUT 3000
-------------------------------------------------------------------------------
-- If we didn't get anything or if there is an error, bail out
-------------------------------------------------------------------------------
IF (@@ROWCOUNT = 0 OR @@ERROR <> 0)
BEGIN
    ROLLBACK TRANSACTION
    GOTO Done
END
ELSE
BEGIN
    IF @message_type_name = '//www.wrox.com/MTCustomerInfo/RequstCustomersCount'
    BEGIN

        ----------------------------------------------------------------------
        --- Your code to process the received message goes here.
        ----------------------------------------------------------------------

        ---Insert what we got into processhistory table.
        INSERT dbo.ProcessHistory(Process, StatusDate,  Status, MessageText, SPID,
UserName)
        SELECT @ProcedureName, GETDATE(),  'Success', @xmlmessage_body, 'ID,
SUSER_NAME()

        SELECT @CustomerCount = COUNT(*)
        FROM AdventureWorks.Sales.Customer

        SET @MessageText = 'Response From Server: \\' + @@SERVERNAME
                        + ', Database: ' + DB_NAME() + ' ** Total Customers: '
                        + CAST(@CustomerCount AS varchar(15)) +  ' **'

        SET @ResponseMessage = N'<message>'+ N'<![CDATA[' + @MessageText + N']]>'
+
N'</message>';

        SEND ON CONVERSATION @conversation_handle
        MESSAGE TYPE [//www.wrox.com/MTCustomerInfo/ResponseTotalCustomers]
        (@ResponseMessage)

        END CONVERSATION @conversation_handle

    END
```

```
        ELSE
        IF @message_type_name = '//www.wrox.com/MTProductInfo/RequestProductsCount'
        BEGIN

            -----------------------------------------------------------------------
------
            --- Your code to process the received message goes here.
            -----------------------------------------------------------------------
------

            ---Insert what we got into processhistory table.
            INSERT dbo.ProcessHistory(Process, StatusDate,  Status, MessageText, SPID,
UserName)
            SELECT @ProcedureName, GETDATE(),  'Success', @xmlmessage_body, 'ID,
SUSER_NAME()

            SELECT @ProductCount = COUNT(*)
            FROM AdventureWorks.Production.Product

            SET @MessageText = 'Response From Server: \\' + @@SERVERNAME
                            + ', Database: ' + DB_NAME()
                            + ' ** Total Products: ' + CAST(@ProductCount AS
varchar(15)) +
' **'

            SET @ResponseMessage = N'<message>'+ N'<![CDATA[' + @MessageText + N']]>'
+
N'</message>';

            SEND ON CONVERSATION @conversation_handle
            MESSAGE TYPE [//www.wrox.com/MTProductInfo/ResponseTotalProducts]
            (@ResponseMessage)

            END CONVERSATION @conversation_handle

        END
        ELSE
        IF (@message_type_name =
'http://schemas.microsoft.com/SQL/ServiceBroker/EndDialog'
            OR @message_type_name =
'http://schemas.microsoft.com/SQL/ServiceBroker/Error')
            -- If the message_type_name indicates that the message is an error
            -- or an end dialog message, end the conversation.
        BEGIN

            END CONVERSATION @conversation_handle

            -----------------------------------------------------------------------
------
            --- Your code to handle the error and do some type of notification
            ---(email etc) goes here
            -----------------------------------------------------------------------
------
            ---Insert what we got into processhistory table.
```

```
          INSERT dbo.ProcessHistory(Process, StatusDate,  Status, MessageText, SPID,
    UserName)
          SELECT @ProcedureName, GETDATE(),  'Error', @xmlmessage_body, 'ID,
    SUSER_NAME()


        END
    END

    COMMIT TRAN

END TRY
BEGIN CATCH

    WHILE (@@TRANCOUNT > 0) ROLLBACK TRAN

    SELECT @ErrorNumber = ERROR_NUMBER(), @ErrorMessage = ERROR_MESSAGE()
                    ,@ErrSeverity = ERROR_SEVERITY(), @ErrorLine = ERROR_LINE()

    SET @comment = 'Error Number: '+ CAST(@ErrorNumber AS varchar(25))
                + ', Error Message: ' + @ErrorMessage
                + ' Error Severity: ' + CAST(@ErrSeverity AS varchar(25))
                + ' Line Number: ' + CAST(@ErrorLine AS varchar(25))

    ---Insert what we got into processhistory table.
    INSERT dbo.ProcessHistory(Process, StatusDate, Status, MessageText, SPID,
    UserName)
    SELECT @ProcedureName, GETDATE(),  'Error', @comment, 'ID, SUSER_NAME()

END CATCH

Done:
```

This code is exactly the same as the one in the stored procedure `CheckRequestFromInitiator` you created in the `SetupTarget.sql` script. You don't want to activate the stored procedure now and pick up the message because you won't know what happened. You need to know some things about the script first.

The command to receive a message from a queue is `RECEIVE`. This is the only way you can retrieve the message from a queue. The `RECEIVE` command can pull one or more messages from a queue. In this case, the code is only pulling one message at a time, which is why `TOP (1)` appears in the `RECEIVE` statement. In the `FROM` clause of the `RECEIVE` statement, you have specified the name of the queue `RequestQueue`. You can also specify a `WHERE` clause in the `RECEIVE` statement, but it is not a full-featured `WHERE` clause. You can only specify a `conversation_handle` or `conversation_group_id`.

The basic `RECEIVE` command returns the messages available at the time the command executes. If the queue is empty, no rows are returned. In some cases, it might be more efficient to wait for messages to appear on the queue, rather than return immediately when the queue is empty. You can use the `WAITFOR` command with the `RECEIVE` command to force the `RECEIVE` command to wait for a message if the queue is empty. The following code shows the `WAITFOR` command:

```
WAITFOR
(
    RECEIVE TOP(1)
```

```
      @xmlmessage_body =  CASE WHEN validation = 'X'
                             THEN CAST(message_body AS XML)
                             ELSE CAST(N'<none/>' AS XML)
                          END
      ,@message_type_name = message_type_name
      ,@conversation_handle = conversation_handle
   FROM dbo.RequestQueue
), TIMEOUT 3000
```

The TIMEOUT clause specifies how many milliseconds the RECEIVE will wait for a message to appear on the queue before returning. In this case it will wait for three seconds.

The RECEIVE statement has three columns: message_body, message_type_name, and conversation_handle. The message_body contains the actual message, and the message_type_name contains the type of the message sent. If you look at the SEND statement in the SendMessageFromInitiator.sql script, you will see that you have sent the message of the type [//www.wrox.com/MTCustomerInfo/RequstCustomersCount]. That's what you will see in the message_type_name column. The last column is conversation_handle, which the target will use to send the message reply back to the initiator.

After the RECEIVE statement, the code checks the row count to make sure it has received something, or to see whether an error occurred. If it has not received anything, you can take any action you like there. If it has received a message, you want to take some action on that message. You use message_type_name in this case to decide what to do with the message. Because you are sending the message type [//www.wrox.com/MTCustomerInfo/RequstCustomersCount], you'll want to count the number of customers. If you had received the message of type //www.wrox.com/MTProductInfoRequest ProductsCount, you would have the count of the products. Now your application may have some complex things to do instead of the simple count(*) you have here. You can call another stored procedure and pass parameters to that stored procedure to execute some tasks. In this case, the code has counted the number of customers, and you are ready to send the reply back to the initiator.

The next command is the SEND, which we have discussed earlier. Notice that here you don't perform the BEGIN DIALOG again. When you sent the message from the initiator, it created a row in the sys .conversation_endpoint view also. Because you are sending a message in the same conversation, you don't need to issue another BEGIN DIALOG, but you do need the conversation handle to send the message, which is why the target received the @conversation_handle in the RECEIVE command. After the SEND statement, you see END CONVERSATION @Conversation_Handle. The END CONVERSATION command ends the conversation, and sends the message of the message type 'http://schemas .microsoft.com/SQL/ServiceBroker/EndDialog' on both sides of the dialog endpoint. In your application you can decide when you want to end the conversation, but it is very important that you do so. Otherwise, you will see thousands of rows in the sys.conversation_endpoints table after your application has run for a while, and that is not good for application performance.

Once the target has received some information, the code has an INSERT statement to insert some information in the ProcessHistory table so you can later look to see what happened. Notice the BEGIN TRAN statement before the target receives the message and the COMMIT TRAN statement after successfully processing the message. You want to do that to maintain transaction consistency in the database. If something bad happens while you are processing the message, you may lose it. Once the message is received from the queue, you cannot put it back without using BEGIN and COMMIT TRAN. Whether you need that in your application or not is up to you when you design the application. If you cannot tolerate losing any messages, then you should consider using BEGIN and COMMIT TRAN.

Run the script `ReceiveMessageOnTarget.sql` now. After that, run the script `ViewInfoOnTarget.sql` in `TargetDB`. The output is shown in Figure 8-5.

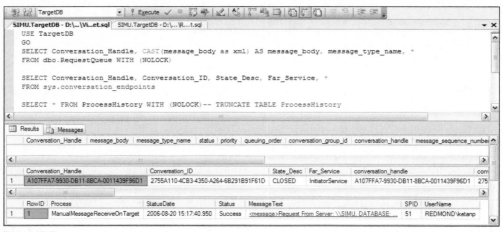

Figure 8-5

You probably noticed that after you ran the `ReceiveMessageOnTarget.sql` script, the message disappeared from the `RequestQueue`. You will still see a row in the conversation table with a `state_desc` of `CLOSED`. The `state_desc` is `CLOSED` because after the message was sent, the script issued `END CONVERSATION`. In addition, the message is inserted into the `ProcessHistory` table after it was received, so now the message is back on `InitiatorDB` with the customer count.

Before we receive the message from the queue `ReceiveAckError` in `InitiatorDB`, take a look at what's currently in the queue. Open the script `ViewInfoOnInitiator.sql` and run it. The output is shown in Figure 8-6.

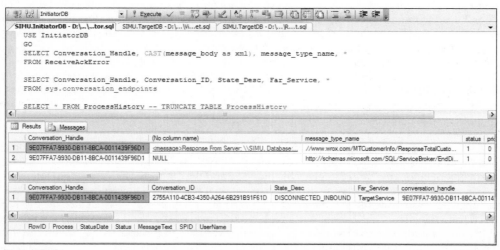

Figure 8-6

Two rows appear in the queue `ReceiveAckError` in `InititatorDB`: One is the customer count sent by the `TargetDB`, and the other is the Service Broker end dialog message. The end dialog message appears because of the `END CONVERSATION` command you ran on the target after sending the message. Also notice that the `state_desc` column in `sys.conversation_endpoint` has the value `DISCONNECTED _INBOUND`. That's because the `'TargetService'` has closed the conversation. You won't see any rows in the `ProcessHistory` table yet, because you have not received the message from the queue yet.

Now you can receive the message from the `ReceiveAckError` queue. Open the script `ReceiveMessage OnInitiator.sql`. You will see that this script is very similar to `ReceiveMessageOnTarget.sql`. The difference is that the `message_type_names` you will see in the `ReceiveMessageOnInitiator.sql` script are `'//www.wrox.com/MTCustomerInfo/ResponseTotalCustomers'` and `'//www.wrox.com/MTProductInfo/ResponseTotalProducts'`. In addition, the `RECEIVE` statement is receiving the message from the `ReceiveAckError` queue. Now run the script `ReceiveMessageOnInitiator.sql`. After that, run the script `ViewInfoOnInitiator.sql` again. Note that you still see a row in the `Receive AckError` queue; that's because you have only run the `ReceiveMessageOnInitiator.sql` script once, and it will receive only one message from the queue because you have set `TOP (1)` in the `RECEIVE` statement. Run the `ReceiveMessageOnInitiator.sql` script again, and then run the `ViewInfoOn Initiator.sql` script one more time. The output is shown in Figure 8-7.

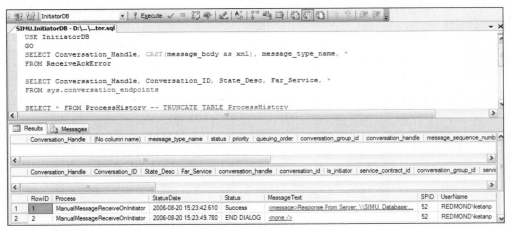

Figure 8-7

Notice that the queue is now empty and that no row exists in the `sys.conversation_endpoints` table. You have to make sure that you end the conversation. Whenever you end the conversation, a row for that conversation is deleted from the `sys.conversation_endpoints` table. You will see two rows in the `ProcessHistory` table, one is the actual message from `TargetDB` and the other is the result of `END CONVERSATION`.

You ended the dialog in the script `ReceiveMessageOnInitiator.sql`, as shown here:

```
        IF (@message_type_name =
  'http://schemas.microsoft.com/SQL/ServiceBroker/EndDialog')
          -- an end dialog message, end the conversation.
```

```
    BEGIN

        END CONVERSATION @conversation_handle

        ---Let's insert what we got into processhistory table.
        INSERT dbo.ProcessHistory(Process, StatusDate,  Status, MessageText, SPID,
UserName)
        SELECT @ProcedureName, GETDATE(),  'END DIALOG', @xmlmessage_body, 'ID,
SUSER_NAME()

    END
```

Run the `ViewInfoOnTarget.sql` script again. You will notice that in the `TargetDB sys`
`.conversation_endpoints` table, you still see a row even though you have ended the conversation.
Those rows will be deleted by the Service Broker after about 33 minutes.

You have just seen how the stored procedure is activated when a message gets into the queue. Activation
is one of the most important things in a Service Broker application. Of course, it is not required, but activation is a tool to make it easier to write services that execute as stored procedures.

Activation

Service Broker *activation* is a unique way to ensure that the right resources are available to process
Service Broker messages as they arrive on a queue. To use activation, you associate a stored procedure
with a queue. The following is a section from the script `SetupTarget.sql`:

```
CREATE QUEUE dbo.RequestQueue
WITH STATUS = ON
    ,RETENTION = OFF
    ,ACTIVATION (
              STATUS = ON
            ,PROCEDURE_NAME = dbo.CheckRequestFromInitiator
            ,MAX_QUEUE_READERS = 5
            ,EXECUTE AS SELF
            )
GO
```

Similar code exists in `SetupInitiator.sql`, with a different queue name and PROCEDURE_NAME. One
thing we have changed here is to set the STATUS parameter to ON in ACTIVATION. This is how you associate the stored procedure activation with a queue. This means that whenever a message arrives in a
`RequestQueue` queue, an instance of a stored procedure CheckRequestFromInitiator will be started
by the Service Broker *only* if an instance of the stored procedure isn't already running. The ACTIVATION
STATUS must be set to ON to activate a stored procedure when a message arrives in the queue.

When a message is written in the queue, the commit process (which writes the message row into the
transaction log) checks to see whether a copy of the activation stored procedure is running. If not, the
activation logic starts a stored procedure. When the activation logic finds that a stored procedure is
already running, it also checks the number of arriving messages against the number of processed messages to determine whether the activated stored procedure is keeping up with the incoming message
rate. If the rate of incoming messages is higher, another copy of the stored procedure is started. This will
continue until either the activated stored procedures are able to keep up with incoming messages or

until the maximum number of stored procedure instances defined by the MAX_QUEUE_READERS parameter is reached. In this case, MAX_QUEUE_READERS is set to five, which mean that no more than five instances of the stored procedure CheckRequestFromInitiator will be started at any given point in time.

If you have five messages in the RequestQueue, will five instances of CheckRequestFromInitiator be started? It depends. When a stored procedure is configured for activation, it creates a queue monitor for the queue. When messages are added to the queue, and after five seconds of inactivity, the queue monitor determines whether a stored procedure should be started. Suppose you sent four messages to the RequestQueue. The Service Broker will start the first instance of the stored procedure Check RequestFromInitiator. Now there are still three messages waiting in the queue RequestQueue to be processed but the Queue Monitor will not start another copy of CheckRequestFromInitiator unless the first message takes more than five seconds to process. Assume that the first message is going to take more than five minutes; in that case, the Queue Monitor will start another second copy of Check RequestFromInitiator. To process the third message, it may or may not start another instance of CheckRequestFromInitiator. When the third message is about to be processed, after waiting for five seconds, the Queue Monitor will check whether any of those instances has finished its work; if one has, the Queue Monitor will use whichever instance completed the work. If not, it will start a third instance of CheckRequestFromInitiator.

When stored procedures are started, they are owned by the Queue Monitor. If one throws an exception, the Queue Monitor will catch it and start a new copy. The Queue Monitor also makes sure that when an activated stored procedure is not receiving any messages, no more copies will be started.

You can see all the Queue Monitors configured in a SQL Server instance by running this query:

```
SELECT * FROM sys.dm_broker_queue_monitors
```

To find out which activated stored procedures are running in a SQL Server instance, execute the following query:

```
SELECT * FROM sys.dm_broker_activated_tasks
```

So far in this example, you have received the messages from the queue manually by running the ReceiveMessageOnTarget.sql script on the TargetDB, and ReceiveMessageOnInitiator.sql on the InitiatorDB. Now try to receive messages using activated stored procedures. As you just learned, to activate a stored procedure on a queue, you have to associate the stored procedure with the queue, and the ACTIVATION STATUS must be ON. In the scripts SetupInitiator.sql and SetupTarget.sql, you associated the stored procedure with the queue, but the activation was not on, which is why you were receiving the messages manually. At this point, set the ACTIVATION STATUS to ON for both the initiator and target queues.

Open the ActivateSPOnInitiator.sql script and run it. That will set the ACTIVATION STATUS to ON for the ReceiveAckError queue. The stored procedure CheckResponseFromTarget will be activated when a message arrives in the queue.

Next open the ActivateSPOnTarget.sql script and run it. That will set the ACTIVATION STATUS to ON for the RequestQueue. The stored procedure CheckRequestFromInitiator will be activated when a message arrives in the queue.

Now you are ready to send the message. Open the `SendMessageFromInitiator.sql` script and run it. What happens?

❑ The script has sent the message from `InitiatorDB` to `TargetDB` in the `RequestQueue`.

❑ The stored procedure `CheckRequestFromInitiator` was activated in `TargetDB`, which received the message and processed it (i.e., counted the number of customers in `AdventureWorks.Sales.Customer`), sent the response back to `InitiatorDB`, and then ended the conversation.

❑ The message came to the `ReceiveAckError` queue on `InitiatorDB`, and the stored procedure `CheckResponseFromTarget` was activated. The stored procedure received the message, put the result in `ProcessHistory`, and ended the conversation.

You can see the content in the `ProcessHistory` table on `TargetDB` by running the script `ViewInfoOnTarget.sql`, and on `InitiatorDB` by running the script `ViewInfoOnInitiator.sql`.

Now take a look at multiple instances of the activation stored procedure in action. Open the `CheckRequestFromInitiator.sql` script and run it. This is the same stored procedure you created in the `SetupTarget.sql` script with one small change: a WAITFOR DELAY of 20 seconds has been added:

```
          IF @message_type_name =
'//www.wrox.com/MTCustomerInfo/RequstCustomersCount'
          BEGIN


               ----------------------------------------------------------------
               --- Your code to process the received message goes here.
               ----------------------------------------------------------------

               ---Insert what we got into the processhistory table.
               INSERT dbo.ProcessHistory(Process, StatusDate,  Status, MessageText,
SPID, UserName)
               SELECT @ProcedureName, GETDATE(),  'Success', @xmlmessage_body, 'ID,
SUSER_NAME()

               SELECT @CustomerCount = COUNT(*)
               FROM AdventureWorks.Sales.Customer

               SET @MessageText = 'Response From Server: \\' + @@SERVERNAME
                              + ', Database: ' + DB_NAME() + ' ** Total Customers: '
                              + CAST(@CustomerCount AS varchar(15)) + ' **'

               SET @ResponseMessage = N'<message>'+ N'<![CDATA[' + @MessageText +
N']]>' + N'</message>';

               WAITFOR DELAY '00:00:20';

               SEND ON CONVERSATION @conversation_handle
               MESSAGE TYPE [//www.wrox.com/MTCustomerInfo/ResponseTotalCustomers]
               (@ResponseMessage)

               END CONVERSATION @conversation_handle

          END
```

We added the delay to simulate the stored procedure doing some work so that when multiple messages arrive in the queue, the Queue Monitor will activate additional stored procedures.

Now open the scripts `CheckResponseFromTarget.sql` and `CheckRequestFromInitiator.sql` and run them both. Next, open the `SendManyMessages.sql` script and run it. This will send four messages to `TargetDB`. Figure 8-8 shows the output on `TargetDB` when you run the `ViewInfoOnTarget.sql` script after all the messages are processed.

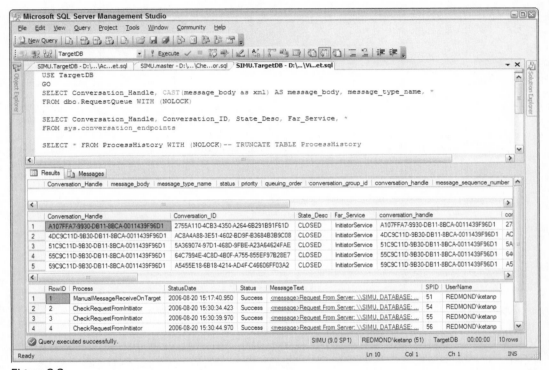

Figure 8-8

Notice that the `RequestQueue` is empty because all the messages are processed. You can also see that all the conversations are `CLOSED`, because you ended the conversation with the `END CONVERSATION` statement. If you look at the `SPID` column in the third result set from `ProcessHistory`, you will see four distinct SPIDs there, which means that four instances of the stored procedure ran to process those four messages. The `StatusDate` column is also interesting: Note the delay of about five seconds before the next instance of `CheckRequestFromInitiator` was activated. That is what the Queue Monitor does.

You will see similar output on `InitiatorDB` if you run the `ViewInfoOnInitiator.sql` script.

> *Because activation procedures run on background threads, there is no user connection on which they can report errors. Therefore, any error or PRINT output for an activated stored procedure is written to the SQL Server error log. When activation doesn't appear to be working, the first thing you want to look at is the SQL error log file.*

Another interesting point to note here is that the reason you will see multiple instances of Check RequestFromInitiator is because you have a distinct conversation_handle for each message (see the second result set in Figure 8-8). The reason you have a different conversation handle is because you have issued the BEGIN DIALOG statement for each new message sent to the target. Take a look at the SendManyMessages.sql script:

```
WHILE (@Count < @NumberOfMessages)
BEGIN
    BEGIN TRY
            BEGIN DIALOG CONVERSATION @Conversation_Handle
            FROM SERVICE [InitiatorService]
            TO SERVICE 'TargetService'
            ON CONTRACT [//www.wrox.com/CTGeneralInfo/ProductCustomer]
            WITH ENCRYPTION = OFF;

            SELECT * FROM sys.conversation_endpoints
            WHERE conversation_handle = @Conversation_Handle;
            ------------------------------------------------------------
            SEND ON CONVERSATION @Conversation_Handle
            MESSAGE TYPE [//www.wrox.com/MTCustomerInfo/RequstCustomersCount]
            (@SendMessage);
            ------------------------------------------------------------
    END TRY
    BEGIN CATCH
        SELECT ERROR_NUMBER() AS ErrorNumber
                ,ERROR_MESSAGE() AS ErrorMessage
                ,ERROR_SEVERITY() AS ErrorSeverity
                ,ERROR_LINE() AS ErrorLine
        BREAK
    END CATCH

    SET @Count = @Count + 1
END
```

The BEGIN DIALOG statement creates a new conversation handle for each message. If you move the BEGIN DIALOG before the WHILE loop, you will get only one conversation handle. In that case, no matter how many messages you send to the target, only one instance of CheckRequestFromInitiator will be created to process all the messages on the same conversation handle.

Conversation Groups

As we just mentioned, in the previous example the SendManyMessages.sql script created a new conversation handle every time you sent the message with the SEND command. This means that only one message is in each conversation group. If you query the sys.conversation_endpoints view after sending a bunch of messages with SendManyMessages.sql, you will notice that the conversation_handle column has distinct values in it. In this case, even though the messages may have arrived in the order they were sent, they will not necessarily be processed in that order. You have just seen that multiple instances of CheckRequestFromInitiator in TargetDB were processing messages, and there is no guarantee that the messages will be processed in the order in which they were received because you indicated that you don't care about the order by sending each message on a different conversation group.

Many messaging applications require that messages be processed in the exact order in which they are received. Although it is reasonably straightforward to ensure that messages are received in order, it is rather more difficult to ensure that they are processed in order. Consider an example in which an order entry application sends messages to credit card validation, inventory adjustment, shipping, and accounts receivable services on four different dialogs. These services may all respond, and it's possible that response messages for the same order may be processed on different threads simultaneously. That could cause a problem because if two different transactions are updating the order status simultaneously without being aware of each other, status information may be lost. To solve this type of problem, the Service Broker uses a special kind of lock to ensure that only one task (one instance of the activation procedure) can read messages from a particular conversation at a time. This special lock is called a *conversation group lock*.

To see how this works, open the Sample1 solution. Run the scripts `CheckResponseFromTarget.sql` and `CheckRequestFromInitiator.sql`. These are the stored procedures that pick up the messages from the initiator and target queues, as explained earlier. Run `ActivateSPOnTarget.sql` and `ActivateSPOnInitiator.sql`, which make sure that both queue status and activation are ON. Open the script `SendMessageOnSameConvGroup.sql`. The code is as follows:

```
USE InitiatorDB
GO

DECLARE @Conversation_Handle UNIQUEIDENTIFIER
       ,@SendMessage xml
       ,@MessageText varchar(255)
       ,@Another_Conversation_Handle UNIQUEIDENTIFIER
       ,@conversation_group_id UNIQUEIDENTIFIER

SET @MessageText =  'Request From Server: \\' + @@SERVERNAME
               + ', DATABASE: ' + DB_NAME()
               + ': ** Please send the total number of customers.'

SET @SendMessage = N'<message>'+ N'<![CDATA[' + @MessageText + N']]>' +
N'</message>'

BEGIN DIALOG CONVERSATION @Conversation_Handle
FROM SERVICE [InitiatorService]
TO SERVICE 'TargetService'
ON CONTRACT [//www.wrox.com/CTGeneralInfo/ProductCustomer]
WITH ENCRYPTION = OFF;


-----------------------------------------------------------------
SEND ON CONVERSATION @Conversation_Handle
MESSAGE TYPE [//www.wrox.com/MTCustomerInfo/RequstCustomersCount]
(@SendMessage);
-----------------------------------------------------------------
SELECT @conversation_group_id = conversation_group_id
FROM sys.conversation_endpoints
WHERE conversation_handle = @Conversation_Handle;

BEGIN DIALOG CONVERSATION @Another_Conversation_Handle
FROM SERVICE [InitiatorService]
TO SERVICE 'TargetService'
```

```
ON CONTRACT [//www.wrox.com/CTGeneralInfo/ProductCustomer]
WITH RELATED_CONVERSATION_GROUP = @conversation_group_id
    ,ENCRYPTION = OFF;

SEND ON CONVERSATION @Another_Conversation_Handle
MESSAGE TYPE [//www.wrox.com/MTCustomerInfo/RequstCustomersCount]
(@SendMessage);
```

This code sends two messages on the same conversation group. When you send the first message, a conversation group is created by default. Before you send the second message, you get the conversation group of the first message from the sys.conversation_endpoints table with the following script:

```
SELECT @conversation_group_id = conversation_group_id
FROM sys.conversation_endpoints
WHERE conversation_handle = @Conversation_Handle;
```

Then you send the second message on the same conversation group by using the RELATED _CONVERSATION_GROUP argument in the BEGIN DIALOG statement.

Run the SendMessageOnSameConvGroup.sql script. Now open the script ViewInfoOnInitiator.sql and run it. You will notice that when you run SELECT * FROM ProcessHistory, the SPID column shows you that only one SPID has worked on both response messages, which indicates that the messages on the same convesation group can only be processed by a single thread.

You've now seen a basic example of how messaging works in the Service Broker. We haven't yet sent a message from one SQL Server instance to another, nor have we sent a message with all the security features the Service Broker provides for a secured application. Next, we will first discuss how security works in the Service Broker. Then we look at an example that sends a message from one SQL Server instance to another, which includes details about how to configure security for safe messaging.

Security Considerations for the Service Broker

Configuring security is probably the most complex piece of the Service Broker application. Nevertheless, the Service Broker is designed to run enterprise applications in very secure environments. In fact, by default, the Service Broker can only send messages within the database. Recall from the first example that in order to send the message to a different database on the same SQL Server instance, you had to set the TRUSTWORTHY bit to 1 for both the databases.

The Service Broker provides two distinct levels of security:

❑   **Transport security**: Secures the TCP/IP connection between two SQL Server instances on different servers

❑   **Dialog Security**: Secures each individual dialog between the two dialog endpoints. This ensures that the services exchanging the messages are who they say they are.

In cases where the highest level of security is required, using both transport and dialog security is appropriate. In addition, the Service Broker uses regular SQL Server security to assign permissions to users to enable them to create and use the various Service Broker objects such as message types, contracts, and services.

Transport Security

Transport security secures the TCP/IP connection. There are two parts to transport security: *authentication* (whereby the two instances of SQL server determine that they are willing to talk) and *encryption* of the data over the network. Note that authentication is not optional, but encryption is. In order for two SQL Server instances to exchange Service Broker messages, you must create an endpoint on each server using the CREATE ENDPOINT or ALTER ENDPOINT statements.

The Service Broker offers two types of authentication: Windows and Certificate. Windows authentication uses the normal Windows authentication protocols — NTLM or Kerberos — to establish a connection between two endpoints. For simplicity, consider an endpoint as an instance of SQL Server. Certificate-based authentication uses the TLS (Transport Layer Security) authentication protocol (SChannel) to authenticate the two endpoints. To establish either of these authentications, you have to use the CREATE ENDPOINT statement on each instance of the SQL Server. More details about this are discussed in the following sections.

Windows Authentication

Suppose you want two instances of SQL Server to exchange Service Broker messages. The first thing you have to do is create an endpoint on each SQL Server instance. At this point, you can start the second example and learn how to create endpoints. Open the folder Sample2 under the Chapter 8 folder and double-click the Sample2 solution file. You need two instances of SQL Server connected on the same domain.

Open the CreateEndPointOnInitiator.sql script and connect it to the initiator SQL Server:

```
CREATE ENDPOINT InitiatorSSBEndPoint
STATE = STARTED
AS TCP(LISTENER_PORT = 5040)
FOR SERVICE_BROKER(AUTHENTICATION = WINDOWS, ENCRYPTION = REQUIRED)
```

You can create only one endpoint for the Service Broker for each instance of SQL Server. This endpoint listens on a specific TCP port. In this example it is port 5040. The default port for the Service Broker is 4022. You can specify any available port number above 1024. Use the netstat -a command in a command window to determine which ports are available on your system.

This script specified WINDOWS for AUTHENTICATION, so the Service Broker will either use NTLM or Kerberos depending on how your network is configured and how the endpoint is configured (Kerberos, NTLM, or both) in the endpoint configuration. Suppose you have two servers, InitiatorServer and TargerServer. If your SQL Server service account is "local system," in order to use Windows authentication, you have to make sure that your network has Kerberos authentication. If not, you will have to change the SQL Server service account to a domain user such as MYDOM\ketanp. If you have permission to run the SQL Server service under the "local system" account and if your network does not have Kerberos, then you must use certificate-based authentication, which is covered in the section "Certificate-Based Authentication." For this exercise, we assume that you are running the SQL Server service using a domain account.

Run the `CreateEndPointOnInitiator.sql` script. After you run the script, run the following SQL statement to view the TCP endpoint you just created:

```
SELECT * FROM sys.tcp_endpoints
```

Open the `CreateEndPointOnTarget.sql` script, connect it to the target machine, and run it. Now you have established endpoints on both ends.

The next step is to grant `CONNECT` permission to these endpoints so that remote machines can connect to them. To do that, first you have to add the login under which the SQL Server service runs on `InitiatorServer` to `TargerServer`, and vice versa.

Open the `AddRemoteLoginOnTarget.sql` script and connect to the `TargetServer` machine:

```
CREATE LOGIN [MYDOM\InitiatorLogin] FROM WINDOWS

GRANT CONNECT ON ENDPOINT::TargetSSBEndPoint TO [MYDOM\InitiatorLogin]
```

You are adding the account `MYDOM\InitiatorLogin` (which runs the SQL Server service on `InitiatorServer`) to `TargetServer`, and you are granting `CONNECT` permission on the endpoint you created on the `TargetServer` to this account. Please note that if you are using the "local system" service account to run the SQL Server, then the login name would be something like `[MYDOM\InitiatorServer$]`.

You need to perform a similar operation on the `InitiatorServer` machine to introduce the `MYDOM\TargetLogin` account and grant `CONNECT` permission. Open the `AddRemoteLoginOnInitiator.sql` script, connect to the `InitiatorServer` machine, and run it:

```
CREATE LOGIN [MYDOM\TargetLogin] FROM WINDOWS

GRANT CONNECT ON ENDPOINT::InitiatorSSBEndPoint TO [MYDOM\TargetLogin]
```

Again, if you are using the "local system" service account to run SQL Server, the login name would be something like `[MYDOM\TargetServer$]`.

If you are running the SQL Server service under the same the domain account on both machines, you do not need to run the `AddRemoteLoginOnTarget.sql` *and* `AddRemoteLoginOnInitiator.sql` *scripts.*

You're done! You have set up the transport security using Windows authentication. You are not yet ready to send the message, however. First you need to understand certificate-based authentication.

Certificate-Based Authentication

In this section, we assume that you know what public and private keys are and how they work. If the endpoints are in different domains, Windows authentication can be complex and slow. In this case, you may choose to use certificate-based authentication. Each endpoint needs two certificates, one with its own private key and another with the opposite endpoint's public key. When one endpoint encrypts the data with the private key, it can only be decrypted with the corresponding public key at the opposite endpoint. The advantage of certificate-based authentication is that authentication only requires certificates. There is no need for the endpoints to contact a domain controller, as there is with Windows authentication, so the endpoints can be in different domains, which is one of the most compelling reasons to use certificates. For more information about how certificates work, please refer to Books Online.

Now you'll use `sample2` to create and install certificates on `InitiatorServer` and `TargerServer`. Open the script `CreateCertOnInitiator.sql` and connect to `InitiatorServer`:

```
USE MASTER
GO
IF NOT EXISTS(SELECT 1 FROM sys.symmetric_keys where name =
'##MS_DatabaseMasterKey##')
CREATE MASTER KEY ENCRYPTION BY PASSWORD = '23%&weq^yzYu2005!'
GO

IF NOT EXISTS (select 1 from sys.databases where
[is_master_key_encrypted_by_server] = 1)
ALTER MASTER KEY ADD ENCRYPTION BY SERVICE MASTER KEY
GO

IF NOT EXISTS (SELECT 1 FROM sys.certificates WHERE name = 'InitiatorDBCert')
CREATE   CERTIFICATE InitiatorDBCert
WITH SUBJECT = 'Initiator Server Certificate'
GO

BACKUP CERTIFICATE InitiatorDBCert TO FILE = 'C:\InitiatorDBCert.cer'
```

For simplicity, here we are using the certificate created by SQL Server, but other ways of creating and distributing certificates will work equally well.

You have created a master key in this script because when you create a certificate, you have to specify the encryption by password. If you don't specify it, the private key will be encrypted using the database master key. This script creates a certificate in the master database. The BACKUP CERTIFICATE statement backs up the public key certificate for this private key.

Now open the script `CreateEndPointWithCertOnInitiator.sql` and connect to `InitiatorServer`:

```
CREATE ENDPOINT InitiatorSSBEndPoint
STATE = STARTED
AS TCP(LISTENER_PORT = 5040)
FOR SERVICE_BROKER(AUTHENTICATION = CERTIFICATE InitiatorDBCert, ENCRYPTION =
REQUIRED)
```

This script creates an endpoint with CERTIFICATE authentication using the certificate you just created on `InitiatorServer`.

Let's do the same on `TargetServer`. Open `CreateCertOnTarget.sql` on `TargetServer` and run it. Then open `CreateEndPointWithCertOnTarget.sql` on `TargetServer` and run it.

So far you have created certificates on both `InitiatorServer` and `TargetServer` and have associated the endpoint on each server with certificates. Now you have to introduce the endpoints to each other by exchanging the public keys. Copy the certificate you backed up using `CreateCertOnInitiator.sql` to `TargetServer` on `C:\`. Also copy the certificate backed up using `CreateCertOnTarget.sql` to `InitiatorServer` on `C:\`.

Once the certificates have been exchanged, all you have to do is associate them with a login that has CONNECT permissions for the endpoint. Open the CreateLoginOnInitiator.sql script and connect to InitiatorServer:

```
CREATE LOGIN TargetServerUser WITH PASSWORD = '32sdgsgy^%$!'

CREATE USER TargetServerUser;

CREATE CERTIFICATE TargetDBCertPub  AUTHORIZATION TargetServerUser
FROM FILE = 'C:\TargetDBCert.cer'

GRANT CONNECT ON ENDPOINT::InitiatorSSBEndPoint TO TargetServerUser
```

This script creates a SQL Server login and creates a user in the master database. You are also importing the certificate you just copied from TargetServer and authorizing the user you created. At the end, you are granting CONNECT permission to the endpoint InitiatorSSBEndPoint to the user TargetServerUser. You still have to do the same on the TargetServer, so open the script CreateLoginOnTarget.sql, connect to TargetServer, and run it.

You have now configured endpoints on both the InitiatorServer and TargetServer to use certificate-based authentication.

Our general recommendation is that if both endpoints are in the same Windows domain, then you should use Windows authentication; if both endpoints are in different domains, then you should use certificate authentication instead. These are recommendations, though, and not rules.

Encryption

When you configured an endpoint on each SQL Server instance, you specified ENCRYPTION = REQUIRED in the CREATE ENDPOINT statement:

```
CREATE ENDPOINT InitiatorSSBEndPoint
STATE = STARTED
AS TCP(LISTENER_PORT = 5040)
FOR SERVICE_BROKER(AUTHENTICATION = WINDOWS, ENCRYPTION = REQUIRED)
```

By default, encryption is required for all transport connections. Along with authentication, all transport messages are checksummed and signed to ensure that the messages are not altered on the wire. Message encryption is required by default, so the endpoints you configured earlier will send the messages encrypted. What if both endpoints are not configured with the same option in the ENCRYPTION clause? The clause has three options: REQUIRED, SUPPORTED, and DISABLED. The following table indicates whether data will be encrypted or not when endpoints are configured with different ENCRYPTION options.

EndpointA	EndpointB	Data Encrypted?
REQUIRED	REQUIRED	Yes
REQUIRED	SUPPORTED	Yes
DISABLED	DISABLED	No
DISABLED	SUPPORTED	No
SUPPORTED	SUPPORTED	Yes

When both endpoints of the dialog are in the same SQL Server instance—either in the same database or different databases (as in Sample1) in the same instance—encryption is never done. The Service Broker message never leaves the server's memory, so there is no reason to encrypt them.

Routing

You are almost ready to send the message from `InitiatorServer` to `TargetServer`. Before we talk about dialog security, we need to introduce routing. This is a required component to send the messages between two instances of SQL Server. Routing isn't really related to the security configuration, but you need to know about it before you can send the message.

When messages are sent, the Service Broker needs to know where to send them. A Service Broker *route* maps a service to a destination where messages can be sent. Four routes are involved in delivering a message to its destination:

1. When the `SEND` command is executed, a route from the local `sys.routes` table is used to determine where the message is sent.

2. When the message arrives at the destination SQL Server instance, a route from the `sys.routes` table in the `msdb` database is used to determine which database will receive the message. Note that whenever a message comes from a remote SQL Server instance, it always goes to the `msdb` database first. Make sure that the `is_broker_enabled` bit is set to 1 in `msdb`, or your messages will not be delivered. Once the message has been successfully committed in the proper queue in the destination database, an acknowledgment is sent back to the sender.

3. A route from the `sys.routes` table is used to determine where to send the acknowledgment message. When the message is sent from the sender, it always goes to the `sys.transmission_queue` table on the sender, and will stay there until the receiver sends the acknowledgment that the message has been received. It is important that you specify the return route.

4. When the acknowledgment message arrives at the sender's SQL Server instance, a route in the `msdb` database is used to route the message to the sending service's queue in the sending database.

You need to create a route on `InitiatorServer` and a return route on `TargetServer` in order to send the messages between these two instances. Let's do that now.

Open `SetupInitiator.sql` on `InitiatorServer` and run it, and then open `SetupTarget.sql` on `TargetServer` and run it. Both of these scripts are taken from `sample1`. Now you can create the route and bind that route to a service. Open the `CreateRouteOnInitiator.sql` script and connect to `InitiatorServer`:

```
USE InitiatorDB
GO
IF EXISTS(SELECT * FROM sys.routes WHERE name = 'RouteToTargetServer')
DROP ROUTE RouteToTargetServer
GO
CREATE ROUTE RouteToTargetServer
WITH
 SERVICE_NAME = 'TargetService'
,ADDRESS = 'TCP://TargetServer:5040'
```

Notice that the route is created in the database from which we are sending the message. In addition, the SERVICE_NAME specified is the TargetService, which is on the TargetServer in the TargetDB database. The ADDRESS argument specifies the name of the server, which is TargetServer, and the port on which it is listening. Remember that when you created the endpoint on TargetServer, you specified the port number. That's the port number you use here.

Now run the script CreateRouteOnTarget.sql.

Remember the BEGIN DIALOG statement you used to send the message? Here's part of it:

```
BEGIN DIALOG CONVERSATION @Conversation_Handle
FROM SERVICE [InitiatorService]
TO SERVICE 'TargetService'
ON CONTRACT [//www.wrox.com/CTGeneralInfo/ProductCustomer]
WITH ENCRYPTION = OFF
```

This tells the Service Broker that the message is being sent to TargetService, but where is TargetService? Remember that Figure 8-2 shows the four points needed to deliver messages successfully. In this case, when the message is sent, the Service Broker on InitiatorServer checks for routes in sys.routes. Because you have set SERVICE_NAME = 'TargetService' in the CREATE ROUTE statement, this says that this service resides on TargetServer, so the message will be sent to TargetServer. Then, on TargetServer, the Service Broker will check in the msdb database route table which database the TargetService exists in, and send the message to the RequestQueue, which is the endpoint for TargetService.

You have to create the route on TargetServer to complete the communication loop. Open the script CreateRouteOnTarget.sql and connect to TargetServer:

```
USE TargetDB
GO
IF EXISTS(SELECT * FROM sys.routes WHERE name = 'RouteToInitiatorServer')
DROP ROUTE RouteToInitiatorServer
GO
CREATE ROUTE RouteToInitiatorServer
WITH
 SERVICE_NAME = 'InitiatorService'
,ADDRESS = 'TCP://InitiatorServer:5040'
```

Here you are defining the route to InitiatorServer, which resides on InitiatorServer.

Now you are ready to send the message. Open the SendMessageFromInitiator.sql script, connect to InitiatorServer, and run it. You can check the status on TargetServer using the ViewInfo OnTarget.sql script, and on InitiatorServer using ViewInfoOnInitiator.sql.

Two addresses have special meaning for Service Broker routes. When the route for a service name has an address of LOCAL, the message classifier will look for the service name in the local instance to find which queue to put the message in. The first priority is the current database where the route exists. If the service does not exist there, the classifier checks the service list, which contains all the services that exist in the local SQL Server instance. The following SQL statement creates a local route:

```
CREATE ROUTE MyLocalRoute
WITH SERVICE_NAME = 'MyService'
    ,ADDRESS = 'LOCAL'
```

If you have services with the same name (in this case `MyService`) in different databases on the local SQL Server instance, the classifier will pick one of the services as the target service and send the messages to that service. To avoid this, use the `BROKER_INSTANCE` parameter in the `CREATE ROUTE` statement to ensure that messages are delivered to the specific database (broker).

When you create a new database, you will find a route called `AutoCreatedLocal` in `sys.routes`. This route has no service name (`remote_service_name` column in `sys.routes` view) or broker identifier (`broker_instance` column in `sys.routes` view), and an address of `LOCAL` (address column in `sys.routes` view). Remember that in the first example in this chapter, you were sending messages from `InitiatorDB` to `TargetDB` without creating a route. `AutoCreatedLocal` is a wildcard route, so the message classifier will use this route for any service that does not have another route available. This route sends messages to local services, so in the first example in this chapter you were able to send the message to `TargetService` using `AutoCreatedLocal`. In a distributed application, it is better to drop this `AutoCreatedLocal` route, because without a wildcard route, you can be sure that messages only go where you intend them to go.

The other special address is called `TRANSPORT`. When you send the message to the target, you need the response from the target back to the initiator, so a route must exist on the target to specify the address of the initiator in order to send the message back. Consider a scenario in which you want to send messages from 100 initiators to one target. You will need 100 routes on the target to send the acknowledgment or messages back to the initiator. Instead, you can use a shortcut with the `TRANSPORT` address, so you just need to create one route on the target instead of 100. When messages are sent back from the target to the initiator, the classifier uses the service name from the dialog as an address.

Here's a small example. Suppose you want to send the message from `InitiatorServer`, which has an endpoint defined on port 4040, to `TargetServer`. On `InitiatorServer`, create this service:

```
CREATE QUEUE [InitiatorQueue]
CREATE SERVICE [TCP://InitiatorServer:4040/ResponseService]
ON QUEUE InitiatorQueue
```

When you send the message to `TargetServer`, you issue the `BEGIN DIALOG` statement as follows:

```
BEGIN DIALOG @Conversation_handle
FROM SERVICE [TCP://InitiatorServer:4040/ResponseService]
TO SERVICE 'TargetService'
ON CONTRACT 'AppContract'
```

You have already created the route on `InitiatorServer`. Now on `TargerServer`, create a wildcard route as follows:

```
CREATE ROUTE RouteToInitiatorServer WITH ADDRESS = 'TRANSPORT'
```

Now when the message needs to be sent back to `InitiatorServer` from `TargetServer`, because no specific route is created for the service [`TCP://InitiatorServer:4040/ResponseService`] on

`TargetServer`, the classifier will look for a wildcard route with the `TRANSPORT` address and attempt to open a connection to `TCP://InitiatorServer:4040`. In this example, it will succeed and the message will be returned successfully to `InitiatorServer`.

The biggest disadvantage of using `TRANSPORT` routes is that the address is hardcoded in the service name, so to move an application to another server you have to destroy all the existing dialogs to the service. You also have to re-create the service with new server name in the address, and you must change your `BEGIN DIALOG` statement if you are not using dymanic SQL in BEGIN DIALOG. We don't recommend using this method of routing unless this disadvantage is acceptable in your environment.

Dialog Security

Dialog security is used to secure the dialogs from the initiator of the dialog to the target of the dialog. You have just learned that the data from one endpoint to another endpoint will be encrypted by default, so why do you need dialog security? The difference is that dialog security works between dialog endpoints instead of transport endpoints (see Figure 8-9).

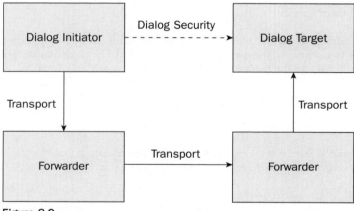

Figure 8-9

What is the Forwarder box in the diagram? The Service Broker uses a concept of message forwarding, so a SQL Server instance can be configured to forward the messages using the following statement:

```
CREATE ENDPOINT ForwarderSSBEndPoint
STATE = STARTED
AS TCP(LISTENER_PORT = 5040)
FOR SERVICE_BROKER
(
    AUTHENTICATION = WINDOWS
   ,MESSAGE_FORWARDING = ENABLED
   ,MESSAGE_FORWARD_SIZE  = 40
)
```

This enables message forwarding and sets the maximum amount of memory to use for forwarding, in this case 40MB. The messages on the forwarding server always stay in memory and aren't persisted in the database. In some scenarios, message forwarding is required. One of those scenarios is the case when two endpoints cannot connect directly, so some kind of gateway is needed to connect the two endpoints. Please refer to Books Online for more details about message forwarding.

Returning to Figure 8-9, when a message is initiated, it travels through two forwarders before it reaches the final destination. If you have used transport security, you know that the messages are decrypted and encrypted at each forwarder, so the message would be encrypted and decrypted three times en route. If you had used dialog security instead, the messages going from the initiator to the target would be encrypted at the initiator and decrypted at the target, rather than at each forwarder. The extra overhead in the first case can cause significant delay and increase processing time. Dialog security has the advantage of encrypting and decrypting a message once, no matter how many Service Brokers the message is forwarded through, so if you have a message forwarder in your network, then you may want to use dialog security. If your network is secure enough that encryption on the wire is not required, or if transport security is sufficient, you may want to turn off dialog security. In the previous examples, we set ENCRYPTION = OFF in the BEGIN DIALOG statement. That's how you turn off dialog security.

Configuring dialog security is similar to configuring certificate-based authentication. Open the script ConfigureDialogSecurityOnTarget.sql and connect to TargetServer:

```
USE TargetDB
GO

IF NOT EXISTS(SELECT 1 FROM sys.symmetric_keys where name =
'##MS_DatabaseMasterKey##')
CREATE MASTER KEY ENCRYPTION BY PASSWORD = '23%&weq^yzYu2005!'
GO

IF NOT EXISTS (select 1 from sys.databases where
[is_master_key_encrypted_by_server] = 1)
ALTER MASTER KEY ADD ENCRYPTION BY SERVICE MASTER KEY
GO


--Create a USER TO own the TargetService.
IF NOT EXISTS(SELECT * FROM sys.sysusers WHERE name = 'TargetServiceOwner')
CREATE USER TargetServiceOwner WITHOUT LOGIN
GO

GRANT CONTROL ON SERVICE::TargetService TO TargetServiceOwner
GO

IF NOT EXISTS (SELECT 1 FROM sys.certificates WHERE name = 'TargetDBDialogCert')
CREATE  CERTIFICATE TargetDBDialogCert
AUTHORIZATION TargetServiceOwner
WITH SUBJECT = 'Target Server Certificate for Dialog Security'
GO

BACKUP CERTIFICATE TargetDBDialogCert TO FILE = 'C:\TargetDBDialogCert.cer'
```

This script creates a user and grants CONTROL permission on TargetService to that user. The script also creates a certificate and makes the TargetServiceOwner user the owner of that certificate. It also backs up the certificate to C:\. Note that you are creating a certificate in the database in which the service resides, and not in the master database.

Now open the script `ConfigureDialogSecurityOnInitiator.sql` and connect to `InitiatorServer`:

```
USE InitiatorDB
GO

IF NOT EXISTS(SELECT 1 FROM sys.symmetric_keys where name =
'##MS_DatabaseMasterKey##')
CREATE MASTER KEY ENCRYPTION BY PASSWORD = '23%&weq^yzYu2005!'
GO

IF NOT EXISTS (select 1 from sys.databases where
[is_master_key_encrypted_by_server] = 1)
ALTER MASTER KEY ADD ENCRYPTION BY SERVICE MASTER KEY
GO

--Create a USER TO own the InitiatorService.
IF NOT EXISTS(SELECT * FROM sys.sysusers WHERE name = 'InitiatorServiceOwner')
CREATE USER InitiatorServiceOwner WITHOUT LOGIN
GO
--Make this user the owner of the InitiatorService.
ALTER AUTHORIZATION ON SERVICE::InitiatorService TO InitiatorServiceOwner
GO

IF NOT EXISTS (SELECT 1 FROM sys.certificates WHERE name = 'InitiatorDBDialogCert')
CREATE  CERTIFICATE InitiatorDBDialogCert
AUTHORIZATION   InitiatorServiceOwner
WITH SUBJECT = 'Initiator Server Certificate for Dialog Security'
GO

BACKUP CERTIFICATE InitiatorDBDialogCert TO FILE = 'C:\InitiatorDBDialogCert.cer'
```

This script creates a user and makes that user the owner of the `InitiatorService`. The script also creates a certificate and makes the `InitiatorServiceOwner` user the owner of that certificate. It also backs up the certificate to `C:\`, just as before.

Now copy the certificate `TargetDBDialogCert.cer` from `C:\` on `TargetServer` to `C:\` on `InitiatorServer`. Similarly, copy the certificate `InitiatorDBDialogCert.cer` from `C:\` on `InitiatorServer` to `C:\` on `TargerServer`.

Now open the script `DialogImportCertOnInitiator.sql` and connect to `InitiatorServer`:

```
USE InitiatorDB
GO
--Create a USER TO own the TargetService.
IF NOT EXISTS(SELECT * FROM sys.sysusers WHERE name = 'TargetServiceOwner')
CREATE USER TargetServiceOwner WITHOUT LOGIN

--Import the certificate owned by above user
IF NOT EXISTS(SELECT * FROM sys.certificates WHERE name = 'TargetDBDialogCertPub')
CREATE CERTIFICATE TargetDBDialogCertPub
AUTHORIZATION TargetServiceOwner
FROM FILE = 'C:\TargetDBDialogCert.cer'
```

This script creates the user `TargetServiceOwner`, the same user you created on `TargetServer`. The script also imports the certificate that you copied from `TargetServer` and made `TargetServiceOwner` the owner of that certificate.

Next, open the script `DialogImportCertOnTarget.sql` on `TargetServer`:

```
USE TargetDB
GO


IF NOT EXISTS(SELECT * FROM sys.sysusers WHERE name = 'InitiatorServiceOwner')
CREATE USER InitiatorServiceOwner WITHOUT LOGIN

--Import the certificate owned by above user
IF NOT EXISTS(SELECT * FROM sys.certificates WHERE name =
'InitiatorDBDialogCertPub')
CREATE CERTIFICATE InitiatorDBDialogCertPub
AUTHORIZATION InitiatorServiceOwner
FROM FILE = 'C:\InitiatorDBDialogCert.cer'

GRANT SEND ON SERVICE::TargetService TO InitiatorServiceOwner
```

This script does the same thing on `TargerServer` that you just did on `InitiatorServer`.

The last thing you have to do is create a `REMOTE SERVICE BINDING` to bind the user TargetServiceOwner you created on `InitiatorServer` to the `TO SERVICE` used in the `BEGIN DIALOG` command. The `TO SERVICE` in this case is `TargetService`. Open the `CreateRemoteBindingOnInitiator.sql` script and connect to `InitiatorServer`:

```
USE InitiatorDB
GO
IF NOT EXISTS(SELECT * FROM sys.remote_service_bindings WHERE name =
'ToTargetService')
CREATE REMOTE SERVICE BINDING ToTargetService
TO SERVICE  'TargetService'
WITH USER = TargetServiceOwner
```

Now the `BEGIN DIALOG` command knows which two certificates to use to authenticate the dialog: the private key certificate associated with the owner of the `FROM SERVICE` (user `InitiatorServiceOwner`) and the certificate owned by the user bound to the `TO SERVICE` (user `TargetServiceOwner`) with the `REMOTE SERVICE BINDING`.

You are now ready to send the first encrypted message to the `TargetServer`. Open the `SendMessage WithEncryption.sql` script. This script is similar to `SendMessageFromInitiator.sql` with a small difference in the `BEGIN DIALOG` statement, as you can see:

```
BEGIN DIALOG CONVERSATION @Conversation_Handle
FROM SERVICE [InitiatorService]
TO SERVICE 'TargetService'
ON CONTRACT [//www.wrox.com/CTGeneralInfo/ProductCustomer]
WITH ENCRYPTION = ON
```

You have turned on encryption, but how do you know the messages are encrypted? Run the script `SendMessageWithEncryption.sql`. Then open `ViewInfoOnTarget.sql`, connect to `TargetServer`, and run it.

Check the output of `SELECT * FROM sys.conversation_endpoints`. You will notice that the `outbound_session_key_identifier` and `inbound_session_key_identifier` columns in the `sys.conversation_endpoints` view have values other than 0, which shows that the messages were encrypted.

Note than when you specify `ENCRYPTION = OFF`, it doesn't mean that encryption is disabled for a dialog. `ENCRYPTION = OFF` means that encryption is not required. If the `TO SERVICE` has the `REMOTE SERVICE BINDING`, the dialog will be secured even when `ENCRYPTION = OFF` is used. Change the `ENCRYPTION = OFF` statement in the script `SendMessageWithEncryption.sql` and run it. You will see that the messages are still encrypted.

If `ENCRYPTION = ON` is used and `REMOTE SERVICE BINDING` is not present, or the dialog security is not configured properly, the `BEGIN DIALOG` statement will fail.

Administering the Service Broker

The Service Broker is integrated with the database engine, so administrating the Service Broker application is a part of your day-to-day activities. In this part of the chapter, we describe the different tasks involved in administering a database that hosts a Service Broker application. Most administrative tasks are part of the normal administration for your database. Of course, there are some special things you have to do for a Service Broker application.

Installing the Service Broker Application

You learned earlier that the key components to develop a Service Broker application are message types, contracts, queues, services, routes, endpoints, and stored procedures. When a development team provides the installation script for a Service Broker application, those scripts will typically include T-SQL statements. A typical Service Broker application will have an initiator, which resides on a server, and a target, which may reside on the same server in the same database, or in a different database, or even on a different server. Obviously, complex Service Broker applications may involve more than a couple of servers communicating with one another. In general, you should have separate scripts, for installation on the initiator and on the target.

Preparing the Databases

When messages are sent from one database to another, the Service Broker uses a unique identifier to route the messages to the correct database. That unique identifier is called the *Service Broker GUID*. The `Service_Broker_Guid` column in the `sys.databases` catalog view shows the Service Broker identifier for each database. This identifier should be unique across all SQL Server instances on the same network to ensure proper message delivery.

Each database also has a setting for message delivery. The `is_broker_enabled` column in the `sys.databases` catalog view shows whether message delivery is enabled or disabled in a database.

Run the following T-SQL statement in the database in which you are going to install the application:

```
SELECT is_broker_enabled, Service_Broker_Guid
FROM sys.databases
WHERE database_id = DB_ID()
```

Make sure that the `is_broker_enabled` bit is set to 1 in order for the database to send and receive messages. If this bit is not 1, you can still install the Service Broker application and even send messages, but you will see an error for that conversation in the `sys.transmission_queue` catalog view. In this case, the error message in the `transmission_status` column would be "The broker is disabled in the sender's database." There are two ways you can set this bit to 1. Both of the following commands requires exclusive database access, so if you have users in the database in which you are running the command, you will be blocked by those connections.

```
ALTER DATABASE database_name SET NEW_BROKER
ALTER DATABASE database_name SET ENABLE_BROKER
```

The `NEW_BROKER` option activates the Service Broker message delivery, creates a new Service Broker identifier for that database, and throws away any existing dialogs and messages. Therefore, you will see a different value in the `Service_Broker_Guid` column in the `sys.databases` view than what was shown before.

The `ENABLE_BROKER` option also activates Service Broker message delivery, but it preserves the Service Broker identifier for that database, so you will see the same value in the `Service_Broker_Guid` column that was there before.

We will talk about when to use these options, as well as `DISABLE_BROKER` and `ERROR_BROKER_CONVERSATIONS`, later in this section. When you create a brand-new database, this bit is set to 1 by default, so Service Broker message delivery is enabled by default in a newly created database.

If you are installing a Service Broker application for which more than one database is involved in the communication on the same instance of SQL Server, you have to set the `is_trustworthy_on` bit to 1 on the initiator database of the dialog. The `is_trustworthy_on` column in the `sys.databases` catalog view shows the bit value for each database. By default this bit is 0 (`OFF`). You can run the following statement to set the bit to 1:

```
ALTER DATABASE database_name SET TRUSTWORTHY ON
```

This statement doesn't require exclusive database access. By default, when you restore or attach a database this bit is set to 0 (`OFF`). Remember that in the first example in this chapter, you set this bit to 1 after creating the databases because that example sends and receives messages between two databases. For information on the `TRUSTWORTHY` bit, please refer to Chapter 9 or BOL.

Running the Scripts to Install the Application

Now that you have set up the database that is going to host the Service Broker application, review the installation script provided by the development team. Of course, the code review should have happened long before the application was released for system test from development. As a best practice, you should have the queue `STATUS OFF` by default, and `ACTIVATION STATUS OFF` by default. As a part of code review with the development team, you should notify them that you want to have these options as a part of the installation script, rather than you munging the installation scripts during deployment.

Another thing to consider is that until installation is completed, do not grant the SEND permission to the queue so that you can complete the internal testing before your application users go wild. You and your team want to ensure that everything looks good before you give the green light. Consider creating a table that lists the objects for which you have to grant permission, and write a stored procedure to grant the permission on those objects. That way, if you have to change the permission on any object involved in your application, you don't have to start searching for those objects. All you have to do is add, change, or remove the object from the table and run the stored procedure to grant the permission. The installation script will only insert the objects in the table where you hold the all the objects for your application and it will not grant any permissions, but you will.

Be sure to keep the installation document up-to-date, because even though your development team has shown due diligence, it is hard to mimic the production environment in your development or test. While you are installing the application, you will certainly find something that is not in the installation document, so you want to make sure that you update the document right away.

Setting Permissions on Service Broker Objects

In the section "Security Considerations for the Server Broker," we explained how to set up transport security using both Windows authentication and certificates. If your application involves more than one instance of SQL Server, you should consider creating a database principal for the application.

CONNECT Permission

Remote authorization is involved when more than one instance of SQL Server is involved in the application. To connect to a remote SQL Server, you have to grant CONNECT permission to the principal connecting to the remote instance.

If the initiator instance is running under a domain account, you have to add that domain account to the target instance and grant CONNECT permission:

```
GRANT CONNECT ON ENDPOINT::TargetSSBEndPoint TO [MYDOM\mssdev1]
```

You'll need to grant the same permission on the initiator instance, so that the target instance can connect to the initiator.

If the initiator instance is running under a "local system" account, you have to add that machine account to the target instance and grant CONNECT permission:

```
GRANT CONNECT ON ENDPOINT::TargetSSBEndPoint TO [MYDOM\InitiatorMachine$]
```

You have to do the same thing on the initiator instance so the target instance can connect to the initiator. Keep in mind that in order for the machine account to be authenticated on the remote instance, you need Kerberos on your network. If Kerberos authentication is not available on your network, this method will not work. You would have to use certificates in that case.

If certificates are used for transport authentication, you have to grant the CONNECT permission on the endpoint on the initiator instance to the user who owns the certificate that corresponds to the private key in the remote database.

See the scripts `CreateLoginOnInitiator.sql` and `CreateEndPointWithCertOnInitiator.sql` in `Sample2`.

```
GRANT CONNECT ON ENDPOINT::InitiatorSSBEndPoint TO TargetServerUser
```

You'll also have to do the same thing on the target instance. See the scripts `CreateLoginOnTarget.sql` and `CreateEndPointWithCertOnTarget.sql` in `Sample2`.

SEND Permission

When you send the message, you send it to a target service. You need `SEND` permission to send the message to a target service. The database principal that owns the initiating service must have `SEND` permissions on the target service.

When you do not configure full-dialog security, you have to grant `SEND` permission on the target service as `public`, because the target service cannot verify the identity of the initiating service. Operations on behalf of the initiating service run as a member of the fixed database role `public` in the target database. This is called *anonymous dialog security:*

```
GRANT SEND ON SERVICE::TargetService TO PUBLIC
```

When you use `FULL` dialog security, you can establish the trust by exchanging the certificates that contain public keys, as discussed in the "Dialog Security" section earlier in this chapter. For better security, you should have a different user who has `SEND` permission to a service than the one who runs the activation on a queue tied to that service.

You don't need either of these steps if your dialog remains in the same SQL Server instance.

RECEIVE Permission

The user executing the `BEGIN DIALOG`, `END CONVERSATION`, `MOVE DIALOG`, `RECEIVE`, or `GET CONVERSATION GROUP` command must have `RECEIVE` permission on the queue associated with the `FROM SERVICE`. The following statement is an example of how you can grant `RECEIVE` permission on a `RequestQueue`:

```
GRANT RECEIVE ON dbo.RequestQueue TO [mydom\mssdev1]
```

In addition, if you have activation specified on a queue, the user specified in `EXECUTE AS` in `ACTIVATION` must have `RECEIVE` permission on the queue.

EXECUTE Permission

When you create a queue and define the `ACTIVATION`, you specify the stored procedure name and `EXECUTE AS` option there. The user you specify there must have permission to execute the stored procedure. Of course, if that stored procedure does some cross-database queries, you have to set those permissions too.

Notice that when you create the stored procedure and you have defined the `EXECUTE AS` clause with some user, the statements in that stored procedure will run under the defined security principal. Therefore, when a stored procedure is activated, it will be under the security context of the database principal you have specified in the `CREATE QUEUE` statement, and after that it will change the security context to the database principal you have specified in the `CREATE PROCEDURE EXECUTE AS` clause.

Managing Service Broker Queues

A Service Broker application that is running well will generally keep the queues fairly small. Make sure you have enough disk space available to handle any problems. The Queue Monitor will try to create enough instances of the activation procedure to process the incoming messages, and the transport layer does a good job of moving messages to their destination as efficiently as possible. What if something goes wrong? If you have a lot of incoming messages in your application, a queue can get pretty big very quickly. Suppose your application has 1,000 messages coming in per second; if your network has to go down or your destination server is down for an hour, the sys.transmission_queue will have 4 million messages in it. You can have an SQL job that monitors for a heavily used queue and a sys.transmission_queue every hour or so and that also sends an e-mail if the messages in the queue exceed a certain threshold.

You can also plan to put the queue on a separate filegroup so it's easy to maintain if it runs out of space. Try putting the queue on a separate filegroup by specifying the filegroup in the CREATE QUEUE statement, or use the ALTER QUEUE statement.

Finally, one of the best things you can do with a queue is to use SELECT * FROM [queuename] to view what's in there.

Poison Message Handling

All transaction messaging systems have to deal with *poison messages*, which are messages that cannot be processed by the destination service. Any message containing data that can force the message processing transaction to roll back can become a poison message. The Service Broker will detect the repeated rollbacks of messages, and disable the queue to keep a poorly handled message from becoming a poison message. When you design the application, make sure all messages are handled correctly, because only the application knows how to handle the messages — that is, whether to roll back or end the conversation.

Open sample1 to simulate a poison message and how to remove it from the queue. Open the script PoisonMessageSimulate.sql and run it. This will compile the stored procedure you created on RequestQueue again. Part of the code is reproduced here:

```
BEGIN TRY
   WHILE (1 = 1)
   BEGIN
      BEGIN TRANSACTION
      -- Receive the next available message
      WAITFOR
      (
         RECEIVE TOP(1)                          -- just handle one message at a time
            @xmlmessage_body =  CASE WHEN validation = 'X'
                                     THEN CAST(message_body AS XML)
                                     ELSE CAST(N'<none/>' AS XML)
                                END
            ,@message_type_name = message_type_name
            ,@conversation_handle = conversation_handle
         FROM dbo.RequestQueue
      ), TIMEOUT 3000
```

```
    -----------------------------------------------------------------------
    -- If we didn't get anything or if there is any error, bail out
    IF (@@ROWCOUNT = 0 OR @@ERROR <> 0)
    BEGIN
        ROLLBACK TRANSACTION
        BREAK
    END
    ELSE
    BEGIN
        IF @message_type_name =
//www.wrox.com/MTCustomerInfo/RequstCustomersCount'
        BEGIN

            ROLLBACK TRAN

        END
    END
  END --WHILE END here.
END TRY
```

The preceding script receives the message and rolls it back. This simulates a problem processing the message, so after the rollback the message will go back to the queue. This will be detected by the Service Broker, which will disable the queue.

Run the script `ActivateSPOnTarget.sql`, which will activate this stored procedure to run when the message arrives. Now open the `SendMessageFromInitiator.sql` script and run it. It will send the message to `RequestQueue` in the `TargetDB` database.

Now open the script `RemovePoisonMessage.sql`:

```
USE TargetDB
GO

SELECT name, is_receive_enabled
FROM sys.service_queues
GO
ALTER QUEUE RequestQueue WITH  ACTIVATION (STATUS = OFF)
GO
ALTER QUEUE RequestQueue
WITH STATUS = ON
GO

DECLARE
    @message_type_name   nvarchar(256)
    ,@xmlmessage_body    xml
    ,@MessageFromTarget  varchar(255)
    ,@MessageText varchar(255)
    ,@conversation_handle UNIQUEIDENTIFIER;

RECEIVE TOP(1)
    @xmlmessage_body = message_body
    ,@message_type_name = message_type_name
```

```
    ,@conversation_handle = conversation_handle
FROM dbo.RequestQueue

END CONVERSATION @conversation_handle
GO
SELECT name, is_receive_enabled
FROM sys.service_queues
GO
```

Because the queue is now disabled, you will see 0 in the `is_receive_enabled` column in the `sys .service_queues` catalog view for the `RequestQueue`.

First, you have to enable the queue, because when queue is disabled, you can not send or receive messages. After the queue is enabled, you receive the first message from the top of the queue, which is the one causing the problem. This assumes that only one message is processed at a time by the application. If this is not the case, the poison message could be any of the messages in the same conversation group as the message at the top of the queue. You can look at the SQL error log for more details on what's causing the message to fail.

You can also subscribe to event called `Broker_Queue_disabled`, which will send the message to a designed queue when a queue is disabled. Here's how you can do that. Open the script `PoisonMessage Notification.sql`.

```
USE TargetDB
GO
CREATE QUEUE dbo.PoisonMessageNotification
GO
CREATE SERVICE ServicePoisonMessageNotification ON QUEUE
dbo.PoisonMessageNotification
([http://schemas.microsoft.com/SQL/Notifications/PostEventNotification])
GO
--below notification will send the message to queue
--when queue PoisonMessageNotification is disabled. The event
--generated is BROKER_QUEUE_DISABLED
CREATE EVENT NOTIFICATION PoisonMessageEvent
ON QUEUE RequestQueue
WITH FAN_IN
FOR BROKER_QUEUE_DISABLED
TO SERVICE 'ServicePoisonMessageNotification', 'current database'

GO
```

Now create a poison message on the `RequestQueue` as we described earlier. Run the following script:

```
USE TargetDB
SELECT CAST(message_body as xml), * FROM PoisonMessageNotification
```

You will notice that an event got generated because the `RequestQueue` got disabled because of poison message, and a message is put into the `PoisonMessageNotification` queue, which shows that `RequestQueue` is disabled. You can do whatever you like with that message in the `PoisonMessage Notification` queue, such as sending an e-mail. In fact, you can send the message to different server, where you are probably monitoring other servers using routing machanism you learned about earlier.

Also, this example above shows the power of Service Broker where you can receive event notifications in a Service Broker queue and take action on that event. Refer to Books Online to see how event notification works.

Moving Service Broker Applications

Sometime you need to move your application from one server to another. Maybe you got lucky, and your management got you bigger, latest-and-greatest hardware, or some other reason. Usually you have to move the database where you are hosting the Service Broker application to some other instance and many aspects of Server Broker application move with the database. Some aspects of the application must be recreated or reconfigured in the new location.

The stored procedure, users, certificates, and outgoing routes will move with the database. But some of the things you have to reconfigure on the new instance. If your Service Broker application sends messages across instances, you will need to reconfigure the endpoint on new instance. Of course, if the server you are moving the application to already has an endpoint configured, you do not need to do anything because endpoint and transport security apply at the server level, not the database level. Make sure that the endpoint is configured according to your application requirement, though. For example, if your application required transport security and the server you are moving the application doesn't have its endpoint configured with transport security, you will have to reconfigure it.

You must configure logins for any users that the application uses.

Most Service Broker databases have a database master key, but if you are using certificates for transport or dialog security, make sure you preserve the password for the master key you have created because you will need the password when you restore the database in the new location. Remember the script `CreateCertOnInitiator.sql` and `ConfigureDialogSecurityOnInitiator.sql` where you created the master key with a password. You have to keep that password in a safe place.

If you have routing configured using `CREATE ROUTE`, and if you have specified the option called `BROKER_INSTANCE` in the statement, you have to make sure that after you restore the database on new location you use the `ALTER DATABASE database_name SET ENABLE_BROKER` statement to preserve the `BROKER_INSTANCE`. If you don't have that issue, or if you can reconfigure the route with a new initiator and target, you may use `ALTER DATABASE database_name SET NEW_BROKER`.

If you use `NEW_BROKER` in the `ALTER DATABASE` statement, it will clean up all the undelivered messages sitting in `sys.transmission_queue` and all the conversations in `sys.conversation_endpoints` view. When you back up the database to restore on the new location, make sure that application has finished processing all the messages, or if you have to process these messages after restoring to the new location, make sure that you do not use `ALTER DATABASE database_name SET NEW_BROKER`.

Also, you should not change the `BROKER_INSTANCE` identifier when you attach a database:

❑   For recovery purposes.

❑   To create a mirrored pair (see Chapter 17).

If you want to keep the same unique identifier for the database but want to ignore all the existing conversations (error them out), you will have to use the following statement.

```
ALTER DATABASE database_name SET ERROR_BROKER_CONVERSATIONS
```

Also remember that the msdb database should have always the is_broker_enabled bit set to 1, especially if you have any incoming or outgoing Service Broker messages. You can run following statement to check that:

```
SELECT name, is_broker_enabled FROM sys.databases WHERE name = 'msdb'
```

Make sure that if you have any routes on your destination, to point back to the new server, otherwise you will not get messages back to your new server.

Copying Service Broker Applications

The Development and Testing groups frequently refresh the environment with new data from production. In that case, as a DBA you provide a back up of the database. Most of the things we discussed in the "Moving Service Broker Applications" section apply here as well with some small changes.

Since the backup is a copy of the original application, make sure to change the unique identifier of that database using following statement because Service Broker routing relies on a unique identifier in each database to deliver messages correctly:

```
ALTER DATABASE database_name SET NEW_BROKER
```

This is the one thing you must not forget to do. Also, you have to change the routing on servers as we described in the previous section.

If you are using the BROKER_INSTANCE option in CREATE ROUTE, we highly recommend that, when you build an application, you store the route name in a table with a server name. (See the following table structure and stored procedure.) You should then write a stored procedure to retrieve the Broker _Instance from the sys.routes table, based on the route name you have stored in the table, to use in your application. That way, when you move or copy your application, you may have to drop and create the route, which may or may not have the same BROKER_INSTANCE, so you do not have to change your application at all.

```
CREATE TABLE ServerRoute
(
 ServerName varchar(50) NOT NULL
,RouteName varchar(100) NOT NULL
);

CREATE PROC GetRouteName
(
 @ServerName varchar(50)
,@Broker_Instance uniqueidentifier OUTPUT
)
AS
----------
SELECT @Broker_Instance = Broker_Instance
FROM sys.routes r
JOIN ServerRoute s
  ON s.RouteName = r.RouteName
 AND s.ServerName = @ServerName
----------
```

Replacing Expired Certificates

By default, certificates expire and become unusable. If you do not specify the expiration date in the `CREATE CERTIFICATE` statement, the expiration date is set to one year from when the certificate is created. When the certificate is about to expire, it must be replaced. To avoid disruptions, you must do this in the correct order. If you change the certificate at the endpoint, all connections to endpoints that do not have the new certificate will fail. However, the dialog won't fail, so when the certificate is replaced, it will continue from where it left off. To avoid this, create a new certificate and send the public key to all the remote connections. The remote Service Broker can associate this certificate with a user who represents the SQL Server instance whose certificate will be changed. Once all the remote endpoints have added the certificate to their users, you can change the local endpoint to the new certificate by using the `ALTER ENDPOINT` command.

Troubleshooting Service Broker Applications

We have learned how the Service Broker works throughout this chapter. In this section, you will learn what to do when it doesn't. You can use DMV, catalog views, and profiler to troubleshoot the problems in Service Broker application.

Design and Code Review

Because the Service Broker is a new technology to both SQL DBAs and developers, we highly recommend that you do code review (if you are not doing one, start now!), and pay close attention to the following issues in the code review process so that any problems will disappear in the earliest stage of your application.

Not Handling All Message Types

You may sometimes wonder why, after sending a message of a particular type, nothing happened. You have probably forgotten to handle that message type in the stored procedure in which you receive the message. In addition to all the application message types, be sure to handle at least the following system message types:

- ❑ `[http://schemas.microsoft.com/SQL/ServiceBroker/Error]`
- ❑ `[http://schemas.microsoft.com/SQL/ServiceBroker/EndDialog]`

You can see how to handle these message types in one of the activation stored procedures we have created in Sample1 or Sample2.

Not Dealing with Poison Messages

We discussed poison messages earlier in this chapter. Make sure you handle them; otherwise, the Service Broker will disable the queue and your application will come a halt.

Not Ending the Conversation

Remember that conversations persist in `sys.conversation_endpoints`, and they are not completely eliminated until both the initiator and target have issued the `END CONVERSATION` command. When to end the conversation is totally up to your application, but make sure that you do.

Service Broker Commands Outside of an Explicit Transaction

The key advantage of the Service Broker is data integrity. When you receive messages from the queue with the RECEIVE command without a BEGIN TRANSACTION before the RECEIVE, your message will be deleted from the queue, which means that if something goes wrong while you are processing the message, you will not get the message back in the queue because you specified otherwise. If you do not see BEGIN TRANSACTION before the RECEIVE statement, carefully examine the logic to ensure that there is an active transaction. It may happen that in your application you may not need the message after you receive it, so in that case you can avoid BEGIN TRANSACTION before RECEIVE.

Using Catalog Views for Service Broker Metadata

There are many catalog views available to look at the metadata objects created for the Service Broker, and some views to look at the data for Service Broker conversations. The following list shows the views you can use. You can refer to Books Online for each and every column in that metadata.

- ❑ sys.service_message_types
- ❑ sys.service_contracts
- ❑ sys.service_contract_message_usages
- ❑ sys.services
- ❑ sys.service_contract_usages
- ❑ sys.service_queues
- ❑ sys.certificates
- ❑ sys.routes
- ❑ sys.remote_service_bindings
- ❑ sys.service_broker_endpoints
- ❑ sys.tcp_endpoints
- ❑ sys.endpoints
- ❑ sys.databases

Not all of these views are for the Service Broker, but they are related to the Service Broker in some way. The following example queries should give you an idea about how you can use these views.

This query will determine which Service Brokers are enabled in the current SQL Server instance:

```
SELECT name, is_broker_enabled, service_broker_guid, is_trustworthy_on
FROM sys.databases
```

The following query will determine the Service Broker endpoint state, port, connection authentication type, encryption algorithm, and whether forwarding is enabled or not:

```
SELECT se.name, te.port, se.protocol, se.state_desc,
se.is_message_forwarding_enabled, se.connection_auth as authentication_method,
se.encryption_algorithm_desc
FROM sys.service_broker_endpoints se
JOIN sys.tcp_endpoints te
  ON se.endpoint_id = te.endpoint_id
```

This query provides all the service names along with their queues, and activation stored procedures and their status:

```
SELECT s.name AS Service, sq.Name AS Queue,
CASE WHEN sq.is_receive_enabled = 1 THEN 'Yes' ELSE 'No' END AS QueueActive,
ISNULL(sq.activation_procedure, 'N/A')
,CASE WHEN sq.is_activation_enabled = 1 THEN 'Yes' ELSE 'No' END  AS
Is_Activation_Enabled
FROM sys.services s
JOIN sys.service_queues sq
  ON s.service_queue_id = sq.object_id
```

This next query will give you the queue and message types associated with that queue. This is helpful when you write the RECEIVE statement in the queue to make sure that you have covered all the message types for that queue:

```
SELECT sq.name AS Queue, mt.Name AS Message_Type_Name
FROM sys.service_queues sq
JOIN sys.services s
  ON s.service_queue_id = sq.object_id
JOIN sys.service_contract_usages scu
  ON s.service_id = scu.service_id
JOIN sys.service_contracts sc
  ON scu.service_contract_id = sc.service_contract_id
JOIN sys.service_contract_message_usages mtu
  ON mtu.service_contract_id = sc.service_contract_id
JOIN sys.service_message_types mt
  ON mt.message_type_id = mtu.message_type_id
GROUP BY sq.name, mt.Name
```

Using Catalog Views for Service Broker Data

The catalog views that expose the queue data and conversation endpoints are the most useful views. The two views we use the most are sys.conversation_endpoints and sys.transmission_queue. In addition, to look at the data in the queue, you can always use SELECT * FROM [queuename], as we mentioned earlier.

Take a look at the sys.conversation_endpoints and sys.transmission_queue views. The query shown in Figure 8-10 will give you the state of some of the dialogs in the sys.conversation_endpoints view. We have selected only a few columns here. For all the column descriptions, please refer to Books Online.

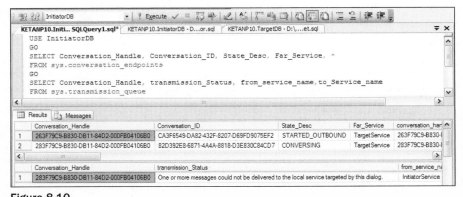

Figure 8-10

In Figure 8-10, the first results set (sys.conversation_endpoints) shows that the first dialog has State_Desc of STARTED_OUTBOUND, which means that the dialog on the initiator side has been started (with BEGIN DIALOG) but no messages have been sent on this dialog yet. The second row in that result set shows that a message has been sent (State_Desc is CONVERSING), but notice in the second result set (sys.transmission_queue) that the message is trying to send to a far service (TargetService) but it has failed because of some connection issue in this case. Conversation_handle is the key to tie messages in the sys.conversation_endpoints and sys.transmission_queue views.

Together, both sys.conversation_endpoints and sys.transmission_queue provide valuable information in troubleshooting problems. Later in this section you will look at the most common errors you get in Service Broker communications, and their solutions using both of these views and the Profiler, described in the following section.

Dynamic Management Views

You can use some Service Broker–related DMVs to get information on activated tasks and queue_ monitors:

❑ sys.dm_broker_queue_monitors: This DMV provides how many Queue Monitors you have in the current instance of SQL Server. For example, the query shown in Figure 8-11 will tell you when messages are being received in the queue, and how many sessions are waiting in a RECEIVE statement for this queue in the TargetDB database.

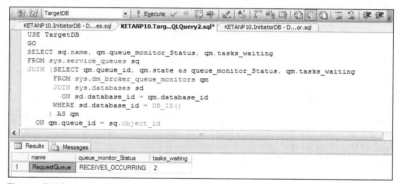

Figure 8-11

❑ sys.dm_broker_activated_tasks: This DMV returns a row for each stored procedure activated by the Service Broker in the current instance of SQL Server. The query in Figure 8-12 will give you the number of stored procedures activated in the database TargetDB for each queue. Notice that five stored procedures are activated on TargetQueue.

❑ sys.dm_broker_connections: Whenever the Service Broker makes network connections, you will see rows in this DMV. If the connection is idle for 90 seconds, the Service Broker will close the connection; otherwise, it will keep it open so messages can be sent using the same connection.

❑ sys.dm_broker_forwarded_messages: When a SQL Server instance is working as a message forwarder, you will see a row for each message in the process of being forwarded on a SQL Server instance.

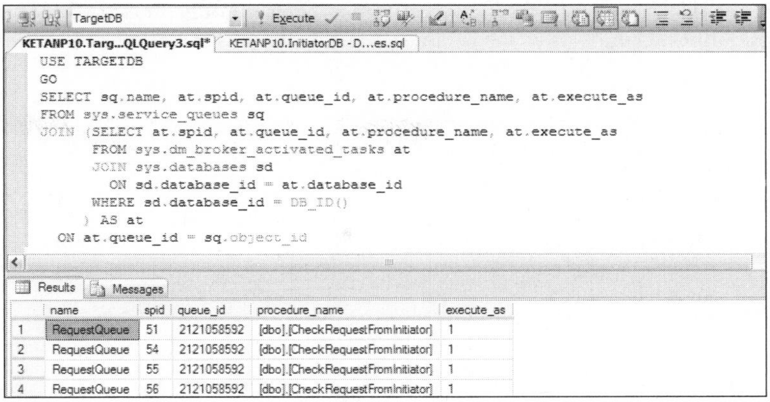

Figure 8-12

Using SQL Profiler to View Service Broker Activities

Most of the activities in the Service Broker happen in the background threads, and are not visible to the user. Many times when you issue BEGIN DIALOG and SEND the message, the Service Broker does it successfully but you later realize that the message never reached the destination! You are left wondering why you are not getting any errors when you send the message. The message is on its way, but because you have forgotten to configure the route properly, or forgot some permissions to set properly, the Service Broker keeps trying to send the message repeatedly until it times out or you end the dialog. The Service Broker guarantees reliable message delivery, so it will keep trying in spite of failure and misconfigurations, which are required when you implement a highly reliable network application; but you are not going to get the errors reported back to your application when things go wrong. You have to determine for yourself what's going on behind the scenes. In most cases the views described in the preceding section provide you with the necessary information to troubleshoot the problem, but sometime you will need more information to diagnose an issue, and that's where you use *traces*.

The Service Broker has a large number of traces that provide enough information about internal performance to enable you to diagnose the problem. Figure 8-13 shows the Service Broker Profiler events.

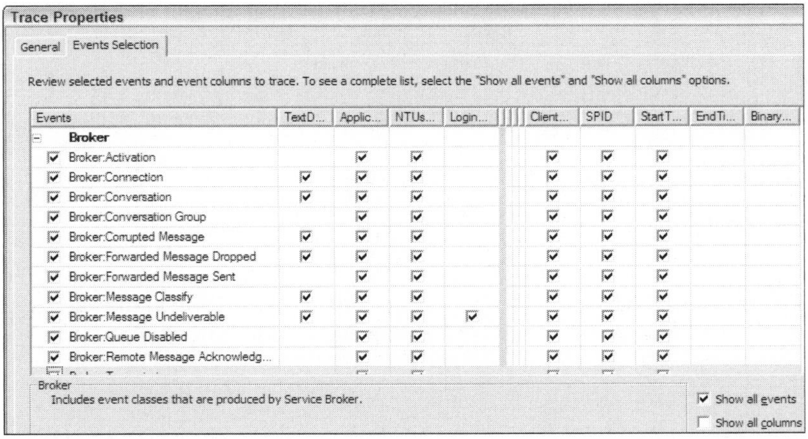

Figure 8-13

Figure 8-14 shows the trace of an event in which a message cannot be delivered to the remote server because the account that connects to the remote server doesn't have permission to connect on this endpoint.

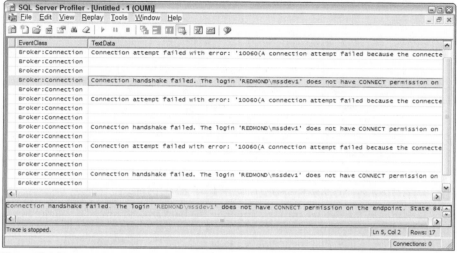

Figure 8-14

This trace was run on the target instance, and the message here shows that the remote login Redmond\mssdev1 does not have connect permission on the endpoint of the target machine. In Figure 8-15, you can also see that the conversation is sitting on sys.transmission_queue on the initiator, so the Service Broker will keep trying to send the message until it times out, the conversation is ended, or you fix the problem. Notice in Figure 8-14 the multiple error messages regarding "connection handshake failed" because the Service Broker keeps trying to send the message. The first retry is after four seconds, and if that does not succeed, the Service Broker resends exponentially up to 64 seconds (4, 8, 16, 32, and 64 seconds). When the Service Broker reaches the maximum resend timeout (64 seconds), it will try once every 64 seconds (about once a minute).

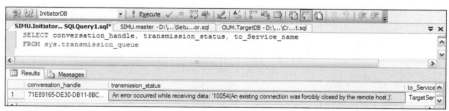

Figure 8-15

As you can see, the Profiler is a great tool for determining what's going in the background. The next several sections describe the most common Service Broker problems and what you can do to resolve them.

No Return Route

You have sent the message and you have verified that it reached the target, but you are expecting something from the target and that message never comes back to the initiator. If you trace the `Message undeliverable` event you will see continuous duplicate message events, as shown in Figure 8-16.

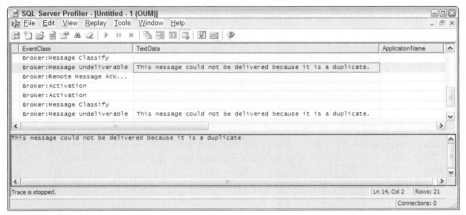

Figure 8-16

The issue is that you have correctly defined the route to the target so that messages are delivered from the initiator to the target, but you have not defined the route back to the initiator on the target. In `sample2`, if you drop the route with `DROP ROUTE` in the `TargetDB` database, and then send the message from the initiator, you will be able to see this error in the Profiler if you connect it to your target instance.

Dropped Messages

When the Service Broker cannot process a message, it will drop it. Some of the reasons why messages are dropped are as follows:

❑   The certificate in the message header doesn't exist or it doesn't have the required permission, or `public` doesn't have send permission on the service.

❑   The service that sent the messages doesn't exist.

❑   The message or header is corrupt or has been altered.

❑   The XML message doesn't validate against the schema for the message type.

If you notice a lot of messages are piling up in `sys.transmission_queue`, you should use SQL Profiler to see why messages are being dropped.

Conversation Endpoint is Not in a Valid State for SEND

As soon as you send the message it will be placed in the queue. If for some reason a message cannot be placed in the queue, you will see an error like the following:

```
Msg 8429, Level 16, State 1, Line 14
The conversation endpoint is not in a valid state for SEND. The current endpoint
state is 'ER'.
```

The most common cause of this error is that the conversation lifetime has expired, but it also happens when the conversation is ended by the far end, or by some other error. If you want to produce this error, then run the following script after you've set up `sample1` or `sample2`:

```
USE InitiatorDB
GO

DECLARE @Conversation_Handle UNIQUEIDENTIFIER
        ,@SendMessage xml
        ,@MessageText varchar(255)

SET @MessageText =  'Request From Server: \\' + @@SERVERNAME
                  + ', DATABASE: ' + DB_NAME()
                  + ': ** Please send the total number of customers.'

SET @SendMessage = N'<message>'+ N'<![CDATA[' + @MessageText + N']]>' +
N'</message>'

BEGIN DIALOG CONVERSATION @Conversation_Handle
FROM SERVICE [InitiatorService]
TO SERVICE 'TargetService'
ON CONTRACT [//www.wrox.com/CTGeneralInfo/ProductCustomer]
WITH ENCRYPTION = OFF
    ,LIFETIME = 5

WAITFOR DELAY '00:00:07';


BEGIN TRY;

SEND ON CONVERSATION @Conversation_Handle
MESSAGE TYPE [//www.wrox.com/MTCustomerInfo/RequstCustomersCount]
(@SendMessage);

END TRY
BEGIN CATCH
    SELECT ERROR_NUMBER() AS ErrorNumber
          ,ERROR_MESSAGE() AS ErrorMessage
          ,ERROR_SEVERITY() AS ErrorSeverity
          ,ERROR_LINE() AS ErrorLine
END CATCH
```

This script starts the dialog, but does not send the message until after seven seconds have passed. You specified the dialog lifetime in the LIFETIME clause to be five seconds, so you are not in a valid state to send the message on the expired `conversation_handle`.

Queue Disabled

If your application suddenly stops working, the first thing you want to check is queue status, using the following query:

```
SELECT name, CASE WHEN is_receive_enabled = 1 THEN 'Yes' ELSE 'No' END AS
QueueEnabled
FROM sys.service_queues
```

You can reenable the queue with the following query:

```
ALTER QUEUE ReceiveAckError WITH  STATUS = ON
```

In addition, make sure that activation is enabled if you have it. After you enable the queue, check the queue status again. If it is disabled again, you have a poison message on the queue. Read the "Poison Message Handling" section earlier in the chapter for details about detecting and handling poison messages.

Service Broker Is Disabled in a Database

If the Service Broker is disabled in the database, your application can still send messages but they will not be delivered. This can be caused by restoring or attaching a database without the Service_Broker_ Enabled option. Any message will sit in the sys.transmission_queue until the Service Broker is enabled. Using the following, you can check whether the database is enabled for the Service Broker or not:

```
SELECT name, CASE WHEN is_broker_enabled = 1 THEN 'Yes' ELSE 'No' END AS
Service_Broker_Enabled
FROM sys.databases
```

See the "Preparing Databases" and "Moving Service Broker Applications" sections of this chapter for more details.

Could Not Obtain Information about Windows NT Group/User

When you log in under your domain account, if you are not connected to the domain, you will get the following error when you try to send the message:

```
Msg 15404, Level 16, State 19, Line 15
Could not obtain information about Windows NT group/user 'MYDOM\ketan', error code
0x54b.
```

Whenever SQL Server needs to authorize a user, it needs to connect to a domain controller if SQL Server doesn't have enough information cached for authorization. The only way to correct this problem is to connect to your domain.

Duplicate Routes

Suppose half the messages you send are lost somewhere. Maybe you forgot to drop a route that is not required and messages are being sent to that. For example, when you refresh your environment with test data, you have the old route, which is pointing to ServerX. After the refresh, you add another route to ServerY and forget to drop the route to ServerX. If the Service Broker finds multiple routes to the same service, then it assumes that you want to do load balancing and it divides the dialogs between the two servers. In this case, half the dialogs will go to ServerX even though you don't want them to go there. The solution is to drop the unnecessary route. You can also specify the BROKER_ID in the BEGIN DIALOG or CREATE ROUTE statement to prevent this, but as long as you are careful about dropping unnecessary routes, you will be fine.

Activation Stored Procedure Is Not Being Activated

Frequently, messages are not picked up from the queue, even though you know that you have defined the activation stored procedure on that queue. The first thing you should check is whether the activation status is ON or not using the following query:

```
SELECT name, CASE WHEN is_activation_enabled = 1 THEN 'Yes' ELSE 'No' END AS
ActivationEnabled
FROM sys.service_queues
```

You can enable the activation using the following query on a RequestQueue:

```
ALTER QUEUE RequestQueue WITH ACTIVATION (STATUS = ON)
```

If activation is enabled, it's possible that you don't have correct permission on the stored procedure for the user you have specified in the EXECUTE AS clause in the CREATE QUEUE statement. Look in the SQL error log, and if that is the case you will see an error like this one:

```
The activated proc [dbo].[CheckResponseFromTarget] running on queue
InitiatorDB.dbo.ReceiveAckError output the following:  'EXECUTE permission denied
on object 'CheckResponseFromTarget', database 'InitiatorDB', schema 'dbo'.'
```

Grant proper permission on the stored procedure to avoid this error.

Performance

If you think that the Service Broker is not performing as well as you expect, look for following things. Keep in mind that the Service Broker uses SQL Server for all data storage, so all the things that affect database performance affect Service Broker performance. Don't worry about the RECEIVE message from the queue, because that is a very well tuned part.

Suppose you send a bunch of messages to a queue and you have defined an activation stored procedure on that queue with MAX_QUEUE_READERS = 10, but you still see only one instance of that stored procedure running. That's happening because all those messages are on the same dialog. In that case, activation would not start an additional instance of the activation stored procedure because all of the messages have to be processed serially. If you want parallelism, you need more than one dialog. You have to use dialogs effectively. If you think that some tasks have to be processed serially, then group them in one dialog. Don't send the messages you want to be processed in parallel on the same dialog.

Not ending the conversation is another performance problem. You know that as soon as you issue BEGIN DIALOG an entry will be made to the sys.conversation_endpoints catalog. This will remain until you end the dialog with END CONVERSATION on both ends of the conversation. Do not assume that specifying LIFETIME in BEGIN DIALOG is sufficient to clear the rows from that catalog. If you forgot END CONVERSATION, you may see millions of rows in the sys.conversation_endpoints view if you have a very active service. Conversations are cached for performance, so millions of expired and useless conversations waste a lot of cache space. If there is not enough cache size available, these conversations are swapped out into tempdb, so tempdb will grow too. Too many conversations are not good because they use a lot of cache size, and too few conversations are not good either because you will get less parallelism, so make sure that you use conversation wisely in your application to get the best possible performance. We believe that the Service Broker excels in many areas, including sending and receiving the messages in the queue, how quickly activation is initiated, and receiving from the queue.

Introduction to CLR Integration

In this section, we discuss what it means to be a .NET runtime host, deploying .NET assemblies, maintaining security for .NET assemblies, and monitoring performance. Also included is a short example demonstrating how to debug a .NET assembly. This section is not about how to write a cool .NET assembly, although we do create a small assembly to further your understanding of how it works. This section focuses more on administration.

> *For more information on SQL Server Integration Services, see Professional SQL Server 2005 Integration Services, by Brian Knight et al (Wrox, 2006); and to learn more about programming in SQL CLR, see Professional SQL Server 2005 CLR Stored Procedures, Functions, and Triggers, by Derek Comingore and Douglas Hinson (Wrox, 2007).*

SQL Server as .NET Runtime Host

A runtime host is defined as any process that loads the .NET runtime and runs code in the managed environment. The database programming model in SQL Server 2005 is significantly enhanced by hosting the Microsoft .NET Framework 2.0 Common Language Runtime (CLR). With CLR integration, also called SQLCLR, SQL Server 2005 enables .NET programmers to write stored procedures, user-defined functions, and triggers in any .NET compatible language, particularly C# and VB.NET.

The .NET code that SQL Server runs is completely isolated from SQL Server itself. Of course .NET code runs in the SQL Server process space, but SQL Server uses a construct in .NET called the *AppDomain (Application Domain)* to completely isolate all resources that the .NET code uses from the resources that SQL Server uses. The AppDomain protects SQL Server from all malicious use of system resources. Keep in mind that SQL Server manages its own thread scheduling, synchronization and locking, and of course memory management. There are other .NET hosts, such as ASP.NET and Internet Explorer, for which these tasks are managed by the CLR. There is no conflict of interest between SQL Server and CLR regarding who manages the resources. Obviously SQL Server wins because reliability, security, and performance are of the utmost importance for SQL Server, and changes have been made in how the managed hosting APIs work as well as in how the CLR works internally.

Figure 8-17 shows how SQL Server hosts the CLR .NET 2.0 hosts want to have hooks into the CLR's resource management and allocations. They achieve that by calling ICLRRunTimeHost. These APIs calls a shim DLL, MSCOREE.DLL, whose job is to load the runtime. The host (SQL Server) then can call ICLRHostRunTime::SetHostControl(). This method points to the IHostControl interface, which contains the method GetHostControl, which the CLR can call to delegate tasks such as thread management and memory management to the host (SQL Server). SQL Server uses this interface to take control of some functions that the CLR calls down to the OS directly.

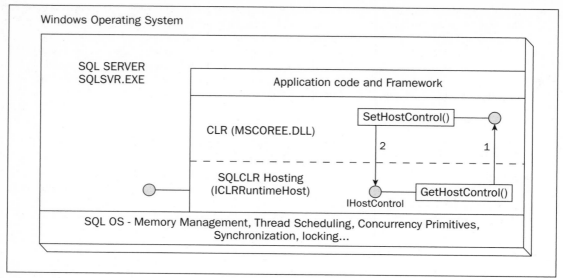

SQLCLR Hosting

Figure 8-17

The CLR calls SQL Server APIs for creating threads, both for running user code and for its own internal use. SQL Server uses a cooperative thread schedule model, whereas managed code uses preemptive thread scheduling. In cooperative thread scheduling, the thread must voluntarily yield control of the processor, while in preemptive thread scheduling the processor takes control back from the thread after its time slice has expired. Some greedy managed code may not yield for a long time and may monopolize the CPU time. SQL Server can identify those "runaway" threads, suspend them, and put them back in the queue. Some threads that are identified repeatedly as runaway threads are not allowed to run for a given period of time, which enables other worker threads to run.

Only one instance of the runtime engine can be loaded into the process space during the lifetime of a process. It is not possible to run multiple versions of the CLR within the same host.

Application Domains

In .NET, processes can be subdivided into execution zones called application domains (AppDomains) within a host (SQL Server) process. The managed code assemblies can be loaded and executed in these AppDomains. Figure 8-18 shows the relationship between a process and AppDomains.

SQL Server isolates code between databases by using AppDomains. This means that for each database, if you have registered an assembly and you invoke some function from that assembly, an AppDomain is created for that database. Only one AppDomain is created per database. Later you will look at some DMVs that you can use to find out information about AppDomains.

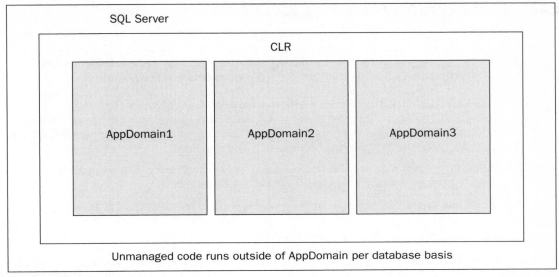

Figure 8-18

T-SQL versus CLR

We mentioned earlier that you can write stored procedures, triggers, and functions using CLR-compatible languages. Does that mean DBAs need to take a crash course on C# or VB.NET? No, but you need to at least understand why code is returned in .NET languages versus T-SQL. You are the one who is going to run the production environments, so you need to be part of the decision regarding which set of tools is chosen for your application.

The data manipulation can be broadly categorized into two parts: a declarative query language and a procedural query language. The declarative query language is composed of SELECT, INSERT, UPDATE, and DELETE statements, while a procedural language is composed of triggers, cursors, and WHILE statements. SQL CLR integration provides an alternative support to the procedural portion of T-SQL. Database applications should look to procedural programming if you cannot express the business logic you need with a query language. T-SQL is best when you perform set-based operations. It can take advantage of the query processor, which is best able to optimize the set operations. Do not write CLR code to start processing row-by-row operations, which you can do best with T-SQL in set operations. However, if your application requires performing complex calculations on a per-row basis over values stored in database tables, you can access the results from your table by first using SELECT and then by performing row-by-row operations using CLR code. Of course, there is a transition cost between the CLR and SQL layer, but if you are performing operations on high-volume data, the transition cost may be negligible.

Extended Stored Procedure versus CLR

To write server-side code with logic that was difficult to write in T-SQL, the only option prior to SQL Server 2005 was to write extended stored procedures (XPs). CLR integration in SQL Server 2005 now provides a more robust way to do those operations with managed code. The following list describes some of the benefits SQL CLR integration provides over extended stored procedures:

❑ **Granular control**: SQL Server administrators have little control over what XPs can or cannot do. Using the Code Access Security model, a SQL Server administrator can assign one of three permission buckets — SAFE, EXTERNAL_ACCESS, or UNSAFE — to exert varying degrees of control over the operations that managed code is allowed to perform.

❑ **Reliability**: There is no possibility of managed, user-code access violations making SQL Server crash, especially with SAFE and EXTERNAL_ACCESS assemblies.

❑ **New Data Types**: The managed APIs support new data types — such as XML, (n)varchar(max), and varbinary(max) — introduced in SQL Server 2005, while the Open Data Services (ODS) APIs have not been extended to support these new types.

These advantages do not apply if you register the assemblies with the UNSAFE permission set. Most extended stored procedures can be replaced, especially considering that Managed C++ is available as a coding option.

Enabling CLR Integration

By default, CLR integration is disabled. You cannot execute any .NET code until you intentionally change the configuration in SQL Server to allow CLR integration. You can do that with the GUI, the Surface Area Configuration tool, or using a T-SQL script. The shortcut to the tool is located in Start⇨All Programs⇨SQL Server 2005⇨Configuration Tools. Select the SQL Server Surface Area Configuration option, and then select Surface Area Configuration for Features. Figure 8-19 shows where you can enable or disable CLR integration within the Surface Area Configuration tool.

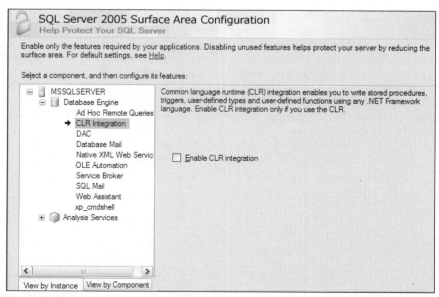

Figure 8-19

If you prefer to use a T-SQL script, the following script will do the same thing:

```
EXEC sp_configure 'clr enabled', 1
GO
RECONFIGURE
GO
SELECT *
FROM sys.configurations
WHERE name = 'clr enabled'
```

You can check serverwide configuration using the catalog view `sys.configuration`. Look in the `value_in_use` column for the current configured value in the `sys.configuration` view.

Creating the CLR Assembly

In this section we will create a small C# Table Valued Function in order to demonstrate how to deploy an assembly, maintain security, and look for CLR objects in the database. The following code will access the specified directory and list all the files and attributes as a tabular result set. This example also illustrates how impersonation works. If you don't have Visual Studio 2005 installed, you can just take the compiled DLL from this book's Web site at www.wrox.com, and register that in the database, as shown later, or you can use the command we provide to compile the DLL from the .cs file using csc.exe (the C# compiler), which ships free with the .NET SDK. The following code will create a Table Valued Function:

```csharp
using System;
using System.Collections;
using System.Collections.Generic;
using System.Text;
using System.IO;
using Microsoft.SqlServer.Server;
using System.Data.SqlTypes;
using System.Security.Principal;

public class FileDetails
{

    [SqlFunction(DataAccess = DataAccessKind.Read, FillRowMethodName =
"FillFileRow"
     ,TableDefinition = "name nvarchar(4000), creationTime datetime, lastAccessTime
datetime, lastWriteTime datetime, isDirectory bit, isReadOnly bit, length bigint"
    )]
    public static IEnumerable GetFileDetails(string directoryPath)
    {
        try
        {
            DirectoryInfo di = new DirectoryInfo(directoryPath);
            return di.GetFiles();
        }
        catch (DirectoryNotFoundException dnf)
        {
            return new string[1] { dnf.ToString() };
        }
        catch (UnauthorizedAccessException ave)
        {
            return new string[1] { ave.ToString() };
```

```
        }
    }

    [SqlFunction(DataAccess = DataAccessKind.Read, FillRowMethodName =
"FillFileRowWithImpersonation", TableDefinition = "name nvarchar(4000),
creationTime datetime, lastAccessTime datetime, lastWriteTime datetime, isDirectory
bit, isReadOnly bit, length bigint")]
    public static IEnumerable GetFileDetailsWithImpersonation(string directoryPath)
    {
        WindowsIdentity clientId = null;
        WindowsImpersonationContext impersonatedUser = null;

        clientId = SqlContext.WindowsIdentity;
        try
        {
            try
            {
                impersonatedUser = clientId.Impersonate();
                if (impersonatedUser != null)
                    return GetFileDetails(directoryPath);
                else return null;
            }
            finally
            {
                if (impersonatedUser != null)
                    impersonatedUser.Undo();
            }
        }
        catch
        {
            throw;
        }
    }
    public static void FillFileRow(object fileData, out SqlString name, out
SqlDateTime creationTime,
        out SqlDateTime lastAccessTime, out SqlDateTime lastWriteTime,
        out SqlBoolean isDirectory, out SqlBoolean isReadOnly, out SqlInt64 length)
    {
        FileInfo info = fileData as FileInfo;
        if (info == null)
        {
            name = "Error, directory list failed: " + fileData.ToString();
            creationTime = SqlDateTime.Null;
            lastAccessTime = SqlDateTime.Null;
            lastWriteTime = SqlDateTime.Null;
            isDirectory = SqlBoolean.Null;
            isReadOnly = SqlBoolean.Null;
            length = SqlInt64.Null;
        }
        else
        {
            name = info.Name;
            creationTime = info.CreationTime;
            lastAccessTime = info.LastAccessTime;
            lastWriteTime = info.LastWriteTime;
```

```
                isDirectory = (info.Attributes & FileAttributes.Directory) > 0;
                isReadOnly = info.IsReadOnly;
                length = info.Length;
        }
    }
    public static void FillFileRowWithImpersonation(object fileData,
        out SqlString name, out SqlDateTime creationTime,
        out SqlDateTime lastAccessTime, out SqlDateTime lastWriteTime,
        out SqlBoolean isDirectory, out SqlBoolean isReadOnly, out SqlInt64 length)
    {
        WindowsIdentity clientId = null;
        WindowsImpersonationContext impersonatedUser = null;

        clientId = SqlContext.WindowsIdentity;
        try
        {
            try
            {
                impersonatedUser = clientId.Impersonate();
                if (impersonatedUser != null)
                    FillFileRow(fileData, out name, out creationTime,
                        out lastAccessTime, out lastWriteTime, out isDirectory,
                        out isReadOnly, out length);
                else
                {
                    FillFileRow("Error: Impersonation failed!",
                        out name, out creationTime, out lastAccessTime,
                        out lastWriteTime, out isDirectory, out isReadOnly,
                        out length);
                }
            }
            finally
            {
                if (impersonatedUser != null)
                    impersonatedUser.Undo();
            }
        }
        catch
        {
            throw;
        }
    }
}
```

The preceding code has two main methods: GetFileDetails and GetFileDetailsWithImpersonation. The method GetFileDetails calls the method FillFileRow. The method GetFileDetailsWith Impersonation calls the methods FillFileRowWithImpersonation, GetFileDetails, FillFile RowWithImpersonation, and FillFileRow, in that order.

Later we will define two SQL TVFs called GetFileDetails and GetFileDetailsWithImpersonation. The function GetFileDetails will call the method GetFileDetails from this code. This method just gets the files list and other details such as creation time and last modified time using the SQL Server service account. The FillFileRow method will get this property and return it to the SQL TVF. The SQL TVF function `GetFileDetailsWithImpersonation` will call the method `GetFileDetailsWith Impersonation`, which sets the impersonation to your login; and when it calls the `GetFileDetails` method, it uses your login identity rather than the SQL Server service account. You'll see how to call these SQL TVF functions later.

Now you need to compile the code and create an assembly called `GetFileDetails.dll`. If you have Visual Studio 2005, you can open the solution `GetFileDetails.sln`. Build the project by clicking Build⇨Build GetFileDetails. That will create the `GetFileDetails.dll` file in the `debug` directory under the `bin` directory in your `solution` directory. You can deploy this assembly using Visual Studio 2005, but we will do that manually so that you know how to write T-SQL script to deploy the assembly in a database.

If you do not have Visual Studio 2005, you can use following command-line utility, `csc.exe`, to build `GetFileDetails.dll`:

```
C:\>C:\WINDOWS\Microsoft.NET\Framework\v2.0.50727\Csc.exe
/reference:C:\WINDOWS\Microsoft.NET\Framework\v2.0.50727\System.Data.dll
/reference:C:\WINDOWS\Microsoft.NET\Framework\v2.0.50727\System.dll /reference:C
:\WINDOWS\Microsoft.NET\Framework\v2.0.50727\System.Xml.dll /keyfile:c:\assembly
\keypair.snk /out:c:\assembly\GetFileDetails.dll /target:library C:\assembly\Get
FileDetails.cs
```

The `/out` parameter specifies the target location where `GetFileDetails.dll` will be created. The `/target` parameter specifies that this is a library (DLL). When you specify `GetFileDetails.cs`, you may have to specify the full path of the file if you are not in the directory where `GetFileDetails.cs` is located. In addition, the option `/keyfile` is used to sign the assembly. You will see why we have used this option when we register the assembly.

Now that you have created the DLL, you need to deploy the assembly and associate it with SQL user-defined functions.

Deploying the Assembly

Managed code is compiled and then deployed in units called *assemblies*. An assembly is packaged as a DLL or executable (.exe). The executable can run on its own, but a DLL needs to be hosted in an existing application. We have created a DLL in this case because SQL Server will host it. You now have to register this assembly using the new DDL statement CREATE ASSEMBLY, like this:

```
CREATE ASSEMBLY assembly_name
[ AUTHORIZATION owner_name ]
FROM { <client_assembly_specifier> | <assembly_bits> [ ,...n ] }
[ WITH PERMISSION_SET = { SAFE | EXTERNAL_ACCESS | UNSAFE } ]
[ ; ]

<client_assembly_specifier> :: =
        '[\\computer_name\]share_name\[path\]manifest_file_name'
  | '[local_path\]manifest_file_name'

<assembly_bits> :: =
{ varbinary_literal | varbinary_expression }
```

The arguments of the CREATE ASSEMBLY statement are as follows:

❏ assembly_name: This is the name of the assembly, and must be unique within the database. It should be a valid SQL identifier.

❏ Authorization: This specifies the name of a user or role as an owner of the assembly. If you do not specify this, then the owner will be the user executing this statement.

❏ client_assembly_specifier: This is the location of the assembly being loaded, with the filename of that assembly. You can specify the local path or a network location (such as a UNC path). SQL Server does not load multimodule assemblies. If the assembly you are loading is dependent on other assemblies, SQL Server will look for those dependent assemblies in the same directory and load them with the same owner as the root-level assembly. The owner of the dependent assemblies must be the same as the root assembly. The user executing the CREATE ASSEMBLY statement must have read permission to the share where the file is located.

❏ assembly_bits: This is the list of binary values that make up the assembly and its dependent assemblies. The value is considered as the root-level assembly. The values corresponding to the dependent assemblies can be supplied in any order.

❏ PERMISSION_SET: Grouped into three categories, the code access security specifies what the assembly can do:.

  ❏ SAFE: The assembly runs under the caller's security context. An assembly with this code access security cannot access any resources outside of the SQL Server instance. This is the default and the most restrictive permission you can set for an assembly.

  ❏ EXTERNAL_ACCESS: Assemblies created with this permission set can access external resources such as the file system, the network, environment variables, the registry, and more.

  ❏ UNSAFE: This permission extends the external_access permission set. This permission allows the assembly to call unmanaged code.

Security Notes

You have just learned about what code access security can be applied to an assembly, but this section provides a bit more detail about the various options.

SAFE is the most restrictive option and the default. If the assembly doesn't need access to external resources, this is the permission you should use when you register the assembly.

You should use EXTERNAL_ACCESS whenever you need access to external resources. Keep in mind that when an assembly with this permission accesses external resources, it uses the SQL Server service account to do so. So make sure during the code review that impersonation is used while accessing the external resource. If impersonation is used, the external resources would be accessed under the caller's security context. Because this code can access external resources, before you register this assembly, you have to either set the TRUSTWORTHY bit in the database to 1, or sign the assembly, as you'll see later. The EXTERNAL_ACCESS assembly includes the reliability and scalability of the SAFE assembly.

We do not recommend using an UNSAFE assembly, because it could compromise SQL Server. It is no better than an extended stored procedure. You should have a very solid reason to use this option and should carefully examine what the assembly does, documenting it exactly. Keep in mind that when an assembly with this permission accesses external resources, it uses the SQL Server service account to do so.

The following table should help clarify how SQL Server applies rules for accessing resources outside of SQL Server when the assembly is created with either with the EXTERNAL_ACCESS or UNSAFE permission sets.

IF	THEN
If the execution context is SQL Server login . . .	attempts to access external resources are denied and a security exception is raised.
If the execution context corresponds to the Windows login and the execution context is the original caller . . .	external resources are accessed under the SQL Server service account.
If the execution context corresponds to the Windows login and the execution context is not the original caller . . .	attempts to access external resources are denied and a security exception is raised.

Registering the Assembly

Now you are ready to register the assembly into a database. Open the solution Sample3.

Open and run the script CreateDB.sql. This will create a database called CLRDB. Now open the script CreateAssembly.sql, shown here:

```
---------------------
USE CLRDB
GO
IF OBJECT_ID('GetFileDetails') IS NOT NULL
DROP FUNCTION [GetFileDetails];
GO
IF OBJECT_ID('GetFileDetailsWithImpersonation') IS NOT NULL
DROP FUNCTION [GetFileDetailsWithImpersonation];
GO
IF EXISTS (SELECT * FROM sys.assemblies WHERE [name] = 'GetFileDetails')
DROP ASSEMBLY [GetFileDetails];
GO
---------------------
USE master
GO
IF EXISTS (SELECT * FROM sys.server_principals WHERE [name] =
'ExternalAccess_Login')
DROP LOGIN ExternalAccess_Login;
GO
IF EXISTS (SELECT * FROM sys.asymmetric_keys WHERE [name] = 'ExternalAccess_Key')
DROP ASYMMETRIC KEY ExternalAccess_Key;
GO
CREATE ASYMMETRIC KEY ExternalAccess_Key
FROM EXECUTABLE FILE = 'C:\Assembly\GetFileDetails.dll'
GO
CREATE LOGIN ExternalAccess_Login FROM ASYMMETRIC KEY ExternalAccess_Key
GO
GRANT EXTERNAL ACCESS ASSEMBLY TO ExternalAccess_Login
GO
```

```
---------------------
USE CLRDB
GO
CREATE ASSEMBLY GetFileDetails
FROM  'C:\Assembly\GetFileDetails.dll'
WITH PERMISSION_SET = EXTERNAL_ACCESS;
GO
```

Before you register the assembly with SQL Server, you must arrange for the appropriate permissions. Assemblies with UNSAFE or EXTERNAL_ACCESS permissions can only be registered and operate correctly if either the database TRUSTWORTHY bit is set (ALTER DATABASE CLRDB SET TRUSTWORTHY ON), or the assembly is signed with a key, that key is registered with SQL Server, a server principal is created from that key, and that principal is granted the external access or unsafe assembly permission. Here you'll use the latter approach so that you can also see how you can sign the assembly and register it, because the first approach is a simple matter of just setting the TRUSTWORTHY bit to ON. The latter approach is also more granular, and therefore safer. You should never register an assembly with SQL Server (especially with EXTERNAL_ACCESS or UNSAFE permissions) without thoroughly reviewing the source code of the assembly to make sure that its actions do not pose an operational or security risk.

In the previous code, you created a login called ExternalAccess_Login from the asymmetric key ExternalAccess_Key. When you created the assembly using the command-line option csc.exe, you specified the /keyfile option. Because of that option, the assembly GetFileDetails.dll was signed. You are now registering that key into SQL Server because in the CREATE ASYMMETRIC KEY statement in this code you specified the EXECUTABLE FILE option to point to the signed DLL. You have granted the EXTERNAL_ACCESS permission to ExternalAccess_Login. Then you create the assembly with the CREATE ASSEMBLY command. The assembly is now registered in the CLRDB database. Remember that once the assembly is registered in the database, you don't need the assembly file .dll, so you can move your database from server to server without worrying about that file. Of course, you have to put the source code from which you have created the DLL into your source control so that in the future, if you need to modify anything, you will do that in the source. If you want to set the TRUSTWORTHY bit to 1 for the database, you do not need to perform any of these steps except for creating the assembly.

Now open the CreateTVF.sql file and run it. The code is shown here:

```
USE CLRDB
GO

IF OBJECT_ID('GetFileDetails') IS NOT NULL
DROP FUNCTION GetFileDetails
GO
CREATE FUNCTION GetFileDetails(@directory nvarchar(256))
RETURNS
TABLE
(
 Name nvarchar(max)
,CreationTime datetime
,LastAccessTime datetime
,LastWriteTime datetime
,IsDirectory bit
,IsReadOnly bit
,Length bigint
)
```

```
AS EXTERNAL NAME [GetFileDetails].[FileDetails].[GetFileDetails]
GO


IF OBJECT_ID('GetFileDetailsWithImpersonation') IS NOT NULL
DROP FUNCTION GetFileDetailsWithImpersonation
GO
CREATE FUNCTION GetFileDetailsWithImpersonation(@directory nvarchar(256))
RETURNS
TABLE
(
 Name nvarchar(max)
,CreationTime datetime
,LastAccessTime datetime
,LastWriteTime datetime
,IsDirectory bit
,IsReadOnly bit
,Length bigint
)
AS EXTERNAL NAME [GetFileDetails].[FileDetails].[GetFileDetailsWithImpersonation]
GO
```

You are creating two Table Value Functions, GetFileDetails and GetFileDetailsWithImpersonation. The T-SQL function GetFileDetails calls the method GetFileDetails of the class FileDetails from the assembly GetFileDetails. The T-SQL function GetFileDetailsWithImpersonation calls the method GetFileDetailsWithImpersonation of the class FileDetails from the assembly GetFile Details. Now you have mapped the T-SQL TVF to the methods in the assembly GetFileDetails.dll.

Now it's time to test these functions. Open the file TestGetFileDetails.sql. The code is shown here:

```
USE CLRDB
GO
DECLARE @TestDir nvarchar(256);
SELECT @TestDir = 'D:\test'

SELECT [Name], CreationTime, LastAccessTime, LastWriteTime,
   IsDirectory, IsReadOnly, Length
FROM GetFileDetails(@TestDir)

SELECT [Name], CreationTime, LastAccessTime, LastWriteTime,
   IsDirectory, IsReadOnly, Length
FROM GetFileDetailsWithImpersonation(@TestDir)
```

In the preceding script, you set the variable @TestDir to 'D:\test' because you want to list all the files in the directory D:\test. You should set the permission on the directory D:\test so that only you have permission to that directory. If you have set the permission correctly, you will see the results shown in Figure 8-20 when you run the script.

The first function, GetFileDetails, fails with an Unauthorized Access exception. Because this assembly is registered with the EXTERNAL_ACCESS permission set, SQL Server uses the SQL Server service account to access the external resource, and because you set the permission on the directory D:\test so that only you can access it, the function failed. Of course, in this case the SQL Server Service account is not running under the security context with which you have run the function.

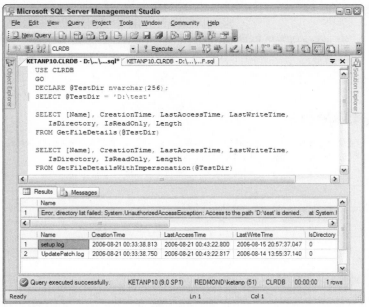

Figure 8-20

The second function, `GetFileDetailsWithImpersonation`, succeeded because you set the impersonation to the user who is connecting to SQL Server to execute the function. Now SQL Server will access the directory `D:\test` under the security context of the user executing the function, rather than the SQL Server service account.

ALTER ASSEMBLY

You can change the properties of an assembly or change the assembly code using the ALTER ASSEMBLY statement. Reload the assembly with the modified code and it will refresh the assembly to the latest copy of the .NET Framework module that holds its implementation, adding or removing files associated with it:

```
ALTER ASSEMBLY GetFileDetails
FROM '\\MyMachine\Assembly\GetFileDetails.dll'
```

If you decide that an assembly should only be called by another assembly and not from outside, you can change the visibility of the assembly as follows:

```
ALTER ASSEMBLY GetFileDetails
SET VISIBILTY = OFF
```

For full syntax details, you can refer to Books Online.

DROP ASSEMBLY

You can drop an assembly using the DROP ASSEMBLY statement. If the assembly is referenced by other objects, such as user-defined functions or stored procedures, you cannot drop the assembly until you drop those dependent objects:

```
DROP ASSEMBLY GetFileDetails
```

There is a NO DEPENDENTS option to the DROP ASSEMBLY statement. If you don't specify this option, all the dependent assemblies will also be dropped:

```
DROP ASSEMBLY GetFileDetails WITH NO DEPENDENTS
```

Cataloging Objects

You can get information about different CLR objects, such as CLR stored procedures and CLR functions, using the queries described in the following sections.

Assemblies

The following are some queries from catalog views you can use to get more information on registered assemblies.

The sys.assemblies view gives you all the registered assemblies in the database:

```
SELECT * FROM sys.assemblies
```

The following view will give you all the files associated with the assembly:

```
SELECT a.Name AS AssemblyName, f.name AS AssemblyFileName
FROM sys.assembly_files f
JOIN sys.assemblies a
  ON a.assembly_id = f.assembly_id
```

The following view will provide information about the assembly, its associated class, the methods in the class, and the SQL object associated with each assembly:

```
SELECT
 a.Name AS AssemblyName
,m.Assembly_Class
,m.Assembly_Method
,OBJECT_NAME(um.object_id) AS SQL_Object_Associated
,so.type_desc AS SQL_Object_Type
,u.name AS Execute_As_Principal_Name
FROM sys.assembly_modules m
JOIN sys.assemblies a
  ON a.assembly_id = m.assembly_id
LEFT JOIN sys.module_assembly_usages um
  ON um.assembly_id = a.assembly_id
LEFT JOIN sys.all_objects so
  ON so.object_id = um.object_id
LEFT JOIN sys.sysusers u
  ON u.uid = m.Execute_As_Principal_id
```

CLR Stored Procedures

This query will give you the CLR stored procedure and other details associated with it:

```
SELECT
 schema_name(sp.schema_id) + '.' + sp.[name] AS [SPName]
,sp.create_date
,sp.modify_date
,sa.permission_set_desc AS [Access]
FROM sys.procedures AS sp
JOIN sys.module_assembly_usages AS sau
  ON sp.object_id = sau.object_id
JOIN sys.assemblies AS sa
  ON sau.assembly_id = sa.assembly_id
WHERE sp.type = 'PC'
```

CLR Trigger Metadata

This query will give you the CLR trigger's details:

```
SELECT
 schema_name(so.schema_id) + '.' + tr.[name] AS [TriggerName]
,schema_name(so.schema_id) + '.' + object_name(tr.parent_id) AS [Parent]
,a.name AS AssemblyName
,te.type_desc AS [Trigger Type]
,te.is_first
,te.is_last
,tr.create_date
,tr.modify_date
,a.permission_set_desc AS Aseembly_Permission
,tr.is_disabled
,tr.is_instead_of_trigger
FROM sys.triggers AS tr
JOIN sys.objects AS so
  ON tr.object_id = so.object_id
JOIN sys.trigger_events AS te
  ON tr.object_id = te.object_id
JOIN sys.module_assembly_usages AS mau
  ON tr.object_id = mau.object_id
JOIN sys.assemblies AS a
  ON mau.assembly_id = a.assembly_id
WHERE tr.type_desc = N'CLR_TRIGGER'
```

CLR Scalar Function

The following query will give you the CLR scalar function:

```
SELECT
 schema_name(so.schema_id) + '.' + so.[name] AS [FunctionName]
,a.name AS AssemblyName
,so.create_date
,so.modify_date
,a.permission_set_desc AS Aseembly_Permission
```

```
FROM sys.objects AS so
JOIN sys.module_assembly_usages AS sau
  ON so.object_id = sau.object_id
JOIN sys.assemblies AS a
  ON sau.assembly_id = a.assembly_id
WHERE so.type_desc = N'CLR_SCALAR_FUNCTION'
```

CLR Table Valued Function

This query will give you all CLR Table Valued Functions:

```
SELECT
  schema_name(so.schema_id) + N'.' + so.[name] AS [FunctionName]
,a.name AS AssemblyName
,so.create_date, so.modify_date
,a.permission_set_desc AS Aseembly_Permission
FROM sys.objects AS so
JOIN sys.module_assembly_usages AS sau
  ON so.object_id = sau.object_id
JOIN sys.assemblies AS a
  ON sau.assembly_id = a.assembly_id
WHERE so.type_desc = N'CLR_TABLE_VALUED_FUNCTION'
```

CLR User-Defined Aggregates

The following query will give you the CLR user-defined aggregates:

```
SELECT
  schema_name(so.schema_id) + N'.' + so.[name] AS [FunctionName]
,a.name AS AssemblyName
,so.create_date
,so.modify_date
,a.permission_set_desc AS Aseembly_Permission
FROM sys.objects AS so
JOIN sys.module_assembly_usages AS mau
  ON so.object_id = mau.object_id
JOIN sys.assemblies AS a
  ON mau.assembly_id = a.assembly_id
WHERE so.type_desc = N'AGGREGATE_FUNCTION'
```

CLR User Defined Types

This query will provide a list of the CLR user-defined types:

```
SELECT
  st.[name] AS [TypeName]
,a.name AS [AssemblyName]
,a.permission_set_desc AS AssemblyName
,a.create_date AssemblyCreateDate
,st.max_length
,st.[precision]
,st.scale
,st.collation_name
,st.is_nullable
FROM sys.types AS st
```

```
JOIN sys.type_assembly_usages AS tau
  ON st.user_type_id = tau.user_type_id
JOIN sys.assemblies AS a
  ON tau.assembly_id = a.assembly_id
```

Application Domains

We talked earlier about application domains. Here we look at some DMVs that will give you more information about AppDomains in your servers. The following DMV will provide information about all the AppDomains currently loaded and their state:

```
SELECT * FROM sys.dm_clr_appdomains
```

Recall that an AppDomain is created for each database. An AppDomain has different states described in the column *state* in the DMV sys.dm_clr_appdomains. The following list describes the different possible AppDomain states:

❑ E_APPDOMAIN_CREATING: An AppDomain is being created. After the AppDomain is created, you will see the following type of entry in the SQL error log:.

```
AppDomain 70 (InitiatorDB.dbo[runtime].69) created.
```

❑ E_APPDOMAIN_SHARED: An AppDomain is ready for use by multiple users. This is the state you will normally see after the AppDomain is loaded.

❑ E_APPDOMAIN_SINGLEUSER: An AppDomain is ready to use by a single user to perform the DDL operations (such as CREATE ASSEMBLY).

❑ E_APPDOMAIN_DOOMED: An AppDomain is about to be unloaded, but cannot be yet because of some threads still executing in it.

❑ E_APPDOMAIN_UNLOADING: SQL is telling the CLR to unload the AppDomain, usually because an assembly is dropped or altered. You will see the following type of message in the SQL error log when this happens:

```
AppDomain 70 (InitiatorDB.dbo[runtime].69) is marked for unload due to common
language runtime (CLR) or security data definition language (DDL) operations.

AppDomain 70 (InitiatorDB.dbo[runtime].69) unloaded.
```

❑ E_APPDOMAIN_UNLOADED: The CLR has unloaded the AppDomain. This is usually the result of an escalation procedure due to ThreadAbort, OutOfMemory, or an unhandled exception in user code. You will see an error message in the error log if any of these conditions occur before unloading the app domain.

❑ E_APPDOMAIN_ENQUEUE_DESTROY: An AppDomain is unloaded in the CLR and ready to be destroyed by SQL.

❑ E_APPDOMAIN_DESTROY: An App Domain is being destroyed by SQL.

❑ E_APPDOMAIN_ZOMBIE: An App Domain has been destroyed but all the references to it have not yet been cleaned up.

This view is helpful when the AppDomain in question is loaded, but it doesn't help much when the AppDomain is unloaded. The following query will give you all the states an AppDomain has gone through so you can see what exactly happened to it:

```
SELECT
 Timestamp
,rec.value('/Record[1]/AppDomain[1]/@address', 'nvarchar(10)') as Address
,rec.value('/Record[1]/AppDomain[1]/@dbId', 'int') as DBID
,d.name AS DatabaseName
,rec.value('/Record[1]/AppDomain[1]/@ownerId', 'int') as OwnerID
,u.Name AS AppDomainOwner
,rec.value('/Record[1]/AppDomain[1]/@type', 'nvarchar(32)') as AppDomainType
,rec.value('/Record[1]/AppDomain[1]/State[1]', 'nvarchar(32)')as AppDomainState
FROM (
      SELECT timestamp, cast(record as xml) as rec
      FROM sys.dm_os_ring_buffers
      WHERE ring_buffer_type = 'RING_BUFFER_CLRAPPDOMAIN'
      ) T
JOIN sys.sysdatabases d
  ON d.dbid = rec.value('/Record[1]/AppDomain[1]/@dbId', 'int')
JOIN sys.sysusers u
  on u.uid = rec.value('/Record[1]/AppDomain[1]/@ownerId', 'int')
ORDER BY timestamp DESC
```

Note that the DMV used in the `sys.dm_os_ring_buffers` query is not documented, so you should not rely on it for future releases of SQL Server. The `DatabaseName` column will indicate which database the AppDomain belongs to and what stages it has gone through.

Performance Monitoring

You can use Windows System Monitor, DMVs, and SQL Profiler for SQLCLR performance monitoring.

System Monitor

You can use Windows System Monitor (`PerfMon.exe`) to monitor CLR activities for SQL Server. Use the counter in the .NET CLR group in System Monitor. Choose the `sqlservr` instance when you monitor CLR counters for SQL Server. Use the following counters to understand the health and activity of the programs running under the SQL-hosted environment:

❑ **.NET CLR Memory:** Provides detailed information about the three types of CLR heap memory, as well as garbage collection. These counters can be used to monitor CLR memory usage and to flag alerts if the memory used gets too large. If code is copying a lot of data into memory, you may have to check the code and take a different approach to reduce memory consumption, or add more memory.

❑ **.NET CLR Loading:** SQL Server isolates code between databases by using an AppDomain. This set of counters enables monitoring of the number of AppDomains and the number of assemblies loaded in the system. You can also use some DMVs for AppDomain monitoring as described in the previous section.

❑ **.NET CLR Exceptions:** The Exceptions/Sec counter provides you with a good idea of how many exceptions the code is generating. The values vary from application to application because sometime developers use exceptions for some functionality, so you should monitor overtime to set the baseline and go from there.

SQL Profiler

SQL Profiler is not much use for monitoring the CLR because it has only one event for the CLR, called *Assembly Load*. This event tells you when an assembly is loaded with the message "Assembly Load Succeeded." If the load fails, it will provide a message indicating which assembly load failed and some error code.

DMVs

The DMVs related to SQL CLR provide very useful information on CLR memory usage, which assemblies are currently loaded, the current requests waiting in CLR, and more. The following sections describe some queries that help in monitoring the CLR.

SQL CLR Memory Usage

You can find out how much memory SQL CLR is using in KB with the following query:

```
SELECT single_pages_kb + multi_pages_kb + virtual_memory_committed_kb
FROM sys.dm_os_memory_clerks WHERE type = 'MEMORYCLERK_SQLCLR'
```

The first column, `single_pages_kb`, is the memory allocated in the SQL buffer pool. The second column, `multi_pages_kb`, indicates the memory allocated by the SQL CLR host outside of the buffer pool. The third column, `virtual_memory_committed_kb`, indicates the amount of memory allocated by the CLR directly through bulk allocation (instead of heap allocation) through SQL server.

Note that you will see a second row with 0 if you don't have a NUMA (non-uniform memory access) system. In a NUMA system, each node has its own memory clerk, so in that case, you would have to add the node totals to get the total memory usage.

Loaded Assemblies

The following query will give you all the currently loaded assemblies:.

```
SELECT
 a.name AS Assembly_Name
,ad.Appdomain_Name
,clr.Load_Time
FROM sys.dm_clr_loaded_assemblies AS clr
JOIN sys.assemblies AS a
  ON clr.assembly_id = a.assembly_id
JOIN sys.dm_clr_appdomains AS ad
  ON clr.appdomain_address = ad.appdomain_address
```

CLR Request Status

The following query will give you current request status in the SQL CLR:

```
SELECT session_id, request_id, start_time, status, command, database_id,
wait_type, wait_time, last_wait_type, wait_resource, cpu_time,
total_elapsed_time, nest_level, executing_managed_code
FROM sys.dm_exec_requests
WHERE executing_managed_code = 1
```

Time Spent in SQL CLR By a Query

The next query provides interesting statistics on a CLR query, such as execution count (how many times that query was executed), logical reads, physical reads, time elapsed, and last execution time:

```
SELECT
(SELECT text FROM sys.dm_exec_sql_text(qs.sql_handle)) AS query_text, qs.*
FROM sys.dm_exec_query_stats AS qs
WHERE qs.total_clr_time > 0
```

Finding the .NET Framework Version in SQL Server

If the .NET Framework is loaded you can use the following query to determine which .NET Framework version is used in SQL Server. (The .NET load is a lazy load in SQL Server. It is only loaded when any CLR assembly is called for the first time.)

```
SELECT value AS [.NET FrameWork Version]
FROM sys.dm_clr_properties
WHERE name = 'version'
```

If the .NET Framework is not loaded and you want to find out which .NET Framework version SQL Server is using, run the following query:

```
SELECT Product_Version AS [.NET FrameWork Version]
FROM sys.dm_os_loaded_modules
WHERE name LIKE N'%\MSCOREE.DLL'
```

Summary

With the SQL Server Service Broker, messaging is now deeply integrated into the database engine. The Service Broker provides an excellent platform on which to build a reliable, scalable, and secure messaging system. You can base your service-oriented application on the Service Broker, which adds reliability and fault tolerance to this approach. The Service Broker also simplifies the design, construction, deployment, and servicing of service-oriented applications. With the Service Broker, you can build asynchronous applications using T-SQL language with reliable message transport. You have learned how to build the messaging application and how to administer it in this chapter.

With CLR integration, SQL Server has now become an application platform along with its usual database engine capabilities. You learned how to create an assembly and register it into SQL Server. You also learned how to set permissions on assemblies and maintain them. The CLR's Framework class libraries are categorized according to degree of safety, which will alleviate some concerns DBAs have.

With the key concepts out of the way, you can now drill into more specific areas to manage, such as security. In the Chapter 9, you will learn much more about securing your SQL Server.

9

Securing the Database Engine

In this chapter, you learn how to secure your data and the core database engine. As you can imagine, security is a huge topic and can easily turn into an entire book by itself. This chapter covers core topics such as setting up your logins and users for the minimal data access to do their job. This is called the *principle of least access*. Also, we cover how to do encryption inside T-SQL, which is now part of SQL Server 2005.

Logins

Logins are the essential element for any person who would like to connect to your SQL Server instance. There is a key differentiating factor when a DBA uses the word *login* versus the word *user*. A login grants you instance-level rights to an instance, and a user gives you database-level rights to a database. It's similar to the login giving you the key to the front door with no access to any room, unless you have the user key. Certain types of rights at server-level roles will grant you rights to do anything you'd like to do, almost like a skeleton key in a building. We'll cover those server roles in a moment.

Windows vs. SQL Server Authentication

There are two types of logins you can enable in SQL Server: Windows and SQL Server authentication. Windows authentication is the most secure solution for most environments, if you have the luxury of using this type of authentication. With Windows authentication, you would grant the rights to the database to the user's Windows login. A better solution would be to create a group that the Windows users can be added to for the application and then grant the Windows group rights to the SQL Server. This way, you have only to create the SQL login and assign rights a single time, and the group will delegate the user administration to the Active Directory administrator.

This will simplify laws such as Sarbanes-Oxley that your company must comply with, since access to the database is controlled through a single mechanism.

The best thing about Windows authentication is the user will have a single user name and password to remember. When the user wishes to log in to the database, his or her Windows credentials are passed to the server automatically, and the user is never prompted for a user name and password. Additionally, the domain policies that you set up for changing the user's login and lockouts apply automatically for SQL Server. You could also use domain policies to lockout the user during certain hours.

With all that said, there are some drawbacks to using Windows authentication. If your server is in a different domain from your users and the two domains don't trust each other, you have to use SQL Server authentication. You now have the ability in SQL Server authentication to lock out logins and force them to change their passwords. Some of these features are only available in Windows 2003 or later.

Creating the Login

Granting a person rights to your SQL Server and the various databases is vastly different from how it was in SQL Server 2000, but the screens do look similar to those of SQL Server 2000. To create a login in the Management Studio interface, connect to the server you wish to add the login to and click the Security group. Right-click Logins and select New Login.

You are first faced with the decision of whether to use Windows or SQL Server authentication. If you want Windows authentication, type the Windows local or domain user account name or the group you wish to grant access to. Type the domain name first and then the user name, separated by a backslash, like this: DomainName\AccountName. Alternatively, you can search for the login by clicking Search. If you wish to add a SQL Server authenticated login, just select that radio box and type the login name and password.

If you have chosen to use SQL Server authentication, as shown in Figure 9-1, you have the option to enforce password policies and expiration. You can also force the user to change his or her password the first time the user connects. If you check Enforce Password Policy, your outcome may vary based on the operating system that you have installed. In Windows 2003, this checkbox enforces the policy using the Windows 2003 NetValidatePasswordPolicy API, which ensures that the password meets the following criteria by default:

❑ Must not contain all or part of the login name

❑ Must be at least eight characters long

❑ Must contain three of the following strong password options:

> ❑ Uppercase letters
>
> ❑ Lowercase letters
>
> ❑ Numbers 0-9
>
> ❑ Special characters like ! or ^.

In Windows 2000 and Windows XP, the criteria for passwords are weaker. The check ensures that your password is not blank and that it does not contain the login or computer name. The last check it makes is to ensure that your password does not contain any obvious passwords like "admin," "administrator," "password," "sa," or "sysadmin." If you type a weak password when setting up the login or when changing the password, you will receive this error:

```
Msg 15118, Level 16, State 1, Line 1
Password validation failed. The password does not meet Windows policy requirements
because it is not complex enough.
```

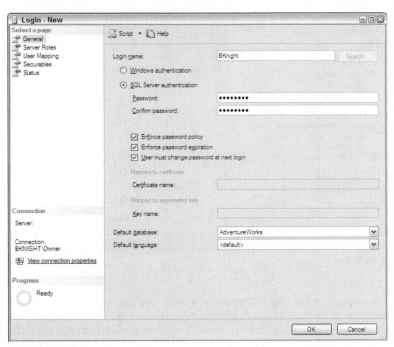

Figure 9-1

It is important to note that passwords are case sensitive in SQL Server 2005 but user names are not. In Windows 2003, you adjust the password policy in the Local System Settings console that can be found in Administrative Tools (shown in Figure 9-2). Most DBAs may not be familiar with the console, but SQL Server password and lockout policies are tied to the console. For example, the default configuration may not have the Account Lockout setting enabled. You set this setting to the number of failed logins that will cause a SQL Server login or Windows login to be locked out of your server. You can then also set how long the account will be locked out by adjusting the Account Lockout Duration setting in the Account Lockout Policy folder, as shown in Figure 9-2.

As a DBA, you can force the user to be unlocked by going to the Status page for the login. The point of the account-lockout feature is to deter hackers from performing a brute-force attack against your system where they rotate through a list of passwords and attempt to break your password. Previously in SQL Server 2000, you could log that you were being brute-force attacked but couldn't do anything about it other than manually remove the login from having access.

In the Password Policy folder of the Local Security Setting console in Windows 2003, you can also enable complex passwords for SQL Server logins. In this folder, you can also specify how long your password must be, how often the password must be reset, and how long password history is kept.

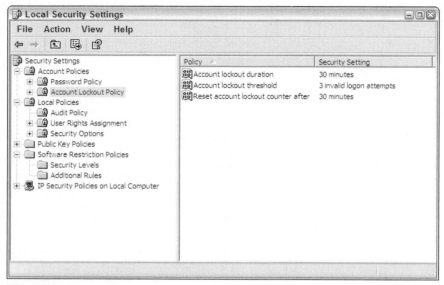

Figure 9-2

Back in the General page of the Login Properties screen, you can set a default database for the login by selecting the database from the Default Database drop-down box. Even though the default database is set to master by default, you should always make it a practice to change this database to the database where the user will spend most of his or her time. This will make it easier for your users, since they will not have to change databases once they log in to the server. It also helps keep clutter out of your master database. Oftentimes, a DBA or user will connect to SQL Server and run a script that they think they're running against the proper database. Instead, they may run the script in the master database, potentially creating objects in that database by accident.

The downside to setting the database to something other than master is that if the login does not have access to the database you selected, the user will not be able to login. For example, consider a user named bknight who connected by default to the database called Reports. If you were to delete the Reports database, or remove bknight's access to the Reports database, he would receive the error shown as follows:

```
Cannot connect to <instance name>
Cannot open user default database. Login failed.
Login failed for user '<user name>'. (Microsoft SQL Server, Error: 4064)
```

The last option on the General page is to set the login's default language. The default language is set to the server's default language by default, but you can change that by selecting the new language from the drop-down box. This option will essentially change the error and informational messages that the SQL Server returns to the user's native language (if available). The SQL Server tools will still have all their menus in English unless you have installed the multilingual SQL Server.

There are other options on this page that relate to certificates and keys, but you can't add those through this screen. Those options give the login a certificate to use for encrypting and decrypting data and can be set through the CREATE LOGIN command, which we'll discuss in a moment.

Defining Server Roles

Technically, you could click OK at this point, and the login would be created. At this stage, though, the login has no rights to do anything in the SQL Server or in the database, since all you've given the user is the key to the door. Next, click the Server Roles page. Server roles give a user the right to perform a universal function across the entire server. For example, the sysadmin role is the equivalent of the skeleton key mentioned earlier. This role gives the user the right to do anything he or she would like to do. If you have this option checked, there's no reason to check any other option, since the sysadmin role trumps all other permissions, including explicit denial of rights. The following table shows all the roles and the rights you give a user by checking each role:

Server Role	Rights Given
bulkadmin	Can run the BULK INSERT statement
dbcreator	Can create, alter, restore, and drop databases
diskadmin	Can manage the disk file
processadmin	Can terminate sessions connecting to your SQL Server
securityadmin	Can create logins and grant logins rights to a database. Can also reset passwords and alter the login.
serveradmin	Can shut down the SQL Server and alter the instance's configuration
setupadmin	Can add and remove linked servers
sysadmin	Can do anything on the server

Granting Database Rights

In the User Mappings page, you grant the login rights to the individual database. To do this, check each database that you wish grant login rights to. Then click the database role that you wish to give the user, if any. Once you check the database to assign the login rights to, the login is automatically granted access to the public role. The public role is special in that every user in the database belongs to it. You can also see in Figure 9-3 that when you assign the login rights to the database, user-defined roles show in the role membership list below the list of databases, as in the role called Test. We'll talk much more about this in a moment. The list of system roles that appears gives users various rights to the database. As you check the database, you can also assign the user a default schema. This, too, will be discussed in this chapter a little later. The following table lists how these rights work.

Database Role	Rights Given
db_accessadmin	Can add or remove access for a login
db_backupoperator	Can back up the specified database
db_datareader	Can read from every table in the database unless the access is explicitly denied
db_datawriter	Explicitly grants the user permission to run an UPDATE, DELETE, or INSERT statement for the database
db_ddladmin	Can run any DDL statement inside the database, including creating stored procedures or tables
db_denydatareader	Explicitly prevents the user from reading data
db_denydatawriter	Explicitly prevents the user from running an UPDATE, DELETE, or INSERT statement for the database
db_owner	Is an administrator of the database and can perform any function

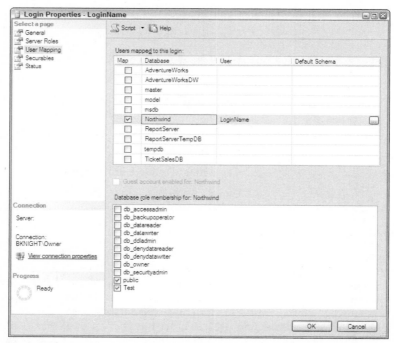

Figure 9-3

Defining Access to Objects

Oftentimes, you need to delegate security to a login without giving them overarching security like sysadmin. For example, you may want a user to be able to run Profiler but not be a sysadmin, which you had to do in SQL Server 2000. You can do this in the Securables page of the Login dialog box (shown in Figure 9-4), where you can secure to a very granular level on almost any type of server-level function that the login can perform.

To grant or deny a login explicit rights, click Add; then select the type of object that you'd like to list in the below grid. For example, if you select "All Objects of the Types," all securables will display. You can then check Grant or Deny to give rights or take rights away from the login. You can also check With Grant. The With Grant option not only grants the login rights but also allows the user to delegate those rights to someone else.

As of service pack 1 of SQL Server 2005, you will not see what was already checked in the Securables page by default. You will have to search for the object again and it will then display as already checked.

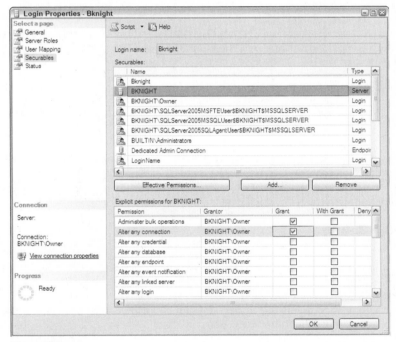

Figure 9-4

The Status Page

The final page is the Status page. In this page, you can unlock someone's login. You can also disable the login from accessing your system temporarily without having to delete the account. You cannot lockout someone's account as a sysadmin. This can only be done by the SQL Server instance. You can, however, unlock an account as a sysadmin by unchecking "Login is locked out."

Logins with T-SQL

You can take the same actions that you applied in Management Studio for creating a login and apply them by using T-SQL. It's often very important to know how to do these T-SQL commands in order to script a reproducible installation. Only the essential commands are covered in this section, rather than each minor detail. First, to create a login, use the CREATE LOGIN command. The command has changed since SQL Server 2000 to handle the additional options. To create a SQL Server authenticated login called LoginName, you can use the following syntax:

```
CREATE LOGIN LoginName WITH PASSWORD = 'StRonGPassWord1', CHECK_POLICY=ON,
CHECK_EXPIRATION=ON;
```

Ultimately, the CHECK_POLICY piece of this syntax (which checks the password's strength) is not required, since it's on by default if not specified. The CHECK_EXPIRATION option, which enables the password to be expired, is not on by default and is required if you want to enable the feature. If you wish to grant access for a Windows account to access your SQL Server, you can use the following syntax:

```
CREATE LOGIN [Domain\AccountName] FROM WINDOWS;
```

To add the login to a given server role, you can use the sp_addsrvrolemember stored procedure. The stored procedure accepts two parameters: the login name and the server role. The following example shows you how to add the login bknight into the sysadmin role.

```
EXEC sp_addsrvrolemember 'bknight', 'sysadmin';
```

Adding a login to a database role and a database as a user is discussed in the "Users" section of this chapter.

Another handy new function in SQL Server 2005 is the LOGINPROPERTY function. With this function, you can determine which properties are turned on for the given login. Developers can use these checks to build functionality into their application to simplify the administration of an application's users. You can use the function with the following syntax:

```
LOGINPROPERTY ( 'login_name' ,
                { 'IsLocked' | 'IsExpired' | 'IsMustChange'
                | 'BadPasswordCount' | 'BadPasswordTime'
                | 'HistoryLength' | 'LockoutTime'
                | 'PasswordLastSetTime' | 'PasswordHash' }
```

For example, if you wish to determine if the login name bknight must change his password the next time he logs in, you can use the following code:

```
SELECT LOGINPROPERTY('bknight', 'IsMustChange');
```

If the login needs to be changed, a boolean 1 will be returned.

The Security Hierarchy

Security can be confusing when you have a conflict between an explicit denial of rights conflicting with an explicit grant of rights. Granting access to an object or a role gives the user rights to a database unless the user has been denied that same access. The main thing to point out is that a denial of access always outweighs a grant of access, with the exception of the sysadmin role at a server. The other type of right that you can perform is a revoke. Revoke essentially removes any rights (grant or deny) from the user and is a neutral position.

For example, say that John has a login into SQL Server called DomainName\John. He is also a part of an Active Directory group called Accounting. John has been granted access to the Salary table, but the Accounting group has explicitly been denied access to the table. In this scenario, he would be denied access to the table. The following table takes this example a bit further and shows you what combinations of permissions would result in denial of granting of access.

Accounting Group	John	Effective Rights for John
Granted access to table	Denied access to table	Denied
Denied access to table	Granted access to table	Denied
db_datareader	No rights	Read access to all tables
db_datawriter	Db_denydatareader	Can write but not read
db_denydatareader	Db_owner	Can do anything except read
db_denydatareader	sysadmin	Can do anything on server
Sysadmin	Denied all access from tables	Can do anything on server

Additionally, it's important to note that if you grant a user rights to the db_datareader database role, he will not have rights to any stored procedures or functions. Typically, if you grant a user access to stored procedures, he will not need access to the underlying tables. The reason we use the word *typically* is that there are exceptions to the rule. The main exception is in the case of dynamic queries inside the stored procedure. In that case, you will need to grant access to the underlying tables. The way around this from a security perspective is context switching, which we will cover momentarily.

The Guest Account

The guest account is a special user in SQL Server that does not exist as a login. Essentially, if you grant the guest account access to your database, anyone who has a login into SQL Server will implicitly have access to your database and be given any rights that the guest account has been granted. Granting the guest account access to your database creates a security hole in your database and should never be done. The only tables that should ever have the guest account enabled are the master, msdb, and tempdb databases. This allows users access to create jobs, create temporary objects, and connect to SQL Server.

BUILTIN\Administrators Login

Another special type of login that could pose some security issues for you is BUILTIN\Administrators. This login grants implicit sysadmin rights to your database server to anyone in the local Administrators group for the Windows machine. In some environments, this may be fine, but in most environments, you don't want a Windows administrator to have access to sensitive data, like salary information. This creates a challenge if you're trying to become HIPAA or Sarbanes-Oxley compliant as well, since you have someone not explicitly given rights to become a sysadmin on your system.

If this is a problem for you, you're better off dropping the login. Before you do this, though, ensure that the SQL Server service accounts have a login to SQL Server and have been given sysadmin rights. These logins should be granted access by default through groups named something like BKNIGHT\SQLServer 2005MSSQLUser$BKNIGHT$MSSQLSERVER (where BKNIGHT is the machine name).

Granting Profiler Access

Previously in SQL Server 2000, you had to be a sysadmin to use the Profiler application. This created a bottleneck for DBAs, since access was not given away lightly and Profiler was sometimes the only tool that could be used to debug certain problems. In SQL Server 2005, you can allow a login access to create a Profiler trace without having to give them high-level authority by granting the user ALTER TRACE rights in the Securables page. You can also use this syntax to grant them the right:

```
GRANT ALTER TRACE TO [LoginName]
```

Credentials

Credentials typically are used to map a SQL Server authenticated account to a Windows account. You can also use this feature to give an account access to items outside the SQL Server instance, like a file share. This is used often in SQL CLR and, most important, to allow SSIS packages to impersonate Windows accounts when running. This is all done through setting up proxy accounts, which will be discussed later.

You can create a credential through Management Studio or through T-SQL. To create a credential in Management Studio, right-click the Credentials folder in the Security tree and select New Credential. In the New Credential dialog box, type a name for the credential, as shown in Figure 9-5, and select which Windows identity you'd like that credential to impersonate. Finally, type the password to protect the credential.

In T-SQL, you use the CREATE CREDENTIAL T-SQL command to create a new credential. The IDENTITY keyword specifies which Windows account you wish to map the credential to, and the SECRET keyword specifies the password. To create the same credential we created in Figure 9-6, use the following syntax:

```
CREATE CREDENTIAL [WindowsAdmin]
WITH IDENTITY = N'BKNIGHT\Administrator',
SECRET = N'password'
```

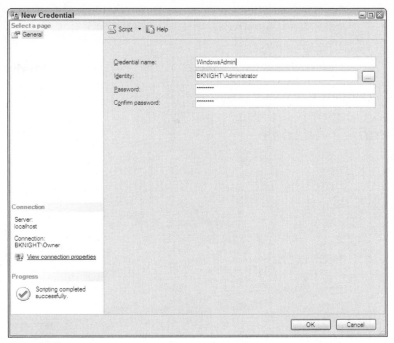

Figure 9-5

Users

When a login is granted access to a database, a user is created in the database with the same name as the login by default. The user is given specific rights to database roles or to granular objects inside the database, such as EXECUTE rights on a stored procedure. One method to create a user shown earlier is through the Login Properties dialog box. In that dialog box, you can go to the User Mappings page to check which databases you wish to add login in and which roles you wish to assign to the user.

A person assigned the db_owner database role would not have access to the Login Properties dialog box, though, unless he or she were a member of a specific server role, like sysadmin. The alternative way to do this, which most DBAs prefer, is to go to the individual database, right-click the Users folder under Security, and select New User. The window shown in Figure 9-6 appears.

First, select the ellipsis button next to the Login Name option. Select the login name that you wish to add to the database. Then type the user name that the login will be mapped to. The Default Schema field specifies the schema that the user's objects will be created in and selected from. If you don't specify for this optional setting, the objects will be created with the user's name, like UserName.TableName. If the user owns a given schema, that will show in the "Schemas Owned By User" grid. (Schemas will be covered much more in a later section of this chapter.) Last in this screen, you must specify which database roles you wish the user to be a member of. (Database roles are discussed in detail in the login section of this chapter.) If you've created user-defined database roles, they'll show up in this list as well.

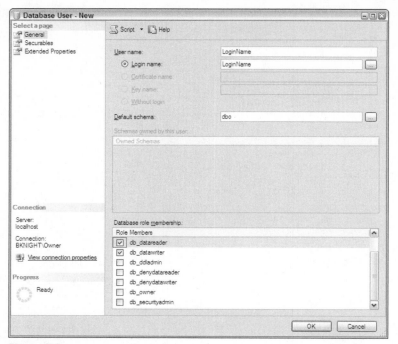

Figure 9-6

Granular Permissions

Let's take a look at a quick common example. If you were to grant a user db_datareader and db_datawriter rights, he would be able to read and write to any table in the database. He would not be able to execute stored procedures, however. Generally speaking, you will want to have all your data access through stored procedures. There are numerous reasons for that, which are listed in Chapters 6 and 7, but one of them is security. If you can encapsulate access through stored procedures, you can add auditing and guarantee that all access to your data will be done a certain way.

If the user had the rights to the database as shown in Figure 9-7 with no EXECUTE rights granted to the stored procedure, the user would receive an error like this if he tried to access any stored procedure:

```
Msg 229, Level 14, State 5, Procedure SelectSproc, Line 1
EXECUTE permission denied on object 'SelectSproc', database 'TicketSalesDB', schema
'dbo'.
```

If the user had stored procedure access, he would likely not need access to the underlying tables. There are exceptions to that rule in the case of dynamic queries. There are ways around that, though, by using context switching. To allow your users access to stored procedures, you need either to grant them access to each stored procedure or grant them overarching rights to the database, but there is no database role for EXECUTE rights. The disadvantage to granting the user access to each stored procedure is that it becomes a bit of a management headache. The disadvantage to granting overarching rights to every stored procedure is that you may have stored procedures you don't wish the user to access.

For the purpose of this example, let's look at both situations. Typically, in an enterprise application environment, a DBA would be granular and would grant a user access to each stored procedure individually. This is usually done when the DDL is originally created.

For either example, you go would go to the Securables tab of the Database User dialog box and click Add. Even if you have already granted granular permissions, they will not display in the permission grid until you click Add. For the overarching permission, you would want to show the database securables. For individual rights to each stored procedure, you would want to display each stored procedure.

Both of these scenarios can be seen in Figure 9-7. By selecting the database securable, you can select Execute from the Grant column, and now the user can execute any stored procedure in the database. If you select an individual stored procedure, you can select Execute to grant rights to execute the single stored procedure. If you check the securable from the With Grant column, the user will be able not only to execute the stored procedure but also to give others rights to do so as well.

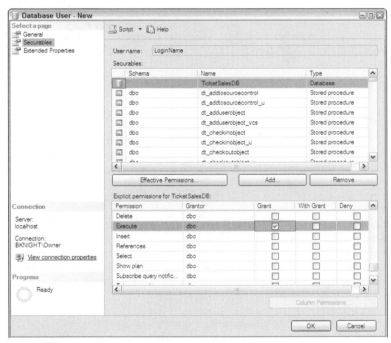

Figure 9-7

On a stored procedure or almost any other database object, there are other securable actions that you may wish to enable. If you wish your developers to be able to see the schema in production but not alter the schema, you could grant them the View Definition permission and deny them Alter rights. The Control permission would enable a person to perform any action on the object, much like a db_owner does but at a granular level.

Roles

We have already discussed system database roles, but you can also create user-defined roles inside of your database. User-defined roles are essentially groups inside SQL Server to group your users together. If you have gone through the trouble of granting permissions for the users to be able to access only a select few stored procedures, you can use roles to ensure that every user thereafter would inherit those rights.

To do this, you would essentially create the database role and then grant the rights to the role just as you do a user. When you grant new login rights to the database, you would then assign them to the role with no other permissions. The user then inherits all rights given to him via the role.

Creating a role is simple in Management Studio. Right-click Database Roles under the database, click Security⇨Roles, and click select New Role. Name the role and then specify who owns the role. You can then go through the same screens that we discussed earlier in the Users section to specify what the role has permissions to do.

In T-SQL, you can use the CREATE ROLE DDL syntax to create a role. Simply name the role and then specify the owner of the role with the AUTHORIZATION keyword, like this:

```
CREATE ROLE [WebUsers] AUTHORIZATION [bknight]
```

Creating Users with T-SQL

To create a user through T-SQL, you can use the CREATE USER DDL. For example, if you wish to grant the login "LoginName" access to the database as a user named "LoginName," you could use the following syntax. The brackets around the login and user name allow the login to have spaces.

```
CREATE USER [LoginName] FOR LOGIN [LoginName]
```

With the user now created, you will want to add the user to various roles. The most common roles to add a user to are db_datareader and db_datawriter, as you'll see. To do this through T-SQL, you would use the sp_addrolemember stored procedure. You would then pass in the role you wish to add the user to, followed by the user name. We prefixed each parameter with an N, since each input parameter is a Unicode value. You can use sp_addrolemember to add the user to user-defined roles like the WebUsers role you created earlier in the previous section.

```
EXEC sp_addrolemember N'db_datawriter', N'LoginName'
EXEC sp_addrolemember N'db_datareader', N'LoginName'
EXEC sp_addrolemember N'WebUsers', N'LoginName'
```

Last, you can grant the user rights to various securables by using the GRANT statement. The syntax will vary based on what you're trying to grant access to. The following three examples show how to grant the user access to create schemas and tables and the ability to execute the SprocName stored procedure.

```
GRANT CREATE SCHEMA TO [LoginName]
GRANT CREATE TABLE TO [LoginName]
GRANT EXECUTE ON SprocName to [LoginName]
```

Schemas

Schemas were a feature in SQL Server 2000 that weren't emphasized as much, but in SQL Server 2005, they're an integral part of the database engine. Schemas allow you to group database objects into a logical group for security, ease of use, and manageability. Whether you have created custom schemas or not, it's a best practice to use schema names in your queries. If you were to query the `Salary` table in the `HumanResource` schema, it may look like this:

```
SELECT FirstName, LastName, Salary, StartDate, EndDate FROM HumanResource.Salary
```

Since the `HumanResource` schema contains information that should be considered more secure, you can allow a user to see all tables with the exception of tables in that schema. You could also give a user a schema that the user owned and could create tables inside it without interfering with the other tables in the database. This is because the user could create tables inside the schema that would be named differently. In effect, the table name `Employees` is different from the table name `SchemaName.Employees`. If a schema is not specified, it is implied that you want the `dbo` schema. So the `Employees` table in the last example without a schema name was actually `dbo.Employees`.

Schema Example

Let's try an example on how to use schemas to both compartmentalize your tables and secure them. First, create an empty database called `SchemaExample`. Next, create a login named `SchemaExampleLogin` and a password of `schemapass08`. Give the login public access to the `SchemaExample` database, and make it the login's default database. Last, grant the login rights at a user-level in the `SchemaExample` database rights to create tables. You'll have to go to the User Properties dialog box to do this under the Securables page. You can use the steps covered in the login section of this chapter to do this, or you can use the following script, downloadable from this book's page on www.wrox.com.

```
USE [master]
GO
CREATE LOGIN [SchemaExampleLogin] WITH PASSWORD=N'schemapass08',
DEFAULT_DATABASE=[SchemaExample],
CHECK_EXPIRATION=ON,
CHECK_POLICY=ON
GO

USE [SchemaExample]
GO
CREATE USER [SchemaExampleLogin] FOR LOGIN [SchemaExampleLogin]
GRANT CREATE TABLE TO [SchemaExampleLogin]
```

With the preparation now complete, it's time to create a schema. In Management Studio, connect to the `SchemaExample` database. Right-click Schemas under the Security tree and select New Schema. In the New Schema dialog box (shown in Figure 9-8), type the name `TestSchema` for the schema name and make the schema owner the `SchemaExampleLogin` that you created earlier. Alternatively, you can use the `CREATE SCHEMA` syntax as shown here to perform the same action:

```
CREATE SCHEMA [TestSchema] AUTHORIZATION [SchemaExampleLogin]
```

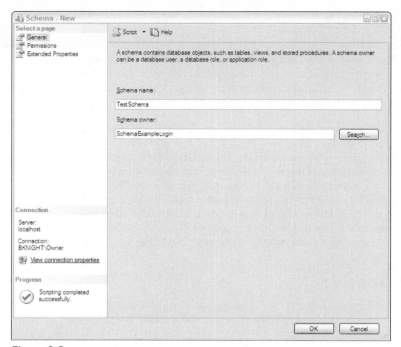

Figure 9-8

Now that the schema has been created, you can try to create a few tables using Management Studio and through T-SQL. Right-click Tables in Management Studio under the SchemaTest database and select New Table. In the Table Designer, create one column called Column1 with an integer data type, as shown in Figure 9-9. Go to the Properties Window of the Table Designer and select TestSchema from the Schema drop-down box. If the Properties Window is not showing, select Properties Window from the View menu (or hit F4). Also in the Properties Window, type **TableDesignerTest** for the table name. Click Save and close the Table Designer.

In Management Studio, expand the tables folder (you may have to right-click and select Refresh to see the table). You should see your newly created table there, and it should be titled TestSchema.TableDesignerTest.

Next, open a new query while connecting with the login of SchemaExampleLogin and a password of schemapass08. Ensure that the database that you're connected to is SchemaExample. Next, try to create a simple test table by using the following syntax:

```
create table TestSchema.TestTable
(column1 int)
```

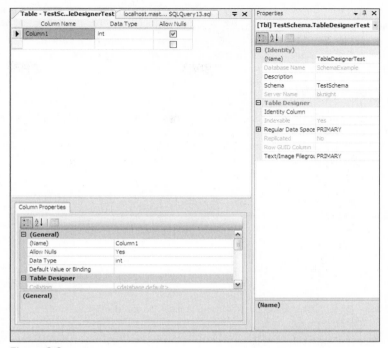

Figure 9-9

Next, try to create another table in the dbo schema by using the following syntax. Remember that since you didn't specify a schema in this syntax, the table will be created in the dbo schema.

```
create table TestTableProblem
(column1 int)
```

Because you don't have rights to create tables in the dbo schema, you will receive the following error message.

```
Msg 2760, Level 16, State 1, Line 1
The specified schema name "dbo" either does not exist or you do not have permission
to use it.
```

To create the table, you must explicitly grant the user rights to create the table in the dbo schema. To do this, you can use Management Studio to grant the user ALTER rights to the dbo schema in the Securables page. You can also use the following syntax to perform the same action. You will need to be logged in as a user with higher authority to do this, though.

```
GRANT ALTER ON SCHEMA::[dbo] TO [SchemaExampleLogin]
GO
```

Once the user has been granted ALTER rights to the schema, he or she will now be able to create the table. This simple example shows you how you can use schemas to control the user's access through grouping tables. Schemas are also handy from a usability perspective. By naming a table HumanResource.Contact, it has an implied meaning that these are human resource contacts, not sales leads.

Changing Ownership

Once a schema has tables inside of it, it cannot be dropped until all the objects have been moved out of it. SQL Server does not want to implicitly assume that you mean to move the tables from the TestSchema schema to the dbo schema. Instead of implicitly doing this, the command will fail until the administrator or owner explicitly moves the tables. The error the user would receive would look like this (where TableDesignerTest is the first table in the schema):

```
Msg 3729, Level 16, State 1, Line 2
Cannot drop schema 'SchemaName' because it is being referenced by object
'TableDesignerTest'.
```

You also cannot drop any login or user that owns a schema. If you were to try to delete a user that owned a schema, you would receive an error like this:

```
Msg 15138, Level 16, State 1, Line 1
The database principal owns a schema in the database, and cannot be dropped.
```

The way around this is to create a new schema (or use an existing one) and move all the objects in the old schema to the new schema. You can do this by using the ALTER SCHEMA syntax followed by the TRANSFER keyword. The following syntax will create a new schema called SecondSchema and then move the TestSchema.TestTable table over to it. Then you could delete the empty schema.

```
CREATE SCHEMA SecondSchema
GO
ALTER SCHEMA SecondSchema TRANSFER TestSchema.TestTable
GO
```

Permission Context

Earlier in this chapter, a classic security problem was brought up. If it's a best practice to always use stored procedures, how do I handle dynamic SQL inside of a stored procedure? To illustrate this problem, let's use the same database and table from the previous section in this chapter. In that example, you had a user named SchemaExampleLogin. This user did not have any rights to the dbo schema other than to add new tables into it. He could not select from any table in the dbo schema, however. This is shown if you login as the SchemaExampleLogin and use a password of schemapass08. Once logged in, attempt to query the dbo.TestTableProblem table:

```
SELECT * FROM dbo.TestTableProblem
```

You will then receive the following error:

```
Msg 229, Level 14, State 5, Line 1
SELECT permission denied on object 'TestTableProblem', database 'SchemaExample',
schema 'dbo'.
```

The best practice mentioned earlier is not to grant the SchemaExampleLogin user access to the TestTableProblem table but instead create a stored procedure. This allows you to tightly control access to your tables through canned queries that you've already approved. More benefits are listed in Chapters 6 and 7. So, to quickly fix the problem, you could create a stored procedure as shown in the following example:

```
CREATE PROC DynamicSQLExample
AS

SELECT * FROM dbo.TestTableProblem
GO
```

The stored procedure would then be called and would return the expected results:

```
EXEC DynamicSQLExample
```

Throughout the example in this section, you will need to flip back and forth from the lower-privileged account SchemaExampleLogin to a database owner or sysadmin. Run the code that will create the stored procedures with the higher privileged account and the execution of the stored procedures with the SchemaExampleLogin user.

The problem crops up when you have a stored procedure with dynamic SQL. Dynamic SQL allows a T-SQL programmer to create a looser stored procedure that can order the data dynamically or only select certain columns. They should always be used sparingly, since the Query Optimizer won't be able to give you the same optimized query plan as with a canned stored procedure. Typically, you will see these types of queries with a search screen in an application where a user may type any number of fields to search. You can alter the previous stored procedure as shown below to make it dynamic.

```
ALTER PROC DynamicSQLExample
@OrderBy Varchar(20)
AS

DECLARE @strSQL varchar(255)

SET @strSQL = 'SELECT * FROM dbo.TestTableProblem '
SET @strSQL = @strSQL + 'ORDER BY ' + @OrderBy
EXEC (@strSQL)
GO
```

If you try to execute the stored procedure like this:

```
DynamicSQLExample 'column1'
```

This will give the same error that you saw before stating that you must have SELECT permission to the underlying table before you can run the stored procedure.

```
Msg 229, Level 14, State 5, Line 1
SELECT permission denied on object 'TestTableProblem', database 'SchemaExample',
schema 'dbo'.
```

The old way to solve this problem in SQL Server 2000 was to go ahead and grant the SchemaExampleLogin user more rights than you wanted and hope they exercised caution when selecting from the table. In SQL Server 2005, you can use context switching to impersonate another user for a short duration.

EXECUTE AS Command

Now that you know the previous problem, context switching will hopefully give you the best relief. Context switching will temporarily give the user executing the stored procedure higher rights but only in the scope of the stored procedure's execution. As soon as the stored procedure has completed executing, the permissions are reverted. Additionally, you can use context switching to troubleshoot permission problems. You can impersonate another login to see what problems they may be seeing and try to reproduce the difficulties.

Context switching is done through the EXECUTE AS command. It's similar to the old SETUSER command, but SETUSER required that you be a sysadmin or db_owner to run. At its simplest form, the syntax would either state EXECUTE AS USER or EXECUTE AS LOGIN. As you can guess, this will either allow you to impersonate a user or a login. In the previous example, you could create an additional user with very minimal rights to given tables that are needed. Then you could impersonate that user in the stored procedure and revert to the old permissions afterward. Some people like to create many new users for each type of access and then do impersonation based on need.

Before you can do this type of context switching, though, the user that you wish to impersonate must grant you access to do the impersonation. Otherwise, you would receive the following error anytime someone tried to run a query with context switching.

```
Msg 15517, Level 16, State 1, Procedure DynamicSQLExample, Line 5
Cannot execute as the database principal because the principal "dbo" does not
exist, this type of principal cannot be impersonated, or you do not have
permission.
```

To grant someone rights to impersonate your user, you can use the GRANT statement or go to the Securables page in the User Properties dialog box. For example, to grant the SchemaExampleLogin user rights to impersonate the dbo account, use the following syntax:

```
GRANT IMPERSONATE ON USER:: dbo TO SchemaExampleLogin;
```

This syntax would be a worst practice, since you're granting the user rights to impersonate a very sensitive account. The dbo user would have rights to do anything you would like inside the database. You should instead grant the user rights to impersonate a lower-privileged account. Since we have no other users for this example, the previous code will work fine, temporarily.

The next step is to alter the previous stored procedure to enable context switching. You can see the EXECUTE AS statement in the following code, right before the SELECT statement. There is also quite a bit of debugging code in the stored procedure to show what context you're currently using. The SUSER_NAME function shows what login you're currently using. The USER_NAME function shows the user name that you're currently using, and the ORIGINAL_LOGIN function shows what your original login was before the context switch. ORIGINAL_LOGIN is a key function to use to help with auditing.

```
ALTER PROC DynamicSQLExample
@OrderBy Varchar(20)
AS

EXECUTE AS USER = 'dbo'
DECLARE @strSQL varchar(255)
```

```
SET @strSQL = 'SELECT * FROM dbo.TestTableProblem '
SET @strSQL = @strSQL + 'ORDER BY ' + @OrderBy
EXEC (@strSQL)
SELECT SUSER_NAME() as LoginNm,
USER_NAME() as UserNm,
ORIGINAL_LOGIN() as OriginalLoginNm;
GO
```

With the stored procedure now modified, go ahead and execute it again while logged in as
SchemaExampleLogin:

```
DynamicSQLExample 'column1'
```

You should now see results from the query. You should also see the login and user names that you're
impersonating. After the stored procedure runs, go ahead and rerun the following chunk of code to see
what user you are currently using:

```
SELECT SUSER_NAME() as LoginNm,
    USER_NAME() as UserNm,
    ORIGINAL_LOGIN() as OriginalLoginNm;
```

Now your user has reverted to the SchemaExampleLogin. This shows that when using context switching in a stored procedure, it reverts as soon as the stored procedure completes running.

If you were to manually connect with the SchemaExampleLogin and run the following query, you could
see another point.

```
EXECUTE AS USER = 'dbo'
GO
USE AdventureWorks
GO
```

When you're switching context to another user (not login), you will receive an error when trying to leave
the database.

```
Msg 916, Level 14, State 1, Line 1
The server principal "BKNIGHT\Owner" is not able to access the database "
AdventureWorks" under the current security context.
```

The solution, if you must do this, is to switch context to a login, not a user, as shown in the following
code. You should not switch to a login context if only database-level items are needed. Otherwise, you
may be giving the user more rights than needed, and you may be opening yourself up to hackers. Use
login context switching very sparingly.

```
EXECUTE AS login  = 'Bknight'
```

The keyword REVERT will revert the user's permissions to the previous context. If you have switched
context multiple times, it will only revert you a single switch, and you may have to issue REVERT several
times before going back to your original user. If you had switched context to a login and then began to
use a different database, you would receive the following message when you tried to issue a REVERT
command. This will force you to then go back to the original database to issue the REVERT.

```
Msg 15199, Level 16, State 1, Line 1
The current security context cannot be reverted. Please switch to the original
database where 'Execute As' was called and try it again.
```

Troubleshooting Permission

As you have seen throughout this chapter, if you don't really configure the permissions appropriately, it can be very tricky to troubleshoot. There is a new function that will help you figure out what permissions a given user has available before you have to dig through many screens in Management Studio. The function is `fn_my_permissions`, and it shows what permissions the caller has by default. For example, if you wish to see what access you have to the `TestSchema` schema, you can use the following syntax:

```
SELECT *
FROM fn_my_permissions('TestSchema', 'SCHEMA')
```

The second input parameter is the type of object, and the first parameter is the name of the specific object. To view what permissions you have for the `dbo.TestTableProblem` table, you can run the following syntax. If nothing is returned, either you have typed the wrong input parameter or you have no permissions. The input parameter `OBJECT` applies for all the basic database objects (tables, stored procedures, views, and so on).

```
SELECT *
FROM fn_my_permissions('dbo.TestTableProblem', 'OBJECT')
```

You can also find out what permissions a user has to the server by passing in the parameter of `SERVER` with an input parameter of `NULL` for the first parameter. In addition, you can use context switching to see what permissions someone else has when trying to debug a problem, as shown here:

```
EXECUTE AS Login = 'Bknight'
SELECT *
FROM fn_my_permissions(NULL, 'SERVER')
REVERT
```

If you're trying to figure out if you can impersonate someone else, you can use the input parameter of `USER` and pass in the user name. The same applies for the parameter of `LOGIN`.

```
SELECT * FROM fn_my_permissions('SchemaExamplelogin', 'USER');
```

Encryption

A common request in the days of SQL Server 2000 was for a way to encrypt data inside the columns. Industries like healthcare and banking would typically have to encrypt their sensitive data. With the advent of laws like Sarbanes-Oxley, all publicly owned companies must encrypt sensitive data such as social security numbers or passwords. Developers would typically push the functionality into the application rather than attempt to write an extended stored procedure. Each application then would have its own logic for the encryption and decryption. In SQL Server 2005, the functionality is built into the core database engine and can be used with minimal effort.

Creating the Certificate and Key

The first question that security individuals ask when encrypting data is where you want to store the keys for encryption. Essentially, the key allows encryption and decryption of the data. SQL Server stores a hierarchy of keys. The top of the hierarchy is a database instance master key, which is protected by the Windows Data Protection API. Beneath that, each database can have a master key that protects all the individual keys that can be created.

Encryption in SQL Server 2005 is done by first creating a certificate, then creating a master key in the database, and finally creating an individual key to do the data encryption that uses a certificate. Last, you would use a series of functions to encrypt the data. The last sentence is worded very carefully because there is not a switch in the table designer that you can use to encrypt a column. Instead, you encrypt the data as it goes into the table using built-in system functions.

In SQL Server 2005, two different types of encryption keys can be used: symmetric and asymmetric. Symmetric key encryption uses the same key to encrypt and decrypt the data. While this is less secure, it performs much faster than asymmetric key encryption, which uses a different key for encryption and decryption. With asymmetric key encryption, you would lock the door with one key and then pass out a different key to anyone who needed to open the door. With symmetric encryption, you would essentially put the same key under the door mat and allow everyone to use it. You should never hand this key to anyone, because it's the only one to the house.

As mentioned earlier, there is a noticeable performance degradation when encrypting and decrypting data. It's not nearly as noticeable with symmetric key encryption, though. There is a compromise to keep your data secure with both types of keys. That solution enables you to encrypt your session key with the asymmetric key and then encrypt your data thereafter with the symmetric key. Because of the slight performance problem, you should never encrypt all of your columns in a table. For example, there's little reason to generally encrypt the data in the FirstName or Gender column.

Let's take an example to walk you through how data is encrypted and decrypted. This example can be downloaded from this book's Web site at www.wrox.com. First, create a fresh database called EncryptionExample. Create a login called LowPrivLogin with a password of encryptdemo08. Then grant the login access to the EncryptionExample database. You can perform all of these steps through the Management Studio interface or by using these three lines of code:

```
CREATE DATABASE [EncryptionExample]
CREATE LOGIN LowPrivLogin WITH PASSWORD = 'encryptdemo08'
CREATE USER LowPrivLogin FOR LOGIN LowPrivLogin
```

Create a table that you'll use throughout this example in the dbo schema. The table will hold fake credit card information. Notice that the credit card number is stored as a variable binary column. This is because you're going to use this column to store encrypted data.

```
CREATE TABLE dbo.CustomerCreditCards
        (CustomerID INT PRIMARY KEY,
         CardNumber varbinary(256))
```

To create the key, you cannot use the Management Studio GUI interface; you have to use T-SQL. You can use Management Studio to delete the key, but that's the only functionality available under the Security tree for a given database. First, create a master key for the database by using the CREATE MASTER KEY syntax:

```
CREATE MASTER KEY ENCRYPTION BY PASSWORD = 'EncryptionExampleMasterKey08$'
```

Next, you will want to protect your other keys with a certificate. While logged in as a dbo, run the CREATE CERTIFICATE statement that follows. The subject is not needed but is handy metadata that can tell an administrator what the use of the key is for. Remember the name of the certificate, because you're going to use it later.

```
CREATE CERTIFICATE [CertSymetricKey]
  WITH SUBJECT = 'User defined subject. This key will protect the secret data.'
```

With the certificate created, create a symmetric key using the CREATE KEY syntax, as shown below. This syntax accepts a number of algorithms, including triple DES, AES 128, and RC4 to name just a few. There are nine algorthims in all, including several variations of the same. Note that in the following syntax the key is protected with the CertSymetricKey certificate. There are other ways of doing this as well. For example, you could encrypt the symmetric key with a password or another key.

```
CREATE SYMMETRIC KEY [SecretSymmetricKey]
   WITH ALGORITHM = TRIPLE_DES --AES_128 Fine too
   ENCRYPTION BY CERTIFICATE [CertSymetricKey]
```

Encrypting the Data

You now are ready to begin encrypting your data. For the purpose of this example, remain logged in as a dbo account that created the keys. If you do not have access to the keys, you will not be able to see data. We'll cover that aspect of encryption momentarily.

The first thing to do is use the symmetric key created earlier by issuing the OPEN SYMMETRIC KEY syntax. You specify the key name and specify that you wish to decrypt the key with the certificate that you created earlier as well. This key will remain open until your session expires or you issue the CLOSE statement.

```
OPEN SYMMETRIC KEY [SecretSymmetricKey]
    DECRYPTION BY CERTIFICATE [CertSymetricKey]
```

The next code block is a little more complex but is still not too bad. In this block you get a unique GUID for the symmetric key created earlier by using the key_guid function. If you did not have permission to access the key, it would return NULL and would be caught by the error trap later in the block of code. The entire point of retrieving the GUID is that it's required for the encryptbykey function later in the code block. This function is actually what does the encryption in our case. You pass to that function the GUID for the key and the data you wish to encrypt.

```
DECLARE @Key_Guid AS UNIQUEIDENTIFIER
SET @Key_Guid = key_guid( 'SecretSymmetricKey')
IF( @Key_Guid is not null )

BEGIN
INSERT INTO dbo.CustomerCreditCards
VALUES ( 1, encryptbykey( @Key_Guid, N'4111-1234-1234-5678'))

INSERT INTO dbo.CustomerCreditCards
VALUES ( 2, encryptbykey( @Key_Guid, N'4111-9876-7543-2100'))
```

```
INSERT INTO dbo.CustomerCreditCards
VALUES ( 3, encryptbykey( @Key_Guid, N'4111-9876-7543-2100'))


END
ELSE
BEGIN
  PRINT 'Error retrieving key GUID'
END
```

This will insert three encrypted credit card numbers. If you select against the table, you will see that the data for that column is all in binary:

```
SELECT * FROM dbo.CustomerCreditCards
```

If you wish to decrypt the data, one of the functions that you can use is decryptbykey, as shown in the following code. This will use the key you opened earlier to decrypt the data. If the key that was opened matches the key that encrypted the data, you will be able to see the data unencrypted.

```
SELECT CustomerId,
       convert( NVARCHAR(100), decryptbykey( CardNumber )) as 'CardNumber'
    FROM dbo.CustomerCreditCards
go
```

To close the key, you can use the CLOSE syntax, naming the key that you wish to close:

```
CLOSE SYMMETRIC KEY SecretSymmetricKey
```

At this point, the data viewed earlier will return NULL. Prove this out by rerunning the same SELECT statement that you ran previously with the decryptbykey syntax. This is also the behavior if you try to open the wrong key to view the data or if you don't have permission to use the key. It's worked for you in this example because you have dbo rights to the database. With the data encrypted, only users that had access to your certificiate and the key would be able to see the data. To grant a user rights to see the data, you would have to use syntax as shown below:

```
GRANT CONTROL on certificate::[CertSymetricKey]
  TO [username]
go
GRANT VIEW DEFINITION on symmetric key::[SecretSymmetricKey]
  TO [username]
```

These may be more permissions than you would be willing to permanently hand out to a user. The method around this is to grant these rights only to a given account and tempoarily escalate the rights to the user by using the EXECUTE AS statement.

Creating a Helper Function Example

For usability, you may decide to create a function to help users decrypt the data. You can use context switching to give the user rights to the certificate and key for a short duration. In the following function, you use the decryptbykeyautocert function to combine the OPEN SYMMETRIC KEY and decryptbykey functionality.

```
CREATE FUNCTION dbo.udfDecryptData ( @InputValue VARBINARY(256))
RETURNS NVARCHAR(20)
WITH EXECUTE AS 'DBO'
AS
BEGIN
RETURN convert( NVARCHAR(50), decryptbykeyautocert( cert_id( 'CertSymetricKey' ),
null, @InputValue ))
END
```

For the purpose of this example, you'll allow the LowPrivUser you created earlier access to the function and to the credit card data by using the following code:

```
GRANT EXECUTE ON [dbo].[udfDecryptData] TO [LowPrivUser]
GRANT SELECT ON [dbo].[CustomerCreditCards] TO [LowPrivUser]
```

You're now ready to use the function. Either sign off as the dbo user and sign back in as the LowPrivUser, or use the EXECUTE AS syntax that follows to simulate the user. The following code should look much like the SELECT statement used earlier, but now you're using the user-defined function you created.

```
EXECUTE AS USER = 'LowPrivUser'
SELECT CustomerId,
       dbo.udfDecryptData( CardNumber ) as 'CardNumber'
    FROM dbo.CustomerCreditCards
REVERT
```

This will display the data unencrypted, and you would simply need to grant users rights to the function to enable them to see the data. As you can imagine, this does open a slight can of worms, though, as it makes the data a little too easy to decrypt, but you did add layers of security and obscurity.

Column-Level Permissions

While you're encrypting data, you may find a table like your credit card data where users should be able to see all columns except the credit card number. If this is the case, you have the option to protect data at the column level. To deny rights to an individual column, you can use the DENY SELECT statement. If you take the earlier example and deny the LowPrivUser rights to the CardNumber column in the dbo.CustomerCreditCards table, it would look like the following code:

```
DENY SELECT (CardNumber) on dbo.CustomerCreditCards  to LowPrivUser
```

If the LowPrivUser attempted to pull the CustomerID column out of the table, he would experience no problem. The minute he tried a larger query, as shown below, he would experience a permission problem:

```
EXECUTE AS USER = 'LowPrivUser'
SELECT CustomerId,
     dbo. CardNumber
    FROM dbo.CustomerCreditCards
REVERT
```

This would return the following error. Any SELECT * statement would also fail with the same error.

```
Msg 230, Level 14, State 1, Line 2
SELECT permission denied on column 'CardNumber' of object 'CustomerCreditCards',
database 'EncryptionExample', schema 'dbo'.
```

Summary

In this chapter, you've learned how to secure your data and your database engine. We covered many ways to secure your data, whether through granular security or roles. Another mechanism is to assume the attacker can get the data but can't read the sensitive data due to encryption. Now that you know how to protect your SQL Server data, Chapter 10 talks more about implementing your changes through various stages of the development lifecycle by using proper change management.

10

Change Management

The challenges of the database administrator have changed drastically since the days of SQL Server 2000. Laws such as HIPAA and Sarbanes-Oxley have caused a DBA's job to become much more ritualistic because of trying to follow policies. In this chapter, you will learn how to create projects for your SQL Scripts and how to integrate those into Source Safe. You'll also learn how to monitor for unauthorized changes by using DDL triggers.

Creating Projects

Visual Studio Projects are generally a foreign concept to DBAs, as the concept originated from the programmer world. The hierarchy in Visual Studio is that you create a *solution,* which could contain many *projects*, which could contain many files for the project. For example, you may have a solution called LoanApplication that contains two projects: one for your C# program and another for the DDL to create the database. In the business-intelligence world, these solutions help you group all the related files together, like SSRS reports, SSAS cubes, and the SSIS packages to load the data.

Inside Management Studio, you can create projects as well to hold your scripts and connections for easy access. When you double-click a script, it will automatically connect to the connection associated with the script. By storing it in a project, it enables you to store files easily into Source Safe. This enables you to be able to check code in and out, allowing for a collaborative development environment where only one DBA could be editing the code at one time. We'll discuss this requirement later in this chapter, but version-controlling your scripts is often a requirement for change management. You could also check all of your administrative scripts into Source Safe and share them out amongst all the other administrators.

You can create a project in Management Studio by selecting File➪New➪Project. Select SQL Server scripts as your project template. Call the project ProjectExampleScripts and name the solution AdminBookExamples (shown in Figure 10-1).

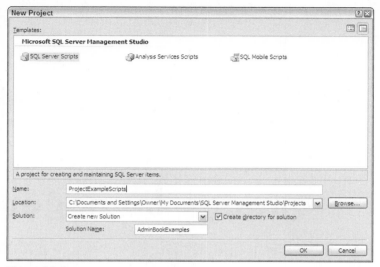

Figure 10-1

When you click OK, a new solution and project will be created. You will see three folders created in the project: Connections, Queries, and Miscellaneous. Your database connections will go into the Connections folder, and all of your queries that you'd like to keep together in the project go into the Queries folder. The Miscellaneous folder holds files that don't have a .SQL extension but are files that you'd like to keep in the project, like a `readme.txt` file that may describe instructions for using the project.

> *If you have a tool like Visual Source Safe installed, there will be a checkbox to automatically check the solution into Source Safe upon creation.*

Creating a Connection

To create a connection, right-click the Connections folder and select New Connection. The Connect to Server dialog box will open. Type your normal server connection information and how you wish to authenticate. Then go to the Connection Properties tab (shown in Figure 10-2) and select AdventureWorks for the Connect to Database option. Note that you can also set the default protocol here if it differs from your default.

When you click OK, the connection will be created in the Connections folder. There are other ways to create this connection as well. If you create a query first, you will be prompted for a connection prior to query creation. This would also create a connection in the Connections folder as well and is normally the easier way to create the connection.

Figure 10-2

Creating a Project Query

The Queries folder is a repository of all the queries for your project. To create a query in the project, right-click the Queries folder and select New Query. You will be prompted to confirm the connection. The default query name will be `SQLQuery1.sql`. Next, type whatever you wish in the Query Window and click File⇨Save. Finally, rename the query to `SampleQuery1.sql` by right-clicking the query and selecting Rename. Click Save All to save the queries and the project.

With the query now saved, you're ready to begin using the query. Close the Query Window and then double-click the query file again. Note that this time, the query opens automatically and does not prompt you for a connection. You can see what connection is associated with the query by right-clicking the query and selecting Properties Window. You then continue to add additional queries until your project is complete.

Again, generally the main point of creating an entire project and solution is for integration with a source-control system. If you are using a source-control system such as Source Safe, each time you add or delete a new script, the entire project will be checked out.

DDL Triggers

After a few public companies collapsed dramatically in 2002, the U.S. government enacted a new law called Sarbanes-Oxley, which demanded, among many other things, good IT practices. One of the big requirements of the law was to have a good change-management process and to know who installed a schema change into production and when it occurred. This required companies to spend hundreds of millions of dollars nationwide on new software to monitor changes and ensure good IT practices. Of course, they had the best motivation ever to be good citizens (if they didn't, they'd be in yellow jump-suits and handcuffs).

Part of those millions of dollars spent was on monitoring software for SQL Server to watch for unautho-rized changes. In this section, you'll learn how to use DDL triggers to alleviate the need for some of these auditing tools. We've had DML triggers since modern-day database systems were conceived, but what are DDL triggers? A DDL event includes any event at a database or server-level that alters or cre-ates a database object or server object (like a login). For example, with a DDL trigger, you can configure the trigger to e-mail you or to log whenever a table is created.

DDL Trigger Syntax

The syntax for a DDL trigger is much like that of a DML trigger. With a DDL trigger, though, instead of monitoring an INSERT statement, you monitor for a CREATE event, for example. The generic syntax looks like this:

```
CREATE TRIGGER <trigger_name>
ON { ALL SERVER | DATABASE }
[ WITH <ddl_trigger_option> [ ,...n ] ]
{ FOR | AFTER } { event_type | event_group } [ ,...n ]
AS { sql_statement   [ ; ] [ ...n ] | EXTERNAL NAME < method specifier >   [ ; ] }
```

Most of this syntax you probably recognize from DML triggers, so we'll focus mostly on the DDL-specific syntax. You have two scopes you can specify in a DDL trigger: ALL_SERVER or DATABASE. As the names imply, the ALL_SERVER scope monitors all server-level events, and the DATABASE option monitors database-level events.

The other important configurable part of the syntax is after the FOR clause. After the FOR clause, you would specify what you'd like to monitor in the database or on the server with the DDL trigger option. Examples of this vary based on what level of DDL trigger you have. The upcoming sections will break down these examples.

Database Triggers

Database DDL triggers are executed when you create, drop, or alter an object at a database-level, like a user, table, stored procedure, Service Broker queue, or view, to name a few. If you want to trap all database DDL events, you use the trigger option in the syntax mentioned earlier for FOR DDL_DATABASE_LEVEL_EVENTS. The events are hierarchical, and the top-level database trigger types are shown in the following list. Under the trigger types mentioned in list, you can get much more granular. For example, rather than trapping all events when any type of table event occurs, you can narrow it down to only raising the DDL event when a table is dropped by using the DROP_TABLE trigger option.

- ❑   DDL_TRIGGER_EVENTS
- ❑   DDL_FUNCTION_EVENTS
- ❑   DDL_SYNONYM_EVENTS
- ❑   DDL_SSB_EVENTS
- ❑   DDL_DATABASE_SECURITY_EVENTS
- ❑   DDL_EVENT_NOTIFICATION_EVENTS
- ❑   DDL_PROCEDURE_EVENTS
- ❑   DDL_TABLE_VIEW_EVENTS
- ❑   DDL_TYPE_EVENTS
- ❑   DDL_XML_SCHEMA_COLLECTION_EVENTS
- ❑   DDL_PARTITION_EVENTS
- ❑   DDL_ASSEMBLY_EVENTS

To create a trigger that would audit for any stored procedure change, deletion, or creation, the CREATE TRIGGER statement would look like the following:

```
CREATE TRIGGER ChangeWindow
ON DATABASE
FOR DDL_PROCEDURE_EVENTS
AS
-- Trigger statement here
```

As mentioned earlier, you can create granular triggers on certain events by using the event type after the FOR keyword. For example, to monitor for anytime a DROP TABLE, CREATE TABLE, or ALTER TABLE statement is issued, you could use the following code:

```
CREATE TRIGGER ChangeWindow
ON DATABASE
FOR CREATE_TABLE, DROP_TABLE, ALTER_TABLE
AS
-- Trigger statement here
```

Finally, you can monitor all changes by using the DDL_DATABASE_LEVEL_EVENTS event type:

```
CREATE TRIGGER ChangeWindow
ON DATABASE
FOR DDL_DATABASE_LEVEL_EVENTS
AS
-- Trigger statement here
```

An important function in your DDL trigger toolbox is the EVENTDATA() system function. The EVENTDATA() system function is raised anytime a DDL trigger is fired at any level and outputs the event type, the user who executed the query, and the exact syntax the user ran. The function outputs this data in XML format:

```
<EVENT_INSTANCE>
  <EventType>CREATE_USER</EventType>
  <PostTime>2006-07-09T12:50:16.103</PostTime>
  <SPID>60</SPID>
  <ServerName>BKNIGHT</ServerName>
  <LoginName>BKNIGHT\Owner</LoginName>
  <UserName>dbo</UserName>
  <DatabaseName>AdventureWorks</DatabaseName>
  <ObjectName>brian</ObjectName>
  <ObjectType>SQL USER</ObjectType>
  <DefaultSchema>brian</DefaultSchema>
  <SID>q7ZPUruGyU+nWuOrlc6Crg==</SID>
  <TSQLCommand>
    <SetOptions ANSI_NULLS="ON" ANSI_NULL_DEFAULT="ON" ANSI_PADDING="ON"
QUOTED_IDENTIFIER="ON" ENCRYPTED="FALSE" />
    <CommandText>CREATE USER [brian] FOR LOGIN [brian] WITH DEFAULT_SCHEMA =
[dbo]</CommandText>
  </TSQLCommand>
</EVENT_INSTANCE>
```

You can then either pull all the data from the EVENTDATA() function and log it into a table as an XML data type or pull selective data out using an XPATH query. To do an XML XPATH query in SQL Server 2005, you would specify the path to the XML node. In DDL triggers, the key elements from the EVENTDATA() function are the following:

❑ EventType — The type of event that caused the trigger

❑ PostTime — The time the event occurred

❑ SPID — The SPID of the user that caused the event

❑ ServerName — The instance name that the event occurred on

❑ LoginName — The login name that performed the action that triggered the event

❑ UserName — The username that performed the action that triggered the event

❑ DatabaseName — The database name the event occurred in

❑ ObjectType — The type of object that was modified, deleted, or created

❑ ObjectName — The name of the object that was modified, deleted, or created

❑ TSQLCommand — The T-SQL command that was executed to cause the trigger to be run

To pull out selective data, you could use code like the following to do an XPATH query. You would first pass in the fully qualified element name, like /EVENT_INSTANCE/TSQLCommand, and the [1] in the following code means to pull out the first record. Since there is only one record in the EVENTDATA() function, you will always pull the first record only. The EVENTDATA() function will only be available to you in the scope of the trigger. If you were to run this query outside the trigger, it would return NULL.

```
CREATE TRIGGER RestrictDDL
ON DATABASE
FOR DDL_DATABASE_LEVEL_EVENTS
AS
```

```
EXECUTE AS USER = 'DBO'

DECLARE @errordata XML
SET @errordata = EVENTDATA()

SELECT  @errordata
GO
```

You can use the ROLLBACK command in a DDL trigger to cancel the command that the user ran. You can also wrap this in a conditional IF statement to conditionally roll the statement back. Typically, though, you'll see DDL triggers log that the event occurred and then potentially roll the command back if the user did not follow the correct change procedures.

We'll now walk through a complete example of how you could use DDL triggers to monitor for changes that occur in a database. The type of triggers that you're trying to monitor for are any database-level events, such as table or security changes. In the event of a change, you wish to log that event into a table. If the user is not logged in as the proper account, you wish to roll the change back. This way, you can prevent users in the sysadmin role from making changes. The table that you want to log the change events into is called DDLAudit. To create the table, use the following syntax or download the complete example on www.wrox.com:

```
CREATE TABLE DDLAudit
(
    AuditID         int             NOT NULL identity
                                    CONSTRAINT DDLAuditPK
                                    PRIMARY KEY CLUSTERED,
    LoginName       sysname         NOT NULL,
    UserName        sysname         NOT NULL,
    PostDateTime    datetime        NOT NULL,
    EventType       varchar(100)    NOT NULL,
    DDLOp           varchar(2500)   NOT NULL
)
```

You're now ready to create the trigger to log into the table. Most SQL Server environments only allow changes to the database between certain maintenance window hours. You can use the following DDL trigger to prevent changes outside the 8 p.m. to 7 a.m. maintenance window. Changes made at any other time will be rolled back. If you are inside the maintenance window, the change will be logged to a DDLAudit table.

```
CREATE TRIGGER ChangeWindow
ON DATABASE
FOR DDL_DATABASE_LEVEL_EVENTS
AS

DECLARE @errordata XML
SET @errordata = EVENTDATA()

INSERT dbo.DDLAudit
        (LoginName,
         UserName,
         PostDateTime,
         EventType,
```

```
        DDLOp)
VALUES   (SYSTEM_USER, ORIGINAL_LOGIN(), GETDATE(),
  @errordata.value('(/EVENT_INSTANCE/EventType)[1]', 'varchar(100)'),
  @errordata.value('(/EVENT_INSTANCE/TSQLCommand)[1]', 'varchar(2500)') )

IF DATEPART(hh,GETDATE()) > 7 AND DATEPART(hh,GETDATE()) < 20
BEGIN

  RAISERROR ('You can only perform this change between 8PM and 7AM. Please try this
change again or contact Production support for an override.', 16, -1)
  ROLLBACK
END
```

Note that in this code, you trap the login being used, as well as the original login to check for context switching (EXECUTE AS). With the trigger now created, test the trigger by running a simple DDL, command such as:

```
CREATE table TriggerTest
(Column1 int)
```

If you executed this command after 7 a.m. and before 8 p.m., you would receive the following error, and the CREATE statement would roll back. You could look at the tables in Management Studio, and you should not see the TriggerTest table.

```
(1 row(s) affected)
Msg 50000, Level 16, State 1, Procedure ChangeWindow, Line 22
You can not perform this action on a production database. Please contact the
production DBA department for change procedures.
Msg 3609, Level 16, State 2, Line 2
The transaction ended in the trigger. The batch has been aborted.
```

If you were to run the statement before 7 a.m. or after 8 p.m., you would only see (1 row(s) affected), meaning that the change was logged but you were able to successfully perform the action. You can test this by changing the server's time in Windows. After you try to create a few tables or make changes, select from the DDLAudit table to see the audited records.

There is little performance effect to this type of trigger, since generally DDL events rarely happen. The trigger can be found in Management Studio by selecting the individual database and then selecting Programmability⇨Database Triggers. You can create a script of the trigger to modify an existing trigger or you can delete the trigger by using Management Studio.

Of course, you are still going to want to occasionally run a DDL statement in production by overriding the trigger. To allow access, you must only temporarily turn off the trigger using the following syntax for database or server-level triggers:

```
DISABLE TRIGGER ALL ON DATABASE
GO
DISABLE TRIGGER ALL ON ALL SERVER
```

After the override, you can enable the triggers again by running the following syntax. You could replace the keyword ALL with the specific trigger name to enable or disable the individual trigger.

```
ENABLE TRIGGER ALL ON  DATABASE
GO
ENABLE Trigger ALL ON ALL SERVER;
```

Server Triggers

Server-level triggers operate the same way as database triggers but are monitored for server configuration, security, and other server-level changes. The following list shows you the top-level events, but these too are hierarchical. For example, you can monitor any login changes, as you'll see in an upcoming example.

- ❏ DDL_DATABASE_EVENTS

- ❏ DROP_DATABASE

- ❏ DDL_ENDPOINT_EVENTS

- ❏ CREATE_DATABASE

- ❏ DDL_SERVER_SECURITY_EVENTS

- ❏ ALTER_DATABASE

We'll walk through another quick example. As we mention in Chapter 9, if you are in the sysadmin role, you will be able to perform any function you wish on the server. With this DDL trigger, you can ensure that only a single login will be able to perform login-type events, like creating logins. If anyone else tries to create, modify, or delete a login, it will be rolled back. Of course, you'd have to implement additional security measures if this is your actual requirement, like protecting the DDL trigger from change, but we'll keep it simple for this example.

```
CREATE TRIGGER PreventChangeTrigger
ON ALL SERVER
FOR DDL_LOGIN_EVENTS

AS

IF SUSER_NAME() != 'BKNIGHT\OWNER'
BEGIN
  RAISERROR ('This change can only be performed by the server owner, Brian Knight.
Please contact him at extension x4444 to follow the procedure.', 16, -1)
ROLLBACK

END
```

If someone other than the BKNIGHT\OWNER login were to attempt a login change, they would receive the following error. You can issue a permission context switch (EXECUTE AS LOGIN) to test out the trigger in your development environment.

```
Msg 50000, Level 16, State 1, Procedure PreventChangeTrigger, Line 9
This change can only be performed by the server owner, Brian Knight. Please contact
him at extension x4444 to follow the procedure.
Msg 3609, Level 16, State 2, Line 1
The transaction ended in the trigger. The batch has been aborted.
```

DDL server triggers can be found in Management Studio under Server Objects⇨Triggers. Like the database triggers, you can only script the trigger for modifications and delete the trigger from Management Studio.

Trigger Views

The Management Studio interface is still slightly lacking in what you can accomplish with DDL triggers, so a DBA must often go T-SQL as a management interface. One of the nice views available to show you all the database-level DDL triggers is `sys.triggers`; for server-level triggers, you can use `sys.server_triggers`. Between these two views, you can quickly see what views your server has installed on it with a query like this one:

```
SELECT type, name, parent_class_desc FROM sys.triggers
WHERE parent_class_desc = 'DATABASE'
UNION
SELECT type, name, parent_class_desc FROM sys.server_triggers
WHERE parent_class_desc = 'SERVER'
```

SQLCMD

Change management is all about creating a reproducible way to deploy and manage your changes. This is simply impossible to do properly by having a DBA execute T-SQL scripts through a Management Studio environment. The main way to create a repeatable change management is by using `sqlcmd` files that may encapsulate that T-SQL logic into output logs. This way, you will know that the change will deploy to each of your environments (test, QA, Production, and so on) and give you a predictable result.

`sqlcmd` is a replacement for `isql` and `osql`. There are two modes you can use to execute a `sqlcmd` command: at a command line or in Management Studio. If you are a SQL Server 2000 DBA, the transition to `sqlcmd` will be an easy one for you, since it's very similar to `osql`, but with some additional switches to simplify your day-to-day job. You probably won't be familiar, though, with executing `sqlcmd` commands from Management Studio. Using Management Studio to execute these types of commands gives you lots of control and replaces many of the old extended stored procedures like `xp_cmdshell`. We cover both solutions in this section.

Sqlcmd from the Command Prompt

Executing `sqlcmd` from the command prompt allows you to run any query from a command prompt and, more important, allows you to wrap these queries into a packaged install batch file for deployments, making it easy for anyone to install the database. There are many switches in `sqlcmd` you can use, but most that you'll find have only a very specialized usage. The following are some of the important switches (they are all case sensitive):

❏ `-U` — User Name

❏ `-P` — Password

❏ `-E` — Use Windows Authentication. If you use this switch, you will not need to pass the `-U` and `-P` switches in.

❑   -S — Instance name to connect to

❑   -d — Database name to start in

❑   -i — Input file that contains the query to run

❑   -o — Output file where you wish to log the output of the query to

❑   -Q — You can also pass in the query with the –Q switch instead of an input file.

We'll start with a few basic examples to show you the commands you'll use on a regular basis. First, create a new SQL file with Notepad or the editor of your choice. Type the following query into the editor and save the file as C:\TestQuery.sql:

```
SELECT * FROM Purchasing.Vendor
```

Go to a command prompt and type the following command. The –i switch represents the input file that contains the file. The –S switch represents the server name to connect to. Finally, the –d switch represents the database name.

```
sqlcmd -i c:\testquery.sql -S localhost -d AdventureWorks
```

The query will retrieve all the records from the Vendor table and display them in the console window. If you do not specify a username and password with the –U and –P switches or the –E switch for Windows Authentication, sqlcmd will default to Windows Authentication.

A variation of this command is to use the –Q switch to pass the query to sqlcmd and then quit sqlcmd after the query is complete. The –q switch can also be used if you do not wish to exit. The other variation in the following query is the use of the –o switch. The –o switch passes the results of the query into an output file and does not display anything in the console.

```
sqlcmd -Q "select * from purchasing.vendor" -d adventureworks -S localhost
-o C:\testoutput.txt
```

Another way you can execute sqlcmd from a command prompt is by just going to a command prompt and typing sqlcmd if you'd like to connect to your local instance or by specifying the instance with the –S switch. You will then be presented with a 1> prompt, where you can type a query. If you want to execute an operating system command from the sqlcmd window, you can type !! in front of the command, like this:

```
1>!!dir
```

To execute a SQL command, type the command. After you hit enter, you will see a 2> and 3> prompt until you finally issue a GO statement to execute the batch. After the GO statement, the batch runs and the prompt resets to 1>.

We've gone through the basic commands, but to simplify matters, it would be great to have a set of commands that executes each time you run sqlcmd. *Initialization files* run a series of commands after you execute sqlcmd but before control is handed over to the user.

To create an initialization file, first create a T-SQL file called `C:\initexample.sql` with Notepad or your favorite editor. This file is going to run a series of commands after you first run `sqlcmd`. The `:setvar` statement can be used to set user variables that can be used later in the script with the $ sign. This example initialization script will create three variables. One holds the database name, the other holds the 60-second timeout, and the last holds the server name. You use the variables later in the script by using `$(variablename)`.

```
:setvar   DBNAME AdventureWorks
:setvar sqlcmdlogintimeout 60
:setvar server "localhost"
:connect $(server) -l $(sqlcmdlogintimeout)
SELECT @@VERSION VersionofSQL;
SELECT @@SERVERNAME as ServerName;
```

Next, go to a command prompt and type the following command to set the `sqlcmdini` environment variable. This will set the environment variable for the profile of the user. After executing this, each time the `sqlcmd` program is executed, the `initexample.sql` script will execute before handing control to the user.

```
SET sqlcmdini=c:\initexample.sql
```

With the environment variable now set, just run `sqlcmd` from a command prompt (shown in Figure 10-3). After you run this, you will see the version of SQL Server and the server name before you're given control to run any query against the database.

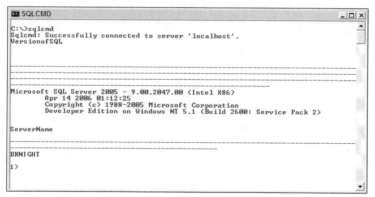

Figure 10-3

Sqlcmd from Management Studio

Eventually, when doing your day-to-day job, you're going to find yourself wanting to integrate `sqlcmd` scripts into your regular T-SQL scripts, or someone may pass you a script that has `sqlcmd` integrated into it. To use this script in Management Studio's query environment, simply click the SQLCMD Mode icon in the Query Window. If you try to execute `sqlcmd` syntax from within the Query Window without being in SQLCMD Mode, you will receive an error like this:

```
Msg 102, Level 15, State 1, Line 3
Incorrect syntax near '!'.
```

`sqlcmd` and T-SQL can intermingle in the same script, and you can go in between script types easily as long as SQLCMD Mode is enabled. Once enabled, any `sqlcmd` syntax will be highlighted in grey. You can also enable the mode each time a query is opened by going to Tools⇨Options in Management Studio. In the SQL Server page of the Query Execution group (shown in Figure 10-4), enable the option "By default, open new queries in SQLCMD mode." After enabling this option, any subsequent query windows will be opened with the mode enabled.

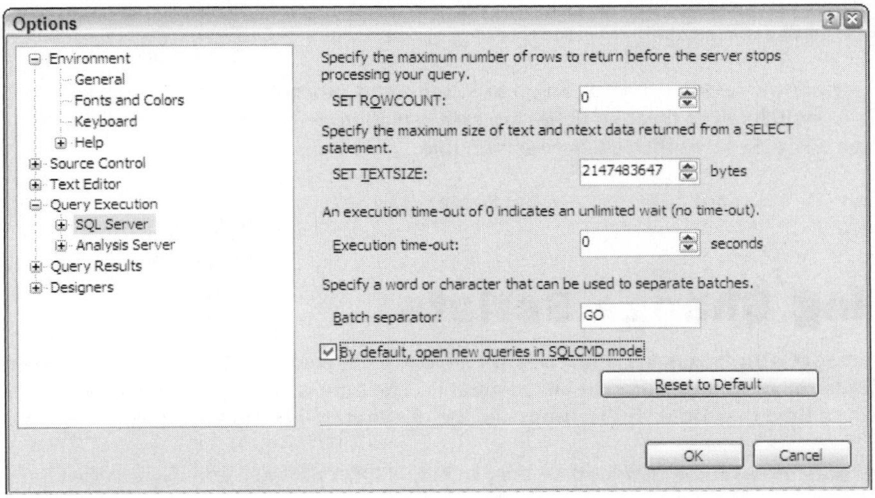

Figure 10-4

By using `sqlcmd` and T-SQL, you can connect to multiple servers from within the same script and run T-SQL statements. For example, the following script will log on to multiple servers and back up the master database of each server. The :CONNECT command is followed by the instance name that you wish to connect to. This is a simple example, but it can be strengthened in a disaster recovery situation to do massive repairing of your databases or SQL Server instances.

```
:CONNECT localhost
BACKUP DATABASE master TO  DISK = N'C:\test.bak'

:CONNECT localhost\sql2k5test
BACKUP DATABASE master TO  DISK = N'C:\test2.bak'
```

You can also use the :SETVAR command inside of `sqlcmd` to create a script variable. This variable allows you to either set the variable from within the :SETVAR command, as shown in the following code, or can set it by passing in the variable through the command prompt. The following example shows you how to set a variable called SQLServer to the value of Localhost. You then use that variable by using the variable name prefixed with a dollar sign and wrapping it in parenthesis. Another variable called DBNAME is also created and used in the T-SQL backup command. As you can see, in `sqlcmd`, you can mix T-SQL and `sqlcmd` easily, and the variables can intermix.

```
:SETVAR SQLServer Localhost
:CONNECT $(SQLServer)
:SETVAR DBNAME Master

BACKUP DATABASE $(DBNAME) TO  DISK = N'C:\test.bak'
```

Now take the preceding script and modify it slightly to look like the following script. Then save it to a file called C:\InputFile.sql (place the file wherever is appropriate on your machine). This script will dynamically connect to a server and back up the master database.

```
:CONNECT $(SQLServer)
BACKUP DATABASE master TO  DISK = N'C:\test.bak'
```

With the script now saved out, you can go to a command prompt and type the following command using the –v switch (all of these switches are case sensitive) to pass in the variable. In this case, you pass in the name localhost to the SQLServer variable.

```
sqlcmd -i c:\inputfile.sql -v SQLServer="localhost"
```

Creating Change Scripts

Creating change scripts is never a fun task for a DBA. That being said, nothing is more satisfying than a perfect deployment to four different environments. The only way to do this "perfect" deployment is to invest a lot of time in good script writing, like the one that will be shown shortly, or to invest in a tool.

There are more tools on the market than ever to help a DBA package and deploy the changes. For example, Red-Gate (http://www.red-gate.com) can compare two databases (test and production, for example) and package the change scripts to move production up to the same level. This same type of tool is available through many vendors such as ApexSQL, Idera, and Quest, to name a few. None of these tools eliminates human intervention entirely. You must have some interaction with the program to ensure that a change that was not meant to be deployed is not sent to production.

A last tool worth mentioning here is Visual Studio Team System for Database Professionals. This is the Microsoft product that aids in the complete change cycle. Visual Studio 2003 used to do this very well, but the deployment feature was removed in Visual Studio 2005 until the Team System version. At the time of the publication of this book, Visual Studio Team System for Database Professionals is still in very early beta. The tool should allow for change detection and simple deployment to environments. If you make a change to a column name, the tool creates a change script to change every stored procedure and view that referenced that column name.

Since this tool isn't generally available yet, let's go over the way you used to do this in Visual Studio 2003 and use SQL Server 2005 technology with it. Visual Studio 2003 had a great way to package all of your scripts and generate a command file to call the scripts. The command file was the key element that ensured a perfect deployment time after time. You can create the command file manually in Notepad or you can download the sample here, called Installv101.cmd, from www.wrox.com. We will break this script into more manageable chunks, but first here's the entire process:

```
@echo off
REM: Authentication type: Windows NT
REM: Usage: CommandFilename [Server] [Database]

if '%1' == '' goto usage
if '%2' == '' goto usage

if '%1' == '/?' goto usage
if '%1' == '-?' goto usage
if '%1' == '?' goto usage
if '%1' == '/help' goto usage

sqlcmd -S %1 -d %2 -E -b -i "Version100.sql"
if %ERRORLEVEL% NEQ 0 goto errors
sqlcmd -S %1 -d %2 -E -b -i "Version101.sql"
if %ERRORLEVEL% NEQ 0 goto errors


goto finish

REM: How to use screen
:usage
echo.
echo Usage: MyScript Server Database
echo Server: the name of the target SQL Server
echo Database: the name of the target database
echo.
echo Example: MyScript.cmd MainServer MainDatabase
echo.
echo.
goto done

REM: error handler
:errors
echo.
echo WARNING! Error(s) were detected!
echo --------------
echo Please evaluate the situation and, if needed,
echo restart this command file. You may need to
echo supply command parameters when executing
echo this command file.
echo.
pause
goto done

REM: finished execution
:finish
echo.
echo Script execution is complete!
:done
@echo on
```

First, the lines with the following `if` statements ensure that the user has passed in the proper variables. If they neglected to pass in a variable, they are sent to a section of code called `usage`. Also, if the user passes in one of many switches such as `/?`, the user is sent to the same section. You can add many more checks for variables, but just keep in mind that variables are ordinal in nature. If you pass in a third variable, just refer to it as `%3`, and then pass it as the third option after calling the command file.

```
if '%1' == '' goto usage
if '%2' == '' goto usage
if '%1' == '/?' goto usage
```

The most important part of the script actually calls the subscripts. There would be two lines here for each script that you wished to call. In some cases, you could have 50 lines on large deployments. This is the script that has been modernized to use `sqlcmd` versus `osql.exe`. You pass in the variables for the server name and the database name. The `-E` switch enforces Windows Authentication. If you wished to use SQL Authentication, you could use the `-U` and `-P` switches. Using these two switches would cause you to have to create two new input parameters (`%3` and `%4`) and write the error checks mentioned earlier.

In the following script, you can also see two input files being called. One is for Version 1.0 of the database and then the other is for 1.0.1 bug fixes. If any error is found in the script, the command file halts and calls the error routine. If the error level is not equal to 0, the error routine is executed.

```
sqlcmd -S %1 -d %2 -E -b -i "Version100.sql"
if %ERRORLEVEL% NEQ 0 goto errors
sqlcmd -S %1 -d %2 -E -b -i "Version101.sql"
if %ERRORLEVEL% NEQ 0 goto errors
```

The error routine looks like the following block of code. The code will display an error message and stop the execution of code. The weakness in this code is that it's not transaction based. The DBA must code this inside each subscript called earlier. The problem there is that the transactions cannot *not* cross subscripts. So, if Script A successfully executed to purge the data but Script B failed to load the data, the data would remain truncated.

```
:errors
echo.
echo WARNING! Error(s) were detected!
echo ----------------
echo Please evaluate the situation and, if needed,
echo restart this command file. You may need to
echo supply command parameters when executing
echo this command file.
echo.
pause
goto done
```

This rather large script is a practical example if you must hand-code your solution. After doing this enough, you'll either become proficient at it or so tired of hand-coding that you decide to buy a tool. There is no wrong answer as long as you get your changes deployed without incident. Before executing this command file against the production database on the final deployment day, try to clone the database (if it is small enough) to ensure that you can execute the script against the clone successfully.

You can call the batch file by using the following syntax. Again, this syntax is only using two variables: the server name and database name. Typically, you will want to name your command files to match a database version number or application version number.

```
InstallV101.cmd localhost adventureworks
```

Version Tables

Another important concept when deploying changes is to add a version number to your changes, much like application developers do in their own version controlling. A table that we've used for years is db_version. This table holds what version of the database is installed now and what versions have been installed over the history of the database.

You can use the table to diagnose if the DBA that deployed the change skipped a build of the database by looking in the history of the changes. If you jump from 2.0 to 2.2, you know you may have an issue. It can also be used in conjunction with the application's version number. For example, you may have a document that says application 2.1 if the application requires 2.1.8 of the database. I've even had developers code the logic into the application at startup. If the application did not match the db_version table, it would throw an error. The table's schema looks like the following. You can download this code, called db_version.sql, from this book's page at www.wrox.com.

```
if not exists (select * from sys.objects where object_id =
object_id(N'[dbo].[DB_VERSION]') and OBJECTPROPERTY(object_id, N'IsUserTable') = 1)
 BEGIN
CREATE TABLE [DB_VERSION] (
  [MajorVersion] [char] (5) NULL ,
  [MinorVersion] [char] (5) NULL ,
  [Build] [char] (5) NULL ,
  [Revision] [char] (5) NULL ,
  [OneOff] [char] (5) NULL,
  [DateInstalled] [datetime] NULL CONSTRAINT [DF__Version__DateIns__0876219E]
DEFAULT (getdate()),
  [InstalledBy] [varchar] (50) NULL ,
  [Description] [varchar] (255) NULL
) ON [PRIMARY]
END
```

For most environments, there are too many columns in this db_version table, but it was created as a catch-all and standard table. Every DBA that works at your company would know to go to the table, regardless of the application, to find the version. The version may match a document of known issues with the database. Typically, you may also find yourself creating views on top of the table to show you the last installed version. The following is a complete data dictionary for the table.

❑ MajorVersion — Major release of the application. In the application version, it would be the following bolded number (**1**.0.5.1).

❑ MinorVersion — Minor release of the application. In the application version, it would be the following bolded number (1.**0**.5.1).

❑   Build — Build number of the application. In the application version, it would be the following bolded number (1.0.**5**.1).

❑   Revision — Also can be called the minor service pack (or patch) position. This number would also refer to bug fixes found in QA. For example, you may have numerous iterations of Portal 2.5.3 as you fix bugs. You could increment this number (Application Build 2.5.3.**2**, for the second iteration). In the application version, it would be the following bolded number (1.0.5.**1**).

❑   OneOff — In some cases, a customization code may be required. For example, Application A has a number of customized versions of Build 2.1.1. In those cases, you could have 2.1.1.0 - **1** to indicate a customization (1 being for Client B for example). This field is only used in specialized situations.

❑   DateInstalled — The date this application was installed in the environment. This is set to getdate() by default, which will set it to today's date and time.

❑   InstalledBy — The name of the installer or creator of the service pack

❑   Description — Description of the service pack. This can be used in an environment where multiple clients are sharing one database (for example, "Upgrade Application A 2.5.1.2 for client."

To insert into the table, you would use the following syntax. You would need to make sure that the deploying DBA is disciplined to place the lines of code to create the table and insert into it at the top of each command file you create.

```
INSERT INTO DB_VERSION  SELECT 1, 5, 0, 2, NULL, getdate(),'Brian Knight', 'Script
to promote zip code changes'
```

A last use for the table is to run a check before you perform a database upgrade. Before applying the database install for version 1.1, you can run an IF statement against the table to ensure that version 1.0 is installed. If it isn't installed, you can throw an error and stop the script from executing.

Summary

In this chapter, we've covered how to become compliant with best practices in change management. You can do this by monitoring for change by using DDL triggers. You can also use Visual Studio to create database projects that integrate into Source Safe. The last key for smoothly creating a change-management process is using sqlcmd for a smooth deployment by using command-line scripts. In Chapter 11, you'll learn how to properly configure a server for optimum performance before installing SQL Server 2005.

11

Configuring the Server for Optimal Performance

The developer DBA needs to know how to optimize performance to ensure that anything he or she designs will perform up to its potential. The developer DBA must ensure that the system will start its life performing well; and that as inevitable changes are made to the system throughout its life cycle, they are made in a way that enables the application to continue to perform. As the system grows in terms of data, users, and functionality, it needs to grow in ways that keep the system operating optimally.

Similarly, the production DBA needs to understand performance so that the system he or she maintains starts out performing well and then continues to do so throughout the system's life cycle. Several different elements factor into this, from getting the server set up correctly, to monitoring the system as it starts working, to implementing a full monitoring strategy to keep the system operating optimally.

The three most important aspects of performance are as follows:

❑   Know what your system can deliver (CPU, Memory, IO)
❑   Find the bottlenecks
❑   Know your target (how many, how fast)

This chapter discusses all of these issues and addresses the most pressing questions regarding performance and configuring a server.

What Every DBA Needs to Know about Performance

In this chapter, we lay out a lot of specific hardware recommendations that will enable you to improve the performance of your system. However, shaving milliseconds off of a transaction time isn't always worth the amount of time and hardware budget you spend to accomplish that goal. Frequently, good planning up front is worth more than clever optimization later. The three things you should know above all else are as follows: start tuning early, define performance, and focus on what's important.

The Performance Tuning Cycle

Performance tuning is an iterative process, and ideally starts at the beginning of the design process. Too often performance and optimization are tacked on at the end. Obtaining optimal performance starts with configuring the server, continuing with designing an efficient schema and specifying optimized queries, which leads to optimal index selection. The monitoring and analysis of performance can then feed back to any point in this process, right back to changes to server configuration or schema design. This system is illustrated in Figure 11-1.

You start with your first best guess about how you think your application is going to work and what resources you think it's going to use, and plan accordingly. Most often, it's only a best guess. At this point in time, you really don't know exactly how the application is going to work.

In the case of a new application, you don't have an existing system to measure. It is hoped that you will have some metrics from either an existing user base or management predictions regarding who the users will be, what they do on a daily basis, and how that would impact the new application.

In the case of an existing system that you are either moving to a new server or to which you are adding functionality, you can measure specific metrics on system resource usage, and use those as a starting point. Then you can add information about any new functionality. Will this increase the user base? Will it increase the processing load on the server? Will it change the data volume?

All this information enables you to make a good estimate of the new system's impact on resources. Even before you have implemented the new system, while testing is taking place, you have a great opportunity to start to evaluate your estimates against the actual resource requirements, and the performance you get from your test servers.

Defining Good Performance

The fundamental question that every DBA has to answer before refining a system is simple: Do we have good performance? Without either a specific target or some baseline to compare against, you will never know. Planning, sizing, testing, and monitoring will provide you with the information you need to be able to start to answer this question. Identify your critical metrics for CPU, memory, and IO; create a baseline; and then after deploying, monitor your critical metrics to answer the question.

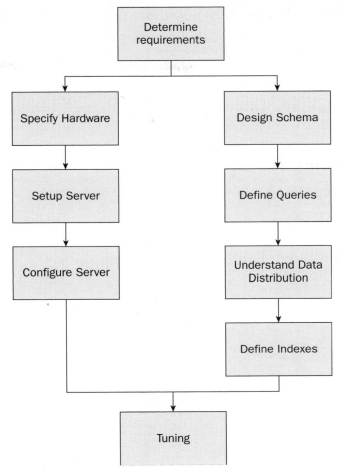

Figure 11-1

For example, consider how performance requirements can vary in the case of an online store. Here, response time to users is critical to keep them shopping. On a database such as this, there are likely to be very clearly defined response times for the most important queries, and maybe a broad requirement that no query can take longer than two or three seconds. On a different database server delivering management reports on warehouse inventory levels, there may be an expectation that these reporting queries take some time to gather the right information, so response times as long as a few minutes may be acceptable, although there may still be some queries that have much shorter response time requirements. In yet another database the key performance criteria might be the time it takes to back up the database. In another database the key criteria might be the time to load or unload data.

The key performance criteria might be defined as a very high level requirement such as "no query must take longer than x seconds." In another system it might be that long-running operations must complete within a specific time window, such as backup must complete in an overnight window of x hours.

Focus on What's Most Important

The final essential aspect of performance is being able to focus on what's really important, knowing what you can measure, how to measure it, and what the limitations of that measurement might be. Consider a typical system. The end users' experience is the net sum of all performance from their client machine through many layers to the database server and back again. Because the focus of this book is the DBA and SQL Server 2005, we are going to focus on measuring SQL Server performance, but it's worthwhile to have a basic understanding of the big picture, where DBAs fit in, and some of the tools and metrics that may be having an impact on your system.

Figure 11-2 shows a schematic diagram of a typical Web-based architecture. This schematic is typical of any enterprise customer using the Microsoft Windows Server System Reference Architecture to implement their enterprise solution. This may be the first time that many DBAs have looked at something like this, and understood where their puzzle piece (the database) fits into the big picture.

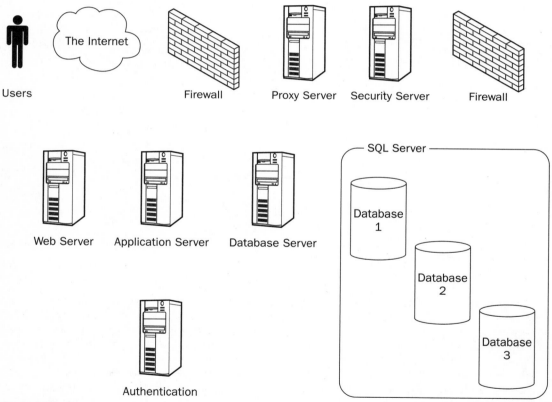

Figure 11-2

One of the first things you notice in the diagram is the number of elements in the bigger picture. When the user calls the help desk and complains of poor performance, finding the culprit involves a lot of possible candidates, so it is important to spend time identifying which piece of the complex system architecture might be guilty.

The important thing to take away from this exercise is an understanding of both the big picture and how to focus in on what's important for you. In this book we are interested in SQL Server, databases, and the server on which SQL runs.

What the Developer DBA Needs to Know about Performance

Good performance is built on a solid foundation, which for a SQL database is the schema. A well-designed schema will provide a solid foundation on which the rest of your application can be implemented. The rules to follow are less simple than traditional concepts such as "normalize to the n Normal form." Instead, they require that you have a solid understanding of the use of the system, including a knowledge of the users, the queries, and the data. The optimal schema for an OLTP system will be less optimal for a DSS system, and of no use at all for a DW system.

Users

You first need to know who is going to use the system, how many users there are, and what they are going to do. The users will usually fall into different groups based on either job function or feature usage. For an e-commerce-based system, for example, the user groups might be browsers, purchasers, order trackers, customers needing help, and others.

Queries

After determining the different groups of users, you need to understand what they do, which queries will be run, and how often each query is run for each user action. In the e-commerce example, a browser might arrive at the site, which invokes the home page, requiring maybe 20 or even 30 different stored procedures to be called. When users click on something on the home page, each action taken will require another set of stored procedures to be called to return the data for the next page. So far it looks like everything has been read-only, but for ASP.NET pages there is the issue of session state, which might be kept in a SQL database. If that's the case, then you may already have seen a lot of write activity just to get to this stage.

Data

The final part of the picture is the data in the database. You need an understanding of the total volume of data in each table. You need to understand how that data gets there and how it changes over time. Going back to the e-commerce example, the main data elements of the site would be the catalog of items available for sale. For example, the catalog could come directly from the suppliers' Web sites through an Internet portal. Once this data is initially loaded, it can be refreshed with updates as each supplier changes their product line, and as prices vary. The overall volume of data won't change much unless you add or remove items or suppliers.

What will change, hopefully very quickly, will be the number of registered users, any click tracking you do based on site personalization, the number of orders placed, the number of line items sold, and the number of orders shipped. Of course, it is hoped that you will sell a lot of items, which will result in a lot of new data growth every day.

A sound knowledge of the data, its distribution, and how it changes helps you find potential hot spots, which could be either frequently retrieved reference data, frequently inserted data, or frequently updated data. All of these could result in bottlenecks that might limit performance.

Robust Schema

An understanding of all the preceding pieces — users, queries, and data — needs to come together to help implement a well-designed and well-performing application. If the foundation stone of your database schema isn't solid, then anything you build on top of that shaky foundation is going to be shaky. Although you are unlikely to achieve an optimal solution, you may be able to achieve something that's acceptable.

How does all this information help you tune the server? You need to understand where the hot spots are in the data to allow the physical design to be implemented in the most efficient manner. If you are going through the process of designing a logical data model, you shouldn't care about performance issues. Only when you come to design the physical model do you take this information into account, and modify the design to incorporate your knowledge of data access patterns.

What the Production DBA Needs to Know about Performance

The production DBA's life is considerably different from that of the developer DBA, in that a production DBA will be dealing with a system that someone else has designed, built, and handed over, either as a new or an already running system. The production DBA may also face challenges with performance on very old systems running legacy applications on old outdated hardware. In this case, the scenario changes from designing an efficient system to making the system you have been given work as well as possible on the hardware you have.

The starting point for this process has to be an understanding of what the hardware can deliver; what resources the system needs; and, finally, what are the expectations of the users. The key elements of understanding the hardware are processor speed and cache size (and type). Next comes memory: How much is there? What is the bus speed? Finally comes IO: How many NICs are there? How many disks? How are they configured? Having answers to these questions is just the start.

The next step is determining how each system is required to perform. Are there any performance-related Service Level Agreements (SLAs)? If there are any performance guidelines specified anywhere, are you meeting them, exceeding them, or failing them? In all cases, you should also know the trend. Have you been maintaining the status quo, getting better, or, as is most often the case, slowly getting worse?

The production DBA needs to understand all of this, and then know how to identify bottlenecks and resolve them to get the system performing at the required level again.

The tools that the production DBA uses to perform these tasks are as follows:

❑ **Task Manager:** Gives a quick, high-level view of server performance and use of resources

❑ **Performance Monitor:** Provides a much more detailed view of server performance

❑   **SQL Profiler:** Enables workload traces to be captured, and can report on long-running queries

❑   **Query Analyzer:** Enables long-running queries to be analyzed, bottlenecks found, and solutions developed

These tools are covered in more detail in Chapter 13.

Optimizing the Server

The rest of this chapter covers optimizing the server. This includes the hardware and operating system configuration to provide SQL Server with the best environment in which to execute. The three key resources that you should consider anytime you discuss optimization or performance are the CPU, memory, and I/O.

Starting with the CPU, there aren't a lot of options to play with here other than the number and type of processors. The only real configuration option to consider once the server is mounted in the data center is whether it is hyperthreading-enabled — that is, should you turn hyperthreading on or off? Other than helping you make the right decision about hyperthreading, most of this part of the chapter is focused on understanding the different processor attributes so you can make the right purchasing decisions.

Memory has more options, and it's a lot easier to add or remove memory (RAM) than it is to change the number or type of processors in a server. When you initially configure the server, you should have some idea of how much memory you might need, and understand the available configuration options. These options are primarily for non-uniform memory access (NUMA) systems. On a NUMA system, you will often have the choice of using *cell local memory* or *interleaved memory*. On most 32-bit systems today, a number of *boot.ini* settings can affect memory configuration. These are settings such as enabling Physical Address Extensions (PAEs), which enables the operating system's kernel to use the PAE version of the kernel, which in turn can take advantage of an additional four address lines on Intel processors that support PAE.

`/3GB` and `/USERVA` are boot.ini settings that alter the way the operating system configures the 32-bit address space. I/O is, by far, the largest and most complex section of this chapter. In many ways I/O performance is perhaps the most important part of the server configuration to get right because everything you do lives on the disk. All the code you run in the operating system, SQL Server, and any other applications start off as files on the disk. All the data you touch in SQL Server lives on the disk. Data starts out life there, is read into memory, and then has to be written back to disk before it becomes a permanent change. Every change you make in SQL Server is written to the SQL log file, which lives on disk. All these factors make a good I/O configuration an essential part of any SQL Server system.

I/O configuration is actually too big a subject to cover in one chapter; it really requires a book of its own. This chapter introduces you to some of the I/O options available, and then walks through several scenarios to provide some insight into how to make the right storage configuration decisions.

Before we start, it will be helpful to put each of the three server resources back into perspective in terms of their relative performance. The following is an outline that's relevant to today's systems. As you refer to this book in the future, you can easily pencil in the current start of processor, memory, and I/O performance to see how the relative speeds of different elements have changed.

Typical speeds and throughput for system resources are as follows:

❑   A CPU speed of 2GHz results in 8GB/sec

❑   Memory speed of 500MHz results in 2GB/sec

❑   Disk speed of 5 to 200MB/sec

Use these numbers to do the math for throughput for a 10GB table:

❑   A 2GHz CPU with a throughput of 8GB/sec would access 10GB of data in 1.2 seconds.

❑   500MHz memory with a throughput of 2GB/sec would access 10GB of data in 5 seconds.

❑   Disks with a throughput of 5MB/sec would access 10GB in 33 minutes.

Graphically, this might look something like what is shown in Figure 11-3.

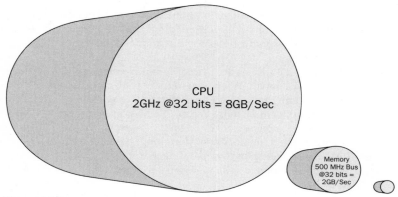

Figure 11-3

Unfortunately, I can't draw the disk small enough, or the CPU big enough, to make this illustration to scale given the relative difference between CPU speed and disk speed. The conclusion here is that disk access is much slower than memory access, which is slower than the CPU. The key, therefore, is to get as much data as you can into memory, and then as much of that onto the CPU as you can.

With SQL Server, there isn't much you can do to alter how much of your data is being operated on by the CPU; that's controlled by the developers who wrote SQL Server. What you can do, though, is specify the processors with larger cache, and a higher speed. Add more memory at a faster speed, and design your storage subsystem to deliver the fastest performance possible within your requirements for speed, size, and cost.

Configuring Server Hardware

On most small to medium-size servers, very little needs to be done to configure the hardware other than make a BIOS change to enable hyperthreading. Once this option is set, most of the remaining tasks are related to physically installing RAM, I/O adapters such as NICs, disk adapters for SCSI or SATA, and that's about it.

On medium to large systems, you will find a variety of management software to help you configure, operate, and maintain the hardware. Most hardware vendors have their own version of this kind of software, offering a wide variety of capabilities and options.

On large enterprise systems such as the HP Superdome, NEC5800 Express, or Unisys ES7000 family, configuring the server hardware has entered a whole new dimension. On these larger enterprise systems, you will find a *management processor (MP)* hiding within the server. The management processor, and its software interface, controls the hardware — from booting a partition, to configuring different hardware partitions, to changing memory layout, to managing the power to different hardware components. The management processor handles all of these tasks.

The tasks that need to be achieved to manage all the large systems are very similar, but the way each hardware vendor implements their interface is unique, from the Java/Web site approach on Unisys to the Telnet-based command-line interface on HP and NEC systems.

Windows Server System Reference Architecture

Anytime you're thinking about building a new server, or are designing a new application, it is worthwhile to refer to the Windows Server System Reference Architecture (WSSRA) to find the latest Microsoft-recommended configurations, and to determine whether a configuration exists that might match closely with what you want to do. If Microsoft has already built a server configuration that matches your requirements, then you can save a lot of time by reusing the work they have already done. The WSSRA is a reference architecture that contains prescriptive guidance for setting up servers for different roles in an enterprise.

Windows Server Catalog

The Windows Server Catalog (www.microsoft.com/windows/catalog/server/) should be your first stop when considering purchasing any new hardware. If the new hardware isn't in the catalog, then it's not supported to run Windows Server 2003 (or Windows 2000) and won't be supported when running SQL Server either.

CPU

SQL Server 2005 operates in a very different environment than previous versions of SQL Server. When SQL Server 2000 was launched, a large server used for SQL might have two, or maybe even four, processors. Now SQL Server 2005 is able to run on the largest servers, with 64 processors, and up to 1TB of RAM running Windows Server 2003 Data Center Edition. Currently, there is a bewildering array of processor options to consider when thinking about a new system. SQL Server 2005 can run on a wide variety of processors:

- ❑ 32-bit processors: X86
- ❑ 32-bit with 64-bit extension processors: X64
- ❑ 64-bit processors: IA64

What follows is a short introduction to these different processor families, along with a short discussion of some of the factors that influence making a decision about which processor you should use.

32-bit X86 Processors

32-bit systems are fast becoming replaced by 64-bit systems. The only reason to purchase a 32-bit system today is cost, and a certainty that the system will never need more than 2 to 4GB of physical memory.

64-bit

If you're considering purchasing new servers today, you should seriously be considering 64-bit processors. Even when the server is only going to run 32-bit applications, the capability to increase memory beyond 4GB without resorting to PAE, and to greater than 64GB at all, means that a 64-bit system should be your first choice.

X64 or IA64

The key factors when deciding between X64 and IA64 are cost, availability, scalability, and processor speed. It's always dangerous to generalize, but today most X64 processors have faster clock speeds than IA64 systems. The current state of processor clock speed is such that X64 processors are running at up to 3GHz, whereas IA64 processors have been stuck at 1.6GHz for some time now, with no sight of an increase in the foreseeable future.

However, processor speed alone can be misleading, as most IA64 processors have larger caches than X64 processors. The larger cache can help minimize the disadvantage of slower processor speeds. X64 processors are typically available in a wider range of servers than IA64 systems, which are increasingly only found in specialized machines, either high-performance workstations or very large highly scalable systems from a few specialist vendors.

Hyperthreading

You want to answer two questions about hyperthreading: First, should you purchase processors with hyperthreading capability? If you do, then the second question is whether you should run with hyperthreading enabled or disabled. This is a very difficult question to answer, and a one-size-fits-all approach will not work. Any answer must involve each customer testing for themselves.

One of the most important factors when considering hyperthreading is to understand the maximum theoretical performance benefit that you might get from hyperthreading. Intel's documentation on hyperthreading reveals that the maximum theoretical performance gain from hyperthreading is 30 percent. Many people running with hyperthreading enabled for the first time expect to see double the performance, because they see two processors. You should understand that hyperthreading is only ever going to give you a maximum performance increase of 1.3 times non-hyperthreaded performance, and in practice it will be closer to 1.1 to 1.15 times. This knowledge helps put any decision about hyperthreading back into perspective.

In some cases hyperthreading, at least theoretically, won't provide any benefit. For example, in any workload where the code is running a tight loop entirely from cache, hyperthreading won't provide any benefit because there is only a single execution engine. In some cases this scenario will result in degraded performance because the OS will try to schedule activity on a CPU that isn't physically there.

Another scenario in which hyperthreading can directly affect SQL Server performance is when a parallel plan might be chosen. One of the things a parallel plan does is split the work across the available processors with the assumption that each processor will be able to complete the same amount of work in the given time. In a hyperthreading-enabled scenario, any thread that's not currently executing will be stalled until the other thread on that processor completes.

No one can yet tell you whether hyperthreading will help or hurt your performance when running your workload. Plenty of theories abound about how it might impact different theoretical workloads, but no one has yet been able to come up with prescriptive guidance that definitely says turn it on here and off over there. Unfortunately, that leaves the customer with the burden of figuring it out for themselves.

That said, however, there are a few things to consider that can help you make your decision. First, the operating system can make a big difference. Windows 2000 wasn't hyperthreading-aware, whereas Windows Server 2003 is, so expect to see better performance on Windows Server 2003 compared to Windows 2000. In addition, Windows Server 2003 Service Pack 1 added additional hyperthreading awareness, so make sure you are running SP1.

Something else to consider is that hyperthreading itself has been evolving, and although we haven't found any concrete evidence of changes in how hyperthreading is implemented on different Intel processors, feedback from the field seems to indicate that it's getting better with each generation of processors that use it. The point here is that if the customer is trying hyperthreading on an older server, then they may not see as much benefit as they would if they used it on a server with the very latest generation of processors.

Microsoft's licensing policy is the opposite of its competitors in that they license by the socket, not by the core or thread. This means that in some configurations it's possible for the operating system (and SQL Server) to recognize up to eight processors (threads) and still run on a low-end system SKU such as Windows Server 2003 Standard Edition.

Because it's so important to our discussion of hyperthreading, we close this section by repeating the following: The maximum theoretical performance improvement with hyperthreading is only 30 percent compared to non-hyperthreaded applications. In practice, this will actually be a maximum of maybe just 10–15 percent. Moreover, for a lot of customers this is going to be very difficult to measure, especially if they are running testing with a workload that doesn't produce consistent results in the first place.

Cache

The reason modern processors need cache is because the processor runs at 2 to 3GHz, and main memory simply cannot keep up with the processor's appetite for memory. To try to alleviate this, processor designers added several layers of cache to keep recently used memory in small, fast memory caches so that if you need to reuse memory it might already be in cache. In addition, because of the way cache works, it doesn't just load the byte requested, but the subsequent range of addresses as well. The amount of memory loaded on each request is determined by the cache line size, and the processor's caching algorithm pre-fetch parameters.

The cache on modern processors is typically implemented as multiple layers (L1, L2, L3). Each subsequent layer is physically farther from the processor core, and becomes larger and slower until we are back at main memory. Some caches are general purpose and hold copies of any memory (L2 and L3). Other caches are very specific and hold only address lookups (TLB), data (L1 data), or instructions (instruction cache). Typically, L1 is smaller and faster than L2, which is smaller and faster than L3. L3 cache is often physically located on a separate chip, and so is farther from the processor core than L1 or L2, but still closer than main memory.

Processor cache is implemented as a transparent look-through cache. This means that controlling functions on the chip manage the process of filling the cache and managing cache entries. At this point, we should consider some SQL Server specifics.

SQL Server 2005 is a considerably more complex product than SQL Server 2000. Building in all this additional complexity is achieved at the cost of additional lines of code, which results in additional bytes in the size of the final exe. Sqlservr.exe. The exe for SQL Server 2000 is 8.9MB; the exe for SQL Server 2005 has grown considerably and is now weighing in at 28MB. Moreover, simply starting the service requires more system resources. SQL Server 2000 runs in about 29MB of memory. (You can easily see this by using the Task Manager and looking at the Mem Usage column for SQL Server. The Mem Usage column provides an approximation of the working set for the process.) Connecting with SQLCMD and issuing a simple query, such as selecting a name from master..sysdatabases, adds another 0.5MB to that number. SQL Server 2005 uses around 50MB of memory just to start. On my test server, the Task Manager Mem Usage column reports 49,604KB. Connecting with SQLCMD and issuing the same command causes that to grow to over 53MB (53,456 KB).

All this increased complexity results in a lot more code to do the same operations in SQL Server 2005 than in SQL Server 2000. This manifests itself as an increase in sensitivity to cache size, so the smaller the cache, the slower you might run, and vice versa. In other words, if you have a choice between two processors running at the same speed, go for the one with the largest cache. Unfortunately, the increased cache usually comes at a price. Whether that additional cost is worthwhile is very difficult to quantify. If you have the capability to run a test on both processors, this is the best way to determine the potential improvement. Try to come up with a test that delivers a specific metric that you can factor against the cost to deliver a clear indication of the cost/benefit of larger cache.

Note one qualification to the information just presented in the preceding paragraph. SQL Server 2005 adds a lot more complexity to how it determines the best plan for executing your query. You will see this in an increase in the time it takes to compile a query, and in most cases a reduction in the query execution time. This means that the first time a new query is run, there is a chance that it may actually take longer to run than in SQL 2000, but future executions of the plan from cache will execute considerably faster.

This is an excellent reason to make use of any feature that enables you to reuse a plan. As long as SQL Server has taken all that time to figure out a fast way to get you your data, reuse that plan as much as you can before it's thrown away. This enables you to optimize your time. One sure way to fail to take advantage of this, and to set yourself up for worse performance, is to issue only ad hoc statements, which ensures there is no plan reuse. In addition, you will spend a lot of time compiling statements that are never reused.

Multi-Core

One of the biggest challenges facing multi-processor system designers is how to reduce the latency caused by the physical limitations of the speed of light and the distance between processors and memory. One solution is to put multiple processors on a single chip. This is what a multi-core system does, and it provides more potential for better performance than a single-core system because of this reduced latency between processors and memory. The big question is, do you need a multi-core system?

The answer to this depends on how many processors you need and how much you are willing to pay. If you need an eight-processor system, you will get a potentially faster system for less money by purchasing a quad-socket dual-core system, rather than an eight-socket single-core system.

In most cases, a multi-core system will deliver 1.6 to 1.8 times the performance of a single-core system. This is pretty much in line with the performance of a dual-socket system, making it a very good option. For the latest information on this issue, check out what the hardware vendors are doing with their Transaction Processing Council numbers (see www.tpc.org). The TPC results are a great way to compare hardware, although some hardware vendors don't publish results for the systems you want to compare.

Another factor to consider is scalability. Rather than purchase a straightforward dual-socket, single-core system, you can purchase a dual-socket system with a single-core processor that is capable of being upgraded to dual-core processors in the future. This way, you can defer the expense of adding dual-core processors when you need to add more processing power.

Before continuing, it's worth defining some clear terminology here to avoid confusion when discussing multi-core systems:

❑   The **socket** is the physical socket into which you plug the processor. Before multi-core systems arrived, there used to be a direct one-to-one relationship between sockets and execution units.

❑   A **core** is equivalent to an execution unit, or what you would previously have considered to be a processor. With a multi-core processor there will be two or more of these per socket.

❑   A **thread** in this context is not the same as the thread you might create in your program, or the operating system threads; it is only relevant in the context of hyperthreading. A hyperthreading thread is not a new execution unit, but a new pipeline on the front of an existing execution unit. See the section "Hyperthreading" for more details on how this is implemented.

Now let's look at a specific example to illustrate what this actually means.

Figure 11-4 shows a single-socket, single-core processor with no hyperthreading, which results in one thread.

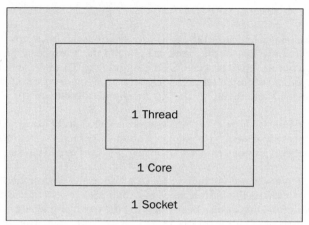

Figure 11-4

Figure 11-5 shows a single-socket, multi-core processor with hyperthreading, which results in four threads, licensed as one processor.

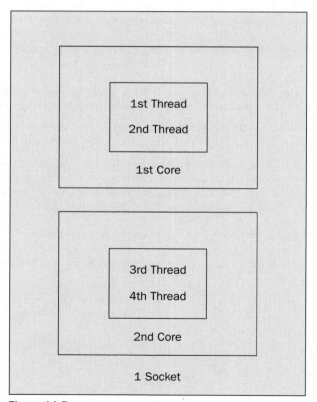

Figure 11-5

Figure 11-6 shows a dual-socket, dual-core processor with hyperthreading, which results in eight threads, licensed as two processors.

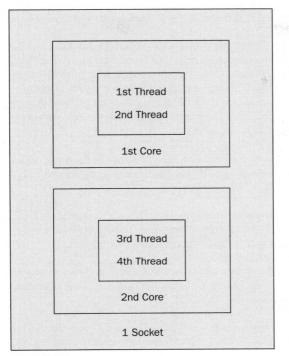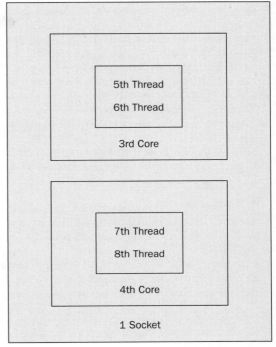

Figure 11-6

System Architecture

Another key purchasing decision has to be made regarding the machine architecture. For systems up to eight processors there really isn't much choice. Single-socket, dual-socket, quad-socket, and even most eight-way systems are only available in a symmetric multi-processor (SMP) configuration. It's only when you move to 16-, 32-, or 64-way systems that you need to consider the options of SMP versus NUMA. This isn't something you actually need to configure, but rather something you should understand as an option when considering the purchase of one type of system versus another.

Symmetric Multi-Processing

A symmetric multi-processor (SMP) system is a system in which all the processors are connected to a system bus in a symmetric manner. All processors have to share access to system resources over a common system bus. This architecture works great for smaller systems in which the physical distance between resources is short, the number of resources is small, and the demand for those resources is small.

NUMA

NUMA stands for non-uniform memory access; this architecture is often also referred to as ccNUMA, meaning a cache-coherent version of NUMA. The main difference between an SMP system and a NUMA system is where the memory is connected to, and how processors are arranged on the system bus.

Whereas on an SMP system the memory is connected to all the processors symmetrically via a shared bus, on a NUMA system each group of four processors has its own pool of "local" memory. This has the advantage that each processor doesn't pay a cost of going to a bus past more than four processors to access memory, provided the data it wants is in the local memory pool. If the data it wants is in the memory pool from another node, then the cost of accessing it is a little higher than on an SMP system. Therefore, one of the objectives with a NUMA system is to try to maximize the amount of data you get from local memory, as opposed to accessing memory on another node.

NUMA systems typically have a four-sockets-per-node configuration, and implement multiple nodes up to the current system maximum of sixteen nodes. This fully populated configuration delivers a full 64 processors to the operating system.

Smaller configurations that are any multiple of a four-socket node can usually be accommodated, allowing for highly configurable servers, and highly scalable servers. For example, a company could start with a single four-socket node and scale up all the way to 16 four-socket nodes, for 64 sockets.

One of the problems with NUMA systems is that as they grow, the issues of maintaining cache coherency also grow, introducing management overhead. Another problem is that as the number of nodes increases, the chance of the data you want being local is reduced.

The operating system must also be NUMA aware to schedule threads and allocate memory local to the node, which is more efficient than allocating nonlocal memory or scheduling a thread to run on a different node. Either of these actions incurs an overhead of node memory access, either to fetch data or to fetch the thread's data from the old node and transfer it to the new node.

Memory

This section looks at memory–specifically, memory on the server, including some of the issues associated with memory, the options you can use, and how they can impact the performance of the server. We'll start with a basic introduction to operating system memory, and then jump straight into the details of how to configure a server for different memory configurations.

Physical Memory

Physical memory is the RAM you install into the server. You are probably already familiar with the SIMMs and DIMMs that go into desktop PCs and servers. This is the *physical memory,* or RAM. This memory is measured in megabytes, or, if you are lucky, in terabytes, as the latest editions of Windows Server 2003 Data Center Edition now support systems with 1TB of RAM. Future editions of the operating system will increase this number as customers demand ever more powerful systems to solve ever more complex business problems.

Physical Address Space

The physical address space is the set of addresses that the processor uses to access anything on its bus. Much of this space is occupied by memory, but some parts of this address space are reserved for things such as mapping hardware buffers, and interface-specific memory areas such as video RAM. On a 32-bit processor, this is limited to a total of 4GB of addresses. On 32-bit Intel server processors with PAE, the address bus is actually 36 bits, which enables the processor to handle 64GB of addresses. You might assume that on a 64-bit processor the address bus would be 64 bits, but because there isn't a need for systems that can address 18 exabytes of memory yet, or the capability to build a system that large, manufacturers have limited the address bus to 40 bits, which is enough to address 1TB.

Virtual Memory Manager

The Virtual Memory Manager (VMM) is the part of the operating system that manages all the physical memory and shares it between all the processes that need memory on the system. Its job is to provide each process with the illusion that it has 4GB of virtual address space, and ensure that it has memory when it needs it, although the limited physical memory is actually shared between all the processes running on the system at the same time.

The VMM does this by managing the virtual memory for each process, and when necessary it will take back the physical memory behind virtual memory, and put the data that resided in that memory into the page file so that it is not lost. When the process needs to use that memory again, the VMM retrieves the data from the page file, finds a free page of memory (either from its list of free pages or from another process), writes the data from the page file into memory, and maps the new page back into the processed virtual address space. The resulting delay or interruption is called a *page fault*.

On a system with enough RAM to give every process all the memory it needs, the VMM doesn't have to do much other than hand out memory and clean up after a process is done with it. On a system without enough RAM to go around, the job is a little more involved. The VMM has to do some work to provide each process with the memory it needs when it needs it. It does this by using the page file to store data in pages that a process isn't using, or that the VMM determines it can remove from the process.

The Page File

On a server running SQL Server, the objective is to try to keep SQL Server running using just the available physical memory. SQL Server itself goes to great lengths to ensure that it doesn't over-allocate memory, and tries to remain within the limits of the physical memory available.

Given this basic objective of SQL Server, in most cases there is limited need for a page file. The only reason for changing the default size of the page file is to aid in diagnosing a system crash. In the event of a system crash, the kernel uses the parameters defined in the system recovery settings to decide what to do. You want the kernel to write some kind of memory dump, and in order to do this the page file size must be large enough to hold the type of memory dump you asked for. In servers with less than 2GB of RAM, a full memory dump is acceptable, so you need a page file that's at least 2GB. On servers with more than 2GB of RAM, a full memory dump can become excessively large, so choosing a smaller dump, such as a kernel dump, makes more sense. The smallest memory dump you can create is a mini-dump. A mini-dump has a lot less information than a kernel memory dump, but in many cases it may still have enough data to enable a system crash to be identified and resolved. If not, then a kernel dump, or in some cases a live kernel debug, is needed to isolate the root cause of the system crash.

In some cases, SQL Server and the OS might not cooperate well on sharing the available memory, and you may start to see system warnings about low virtual memory. If this starts to occur, then ideally add more RAM to the server, reconfigure SQL to use less memory, or increase the size of the page file. It's better to reconfigure SQL Server to remain within the available physical memory than it is to increase the size of the page file.

Page Faults

Page faults are generally bad for SQL Server, but not all page faults are the same. Some are unavoidable, and some have limited impact on performance, while others can cause severe performance degradation and are the kind we want to avoid.

SQL Server is designed to work within the available physical memory so that it won't experience the bad kind of page faults. Unfortunately, the Performance Monitor page fault counter doesn't indicate whether you are experiencing the benign or bad kind of page fault; and because of this, it doesn't tell you whether you are experiencing good or bad performance.

Soft Page Faults

The most common kind of page fault you will experience is the *soft page fault*. These occur when a new page of memory is required. Anytime SQL Server wants to use more memory, it asks the VMM for another page of memory. The VMM then issues a soft page fault to bring that memory into SQL Server's virtual address space. This actually happens the first time SQL Server tries to use the page, and not when SQL Server first asks for it. For the programmers among you, this means that SQL Server is calling `VirtualAlloc` to commit a page of memory. The page fault only occurs when SQL tries to write to the page the first time.

Hard Page Faults

Hard page faults are the ones you want to try to avoid. A hard page fault occurs when SQL Server tries to access a page of its memory that has been paged out to the page file. When this happens, the VMM has to step in and take some action to get the needed page from the page file on disk, find an empty page of memory, read the page from disk, write it to the new empty page, and then map the new page into SQL Server's address space. All the while, the SQL Server thread has been waiting. Only when the VMM has replaced the missing page of memory can SQL Server continue with what it was doing.

Why Page Faults Are Bad

If you look back to the section "Optimizing the Server," where I discussed the relative difference in speed between the CPU, memory, and disks, you can see that disk speeds can be as slow as 5MB/Sec, whereas memory speeds are likely to be around 2GB/sec. Whenever a hard page fault occurs, the thread that incurs the hard page fault will be waiting for a relatively long time before it can continue. If the thread running your query incurs a series of hard page faults, then your query will appear to run very slowly.

The most common symptom of this is intermittently slow-running queries. The resolution is to either add more memory to the server, reduce the memory used by other applications on the server, or tune your SQL Server queries to reduce the amount of memory the queries need.

Virtual Address Space

On a 32-bit system, each process running on the system has a total of 4GB of virtual address space (VAS). Note two important things about this: It's virtual memory, not physical memory, and it's only space, not actual memory.

The 4GB of VAS is shared between the kernel and your process, split in the middle at address 0x7FFFFFFFh, with user-mode address space from 0x00000000h through 0x7FFFFFFFh, and the kernel from 0x80000000h to 0xFFFFFFFFh. However, if you enable /3GB or /USERVA, the boundary can be moved from 2GB up to 3GB.

What this means is that there is no memory in the virtual address space until you either ask for memory or try to load something. In both cases, the OS takes your request and fills in a block of virtual address space with actual memory. Note that the actual memory isn't guaranteed to always be there, as the VMM can take the memory away and put it into the page file. This behavior is completely transparent; you know nothing except that the next time you try to access that piece of memory, it's very slow because you have to wait for the VMM to read the page from the page file, put it back into a page of memory, and then map that page back into your virtual address space.

32-Bit System Memory Configuration

Several options with 32-bit systems have been introduced over the years as ways to get around the basic limitations of a 32-bit system — that is, a 4GB address space evenly divided into 2GB of user address space and 2GB of kernel address space.

Physical Address Extensions

Intel introduced a way to get around the 4GB limitation of a 32-bit address bus by physically extending the address bus to 36 bits. This extension is called PAE, or Physical Address Extensions. It enables a 32-bit operating system to access up to 64GB of memory.

PAE is also a flag you can set in the `boot.ini` file to tell the operating system to use the version of the kernel that can take advantage of those extra four bits of address bus, and it enables a 32-bit Windows system to use more than 4GB of memory.

There are some scenarios in which you will end up running the PAE kernel even if you don't enable it in `boot.ini`. This is the case if you are running a DataCenter edition of the OS and the hardware is hot-swap-memory-enabled. In this case, because the server may have additional memory added at any time that could exceed the 4GB limit of 32-bit addresses, the OS always uses the PAE kernel, just in case it ever has to deal with more than 4GB of physical memory.

3GB

One way to increase the amount of memory a 32-bit process can use is to take some of the space assigned to the kernel and use it for user mode address space. You can do this by specifying either the /3GB or /USERVA options in the `boot.ini` file.

The /3GB option moves the boundary to be at 3GB, giving each process an additional 1GB of address space. This does mean that the kernel now only has 1GB of memory to use, however, which can sometimes be a problem that results in the server crashing with a bug check.

The /USERVA option enables you to specify a different amount of address space to be taken from the kernel. You can specify any value between 2GB and 3GB as the boundary between user and kernel address space. This has the same effect of increasing each process's virtual address space, and reducing the kernel's address space, as the setting /3GB, and can have the same consequences if the kernel ends up running out of memory space.

One of the limitations of reducing the amount of memory available for the kernel is that it reduces the amount of memory available for the kernel to track physical memory. This is why when you turn on /3GB or /USERVA, the OS is limited to using a maximum of 16GB of RAM. Therefore, if your server has more than 16GB of RAM installed, you wouldn't want to use /3GB or /USERVA.

AWE

Another way for a 32-bit process to use more memory is Address Window Extensions (AWE). AWE is a Windows API that enables a 32-bit process to create a small window in its virtual address space and then to use this to map physical memory directly into its virtual address space. This enables any 32-bit process to use more than 2 or 3GB of memory. SQL Server is a process that has been written to use the Windows AWE APIs. You can enable this on 32-bit editions of SQL Server by setting the SQL Server configuration option AWE enabled to 1.

Given what we know about memory, and AWE, it would seem that there is no reason to use AWE on a 64-bit system. After all, a 64-bit system has enough address space to address as much memory as it needs, so why would you consider using AWE on a 64-bit system? In fact, you can't enable AWE in a 64-bit version of SQL; the option is disabled in the UI.

However, it turns out that there are some great reasons for using AWE to access your memory, even on a 64-bit system. The SQL Server team realized that on 64-bit systems they could improve overall performance by using AWE in a 64-bit environment. They found that using AWE memory enables memory to be allocated a lot faster, and each access is faster. In addition, there is a more direct route to the memory, so every access is slightly faster.

Because of this, they changed the way 64-bit SQL Server works, so although you can't enable AWE on a 64-bit system, if the account used to run SQL Server has the "lock pages in memory" privilege, then SQL Server will automatically use AWE to access buffer pool memory.

/3GB or AWE?

This is a question you end up answering pretty frequently. A customer has a system with somewhere between 2GB and 4GB of RAM, and they want to know whether they should use /3GB, or AWE, or maybe both. One thing to remember is that this has to be a 32-bit operating system running 32-bit SQL server 2005. In any other scenario, this question just isn't relevant because SQL Server will have 4GB of virtual address space (32-bit SQL Server on an X64 OS), or it will have a 16 EB virtual address space (64-bit SQL Server on a 64-bit OS).

The /3GB option enables SQL server to use more memory for anything it needs. It can use the additional 1GB of virtual address space for the buffer pool, the procedure cache, or any other operation for which it needs memory.

AWE enables the SQL Server to use more memory, but only for the buffer pool. In most cases this is what SQL needs more memory for, but in some special cases the SQL may need more memory for the procedure cache, or connections, or something else that can't be allocated from the buffer pool.

These situations in which SQL can't use the extra memory for the buffer pool are very few and far between, but they do occur, so you need to know how to spot this situation. For more details, refer to Chapter 13, which includes ways to determine the amount of memory SQL Server is using for stored procedures versus the buffer pool.

64-bit Systems

This section applies to both X64 and IA64 systems. With X64 systems, you can install a 32-bit operating system. If you have installed a 32-bit operating system onto an X64 system, even though the processor is 64-bit capable, it's running as a 32-bit processor, so everything we said about 32-bit systems from the preceding section applies.

Each flavor of 64-bit operating system has a slightly different memory layout, and provides each process with a slightly different amount of virtual address space. This is currently 7,152GB for IA64, and 8,192GB with X64. Note that Windows Server 2003 SP1 currently supports a maximum of 1TB of physical memory.

What this means for SQL Server is that you don't have to worry about using PAE or /3GB as a workaround for the 2GB limit imposed by 32-bit Windows.

You do still have to consider AWE, though. This is because using AWE even in a 64-bit environment can provide you with a boost to performance at startup, when you need to take memory, and during normal operation. Using memory through AWE enables SQL to take a number of shortcuts and avoid going through the VMM. For these reasons, on a 64-bit system, if the account used to run SQL Server has the "Lock pages in memory" privilege, then SQL Server will default to using AWE memory.

Memory Configuration Scenarios

Now that you understand the various memory options, this section examines the key scenarios and makes specific recommendations regarding the various memory options:

❑ **32-bit OS and SQL with less than 2GB of RAM:** This is the simple case. There isn't enough memory to require you to use PAE, /3GB, /USERVA, or AWE.

❑ **32-bit OS and SQL with 2-4GB of RAM:** In this case, you don't need to use PAE, as you haven't exceeded the 32-bit address space limit. You might want to consider using /3GB, /USERVA, or AWE. This means either AWE *or* /3GB, not both, and the decision would depend on what the application is doing, which dictates what memory demands it will place on SQL.

If you find that your 32-bit SQL Server system needs to use more than 2 to 4GB of memory, then rather than struggle with PAE, AWE, and /3GB, you should really be considering moving to a 64-bit system, which will provide immediate relief to many of the challenges we have to overcome in a 32-bit environment.

❏ **Special case — 32-bit OS with 2 to 4GB of RAM:** Use 3GB/ USERVA or AWE? A frequently asked question for customers in this space is whether should they use AWE to get to memory above the 2GB limit, or use /3GB or /USERVA to give SQL Server more memory. We have asked many people in the SQL Server developer team, and PSS, this question, and it seems that they all have a different answer. However, after asking a few more pointed questions, the answer becomes a little clearer.

When SQL Server uses AWE memory, it can only be used by the buffer pool for data pages. In most cases this is just fine, as that's what you need the extra memory for. In a few very special cases, however, SQL Server needs to use the extra memory for other things, such as the stored procedure cache, the memory for user connections, or other internal memory that SQL needs to do its work. In these cases, SQL Server won't be able to use the extra memory if it's provided through AWE, so you would have to use /3GB.

❏ **Special Case — 32-bit OS with 4GB of RAM:** A couple of special cases aren't covered in the previous points. One of these is the odd situation that occurs when you actually try to fit 4GB of RAM into a 32-bit server. Initially this would seem to be pretty straightforward — after all, 4GB is the maximum amount of memory that a 32-bit operating system can address, so it should be just fine.

Unfortunately, the operating system uses of some of that 4GB address space to do things such as map hardware into the address space, so before you even fit your first byte of RAM into the system, there is already a load of stuff there taking up some of your 4GB of available physical addresses. One of the biggest chunks of this memory is for mapping memory from video cards. On most server systems, there won't be a lot of memory here, but it's quite easy to take a reasonably mid-range workstation video card with 256 to 512MB of memory installed and slot that into a server. That's going to be another 256 to 512MB of your precious 4GB of addresses that have been eaten up by the video card's memory.

What this means is that the operating system can't fit your 4GB of memory into the available space. To actually be able to use all your 4GB of memory, you need to enable PAE. This is the bit that seems so strange at first, until you look at the math and realize that you don't have to just account for the RAM you install, but for all those other areas of memory you never even thought about before. After you do the calculations, it becomes clear why you need to enable PAE to use all 4GB of RAM.

To see this for yourself, open the Device Manager, switch the view to Resource View, and then expand the Memory node. You will see a window similar to the one shown in Figure 11-7.

Initially this looks pretty confusing, but with a little explanation it starts to make more sense. The key to interpreting this window is to understand that most memory areas appear in this view multiple times. First there will be big chunks of memory allocated to the PCI bus. These areas are then duplicated in more detail, with specific memory allocations within each chunk of PCI bus memory. A good example of this is the area of memory shown in Figure 11-8.

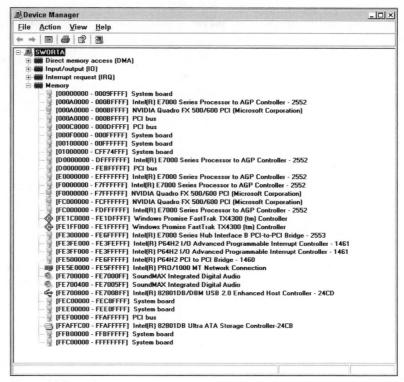

Figure 11-7

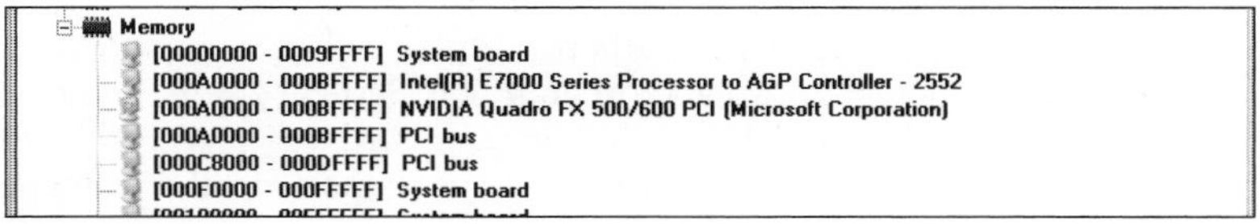

Figure 11-8

In this figure you can see three things mapped into the memory at 000A0000–000BFFFF: two named AGP graphics controllers, and a third mapping for PCI bus. All this is indicating is that this is the AGP graphics aperture, that there are multiple AGP cards installed, and that this area of memory is on the PCI bus.

There is one more twist to this story. When enabling PAE as mentioned earlier, the BIOS must be able to map the physical memory into addresses above the 4GB limit. In some cases, the BIOS doesn't do this. In other cases, the hardware might not implement 36 address lines on the motherboard. Either of these reasons can prevent your server from mapping the additional memory above 4GB, preventing you from using a full 4GB of physical memory.

❑ **32-bit OS and SQL with 4 to 16GB of RAM:** In this case, you need PAE to enable the system to access more than 4GB of RAM. You will also want to use AWE to enable SQL to access as much memory as possible. You might want to consider turning on /3GB as well.

❑ **32-bit OS and SQL with more than 16GB of RAM:** Again, you need to use PAE to enable the OS to access more than 4GB of RAM. You also need to enable AWE to allow SQL to use all the additional memory above 2GB. You can't use /3GB in this case because it would restrict your memory to just 16GB.

❑ **X64 system with 64-bit OS and 32-bit SQL with less than 4GB of RAM:** If your system is running on a 64-bit OS, you don't need PAE because the OS can already access up to 16 exabytes of RAM. You don't need /3GB or /USERVA either, because on an X64 system every 32-bit process gets a full 4GB of user mode address space.

❑ **X64 system with 64-bit OS and 32-bit SQL with more than 4GB of RAM:** In this scenario, you still don't need PAE. You also don't need /3GB, or /USERVA. What you do need is AWE to enable SQL to use memory above 4GB. However, as you are running in a 32-bit process, although the server may have much more than 64GB of RAM available, your 32-bit process can only map a maximum of 64GB using AWE.

❑ **64-bit SQL on a 64-bit OS:** In this case, SQL Server, like every other 64-bit process, gets 7152 to 8192GB of memory space by default. If the "lock pages in memory" privilege is granted, SQL will use AWE as a more efficient way for it to access memory than through the OS VMM.

I/O

I/O encompasses both network I/O and disk I/O. In most cases with SQL Server, you are primarily concerned with disk I/O, as that's where the data lives. However, you also need to understand the effect that poor network I/O can have as a bottleneck to performance.

Configuring I/O for a server storage system is perhaps the place where you have the most options, and it can have the largest impact on the performance of your SQL Server system. When you turn off your computer, the only thing that exists is the data stored on your hard drive. When you turn the power on, the processor starts running, the OS is loaded, and SQL Server is started; all this happens by reading data and code from the storage subsystem.

This basic concept is true for everything that happens on a computer. Everything starts its life on the disk, and has to be read from the disk into memory, and from there through the various processor caches before it reaches the processor and can be used as either code or data. Any results the processor arrives at have to be written back to disk to persist any system event, e.g., shutdown, failure, maintenance, etc.

SQL Server 2005 is very sensitive to disk performance, more so than many applications, because of the manner in which it manages large amounts of data in user databases. Many applications have the luxury of being able to load all their data from disk into memory and then being able to run for long periods of time without having to access the disk again. SQL Server strives for that model, as it is by far the fastest way to get anything done. Unfortunately, when the requested operation requires more data than can fit into memory, SQL Server has to do some shuffling around to keep going as fast as it can, and it has to start writing data back to disk so it can use that memory to generate some new results.

At some point in the life of SQL Server data, every piece of data that SQL server uses has to come from disk, and must be written back to disk.

Network

Referring back to Figure 11-2, you can see that the network is a key component in any SQL Server system. The network is the link over which SQL Server receives all its requests to do something, and by which it sends all its results back to the client. In most cases, today's high-speed networks provide enough capacity to enable a SQL Server system to use all its other resources (CPU, memory, disk) to their maximum before the network becomes a bottleneck.

In some systems the type of work being done on the SQL Server is relatively small compared to the number of requests being sent to the server, or to the amount of data being returned to the client. In either of these cases, the network can be a bottleneck. Network bottlenecks can occur anywhere in the network. They can be on the NIC of the client, where the client is an application server that's serving the database server with hundreds of thousands of requests per second. Bottlenecks can occur on the fabric of the network between the NIC or the client (application server, Web server, or the user's workstation). This network fabric can consist of many pieces of network infrastructure, from the simplest system in which two machines are connected over a basic local area network to the most complex network interconnected systems in either the Internet or a global corporate WAN. In these larger more complex interconnected systems, much of the network can be beyond your control, and may introduce bandwidth or latency issues outside of acceptable limits, but that we have no control over. In these cases you can do little more than investigate, document, and report your findings.

The parts of networking that we are going to examine here are those that you may have direct control over, and all are on the SQL Server system. We are making the assumption that the remainder of the network fabric is up to the job of supporting the number of requests we receive, and of passing the results back to the client in a timely manner.

It's beyond the scope of this book to go into the details of monitoring and tuning the network outside of the SQL Server system.

Disks

The other piece of I/O is disk IO. With earlier versions of SQL Server, disks were pretty simple, leaving you with limited options. In most cases you had a couple of disks at most to deal with. Large enterprise systems have long had the option of using SAN storage, while medium to large business systems have been able to use external disk subsystems using some form of RAID, and most likely utilizing a SCSI interface that enables you to build disk subsystems with hundreds if not thousands of disks.

Take a moment to consider some of the basic physics involved in disk performance. It's important to understand the fundamental differences between different types of disks, as they explain differences in performance. This in turn helps you make an informed decision about what kind of disks to use. The following table demonstrates some fundamental disk information.

Disk Rotational Speed	Rotational Latency	Track-to-Track Latency	Seek Time	Data Transfer Rate	Transfer Time for 8KB	Total Latency
5,400 rpm	5.5 mS	6.5 mS	12 mS	90MB/Sec	88 >S	12.1 mS
7,200 rpm	4.1 mS	6.5 mS	10.7 mS	120MB/Sec	66 >S	10.8 mS
10,000 rpm	3 mS	1.5 mS	4.5 mS	166MB/Sec	48 >S	4.6 mS
15,000 rpm	2 mS	1.5 mS	3.5 mS	250MB/Sec	32 >S	3.5 mS

Rotational latency is the time it takes the disk to make a half-rotation. This figure is given for just half a rotation rather than a full rotation because on average the disk makes only a half rotation to find the sector you want to access. It is calculated quite simply as rotational speed in rpm divided by 60 (to give revolutions per second) and then divided by the number of rotations per second.

Track-to-track latency is the time it takes the disk head to move from one track to another. In the table, the number for 5,400 and 7,200 rpm disks is considerably slower than for the 10,000 and 15,000 rpm disks. This indicates that the slower disks are more likely to be ATA disks rather than SCSI disks. ATA disks have considerably slower internals than SCSI disks, which accounts for the considerable difference in price and performance between the two disk types.

Seek time is the magic number disk manufacturers publish and it's their measure of rotational latency and track-to-track latency. This is calculated in the preceding table as the sum of rotational latency and track-to-track latency.

Data transfer rate is the average rate of throughput. This is usually calculated as the amount of data that can be read from a single track in one revolution, so for a modern disk with a data density of around 1MB/track, and for a 7,200 rpm disk, rotating at 120 revs per second, that equates to around 1MB per track × 120 revolutions per sec = 120MB/sec of data that can be read from the disk.

Transfer time for 8KB is the time it takes to transfer a given amount of data at that transfer rate. To see how long it takes to transfer an 8KB block, you simply divide the amount of data you want to move by the transfer rate, so 8KB/120MB = 66 micro secs (or >S)

Total latency for a given amount of data is the sum of rotational latency, track-to-track latency, and disk transfer time.

In the table you can clearly see that for a single 8KB transfer, the largest amount of time is spent moving the head to the right position over the disk's surface. Once there, reading the data is a tiny percentage of the time.

Latency limits the disk's ability to service random read requests. Sequential read requests will have an initial latency, and are then limited by the disk's ability to read the data from the disk surface and get each I/O request back through the many layers, before reading the next sector from the disk's surface.

Write requests will often be buffered to cache, which is bad for SQL Server. You always want to turn disk caching off, unless you are using a storage array with a battery backup that can guarantee writing the cache to disk in the event of a power failure.

Throughput in MB/sec is a measure of how many bytes the disk can transfer to or from its surface in a second. This is usually quoted as a theoretical number based on the disk's bus.

Throughput in IOs/sec is a measure of how many I/Os the disk can service per second. Most often this is quoted as a theoretical number based on the disk's bus.

Storage Design

After all that talk about the different pieces of a storage system, it's time to get serious about figuring out how best to configure your storage system. This is a pretty difficult thing to do, so we have come up with a set of guidelines, and then go into the details of how you can figure this out for yourself.

No Silver Bullet in Storage Design

Simply put, there is no single simple way to configure storage that's going to suit every purpose. SQL Server systems can be required to do dramatically different things, and each implementation could require a radically different storage configuration to suit its peculiar I/O requirements.

Use the Vendors' Expertise

The vendors of each piece of hardware should be the people you turn to for expertise in how to configure their hardware. They may not necessarily know how to configure it best for SQL Server, however, so this is where you have to be able to convey SQL Server's requirements in a manner the hardware vendor might understand. This is best done by being able to quote specific figures of reads versus writes, sequential versus random I/O, block sizes, I/O's per second, MB/sec for throughput, and minimum and maximum latency figures. This information will help the vendor provide you with the optimal settings for their piece of the hardware, be it disks, an array controller, fiber, networking, or some other piece of the storage stack.

Every System Is Different

Each SQL Server system may have very different I/O requirements. Understand this and don't try to use a cookie-cutter approach to I/O configuration (unless you have already done the work to determine that you really do have SQL systems with the exact same IO requirements).

Simple Is Better

It is an age-old engineering concept that simpler solutions are easier to design, easier to build, easier to understand, and hence easier to maintain. In most cases, this holds true for I/O design as well. The simpler solutions invariably work faster, are more robust and reliable, and take less maintenance than more complex designs. Unless you have a very compelling, specific reason for using a complex storage design, keep it simple.

More Disks

More disks are invariably faster than fewer disks. For example, if you have to build a 1TB volume, it's going to deliver higher performance if it's built from a lot of small disks (ten 100GB disks) versus a few larger disks (two 500GB disks). This is true for various reasons. First, smaller disks are usually faster than larger disks. Second, you stand a better chance of being able to utilize more spindles to spread read and write traffic over multiple disks when you have more disks in the array. This gives you throughput that in some cases is the sum of individual disk throughput. For example, if those 100GB disks and the

500GB disks all delivered the same throughput, which was, say 20MB/Sec, then you would be able to sum that for the two 500GB disks to achieve just 40MB/sec. However, with the ten smaller disks, you would sum that to arrive at 200MB/sec, or five times more.

Faster Disks

Not surprisingly, faster disks are better for performance than slower disks. However this doesn't just mean rotational speed, which is just one factor of overall disk speed. What you are looking for is some indicator of the disk's ability to handle the I/O characteristics of the workload you are specifically interested in. Unfortunately, disk manufacturers rarely, if ever, provide any information other than rotational speed and theoretical disk bus speeds. For example, you will often see a 10K or 15K rpm SCSI disk rated as being able to deliver a maximum throughput of 300MB/sec because it's on a SCSI 320 bus. However, if you hook up that disk and start running some tests using a tool such as SQLIO, then chances are good that for small-block-size non-queued random reads you will be lucky to get much more than 2–4MB/sec from that disk. Even for the fastest I/O types, large-block sequential I/O, you will be lucky to get more than 60–70 MB/sec. That's a long way from 300MB/sec.

Test

Testing is an absolutely essential part of any configuration, optimization, or performance tuning exercise. Too often we have spoken with customers who have been convinced that black is white based on absolutely nothing more than a gut feeling, or some half-truth overheard in a corridor conversation.

Until you have some test results in your hand, you don't truly know what the I/O system is doing, so forget all that speculation, which is really nothing more than poorly informed guesswork, and start testing your I/O systems to determine what's really going on.

Monitor

Once you have set up the system and tested it, you need to keep monitoring it to ensure that you are aware of any changes to the workload or I/O system performance as soon as it starts. If you have a policy of monitoring, you will also build a history of system performance that can be invaluable for future performance investigations. Trying to track down the origins of a slow-moving trend can be very hard without a solid history of monitoring data. See Chapter 14 for more specifics on what and how to monitor.

Designing a Storage System

Now let's run through the steps you need to take when designing a storage system. The following sections introduce each of the different parts of a storage system, providing some guidance on key factors, and offering recommendations where they are appropriate.

The first questions you have to answer when designing a new storage system are about the disks. How many disks do you need? What size should they be? How fast should they be?

Space

The first thing you really need to determine is how much space you need. Once you have sized the data, you need to factor in index space, growth, room for backups, and recovery. All of these factors will increase the amount of space required.

How Many Disks

The number of disks you need is going to be driven by the amount of space you need, the performance you want, and how robust the storage needs to be. As an example, here are several alternative ways to build a 1TB disk subsystem:

❑ **Two 500GB SATA disks with a basic SATA controller:** This is the simplest and cheapest option. Use two of the latest 500GB disks. However, this is also the slowest option, and the least robust.

❑ **Four 500GB SATA disks with a RAID 1 controller:** This is twice the cost of the previous system, and isn't any faster, but it provides a robust solution using a mirroring controller to provide redundancy.

❑ **Four 250GB SATA disks with a RAID 0 controller:** This system is a non-robust step to improve performance. You've increased the number of disks by reducing their size. Using a striping controller, you can get some performance improvement by writing and reading from more disks at the same time.

❑ **Eight 125GB SCSI disks with a RAID 0 controller:** Now you're starting to get into a more serious performance configuration. This uses more, smaller disks, which will provide a significant performance improvement.

With all of these configurations you need to be aware of other bottlenecks in the I/O path. The first thing to consider is the PC's bus bandwidth, and then the disk adapter's bus bandwidth. If your server is using a basic PCI bus, then this will likely be limited to around 200MB/sec, so anytime you need to do large sequential I/O to more than two to four disks, you may be limited by the PCI bus. Next is the disk bus. For example, with a SCSI 320 bus, you can max out the bandwidth with around six disks at about 260MB/sec. If you need a system able to deliver higher than 250MB/sec, you should consider using an adapter with multiple channels.

Cost

Much as we would all like to have an unlimited budget, that's unlikely to be the case in most environments, so the ideal design will have to be modified to bring it in line with the available budget. This often results in less than optimal designs, but it's a necessary factor when designing any system.

Desired I/O Characteristics

The first thing you need to consider here are the I/O characteristics of the operations you are going to perform in SQL Server. This can be a complex issue to resolve, and in many cases the easiest way to determine this is through testing and monitoring of an existing system so that you can identify the exact types and volume of I/O that each major feature or function requires.

If you don't have an existing system, then you may be able to use the information in the following table as a guideline to get you started.

Operation	Random/Sequential	Read/Write	Size Range
CREATE DATABASE	Sequential	Write	512KB (Only the log file is initialized in SQL Server 2005)
Backup	Sequential	Read/Write	Multiple of 64K (up to 4MB)
Restore	Sequential	Read/Write	Multiple of 64K (up to 4MB)
DBCC – CHECKDB	Sequential	Read	8K–64K
DBCC – DBREINDEX (Read Phase)	Sequential	Read	(see Read Ahead)
DBCC – DBREINDEX (Write Phase)	Sequential	Write	Any multiple of 8K up to 128K
DBCC – SHOWCONTIG	Sequential	Read	8K–64K

It is not necessary for all of the space you need to have the same storage characteristics. The SQL Data Log, and tempdb should go onto the fastest, most robust storage you can afford, while space for backup and recovery and other repeatable tasks can be slower and less robust.

In some cases, where your database is a copy of some other master system, you might decide to build the whole system on cheap, non-robust storage. In the event of a failure, you could rebuild the whole system from the master system. However, if your copy has an SLA that requires minimal downtime and doesn't allow for a full rebuild, even though the data is only a copy, you have to implement some form of robust storage so that you never have to take the unacceptable hit of rebuilding from the master.

RAID

As part of the "How many disks do you need?" question, you must consider the RAID level you require, as this will influence the total number of disks required to build a storage system of a certain size and with the I/O characteristics you require:

❑ **Availability:** The first factor when thinking about RAID is the level of availability you need from the storage.

❑ **Cost:** An important part of any system is meeting any cost requirements. It's no good specifying the latest greatest high-performance system if it costs 10, 100, or 1,000 times your budget.

❑ **Space:** Another major factor in combination with cost is how much space you need to provide.

❑ **Performance:** The performance of the storage is another major factor that should help you determine what level of RAID you should choose.

Mirror with Stripe

This is the fastest, most robust option, but it also costs the most to implement. It may be overkill in some cases. Backups, data load, and read-only copies may not require this level of protection.

Striping with Parity

Striping with parity is a more cost-effective option to provide a degree of robustness, with some increase in performance. The downside with RAID 5 is that it's a bit of a compromise all round, and in the event of a disk failure system, performance can be seriously degraded when rebuilding the array with the new disk.

RAID-Level Recommendations

You need to use the fastest most robust storage for SQL data files. The recommendation is to use *striping with mirroring*.

You also need to use the fastest most robust storage for SQL log files. As for SQL data files, the recommendation is to use striping with mirroring.

If you know your application is going to make extensive use of `tempdb`, use the fastest most robust storage for `tempdb`. This might seem a little strange because the data in `tempdb` is always transitory, but the requirement for robustness comes from the need to keep the system running, not from a concern about losing data. If the rest of the system is using robust storage but `tempdb` isn't, then a single disk failure will prevent everything from working.

The operating system and SQL files can live on a simple mirror, although in many cases the time to rebuild the OS and SQL may be within acceptable downtime, so then a single disk will suffice.

For critical systems, the OS and SQL files should be on a mirrored disk array, but it only needs to be a single mirrored pair. OS and SQL files don't have high I/O requirements; they are typically read once when the application is loaded, and then not touched until new code paths may be used, and then a few more 4K random reads are issued. These files just don't require high-performance storage.

Isolation

Isolation is needed at several levels. You want to isolate the different types of I/O SQL generates to optimize each storage system. You don't want the heavy random I/O generated by a high-volume OLTP system from the highly sequential write access to the log file.

At the same time, on a shared storage system such as a SAN, you want to ensure that your storage is isolated from the I/O generated by other systems using the same shared storage. Isolation is primarily concerned with the sharing of disks that results from virtualization on a SAN system, but the principle can also apply to other parts of the storage subsystem, specifically the ports, fiber, and switches that make up the SAN fabric.

Separate SQL Data from the Log

I/O to SQL data files is very different in nature from I/O to the SQL log file. SQL data traffic is random in nature with relatively larger block sizes, occasionally becoming large sequential I/O for large table scans. SQL log traffic is sequential in nature, and is predominantly write until a checkpoint occurs, when you will see some read activity.

Because of this, it's important to separate data files and log files onto separate disks. Doing this enables the heads on the log disks to track sequentially, matching the log write activity. The heads on the data traffic will have a lot of seeks, as they need to get the next random disk block, but this won't impact log performance, nor will it be further randomized by having to intersperse random data reads and writes with sequential log writes.

Group Similar I/O Workloads

Going one step further, if you have multiple databases, or SQL instances, or tables within your database with very different access patterns, then wherever possible you should try to group similar I/O patterns together on the same set of disks. Identify read-only data access, write-only data access, and frequent read/write accesses, and then separate each group onto its own set of spindles.

Using tempdb

SQL Server 2005 makes much more extensive use of `tempdb` than previous versions, so it's very important to know how often you need to use this database. See Chapter 14 for more details on monitoring. If after monitoring you find that your system uses `tempdb` extensively, you should consider placing it on separate disks.

Another option considered by some users is placing `tempdb` on a RAM disk, or other high-performance solid state disk. Because of the lightning-fast response times of these kinds of disks, this can provide a considerable performance boost for systems that make extensive use of `tempdb`.

> *Although it's OK to place* `tempdb` *on volatile disks such as RAM disks, it's not OK to put any other SQL files on these kinds of volatile storage. SQL Server has very specific requirements for its storage to ensure the integrity of data.*

`tempdb` is discussed in more detail in Chapter 2 and Chapter 12.

Large Storage System Considerations: SAN Systems

More and more SQL Server systems are using storage provided by an external storage array of some kind. Frequently, these large external systems are called a *SAN system,* but they could be NAS or some other storage array technology such as iSCSI. This terminology doesn't refer to the storage but to the technology used to connect your SQL Server to the box of disks on a network of some kind.

In the case of a SAN system, the network is a dedicated storage network, frequently built using fiber. For an iSCSI system, the network is an IP network (the IP part of TCP/IP) built with compatible network cards but using a private network dedicated to storage traffic. For a NAS system, the network is not dedicated; it is shared with all your other network traffic.

Any discussion on SQL storage configuration has to include information on the concepts involved in configuring an external storage array.

Disk Virtualization

SAN systems have many challenges to face when you are placing large numbers of fast, high-capacity disks in a single box. One of these problems is how to provide the fastest storage to the largest number of people. You know that to increase disk performance, you need to stripe across as many spindles as possible, but many users of the SAN may require as little as 250GB or less of storage. If your SAN system is filled with 76GB disks, you could deliver that 250GB using three or four disks. Unfortunately, delivering 250GB from just four disks isn't going to provide much performance. Step back and consider that the SAN itself may have as many as 140 of these 76GB disks. If you could take a small piece of a larger number of disks, you could build the same 250GB chunk of storage, but it would be much faster.

Now consider the situation in which you can take a 2GB chunk from each of those 140 76GB disks. When you combine all those 2GB chunks together, you end up with 280GB of raw disk space. After subtracting some system overhead, that would probably end up at around 250GB. Sure, you wasted a little bit of space for the overhead of managing 140 disks, but now you have a 250GB chunk of storage that has the potential to deliver I/O at the rate of the sum of 140 disks; or if each disk were capable of 50MB/sec for sequential 64K reads, you would have a combined I/O throughput of run around 7,000 MB/Sec (7GB/sec). In practice, you won't get anywhere near that theoretical I/O rate, but you will see considerably higher I/O rates than you would if you just combined three or four disks together.

Disk virtualization is a technique that SAN vendors use for doing this. All the large SAN vendors have their own unique method, but they are all based around the same basic concept: Slice each disk up into uniform slices, recombine these small slices into larger chunks of storage, and present these virtualized chunks to each application.

1. Start with a single disk, and create multiple slices on the disk.

2. Do the same thing across multiple disks.

3. Group a collection of these disk slices together using some level of RAID, and present it to the server as a logical unit number (LUN).

LUNs

When considering the LUNs that the storage is going to present to the OS, you have to answer two questions. How big should each LUN be, and how many should you have? The starting point for answering these questions is to determine how much you need. If you have differing storage requirements, you also need to know how much of each different type you require. Different types of storage might range from high speed, high reliability for data and log; low speed, high reliability for archive data; high speed, low reliability for backup staging (before writing to tape); and low speed, low reliability for "other" storage that doesn't have tight performance criteria or present reliability concerns.

LUN Size

The next factor to be considered is LUN size. For a SAN-based system, or large local storage array, this equates to how big you make each chunk of storage presented to the operating system. These LUN-sized chunks of storage are the first time the OS sees the storage. You can tell from the amount of work you have already done with virtualization that the OS has no way of knowing how many disks, or how much from each disk, each LUN represents.

A number of factors can influence your decision regarding LUN size. You need to consider how the storage is going to be mounted in the OS. If you are going to mount each LUN as its own volume, then you can make them a little larger, although you need to remain far below the single-volume limit of 2TB. You want to stay well below this limit due to backup, restore, and startup times. On startup, the OS will run a basic check of each volume. Basically, the OS runs *Check Disk (CHKDSK)* at startup to validate each volume. If the volume is very large, the time taken to run chkdsk can become long — in some cases, very long, which can start to have a large impact on system startup time. For large enterprise servers with less than one server restart scheduled per year, this isn't a major problem, except when it's time to set everything up—installing the OS and drivers, and configuring the server; many reboots may be required. If each reboot takes one or two hours, restarting the server eight or more times becomes a two or three day labor, rather than something you do while getting another coffee refill.

In most cases, the storage array vendor will have specific recommendations regarding how big each LUN should be. These are based upon their extensive experience with their storage systems. Be cautious here because much of the storage vendor's experience will have come from storage arrays, not running SQL Server, whose I/O requirements are completely different. Make sure they understand the unique nature of the storage I/O characteristics you have for your system.

Number of LUNs

If there are no clear criteria that set an ideal size for each LUN, then there may be factors that dictate a specific number of LUNs. The simplest way to determine the number of LUNs you need is to divide the total storage volume required by the size of LUN you want, which gives you the ideal number of LUNs. That's not a very informed way of determining the number, however, and in many ways the calculation should start from the number of LUNs. The starting point for this is the storage vendor's recommendations. They should be able to provide guidance on how best to configure their storage, but their expertise might not include experience with SQL Server.

Server Configuration

After spending a lot of time configuring the storage, you still have to configure the server. The main configuration options on the server are related to the number, placement, and configuration of the *host bus adapter (HBA)*, and then you're into the details of the operating system, and more specifically the device manager and the file system.

Disk Adapters

The disk adapter is the interface card that you plug into the PCI bus inside your server to enable the PCI bus to connect to the ATA, SCSI, iSCSI, or fiber channel cabling required to connect to the disks. Several factors should be considered with disk adapters.

Number of Adapters

When determining the number of disk adapters, you first have to consider how many disks you need to support. On some interfaces, such as ATA and SCSI, there are physical limits to the number of disks allowed per bus. This is two disks per ATA bus (one master, one slave) and either eight or sixteen per SCSI bus (depending on which version of SCSI is in use). If you need an ATA-based system with eight disks, you need to have enough disk adapters to provide four ATA buses. If you need a SCSI-based system with 32 disks, and you are using a version of SCSI that supports 16 disks per bus, you would need two buses.

One adapter can provide more than one bus. You might find an ATA adapter that implements two or maybe four ATA buses, so your eight-disk system might only need a single adapter. In the case of SCSI adapters, many are multi-bus, so you should be able to deliver two SCSI buses from a single adapter card.

Placement

In larger servers, the physical placement of the adapter card in the PCI slots can have an impact on performance. There are two ways placement can affect performance. On a large system, the physical distance between the furthest PCI slot and the CPU can increase latency and reduce overall bandwidth.

On some systems the PCI slots are not all of the same type. It is increasingly common for systems to have a few PCI-X or fast 64-bit PCI slots with the remainder being slower slots. Placing a high-speed 64-bit, PCI-X, or PCI-Express disk adapter into a slow-speed PCI slot (some won't physically fit, but some will) can force the whole bus to run at a considerably slower speed than expected.

Firmware

Most disk adapters have firmware that can be upgraded. Even when you first purchase a new disk adapter, you should check the vendor's Web site to make sure you have the very latest firmware version. Vendors will change their firmware to fix bugs, improve performance, and match specific drivers, so you must always confirm that you have the latest firmware to ensure optimal performance.

Drivers

Even though the disk adapter probably comes with drivers, there is a very good chance that they are outdated by the time you purchase the adapter, so even before installing anything you should check the vendor's Web site for the very latest signed drivers.

In most cases, you should only ever run the latest signed driver, because this is the one that has been through full certification testing. Sometimes the vendor's Web site will offer a new version of a driver that fixes a specific problem you are encountering, but which hasn't been signed yet. In this very specific case, it's acceptable to take the risk of using the unsigned driver, provided you understand that you may encounter system crashes as a result of unfound bugs. If this happens, then the unsigned driver should be removed or rolled back immediately while further troubleshooting is performed to determine the true cause of the system crash.

Configuration

Many disk adapters have options that can be set to change the way they work in different environments, or for different types of disks to which they may be attached. For ATA and SCSI adapters, this configuration is usually pretty minimal, unless the adapter includes RAID, which is another topic altogether. In most cases the configuration involves fiber channel options on HBAs. iSCSI adapters that are network interface cards (NICs) also have configuration options, but these are the same settings you may have used to configure any IP-based network adapter, and were covered earlier in the material on NICs.

Partitioning

After installing the disks, you need to configure the disks themselves, and the first step with a new disk is to consider the disk partitions. What kind of partition do you want to create on the disk? There are two main options: an MBR partition or a GPT partition. Unless you have a specific requirement that forces the use of GPT, you should use an MBR partition.

Mounting Volumes

After you have partitioned the disks, you have to decide what kind of volumes you want. The choice here is between using a basic volume or a dynamic volume. We recommend using basic volumes, unless you need specific features that only a dynamic volume can provide. If you are running in a clustered environment, there are limitations on using dynamic volumes. This may result in having to resize your LUNs, or using an alternate option such as mount points.

Start Sector Alignment

Start sector alignment is a topic that frequently comes up for discussion. When dealing with storage arrays, the value you use for start sector alignment is driven by the cache line size. You need to ensure that the start sector on the partition is aligned with the start of the cache line on the SAN. If you're not familiar with the intricacies of cache lines, ask your SAN vendor.

The value to use for start sector alignment will come from the storage vendor. After obtaining a value, check to see if the vendor specified this in sectors (each sector is 512 Bytes) or KB. The Start Sector Offset is set using either `diskpar` or `diskparT`. Note the difference, as one has a T at the end, the other doesn't. `diskpar` is the older tool. `diskparT` started shipping with WS03 SP1. `diskpar` takes the disk offset as a number of clusters, whereas `diskparT` takes its offset as a number of KB. A value specified in `diskpar` of 64 (clusters) results in a start sector offset of 32K. Using 32 (KB) in `diskparT/align` will also give you a 32K offset.

File Systems — NTFS versus FAT

This shouldn't even be an issue anymore: Always use NTFS. The reliability offered by NTFS, and the speed and functional improvements of NTFS over FAT, make it the only real choice for your file system.

NTFS Allocation Unit Size

Another topic that frequently comes up is the NTFS *allocation unit size,* also known as NTFS *cluster size.* In testing, we ran with SQL Server 2005, and found that changing the NTFS cluster size has no impact on SQL performance. This is due to the small number and large size of the files that SQL uses. The recommendation that results from this is to continue to use an allocation unit size of 64K. Whatever you decide to use, test to confirm that you are getting the I/O characteristics you expected.

Fragmentation

Any discussion on disks would not be complete without a discussion of fragmentation. Fragmentation can occur in several forms with SQL Server:

❑ Internal fragmentation occurs when data gets old, i.e., it has been subject to many inserts, updates, and deletes. This is covered in Chapter 16.

❑ External fragmentation, which we are interested in here, can take two forms:

    ❑ Classic file fragmentation occurs when a file is created and the file system doesn't have enough contiguous disk space to create the file in a single fragment. You end up with a single file spread across multiple file fragments.

    ❑ Autogrow fragmentation is the fragmentation that occurs when you enable autogrow and the database size continuously grows with the addition of more files. These files may or may not have classic file fragmentation as well, but SQL Server has to manage multiple data and/or log files, which creates additional overhead. In some cases the number of files can be in the thousands.

One important point to consider here is that SQL files don't become more fragmented once they have been created. If files are created when there isn't enough contiguous free space, they are created in multiple fragments. If the disk is defragmented (and the OS has enough space to fully defragment all files) right after the files are created, then the files are no longer fragmented, and won't ever become fragmented.

The ideal scenario is that you have dedicated disks for your SQL files, and can size each file correctly, create the files, and disable autogrow. In this situation, you start with clean disks, create one or two files that aren't fragmented, and they stay that way forever. That way, you only need to deal with internal fragmentation.

The next scenario is when you start from the previous situation but allow autogrow at some tiny size or percentage, so you end up adding hundreds or thousands of small files. In this case, those files may or may not be fragmented, depending on how much free space is available on the disk when each auto-grow operation occurs. Your only solution here to remove the fragmentation is to schedule server down-time to rebuild each DB using a few large files, sized correctly for the expected DB growth, and then disable autogrow. Doing this will resolve any disk fragmentation that occurs, and by disabling autogrow you will prevent external fragmentation from ever occurring.

The worst case is that you don't have dedicated disks, you used the default DB sizes, and enabled auto-grow. Now you may have several problems to resolve. Your SQL files are competing for I/O capacity with the OS, and anything else running on the server. Until you add dedicated disks for SQL this won't be resolved. In addition, you may also end up with a lot of file fragments, as each autogrow operation adds another data or log file. As each new file is created by autogrow, it might be fragmented over the disk surface. As more files are added and the disk fills up, the chances of created fragmented files increases.

The best way to avoid problems is as follows:

1. Install the OS.
2. Defragment the disk.
3. Install any applications (SQL Server).
4. Defragment the disk.
5. Create data and log files at maximum size.
6. Check for fragmentation and defragment if necessary.
7. Disable autogrow.
8. Routinely defragment the disk to clean up fragmentation caused by other applications. This pre-serves the free space should you ever need to add more SQL data or log files.

In most cases, the operating system's disk defragmenter does a great job and is all you need. In some cases, however, you may need to consider purchasing a third-party disk defragmentation utility.

Summary

In this chapter we covered a lot of ground — from introducing performance to the various resources you need to consider when configuring a server.

We started by looking at the key things any DBA needs to know about performance, before discussing the performance tuning process. Then we dug into the specifics of server hardware, looking at the differ-ent attributes of CPUs, memory, networks, and disk I/O.

The discussion on CPUs examined the different types of processors you might encounter, and explained the differences between processor types and the various options available. The memory section looked at the different memory settings you might need to use, and covered all the scenarios you might encounter, including how to set the server to enable SQL Server to utilize the available memory. The disk I/O section examined the many details involved in storage subsystem configuration. You looked at how to design a storage system, and at some of the considerations necessary when working with large SAN systems. Finally, you learned how to configure the server side of the storage system.

In the next chapter you will learn how to optimize your T-SQL/SQL Server configuration.

12

Optimizing SQL Server 2005

Since the inception of SQL Server 7.0, the database engine has been enabled for self-tuning and managing. With the advent of SQL Server 2005, these concepts have reached new heights. When implemented on an optimized platform (as described in Chapter 11) with a properly configured SQL Server instance that has also been well maintained, SQL Server 2005 remains largely self-tuning and healing. In this chapter we introduce and discuss the SQL Server 2005 technologies needed to accomplish this feat.

Application Optimization

The first order of business for scaling SQL Server 2005 on Windows Server platform is optimizing the application. Chapter 33 of the SQL Server 2000 Resource Kit refers to this optimization as the *Pareto Principle*, which states that only a few vital factors are responsible for producing most of the problems in scaling such an application. If the application is not well written, getting a bigger hammer will only postpone your scalability issues rather than resolve them. Tuning an application for performance is beyond the scope of this chapter.

The goal of performance tuning SQL Server 2005 is to minimize the response time for each query and increase system throughput. This will maximize the scalability of the entire database server by reducing network-traffic latency, optimizing disk I/O throughput and CPU processing time.

Defining a Workload

A prerequisite to tuning any database environment is a thorough understanding of basic database principles. Two critical principles are the logical and physical structure of the data and the inherent differences in the application of the database. For example, different demands are made by an online transaction processing (OLTP) environment than are made by a decision support (DSS) environment. A DSS environment often needs a heavily optimized I/O subsystem to keep up with the massive amounts of data retrieval (or reads) it will perform. An OLTP transactional environment will need an I/O subsystem optimized for more of a balance between read and write operations.

In many customer environments, testing to scale with the actual application while in production is not possible. We recommend using an application load generator such as Quests' Benchmark Factory, Idera's SQLscaler, or MS TPC-B Benchmark Kit (ftp://ftp.microsoft.com/bussys/sql/unsup-ed/benchmark-kit) to simulate the loads of the targeted production data-tier environment. This technique allows offline measuring and tuning the system before you introduce it into the production environment.

Further, the use of this technique in a troubleshooting environment will allow you to compartmentalize specific pieces of the overall system to be tested individually. As an example, using the load-generator approach lets you reduce unknowns or variables from a performance-tuning equation by addressing each component on an individual basis (hardware, database, and application).

System Harmony is the Goal

Scaling an application and its database is dependent on the harmony of the memory, disk I/O, network, and processors, as shown in Figure 12-1. A well-designed system balances these components and should allow the system (the application and data tiers) to sustain a run rate of greater than 80-percent processor usage.

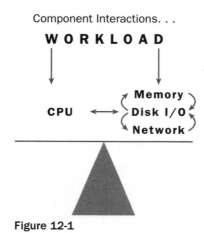

Figure 12-1

Of these resource components, a processor bottleneck on a well-tuned system (application\database) is the least problematic because it has the simplest resolution: Add more processors or upgrade the processor speed/technology.

The Silent Killer: I/O Problems

Many times, customers complain about their SQL Server performance and point to the database because the processors aren't that busy. After a discussion and a little elbow grease, frequently the culprit is an I/O bottleneck. The confusion comes from the fact that disk I/O is inversely proportional to CPU. In other words, over time, the processors are waiting for outstanding data requests that are queued on an overburdened disk subsystem. This section is about laying out the SQL Server shell or container on disk and configuring it properly to maximize the exploitation hardware resources. Scaling any database is a balancing act based on moving the bottleneck to the least affecting resource.

SQL Server I/O Process Model

Windows Server 2003 and SQL Server 2005 storage engine work together to mask the high cost of a disk I/O request. The Windows 2003 I/O Manager handles all I/O operations. The I/O Manager fulfills all I/O (read or write) requests by means of *scatter-gather* or asynchronous methods. For examples of scatter-gather or asynchronous methods, refer to Books Online under "I/O Architecture."

The SQL Server storage engine manages when, how, and the number of disk I/O operations performed. However, the Windows operating system (I/O Manager Subsystem) performs the underlying I/O operations and provides the interface to the physical media. That is why we always recommend running SQL Server 2005 on the latest version of Windows. There are behavioral differences in Windows Server 2003, Windows Server 2003 with SP1, and Windows Server 2003 R2 that SQL Server 2005 can take advantage of. See the http://www.microsoft.com/windowsserver2003/ site under the "Compare the Editions of Windows Server 2003" heading for more specifics. Definitely have a look at the Symmetric Multiprocessing (SMP) under the "Hardware Specifications" section.

The job of the storage engine is to manage or mitigate as much of the cost of these I/O operations as possible. For instance, the storage engine allocates much of its virtual space to a buffer cache. This cache is managed via cost-based analysis to ensure that memory is optimized to efficiently use its space for content. Data that is frequently updated or requested is maintained in memory. This benefits the user's request by performing a logical I/O and avoiding expensive physical I/O requests.

Database File Placement

SQL Server stores its database on the operating system files (physical disks or LUNS). The database is made up of three file types: a primary data file (MDF), one or more secondary data file(s) (NDF), and a transaction log (LDF).

Database (file) location is critical to the performance of the DBMS and its corresponding I/O. Using a fast and independent I/O subsystem for database primary data files is the right thing to do. As described in Chapter 11, available disk space does not equate better performance. Rather, the more physical spindles there are, including LUNS, the better your system will perform. Data can be stored according to usage across data files and filegroups that span many physical disks. A filegroup is a collection of data files used in managing database primary data-file placement.

Read-only filegroups are a new SQL Server 2005 feature. They allow for reference data that rarely gets updated (or archived data) to be placed in a read-only filegroup. This filegroup, along with additional filegroups, can be part of an updatable database.

In SQL Server 2005, the use of MDF, NDF, and LDF file extensions is now optional.

There are functional changes to tempdb to take into consideration when doing your primary data-file placement strategy.

Tempdb considerations

When SQL Server is restarted, `tempdb` is the only database that returns to the default size of 8MB, and it will continue to grow based on requirements. During the autogrow operation worker, threads can lock database resources during the database-growth operation, affecting server concurrency. To avoid time-outs, the autogrow operation should be limited to under two minutes.

In SQL Server 2005, `tempdb` has taken on support for a whole new set of features. `tempdb` still consists of a primary data and log file, but it also has two version stores. A version store is a collection of data pages that hold data rows required to support a particular feature. A "common" version store is used by numerous features:

- ❑ Optimizing Bulk Import Performance
- ❑ Using Common Table Expressions
- ❑ WITH `common_table_expression` (Transact-SQL)
- ❑ About Choosing a Cursor Type
- ❑ Database Mail
- ❑ DBCC CHECKDB (Transact-SQL)
- ❑ Optimizing DBCC CHECKDB Performance
- ❑ Understanding Event Notifications
- ❑ tempdb and Index Creation
- ❑ Special Guidelines for Partitioned Indexes
- ❑ Disk Space Requirements for Index DDL Operations
- ❑ Index Disk Space Example
- ❑ How Online Index Operations Work
- ❑ Using Large-Value Data Types
- ❑ Using Multiple Active Result Sets (MARS)
- ❑ Using Query Notifications
- ❑ Execution Plan Caching and Reuse
- ❑ Understanding Row Versioning Isolation Levels
- ❑ Row Versioning Resource Usage

There is also a dedicated "online-index-build" version store for the online index building process.

Placing the `tempdb` database on an isolated and fast I/O subsystem to ensure good performance is a good place to start. Unfortunately, it probably will not be enough. As we just mentioned, the `tempdb` database now supports user objects (like temporary tables), internal objects (intermediate sort results), and functionality-based requirements on the version stores. There has been a ton of work performed on `tempdb` internals to improve scalability.

Consider reading BOL under "Capacity Planning for tempdb" for additional information and functionality details regarding `tempdb` *usage.*

We recommend that you do some type of capacity planning for `tempdb` to ensure that it's properly sized and can handle the needs of your enterprise. At a minimum, we recommend the following:

1. Take into consideration the size of your existing `tempdb`.

2. Monitor `tempdb` while running your largest-known affecting process.

3. Rebuild the index of your largest table online while monitoring `tempdb`. Don't be surprised if this number turns out to be two times the table size, as this process now takes place in `tempdb`.

The SQL Team recommended the following query to monitor `tempDB` at PASS last year, and we think you should use it. This query identifies and expresses `tempdb` space used, in kilobytes, by internal objects, free space, version store, and user objects.

```
select sum(user_object_reserved_page_count)*8 as user_objects_kb,
    sum(internal_object_reserved_page_count)*8 as internal_objects_kb,
    sum(version_store_reserved_page_count)*8  as version_store_kb,
    sum(unallocated_extent_page_count)*8 as freespace_kb
from sys.dm_db_file_space_usage
where database_id = 2
```

The output of this query looks like this:

```
user_objects_kb      internal_objects_kb  version_store_kb     freespace_kb
-------------------- -------------------- -------------------- --------------------
256                  640                  0                    6208
```

If any of these stores run out of space, `tempdb` *operations will cease.*

Taking into consideration the preceding results, the following steps are recommend:

1. Avoid autogrow. Preallocate space for `tempdb` files based on the results of your testing, but leave autogrow enabled in case `tempdb` runs out of space.

2. Create one database file per system CPU or processor core (all equal in size).

3. Set `tempdb` to simple recovery model (allows for space recovery).

4. Set autogrow to 10 percent.

5. Place `tempdb` on its own fast and independent I/O subsystem.

6. Create alarms that monitor the environment by using SQL Server agent or Microsoft Operations Manager with SQL Pack to ensure that you never get error 1101 or 1105 (`tempdb` is full). This is crucial because the server stops processing inserts. Right-click SQL Server Agent in the SQL Server Management Studio and fill in the screen, as shown in Figure 12-2.

7. Use instant file initialization. If you are not running the SQL Server (`MSSQLSERVER`) Service account with admin privileges, make sure that the `SE_MANAGE_VOLUME_NAME` permissions have been assigned to the services account. This feature can take a 15-minute file-initialization process down to about a second for the same process.

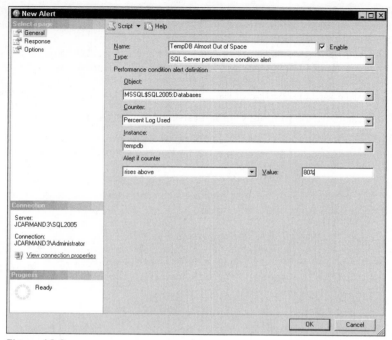

Figure 12-2

Another great tool is the `sys.dm_db_task_space_usage` DMV, which provides insight into `tempdb`'s space consumption on a per-task basis. Keep in mind that once the task is complete, the counters reset to zero.

In addition, you should monitor the disk per Avg. Sec/ Reads; numbers consistently above 30MS are a serious I/O bottleneck issue. If you have very large `tempdb` requirements, look at Q-917047, "Microsoft SQL Server I/O subsystem requirements for tempdb database" or in BOL for "Optimizing tempdb Performance." We are not trying to scare anyone with SQL Server 2005 `tempdb` requirements, but we are trying to convey the fact that you may have to put some serious work into `tempdb` capacity planning.

A concurrency enhancement for `tempdb` *is available via trace flag database T1118. See Q328551 for additional information.*

Table and Index Partitioning

Simply stated, partitioning is the breaking up of a large object, such as a table, into smaller, manageable pieces. Partitioning has been around for a while. The feature received lots of attention once it supported the ability to use constraints with views. This provided the ability for the optimizer to eliminate partitions (or tables) joined by a union of all statements on a view. These partitions could also be distributed across servers. This technology was introduced as a distributed partitioned view (DPV) during the SQL 7.0 launch.

New to SQL Server 2005 is the capability of partitioning database tables and their indexes over filegroups. This type of partitioning has many benefits over DPV, such as being transparent to the application (meaning no application code changes are necessary). Other benefits include database recoverability, simplified maintenance, and manageability.

Although we're discussing partitioning as part of this performance-tuning chapter, partitioning is first and foremost a manageability and scalability tool. In most situations, implementing partitioning will also have performance improvements as a byproduct of scalability. These benefits are highlighted throughout this section.

Why Consider Partitioning?

For a variety of reasons, you may have very large tables. When these tables (or databases) reach a certain size, it becomes painful for activities such as database maintenance, backup, or restore operations that consume a lot of time. Environmental issues such as poor concurrency due to a large number of users on a sizable table result in lock escalations, which also translates into more pain. If archiving the data is not possible because of regulatory compliances, ISV requirements, or cultural requirements, partitioning is most likely the tool for you. If you are still unsure whether or not to implement partitioning, run your workload through the Database Tuning Advisor (DTA). DTA will make recommendations for partitioning and will also generate the code for you. DTA is covered in detail in Chapter 14. DTA can be found under the "Performance Tools" section of the Microsoft SQL Server 2005 program menu.

> *Partitioning is covered through the book's various chapters to ensure that details are presented in their appropriate contexts.*

Here is a high-level process for partitioning:

1. Create a partition function to define a data-placement strategy.
2. Create filegroups to support the partition function.
3. Create a partition scheme to define the physical data distribution strategy (map the function data to filegroups).
4. Create a table or index on the partition function.
5. Enjoy redirected queries to appropriate resource.

After implementation, partitioning will positively affect your environment and most of your processes. The following are a few processes that partitioning your environment can affect. Be careful to understand this new technology to ensure that *every process benefits from it*:

- ❑ Database backup and restore strategy (support for partial database availability)
- ❑ Index maintenance strategy (rebuild and defragmentation), including index views
- ❑ Data management strategy (large insert or truncates)
- ❑ End-user workload (queries)
- ❑ Concurrency
  - ❑ Enhanced lock-escalation story
  - ❑ Enhanced distribution or isolated query workloads

Implementing Partitioning

Partitioning breaks a physical object, such as a large table, into multiple manageable pieces. A *row* is the unit that partitioning is based on. Unlike DPVs, all partitions must reside within a single database.

Creating a partition function

Simply stated, a *partition function* is your primary data-partitioning strategy. The first order of business is to determine your partitioning strategy. Identifying and prioritizing challenges is the best way to decide on a partitioning strategy. Whether it's to move old data within a table to a slower disk (or SAN), enhance workload concurrency, or simplify maintenance of a very large database, identifying and prioritizing is essential. Once you've selected your strategy, you will need to create a partitioning function that matches that strategy.

Remember to evaluate a table for partitioning, as the partition function is based on the distribution of data (selectivity of a column and the range or breath of that column). The range supports the number of partitions that the table can be partitioned by. There is a product limit of a 1000 partitions per table. This range should also match up with the desired strategy. For example, spreading out (or partitioning) a huge customer table by customer last name or by geographical location for better workload management is a sound strategy. Another example of a sound strategy is to partition a table by date for the purpose of archiving data based on date range for a more efficient environment.

> User-defined data types, alias data type, timestamps, images, XML, varchar(max), nvarchar(max), or varbinary(max) cannot be evaluated as partitioning columns.

As an example, we will partition a trouble-ticketing system for a telephone company. When a trouble ticket is generated based on an outage, it hits the database. At this point, many activities get kicked off. Technicians get dispatched, parts are replaced or reordered, and service can be rerouted within the network. SLA's are monitored and escalations are initiated. All of these activities take place because of the trouble ticket. In this system, the activities table and ticketing table have hot spots, as shown in Figure 12-3.

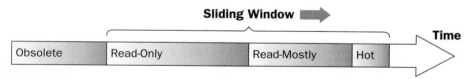

Figure 12-3

In Figure 12-3 the information marked as "hot" is the new or recent data, and it is only relevant or of interest during the outage. The information marked as "Read-Only" and "Read-Mostly" is usually used for minor analysis during postmortem processes and then for application reporting. Eventually, the data becomes obsolete and should be moved to a warehouse. Unfortunately, because of internal regulatory requirements, this database has to be online for seven years. Partitioning this environment will provide sizable benefits. Under the sliding-windows scenario, every month (or quarter) a new partition would be introduced to the environment as a retainer for the current data (hot data) for the tickets and activities tables. As part of this process, a partition with data from these tables that is older than seven years would also be retired.

As we described, there is a one-to-many relationship between tickets and activities. Although there are obvious size differences between these tables, it is important to put them through identical processes. This allows you to run processes that will affect resources shared and limited to these objects. To mitigate the impact of doing daily activities such as backups and index maintenance on all this data, these tables will be partitioned based on date ranges. We will create a left partition function based on the ticketdate column, as outlined below:

```
CREATE PARTITION FUNCTION
PFL_Years (smallint)
AS RANGE LEFT
FOR VALUES ('19991231 23:59:59.997', '20011231 23:59:59.997', '20031231
23:59:59.997', '20051231 23:59:59.997', '20061231 23:59:59.997')
```

SQL Server rounds time to .003 seconds, meaning that a time of .997 would be rounded up to 1.0 second.

❑ The boundary value '19991231 23:59:59.997' is the leftmost partition and includes all values less than or equal to '19991231 23:59:59.997'.

❑ The boundary value '20011231 23:59:59.997' is the second partition and includes all values greater than '19991231 23:59:59.997' but less than or equal to '20011231 23:59:59.997'.

❑ The boundary value '20031231 23:59:59.997' is the third partition and includes all values greater than '20011231 23:59:59.997' but less than or equal to '20031231 23:59:59.997'.

❑ The boundary value '20051231 23:59:59.997' is the fourth partition and includes all values greater than '20031231 23:59:59.997' but less than or equal to '20051231 23:59:59.997'.

❑ The boundary value '20061231 23:59:59.997' is the fifth partition and includes all values greater than '20051231 23:59:59.997' but less than or equal to '20061231 23:59:59.997'.

❑ Finally, the sixth partition includes all values greater than '20061231 23:59:59.997'.

The range partition function specifies the boundaries of the range. The `left` or `right` keyword specifies the interval of the boundary that the value belongs to. There can be no holes in the partition domain; all values must be obtainable. In this code sample, all transactions must fall within a date specified by the sample value range.

Creating Filegroups

You should create filegroups to support the strategy set by the partition function. As a best practice, user objects should be created and mapped to a filegroup outside of the default filegroup, leaving the default filegroup for system objects. This will ensure database availability in the event of an outage that affects the availability of any filegroup outside of the default filegroup.

Creating a Partition Scheme

A partition scheme is what maps database objects such as a table to a physical entity such as a file or filegroups. There are definitely backup, restore, and data-archival considerations when making this decision. (These are discussed in Chapter 18.) The following sample code maps the partition functions or dates to individual filegroups.

```
CREATE PARTITION SCHEME CYScheme
AS
PARTITION PFL_Years
TO ([CY00], [CY02], [CY04], [CY05], [CY06], [Default])
```

This supports the placement of filegroups on individual and distinct disk subsystems. Such an option also supports the capability to move old data to an older disk subsystem and to reassign spindles to support hot data (CY06). When the old data has been moved to the old SAN, filegroups can be marked as read-only. Once this data has been backed up, it no longer needs to be part of the backup process. SQL Server will also automatically ignore these filegroups as part of index maintenance.

The other option for a partition-function scheme allows for the mapping of the partition scheme to map the partition function to individual files within a single filegroup. The following sample code maps the partition function to the default filegroup.

```
CREATE PARTITION SCHEME CYScheme
AS
PARTITION PFL_Years
TO ([Default])
```

This choice provides for the ability to introduce or delete GB of data to this 500+ GB table with a simple metadata switch (in seconds). The process utilized to accomplish this is called *sliding window*. Normally, this process would have taken hours because of lock escalation and index resynchronization. From a high-level, the sliding-window process consists of three types of actions. An empty partition would be created and indexed outside of the environment. It would then be switched with the partition that contains the targeted data. At the conclusion of this process, the partition with the data is now outside of the environment and can then be dropped without impact to the environment. This process would be repeated to introduce a new partition into this table structure as the repository for the "hot" data. The only impact to the environment was a brief pause while a schema lock was in place during the partition swaps, which took seconds. If you wanted to load data into the partitioned table instead of dropping it, the data would be loaded and indexed outside of the environment. To load the data, repeat the previous process. This beneficial process is only available to perform on files or partitions within a filegroup. Implementation details and best practices are covered later in this chapter and in upcoming chapters.

Create Tables and Indexes

As the following code shows, the syntax for creating a table is accomplished as it has always been. The only exception is that it is created on a partition schema instead of a specific or default filegroup. New to SQL Server 2005 is the ability to create tables, indexes, and indexed views on partition schemes. This supports the distribution of database objects across several filegroups. This is different from the existing ability to create an entire object within a filegroup (which is still available in SQL Server 2005).

```
CREATE TABLE [dbo].[Tickets]
(       [TiketID] [int] NOT NULL,
        [CustomerID] [int] NULL,
        [State] [int] NULL,
        [Status] [tinyint] NOT NULL,
        [TicketDate] [datetime] NOT NULL
        CONSTRAINT TicketYear
        CHECK ([TicketDate] >= '19991231 23:59:59.997' AND [TicketDate] <= '20061231
```

```
23:59:59.997'))
ON CYScheme (TicketDate)
GO

CREATE TABLE [dbo].[activities]
(       [TiketID] [int] NOT NULL,
        [Activity detail] [varchar 255] NULL,
        [ActivityDate] [datetime] NOT NULL
        CONSTRAINT ActivityYear
        CHECK ([Activity Date] >= '19991231 23:59:59.997' AND [ActivityDate] <=
'20061231 23:59:59.997'))
ON CYScheme (TicketDate)
GO
```

We will cover two areas of best practices here: index alignment and storage alignment.

Index Alignment

An "aligned" index uses an equivalent partition function and the same partitioning columns as its table (as shown in Figure 12-4). They actually don't have to use the identical partition function or scheme, but there has to be a one-to-one correlation of data-to-index entries within a partition.

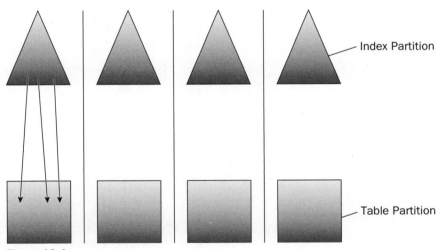

Index Partition

Table Partition

Figure 12-4

A benefit derived from index alignment is the ability to switch partitions in or out of a table with a simple metadata operation. In the trouble-ticket example, you would be able to programmatically add a new partition for the new month (or current month) and delete the outgoing month from the table as part of the seven-year cycle.

Storage alignment

Index alignment is the first requirement of a storage-aligned solution. There are two options for storage alignment. The big differentiator is the ability to use the same partition scheme, or a different one, as long as both tables and indexes have an equal number of partitions. The first option, shown in Figure 12-5, demonstrates a storage-aligned solution with index and relevant data in distinct and isolated filegroups. If a query to compare data in CY04 and CY02 is executed on aligned index and data, the query would be localized to the aligned environment. This would benefit users working in other partitions isolated from the ongoing work within these two partitions.

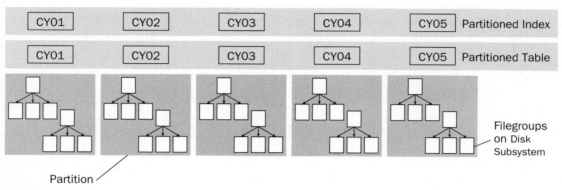

Figure 12-5

Figure 12-6 shows the same query executed on a different architecture. Because of the alignment of index and data, the query will still be localized but will run in parallel on both relevant index and data partitions. This would still benefit users working in other partitions isolated from the ongoing work within these four partitions.

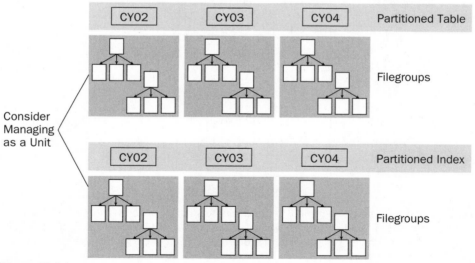

Figure 12-6

Additional benefits derived from storage alignment are partial database availability and piecemeal restores. For instance, in the example scenario, the CY04 partition could be offline, and the application would still be processing trouble tickets. This would occur regardless of what partition went down, as long as the default partition that contains only system-table information (as is the best practice) and the partition that contains the current month's data are online. Considerations that will affect query parallelism of this environment are discussed later in the processor section of this chapter.

Memory Considerations AND Enhancements

Since memory is fast relative to Disk I/O, using this system resource effectively can have a large impact on the system's overall ability to scale and perform well. Most 32-bit systems available on the market today support Intel's 32-bit Intel (IA-32) microprocessor PAE or "physical address extensions" technology. This technology allows the operating system or application to address up to 32GB for Enterprise Edition (EE) and 64GB for Datacenter Edition of physical memory. With the release of Windows Server 2003, SP1, X64, and IA64 platforms are fully supported. The platform of choice is expected to shift from 32-bit to 64-bit in the near future. The hardware aspects of all of these issues are discussed in Chapter 11.

SQL Server 2005 memory architecture and capabilities vary greatly from those of SQL Server 2000. Changes include the ability to consume and release memory-based, internal-server conditions dynamically using the AWE mechanism. In SQL Server 2000, all memory allocations above 4GB were static. Additional memory enhancements include the introduction of hierarchical memory architecture to maximize data locality and improve scalability by removing a centralized memory manager. SQL Server 2005 also introduced resource monitor, Dynamic Management View (DMV), and a common caching framework. We discuss these concepts throughout this chapter.

Tuning SQL Server Memory

The SQL Server Cache Hit Ratio signifies the balance between servicing user requests from data in the data cache and having to request data from disk. Accessing data in RAM (or data cache) is much faster than accessing the same information from disk; thus, the desired state is to load all active data in RAM. Unfortunately, RAM is a limited resource. A desired cache hit ratio average hovers around 98 percent or higher. This does not mean that the environment would not benefit from additional memory. A lower number signifies that the system memory or data cache allocation is below desired size. Another reliable indicator of instance memory pressure is the page-life-expectancy counter. This counter indicates the amount of time that a buffer page remains in memory in seconds. The ideal number should be above 300 seconds or five minutes; anything lower signifies memory pressure.

Be careful not to underallocate total system memory, as it will force the operating system to start hard-paging to disk. Hard-paging is a phenomenon that occurs when the operating system goes to disk to resolve memory references. The operating system will always incur some paging. However, when excessive paging takes places, it uses disk I/O and CPU resources, which can introduce latency in the overall server, resulting in slow database performance. You can identify a lack of adequate system memory by monitoring the Memory: Pages/sec performance counter. It should be as close to 0 as possible, since a higher value indicates that more hard-paging is taking place.

SQL Server 2005 has several new features that should help with this issue. With the assistance of Windows Server 2003, SQL Server 2005 now has support for dynamic address windowing extensions (AWE) memory allocation, Hot Add Memory, a manager framework, and other enhancements. The SQL Server operating system (SQL OS) layer is the new and improved version of the User Mode Scheduler

(UMS), now simply called *scheduler*. Consistent with its predecessor, SQL OS is a user-mode cooperative and on-demand thread-management system. An example of a cooperative workload is one that yields the processor during a periodic interval or while in a wait state, meaning that if a batch request does not have access to all of the required data for its execution, it will request its data and then yield its position to a process that needs processing time.

SQL OS is a thin layer that sits between SQL Server and Windows to manage the interaction between these environments and enables SQL Server to scale on any hardware. This was accomplished by moving to a distributed model and by bringing about an architecture that would foster locality of resources in getting rid of global resource management bottlenecks. The issue with global resource management is that in large hardware design, global resources cannot keep up with the demands of the system, slowing overall performance. Figure 12-7 highlights the SQLOS components that perform thread scheduling and synchronization, perform SQL Server memory management, provide exception handling, and host the Common Language Runtime (CLR).

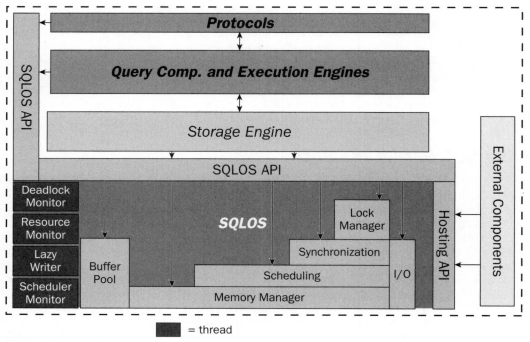

Figure 12-7

The goal of this environment is to empower the SQL Server platform to exploit all of today's hardware innovation across the X86, X64, and IA64 platforms. SQL OS was built to bring together the concepts of data locality, support for dynamic configuration, and hardware workload exploitation. This architecture also enables SQL Server 2005 to better support both Cache Coherent Nonuniform Memory Access (CC-NUMA), Interleave NUMA (NUMA hardware with memory that behaves like an SMP system), Soft-NUMA architecture (registry-activated, software-based emulated NUMA architecture used to partition a large SMP system), and large SMP systems, by affinitizing memory to a few CPUs.

The architecture introduces the concept of a *memory node*, which is one hierarchy between memory and CPUs. There will be a memory node for each set of CPUs to localize memory and its content to these CPUs. On an SMP architecture, a memory node shares memory across all CPUs, while on a NUMA architecture, there will be a memory node per NUMA node. As shown in Figure 11-8, the goal of this design is to support SQL Server scalability across all hardware architectures by enabling the software to adapt to or emulate various hardware architectures.

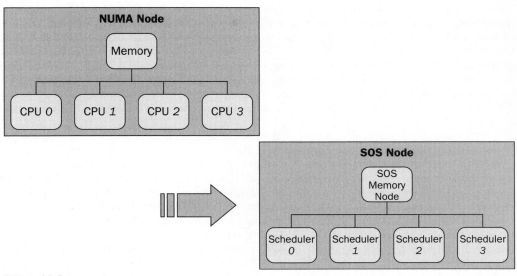

Figure 12-8

Schedulers will be discussed later in this chapter, but for the purposes of this discussion, they manage the work being executed on a CPU.

Memory nodes share the memory allocated by "Max Server Memory," setting evenly across a single memory node for SMP system and across one or more memory nodes for NUMA architectures. Each memory node has its own lazy writer thread that manages its workload based on its memory node. As seen in Figure 12-9, the CPU node is a subset of memory nodes and provides for logical grouping for CPUs.

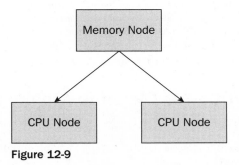

Figure 12-9

A CPU node is also a hierarchical structure designed to provide logical grouping for CPUs. The purpose is to localize and load-balance related workloads to a CPU node. On an SMP system, all CPUs would be grouped under a single CPU node, while on a NUMA based system, there would be as many CPU nodes as the system supported. The relationship between CPU node to memory node is explicit. There can be many CPU nodes to a memory node, but there will never be more that one memory node to a CPU node. Each level of this hierarchy provides localized services to the components that it manages in a hierarchy, resulting in the ability to process and manage workloads in such a way to exploit the scalability of whatever hardware architecture SQL Server is running on. SQL OS also enables services such as dynamic affinity, load-balancing workloads, dynamic memory capabilities, Dedicated Admin Connection (DAC), and support for partitioned resource management capabilities.

SQL Server 2005 leverages the common caching framework (also part of SQL OS) to have fine-grain control to manage the increasing number of cache mechanisms (Cache Store, User Store, and Object Store). This framework improves the behavior of these mechanisms by providing a common policy that can be applied to internal caches to manage them in a wide range of operating conditions. For additional information about these caches, refer to BOL.

SQL Server 2005 also features a memory-tracking enhancement called the Memory Broker, which enables the tracking of operating system-wide memory events. Memory Broker manages and tracks the dynamic consumption of internal SQL Server memory. Based on internal consumption and pressures, it automatically calculates the optimal memory configuration for components such as buffer pool, optimizer, query execution, and caches. It propagates the memory configuration information back to these components for implementation. SQL Server 2005 also supports dynamic management of conventional, locked, and large-page memory, as well as the Hot Add Memory feature. New to SQL Server 2005 Standard Edition (32-bit) is the introduction of support for the AWE memory mechanism. The Windows property, Lock Pages in Memory, is disabled by default and is only available to local administrative accounts. To ensure that the AWE enabled Memory runs as expected, it needs this privilege to allow SQL Server to manage which pages are being flushed out of memory.

Hot Add Memory offers the ability to introduce additional memory in an operational server without taking it offline. In addition to OEM vendor support, Windows Server 2003 and SQL Server 2005 EE are required to support this feature. Although there is a sample implementation script in the following section, refer to BOL for additional implementation details.

64-bit Version of SQL Server 2005

If your platform is IA64 or X64, you are in luck. SQL Server 2005 64-bit supports 1 TB of RAM, and all of it is flat (no need for /3GB or /AWE switches in your boot.ini file). The mechanism used to manage AWE Memory in 32-bit systems is also used to manage memory on 64-bit systems. Specifically, this mechanism is used to ensure that SQL Server manages what is flushed out of its memory. For this feature to work properly, the SQL Server service account requires the "lock pages in memory" privilege.

Configuring SQL 2005 for Dynamic Memory on an X86 platform

Although some of these concepts are covered in Chapter 11, we will reintroduce them as part of this chapter to bring all of these concepts together. PAE and 3GB technologies can be used independently or together. You use a boot.ini switch to activate either feature. The following provides guidelines on their use with SQL Server 2005.

Insert both the /PAE and /3GB switches into the boot.ini file to boot with the PAE-enabled kernel and give SQL Server (and other applications) 3GB of virtual memory. This allows the system to recognize up to 16GB of physical memory.

❑ Use only the /PAE switch with more than 16GB memory.

❑ SQL Server setting "AWE enabled" must be enabled for SQL Server to access memory beyond 3GB.

❑ Use only the /3GB switch where physical memory is greater than 4GB or less than 16GB.

See the following table for clarification:

System Memory	less than 3GB	More than 3GB	More than 16GB
PAE	NO	YES	YES
/3GB	NO	YES	NO
AWE	NO	YES	YES

To activate the AWE mapped memory feature with the ability to lock pages in memory, follow these steps. The PAE kernel must be booted by adding boot.ini and AWE must be enabled in SQL Server with the sp_configure directive.

First, add this entry to your boot.ini file:

```
[boot loader]
timeout=30
default=multi(0)disk(0)rdisk(0)partition(1)\WINNT
[operating systems]
multi(0)disk(0)rdisk(0)partition(1)\WINNT="Microsoft Windows 2003 Datacenter Server
/PAE /3GB" /fastdetect /PAE /3GB
multi(0)disk(0)rdisk(0)partition(1)\WINNT="Microsoft Windows 2003 Datacenter
Server" /fastdetect
```

Next, issue the following sp_configure statements:

```
sp_configure 'show advanced options', 1
RECONFIGURE
GO
sp_configure 'awe enabled', 1
RECONFIGURE
GO
sp_configure 'min server memory', 15360 (15 GB)
RECONFIGURE
GO
sp_configure 'max server memory', 30720 (30 GB)
RECONFIGURE
GO
```

Unlike its predecessor, SQL Server 2005 will not go beyond this setting even if memory is available and the system is under memory pressure. Ensure that this is the desired limit. Once enabled, memory is dynamically allocated in SQL Server 2005 Standard and Enterprise Editions running and any versions of Windows Server 2003.

Next, configure your SQL Server for Hot Add memory. In the SQL Server Configuration Manager, click SQL Server 2005 Services. In the right pane, right-click SQL Server service, and then click Properties. Select the advanced tab, and add ; -h in the Startup Parameters box. The semicolon is used as a separator for startup options. The server must be restarted to enable this feature.

A 500MB memory cost to this feature is reserved for administrative purposes.

Finally, enable lock pages in memory like this:

1. Click Start⇨Run, type **gpedit.msc**, and then click OK. The Group Policy window appears.

2. In the left pane, expand Computer Configuration, and then expand Windows Settings.

3. Expand Security Settings, and then expand Local Policies.

4. Click User Rights Assignment. The policies appear in the right pane.

5. In the right pane, double-click Lock pages in memory.

6. In the Local Security Policy Setting dialog box, click Add User or Group.

7. In the Select Users or Groups dialog box, add the account that has permissions to run Sqlservr.exe, and then click OK (see Figure 12-10).

8. Close the Group Policy window, and then restart the SQL Server service.

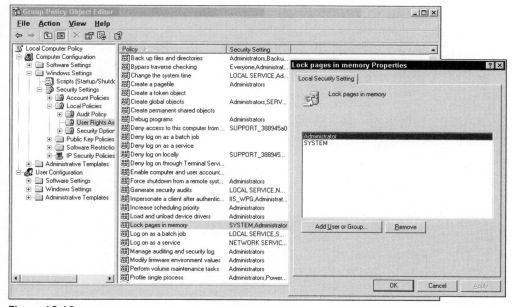

Figure 12-10

Remember that when allocating SQL Server memory on a system with more than 16GB, Windows 2003 will require at least 2GB of available memory to manage the remaining RAM). Therefore, when you start an instance of SQL Server with AWE mechanism enabled, you should not use the default max server memory setting, but instead limit it to 2GB less than the total available memory. Additional information can be found in BOL, or refer to article Q 283037.

AWE mapped memory cannot be managed or monitored through the task manager; this will have to be accomplished through `sys.dm_os_memory_clerks` DMV:

```
select sum(awe_allocated_kb)/1024 as [AWE Allocated Memory in MB] from
sys.dm_os_memory_clerks
```

Removing memory from the server will still require rebooting the system.

Memory-Friendly Applications

You need to identify the type of application driving the database and verify that it can benefit from a large SQL Server data-cache allocation. In other words, is it memory friendly? Simply stated, a database that does not need to keep its data in memory for an extended length of time will not see benefits from a larger memory allocation. For example, a call-center application where no two operators handle the same customer's information and where no relationship exists between customer records has no need to keep data in memory, since data won't be reused. In this case, the application is not deemed memory friendly; thus, keeping customers' data in memory longer than required would not benefit performance. Another type of inefficient memory use occurs when an application brings into memory excessive amounts of data, beyond what is required by the operation. This type of operation suffers from the high cost of data invalidation. (Larger amounts of data than are unnecessary are read into memory; thus, they must be flushed out.)

CPU Considerations

The challenge in building a large SMP is that, because CPUs have increased performance through technology upgrades and through the use of increasingly larger caches, the performance gains achieved through leveraging these caches are significant. Consequently, you need to cache relevant data whenever possible, to allow processors to have relevant data available and resident in their caches. Chip and hardware vendors have attempted to capitalize on this phenomenon through expansion of the processor and system cache.

As a result of this phenomenon, new system architectures such as Cellular Multiprocessing (CMP), CC-NUMA, as seen in Figure 12-11, and NUMA (noncache coherent) have been introduced to the market.

Although this has been successful, it has produced two new challenges: the need to manage data locality and cache coherency.

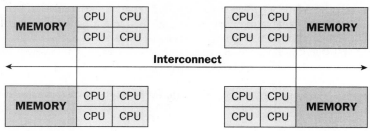

Figure 12-11

Data Locality

Data locality is the concept of having all relevant data locally available to the processor while it's processing a request. All memory within a system is available to any processor on any cell. This introduces the concept of near and far memory. Near memory is the preferred method, since it is accessed by a processor on the same cell. As shown in Figure 12-12, accessing far memory is expensive because the request has to leave the cell and traverse the system interconnect crossbar to get the cell that holds the required information in its memory.

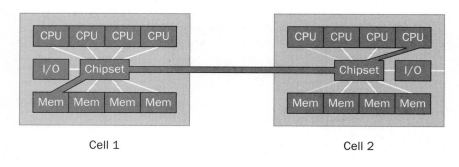

Figure 12-12

The cost of accessing objects in far memory versus near memory is often threefold or more. If data locality is left unmanaged in a large SMP system, it can prevent an application from scaling due to data-locality issues. SQL Server 2000 SP4 (Post SP3 QFE available) introduced innovations to better scale on this platform.

Cache Coherency

For reasons of data integrity, only one processor can update any piece of data at a time; other processors that have copies in their caches will find out that their local copy is "invalidated" and thus must be reloaded. This mechanism is referred to as *cache coherency*. Cache coherency requires that all the caches are in agreement as to the location of all copies of the data and which CPU currently has permission to perform the update. Supporting coherency protocols is one of the major scaling problems in designing big SMPs, particularly if there is a lot of update traffic. This was also addressed with the introduction of NUMA and CMP architectures.

SQL Server 2005 has been optimized to take advantage of NUMA advancements exposed by both Windows and the hardware itself. As discussed in the "Memory Consideration" section, SQL OS is the technology the SQL Server leverages to exploit these advances.

Affinity mask

The affinity mask configuration option restricts SQL Server (or an instance) to run on a subset of the processors. If SQL Server 2005 is running on a dedicated server (and nothing else), allowing SQL Server to use all processors will ensure best performance. In a server consolidation or multiple- instance environment, SQL Server should always be configured to dedicated hardware resources (affinitizing processors by instances).

The benefits of Hyper-Threading in SQL Server workloads have been a matter of heated discussion. To ensure predictability of the environment, I recommend that this feature be disabled. When configuring SQL Server 2005, processor affinity should coincide with the number of processors or cores available to SQL Server. Hyperthreading is discussed in greater detail in Chapter 11.

> *If Hyperthreading is enabled, be sure to set affinity on CPUs, always setting the affinity on both logical processors on a physical processor to the same SQL Server instance.*

SQL Server Processor Affinity Mask

SQL Server's mechanism for scheduling work requests is handled through a data structure concept called a scheduler. There scheduler is created for each processor assigned to SQL Server through the affinity mask configuration setting at startup time. "Worker" threads (a subset of the max worker threads configuration setting) are dynamically created during a batch request and are evenly distributed between each CPU node and load-balanced across its schedulers (refer to Figure 12-13).

Incoming connections are assigned to the CPU node. SQL Server assigns the batch request to a task or tasks, and the tasks are managed across schedulers. Only one task at a time can be scheduled for execution by a scheduler on a CPU. A task is a unit of work scheduled by the SQL Server. This architecture guarantees an even distribution of the hundreds of connections or, in many cases, thousands of connections that can result from a large deployment.

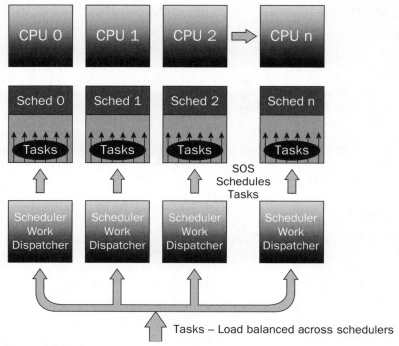

Figure 12-13

Default SQL Server Work Scheduling

The default setting for affinity mask is 0, which enables the Windows scheduler to schedule and move schedulers across any available CPU within a CPU node to execute its worker threads. SQL 2005 in this configuration has its processes controlled and scheduled by the Windows scheduler. For example, a client requests a connection, and the connection is accepted. If no threads are available, one is dynamically created and associated with a task. The work assignments from the scheduler to the CPUs are managed through the Windows scheduler, which has its work distributed among all processors within a CPU node. This is the preferred method of execution, since Windows load-balances the schedulers evenly to all processors.

SQL Server Work Scheduling using Affinity Mask

The affinity mask configuration setting can be used to assign a subset of the available CPUs to the SQL Server process. SQL Server worker threads are scheduled preemptively by the scheduler. A worker thread will continue to execute on its CPU until it is forced to wait for a resource, such as locks or I/O, to become available. If the time slice expires, the thread will voluntarily yield, at which time the scheduler will select another worker thread to begin execution. If it cannot proceed without access to a resource such as disk I/O, it sleeps until the resource is available. Once access to that resource is available, the process is placed on the run queue before being put on the processor. When the kernel transfers control of the CPU from an executing process to another that is ready to run, this is referred to as a context switch.

Context switching

Context switching is expensive because of the associated housekeeping required to move from one running thread to another. Housekeeping is the maintenance of keeping the context or the set of CPU register values and other data that describes the process state. The kernel then loads the context of the new process, which then starts to execute. When the process taken off the CPU next runs, it resumes from the point at which it was taken off the CPU. This is possible because the saved context includes the instruction pointer. Also, context switching takes place in kernel or privileged mode.

The total CPU processing time is equal to the privileged mode time plus the user mode time.

Privileged mode

Privileged mode is a processing mode designed for operating system components and hardware-manipulating drivers. It allows direct access to hardware and all memory. Privileged time includes time-servicing interrupts and deferred process calls (DPC).

User mode

User mode is a restricted processing mode designed for applications such as SQL Server, Exchange, and other application and integral subsystems. The goal of performance tuning is to maximize user mode processing by reducing privilege mode processing. This can be monitored with the Processor: % Privileged Time counter, which displays the average busy time as a percentage of the sample time. A value above 15 percent may indicate that a disk array is being heavily utilized or a high level of network traffic requests. In some rare cases, a high rate of privileged time might even be attributed to a large number of interrupts generated by a failing device.

Priority Boost

By enabling Priority boost, SQL Server runs at a priority base of 13 in the Windows 2003 scheduler rather than its default of 7. On a dedicated server, this might improve performance, although it can also cause priority imbalances between SQL Server functions and operating system functions, leading to instability. Improvements in SQL Server 2005 and Windows Server 2003 make the use of this option unnecessary.

Priority boost should not be used when implementing failover clustering.

SQL Server Lightweight Pooling

Typically, context switching does not become problematic until it reaches about 40,000 switches per second. The SQL Server Lightweight Pooling option provides relief for this by enabling tasks to use NT "fibers" rather than threads as workers.

A fiber is an executable unit that is lighter than a thread and operates in the context of user mode. When light-weight pooling is selected, each scheduler uses a single thread to control the scheduling of work requests by multiple fibers. A fiber can be viewed as a "lightweight thread," which under certain circumstances takes less overhead than standard worker threads to context switch. The number of fibers is controlled by the max worker threads configuration setting.

Max degree of parallelism (MAXDOP)

By default, this setting is set to 0, which enables the SQL Server to consider all processors when creating an execution plan. In some systems, based on application-workload profiles, it is recommended to set this setting to 1 (recommended for SAP & Siebel); this prevents the query optimizer from choosing parallel query plans. Using multiple processors to run a query is not always desirable in an OLTP environment, although desirable in a data warehousing environment.

In SQL Server 2005, you can now assign query hints to individual queries to control the degree of parallelism.

Partitioned table parallelism is also affected by the MAXDOP setting. Returning to the example used in the "Storage Alignment" section, a thread would have been leveraged across each partition also. Had the query been limited to a single partition, multiple threads would be spawned (up to MAX DOP setting) within that partition.

Affinity I/O mask

The affinity I/O mask feature, shown in Figure 12-14, was introduced with SP1 of SQL Server 2000. This option defines the specific processors on which SQL Server I/O threads can execute. The affinity I/O mask option has a default setting of 0, indicating that SQL Server threads are allowed to execute on all processors. The performance gains associated with enabling the affinity I/O mask feature are achieved by grouping the SQL threads that perform all I/O tasks (Nondata Cache retrievals, specifically physical I/O requests) on dedicated resources. This keeps I/O processing and related data in the same cache systems, maximizing data locality and minimizing unnecessary bus traffic.

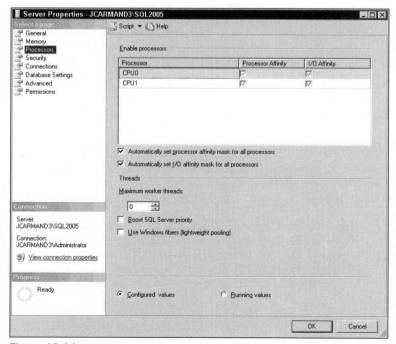

Figure 12-14

When using affinity masks to assign processor resources to the operating system, either SQL Server processes (non-I/O) or SQL Server I/O processes, care must be exercised not to assign multiple functions to any individual processor.

You should consider SQL I/O affinity when there is high privileged time on the processors that aren't affinitized to SQL Server. For example, consider a 32-processor system running under load with 30 of the 32 processors affinitized to SQL Server (leaving two processors to the Windows O/S and other non-SQL activities). If the Processor: % privileged time is high (greater than 15%), SQL I/O affinity can be incorporated to help reduce the privileged-time overhead in processors associated with SQL Sever.

The following is the process for determining what values to set for SQL I/O affinity.

1. Add I/O capability until there's no I/O bottleneck (Disk Queue length has been eliminated) and all unnecessary processes have been stopped.

2. Add a processor designated to SQL I/O Affinity.

3. Measure the CPU utilization of these processors under heavy load.

4. Increase the number of processors until the designated processors are no longer peaked. Make sure you select processors that are in the same cell.

Max Server Memory

When max server memory is kept at the default setting, SQL Server acquires and frees memory in response to internal pressure and external pressure. Dynamic AWE is only supported on Windows Server 2003. For SQL Server implementations based on Windows Server 2003, a max server memory setting is optional but recommended. For Windows 2000 implementations, the setting max memory value is strongly recommended.

Index Creation Memory Option

The index creation memory setting, shown in Figure 12-15, determines how much memory can be used by SQL Server for sort operations during the index-creation process. The default value of "0" allows the SQL Server to automatically determine the ideal value as seen in the figure below. In conditions where index creation is performed on very large tables, preallocating space in memory will allow for a faster index-creation process.

Remember that once memory is allocated it is reserved exclusively for the index-creation process, and values are set in KB of memory.

Min Memory per Query

You can use the 'min memory per query' option to improve the performance of queries that use hashing or sorting operations. The SQL Server automatically allocates the minimum amount of memory set in this configuration setting. The default 'min memory per query' option setting is equal to 1024 KB, which can be seen in Figure 12-15. It is important to ensure that SQL Server environment has plenty of memory available. In an environment with high query-execution concurrency, if the setting is set too high, the server will wait for a memory allocation to meet the minimum memory level before executing a query.

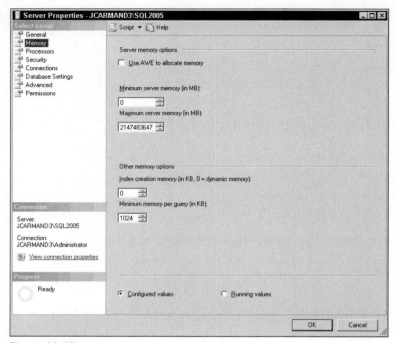

Figure 12-15

Summary

Starting from the hardware specifications you learned in Chapter 11, this chapter provided the necessary steps for setting and configuring SQL Server 2005. If these lessons are applied correctly, SQL Server 2005 is more than capable of autotuning itself to predictably provide the availability and performance to support the needs of your enterprise. Chapter 13 discusses proactive monitoring on this environment, and Chapter 14 discusses how to tune T-SQL code for this environment.

13

Monitoring Your SQL Server

The goal of monitoring databases is to assess how your server is performing. SQL Server 2005 provides a comprehensive set of tools for monitoring events in SQL Server. Both SQL Server and the Windows operating system provide tools to view the current condition of the database system and to track performance as the system parameters change. When you optimize and tune the performance of SQL Server, you're trying to minimize the response time for database queries, and maximize SQL Server throughput. In this chapter, we will concentrate on out-of-the-box tools for monitoring SQL Profiler, Performance Monitor (also called System Monitor), Dynamic Management Views (DMVs), and Dynamic Management Functions (DMFs).

Why Should You Monitor?

SQL Server provides service in a dynamic environment. There are many variables in this environment: The types of access that the users require change, data in the application changes, new requirements crop up in your applications, and more. With growing frequency, SQL Server database systems are being chosen as the preferred backend database solution for large and complex business-critical systems. As a responsible DBA, it's your job to know the health of your SQL Server so that you can take proactive actions. This will help you spot potential problems not yet visible to the end-user. For example, if a certain query has slowed down from 50 ms to 250 ms, then the end-user will not be alarmed, but you should be. As a system administrator, you must identify performance goals and factors that affect the performance of Microsoft SQL Server.

Determining Your Monitoring Goals

Before you start monitoring you must first clearly identify your reasons for monitoring. Some of these reasons are as follows:

- ❑ Identify performance changes over time.
- ❑ Audit user activity.

❑   Establish a baseline for a performance.

❑   Diagnose a specific performance problem.

Choosing the Appropriate Monitoring Tools

Once you define your monitoring goals you should select the appropriate tools for monitoring. The following list introduces you to the basic monitoring tools. The rest of the chapter discusses these tools in detail.

❑   **SQL Profiler**: All database engine process events are tracked by this tool, which has a graphical user interface. You can also store the data into a SQL table or file for later analysis, and you can replay the captured event on SQL Server step by step to see exactly what happened. It can monitor a SQL server instance locally or remotely. The Profiler works well for trend analysis, and is the only tool that can replay captured events. You can also use the Profiler within a custom application, by using the Profiler system stored procedures.

❑   **Performance Monitor**: Performance Monitor tracks resource use on Microsoft Windows Server and Windows operating systems. It can monitor a SQL Server instance, locally or remotely, on Windows OS (4.0 or later). The Performance Monitor is useful in trend analysis, and it can generate alerts, but it's not useful for ad-hoc monitoring.

The key difference between Profiler and Performance Monitor is that Performance Monitor monitors resources (CPU, memory, disk I/O, etc.) related to server processes, whereas Profiler monitors database engine events.

❑   **Activity Monitor in SQL Server Management Studio**: This tool graphically displays the following information:

   ❑   Processes running on an instance of SQL Server

   ❑   Locks

   ❑   User activity

   ❑   Blocked processes

Activity Monitor works best for ad-hoc monitoring, but not very well for trend analysis.

To open Activity Monitor in SQL Server Management Studio, connect to the server with Object Explorer, expand Management, and then double-click Activity Monitor.

❑   **Dynamic Management Views**: Dynamic Management Views and Functions return server state information that can be used to monitor the health of a server instance, diagnose problems, and tune performance. This is one of the best tools added to SQL Server 2005 for ad-hoc monitoring. Of course, you have to save the result from the DMVs for later analysis.

❑   **Transact-SQL**: Some system stored procedures provide useful information for SQL Server monitoring, such as `sp_who`, `sp_who2`, `sp_lock`, and several others. These stored procedures are best for ad-hoc monitoring, not trend analysis.

Evaluating Performance

For many reasons, it is very difficult and sometimes impossible to emulate the production environment in a development or system test for complex systems. Of course, "money matters" is one of the reasons, but other reasons include the load on the system at different times of the day, the numbers of users, differing application use scenarios, and everyday data changes. It is also difficult to have the same hardware in all the environments. Typically, your production system has the best hardware, so application performance changes a lot from development to deployment. Once your application is deployed in production, it is very important that you establish a *performance baseline*. We don't mean that you shouldn't establish a baseline in other environments. In fact, you should be thinking about application performance right from the requirements gathering and database design stages. Ongoing evaluation of database system performance helps you minimize response time and maximize throughput to yield optimal performance.

To determine whether your SQL Server system is performing optimally, take performance measurements at a regular interval over time, even when no problem occurs, to establish a server performance baseline. At a minimum, use baseline performance to determine the following:

- ❑ Peak and off-peak hours of operation
- ❑ Query or batch response time

After you establish the baseline, compare the statistics to current performance. Look for numbers far above or below your baseline, as these warrant further investigation.

Performance Monitor

Performance Monitor is an important tool because not only does it enable you to know how SQL Server is performing, it is also the tool that indicates how Windows is performing. Performance Monitor provides a huge set of counters. Probably no one understands all of them, so don't be daunted.

This section is not about how to use Performance Monitor. Instead, the focus here is on how you can use the capabilities of this tool to diagnose performance problems in your system. For general information about using Performance Monitor, look at the Windows 2000 or Windows 2003 Server Operation Guide in the server resource kit.

You should concentrate your initial efforts on three main areas when investigating performance-related issues:

- ❑ Processor usage
- ❑ Disk activity
- ❑ Memory usage

Monitor these key counters over a "typical" 24-hour period. Pick a typical business day, not a weekend or holiday, so you get an accurate picture of what's happening.

Processor Usage

Processor bottlenecks occur when the processor is so busy that it cannot respond to a request for some time. Processor bottlenecks that happen suddenly and unexpectedly, without additional load on the server, are commonly caused by a non-optimal query plan, a poor configuration, or a design factor, and not insufficient hardware. Nonetheless, always look at the big picture first. Before jumping to conclusions, monitor other counters such as disk, memory, process, and network. That will help you pinpoint the source of the processor activities.

The following sections outline the key Performance Monitor counters to monitor CPU utilization. Remember that it is normal for the trace to show a sharp increase when any program executes; you can safely ignore these spikes.

Object: Processor - Counter: % Processor Time

This counter determines the percentage of time the processor is busy by measuring the percentage of time the thread of an idle process is running and then subtracting from 100 percent. Measuring the processor activity of your SQL Server is key to identifying the potential CPU bottlenecks. For multiprocessor systems, a separate instance of this counter should be monitored for each processor. In such systems, we recommend that you use the System: % Total Processor Time counter to determine the average for all processors.

Object: System - Counter: % Total Processor Time

This counter measures the average of all the CPUs in your server. Obviously this is a key counter to watch for average CPU utilization. A rule of thumb is that if the % Total Processor Time counter exceeds 90% for a continuous period (over 20 minutes or so) on a busy database server, you *may* have a CPU bottleneck on your server.

The value that characterizes high processor usage depends greatly on your system and workload. You can define your target maximum usage at a higher or lower value than we have specified here. You have to monitor the response time of transactions to ensure that they are within reason; if not, CPU usage greater than 90 % may simply mean that the workload is too much for the available CPU resources, and either CPU resources have to be increased or workload has to be reduced or tuned.

While the % Total Processor Time counter is important, you probably don't want to jump to the conclusion that you have a CPU bottleneck based on just this one counter. Another indicator of CPU performance is the System Object: Processor Queue Length.

Object: System - Counter: Processor Queue Length

A collection of one or more threads that is ready but not able to run on the processor due to another active thread that is currently running is called the *processor queue*. This counter corresponds to the number of threads waiting for the processor cycle. If the Processor Queue Length counter exceeds two per CPU for a continuous period (over 20 minutes or so), then you *may* have a CPU bottleneck. For very busy multiprocessor systems, the queue length should range from one to three. For example, if you have eight CPUs in your server, the expected range of Processor Queue Length on a busy database server with high CPU activity is 8 to 24.

Object: Processor - Counter: % Privileged Time

This is another important counter you should monitor when you see high CPU utilization. The Intel x86 family of processors supports four operating modes, called *rings*. These are numbered from 0 through 3 and each is isolated from the others by the hardware, although Windows uses only two of these modes: ring 0 for the kernel and ring 3 for user modes. OS code and device drivers run in kernel mode. This counter represents the percentage of time the CPU spends executing kernel code — for example, processing SQL Server I/O requests. If this counter exceeds 80% to 90% for a continuous period (over 20 minutes or so), and at the same time the Physical Disks counters (discussed in the "Disk Activity" section later in the chapter) are high, you may have a disk bottleneck, rather than a CPU bottleneck.

Object: Processor - Counter: % User Time

This counter measures the amount of time consumed by non-kernel-level applications such as SQL Server or your anti-virus software. The sum of % User Time and % Privileged Time is normally equal to the % Processor Time. This is also a very important counter to look at when you see high CPU usage, especially if you are running multiple processes on a server. You may want to investigate further by looking at the instance of the counter Process: % User Time.

Object: Processor - Counter: Interrupts/Sec

This counter measures the numbers of interrupts the processor was asked to respond to per second. Interrupts are generated from hardware components such as hard-disk controller adapters and network interface cards. A sustained value over 1,000 is usually an indication of a problem. Causes of problems can include poorly configured drivers, errors in drivers, excessive use of a device, or hardware failure. If the Interrupts/sec is much larger over a sustained period, you probably have a hardware issue.

Isolating Processor Activity Created by SQL Server

After you have identified a processor bottleneck, you next need to determine whether SQL Server is using the processor or whether the processor is being consumed by running many other processes. To do this, log processor time used by SQL Server on your system, as follows:

❑ Select the `Process` object.

❑ Select the % Processor Time counter.

❑ Select the `SqlServr` instance. (If you have multiple instances of SQL Server running on a single box, Performance Monitor will list them as `sqlservr#1`, `sqlservr#2`, etc. Make sure that you pick the correct instance. You can use the Process: ID Process counter to do this. That counter lists the ProcessID and the instance name in Performance Monitor.)

Object: Process - Counter: % Processor Time

This counter gives you the percentage of time a CPU spends serving non-idle threads for all processes on your server. It does the same thing as Processor: % Processor Time, but it will give you the percentage of time for a specific process you have chosen, in this case SQL Server. If you suspect that SQL Server is not bottlenecking the CPU, you might want to add some other processes to find out which process is causing the problem. You can also quickly look at Task Manager and sort the activity by CPU, which will indicate what process is consuming the most CPU.

Object: Process - Counter: % User Time

This counter will give you the amount of time each individual process is consuming CPU cycles. It may be that you have just installed the new anti-virus software and it is eating all your CPU cycles. You can determine the culprit through analyzing Process: % User Time for the anti-virus software.

Resolving Processor Bottlenecks

With the help of all these counters, you can pretty much come to a conclusion about whether you have a CPU bottleneck in your system or not. If you do, the performance trends analyses of these counters will be very useful. Even though these counters may be well within the limits now, if you notice an increase each month (provided you are doing trends analysis every month), this is a good indication that you will run out of CPU cycle soon.

Analyze Your Application

You can use SQL Profiler and DMVs to gather the data for application analysis. We discuss both of these later in this chapter. Many CPU-intensive operations occur in SQL Server, such as excessive compilations and recompilations. It is also possible that just one or two problematic queries in your application are causing high CPU usage. The queries might get a high cache hit ratio (described in the "Memory Usage" section), but still require a large amount of logical I/O. Try to tune those queries or add indexes if necessary. The methods you can use to make such adjustments are varied and vast — from redesigning your application to reworking some queries, adding indexes, and more. If you have the money, you can buy bigger hardware, but you certainly don't want to kill a mouse with a bazooka. In addition, as a best practice, do not run OLTP and OLAP applications on the same server. To get the best performance, different types of applications should have their own dedicated servers, each one using the configuration required for the type of application you are running.

Server Configuration

Make sure that your server is properly configured. For more details on this topic please refer to Chapters 11 and 12.

After looking at the preceding options, if you still have high CPU usage you might want to consider purchasing a faster processor or adding a processor to your existing system. Make sure you use a faster processor with the largest processor cache that is practical.

Disk Activity

SQL Server relies on the Windows operating system to perform I/O operations. The disk system handles the storage and movement of data on your system, giving it a powerful influence on your system's overall responsiveness. Disk I/O is frequently the cause of bottlenecks in a system. You need to observe many factors in determining the performance of the disk system. These include the level of usage, the rate of throughput, the amount of disk space available, and whether a queue is developing for the disk systems. Unless your database fits into physical memory, SQL Server constantly brings database pages into and out of the buffer pool. This generates substantial I/O traffic. Similarly, log records need to be flushed to the disk before a transaction can be declared committed.

Many of these factors are interrelated. For example, if disk utilization is high, disk throughput might peak, and a queue might begin to form. These conditions might result in increased response time, and cause performance to slow. In addition, when disk space is extremely low, it can have an influence on response time. We have seen some cases where overall system response was very slow and it turned out that the C: drive had only 2 MB of free space left! Make sure you monitor for free disk space and take action when it falls below certain a given threshold.

The operating system enables a driver called `diskperf.sys` to activate disk monitoring. Keep in mind that by default the operating system activates only the physical performance counters. You must activate the Logical Disk counters manually using the `diskperf` command. To enable Logical Disk counters, run the following commands at the command prompt. Be sure to reboot the server after you run them.

```
Diskperf -yv
Diskperf -ye (when monitoring RAID disks)
```

We strongly recommend that you enable all disk performance data collection on any system for which you care about performance. The `diskperf` measurement layer does add some code to the I/O manager stack, so there is added latency associated with each I/O request that accesses a physical disk when measurement is tuned on. However, the overhead is trivial. In a benchmark environment where a 700MHz, eight-way Windows 2003 server was handling 50K I/O per second, enabling the `diskperf` measurements reduced its I/O capacity by about 4 percent, to 48K I/O per second. Let's say you haven't turned on the disk performance counters and some performance problem arises, which happened to be disk-related (and trust us, many are), you won't be able to gather the data because loading the `diskperf` requires a server reboot.

When it comes to I/O-related information under Windows, Performance Monitor is the undisputed king. We have listed the key I/O-related Performance Monitor counters in this section. The following sections describe the Physical Disk counters because they are the ones that truly provide value.

Object: Physical Disk - Counter: % Avg. Disk Sec/Transfer

This counter reports how fast data is being moved (in seconds). It measures the average time of each transfer, regardless of number of bytes read or written. The Avg. Disk Sec/Transfer measurement reported is based on the complete round-trip time of a request. Strictly speaking, it is a direct measurement of the disk response time, which means it includes the queue time. Queue time is the time spent waiting for the device because it is busy with another request, or waiting for the SCSI bus to the device because it is busy. A high value (for most disks, greater than 0.3 seconds) for this counter might mean that the system is retrying the requests due to lengthy queuing, or, less commonly, disk failures. To further analyze the data use Physical Disk: Avg. Disk Sec/Read and Physical Disk: Avg. Disk Sec/Write.

Object: Physical Disk - Counter: Avg. Disk Sec/Read

Because this counter reports how fast data is being read from your disk (in seconds), it gives you a good idea of disk read operation response time. If you are running a RAID configuration, this counter may signal that you should change your RAID configuration to a different one to get a better response time.

Object: Physical Disk - Counter: Avg. Disk Sec/Write

This counter is nearly the same as the previous one, but it reports how fast data is written to your disk, instead of read from it.

Object: Physical Disk - Counter: % Disk Time

This counter reports the percentage of time that the selected disk drive is busy servicing read or write requests. The % Disk Time counter is not measured directly. It is the value derived by the diskperf filter driver that provides the disk performance statistics. Diskperf is the layer of software sitting in the disk driver stack, as discussed earlier (see Figure 13-1).

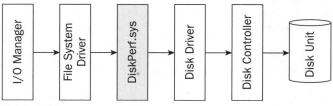

Figure 13-1

As I/O request packets (IRPs) pass through the Diskperf.sys layer, it keeps track of the time the I/O starts and finishes. On the way to the device, diskperf records a timestamp for the IRP. On the way back from the device, the completion time is recorded. The difference is the duration of the I/O request. Averaged over a collection interval, this becomes the Avg. Disk Sec/Transfer, a direct measure of the disk response time from the point of view of the device driver. Diskperf also maintains byte counts and separate counters for reads and writes at both Logical and Physical Disk level. This enables Avg. Disk Sec/Transfer to be broken out into reads and writes.

% Disk Time is the value derived by diskperf from the sum of all the IRP round-trip times (Avg. Disk Sec/Transfer) multiplied by Disk Transfer/Sec (this counter is described later in this section), and divided by duration, or essentially the following:

% Disk Time = Avg. Disk Sec/Transfer × Disk Transfer/Sec

Because the Avg. Disk Sec/Transfer that diskperf measures includes disk queuing, % Disk Time can grow greater than 100 percent if there is significant queuing. The formula used in the calculation to derive % Disk Time corresponds to *Little's Law*, a well-known equivalence relation that shows the number of requests in the system as a function of the arrival rate and service time. According to the law, Avg. Disk Sec/Transfer times Disk Transfer/Sec properly yields the average number of requests in the system, formally known as the *Average Queue Length*. The Average Queue Length value calculated in this fashion includes both the IRPs queued for service and those actually in service.

As a general guideline, if this counter is high (more than 90%), then you should start looking at potential I/O bottlenecks. Use the Physical Disk: Current Disk Queue Length counter together with % Disk Time for potential I/O bottlenecks. Even after looking at these two counters, though, you should not jump to the conclusion that you have an I/O bottleneck. We will discuss later which other counters you should look at before concluding that you have a disk I/O bottleneck. If you are using a RAID device, the % Disk Time counter can indicate a value greater than 100 percent. If it does, use the Avg. Disk Queue Length counter to determine how many system requests on average are waiting for disk access.

Object: Physical Disk - Counter: Avg. Disk Queue Length

This counter tracks the number of requests that are queued and waiting for a disk during the sample interval, as well as the requests in service. The Avg. Disk Queue Length counter is derived from the product of Avg. Disk Sec/Transfer multiplied by Disk Transfer/Sec, which is the average response of the device times the I/O rate, as described previously. The number of waiting I/O requests (Avg. Disk Queue Length) should be sustained at no more than 1.5 to 2 times the number of spindles that make up the physical disk. Most disks have one spindle, although RAID devices usually have more than one. A hardware RAID device appears as one physical disk in Performance Monitor. RAID devices created through software appear as multiple instances in Performance Monitor.

Object: Physical Disk - Counter: Current Disk Queue Length

This counter tracks the number of requests that are waiting as well as the requests currently being serviced. This counter gives an instantaneous value or snapshot of the current queue length, unlike Avg. Disk Queue Length, which reports averages. The Avg. Disk Queue Length counter is an estimate of the number of outstanding requests in the disk (Logical and Physical). This includes any requests that are currently in service at the device, plus any requests that are waiting for the service. If the requests are currently waiting for the device inside the SCSI device driver layer of the software below the `diskperf` filter driver (refer to Figure 13-1), the Current Disk Queue Length counter will have a value greater than 0. If the requests are queued in the hardware, which is usual for SCSI disks and RAID controllers, the Current Disk Queue Length counter will show a value of 0 even though requests are queued.

Object: Physical Disk - Counter: % Disk Read Time

This counter reports the percentage of time that the selected disk drive is busy servicing read requests. When the % Disk Time counter is high, you should add this counter to your watch list because it will give you more information about whether read activity is causing a bottleneck or not. In addition, this counter, along with % Disk Write Time, provides a high-level view of the type of disk activity for which you must plan.

Object: Physical Disk - Counter: % Disk Write Time

This counter reports the percentage of time that the selected disk drive is busy servicing write requests. When the % Disk Time counter is high, you should add this counter to your watch list because it will give you more information about whether write activity is causing a bottleneck or not.

Object: Physical Disk - Counter: % Idle Time

This counter reports the percentage of time that the disk system was not processing requests and no work was queued. This counter, when added to % Disk Time, might not equal 100 percent, because % Disk Time can exaggerate disk usage. Having a measure of disk idle time enables you to calculate whether the % Disk Busy measurement equals 100 minus the % Idle Time, which is a valid measure of disk usage.

Object: Physical Disk - Counter: Avg. Disk Bytes/Transfer

This counter measures the size of input/output operations. The disk is efficient if it transfers large amount of data relatively quickly. This counter shows how many items are processed, on average, during an operation. It displays a ratio of the bytes sent to the number of transfers completed. The ratio is calculated by comparing the number of bytes sent during the last interval to the number of transfers completed during the last interval. If you want to drill down further, use the Physical Disk: Avg. Bytes/Read and Physical Disk: Avg. Bytes/Write counters.

Object: Physical Disk - Counter: Disk Bytes/Sec

This counter measures the rate at which bytes are transferred; it is the primary measure of disk throughput. To analyze the data based on reads and writes, use the Physical Disk: Disk Bytes/Read and Physical Disk: Disk Bytes/Write counters.

Isolating Disk Activity Created by SQL Server

We have discussed all the counters you should monitor to find disk bottlenecks. However, you may have multiple applications running on your servers, and it is very possible that they could cause a lot of disk I/O, or you may have memory bottlenecks in your system. You should isolate the disk activities created by SQL Server. Monitor the following counters to verify whether the disk activity is caused by SQL server or not:

❑ SQL Server: Buffer Manager: Page reads/sec

❑ SQL Server: Buffer Manager: Page writes/sec

Sometime your application is too big for the hardware you have, and a problem that appears to be related to disk I/O may be resolved by adding more RAM. Make sure you do a proper analysis before making a decision. That's where trend analysis is very helpful because you can see how the performance problem evolved.

Is Disk Performance the Bottleneck?

With the help of the disk counters, you can come to a conclusion regarding whether you have disk bottlenecks in your system or not. Several conditions must exist in order for you to determine that a disk bottleneck exists in your system, including a sustained rate of disk activity well above your baseline, persistent disk queue length longer than two per disk, and the absence of a significant amount of paging. Without this combination of factors, it is unlikely that you have a disk bottleneck in your system.

Note here that sometimes your disk hardware may be faulty, and that could cause a lot of interrupts to the CPU. It is a processor bottleneck caused by a disk subsystem, which can have a systemwide performance impact (see the description of counter interrupts/sec in the "Processor Utilization" section). Make sure you consider this when you analyze the performance data.

Data Analysis

When interpreting log data, remember the limitations of the performance counters that report sums or disk time. The counters sum the totals rather than calculate them over the number of disks. For example, if you want to calculate the I/Os per disk in different RAID configurations, you have to use the following formulas:

❑ RAID 0 – I/Os per disk = (Reads + Writes) / Number of disks

❑ RAID 1 – I/Os per disk = [Reads + (2 × Writes)] / 2

❑ RAID 5 – I/Os per disk = [Reads + (4 × Writes)] / Number of disks

❑ RAID 10 – I/Os per disk = [Reads + (2 × Writes)] / Number of disks

As explained earlier, % Disk Time can sometime exceed 100 percent, which it should not. If that is the case, use the Avg. Disk Queue Length, Avg. Disk Write Queue Length, and Avg. Disk Read Queue Length counters to display disk activity and usage as decimals, rather than as a percentage. Don't forget to recalculate the values over the whole disk configuration.

Resolving Disk Bottlenecks

If, after monitoring your system, you came to the conclusion that you have a disk bottleneck, you need to be able to resolve the problem. The following sections outline some steps you can take to return your system to optimal performance.

Analyze Your Application

You can use SQL Profiler and DMVs to gather the data for analysis, which is discussed later in this chapter. In addition, look at the execution plans and see which plans led to more I/O being consumed. It is possible that a better plan (for example, a plan using the right indexes) can minimize the I/O. Query plan analysis is described in detail in Chapter 14. If there are missing indexes, you may want to run the Database Engine Tuning Advisor to find them (see Chapter 15 for details).

Disk Configuration and File Layout

If you are using RAID, make sure that it is properly configured. For more details on this topic refer to Chapter 11. In addition, after looking at the Avg. Disk Queue Length and Current Disk Queue Length counters for each physical disk, make sure that one single disk doesn't get too much queue compared to the others.

Increase I/O Bandwidth

If after looking at these options you still have disk bottlenecks, you should consider adding more physical drives to the current disk array controller, or replacing your current disks with faster drives. That will help boost both read and write access time. In addition, you can add faster or additional I/O controllers. Try to get I/O controllers with more cache on them. Finally, adding more memory can help reduce disk I/O.

Disk Performance Counters

The following table lists the counters you should monitor for disk performance data.

Counter Type	Counters
Queue-Length Counters (Physical Disk Object)	Avg. Disk Queue Length Avg. Disk Read Queue Length Avg. Disk Write Queue Length Current Disk Queue Length
Throughput Counters (Physical Disk Object)	Disk Bytes/Sec Disk Read Bytes/Sec Disk Write Bytes/Sec

Table continued on following page

Counter Type	Counters
Usage Counters (Physical Disk Object)	% Disk Time % Disk Read Time % Disk Write Time % Idle Time Disk Reads/Sec Disk Writes/Sec Disk Transfers/Sec
Paging Counters (Memory Object)	SQL Server: Buffer Manager: Cache Hit Ratio SQL Server: Buffer Manager: Page Life Expectancy SQL Server: Buffer Manager: Checkpoint Pages/Sec SQL Server: Buffer Manager: Lazy Writes/Sec Memory: Pages/Sec Memory: Page Reads/Sec Memory: Page Writes/Sec

Memory Usage

Low memory conditions can slow the operation of the applications and services on your system. Monitor an instance of SQL Server periodically to confirm that the memory usage is within typical ranges. When your server is low on memory, paging — the process of moving virtual memory back and forth between physical memory and the disk — can be prolonged, resulting in more work for your disks. The paging activity might have to compete with other transaction being performed, intensifying disk bottleneck. Monitor the following counters to identify memory bottlenecks.

Object: Memory - Counter: Available Mbytes

This counter reports how many megabytes of memory are currently available after the working set of running processes and the cache have been served. It is calculated by adding the amount of space on the Zeroed, Free, and Standby memory lists. Free memory is ready for use; Zeroed memory are pages of memory filled with zeros to prevent later processes from seeing data used by a previous process; and Standby memory is memory removed from a process' working set (its physical memory) en route to disk, but still available to be recalled. If the memory amount is low, external memory pressure may be present. The exact value depends on many factors; however, you can start looking into this when memory drops below 50–100MB. External memory pressure is clearly present when the value drops below 10MB.

Please keep in mind that when RAM is in short supply (when committed bytes is greater than installed RAM), the operating system will attempt to keep a certain fraction of installed RAM available for immediate use by copying virtual memory pages that are not in active use to the page file. For this reason, this counter will not go to zero, and is not necessarily a good indication of whether your system is short of RAM.

Object: Memory - Counter: Pages/Sec

This counter reports the number of requested pages that were not immediately available in RAM and had to be read from the disk or had to be written to the disk to make room in RAM for other pages.

This counter is the sum of Memory: Pages Input/Sec and Memory: Pages Output/Sec. Pages Input/Sec is the rate at which pages are read from disk to resolve hard page faults. Hard page faults occur when a process refers to a page in virtual memory that is not in its working set or elsewhere in physical memory, and must be retrieved from disk. When a page is faulted, the system tries to read multiple contiguous pages into memory to maximize the benefit of the read operation. Compare the value of Memory: Pages Input/Sec to the value of Memory: Page Reads/Sec to determine the average number of pages read into memory during each read operation. Pages Output/Sec is the rate at which pages are written to disk to free up space in physical memory. Pages are written back to disk only when they are changed in physical memory, so they are likely to hold data, not code. A high rate of pages output might indicate a memory shortage. Windows writes more pages back to disk to free up space when physical memory is in short supply.

If your system experiences a high rate of hard page faults, the value for Memory: Pages/Sec can be high. A high value for this counter is not necessarily indicative of memory pressure. If you happen to have an application running on your server along with SQL Server that is doing sequential reading of memory-mapped files, whether cached or not, this counter will report that too. Therefore, it is necessary to monitor other counters such as Memory: Pages Output/Sec and Memory Pages: Input/Sec in order to understand the big picture.

Object: Memory - Counter: Committed Bytes

Committed Bytes is the amount of committed virtual memory, in bytes. Committed memory is the physical memory that has space reserved on the disk paging file(s). There can be one or more paging files on each physical drive. This counter displays the last observed value only; it is not an average. As Committed Bytes grows above the amount of available RAM, paging will increase and the size of the page file in use will also increase. At some point, paging activity will start to significantly impact perceived performance.

Object: Memory - Counter: Committed Limit

Commit Limit is the amount of virtual memory that can be committed without having to extend the paging file(s). It is measured in bytes. Committed memory is the physical memory that has space reserved on the disk paging files. There can be one paging file on each logical drive. If the paging file(s) are expanded, this limit increases accordingly. This counter displays the last observed value only; it is not an average.

Isolating Memory Used by SQL Server

After you have identified a memory bottleneck, you next need to isolate the memory used by SQL Server. By default, SQL Server changes its memory requirements dynamically, on the basis of available system resources. If SQL Server needs more memory, it queries the operating system to determine whether free physical memory is available and uses the available memory. If SQL Server does not need the memory currently allocated to it, it releases the memory to the operating system if the OS asks for it. To monitor the amount of memory SQL Server uses, examine the following Performance Monitor counters.

Object: Process - Counter: Working Set

The Working Set counter reports the amount of committed memory allocated to the process. This might include shared and private bytes currently residing in physical memory. The Private Bytes counter reports memory allocated exclusively to the process. Working set monitoring is important because when memory is in short supply, the operating system trims the working sets of processes, and paging occurs. As long as no trimming has occurred, Working Set is the best counter for seeing how much memory has been allocated within the SQL Server process space.

Object: Process - Counter: Private Bytes

This counter shows the current number of bytes allocated to a process that cannot be shared with other processes. It is probably the best counter in Performance Monitor for viewing the approximate amount of memory consumed by any threads within the sqlservr.exe process space.

Object: Process - Counter: Virtual Bytes

You can use this counter to see the total virtual memory being used by SQL Server. Virtual Bytes is the current size, in bytes, of the virtual address space the process is using. Use of virtual address space does not necessarily imply corresponding use of either disk or main memory pages.

Object: SQL Server: Buffer Manager - Counter: Buffer Cache Hit Ratio

This counter reports the percentage of pages found in the buffer cache without having to read from disk. The ratio is the total number of cache hits divided by the total number of cache lookups since an instance of SQL Server was started. After a long period of time, the ratio moves very little. Because reading from the cache is much less expensive than reading from disk, you want this ratio to be high (90 percent or higher is desirable).

Object: SQL Server: Buffer Manager - Counter: Total Pages

This counter indicates the total number of pages in the buffer pool, which includes database pages, and free and stolen pages.

Object: SQL Server: Memory Manager - Counter: Total Server Memory (KB) and Target Server Memory (KB)

The first counter, SQL Server: Memory Manager: Total Server Memory (KB), tells you how much memory the Sqlservr service is currently using. This includes the total of the buffers committed to the SQL Server buffer pool and the OS buffers. The second counter, SQL Server: Memory Manager: Target Server Memory (KB), tells you how much memory SQL Server would like to have in order to operate efficiently. This is based on the number of buffers reserved by SQL Server.

If, over time, the SQL Server: Memory Manager: Total Server Memory (KB) counter is less than the SQL Server: Memory Manager: Target Server Memory (KB) counter, then SQL Server has enough memory to run efficiently. Conversely, if the SQL Server: Memory Manager: Total Server Memory (KB) counter is more than or equal to the SQL Server: Memory Manager: Target Server Memory (KB) counter, then SQL Server may be under memory pressure and could use access to more physical memory.

Resolving Memory Bottlenecks

The easy solution to memory bottlenecks is to add more memory, but as we said earlier, tuning your application always comes first. Try to find queries that are memory intensive, such as queries with large worktables — such as hashes for joins and sorts — and see if you can tune them. You will learn more about tuning T-SQL queries in Chapter 14.

In addition, refer to Chapter 11 to ensure that you have configured your server properly. After adding more memory, if you are still running into memory bottlenecks and you are running a 32-bit machine, then look into a 64-bit system. For an analysis (reporting queries) type of application, whereby you have a lot of aggregation and sorts and hash joins, consider a 64-bit platform. Of course, we are talking about big applications with tens of thousands of users running complex reports and pulling a lot of data, and not like Adventure Works.

Monitoring Events

SQL Trace and *event notifications* are the two ways you can monitor events that happened in the database engine. SQL Trace records the specified events and stores them in a file (or files) that you can use later to analyze the data. You have to specify which database engine events you want to trace when you define the trace. There are two ways to access the trace data: using SQL Server Profiler, a graphical user interface, or through T-SQL system stored procedures. SQL Server Profiler exploits all of the event-capturing functionality of SQL Trace, and adds the capability to trace information to or from a table, save the trace definitions as templates, extract query plans and deadlock events as separate XML files, and replay trace results for diagnosis and optimization.

Event notifications send information to a Service Broker service about many of the same events (not all) that are captured by SQL Trace. Unlike traces, event notifications can be used to perform an action inside SQL Server in response to events. Because event notifications execute asynchronously, these actions do not consume any resources defined by the immediate transaction — meaning, for example, if you want to be notified when a table is altered in a database, then the ALTER TABLE statement would not consume more resources or be delayed because you have defined event notification.

There are number of reasons you want to monitor what's happening inside your SQL Server:

❏ **Find the worst performing queries or stored procedures.** We have provided a trace template on this book's Web site at www.wrox.com, which you can import into your SQL Server Profiler to capture this scenario. We have included the Showplan Statistics Profile, Showplan XML, and Showplan XML Statistics Profile under Performance event groups. We included these events because after you determine the worst-performing queries, we are sure that you will want to see what query plan was generated by them. Just looking at the duration of the T-SQL batch or stored procedure does not get you anywhere. You should consider filtering the trace data by setting some value in the Duration column to only retrieve those events that are longer than a specific duration so that you minimize your dataset for analysis.

❏ **Audit user activities.** You can create a trace with Audit Login events; and by selecting the EventClass (the default), EventSubClass, LoginSID, and LoginName data columns, you can audit use activities in SQL Server. You may add more events from the Security Audit event group or data columns based on your need. You may someday need this type of information for legal purposes in addition to your technical purposes.

❏ **Identify the cause of a deadlock.** We highly recommend that you set the startup trace flags for tracing deadlocks. SQL Trace doesn't persist between server cycles unless you use SQL Job to achieve this. You can use startup trace flag 1204 or 1222 (1222 returns more verbose information than 1204 and resembles an XML document) to trace a deadlock anytime it happens on your SQL Server. Refer to Chapter 4 to learn more about these trace flags and how to set them. To capture deadlock information using SQL Trace, you need to capture these events in your trace: `Start with Standard trace` template and add the Locks event classes (Locks: Deadlock graph, Lock: Deadlock, or Lock: Deadlock Chain). If you specify the Deadlock graph event class, SQL Server Profiler produces a graphical representation of the deadlock.

❑ **Collect a representative set of events for stress testing.** For some benchmarking, you want to reply the trace generated. SQL Server provides the standard template `TSQL_Replay` to capture a trace that can be replayed later. If you want to use a trace to replay later, make sure that you use this standard template because in order to replay the trace, SQL Server needs some specific events captured and this template does just that. Later you will look at how to replay the trace.

❑ **Create a workload to use for the Database Tuning Adviser.** SQL Server Profiler provides a predefined `Tuning` template that gathers the appropriate Transact-SQL events in the trace output so it can be used as a workload for the Database Engine Tuning Advisor.

❑ **Take a performance baseline.** Earlier you learned that you should take a baseline and update it at regular intervals to compare with previous baselines to find out how your application is performing. For example, let's say you have a batch process that loads some data once a day and validates it, does some transformation, and so on, and puts it into your warehouse after deleting the existing set of data. After some time there is an increase in data volume and suddenly your process starts slowing down. You would guess that an increase in data volume would slow the process down, but is that the only reason? In fact, there could be more than one reason. The query plan generated may be different, because the stats may be incorrect, because your data volume increased, and so on. If you have a statistic profile for the query plan taken during the regular baseline, with other data (such as perf logs) you can quickly identify the root cause.

SQL Trace

As mentioned earlier, you have two ways to define the SQL Trace: using T-SQL system stored procedures and SQL Server Profiler. We will first explain the SQL Trace architecture and then we will study an example to create the server-side trace using the T-SQL system stored procedure.

Before we start, you need to know some basic trace terminology. For all the terminology related to Trace, please refer to the Books Online section "SQL Trace Terminology."

❑ **Event:** The occurrence of an action within an instance of the Microsoft SQL Server database engine or the SQL Server 2005 database engine, such as the Audit: Logout event, which happens when a user logs out of SQL Server.

❑ **Data column:** An attribute of an event, such as the `SPID` column for the Audit:Logout event, which indicates the SQL SPID of the user who logged off. Another example is the `ApplicationName` column, which gives you an application name for the event.

In SQL Server 2005, trace column values greater than 1GB return an error and are truncated in the trace output.

❑ **Filter:** Criteria that limit the events collected in a trace. For example, if you are interested only in the events generated by the SQL Server Management Studio – Query application, you can set the filter on the `ApplicationName` column to SQL Server Management Studio – Query and you will only see events generated by this application in your trace.

❑   **Template:** In SQL Server Profiler, a file that defines the event classes and data columns to be collected in a trace. Many default templates are provided with SQL Server and these files are located in the directory `\Program Files\Microsoft SQL Server\90\Tools\Profiler\Templates\Microsoft SQL Server\90`.

SQL Trace Architecture

You should understand how SQL Trace works before looking at an example. Figure 13-2 shows the basic form of the architecture. Events are the main unit of activity for tracing. When you define the trace, you specify which events you want to trace. For example, if you want to trace the SP: Starting event, SQL Server will trace only this event (with some other default events that SQL Server always captures). The event source can be any source that produces the trace event, such as a T-SQL statement, deadlocks, other events, and more.

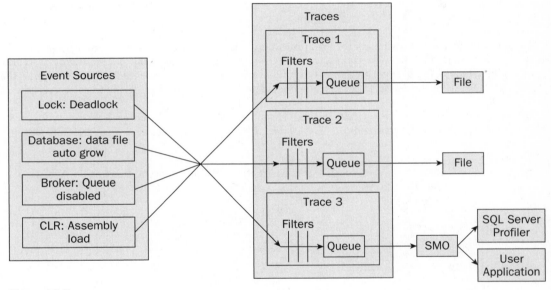

Figure 13-2

After an event occurs, if the event class has been included in a trace definition, the event information is gathered by the trace. If filters have been defined for the event class (for example, if you are only interested in the events for LoginName = 'foo') in the trace definition, the filters are applied and the trace event information is passed to a queue. From the queue, the trace information is written to a file or it can be used by SMO in applications, such as SQL Server Profiler.

Creating a Server-Side Trace Using T-SQL Stored Procedures

If you have used SQL Profiler before, you know that creating a trace using SQL Profiler is very easy. Creating a trace using T-SQL system stored procedures requires some extra effort because it uses internal IDs for events and data column definitions. Fortunately, the `sp_trace_setevent` article in SQL Server Books Online (BOL) documents the internal ID number for each event and each data column. You need four stored procedures to create and start a server-side trace:

❑ `sp_trace_create`: Creates a trace definition. The new trace will be in a stopped state.

❑ `sp_trace_setevent`: Once you define trace using `sp_trace_create`, this stored procedure adds or removes an event or event column to a trace. `sp_trace_setevent` may be executed only on existing traces that are stopped (whose status is 0). An error is returned if this stored procedure is executed on a trace that does not exist or whose status is not 0.

❑ `sp_trace_setfilter`: Applies a filter to a trace. `sp_trace_setfilter` may be executed only on existing traces that are stopped. SQL Server returns an error if this stored procedure is executed on a trace that does not exist or whose status is not 0.

❑ `sp_trace_setstatus`: Modifies the current state of the specified trace.

Now you'll create a server-side trace. This trace will capture the events Audit Login and SQL:StmtStarting. It will capture the data columns `SPID`, `DatabaseName`, `TextData`, and `HostName` for the Audit Login event. It will capture the data columns `ApplicationName`, `SPID`, `TextData`, and `DatabaseName` for the SQL: StmtStarting event.

You want to capture the trace data for the application SQL Server Management Studio – Query only. Save the trace data in a file located on some remote share. The maximum file size should be 6MB and you need to enable file rollover so that another file is created when the current file becomes larger than 6MB. You also want the server to process the trace data, and you want to stop the trace at a certain time.

Server-side traces are much more efficient than client-side tracing with SQL Server Profiler. Defining server-side traces using stored procedures is a bit hard but there is an easy way to do it, which we will look at soon.

Open the sample `SQLTrace-ServerSide` in the Chapter 13 folder found on this book's Web site at www.wrox.com. Open the file `CreateTrace.sql`, which is shown here:

```
-- Create a Queue
declare @rc int
declare @TraceID int
declare @maxfilesize bigint
declare @DateTime datetime

set @maxfilesize = 10
set @DateTime = '2006-06-05 14:00:00.000'
--------------------
-- The .trc extension will be appended to the filename automatically.
-- If you are writing from remote server to local drive,
-- please use UNC path and make sure server has write access to your network share
exec @rc = sp_trace_create @traceid = @TraceID output
,@options = 2
,@tracefile = N'\\cipher\trace\ServerSideTrace'
,@maxfilesize  = @maxfilesize
,@stoptime  = @Datetime
,@filecount = NULL
if (@rc != 0) goto error

-- Set the events
declare @on bit
set @on = 1
exec sp_trace_setevent
```

```
 @traceid = @TraceID
,@eventid  = 14
,@columnid = 8
,@on = @on

exec sp_trace_setevent @TraceID, 14, 1, @on
exec sp_trace_setevent @TraceID, 14, 35, @on
exec sp_trace_setevent @TraceID, 14, 12, @on
exec sp_trace_setevent @TraceID, 40, 1, @on
exec sp_trace_setevent @TraceID, 40, 10, @on
exec sp_trace_setevent @TraceID, 40, 35, @on
exec sp_trace_setevent @TraceID, 40, 12, @on


-- Set the Filters
declare @intfilter int
declare @bigintfilter bigint

exec sp_trace_setfilter
 @traceid = @TraceID
,@columnid = 10
,@logical_operator = 1
,@comparison_operator = 6
,@value = N'SQL Server Management Studio - Query'

-- Set the trace status to start
exec sp_trace_setstatus @traceid = @TraceID, @status = 1

-- display trace id for future references
select TraceID=@TraceID
goto finish

error:
select ErrorCode=@rc

finish:
go
```

Now we'll take a look at this stored procedure. The @traceid parameter returns an integer that you must use if you want to modify the trace, stop or restart it, or look at its properties.

The second parameter, @options, lets you specify one or more trace options. A value of 1 tells the trace to produce a rowset and send it to Profiler. You can't use this option value if you capture to a server-side file. Typically, only Profiler-created traces have this option value. Traces that use the sp_trace_create stored procedure should never have an option value of 1, because this value is reserved for Profiler-defined traces. Because the value for the @options parameter is a bitmap, you can combine values by adding them together. For example, if you want a trace that enables file rollover and shuts down SQL Server if SQL Server can't write to the trace file, the option value is 6 (4 + 2). Note that not all option values can be combined with the others (option value 8 by definition doesn't combine with any other option value). In this case, the option value 2 means that when the trace file reaches the size specified by the value in the parameter @maxfilesize, the current trace file is closed and a new file is created. All new records will be written to the new file. The new file will have the same name as the previous file, but an integer will be appended to indicate its sequence. For details about other @option values, please refer to the sp_trace_setevent article in SQL Server Books Online (BOL).

In the @tracefile parameter, you can specify where you want to store the trace results. You can specify either a local directory (such as N 'C:\MSSQL\Trace\trace.trc') or a UNC to a share or path (N'\\Servername\Sharename\Directory\trace.trc'). The extension .trc will be added automatically, so you don't need to specify that. Note that you cannot specify the @tracefile if you set the @option value to 8; in that case, the server will store the last 5MB of trace information.

You can specify the maximum size of the trace file before it creates another file to add the trace data using the @maxfilesize parameter, in MB. In this case we have specified 10MB, which means that once the trace file size exceeds 10MB, SQL Trace will create another file and start adding data there. We recommend using this option because if you create one big file, it's not easy to move it around, and if you have multiple files, then you can start looking at the older files while trace is writing to the new file. In addition, if disk space issues arise while gathering the trace data, you can move files to different drives or servers.

You can optionally specify the trace stop time using the @stoptime parameter, which is of the datetime type.

The @filecount parameter is used to specify the maximum number of trace files to be maintained with the same base filename. Please refer to Books Online for a detailed description of this parameter.

Now let's see how to set up the events and choose the data columns for those events. The stored procedure sp_trace_setevent will do that job. The first parameter is the traceid, which you got from the sp_trace_create stored procedure. The second parameter, @eventid, is the internal ID of the event you are trying to trace. The first call of the stored procedure specifies 14, which is the Audit Login event. In the third parameter you have to specify which data column you want to capture for the event indicated. In this case, we have set @columnid to 8, which is the data column HostName. You have to call this stored procedure for each data column you want for a particular event. We called this stored procedure multiple times for @eventid 14 because we want multiple data columns. The last parameter is @ON, which is a bit parameter used to specify whether you want to turn the event on or off. As mentioned earlier, the sp_trace_setevent article in SQL Server Books Online (BOL) documents the internal ID number for each event and each data column.

Once the event is established you want to set the filter on it. You use the stored procedure sp_trace_setfilter to set the filter on a particular event and the data column. The article sp_trace_setfilter in BOL documents the internal ID number for the @comparison_operator and @logical_operator parameters. In this case, you want only the trace generated by the application name SQL Server Management Studio - Query.

To start the trace you have to use the stored procedure sp_trace_setstatus. You can specify the trace ID you want to take action on with the option 0, 1, or 2. Because we want to start the trace, we have specified 1. If you want to stop, specify 0. If you specify 2, it closes the specified trace and deletes its definition from the server.

You're all set to run the server-side trace. Note that we have specified the @datetime option to stop the trace. You have to change the datetime value as your needs dictate. Make sure that if you specify the UNC path for the trace file, the SQL Server service account has write access to the share. Run the script now.

It seems like plenty of work to get these internal IDs right when you create the server-side trace. Fortunately, there is an easy way to create the server-side trace using SQL Server Profiler, as you'll see in a moment.

You can define all the events, data columns, filters, filenames (you have to select the option to save to the file, as you cannot store to a table when you create a server-side trace) and size using SQL Server Profiler and then click Run. After that, select File➪Export➪Script Trace Definition ➪For SQL Server (2005 or 2000) and save the script. Now you have the script to create the server-side trace. You may have to check the @maxfilesize *to ensure that it has the correct value if you have changed something other than the default, which is 5MB.*

When you define the server-side trace, you cannot store the trace result directly into the table. You have to store it into the file; later you can use a function, discussed next, to put the trace data into a table.

Retrieving the Trace Metadata

Now that you have defined the trace, you also need to understand how to get the information about the trace. There are built-in functions you can use to do that. The function fn_trace_getinfo (trace_id) is used to get the information about a particular trace. If you do not know the trace_id, specify DEFAULT as the function argument and it will list all the traces.

Open the script GetTraceDetails.sql and run it. Be sure to change the trace_id parameter value to whatever trace_id you got when you ran the script CreateTrace.sql. Figure 13-3 shows the output.

Figure 13-3

In Figure 13-3, the Property 1 row contains the @options parameter value. A trace with a Property 1 value of 1 is most likely a trace started from Profiler. The Property 2 row contains the trace filename, if any. The Property 3 row contains the maximum file size, which is 10MB in this case; and the Property 4 row contains the stop time, which has some value for this trace. The Property 5 row shows the trace's status — in this case 1, which means that Trace is running.

The function Fn_trace_geteventinfo() shows you the events and data columns that a particular trace captures, but the function returns the data with the event and data column IDs, instead of a name or explanation, so you must track down their meaning. The function Fn_trace_getfilterinfo() returns information about a particular trace's filters:

```
SELECT * FROM fn_trace_geteventinfo (2)
```

423

Retrieving Data from the Trace File

There are two ways you can retrieve the trace data from the file: using the function `fn_trace_gettable` or with SQL Server Profiler. The function `fn_trace_gettable` is a Table Valued Function, so you can read directly from the file using this function and insert data into a table to analyze:

```
SELECT * FROM fn_trace_gettable ( '\\cipher\trace\ServerSideTrace.trc' , DEFAULT)
```

You can also use `SELECT INTO` in this query to store the result in a table. We like to put the trace data into a table because then you can write a T-SQL statement to query the data. For example, the `TextData` column is created with the `ntext` data type. You can alter the data type to `nvarchar(max)` so that you can use the string functions. You should not be using the `ntext` or `text` data types anyway, because they will be deprecated in a future SQL Server release; use `nvarchar(max)` or `varchar(max)` instead. Note that even though the trace is running, you can still read the data from the file to which Trace is writing. You don't have to stop the trace for that. The only gotcha in storing the trace data into a table is that the EventClass value is stored as an `int` value and not as a friendly name. We have provided a script, `EventClassID_Name.sql`, that creates a table and inserts the `eventclassid` and its name in that table. You can then use this table to get the event class name when you analyze the trace result stored in the table. You can write a query like the following to do that, assuming that you have stored the trace result in the table `TraceResult`:

```
SELECT ECN.EventClassName, TR.*
FROM TraceResult TR
LEFT JOIN EventClassIdToName ECN
  ON ECN.EventClassID = TR.EventClass
```

SQL Server Profiler

SQL Server Profiler is a rich interface to create and manage traces and analyze and replay trace results. SQL Server Profiler shows how SQL Server resolves queries internally. This enables you to see exactly what Transact-SQL statements or multi-dimensional expressions are submitted to the server and how the server accesses the database or cube to return result sets.

SQL Server 2005 added plenty of new features in Profiler, including the following:

❑ **Profiling of Microsoft SQL Server 2005 Analysis Services (SSAS).** SQL Server Profiler now supports capturing and displaying events raised by SSAS.

❑ **Rollover trace files.** SQL Server Profiler can replay one or more collected rollover trace files continuously and in order.

❑ **Saving the traced Showplan as XML.** Showplan results can be saved in an XML format, which can be loaded later for graphical Showplan display in SQL Server Management Studio without the need for an underlying database. SQL Server Profiler will also display a graphical representation of Showplan XML events at the time they are captured by SQL Server Profiler.

❑ **Save trace results as XML.** Trace results can be saved in an XML format in addition to the standard save formats of ANSI, Unicode, and OEM. Results saved in this fashion can be edited and used as input for the replay capability of SQL Server Profiler.

❑ **Aggregate view.** Users can choose an aggregate option and select a key for aggregation. This enables users to see a view that shows the column on which the aggregation was performed, along with a count of the number of rows that make up the aggregate value.

❑ **Correlation of Trace events to Performance Monitor counters.** SQL Server Profiler can correlate Performance Monitor counters with SQL Server or SSAS events. Administrators can select from a predefined set of Performance Monitor counters and save them at specified time intervals while also collecting a SQL Server or SSAS trace.

❑ **New extensibility standard.** SQL Server Profiler uses an XML-based definition that enables SQL Server Profiler to more easily capture events from other types of servers and programming interfaces.

If you do not know how to create a trace using Profiler, please refer to the BOL topic "Using SQL Server Profiler." Here I explain how to use Showplan XML and how to correlate the trace events to Performance Monitor counters. I also discuss how to capture the trace for replay and how to replay the trace.

You can read the trace file created using a T-SQL stored procedure with SQL Profiler. To use SQL Profiler to read the trace file, just go to the File menu and open the trace file you are interested in.

> *In SQL Server 2005, the server reports the duration of an event in microseconds (one millionth of a second) and the amount of CPU time used by the event in milliseconds (one thousandth of a second). In SQL Server 2000, the server reported both duration and CPU time in milliseconds. In SQL Server 2005, the SQL Server Profiler graphical user interface displays the Duration column in milliseconds by default, but when a trace is saved to either a file or a database table, the Duration column value is written in microseconds. If you want to display the duration column in microseconds in SQL Profiler, go to Tools⇨Options and select the option "Show values in Duration column in microseconds (SQL Server 2005 only)."*

Showplan XML

In SQL Server 2005 you can get the query plan in an XML document. You can use this document later to generate the graphical query plan. Showplan output in XML format can be moved from one computer to another and thus rendered on any computer, even on computers where SQL Server is not installed. Showplan output in XML format can also be programmatically processed using XML technologies, such as XPath, XQuery, and so on. XML Showplan processing is supported in SQL Server 2005, which contains a built-in query evaluation engine for XPath and XQuery.

You can generate XML Showplan output using the following means:

❑ Selecting Display Estimated Execution Plan or Include Actual Execution Plan from the query editor toolbar in SQL Server Management Studio

❑ Using the Transact-SQL Showplan SET statement options SHOWPLAN_XML and STATISTICS XML

❑ Selecting the SQL Server Profiler event classes Showplan XML, Showplan XML for Query Compile, and Showplan XML Statistics Profile for tracing

❑ Using the sys.dm_exec_query_plan dynamic management view

XML Showplans are returned in the nvarchar (max) data type for all of these methods, except when you use sys.dm_exec_query_plan. XML Showplans are returned in the xml data type when you use this dynamic management view.

You can visit http://schemas.microsoft.com/sqlserver/2004/07/showplan/showplanxml.xsd for the XML Showplan schema or you can look in the directory where SQL Server is installed, \Program Files\Microsoft SQL Server\90\Tools\Binn\schemas\sqlserver\2004\07\showplan.

We explain how to read the query plan in Chapter 14. Figure 13-4 shows what a query plan looks like in SQL Profiler when you choose the Showplan XML event.

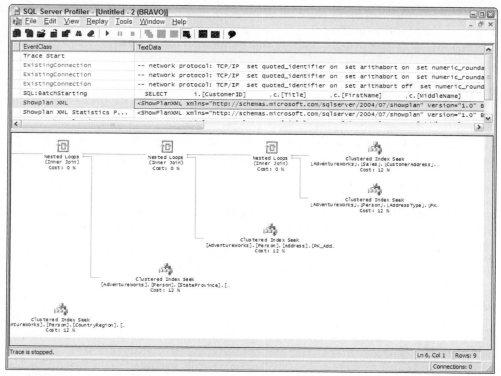

Figure 13-4

If you right-click on the Showplan XML event, you will see a menu item Extract Event Data. This will save the query plan with a `.sqlplan` extension. You can later open that file with SQL Server Management Studio or Profiler and it will display the graphical plan exactly as shown in Figure 13-4. You can also use File➪Export➪Extract SQL Server Event in SQL Profiler to achieve the same results.

When you set up the trace using Profiler, and if you choose Showplan XML or Showplan Statistics Profile or Showplan XML for Query Compile, a tab will show up in the Trace Properties dialog, shown in Figure 13-5.

You can also see in Figure 13-5 that there is a Deadlock XML option to store the deadlock graph in an XML document, which you can view later in SQL Management Studio or Profiler. This option is enabled only if you choose the Deadlock Graph event.

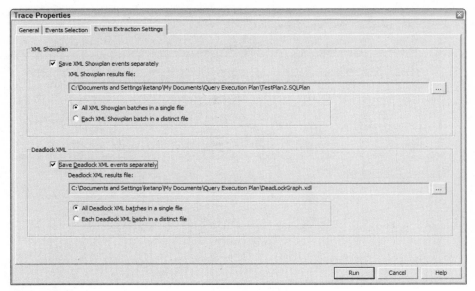

Figure 13-5

You can also use SET SHOWPLAN_XML ON before you execute the query, which will give you an estimated execution plan in XML without executing it. You can also use SET STATISTICS XML ON, which will give you an execution plan in XML format, as shown in Figure 13-6. You can click on the link in the XML Showplan and it will open an XML editor within SQL Server Management Studio.

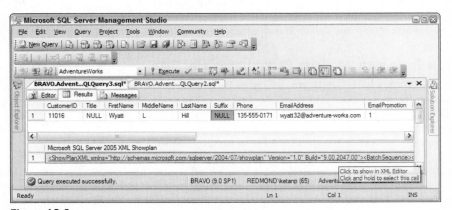

Figure 13-6

If you want to see the graphical execution plan from this XML document, you can save this XML document with a .sqlplan extension. Open that file in SQL Server Management Studio and you will get the graphical execution plan. See Figure 13-7 for the graphical execution plan generated from the XML document.

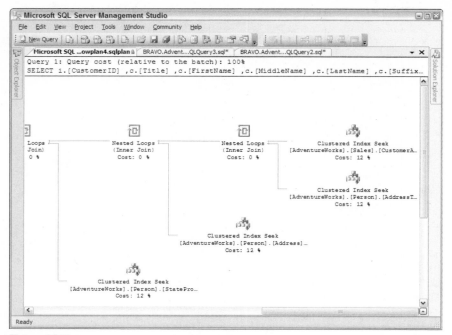

Figure 13-7

When the Showplan XML event class is included in a trace, the amount of overhead will significantly impede performance. Showplan XML stores a query plan that is created when the query is optimized. To minimize the overhead incurred, limit the use of this event class to traces that monitor specific problems for brief periods of time, and be sure to use the data column filter based on specifics you are going to trace.

Correlating a Trace with Windows Performance Log Data

In SQL Server 2005, a new feature was added to correlate the trace data with Performance Monitor log data based on the `StartTime` and `EndTime` data columns in the SQL trace file. If you have taken Trace and Performance Monitor data at the same time, you can relate the events that happened in SQL Server with the server activities such as processor time, disk activity, and memory usage. Figures 13-8 and 13-9 show an example of correlating trace and Performance Monitor log data.

To bring up the performance data after you open a trace file, click File⇨Import Performance Data. That will bring up the dialog box shown in Figure 13-8. You can select the performance counters you are interested in and then click OK. That will bring the performance counters inside the Profiler to correlate the SQL Server activity during a specific time, as shown in Figure 13-9. You can move the red vertical bar to select a particular time you are interested in to see what was happening during that time in SQL Server.

If you look at the peak value for a performance counter — for example, avg. disk queue length — that will bring up whatever query SQL Server was executing at the time. However, that doesn't mean that the query caused the disk queue length to increase exactly at that time. It's possible that the query started a little earlier, and is now requesting a lot of data from disk, and that may be causing the average disk queue length to shoot up. In short, be careful before you jump to conclusions and make sure you have looked at the whole picture.

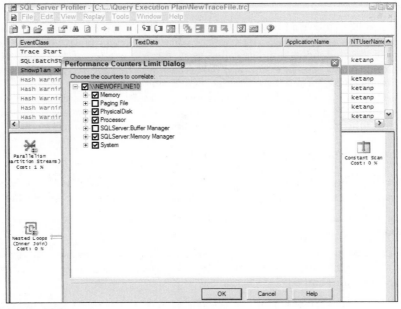

Figure 13-8

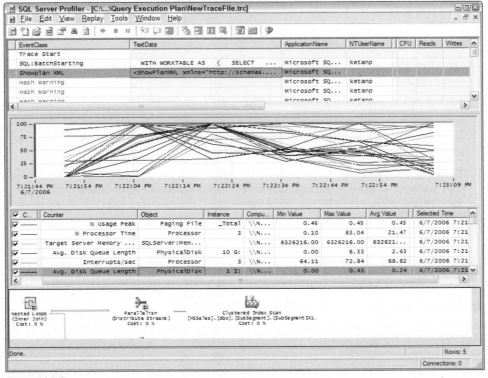

Figure 13-9

Replaying a Trace

Replay is the capability to save a trace and replay it later. This functionality enables you to reproduce the activity captured in a trace. When you create or edit a trace, you can save the trace to replay it later. Be sure to choose the predefined template called `TSQL_Replay` when you create the trace using SQL Profiler. SQL Server needs specific events and data columns to be captured in order to replay the trace later. If you miss those events and data columns, SQL Server will not replay the trace. Trace replay supports debugging by using the Toggle Breakpoint and the Run to Cursor options on the SQL Server Profiler Replay menu. These options especially improve the analysis of long scripts because they can break the replay of the trace into short segments so they can be analyzed incrementally.

The following types of trace are ignored when you replay the trace:

❑ Traces that contain transactional replication and other transaction log activity. These events are skipped. Other types of replication do not mark the transaction log so they are not affected.

❑ Traces that contain operations that involve globally unique identifiers (GUID). These events are skipped.

❑ Traces that contain operations on `text`, `ntext`, and `image` columns involving the `bcp` utility, the `BULK INSERT`, `READTEXT`, `WRITETEXT`, and `UPDATETEXT` statements, and full-text operations. These events are skipped.

❑ Traces that contain session binding: `sp_getbindtoken` and `sp_bindsession` system stored procedures. These events are skipped.

❑ SQL Server Profiler does not support replaying traces collected by Microsoft SQL Server version 7.0 or earlier.

In addition, some requirements must be met in order to replay the trace on the target server:

❑ All logins and users contained in the trace must be created already on the target and in the same database as the source.

❑ All logins and users in the target must have the same permissions they had in the source.

❑ All login passwords must be the same as those of the user who executes the replay. You can use the Transfer Login task in SSIS to transfer the logins to the target server on which you want to replay the trace.

❑ The database IDs on the target ideally should be the same as those on the source. However, if they are not the same, matching can be performed based on the database name if it is present in the trace, so make sure that you have the `DatabaseName` data column selected in the trace.

❑ The default database on the target server for a login should be the same as on the source when the trace was taken.

❑ Replaying events associated with missing or incorrect logins results in replay errors, but the replay operation continues.

Performance Considerations When Using Trace

SQL Server tracing incurs no overhead unless it captures an event, and most events need very few resources. Profiler becomes expensive only if you trace more than 100 event classes and capture all the data from those events. Normally, you will see a maximum of 5 percent to 10 percent overhead if you capture everything. Most of the performance hit is because of a longer code path; the actual resources that the trace needs in order to capture event data aren't particularly CPU-intensive. In addition, to minimize the performance hit, you can define all your traces as server-side traces and avoid the overhead of producing rowsets to send to the Profiler client.

Event Notification

Event notifications are special database objects that send messages to the Service Broker service (see Chapter 8 for details on the Service Broker) with information regarding server or database events. Event notifications can be programmed against many of the same events captured by SQL Trace, but not all. Unlike creating traces, event notifications can be used to perform an action inside an instance of SQL Server 2005 in response to events. Later in this chapter you'll see an example that shows how to subscribe to those events and take actions if needed.

To subscribe to an event, you have to create the Service Broker queue that will receive the details regarding the events. In addition, a queue requires the Service Broker service in order to receive the message. Then you need to create an event notification. You can create a stored procedure and activate it when the event message is in the queue to take a certain action. This example assumes you know how the Service Broker works, so be sure to read Chapter 8 if you don't already know about the Server Broker.

Event notifications are created at the server or database level.

We will create an event notification in a database whereby you will be notified when a new table is created. Open the project `EventNotification` using SQL Server Management Studio. Open the `CreateDatabase.sql` script. This script will create a database called `StoreEvent` for the example. Run this script.

Next, open the `CreateQueue.sql` script, shown here:

```
USE StoreEvent
GO

--CREATE QUEUE to receive the event details.
IF OBJECT_ID('dbo.NotifyQueue') IS NULL
CREATE QUEUE dbo.NotifyQueue
WITH STATUS = ON
    ,RETENTION = OFF
GO

--create the service so that when event happens
--server can send the message to this service.
--we are using the pre-defined contract here.
IF NOT EXISTS(SELECT * FROM sys.services WHERE name = 'EventNotificationService')
CREATE SERVICE EventNotificationService
ON QUEUE NotifyQueue
([http://schemas.microsoft.com/SQL/Notifications/PostEventNotification])

IF NOT EXISTS(SELECT * FROM sys.routes WHERE name = 'NotifyRoute')

CREATE ROUTE NotifyRoute
WITH SERVICE_NAME = 'EventNotificationService',
ADDRESS = 'LOCAL';
GO
```

This script creates a queue in the `StoreEvent` database to store the event data when a table is created in the `StoreEvent` database. It creates a Service Broker service `EventNotificationService` such that SQL Server can send the message when a subscribed event happens. The route `NotifyRoute` will help route the message to a local SQL server instance. Run this script.

Now you need to create the event notification. Open the script `CreateEventNotification.sql`, shown here:

```
USE StoreEvent
GO
CREATE EVENT NOTIFICATION CreateTableNotification
ON DATABASE
FOR CREATE_TABLE
TO SERVICE 'EventNotificationService', 'current database' ;
```

This script creates an event notification called `CreateTableNotification` to notify you when a table is created in the `StoreEvent` database.

Note that messages are sent from one service to another, as discussed in Chapter 8. In this case, you have created the target end of the service, which is `EventNotificationServer`; the initiator end of the service is SQL Server itself.

When a table is created in the `StoreEvent` database, you will get the message in the queue `NotifyQueue`, so create a table and run the following script to see what's in the queue:

```
SELECT CAST(message_body AS xml)
FROM NotifyQueue
```

Here is what the XML message in the queue looks like:

```
<EVENT_INSTANCE>
  <EventType>CREATE_TABLE</EventType>
  <PostTime>2006-06-11T21:53:14.463</PostTime>
  <SPID>56</SPID>
  <ServerName>CIPHER</ServerName>
  <LoginName>REDMOND\ketanp</LoginName>
  <UserName>dbo</UserName>
  <DatabaseName>StoreEvent</DatabaseName>
  <SchemaName>dbo</SchemaName>
  <ObjectName>TestTable1</ObjectName>
  <ObjectType>TABLE</ObjectType>
  <TSQLCommand>
    <SetOptions ANSI_NULLS="ON" ANSI_NULL_DEFAULT="ON" ANSI_PADDING="ON"
QUOTED_IDENTIFIER="ON" ENCRYPTED="FALSE" />
    <CommandText>CREATE TABLE TestTable1 (col1 int, col2 varchar(100), col3 xml)
</CommandText>
  </TSQLCommand>
</EVENT_INSTANCE>
```

You can take some action with this event if you create a stored procedure and have it activated when a message arrives in the queue. Refer to Chapter 8 for details on stored procedure activation.

You create the server-wide event in the same way. For a full list of the events for which you can be notified, you can query the `sys.event_notification_event_types` view. Please refer to the script `Metadata_EventNotification.sql` to get the catalog view list that stores the metadata about event notifications.

Note that you can also be notified for grouped events. For example, if you want to be notified when a table is created, altered, or dropped, you don't have to create three separate event notifications. You can use the group event called `DDL_TABLE_EVENTS` and just create one event notification to achieve the same thing. Another example is related to monitoring all the locking events using the event group `TRC_LOCKS`. When you create an event notification with this group, you can be notified for the following events: `LOCK_DEADLOCK`, `LOCK_DEADLOCK_CHAIN`, `LOCK_ESCALATION`, and `DEADLOCK_GRAPH`.

Please refer to the BOL topic "DDL Event Groups for Use with Event Notifications" for all the event groups.

Event notifications can be used to do the following:

❑   Log and review changes or activity occurring on the database or server.

❑   Perform an action in response to an event in an asynchronous, rather than synchronous, manner.

Event notifications can offer a programming alternative to DDL triggers and SQL Trace.

Monitoring with Dynamic Management Views and Functions

Dynamic Management Views (DMVs) and Dynamic Management Functions (DMFs) are a godsend to the DBA. They provide plenty of information about server and database state. DMVs are designed to give you a window into what's going on inside SQL Server 2005. They return server state information that you can use to monitor the health of a server instance, diagnose problems, and tune performance. There are two types of DMVs and functions:

❑   Server-scoped dynamic management views and functions

❑   Database-scoped dynamic management views and functions

All DMVs and functions exist in the `sys` schema and follow the naming convention `dm_*` and `fn*`, respectively. To view the information from a server-scoped DMV, you have to grant the SERVER VIEW STATE permission to the user. For database-scoped DMVs and functions, you have to grant the VIEW DATABASE STATE permission to the user. Once you grant the VIEW STATE permission, the user can see all the views, so in order to restrict the user, deny the user SELECT permission on the dynamic management views or functions that you do not want them to access. Here is an example to grant the VIEW SERVER STATE permission to the user Aish:

```
GRANT VIEW SERVER STATE TO [MyDom\Aish]
```

Now if you want user [MyDom\Aish] to be restricted from viewing information in the view sys.dm_os_wait_stats, you need to DENY SELECT as follows:

```
DENY SELECT ON sys.dm_os_wait_stats TO [MyDom\Aish]
```

DMVs and functions are generally divided into the following categories:

- ❑ CLR-related Dynamic Management Views
- ❑ I/O-related Dynamic Management Views and Functions
- ❑ Database mirroring–related Dynamic Management Views
- ❑ Query notifications–related Dynamic Management Views
- ❑ Database-related Dynamic Management Views
- ❑ Replication-related Dynamic Management Views
- ❑ Execution-related Dynamic Management Views and Functions
- ❑ Service Broker–related Dynamic Management Views
- ❑ Full-Text-Search-related Dynamic Management Views
- ❑ SQL Server Operating System–related Dynamic Management Views
- ❑ Index-related Dynamic Management Views and Functions
- ❑ Transaction-related Dynamic Management Views and Functions

We won't describe all the views here, but we will look at examples for the common tasks a DBA would do to monitor a SQL Server. To find the details of all the DMVs and functions, please refer to the Books Online topic "Dynamic Management Views and Functions."

Following are some of the scenarios in which you can use DMVs and functions. You can also open a sample DMV to get all the scripts. Here we will just provide some examples, but in the sample DMV solution you will find many examples for monitoring your SQL Server.

Viewing the Locking Information

The following query will help you get the locking information in a particular database:

```
SELECT l.resource_type, l.resource_associated_entity_id
,OBJECT_NAME(sp.OBJECT_ID) AS ObjectName
,l.request_status, l.request_mode,request_session_id
,l.resource_description
FROM sys.dm_tran_locks l
LEFT JOIN sys.partitions sp
  ON sp.hobt_id = l.resource_associated_entity_id
WHERE l.resource_database_id = DB_ID()
```

Viewing Blocking Information

The following query will show blocking information on your server:

```
SELECT
t1.resource_type
,t1.resource_database_id
,t1.resource_associated_entity_id
,OBJECT_NAME(sp.OBJECT_ID) AS ObjectName
,t1.request_mode
,t1.request_session_id
,t2.blocking_session_id
FROM sys.dm_tran_locks as t1
JOIN sys.dm_os_waiting_tasks as t2
  ON t1.lock_owner_address = t2.resource_address
LEFT JOIN sys.partitions sp
  ON sp.hobt_id = t1.resource_associated_entity_id
```

Index Usage in a Database

The following query will give you index usage for the database in which you run the query. It will create a table and store the results in that table so that later you can analyze it. This query can be very helpful for determining which indexes are truly useful in your application and which are not. If certain indexes are not used, then you should consider dropping them because they will take unnecessary time to create or maintain. The results stored in the second table, NotUsedIndexes, will indicate which indexes are not used. Make sure you run these queries for several days, which will give you a better idea of the overall picture than looking at data for just a day. Remember to keep in mind that dynamic management views are volatile, and whenever SQL Server is restarted, these views are initialized again.

```
---------------------------------------------------------------------------------
IF OBJECT_ID('dbo.IndexUsageStats') IS NULL
CREATE TABLE dbo.IndexUsageStats
(
 IndexName sysname NULL
,ObjectName sysname NOT NULL
,user_seeks bigint NOT NULL
,user_scans bigint NOT NULL
,user_lookups bigint NOT NULL
,user_updates bigint NOT NULL
,last_user_seek datetime NULL
,last_user_scan datetime NULL
,last_user_lookup datetime NULL
,last_user_update datetime NULL
,StatusDate datetime NOT NULL
,DatabaseName sysname NOT NULL
)

GO
----Below query will give you index USED per table in a database.
INSERT INTO dbo.IndexUsageStats
(
```

```
  IndexName
,ObjectName
,user_seeks
,user_scans
,user_lookups
,user_updates
,last_user_seek
,last_user_scan
,last_user_lookup
,last_user_update
,StatusDate
,DatabaseName
)
SELECT
 si.name AS IndexName
,so.name AS ObjectName
,diu.user_seeks
,diu.user_scans
,diu.user_lookups
,diu.user_updates
,diu.last_user_seek
,diu.last_user_scan
,diu.last_user_lookup
,diu.last_user_update
,GETDATE() AS StatusDate
,sd.name AS DatabaseName
FROM sys.dm_db_index_usage_stats  diu
JOIN sys.indexes si
  ON diu.object_id = si.object_id
 AND diu.index_id = si.index_id
JOIN sys.all_objects so
  ON so.object_id = si.object_id
JOIN sys.databases sd
  ON sd.database_id = diu.database_id
WHERE is_ms_shipped <> 1
  AND diu.database_id = DB_ID()


--------------------------------------------------------------------------------
--This will store the indexes which are not used.
IF OBJECT_ID('dbo.NotUsedIndexes') IS NULL
CREATE TABLE dbo.NotUsedIndexes
(
 IndexName sysname NULL
,ObjectName sysname NOT NULL
,StatusDate datetime NOT NULL
,DatabaseName sysname NOT NULL
)

----Below query will give you index which are NOT used per table in a database.
INSERT dbo.NotUsedIndexes
(
 IndexName
,ObjectName
,StatusDate
```

```
,DatabaseName
)
SELECT
 si.name AS IndexName
,so.name AS ObjectName
,GETDATE() AS  StatusDate
,DB_NAME()
FROM sys.indexes si
JOIN sys.all_objects so
  ON so.object_id = si.object_id
WHERE si.index_id NOT IN (SELECT index_id
                          FROM sys.dm_db_index_usage_stats diu
                          WHERE si.object_id = diu.object_id
                            AND si.index_id = diu.index_id
                          )
    AND so.is_ms_shipped <> 1
```

View Queries Waiting for Memory Grants

The following query will indicate the queries that are waiting for memory grants. SQL Server will analyze a query and determine how much memory it needs based on the estimated plan. If memory is not
available at that time, the query will be suspended until the memory required is available. If a query is
waiting for a memory grant, an entry will show up in the DMV `sys.dm_exec_query_memory_grants`.

```
SELECT
 es.session_id AS SPID
,es.login_name
,es.host_name
,es.program_name, es.status AS Session_Status
,mg.requested_memory_kb
,DATEDIFF(mi, mg.request_time, GETDATE()) AS [WaitingSince-InMins]
FROM sys.dm_exec_query_memory_grants mg
JOIN sys.dm_exec_sessions es
  ON es.session_id = mg.session_id
WHERE mg.grant_time IS NULL
ORDER BY mg.request_time
```

Connected User Information

The following query will tell you which users are connected, and how many sessions each of them
has open:

```
SELECT login_name, count(session_id) as session_count
FROM sys.dm_exec_sessions
GROUP BY login_name
```

Query Plan and Query Text for Currently Running Queries

Use the following query to find out the query plan in XML and the query text for the currently running
batch for a particular session. Make sure that you are using a grid to output the result in SQL Server
Management Studio. When you get the result, you can click the link for the XML plan, which will open

an XML editor inside Management Studio. If you want to look at the graphical query plan from this XML plan, save the XML plan with the .sqlplan extension. Then open that file in SQL Server management studio and you will see the graphical execution plan. Here is the query:

```
SELECT
  er.session_id
 ,es.login_name
 ,er.request_id
 ,er.start_time
 ,QueryPlan_XML = (SELECT query_plan FROM sys.dm_exec_query_plan(er.plan_handle))
 ,SQLText = (SELECT Text FROM sys.dm_exec_sql_text(er.sql_handle))
FROM sys.dm_exec_requests er
JOIN sys.dm_exec_sessions es
  ON er.session_id = es.session_id
WHERE er.session_id >= 50
ORDER BY er.start_time ASC
```

Memory Usage

The following query will indicate the memory used, in KB, by each internal SQL Server component:

```
SELECT
  name
 ,type
 ,SUM(single_pages_kb + multi_pages_kb) AS MemoryUsedInKB
FROM sys.dm_os_memory_clerks
GROUP BY name, type
ORDER BY SUM(single_pages_kb + multi_pages_kb) DESC
```

Summary

Monitoring SQL Server regularly and gathering the performance data is the key to identifying performance problems. You have learned which counters in Performance Monitor you need to watch to discover performance problems. This chapter also covered how to create a SQL trace on the server side to reduce the impact of gathering events inside SQL Server. You have also learned how to use the Showplan XML to get the graphical query plan using SQL Profiler or SQL Server Management Studio. As you have noticed, Dynamic Management Views and functions are extremely helpful, gathering a lot of useful information about the SQL Server and the operating system. You will learn more about performance tuning T-SQL in the next chapter.

14

Performance Tuning T-SQL

Performance tuning T-SQL is very interesting, but also quite frequently frustrating. It is interesting because there is so much involved in tuning that knowledge of the product's architecture and internals plays a very large role in doing it well. Of course, knowledge alone is not sufficient without the right tools, which you will learn about in this chapter. If you have tuned a query and reduced its runtime, you may have jumped up and down, but sometimes you cannot achieve that result even after losing sleep for many nights, and that's when you get frustrated. In this chapter you will learn how to gather the data for query tuning, the tools for query tuning, the stages a query goes through before execution, and how to analyze the execution plan. It is very important to understand which stages a query passes through before actually being executed by the execution engine, so we'll start with physical query processing.

Physical Query Processing

SQL Server performs two main steps when a query is fired to produce the desired result. As you would guess, the first step is query compilation, which generates the query plan; and the second step is the execution of the query plan. The compilation phase in SQL Server 2005 goes through three steps: parsing, algebrization, and optimization. In SQL Server 2000, there was a *normalization* phase, which has been replaced with the algebrization piece in SQL Server 2005. The SQL Server team has spent much effort to re-architect and rewrite several parts of SQL Server. Of course, the goal is to redesign logic to serve current and future expansions of SQL Server functionality. Having said that, after the three steps just mentioned are completed, the compiler stores the optimized query plan in the plan cache. The execution engine takes over after that, copies the plan into its executable form, and of course executes the steps in the query plan to produce the desired result. If the same query or stored procedure is executed again, the compilation phase is skipped and the execution engine uses the same cached plan to start the execution.

You can see this in action with an example. The goal is to determine whether the stored procedure plan is reused or not. We will also use SQL Profiler and the DMV `sys.dm_exec_cached_plans` to examine some interesting details. In order to determine whether a compiled plan is reused or not, you have to monitor the events SP:CacheMiss, SP:CacheHit, and SP:CacheInsert under the Stored Procedures event class. Figure 14-1 shows these stored procedure plan compilation events in SQL Profiler.

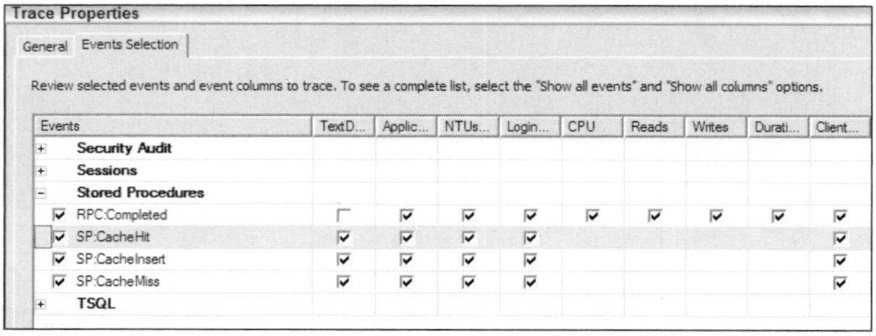

Figure 14-1

Download the sample code for this chapter from this book's web page at www.wrox.com. Open the sample solution QueryPlanReUse and then open the script ExecuteSP.sql. Connect to the SQL Server on which you have the AdventureWorks database. Please don't do this exercise on a production server! Compile the stored procedure TestCacheReUse in AdventureWorks. The code is as follows:

```
USE AdventureWorks
GO
IF OBJECT_ID('dbo.TestCacheReUse') IS NOT NULL
    DROP PROC dbo.TestCacheReUse
GO
CREATE PROC dbo.TestCacheReUse
AS
SELECT EmployeeID, LoginID, Title
FROM HumanResources.Employee
WHERE EmployeeID = 109
GO
```

Connect the Profiler to your designated machine and start the SQL Profiler after selecting the events, as shown in Figure 14-1. Now execute the stored procedure TestCacheReUse as follows:

```
USE AdventureWorks
GO
EXEC dbo.TestCacheReUse
```

Note that in SQL Server Profiler you will find the SP:CacheMiss and SP:CacheInsert events, as shown in Figure 14-2.

As you can see in Figure 14-2, the SP:CacheMiss event indicates that the compiled plan is not found in the plan cache. The stored procedure plan is compiled and inserted into the plan cache indicated by SP:CacheInsert, and then the procedure TestCacheReUse is executed.

Execute the same procedure again. This time SQL Server finds the query plan in the plan cache, as shown in Figure 14-3.

As you can see in Figure 14-3 the plan for the stored procedure TestCacheReUse was found in the plan cache, which is why you see the event SP:CacheHit.

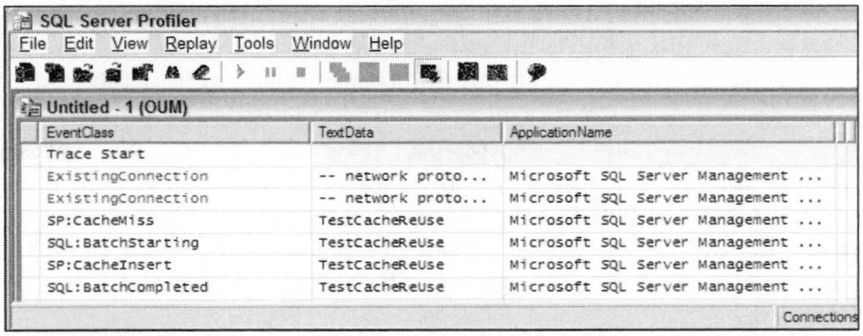

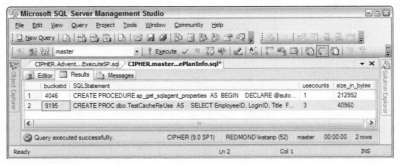

Figure 14-2

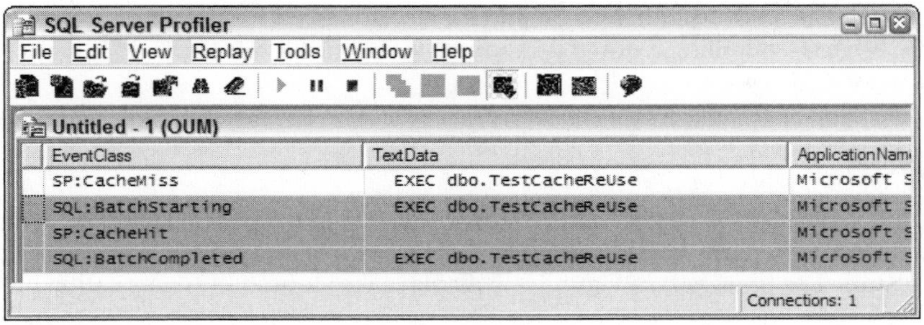

Figure 14-3

The DMV `sys.dm_exec_cached_plans` also provides information about the plans that are currently cached, along with some other information. Open the script `DMV_cachePlanInfo.sql` from the solution, shown here (note that the syntax in the following query is valid only when the database is in 90 compatibility mode):

```
SELECT  bucketid, (SELECT Text FROM sys.dm_exec_sql_text(plan_handle)) AS
SQLStatement, usecounts
,size_in_bytes, refcounts
FROM sys.dm_exec_cached_plans
WHERE cacheobjtype = 'Compiled Plan'
  AND objtype = 'proc'
```

Run this script; you should see output similar what is shown in Figure 14-4.

Figure 14-4

In this script, we used the DMF sys.dm_exec_sql_text to get the SQL text from plan_handle. In Figure 14-4, you can see that the compiled plan for the stored procedure TestCacheReUse that you executed earlier is cached. The column UseCounts in the output shows how many times this plan has been used since its inception. The first inception of the plan for this stored procedure was created when the SP:CacheInsert event happened, as shown in Figure 14-2. You can also see the number of bytes consumed by the cache object in Figure 14-4. In this case, the cache plan for the stored procedure TestCacheReUse has consumed 40KB in the plan cache. If you run DBCC FREEPROCCACHE now, and then run the query in the DMV_cachePlanInfo.sql script, you will notice that the rows returned are 0 because DBCC FREEPROCCACHE cleared the procedure cache.

If you use WITH RECOMPILE in the stored procedure TestCacheReUse (CREATE PROC TestCacheReUse WITH RECOMPILE AS ...) and run the stored procedure, you will notice that the plan will not be cached in the procedure cache because you are telling SQL Server (with the WITH RECOMPILE option) not to cache a plan for the stored procedure, and to recompile the stored procedure every time you execute it. Use this option wisely, because compiling a stored procedure every time it executes could be very costly, and compilation eats many CPU cycles.

Compilation

As we have discussed, before a query, batch, stored procedure, trigger, or dynamic SQL statement begins execution on a SQL Server, the batch is compiled into a plan. The plan is then executed for its effects or to produce results. The flowchart in Figure 14-5 displays the steps in the compilation process in SQL Server 2005.

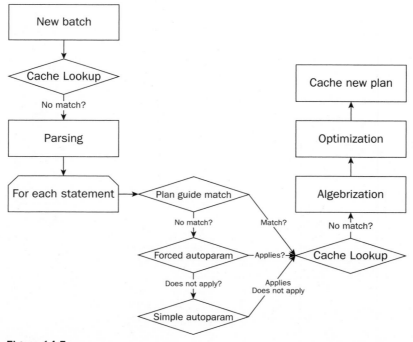

Figure 14-5

When a batch starts, the compilation process will try to find the cached plan in the plan cache. If it finds a match, the execution engine will take over. If a match is not found, the parser starts parsing (explained later in this section). The new plan guide match feature in SQL Server 2005 determines whether an existing plan guide for a particular statement exists (you will learn how to create the plan guide later). If it exists, it uses the plan guide for that statement for execution. (The concepts of forced autoparam and simple autoparam are described later in the chapter.) If a match is found, the parse tree is sent to the algebrizer (explained later in this section), which creates a logical tree for input to the optimizer (also explained later in this section). The plan is then cached in the plan cache. Of course, not all the plans are cached; for example, when you create a stored procedure with WITH RECOMPILE, the plan will not be cached.

Often, the cache plan needs to be recompiled because it is not valid for some reason. Suppose that a batch has been compiled into a collection of one or more query plans. SQL Server checks for validity (correctness) and optimality of that query plan before it begins executing any of the individual query plans. If one of the checks fails, the statement corresponding to the query plan or the entire batch is compiled again, and a possibly different query plan is produced. Such compilations are known as *recompilations*.

Note that when a batch is recompiled in SQL Server 2000, all of the statements in the batch are recompiled, not just the one that triggered the recompilation. In SQL Server 2005, if a statement in a batch causes the recompilation, then only that statement will be recompiled, not the whole batch. This *statement-level recompilation* has some advantages. In particular, SQL Server 2005 spends less CPU time and memory during batch recompilations, and obtains fewer compile locks. In addition, if you have a long stored procedure, then you do not need to break it into small chunks just to reduce compile time (as you would probably do in SQL Server 2000).

The reasons for recompilation can be broadly classified in two categories:

Correctness-Related Reasons

If the query processor decides that the cache plan would produce incorrect results, it will recompile that statement or batch. There are two possible reasons why the plan would produce incorrect results.

Schemas of Objects

Your query batch could be referencing many objects such as tables, views, UDFs, or indexes; and if the schemas of any of the objects referenced in the query have changed since your batch was last compiled, your batch must be recompiled for statement-correctness reasons. Schema changes could include many things — for example, adding an index on a table or in an indexed view, or adding or dropping a column in a table or view.

In SQL Server 2005, manually dropping or creating a statistic on a table causes recompilation. Manually updating statistics does not change the schema version. This means that queries that reference the table but do not use the updated statistics are not recompiled. Only queries that use the updated statistics are recompiled.

Batches with unqualified object names result in non-reuse of query plans. For example, in "SELECT * FROM MyTable", MyTable may legitimately resolve to Aish.MyTable if Aish issues this query and she owns a table with that name. Similarly, MyTable may resolve to Joe.MyTable. In such cases, SQL Server does not reuse query plans. If, however, Aish issues "SELECT * FROM dbo.MyTable", there is no ambiguity because the object is uniquely identified, and query plan reuse can happen. (See the uid column in sys.syscacheobjects. It indicates the user ID for the connection in which the plan was generated.

Only query plans with the same user ID are candidates for reuse. When uid is set to -2, it means that the query does not depend on implicit name resolution, and can be shared among different user IDs.)

SET Options

Some of the SET options affect query results. If the setting of a SET option affecting plan reuse is changed inside of a batch, a recompilation happens. The list of SET options that affect plan reusability is ANSI_NULLS, ANSI_NULL_DFLT_ON, ANSI_PADDING, ANSI_WARNINGS, CURSOR_CLOSE_ON_COMMIT, IMPLICIT_TRANSACTIONS, and QUOTED_IDENTIFIER.

These SET options affect plan reuse because SQL Server 2000 and SQL Server 2005 perform *constant folding*, evaluating a constant expression at compile time to enable some optimizations, and because the settings of these options affect the results of such expressions.

> *To avoid SET option–related recompilations, establish SET options at connection time, and ensure that they do not change for the duration of the connection.*

The following example demonstrates how SET options cause recompilation:

```
USE AdventureWorks
go

CREATE RecompileSetOption
AS
SET ANSI_NULLS OFF

SELECT s.CustomerID, COUNT(s.SalesOrderID)
FROM Sales.SalesOrderHeader s
GROUP BY s.CustomerID
HAVING COUNT(s.SalesOrderID) > 8
GO

exec RecompileSetOption     -- causes a recompilation
GO
exec RecompileSetOption     -- does not cause a recompilation
GO
```

By default, the SET ANSI_NULLS option is ON, so when you compile this stored procedure it will compile with SET ANSI_NULLS ON. Inside the stored procedure, you have set ANSI_NULLS to OFF, so when you begin executing this stored procedure the compiled plan is not valid, and will recompile with SET ANSI_NULLS OFF. The second execution does not cause a recompilation because the cached plan is compiled with "ansi_nulls" set to OFF.

Plan Optimality–Related Reasons

SQL Server is designed to generate the optimal query execution plan as data changes in your database. As you know, data distributions are tracked with statistics (histograms) in the SQL Server query processor. The table content changes because of INSERT, UPDATE, and DELETE operations. Table contents are tracked directly using the number of rows in the table (cardinality), and indirectly using statistics (histograms) on table columns (we explain this in detail later in the chapter). The query processor checks the threshold to determine whether it should recompile the query plan or not, using the following formula:

```
[ Colmodctr (snapshot) - Colmodctr (current) ] >= RT
```

In SQL Server 2005, the table modifications are tracked using `Colmodctr` (explained shortly). In SQL Server 2000, the counter was `Rowmodctr`. The `Colmodctr` is stored for each column, so changes to a table can be tracked with a finer granularity in SQL Server 2005. Note that `Rowmodctr` is available in SQL Server 2005 servers, but its value is always 0.

In this formula, `colmodctr (snapshot)` is the value stored at the time the query plan was generated, and `colmodctr (current)` is the current value. If the difference between these counters as shown in the formula is greater or equal to RT (Recompilation Threshold), then recompilation happens for that statement. RT is calculated as follows for permanent and temporary tables. Note that n refers to a table's cardinality (the number of rows in the table) when a query plan is compiled.

For a permanent table, the formula is as follows:

```
If n <= 500, RT = 500
If n > 500, RT = 500 + 0.20 * n
```

For a temporary table, the formula is as follows:

```
If n < 6, RT = 6
If 6 <= n <= 500, RT = 500
If n > 500, RT = 500 + 0.20 * n
```

For a table variable, RT does not exist. Therefore, recompilations do not happen because of changes in cardinality to table variables. It is interesting to note that if you are using a table variable and you add a large number of rows, the query plan generated may be not optimal if you have already cached the plan before adding a large number of rows.

The following table shows how the `Colmodctr` is modified in SQL Server 2005 because of different DML statements.

Statement	Colmodctr
INSERT	All `colmodctr += 1` (`colmodctr` is incremented by 1 for each column in the table for each insert.)
DELETE	All `colmodctr += 1`
UPDATE	If the update is to non-key columns: `colmodctr += 1` for all of the updated columns. If the update is to key columns: `colmodctr += 2` for all of the columns.
Bulk Insert	Like n INSERTs. All `colmodctr += n`. (n is the number of rows bulk inserted.)
Table truncation	Like n DELETEs. All `colmodctr += n`. (n is the table's cardinality.)

Tools and Commands for Recompilation Scenarios

You can use the following tools to observe or debug the recompilation-related events.

SQL Profiler

Capture the following events under the event classes `Stored Procedure` and `TSQL` to see the recompilation events. Be sure to select the column `EventSubClass` to view what caused the recompilation:

❑ SP:Starting

❑ SP:StmtCompleted

❑ SP:Recompile

❑ SP:Completed

❑ SP:CacheInsert

❑ SP:CacheHit

❑ SP:CacheMiss

You can also select the `AutoStats` event under the `Performance` event class to detect recompilations related to statistics updates.

Sys.syscacheobjects Virtual Table

Although this virtual table exists in the `resource` database, you can access it from any database. Note that the `resource` database is a new system database introduced in SQL Server 2005. The `resource` database is a read-only database that contains all the system objects included with SQL Server 2005. SQL Server system objects, such as `sys.objects`, are physically persisted in the `resource` database, but they logically appear in the `sys` schema of every database. The `resource` database does not contain user data or user metadata. The `cacheobjtype` column of this virtual table is particularly interesting. When `cacheobjtype = "Compiled Plan"`, the row refers to a query plan. When `cacheobjtype = "Executable Plan"`, the row refers to an execution context. Note that each execution context must have its associated query plan, but not vice versa. The `objtype` column indicates the type of object whose plan is cached (for example, `"proc"` or `"Adhoc"`). The `setopts` column encodes a bitmap indicating the `SET` options that were in effect when the plan was compiled. Sometimes, multiple copies of the same compiled plan (that differ in only their `setopts` columns) are cached in a plan cache. This indicates that different connections are using different sets of `SET` options (an undesirable situation). The `usecounts` column stores the number of times a cached object has been reused since the time the object was cached.

DBCC FREEPROCCACHE

This command will clear the cached query plan and execution context. We recommend using this *only* in development or test environment. Avoid running it in a production environment.

DBCC FLUSHPROCINDB (db_id)

This command is the same as `DBCC FREEPROCCACHE` except it only clears the cached plan for a given database. The recommendation for use is the same as `DBCC FREEPROCCACHE`.

Parser and Algebrizer

Parsing is the process of checking the syntax and transforming the SQL batch into a parse tree. Parsing includes, for example, whether a nondelimited column name starts with a digit or not. Parsing does not check whether the columns you have listed in a WHERE clause really exist or not in any of the tables you have listed in the FROM clause. That is taken care of by the *binding* process (algebrizer). Parsing turns the SQL text into logical trees. One logical tree will be created per query.

The *algebrizer* is a new component in SQL Server 2005. This component replaces the *normalizer* in SQL Server 2000. The output of the parser — a parse tree — is the input to the algebrizer. The major function of the algebrizer is *binding,* so sometimes the whole algebrizer process is referred as *binding*. The binding process checks whether the semantics are correct. For example, if you are trying to JOIN table A with trigger T, then the binding process will error this out even though it may be parsed successfully. Other tasks performed by the algebrizer are covered in the following sections.

Name Resolution

The algebrizer perform the tasks of checking whether every object name in the query (the parse tree) actually refers to a valid table or column that exists in the system catalog, and whether it is visible in the query scope.

Type Derivation

The algebrizer determines the type for each node in the parse tree. For example, if you are issuing a UNION query, the algebrizer figures out the type derivation for the final data type. (The columns' data types could be different when you are unioning queries.)

Aggregate Binding

The algebrizer binds the aggregate to the host query and it makes its decisions based on query syntax. Consider the following query:

```
SELECT s.CustomerID
FROM Sales.SalesOrderHeader s
GROUP BY s.CustomerID
HAVING EXISTS(SELECT * FROM Sales.Customer c
             WHERE c.TerritoryID > COUNT(s.ContactID))
```

In this query, although the aggregation is done in the inner query that counts the ContactID, the actual operation of this aggregation is performed in the outer query. See the query plan in Figure 14-6.

You can see in the query plan shown in Figure 14-6 that the aggregation is done on the result from the SalesOrderHeader table, although the aggregation is performed in the inner query. The outer query is converted something like this:

```
SELECT s.CustomerID, COUNT(s.ContactID)
FROM Sales.SalesOrderHeader s
GROUP BY s.CustomerID
```

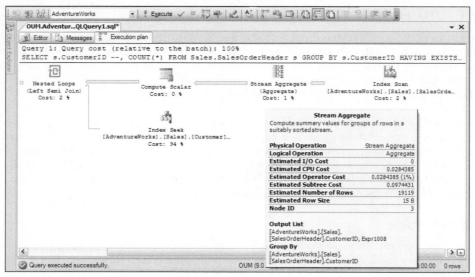

Figure 14-6

Grouping Binding

This is probably the obvious one. Consider this query:

```
SELECT s.CustomerID, SalesPersonID, COUNT(s.SalesOrderID)
FROM Sales.SalesOrderHeader s
GROUP BY s.CustomerID, s.SalesPersonID
```

If you do not add the CustomerID and SalesPersonID columns in the GROUP BY list, the query will error out. The grouped queries have different semantics than the nongrouped queries. All non-aggregated columns or expressions in the SELECT list of a query with GROUP BY must have a direct match in the GROUP BY list. The process of verifying this via the algebrizer is known as *grouping binding*.

Optimization

Optimization is probably the most complex and important piece to processing your queries. The logical tree created by the parser and algebrizer is the input to the optimizer. The optimizer needs the logical tree, metadata about objects involved in the query, such as columns, indexes, statistics, and constraints, and hardware information. The optimizer uses this information optimizer to create the compiled plan, which is made of physical operators. Note that the logical tree includes logical operators that describe *what to do,* such as "read table," "join," and so on. The physical operators produced by the optimizer specify algorithms that describe *how to do,* such as "index seek," "index scan," "hash join," and so on. The optimizer tells SQL Server how to exactly carry out the steps in order to get the results efficiently. Its job is to produce an efficient execution plan for each query in the batch or stored procedure. Figure 14-7 shows this process graphically.

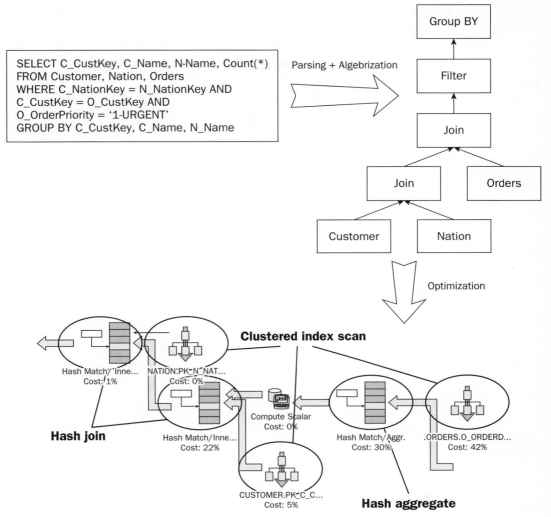

```
SELECT C_CustKey, C_Name, N-Name, Count(*)
FROM Customer, Nation, Orders
WHERE C_NationKey = N_NationKey AND
C_CustKey = O_CustKey AND
O_OrderPriority = '1-URGENT'
GROUP BY C_CustKey, C_Name, N_Name
```

Figure 14-7

As you can see in Figure 14-7, parsing and the algebrizer describe "what to do," and the optimizer describes "how to do it." SQL Server's optimizer is a cost-based optimizer, which means it will come up with the plan that costs the least. Complex queries may have millions of possible execution plans, so the optimizer does not explore them all, but tries to find an execution plan that has a cost reasonably close to the theoretical minimum, because it has to come up with a good plan in a reasonable amount of time. Keep in mind that the lowest estimated cost doesn't mean the lowest resource cost. The optimizer chooses the plan to get the results quickly to the users. Suppose the optimizer chooses a parallel plan for your queries that uses multiple CPUs, which typically uses more resources than the serial plan but offers faster results. Of course, the optimizer cannot always come up with the best plan, and that's why we have a job — for query tuning.

Optimization Flow

The flowchart in Figure 14-8 explains the steps involved in optimizing a query. These steps are simplified for explanation purposes. We don't mean to oversimplify the state-of-the-art optimization engine written by the SQL Server development team.

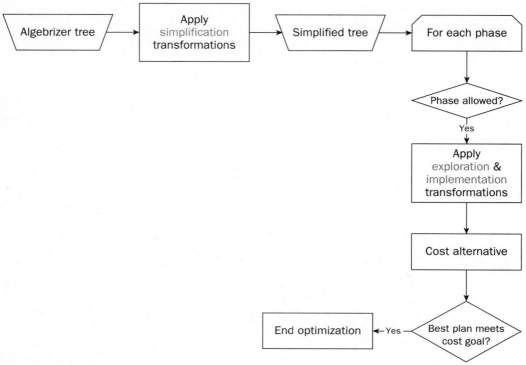

Figure 14-8

As you can see in Figure 14-8, the input to the optimizer is a logical tree produced by the algebrizer. The query optimizer is a transformation-based engine. These transformations are applied to fragments of the query tree. Three kinds of transformation rules are applied, discussed here.

Simplification

The simplification process creates an output tree that is better than the input tree. For example, it might push the filter down in the tree, reduce the group by columns, or perform other transformations. Figure 14-9 shows an example of simplification transformation (filter pushing).

In Figure 14-9, you can see that the logical tree on the left has the filter after the join. The optimizer pushes the filter further down in the tree to filter the data out from Orders table with a predicate on O_OrderPriority. This optimizes the query by performing the filtering early in the execution.

Figure 14-10 is another example of the simplification transformation (aggregate reduction). It includes reducing the number of group by columns in the execution plan.

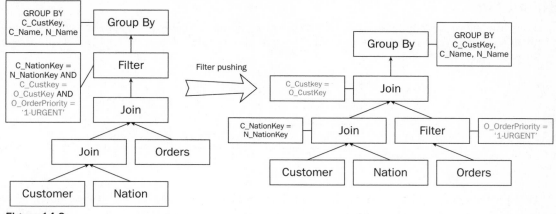

Figure 14-9

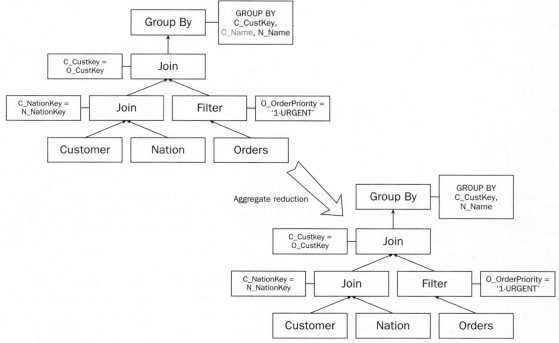

Figure 14-10

Figure 14-10 shows that the C_Name is removed from the Group By clause because it contains the column C_Custkey (refer to Figure 14-7 for the T-SQL statement), which is unique on the Customer table, so there is no need to include the C_Name column in the Group By clause. That's exactly what the optimizer does.

Exploration

As mentioned previously, SQL Server uses a cost-based optimizer implementation. Therefore, the optimizer will look at alternative options to come up with the cheapest plan. It makes a global choice using the estimated cost (see Figure 14-11).

Figure 14-11

The optimizer explores the options related to which table should be used for inner versus outer. This is not a simple determination because it depends on many things, such as the size of the table, the available indices, and operators higher in the tree. It is not a clear choice like the examples you saw in the simplification transformation.

Implementation

The third transformation is implementation. Refer to Figure 14-12 for an example.

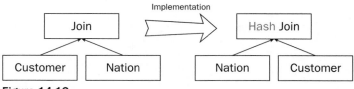

Figure 14-12

As explained earlier, the implantation transforms the "what to do" part into the "how to do" part. In this example, the JOIN logical operation is transformed into a HASH JOIN physical operation. The query cost is derived from physical operators based on model-of-execution algorithms (IO and CPU) and estimations of data distribution, data properties, and size. Needless to say, the cost also depends on hardware such as the number of CPUs and the amount of memory available at the time of optimization.

Refer back to figure 14-8. If the optimizer compared the cost of every valid plan and chose the least costly one, the optimization process could take a very long time, and the number of valid plans can be huge. Therefore, the optimization process is broken up into three *search phases*. As discussed earlier, a set of transformation rules is associated with each phase. After each phase, SQL Server evaluates the cost of the cheapest query plan to that point. If the plan is cheap enough, then the optimizer stops there and chooses that query plan. If the plan is not cheap enough, the optimizer runs through the next phase, which has an additional set of rules that are more complex.

The first phase of the cost-based optimization, Phase 0, contains a limited set of rules. These rules are applied to queries with at least four tables. Because JOIN reordering alone generates many valid plans, the optimizer uses a limited number of join orders in Phase 0 and it considers only hash and loop joins in this phase. In other words, if this phase finds a plan with an estimated cost below 0.2 (internal cost unit), the optimization ends there.

The second phase, Phase 1, uses more transformation rules and different join orders. The best plan that costs less that 1.0 would cause optimization to stop in this phase. Note that until Phase 1, the plans are nonparallel (serial query plans). What if you have more than one CPU in your system? In that case, if the cost of the plan produced in Phase 1 is more than the *cost threshold for parallelism* (see `sp_configure` for this parameter, the default value is 5), then Phase 1 is repeated to find the best parallel plan. Then the cost of the serial plan produced earlier is compared with the new parallel plan, and the next phase, Phase 2 (the full optimization phase), is executed for the cheaper of the two plans.

Tuning Process

There is always room for tuning, but it is very important that you have enough data to start with. Therefore, you need to take a baseline of the system's performance and compare against that baseline so that you know where to start. Chapter 13 has details on getting the baseline. Just because a process is slow doesn't mean that you have to start tuning SQL statements. There are many basic things you need to do first, such as configuring the SQL Server database, and making sure `tempdb` and the log files are on their own drives. It is very important to get the server configuration correct. See Chapters 11 and 12 for details about configuring your server and database for optimal performance. There is also a white-paper on `tempdb` that we recommend you read as well: `http://download.microsoft.com/download/4/f/8/4f8f2dc9-a9a7-4b68-98cb-163482c95e0b/WorkingWithTempDB.doc`.

Don't overlook the obvious. For example, suppose you notice that performance is suddenly pretty bad on your server. If you have done a baseline and that doesn't show much change in performance, then it is unlikely that the sudden performance change was caused by an application in most cases (unless there is a new patch for your application that caused some performance changes). In this case, look at your server configuration and see if that changed recently. Sometimes you merely run out of disk space, especially on drives where your page files reside, and that will bring the server to its knees.

> We assume here that you already know what clustered and nonclustered indexes are, including how they work and how they are physically structured, and what a heap is.

Database I/O Information

Normally, an enterprise application has one or two databases residing on the server, in which case you would know that you have to look into queries against those databases. However, if you have many databases on the server and you are not sure which database is causing a lot of I/O and may be responsible for a performance issue, you have to look at the I/O activities against the database and find out which causes the most I/O and stalls on I/O. In SQL Server 2005, the DMF called `sys.dm_io_virtual_file_stats` comes in handy for this purpose.

You can use the following script to find out this information. The script is provided in the subfolder `DatabaseIO` in the sample folder for this chapter, which you can download from this book's Web site at `www.wrox.com`.

```
-- Database IO analysis.
WITH IOFORDATABASE AS
(
SELECT
  DB_NAME(VFS.database_id) AS DatabaseName
```

```
,CASE WHEN smf.type = 1 THEN 'LOG_FILE' ELSE 'DATA_FILE' END AS DatabaseFile_Type
,SUM(VFS.num_of_bytes_written) AS IO_Write
,SUM(VFS.num_of_bytes_read) AS IO_Read
,SUM(VFS.num_of_bytes_read + VFS.num_of_bytes_written) AS Total_IO
,SUM(VFS.io_stall) AS IO_STALL
FROM sys.dm_io_virtual_file_stats(NULL, NULL) AS VFS
JOIN sys.master_files AS smf
  ON VFS.database_id = smf.database_id
 AND VFS.file_id = smf.file_id
GROUP BY
 DB_NAME(VFS.database_id)
,smf.type
)
SELECT
 ROW_NUMBER() OVER(ORDER BY io_stall DESC) AS RowNumber
,DatabaseName
,DatabaseFile_Type
,CAST(1.0 * IO_Read/ (1024 * 1024) AS DECIMAL(12, 2)) AS IO_Read_MB
,CAST(1.0 * IO_Write/ (1024 * 1024) AS DECIMAL(12, 2)) AS IO_Write_MB
,CAST(1. * Total_IO / (1024 * 1024) AS DECIMAL(12, 2)) AS IO_TOTAL_MB
,CAST(IO_STALL / 1000. AS DECIMAL(12, 2)) AS IO_STALL_Seconds
,CAST(100. * IO_STALL / SUM(IO_STALL) OVER() AS DECIMAL(10, 2)) AS IO_STALL_Pct
FROM IOFORDATABASE
ORDER BY IO_STALL_Seconds DESC
```

Figure 14-13 shows sample output from this script.

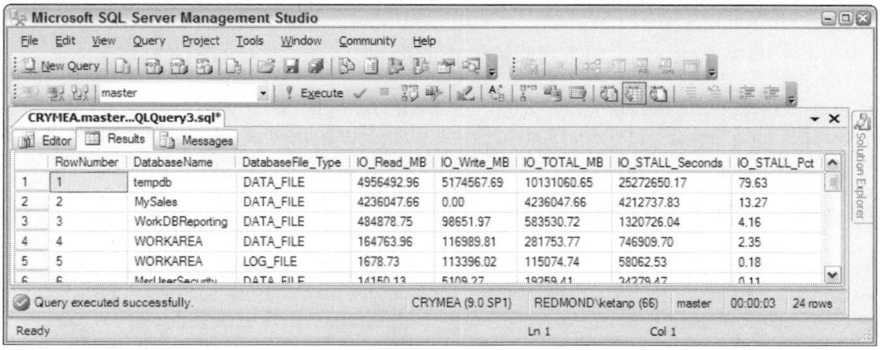

Figure 14-13

Keep in mind that the counters show the value from the time the instance of SQL Server is started, but it gives you a good idea of which database is getting hammered. In this example, you can see that tempdb is being hit hard, but that is not your primary application database, so look at the following row and you'll see that the MySales database is next. It's likely that queries against the MySales database are causing the heavy tempdb usage. This query will give you a good starting point to further investigate the process level (stored procedures, ad-hoc T-SQL statements, etc.) for the database in question.

Next we will look at how to gather the query plan and analyze it. We will also look at the different tools you would need in this process.

Working with the Query Plan

Looking at the query plan is the first step you would take in the process of query tuning. The SQL Server query plan comes in different flavors: textual, graphical, and, with SQL Server 2005, XML format. *Showplan* is the term used to describe any of these query plan flavors. Different types of Showplans have different information. SQL Server can produce a plan with operators only, with cost information, and with XML format some additional runtime details. The following table summarizes the various Showplan formats.

Plan Contents	Text Format	Graphical Format	XML Format
Operators	`SET SHOWPLAN_TEXT ON`	N/A	N/A
Operators and estimated costs	`SET SHOWPLAN_ALL ON`	Displays the estimated execution plan in SQL Server Management Studio	`SET SHOWPLAN_XML ON`
Operators + estimated cardinalities and costs + runtime information	`SET STATISTICS PROFILE ON`	Displays actual execution plan in SQL Server Management Studio	`SET STATISTICS XML ON`

Estimated Execution Plan

This section describes how to get the *estimated* execution plan. In the next section you will learn how to get the *actual* execution plan. There are five ways you can get the estimated execution plan: `SET SHOWPLAN_TEXT`, `SET SHOWPLAN_ALL`, `SET SHOWPLAN_XML`, a graphical estimated execution plan using SQL Server Management Studio (now on SSMS), and SQL Trace. The SQL Trace option is covered in a separate section; the other options are described here.

SET SHOWPLAN_TEXT and SET SHOWPLAN_ALL

We start with a simple query to demonstrate how to read the query plan. Open the script `SimpleQuery Plan.sql` from the `Queryplans` solution in the sample folder for this chapter. The code for the query is shown here:

```
USE AdventureWorks
GO
SET SHOWPLAN_TEXT ON
GO
SELECT sh.CustomerID, st.Name, SUM(sh.SubTotal) AS SubTotal
FROM Sales.SalesOrderHeader sh
JOIN Sales.Customer c
  ON c.CustomerID = sh.CustomerID
JOIN Sales.SalesTerritory st
  ON st.TerritoryID = c.TerritoryID
GROUP BY sh.CustomerID, st.Name
HAVING SUM(sh.SubTotal) > 2000.00
GO
SET SHOWPLAN_TEXT OFF
GO
```

When you SET the SHOWPLAN_TEXT ON, the query will not be executed; it will just produce the estimated plan. The textual plan is shown here:

```
StmtText
-------------------------------------------------------------------------------
------
|--Filter(WHERE:([Expr1006]>(2000.00)))
        |--Hash Match(Inner Join, HASH:([sh].[CustomerID])=([c].[CustomerID]))
             |--Hash Match(Aggregate, HASH:([sh].[CustomerID])
DEFINE:([Expr1006]=SUM(
                     [AdventureWorks].[Sales].[SalesOrderHeader].[SubTotal] as
                     [sh].[SubTotal])))
             |      |--Clustered Index Scan(OBJECT:(
                         [AdventureWorks].[Sales].[SalesOrderHeader].
                         [PK_SalesOrderHeader_SalesOrderID] AS [sh]))
             |--Merge Join(Inner Join,
MERGE:([st].[TerritoryID])=([c].[TerritoryID]),
                     RESIDUAL:([AdventureWorks].[Sales].[SalesTerritory].[TerritoryID]
as

[st].[TerritoryID]=[AdventureWorks].[Sales].[Customer].[TerritoryID] as
                     [c].[TerritoryID]))
                  |--Clustered Index Scan(OBJECT:(
                      [AdventureWorks].[Sales].[SalesTerritory].
                      [PK_SalesTerritory_TerritoryID] AS [st]), ORDERED FORWARD)
                  |--Index Scan(OBJECT:(
                      [AdventureWorks].[Sales].[Customer].
                      [IX_Customer_TerritoryID] AS [c]), ORDERED FORWARD)
```

I would suggest that you use SSMS to view the plan output because the formatting here doesn't look that good. You can run this query in the AdventureWorks database. Note that in this plan all you have is operators' names and their basic arguments. For more details on the query plan, other options are available. We will explore them soon.

The output tells you that there are seven operators: Filter, Hash Match (Inner Join), Hash Match (Aggregate), Clustered Index Scan, Merge Join, Clustered Index Scan, and Index Scan. They are shown in bold in the query plan.

To analyze the plan you read branches in *inner levels* before outer ones (bottom to top), and branches that appear in the *same level* from top to bottom. You can see which branches are inner and which are outer branch based on the position of the pipe (|) character. When the plan is executed, the general flow of the rows is from the top down and from right to left. An operator with more indentation produces rows consumed by an operator with less indentation, and it produces rows for the next operator above, and so forth. For the JOIN operators, there are two input operators at the same level to the right of the JOIN operator denoting the two row sets. The higher of the two (in this case, clustered index scan on the object Sales.SalesTerritory) is referred as the *outer table* (so Sales.SalesTerritory is the outer table) and the lower (Index Scan on the object Sales.Customer) is the *inner table*. The operation on the outer table is initiated first, and the one on the inner table is repeatedly executed for each row of the outer table that arrives to the join operator. Please note that the join algorithms are explained in detail later.

Now you can analyze the plan for the query. As you can see in the plan, the hash match (inner join) operation has two levels: hash match (aggregate) and merge join. Now look at the merge join. The merge join has two levels: The first is the clustered index scan on `Sales.Territory`, and the index scanned on this object is `PK_SalesTerritory_TerritoryID`. We will talk more about index access methods a little later in the chapter. That is the outer table for the merge join. The inner table `Sales.Customer` is scanned only once because of the merge join, and that physical operation is done using index scan on index `IX_Customer_TerritoryID` on the `sales.Customer` table. The merge join is on the `TerritoryID`, as per the plan `Merge Join(Inner Join, MERGE:([st].[TerritoryID])=([c].[TerritoryID])`. Because the `RESIDUAL` predicate is present in the merge join, all rows that satisfy the merge predicate evaluate the residual predicate, and only those rows that satisfy it are returned.

Now the result of this merge join becomes the inner table for hash match (inner join): `Hash Match (Inner Join, HASH:([sh].[CustomerID])=([c].[CustomerID]))`. The outer table is the result of `Hash Match (Aggregate)`. You can see that the `CustomerID` is the hash key (`HASH:([sh].[CustomerID])`) in the hash aggregate operation. Therefore, the aggregation is performed and as per the query, the `SUM` operation is done on the column `SubTotal` from the `Sales.SalesOrderHeader` table (defined by the `DEFINE:([Expr1006])`). Now the `Hash Match (Inner join)` operation is performed on `CustomerID` (the result of the merge join) repeatedly for each row from the outer table (the result of hash match [aggregate]). Finally, the filter is done for `SubTotal > 2000.00` with the filter physical operator with the predicate (`WHERE:([Expr1006]>(2000.00))`).

The merge join itself is very fast, but it can be an expensive choice if sort operations are required. However, if the data volume is large and the desired data can be obtained presorted from existing B-tree indexes, merge join is often the fastest available join algorithm. In addition, merge join performance can vary a lot based on one-to-many or many-to-many joins.

In the query file, we have set the `SET SHOWPLAN_TEXT OFF` following the query. This is because `SET SHOWPLAN_TEXT ON` is not only causing the query plan to show up, it is also turning off the query execution for the connection. The query execution will be turned off for this connection until you execute `SET SHOWPLAN_TEXT OFF` on the same connection. The `SET SHOWPLAN_ALL` command is similar to `SET SHOWPLAN_TEXT`. The only difference is the additional information about the query plan produced by `SET SHOWPLAN_ALL`. It adds the *estimated* number of rows produced by each operator in the query plan, the estimated CPU time, the estimated I/O time, and the total cost estimate that was used internally when comparing this plan to other possible plans.

SET SHOWPLAN_XML

This is a new feature in SQL Server 2005 to retrieve the Showplan in XML form. The output of the `SHOWPLAN_XML` is generated by a compilation of a batch, so it will produce a single XML document for the whole batch. You can open the `ShowPlan_XML.sql` from the solution `QueryPlans` to see how you can get the estimated plan in XML. The query is shown here:

```
USE AdventureWorks
GO
SET SHOWPLAN_XML ON
GO
SELECT sh.CustomerID, st.Name, SUM(sh.SubTotal) AS SubTotal
FROM Sales.SalesOrderHeader sh
JOIN Sales.Customer c
  ON c.CustomerID = sh.CustomerID
JOIN Sales.SalesTerritory st
  ON st.TerritoryID = c.TerritoryID
GROUP BY sh.CustomerID, st.Name
```

```
HAVING SUM(sh.SubTotal) > 2000.00
GO
SET SHOWPLAN_XML OFF
GO
```

When you run this query in Management Studio, you will see a link in the result tab. Clicking the link opens the XML document inside Management Studio. You can also save that document with the extension .sqlplan. When you open that file using Management Studio, you will get a graphical query plan. The graphical plan from the XML document generated by this query is shown in Figure 14-14.

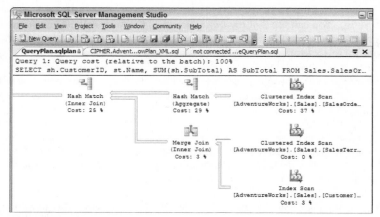

Figure 14-14

XML is the richest format of the Showplan. It contains some unique information not available in other Showplan formats. The XML Showplan contains the size of the plan in cache (the CachedPlanSize attributes) and parameter values for which the plan has been optimized (the Parameter sniffing element). When a stored procedure is compiled for the first time, the values of the parameters supplied with the execution call are used to optimize the statements within that stored procedure. This process is known as *parameter sniffing*. Also available is some runtime information, which is unique to the XML plan and is described further in the section "Actual Execution Plan."

You can write code to parse and analyze the XML Showplan. This is probably the greatest advantage it offers, as this task is very hard to achieve with other forms of the Showplan.

Refer to the whitepaper at http://msdn.microsoft.com/sql/learning/prog/xml/default .aspx?pull=/library/en-us/dnsql90/html/xmlshowplans.asp. This paper describes how you can extract the estimated execution cost of a query from its XML Showplan using CLR functions. You can use this technique to ensure that users can submit only those queries costing less than a predetermined threshold to a server running SQL Server 2005, thereby ensuring it is not overloaded with costly, long-running queries.

Graphical Estimated Showplan

You can view a graphical estimated plan in Management Studio. To access the plan, either use the shortcut key Ctrl+L or select Query➪Display Estimated Execution plan. You can also select the button shown in Figure 14-15.

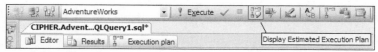

Figure 14-15

If you use any of these options to display the graphical estimated query plan, it will display the plan as soon as compilation is completed, because compilation complexity can vary according to the number and size of the tables. Right-clicking the graphical plan area in the Execution Plan tab reveals different zoom options and properties for the graphical plan.

Actual Execution Plan

This section describes the four options you can use to get the actual execution plan: SET STATISTICS XML ON|OFF, SET STATISTICS PROFILE ON|OFF, using the graphical actual execution plan option in Management Studio, and using SQL Trace.

SET STATISTICS XML ON|OFF

There are two kinds of runtime information in the XML Showplan: per SQL statement and per thread. If a statement has a parameter, the plan contains the parameterRuntimeValue attribute, which shows the value of each parameter when the statement was executed. The degreeOfParallelism attribute shows the actual degree of parallelism. The degree of parallelism shows the number of concurrent threads working on the single query. The compile time value for degree of parallelism is always half the number of CPUs available to SQL Server unless there are two CPUs in the system. In that case, the value will be 2 as well. The XML plan may also contain warnings. These are events generated during compilation or execution time. For example, missing statistics are a compiler-generated event. One important new feature in SQL Server 2005 is the USE PLAN hint. This feature requires the plan hint in XML format so you can use the XML Showplan. Using the USE PLAN hint, you can force the query to be executed using a certain plan. For example, suppose you found out that a query was running slowly in the production environment, but the same query runs faster in the pre-production environment. You also found out that the plan generated in the production environment is not optimal for some reason. In that case, you can use the better plan generated in the pre-production environment and force that plan in the production environment using the USE PLAN hint. For more details on how to implement it, please refer to the BOL topic "Using the USE PLAN Query Hint."

SET STATISTICS PROFILE ON|OFF

We like this option better, and we always use it for query analysis and tuning. Run the query from earlier as follows. Use the script Statistics_Profile.sql in the QueryPlans solution. The code is shown here. If you don't want to mess with your AdventureWorks database, you can back up and restore the AdventureWorks database with a different name. If you do that, be sure to change the USE <DatabaseName> line in the script. Here is the code:

```
USE AdventureWorks
GO
SET STATISTICS PROFILE ON
GO
SELECT p.name AS ProdName, c.TerritoryID, SUM(od.OrderQty)
FROM Sales.SalesOrderDetail od
JOIN Production.Product p
```

```
  ON p.ProductID = od.ProductID
JOIN Sales.SalesOrderHeader oh
  ON oh.SalesOrderID = od.SalesOrderID
JOIN Sales.Customer c
  ON c.CustomerID = oh.CustomerID
WHERE OrderDate >= '2004-06-09'
  AND OrderDate <= '2004-06-11'
GROUP BY p.name, c.TerritoryID
GO
SET STATISTICS PROFILE OFF
```

After you run the query you will get output similar to what is shown in Figure 14-16.

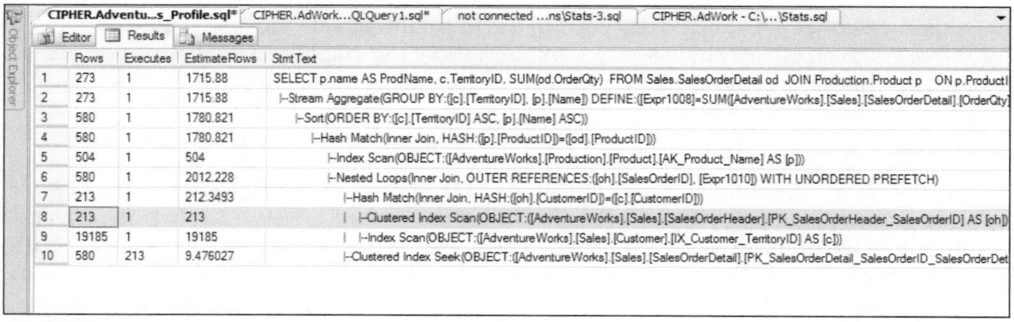

	Rows	Executes	EstimateRows	StmtText
1	273	1	1715.88	SELECT p.name AS ProdName, c.TerritoryID, SUM(od.OrderQty) FROM Sales.SalesOrderDetail od JOIN Production.Product p ON p.ProductI
2	273	1	1715.88	|--Stream Aggregate(GROUP BY:([c].[TerritoryID], [p].[Name]) DEFINE:([Expr1008]=SUM([AdventureWorks].[Sales].[SalesOrderDetail].[OrderQty]
3	580	1	1780.821	|--Sort(ORDER BY:([c].[TerritoryID] ASC, [p].[Name] ASC))
4	580	1	1780.821	|--Hash Match(Inner Join, HASH:([p].[ProductID])=([od].[ProductID]))
5	504	1	504	|--Index Scan(OBJECT:([AdventureWorks].[Production].[Product].[AK_Product_Name] AS [p]))
6	580	1	2012.228	|--Nested Loops(Inner Join, OUTER REFERENCES:([oh].[SalesOrderID], [Expr1010]) WITH UNORDERED PREFETCH)
7	213	1	212.3493	|--Hash Match(Inner Join, HASH:([oh].[CustomerID])=([c].[CustomerID]))
8	213	1	213		|--Clustered Index Scan(OBJECT:([AdventureWorks].[Sales].[SalesOrderHeader].[PK_SalesOrderHeader_SalesOrderID] AS [oh])
9	19185	1	19185		|--Index Scan(OBJECT:([AdventureWorks].[Sales].[Customer].[IX_Customer_TerritoryID] AS [c]))
10	580	213	9.476027	|--Clustered Index Seek(OBJECT:([AdventureWorks].[Sales].[SalesOrderDetail].[PK_SalesOrderDetail_SalesOrderID_SalesOrderDet

Figure 14-16

The four most important columns in the output of SET STATISTICS PROFILE are Rows, EstimateRows, Executes and of course the StmtText. The Rows column contains the number of rows actually returned by each operator. Now read the plan. We can't fit the whole plan on the page, so run this query on your test machine and look at the output on your screen as you follow along. Start from the inner level, bottom to top. Look at line (or row number) #8 and #9. They are at the same level as the hash match (line #7), so line #8 is the clustered index scan on index PK_SalesOrderHeader_SalesOrderID on the table SalesOrderHeader. This is outer table for the hash match. It scans the clustered index in range, as shown here, although you can't see the entire example in Figure 14-16:

```
WHERE:([AdventureWorks].[Sales].[SalesOrderHeader].[OrderDate] as
[oh].[OrderDate]>='2004-06-09 00:00:00.000' AND
[AdventureWorks].[Sales].[SalesOrderHeader].[OrderDate] as [oh].[OrderDate]<='2004-
06-11 00:00:00.000'))
```

The entire table is scanned for the WHERE clause on the OrderDate column. The estimated rows from this operator are 213, which shows in the EstimatedRows column. The output of this operator is the SalesOrderID and CustomerID columns (not shown in Figure 14-16). Notice that the smaller table (SalesOrderHeader — the table itself is not smaller, but because we have criteria on the OrderDate the result set is smaller) is on the outer side of the hash match because the hash key, CustomerID in this case, is stored in memory after that hash and fewer hashes is better because it requires less memory. Therefore, if you see a hash join in your query and you notice that the outer side table's result set is bigger than the inside table, there may be some plan issue, the supporting indexes don't exist, or the statistics are outdated on these tables, which led the optimizer to estimate an incorrect number of rows. We will look at different index access methods and join algorithms a little later in the chapter.

Now the `Sales.Customer` table is scanned on the nonclustered index `IX_Customer_TerritoryID` for `CustomerID` (see line #9) for the hash match. Why does optimizer choose the nonclustered index `IX_Customer_TerritoryID` on the `Sales.Customer` table for scanning `CustomerID` when it has a clustered index on `CustomerID`? Look at the query for this example. You have selected the `TerritoryID` column from the `Customer` table, and because the leaf level in the nonclustered index also has a clustering key (`CustomerID`) in this case, the nonclustered index `IX_Customer_TerritoryID` has necessary information (`TerritoryID` and `CustomerID`) at its leaf level for this query. Remember that the leaf level of a nonclustered index has fewer pages than a clustered index of leaf pages (because leaf pages of a clustered index hold the actual data row) so traversing the nonclustered index in this case would cause less I/O (because it needs to access fewer pages). As you can see, the hash match operation has produced 213 rows (see the `Rows` column for the actual rows produced).

Now let's move up. The hash match (line #7) and clustered index seek (line #10) are at the same level as the nested loop inner join (line #6). The result of the hash match physical operation was 213 rows and the output columns were `SalesOrderID` and `TerritoryID` (line #7). You have a join on the `Sales.Sales OrderDetail` table on the `SalesOrderID` column, so the `SalesOrderID` from the hash match operation is now the outer side of the nested loop join; and the clustered index seek on `PK_SalesOrderDetail_SalesOrderID_SalesOrderDetailID` in the `Sales.SalesOrderDetail` table is the inner side of the nested loop. The nested loop will look into the inner table for each row from the outer table. Therefore, for 213 `SalesOrderID`s (the output of the hash match in line # 7), there will be 213 clustered index seeks performed on the index `PK_SalesOrderDetail_SalesOrderID_SalesOrderDetailID`. You can see that line #10 indicates 213 in the `Executes` column, which means that the clustered index on the `Sales.SalesOrderDetail` table was sought for 213 times, and 580 rows were qualified because of this operation (see the `Rows` column in line #10). As a result, the nested loop physical operation has produced 580 rows (see line # 6).

Moving up again, the hash match operation (line #4) has two levels: the Index scan on the `Product` table (line #5) and a nested loop (line #6). The unordered nonclustered index scan on the index `AK_Product_Name` on the `Product` table is performed and a hash key is created on the `ProductID`. Because the `Product` table has 504 rows, this operation produces 504 rows (see the `Rows` column in line #5). The inner table (the result of the nested loop join) is probed on the `ProductID` (remember that the OutputList of the nested loop operation produces columns `[od].[OrderQty]`, `[od].[ProductID]`, and `[c].[TerritoryID]`). Therefore, the result of the hash match operation is 580 rows (line #4).

Let's move up. Note the `Sort` operation in line #3. Why is sorting required when you have not asked for it? Because you asked for `GROUP BY` (a logical operation), and if the optimizer chooses the Stream Aggregate physical operation, then it requires the input to be sorted, which is why you are seeing the `Sort` operation. The sort is done on `TerritoryID` and `Name` in ASC order.

> `Sort` *is a STOP and GO operator. Nothing will come out (to left side of operator) of the* `Sort` *operator until all the input rows are processed, so* `Sort` *is usually slow. If you don't need sorted data, never add the* `ORDER BY` *clause. In this case, because we asked for* `GROUP BY`*, we will get* `ORDER BY` *for free because of the stream aggregate, so the data already comes sorted.*

Let's move up once again. In line #2, the stream aggregate operation is a result of `GROUP BY`. This operator will remove the duplicate rows. The number of rows produced by this operator is 273 (the `Rows` column in line #2). In other words, 307 duplicate rows (580–273) were removed by this operation. In this stream aggregation, the physical operation is chosen by the optimizer. If the optimizer had chosen the hash aggregate option, the `Sort` operation would have been omitted because hash aggregation doesn't required sorted input. That's it, the result is returned.

Graphical Actual Execution Plan

You can use Management Studio to view the graphical actual execution plan. Again, either use the short-cut key Ctrl+M, select Query⇨Include Actual Execution plan, or select the button shown in Figure 14-17.

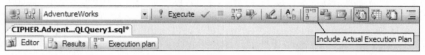

Figure 14-17

If you use any of these options to display the graphical actual query plan, nothing will happen. After query execution, the actual plan is displayed in a separate tab.

Join Algorithms

You saw earlier the different type of joins in the query plans. Here we will discuss the physical strategies SQL Server can use to process joins. Before SQL Server 7.0, there was only one join algorithm, called *nested loops*. Since version 7.0, SQL Server supports hash and merge join algorithms. This section describes each of them here and where and when they provide better performance.

Nested Loop or Loop Join

The nested loop join, also called *nested iteration*, uses one join input as the outer input table (shown as the top input in the graphical execution plan; see Figure 14-18) and the other input as the inner (bottom) input table. The outer loop consumes the outer input table row by row. The inner loop, executed for each outer row, searches for matching rows in the inner input table. You can use the `Join.sql` script from the `QueryPlans` solution for the following exercises. The following query is an example that produces a nested loop join:

```
--Nested Loop Join

SELECT C.CustomerID, c.TerritoryID
FROM Sales.SalesOrderHeader oh
JOIN Sales.Customer c
  ON c.CustomerID = oh.CustomerID
WHERE c.CustomerID IN (10,12)
GROUP BY C.CustomerID, c.TerritoryID
```

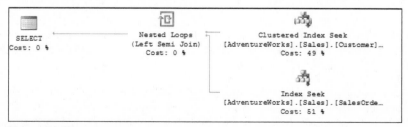

Figure 14-18

A nested loop join is particularly effective if the outer input is small and the inner input is preindexed and large. In many small transactions, such as those affecting only a small set of rows, index nested loop joins are superior to both merge joins and hash joins. In large queries, however, nested loop joins are often not the optimal choice. Of course, the presence of a nested loop join operator in the execution plan doesn't indicate whether it's an efficient plan or not. A nested loop join is the default algorithm, so it can always be applied if another algorithm does match the specific criteria. For example, the "requires join" algorithm must be *equijoin* (the join condition is based on the equality operator).

In the example query, a clustered index seek is performed on the outer table `Customer` for `CustomerID` 10 and 12, and for each `CustomerID`, an index seek is performed on the inner table `SalesOrderHeader`. Therefore, `Index IX_SalesOrderHeader_CustomerID` is sought two times (one time for `CustomerID` 10 and one time for `CustomerID` 12) on the `SalesOrderHeader` table.

Hash Join

The hash join has two inputs like every other join: the build input (outer table) and the probe input (inner table). The query optimizer assigns these roles so that the smaller of the two inputs is the build input. A variant of the hash join (Hash Aggregate physical operator) can do duplicate removal and grouping, such as `SUM (OrderQty) GROUP BY TerritoryID`. These modifications use only one input for both the build and probe roles.

The following query is an example of a hash join, and is shown in Figure 14-19:

```
--Hash Match

SELECT p.Name As ProductName, ps.Name As ProductSubcategoryName
FROM Production.Product p
JOIN Production.ProductSubcategory ps
  ON p.ProductSubcategoryID = ps.ProductSubcategoryID
ORDER BY p.Name,  ps.Name
```

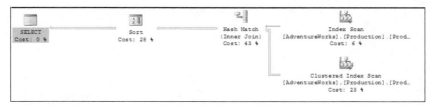

Figure 14-19

As discussed earlier, the hash join first scans or computes the entire build input and then builds a hash table in memory if it fits the memory grant (in Figure 14-19, it is the `Production.ProductSubCategory` table). Each row is inserted into a hash bucket depending on the hash value computed for the hash key, so building the hash table needs memory. If the entire build input is smaller than the available memory, all rows can be inserted into the hash table (you will see what happens if there is not enough memory shortly). This build phase is followed by the probe phase. The entire probe input (in Figure 14-19, it is the `Production.Product` table) is scanned or computed one row at a time, and for each probe row (from the `Production.Product` table), the hash key's value is computed, the corresponding hash bucket (the one created from the `Production.ProductSubCategory` table) is scanned, and the matches are produced. This strategy is called an *in-memory hash join*.

If you're talking about the AdventureWorks database running on your laptop with 1GB RAM, you won't have the problem of not fitting the hash table in memory. In the real world, however, with millions of rows in a table, it's possible there won't be enough memory to fit the hash table. If the build input does not fit in memory, a hash join proceeds in several steps. This is known as a *grace hash join*. In this hash join strategy, each step has a build phase and a probe phase. Initially, the entire build and probe inputs are consumed and partitioned (using a hash function on the hash keys) into multiple files. Using the hash function on the hash keys guarantees that any two joining records must be in the same pair of files. Therefore, the task of joining two large inputs has been reduced to multiple, but smaller, instances of the same tasks. The hash join is then applied to each pair of partitioned files. If the input is so large that the preceding steps need to be performed many times, multiple partitioning steps and multiple partitioning levels are required. This hash strategy is called a *recursive hash join*.

> *SQL Server always starts with an in-memory hash join and changes to other strategies if necessary.*

Recursive hash joins or hash bailouts cause reduced performance in your server. If you see many Hash Warning events in a trace (the Hash Warning event is under the Errors and Warnings event class), update statistics on the columns that are being joined. You should capture this event if you see that you have many hash joins in your query. This will ensure that hash bailouts are not causing performance problems on your server. When good indexes on join columns are missing, the optimizer normally chooses the hash join.

Merge Join

The merge join relies on sorted input and is a very efficient algorithm if both inputs are available sorted (see Figure 14-20):

```
SELECT oh.SalesOrderID, oh.OrderDate,od.ProductID
FROM Sales.SalesOrderDetail od
JOIN Sales.SalesOrderHeader oh
  ON oh.SalesOrderID = od.SalesOrderID
```

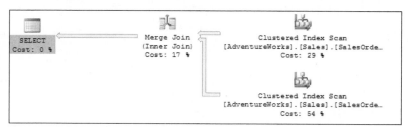

Figure 14-20

With a one-to-many join, a merge join operator scans each input only once, which is why it is superior to other operators if the predicate is not very selective. For sorted input, the optimizer can use a clustered index. If there is a nonclustered index covering the join and select columns, the optimizer would probably choose that option because it will have to fetch fewer pages. A many-to-many merge join is little more complicated. A many-to-many merge join uses a temporary table to store rows. If there are duplicate values from each input, one of the inputs will have to rewind to the start of the duplicates as each duplicate from the other input is processed.

In this query, both tables have a clustered index on the `SalesOrderID` column, so the optimizer chooses a merge join. Sometimes the optimizer chooses the merge join, even if one of the inputs is not presorted by an index, by adding a sort to the plan. The optimizer would do that if the input were small. If the optimizer chooses to sort before the merge, check whether the input has many rows and is not presorted by an index. To prevent the sort, you will have to add the required indexes to avoid a costly operation.

Index Access Methods

This section describes different index access methods. You can use this knowledge when you tune the query and decide whether a query is using the correct index access method or not and take the appropriate action.

In addition, you should make a copy of the AdventureWorks database on your machine so that if you drop or create indexes on it, the original AdventureWorks database stays intact. The copy database is AdWork in these examples.

Table Scan

A table scan involves a sequential scan of all data pages belonging to the table. Run the following script in the AdWork database:

```
SELECT * INTO dbo.New_SalesOrderHeader
FROM Sales.SalesOrderHeader
```

Once you run this script to make a copy of the `SalesOrderHeader` table, run the following script:.

```
SELECT SalesOrderID, OrderDate, CustomerID
FROM dbo.New_SalesOrderHeader
```

Because this is a heap, this statement will cause a table scan. If you want you can always get the actual textual plan using `SET STATISTICS PROFILE ON`. Figure 14-21 displays the graphical plan.

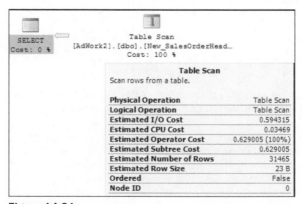

Figure 14-21

In a table scan, SQL Server uses Index Allocation Map (IAM) pages to direct the disk arm to scan the extents belonging to the table by their physical order on disk. As you might guess, the number of logical reads would be the same as the number of pages for this table.

SET STATISTICS IO ON|OFF

Let's look at the STATISTICS IO output for the example query. This is a session-level setting. STATISTICS IO provides you with I/O-related information for the statement you run.

> SET STATISTICS IO *is set at runtime and not at parse time. This is an important tool in your query-tuning arsenal, as disk I/Os are normally a bottleneck on your system, so it is very important to identify how many I/Os your query generates and whether they are necessary or not.*

```
DBCC DROPCLEANBUFFERS
GO
SET STATISTICS IO ON
GO
SELECT SalesOrderID, OrderDate, CustomerID
FROM dbo.New_SalesOrderHeader
GO
SET STATISTICS IO OFF

Table 'New_SalesOrderHeader'. Scan count 1, logical reads 799, physical reads 0,
read-ahead reads 798, lob logical reads 0, lob physical reads 0, lob read-ahead
reads 0.
```

The scan count tells you how many times the table was accesses for this query. If you have multiple tables in your query, you will see statistics showing I/O information for each table. In this case, the New_SalesOrderHeader table was accessed once.

The logical reads counter indicates how many pages were read from the data cache. In this case, 799 reads were done from cache. As mentioned earlier, because of the whole table scan, the number of logical reads equals the number of pages allocated to this table. You can also run the following query to verify the number of pages allocated to the table. Note the resulting number in the dpages column.

```
SELECT dpages, *
FROM sys.sysindexes
WHERE ID = OBJECT_ID('New_SalesOrderHeader')
```

The physical reads counter indicates the number of pages read from the disk. It shows 0 in the preceding code. Does that mean that there were no physical reads from disk? No; keep reading.

The read-ahead reads counter indicates the number of pages from the physical disk that were placed into the internal data cache when SQL Server guesses that you will need them later in the query. In this case, this counter shows 798, which means that many physical reads. Both the physical reads and read-ahead reads counters indicate the amount of physical disk activity.

The lob logical reads, lob physical reads, and lob read-ahead reads are the same as the other reads, but these counters indicate reads for the large objects — for example, if you read a column with the data type varchar(max), nvarchar(max), xml, or varbinary(max). Note that when T-SQL statements retrieve LOB columns, some LOB retrieval operations might require traversing the LOB tree multiple times. This may cause SET STATISTICS IO to report higher than expected logical reads.

Clearing Caches

The first statement in the example query is DBCC DROPCLEANBUFFERS. In a query-tuning exercise, this command is very handy to clear the data cache globally. If you run the query a second time but comment out the DBCC DROPCLEANBUFFERS statement first, the read-ahead reads counter will be 0, which means that the data pages you have asked for are already in the data cache (buffer pool). In your query-tuning exercises, make sure that when you run your query a second time after making some changes, you clear the data cache so that you get the correct I/O information and so does the query runtime.

The other important command to clear the plan cache (not data cache) is DBCC FREEPROCCACHE. It will clear the execution plan from cache globally.

If you want to clear the execution plans for a particular database, you can run the following undocumented command:

```
DBCC FLUSHPROCINDB(<db_id>)
```

Please do not run these commands in your production system because clearing the cache will obviously have a performance impact. When you do query tuning in your development/test environment, be aware of this effect.

Clustered Index Scan (Unordered)

Try creating a clustered index on the New_SalesOrderHeader table. A clustered index is structured as a balanced tree (all indexes in SQL Server are structured as balanced trees). A balanced tree is one in which "no leaf is much farther away from the root than any other leaf" (adopted from www.nist.gov). Different balancing schemes allow different definitions of "much farther" and different amounts of work to keep them balanced. A clustered index maintains the entire table's data in its leaf level (a clustered index is not a copy of the table's data; it *is* the data).

Let's run a query to see the effect of adding a clustered index. Run the following script, which is available in the QueryPlans solution as IndexAccess.sql:

```
CREATE CLUSTERED INDEX IXCU_SalesOrderID ON New_SalesOrderHeader(SalesOrderID)
```

Now run this script:

```
DBCC DROPCLEANBUFFERS
GO
SET STATISTICS IO ON
GO
SELECT SalesOrderID, RevisionNumber, OrderDate, DueDate
FROM New_SalesOrderHeader
GO
SET STATISTICS IO OFF
```

The results of Statistics IO is shown here, and the query plan is shown in Figure 14-22.

```
Table 'New_SalesOrderHeader'. Scan count 1, logical reads 805, physical reads 1,
read-ahead reads 801, lob logical reads 0, lob physical reads 0, lob read-ahead
reads 0.
```

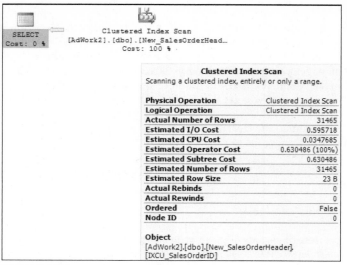

Figure 14-22

As you can see in the Statistics IO output, the number of pages read was 805 (logical reads), which is the same as the table scan (a little more because the leaf level in a clustered index also contains unique row information, and a link to the previous and next page in a doubly linked list, so more space is required to hold that information). As you can see, even though the execution plan shows a clustered index scan, the activities are the same as the table scan, so unless you have a predicate on a clustered index key, the whole clustered index will be scanned to get the data, which is the same as a table scan. You can also see in Figure 14-22, in the information box of the clustered index scan operators, that the scan was not ordered (Ordered = False), which means that the access method did not rely on the linked list that maintains the logical order of the index. Let's see what happens if we create a covering nonclustered index on the table.

Covering Nonclustered Index Scan (Unordered)

A covering index means that a nonclustered index contains all the columns specified in a query. Let's look at this using the same query used in the previous example:

```
CREATE NONCLUSTERED INDEX IXNC_SalesOrderID ON New_SalesOrderHeader(OrderDate)
INCLUDE(RevisionNumber, DueDate)
GO
DBCC DROPCLEANBUFFERS
GO
SET STATISTICS IO ON
GO
SELECT SalesOrderID,RevisionNumber, OrderDate, DueDate
FROM New_SalesOrderHeader
GO
SET STATISTICS IO OFF
```

This script creates a nonclustered index on the OrderDate column. Notice the INCLUDE clause with the column names RevisionName and DueDate. INCLUDE is a new feature in SQL Server 2005 whereby you can specify the non-key columns to be added to the leaf level of the nonclustered index. The `RevisionName` and `DueDate` columns are included because your query needs these columns. The non-clustered index is chosen for this operation so that the data can be served directly from the leaf level of the nonclustered index (because the non-clustered index has the data for these included columns). See the `CREATE INDEX` topic in BOL for details on the `INCLUDE` clause. The statistics I/O information for the query is shown here:

```
Table 'New_SalesOrderHeader'. Scan count 1, logical reads 96, physical reads 1,
read-ahead reads 94, lob logical reads 0, lob physical reads 0, lob read-ahead
reads 0.
```

The query plan is shown in Figure 14-23.

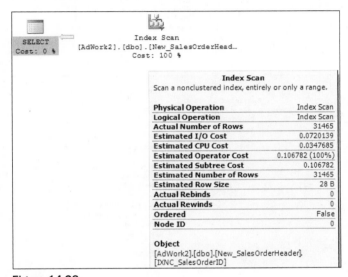

Figure 14-23

As you can see from the statistics I/O result, only 96 logical reads were done to fulfill this query. Notice that the results returned by the clustered index query in and by the covering nonclustered index query are identical (in the number of columns and number of rows), but there were 805 logical reads in the clustered index and only 96 logical reads in the nonclustered scan, because the nonclustered index has covered the query and served the data from its leaf level.

The clustered index leaf level contains the full data rows (all columns), whereas the nonclustered index has only one key column and two included columns. That means the row size is smaller for a nonclustered index, and the smaller row size can hold more data and requires less I/O.

Clustered Index Scan (Ordered)

An ordered clustered index scan is also a full scan of the clustered index, but the data is returned in order by the clustering key. This time, you'll run the same query as before, but ordered by the `SalesOrderID` column:

```
DBCC DROPCLEANBUFFERS
GO
SET STATISTICS IO ON
GO
SELECT SalesOrderID,RevisionNumber, OrderDate, DueDate
FROM New_SalesOrderHeader
ORDER BY SalesOrderID
GO
SET STATISTICS IO OFF
```

The statistics IO information is as follows:

```
Table 'New_SalesOrderHeader'. Scan count 1, logical reads 805, physical reads 1,
read-ahead reads 808, lob logical reads 0, lob physical reads 0, lob read-ahead
reads 0.
```

The query plan is shown in Figure 14-24.

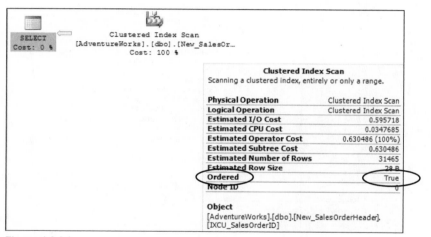

Figure 14-24

As you can see, the query plan is the same as the one in Figure 14-22, but here we have `Ordered = True`, as highlighted in Figure 14-24. The `statistics IO` information is also the same as the unordered clustered index scan. Note that unlike the unordered clustered index scan, the performance of the ordered clustered index scan depends on the fragmentation level of the index. *Fragmentation* is out-of-order pages, which means that although Page 1 appears *logically* after Page 2 according to the linked list, *physically* Page 2 comes before Page 1. The percentage of fragmentation is greater if more pages in the leaf level of the index are out of order with respect to the total number of pages. Note that moving the disk arm sequentially is always faster than random arm movement, so if the fragmentation is higher than for ordered data, there will be more random arm movement, resulting in slower performance.

If you do not need the data sorted, then do not include the ORDER BY *clause.*

Also note that even though you have a covering nonclustered index, the optimizer did not choose it this time (as in Figure 14-23) because you asked that the data be sorted on the SalesOrderID column (which is obviously not sorted on the leaf level of the nonclustered index).

Covering Nonclustered Index Scan (Ordered)

If you run the previous query with OrderDate in the ORDER BY clause, the optimizer would choose the covering nonclustered index. The query plan would be exactly same as shown in Figure 14-23, except that you would see Ordered = True in the information box. The statistics IO information will also be the same as for the non-ordered covering nonclustered index scan. Of course, an ordered index scan is not only used when you explicitly request the data sorted; the optimizer can also choose to sort the data if the plan uses an operator that can benefit from sorted data.

Nonclustered Index Seek with Ordered Partial Scan and Lookups

To demonstrate this access method, you first have to drop the clustered index on the New_SalesOrder Header table. Now run the following script:

```
DROP INDEX New_SalesOrderHeader.IXCU_SalesOrderID
GO
DBCC DROPCLEANBUFFERS
GO
SET STATISTICS IO ON
GO
SELECT SalesOrderID,RevisionNumber, OrderDate, DueDate
FROM New_SalesOrderHeader
WHERE OrderDate BETWEEN '2001-10-08 00:00:00.000' AND '2001-10-10 00:00:00.000'
GO
SET STATISTICS IO OFF
```

The statistics IO looks like this:

```
(25 row(s) affected)
Table 'New_SalesOrderHeader'. Scan count 1, logical reads 27, physical reads 3,
read-ahead reads 0, lob logical reads 0, lob physical reads 0, lob read-ahead reads
0.
```

The query execution plan is shown in Figure 14-25.

Remember that you don't have a clustered index on this table. This is called a *heap*. In the query, you have requested the SalesOrderID, RevisionNumber, OrderDate, DueDate, and SalesOrderNumber columns, and added a predicate on the OrderDate column. Because of the predicate on the key column in the IXNC_SalesOrderID index, the optimizer will choose this index and look for all the rows that have the OrderDate specified in the WHERE clause. This index also has all the columns at its leaf level except for SalesOrderID. To find the SalesOrderID column value, SQL Server performs RID lookups of the corresponding data row for each key. As each key is found, SQL Server can apply the lookup. In addition, because this is a heap table, each lookup translates to a single page read. Because there are 25 rows qualified by the WHERE clause, there will be 25 reads for data row lookup. If you look at the statistics IO information, there are 27 logical reads, which means that out of those 27 logical reads, 25 are the result of the RID lookup. You can probably guess that most of the cost in this query is in the RID lookup, which is also evident in the query plan, where you can see that the cost of the RID lookup operation is 94%. Lookups are always random I/Os (as opposed to sequential), which are more costly. When seeking many times, however, SQL Server often sorts to make I/Os more sequential.

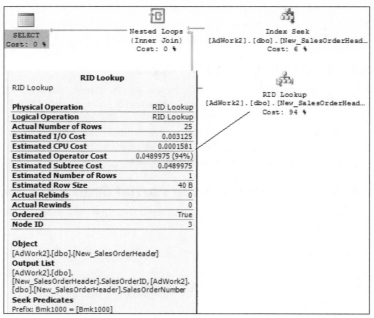

Figure 14-25

This query plan was an RID lookup on a heap. Create your clustered index and run the same query again:

```
CREATE CLUSTERED INDEX IXCU_SalesOrderID ON New_SalesOrderHeader(SalesOrderID)
GO
DBCC DROPCLEANBUFFERS
GO
SET STATISTICS IO ON
GO
SELECT SalesOrderID,RevisionNumber, OrderDate, DueDate, SalesOrderNumber
FROM New_SalesOrderHeader
WHERE OrderDate BETWEEN '2001-10-08 00:00:00.000' AND '2001-10-10 00:00:00.000'
GO
SET STATISTICS IO OFF
```

The following code shows the statistics IO output for this query:

```
(25 row(s) affected)
Table 'New_SalesOrderHeader'. Scan count 1, logical reads 77, physical reads 4,
read-ahead reads 0, lob logical reads 0, lob physical reads 0, lob read-ahead reads
0.
```

Figure 14-26 shows the query plan for this query.

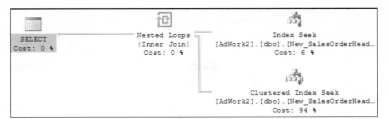

Figure 14-26

The query plans in Figure 14-25 and Figure 14-26 are almost identical except that in Figure 14-26 a clustered index is sought for each row found in the outer reference (the nonclustered index). Once again, you can see in Figure 14-26 that the clustered index seek incurs most of the cost (94%) for this query, but take a look at the `statistics IO` information for the two queries. The logical reads in the clustered index seek query plan are a lot higher than those in the RID lookup plan. Does that mean that a clustered index on the table is not so good? No. This index access method is efficient only when the predicate is highly selective, or a point query. *Selectivity* is defined as the percentage of the number of rows returned by the query out of the total number of rows in the table. A *point query* is one that has an equals (=) operator in the predicate. Because the cost of the lookup operation is greater, the optimizer decided to just do the clustered index scan. For example, if you change the `WHERE` clause in the query to `WHERE OrderDate BETWEEN '2001-10-08 00:00:00.000' AND '2001-12-10 00:00:00.000'`, then the optimizer would just do the clustered index scan to return the result for that query. Remember that the *nonleaf* levels of the clustered index typically reside in cache because of all the lookup operations going through it, so you shouldn't concern yourself too much about the higher cost of the query in the clustered index seek scenario shown in Figure 14-26.

Clustered Index Seek with Ordered Partial Scan

This is a simple one. The optimizer normally uses this technique for range queries, in which you filter based on the first key column of the clustered index. Run the following query:

```
DBCC DROPCLEANBUFFERS
GO
SET STATISTICS IO ON
GO
SELECT SalesOrderID,RevisionNumber, OrderDate, DueDate, SalesOrderNumber
FROM New_SalesOrderHeader
WHERE SalesOrderID BETWEEN 43696 AND 45734
GO
SET STATISTICS IO OFF
```

The `statistics IO` output is as follows:

```
(2039 row(s) affected)
Table 'New_SalesOrderHeader'. Scan count 1, logical reads 56, physical reads 1,
read-ahead reads 53, lob logical reads 0, lob physical reads 0, lob read-ahead
reads 0.
```

The query plan is show in Figure 14-27.

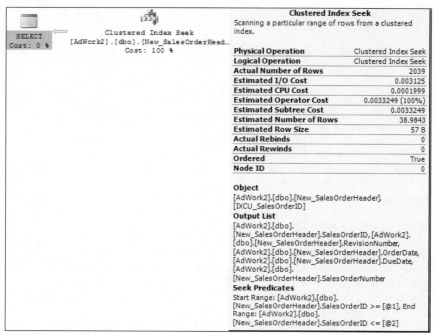

Clustered Index Seek	
Scanning a particular range of rows from a clustered index.	
Physical Operation	Clustered Index Seek
Logical Operation	Clustered Index Seek
Actual Number of Rows	2039
Estimated I/O Cost	0.003125
Estimated CPU Cost	0.0001999
Estimated Operator Cost	0.0033249 (100%)
Estimated Subtree Cost	0.0033249
Estimated Number of Rows	38.9843
Estimated Row Size	57 B
Actual Rebinds	0
Actual Rewinds	0
Ordered	True
Node ID	0

Object
[AdWork2].[dbo].[New_SalesOrderHeader].
[IXCU_SalesOrderID]
Output List
[AdWork2].[dbo].
[New_SalesOrderHeader].SalesOrderID, [AdWork2].
[dbo].[New_SalesOrderHeader].RevisionNumber,
[AdWork2].[dbo].[New_SalesOrderHeader].OrderDate,
[AdWork2].[dbo].[New_SalesOrderHeader].DueDate,
[AdWork2].[dbo].
[New_SalesOrderHeader].SalesOrderNumber
Seek Predicates
Start Range: [AdWork2].[dbo].
[New_SalesOrderHeader].SalesOrderID >= [@1], End
Range: [AdWork2].[dbo].
[New_SalesOrderHeader].SalesOrderID <= [@2]

Figure 14-27

This index access method first performs a seek operation on the first key (43696 in this case) and then performs an ordered partial scan at the leaf level, starting from first key in the range and continuing until the last key (45734). Because the leaf level of the clustered index is actually the data rows, no lookup is required in this access method.

Look at Figure 14-28 to understand the I/O cost for this index access method. To read at least a single leaf page, the number of seek operations required is equal to the number of levels in the index.

How do you find the level in the index? Run the INDEXPROPERTY function with the IndexDepth property:

```
SELECT INDEXPROPERTY (OBJECT_ID('New_SalesOrderHeader'), 'IXCU_SalesOrderID',
'IndexDepth')
```

In this case, the index depth is 3, and of course the last level is the leaf level where the data resides. As shown in Figure 14-28, the cost of the seek operation (three random reads in this case, because that is the depth of the index) and the cost of the ordered partial scan within the leaf level to get the data (in this case 53, according to the read-ahead reads) add up to 56 logical reads, as indicated in the statistics IO information. As you can see, an ordered partial scan typically incurs the bulk of the cost of the query because it involves most of the I/O to scan the range (53 in this case). As mentioned earlier, index fragmentation plays an important role in ordered partial scan operations, so when there is high fragmentation in the index, the disk arm needs to move a lot, which results in degraded performance.

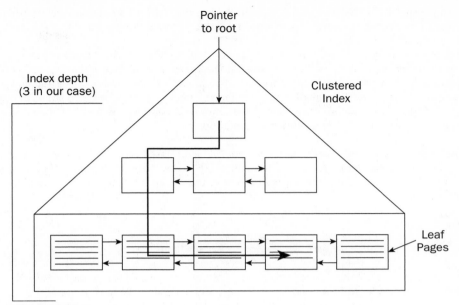

Figure 14-28

Note that this plan is called a *trivial plan*, which means that there is no better plan than this, and the plan does not depend on the selectivity of the query. As long as you have a predicate on the `SalesOrderID` columns, no matter how many rows are sought, the plan will always be the same *unless* you have a better index that the plan chooses in this case. Try adding the following index on this table. Then run the query again and see what happens and why. Notice which index is chosen by the optimizer, and the number of logical reads compared to that in Figure 14-27:

```
CREATE NONCLUSTERED INDEX IXNC_SalesOrderID_2 ON New_SalesOrderHeader(SalesOrderID,
OrderDate)
INCLUDE(RevisionNumber, DueDate, SalesOrderNumber)
```

Now drop the index after you are done with the exercise:

```
DROP INDEX New_SalesOrderHeader.IXNC_SalesOrderID_2
```

Note that you cannot keep adding indexes on your table, because maintaining those indexes is not free. Maintaining a balance tree is a costly operation because of the physical data movement involved when you modify data. Proceed cautiously and analyze the cost of adding indexes for data modification operations, especially on an OLTP system.

Fragmentation

This section elaborates on the topic of index fragmentation covered earlier. There are two types of fragmentation: *logical scan fragmentation* and *average page density*. Logical scan fragmentation is the percentage of out-of-order pages in the index in regard to their physical order as opposed to their logical order in the linked list. This fragmentation has a substantial impact on ordered scan operations like the one shown in Figure 14-27. This type of fragmentation has no impact on operations that do not rely on an ordered scan, such as seek operations, unordered scans, or lookup operations.

The average page density is the percentage of pages that are full. A low percentage (fewer pages full) has a negative impact on the queries that read the data because these queries end up reading more pages than they could were the pages better populated. The upside of having free space in pages is that insert operations in these pages do not cause page splits, which are very expensive. In short, free space in pages is bad for a data warehouse type of system (more read queries), whereas it is good for an OLTP system that involves many data modification operations.

Rebuilding the indexes and specifying the proper fill factor based on your application will reduce or remove the fragmentation. You can use following DMF to find out both types of fragmentation in your index. For example, to find out the fragmentation for indexes on the New_SalesOrderHeader table, run the following query:

```
SELECT *
FROM sys.dm_db_index_physical_stats (DB_ID(),
OBJECT_ID('dbo.New_SalesOrderHeader'), NULL, NULL, NULL)
```

Look for the avg_fragmentation_in_percent column for logical fragmentation. Ideally, it should be 0, which indicates no logical fragmentation. For average page density, look at the avg_page_space_used_in_percent column. It shows the average percentage of available data storage space used in all pages.

> DBCC SHOWCONTIG *was another way to get this information in SQL Server 2000.* DBCC SHOWCONTIG *will be deprecated in a future release of SQL Server, so do not use it.*

There is new feature in SQL Server 2005 to build the indexes online. This feature enables you to create, drop, and rebuild the index online. See Chapter 15 for more details. The following is an example of rebuilding the index IXNC_SalesOrderID on the New_SalesOrderHeader table:

```
ALTER INDEX IXNC_SalesOrderID ON dbo.New_SalesOrderHeader REBUILD WITH (ONLINE =
ON)
```

Statistics

Microsoft SQL Server 2005 collects statistics about individual columns (single-column statistics) or sets of columns (multi-column statistics). Note that a histogram is only collected for the leading column. The query optimizer uses these statistics to estimate the selectivity of expressions, and thus the size of intermediate and final query results. Good statistics enable the optimizer to accurately assess the cost of different query plans, and choose a high-quality plan. All information about a single statistics object is stored in several columns of a single row in the sysindexes table, and in a statistics binary large object (statblob) kept in an *internal-only* table.

If you see in your execution plan that there is a large difference between the estimated row count and the actual row count, the first thing you should check are the statistics on the join columns and the column in the WHERE clause for that table (be careful with the inner side of loop joins; the row count should match the estimated rows multiplied by the estimated executions). Make sure that the statistics are current. Check the UpdateDate, Rows, and Rows Sampled columns (DBCC SHOW_STATISTICS). It is very important that you keep up-to-date statistics. You can use the following views and command to get the details about statistics.

To see how many statistics exist in your table you can use the sys.stats view. To view which columns are part of the statistics, use the sys.stats_columns view. To view the histogram and density information, you can use DBCC SHOW_STATISTICS. For example, to view the histogram information for the IXNC_SalesOrderID index on the New_SalesOrderHeader table, run the following command:

```
DBCC SHOW_STATISTICS ('dbo.New_SalesOrderHeader', 'IXNC_SalesOrderID')
```

Data Modification Query Plan

When you execute data modification plans, the plan has two stages. The first stage is read-only, and determines which rows need to be inserted, updated, or deleted. It generates the data stream to describe the changes. For INSERT statements you will have column values, so the data stream contains the column values. DELETE statements have key column(s), and UPDATE statements have both data streams, the changed columns' values, and the table key. If you have foreign keys, the plan includes doing constraint validation. It also maintains indexes; and if any triggers exist, it fires these triggers as well.

There are two strategies for INSERT, UPDATE, and DELETE statements: per-row and per-index maintenance. Consider the following DELETE query, which has a per-row query plan:

```
DELETE FROM New_SalesOrderHeader
WHERE OrderDate = '2001-07-01 00:00:00.000'
```

The query plan is shown in Figure 14-29.

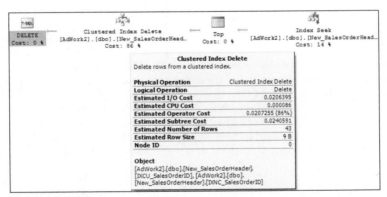

Figure 14-29

With a per-row plan, SQL Server maintains the indexes and the base table together for each row affected by the query. The updates to all nonclustered indexes are performed in conjunction with each row update on the base table. Note that the base table could be a heap or a clustered index. If you look at the Clustered Index Delete information box in Figure 14-29, in the Object information you will notice that both the clustered index and the nonclustered index are listed, which indicates that the indexes are maintained with a per-row operation.

Because of the short code path and update to all indexes and tables together, the per-row update strategy is more efficient in term of CPU cycles.

Now consider another query plan with the following query. The change in this query is to the WHERE clause (changed to <=). We're using the Sales.SalesOrderHeader table to produce the plan for this example:

```
DELETE FROM Sales.SalesOrderHeader
WHERE OrderDate < '2003-07-01 00:00:00.000'
```

The query plan is shown in Figure 14-30. Note that this figure only shows part of the plan because there are so many indexes on this table in the AdventureWorks database.

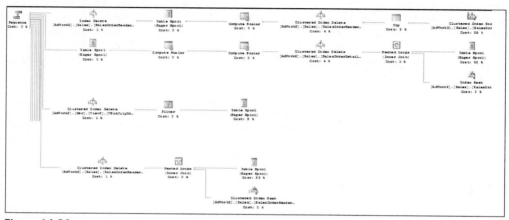

Figure 14-30

This query plan is performing per-index maintenance. The plan first deletes qualifying rows from the clustered index and at the same time builds the temporary spool table containing the clustering key values for the other nonclustered indexes that must be maintained. SQL Server reads the spool data as many times as the number of nonclustered indexes on the table. The sort operator between the index delete operator and the spool operator indicates that SQL Server sorts the data according to the key column of the index it is about to delete so that the index pages can be accessed optimally. The sequence operator enforces the execution order of each branch. SQL Server updates the indexes one after another from the top of the plan to the bottom.

As you can see from the query plan, per-index maintenance is more complicated, but because it maintains individual indexes after sorting the key (Sort operator), it will never visit the same page again, saving in I/O. Therefore, when you are updating many rows, the optimizer usually chooses the per-index plan.

> *Your disk configuration is also important in designing write/read-intensive operations. See Chapter 11 for more information.*

Partitioned Table Query Plan

If you have a predicate on the partition key when you query a partition table, make sure that partitioning pruning is on. (For details on partitioned tables, please refer to Chapter 15, "Indexing Your Database.") See the partition table query in Figure 14-31.

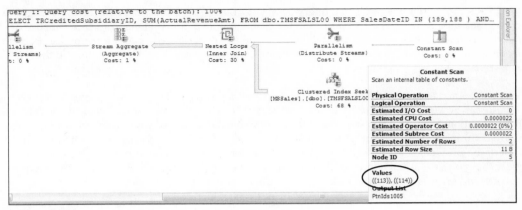

Figure 14-31

In Figure 14-31, notice in the Constant Scan details the Values field at the end of the information box. These values show how many partitions your query will read to look for data you have requested. In this case, it is reading two partitions numbered 113 and 114. If you do not see any values, your query is looking into all the available partitions for the data you have requested. In that case, you want to verify that you have the correct predicate on this query. If the query scans all the partitions, which you may not want, it could generate a lot of I/O and slow your query down.

Gathering Query Plans for Analysis with SQL Trace

Earlier you examined the query plans with different option such as SET STATISTICS PROFILE ON and SET STATISTICS XML ON. This technique does not work when you want to gather the query plans in your production environment. You have to use SQL Trace to get the query plan for analysis. We have provided the trace file you can import into your SQL Trace to gather data for query plan analysis. You can create a server-side trace from this template. See Chapter 13 for details about how to create server-side traces and import the trace data into a database table. We recommend that you create a server-side trace so that you don't miss any events. In addition, import the data into a database table for analysis rather in SQL Profiler because SQL Profiler doesn't have as many options to play with data.

The template for query plan gathering in your environment is in the samples folder for this chapter. The trace template name is QueryPlanAnalysis.tdf. Please make sure that you set filters for your criteria to gather the data, because the file size will grow very quickly. In addition, depending on whether you prefer a textual execution plan or XML, you can check one of the events Showplan Statistics Profile or Showplan XML Statistics Profile.

Summary

In this chapter you learned how query parsing, compiling, and optimization are done in SQL Server 2005. You also learned how to read the query plan. Keep in mind that when you read the query plan (using STATISTICS PROFILE, for example) the most important columns you want to look at are Rows, Executes, and EstimatedRows. If you see a big discrepancy between Rows (the actual row count) and

`EstimatedRows`, remove that small query from your main query and start your analysis there. Note that we are not suggesting that every performance problem with a query stems from bad statistics or cardinality estimations. In the real world, where users are less experienced, most performance problems result from user errors (lack of indexes and such). Check the statistics on the columns in the `JOIN` and `WHERE` clauses.

You also leaned about the different index access methods and join algorithms. Normally, I/O is the slowest process, so your goal in query tuning is to reduce the number of I/Os and balance the data modification operation (in an OLTP system), and for that knowledge of index access methods and join algorithms is vital. Tuning is not easy, but with patience and attention to details, we are sure that you will get to the root of the problem. Of course, make sure that your server and disk configuration are done properly. Now that you've learned about configuring your server, optimizing SQL Server, and tuning queries, you can move on to learn about indexing your database in the next chapter.

Indexing Your Database

Indexes are the solution to many performance problems, but may also be the root of so many more. A good understanding of indexes is essential for the survival of any DBA, yet as with most things in SQL Server, each new version brings about change, and many new features. In this chapter we begin by reviewing the new index-related features in SQL Server 2005, and then touch on the basics to make sure you have a full understanding of indexing before going into the details of those new indexing features.

As with most things in SQL Server, the ultimate reference is Books Online, so we won't be duplicating the reference material available there. What we will do is try to make sense of it, and put that information into a context you can use. This chapter does not cover the internal details of indexes, so it doesn't include a detailed discussion of the new allocation unit types. For the latest information on index internals for SQL Server 2005, read the SQL Storage Engine blog at `http://blogs.msdn.com/sqlserverstorageengine/default.aspx`.

What's New for Indexes in SQL Server 2005

SQL Server 2005 has so many new features it's an absolute garden of delight for any DBA, but at the same time it can be challenging to find the exact information relevant to what you want to do. This section highlights the new index-related features in SQL Server 2005, and provides a very brief overview of each.

Partition Tables and Indexes

You can now create tables on multiple partitions, and indexes on each partition. This enables you to manage operations on very large datasets, such as loading and unloading a new set of data, more efficiently by indexing just the new partition, rather than having to re-index the whole table. You will find a lot more information about partition tables and indexes later in this chapter.

Online Index Operations

Online index operations are a new availability feature. They enable users to continue to query against a table while indexes are being built or rebuilt. The main scenario for using this new feature is when you need to make index changes during normal operating hours. The new syntax for using online index operations is the addition of the ONLINE = ON option with the CREATE INDEX, ALTER INDEX, DROP INDEX, and ALTER TABLE operations.

Parallel Index Operations

Parallel index operations are another new feature. They are available only in Enterprise Edition, and only apply to systems running on multi-processor machines. The key scenario for using this new feature is when you need to restrict the amount of CPU resources that index operations consume. This might be either for multiple index operations to coexist, or more likely when you need to allow other tasks to complete while performing index operations. They enable a DBA to specify the MAXDOP for an index operation. This is very useful on large systems, allowing you to limit the maximum number of processors to be used in index operations. It's effectively a MAXDOP specifically for index operations, and it works in conjunction with the server-configured MAXDOP setting. The new syntax for parallel index operations is the MAXDOP=n option, which can be specified on CREATE INDEX, ALTER INDEX, DROP INDEX (for clustered indexes only), ALTER TABLE ADD (constraint), ALTER TABLE DROP (clustered index), and CONSTRAINT operations.

Asynchronous Statistics Update

This is a new performance SET option — AUTO_UPDATE_STATISTICS_ASYNC. When this option is set, outdated statistics are placed on a queue and will be automatically updated by a worker thread at some later time. The query that generated the auto update request will continue before the stats are updated. Note that asynchronous statistics update cannot occur if any data definition language (DDL) statements such as CREATE, ALTER, or DROP occur in the same transaction.

Full Text Indexes

Full Text Search now supports the creation of indexes on XML columns. It has also been upgraded to use MSSearch 3.0, which includes additional performance improvements for full text index population. It also means that there is now one instance of MSSearch for each SQL Server instance.

Non-Key Columns in Nonclustered Indexes

With SQL Server 2005, non-key columns can be added to a nonclustered index. This has several advantages. It enables queries to retrieve data faster, as the query can now retrieve everything it needs from the index pages without having to do a bookmark lookup into the table to read the data row. The non-key columns are not counted in the limits for the nonclustered index number of columns (16 columns), or key length (900 bytes). The new syntax for this option is INCLUDE (Column Name, . . .), which is used with the CREATE INDEX statement.

Index Lock Granularity Changes

The `CREATE INDEX` and `ALTER INDEX` T-SQL statements have been enhanced by the addition of new options to control the locking that occurs during the index operation. `ALLOW_ROW_LOCKS` and `ALLOW_PAGE_LOCKS` specify the granularity of the lock to be taken during the index operation.

Indexes on XML Columns

This is a new type of index on the XML data in a column. It enables the database engine to find elements within the XML data without having to shred the XML each time.

Dropping and Rebuilding Large Indexes

The database engine has been modified to treat indexes occupying over 128 extents in a new, more scalable way. If a drop or rebuild is required on an index larger than 128 extents, then the process is broken into logical and physical stages. In the logical phase, the pages are simply marked as deallocated. Once the transaction commits, the physical phase of deallocating the pages occurs. The deallocation takes place in batches occurring in the background, thereby avoiding taking locks for a long period of time.

Indexed View Enhancements

Indexed views have been enhanced in several ways. They can now contain scalar aggregates, and some user-defined functions (with restrictions). In addition, the query optimizer can now match more queries to indexed views if the query uses scalar expressions, scalar aggregates, user-defined functions, interval expressions, and equivalency conditions.

Version Store

The *version store* is a major enhancement for SQL Server 2005. It provides the basis for the row versioning framework that is used by Online Indexing, MARS, triggers, and the new row versioning–based isolation levels.

Database Tuning Advisor

The Database Tuning Advisor (DTA) replaces SQL Server 2000's Index Tuning Wizard (ITW). DTA now offers the following new features:

❑ **Time-bound tuning:** Allows you to limit the amount of time spent analyzing a workload. The more time spent, the better the analysis, but the higher the load on the system.

❑ **Tune across multiple DBs:** You can now tune workloads that run across multiple databases.

❑ **Tune a broader class of events and triggers:** DTA adds the capability to tune using workloads with a larger range of events than was possible with the ITW.

❑ **Tuning log:** DTA writes a log of any events it is unable to tune, along with the reason why it cannot tune that event.

❑ **What-if analysis:** DTA enables you to specify a theoretical server configuration in an input XML file, and provides tuning recommendations for the given workload based on the theoretical server configuration. This enables you to model how changing the server configuration will change the tuning required for optimal performance. Unfortunately, using this option requires manually editing an XML configuration file.

❑ **More control over tuning options:** DTA adds more options to control tuning recommendations.

❑ **XML file support:** DTA adds support for input and output XML files. The input file enables you to provide a different server configuration. The output file enables you to store the DTA recommendations in an XML file. Again, in most cases using this and other XML file–based features requires manual editing of the XML file.

❑ **Partitioning support:** One of the new tuning options is the capability to ask for partitioning recommendations.

❑ **Offloading tuning load to lower-spec hardware:** DTA uses just the metadata and statistics from a server to perform its tuning analysis. Because it doesn't need all the data as well, it can easily be run on lower-spec hardware without affecting the quality or speed of delivery of the tuning recommendations. However, during the tuning process, the test server must have access to the production server so that metadata about the server configuration can be captured. It would be nice if this metadata could be persisted to an XML file that you could edit for further what-if analysis, but this doesn't seem to be possible yet.

❑ **Db_owners can now play too:** With ITW, only members of the sysadmin role could execute the wizard. With DTA, members of the db_owners role now have the rights to get the same recommendations. Note that the first time DTA is run, it must be run by a member of the sysadmin role before a member of the db_owners role can use it.

Sample Database

For this chapter, and the example walkthroughs, we looked at the various sample databases available; and after playing with most of them we decided that a simpler case would work just as well, be easier for readers to reproduce in their own environment, and be simpler to use to illustrate how each feature works.

The sample workload consists of a key table called people that we want to insert into as fast as we can. Each insert into this table has to do lookups in three reference tables, and then perform some calculations to determine the rest of the data to be inserted. The three reference tables are a list of male names, a list of female names, and a list of last names.

There is a procedure that can be used to randomly generate names, MakeNames, which has two arguments. The first is the number of names to insert (the default is 100). The second indicates which type of name to insert: a male name ("B" for Boys), a female name ("G" for Girls), or a last name (the default, or "L" for Lastnames)

There are two ways to inserts rows in the people table. The first is used to randomly distribute data over the time period of the database. This simulates an existing data set distributed over a time period. This insert procedure does random number lookups to find a male and female first name, and then a last name. It then randomly generates a date of birth for a date between today and 110 years ago. Then, with all this new data, two rows are inserted into the `people` table: one `male`, one `female`. This is the data load procedure that can be run to initially populate the `people` table.

The other data insert procedure is used primarily for the partitioning example, and is called `Birth`. This procedure does the same male and female name lookup, but then inserts two records using the current date/time as the DOB. This simulates inserting new records into one end of the table.

The update part of the workload consists of several procedures. One is called `marriage`, which finds a male entry and a female entry, and updates the female last name to match the male last name. Another stored procedure is called `death`. This finds the oldest record in the database and sets its DOD to be the current date/time.

All the individual procedures also have other procedures that call them in a loop to make it easier to apply a load to the system. These looping procedures are called `do<something>` where *something* will either be people, births, marriages, or deaths. The `do<something>` procedures all take two arguments, both of which are defaulted. The first argument is the number of times to call the underlying procedure (defaults to 10,000). The second indicates how frequently to report stats on the number of inserts, and time taken (defaults to 500)

To help clarify the simplicity of this database design, here are the only tables:

```
create table people
(
  personID uniqueidentifier DEFAULT NEWSEQUENTIALID(),
  firstName varchar(80) not null,
  lastName varchar(80) not null,
  DOB datetime not null,
  DOD datetime null,
  sex char(1) not null
)

create table BoysNames
  (
  ID int identity(0,1) not null,
  Name varchar(80) not null
  )

create table GirlsNames
  (
  ID int identity(0,1) not null,
  Name varchar(80) not null
  )

create table LastNames
  (
  ID int identity(0,1) not null,
  Name varchar(80) not null
  )
```

You can find scripts to create the database, tables, indexes, stored procedures, and scripts for partitioning on the Web site for this book at www.wrox.com.

Partition Tables and Indexes

Now we'll get started with digging into the details of some of these awesome new features, starting with one that we're particularly excited about: the new partition tables and partition indexes. First you'll learn why you would need to use this new feature, and then how you should use it. As we're doing that, you'll discover more about what partition tables and indexes are, and then find out more about how you use them.

Why Use Partition Tables and indexes?

Partition tables are a way to spread a single table over multiple partitions, and while doing so each partition can be on a separate filegroup. There are several reasons for doing this, described in the following sections.

Faster and Easier Data Loading

If your database has a very large amount of data to load, you might want to consider using a partition table. Anytime we're talking about a very large amount of data, this isn't a specific amount of data, but any case in which the load operation takes longer than is acceptable in the production cycle. A partition table enables you to load the data to an empty table that's not in use by the "live" data, so it has less impact on concurrent live operations. Clearly, there will be an impact to the I/O subsystem, but if you also have separate filegroups on different physical disks, even this has a minimal impact on overall system performance.

Once the data is loaded to the new table, you can perform a switch to add the new table to the live data. This switch is a simple metadata change that executes very quickly, so partition tables are a great way to load large amounts of data with limited impact on users touching the rest of the data in the table.

Faster and Easier Data Deletion or Archival

For the very same reasons, partition tables also help you to delete or archive data. If your data is partitioned on boundaries that are also the natural boundaries on which you add or remove data, then the data is considered to be *aligned*. When your data is aligned, deleting or archiving data is as simple as switching a table out of the current partition, after which you can unload or archive it at your leisure.

There is a bit of a catch to this part: With archival, you often want to move the old data to slower or different storage. The switch operation is so fast because all it does is change metadata; it doesn't move any data around, so to actually move the data from the filegroup where it lived to the old. slow disk archival filegroup, you actually have to move the data, but you are moving it when the partition isn't attached to the existing partition table. Therefore, although this may take quite some time, it will have minimal impact on any queries executing against the live data.

Faster Queries

We're sure the opportunity to get faster queries has you very interested. One thing that the Query Optimizer can do when querying a partition table is eliminate searching through partitions that it knows won't hold any results. This is referred to as *partition elimination*. This only works if the data in the partition table or index is aligned with the query. That is, the data has to be distributed among the partitions in a way that matches the search clause on the query. You will learn more details about this as we cover how to create a partition table.

Sliding Windows

A *sliding window* is basically what we referred to earlier in the discussion about adding new data and then deleting or archiving old data. What we did was fill a new table, switch it into the live table, and then switch an existing partition out of the live table for archival or deletion. It's kind of like sliding a window of new data into the current partition table, and then sliding an old window of data out of the partition table.

Prerequisites for Partitioning

Before you get all excited about partition tables, you should remember that partitioning is only available with SQL Server 2005 Enterprise Edition. There are also some expectations about the hardware in use, in particular the storage system, although these are implicit expectations, and you can store the data anywhere you want. You just won't get the same performance benefits you would if you had a larger enterprise storage system with multiple disk groups dedicated to different partitions.

Creating Partition Tables

When you decide to create a partition table for the first time, you can get pretty lost in the documentation for partition functions, range left versus range right, partition schemes, and how to actually create something that would work, so we'll walk you through the steps for this process.

Creating a Partition Table from an Existing Table

Suppose that you're starting out with an existing table, and you want to turn it into a partition table. You will face a bit of a limitation in that you can't spread the table over multiple filegroups, as that would require you to physically move all the data around, so this system partitions a table onto a partition scheme on a single set of filegroups.

The partition function is the function that determines how your data is split between partitions, so the first step is to create the partition function. Here is the code for a partition function that splits a table called People into multiple partitions based on the DOB field:

```
-- Range partition function for the People table,
-- every 10 years from 2006 - 110 = 1896,
-- start the first partition at everything before 1 Jan 1900

-- 1890-1900, 1900-1910, 1910 - 1920, 1920-1930, 1930-1940, 1940-1950, 1950-1960,
-- 1960-1970, 1970-1980, 1980-1990, 1990-2000, 2000 onwards
CREATE PARTITION FUNCTION [PeopleRangePF1] (datetime)
AS RANGE RIGHT FOR VALUES ('01/01/1900', '01/01/1910', '01/01/1920', '01/01/1930',
  '01/01/1940', '01/01/1950','01/01/1960', '01/01/1970', '01/01/1980',
  '01/01/1990', '01/01/2000', '01/01/2005', '01/01/2006'
  );
GO
```

Most of this will look pretty familiar, but there is one new bit of syntax that's particularly perplexing, and that's the *range right for values*. According to BOL, it's there to determine how the boundary condition is applied at the actual range value, so it tells the function what to do with data that exactly matches the range boundary. In this case, the first range boundary is '01/01/1900'. What should the function do with data that matches that value—does it go above or below? `Range Right` tells the function to put the matching data into the right side (higher values, or above the range boundary) of the data, whereas `range left` tells the function to put the data into the left side (lower values, or below the range boundary) of the data.

Something else to watch for here when using `datetime` fields is the precise `datetime` you're matching on. In this example, you have the luxury of not worrying about the exact placement of a few values close to the boundary, which may get into the next partition. In a production system, you want to ensure that the partition holds exactly the values you want. In that case, you need to pay particular attention to the exact `datetime` constant you specify for the range boundary.

The second step is to create the partition scheme, as follows:

```
CREATE PARTITION SCHEME [PeoplePS1]
AS PARTITION [PeopleRangePF1]
TO ([PRIMARY], [PRIMARY], [PRIMARY]
, [PRIMARY], [PRIMARY], [PRIMARY]
, [PRIMARY], [PRIMARY], [PRIMARY]
, [PRIMARY], [PRIMARY], [PRIMARY]
, [PRIMARY], [PRIMARY]);
GO
```

This is pretty simple syntax. The main thing you need to look out for is the exact number of partitions to be created. This partition function created 13 boundaries, so you need to have 13+1 = 14 partitions for the data to go into.

Because you are partitioning an existing table, you have to keep all the data on the existing filegroup. For cases where you need to physically move the data to different filegroups, see the details on deleting or archiving for information about how to move data around most efficiently.

The third step is applying the partition by creating a clustered index on the partition scheme. As the comment says, you already have data in your table, so now you have to spread it across the partitions, which you do by using a clustered index:

```
-- we already have data in the table, so we have to partition it using a
-- clustered index
create clustered index cix_people on people (dob) on peoplePS1 (DOB)
go
```

The fourth and final step is to check the system metadata to confirm that you have partitioned correctly. To do this there is some new syntax you can use to determine the partition on which that data lives: `$partition`. Here is an example of using this to see how many rows are on each partition:

```
-- How many people do we have in the whole table?
select count (*) from people
-- 17,391,302

--  this will tell us how many entries there are in each partition?
select $partition.PeopleRangePF1(dob) [Partition Number], count(*) as total
from people
group by $partition.PeopleRangePF1(dob)
order by $partition.PeopleRangePF1(dob)
```

```
/*
Partition Number total
---------------- -----------
1                630366
2                1575914
3                1574769
4                1573157
5                1573374
6                1574617
7                1575106
8                1577206
9                1578043
10               1575668
11               1576848
12               788732
13               157508
14               59994
*/
```

Using this syntax, you can see the number of rows on each partition to confirm that the data is distributed as you planned.

Adding New Data to the Partition Table

Now that your table is partitioned, you need a way to add new data offline, and to switch that new data into the partition table. The first step creates a table to hold all the new data to be loaded. This needs to have an identical layout to the partitioned table:

```
-- Now go create a new People table to hold any births after 7/11/2006
-- MUST BE IDENTICAL to People
create table newPeople (
   [personID] [uniqueidentifier] NULL DEFAULT (newsequentialid()),
   [firstName] [varchar](80) NOT NULL,
   [lastName] [varchar](80) NOT NULL,
   [DOB] [datetime] NOT NULL,
   [DOD] [datetime] NULL,
   [sex] [char](1) NOT NULL
) on [PRIMARY]      -- Must be on the same filegroup as the target partition!
```

After doing this, you need to create modified versions of the Birth and doBirths stored procedures to insert rows to the newPeople table, rather then inserting to the People table. We called this new procedure doNewBirths. This change is shown as follows to make it clear that all we are doing is changing the table name we insert to from People to newPeople.

Change the lines

```
    insert people ( firstName, lastname, dob, sex)
                 values ( @BoysName, @lastName, getdate(), 'M')
    insert people ( firstName, lastname, dob, sex)
                 values ( @GirlsName, @lastName, getdate(), 'F')
```

to these two lines:

```
insert newPeople ( firstName, lastname, dob, sex)
                    values ( @BoysName, @lastName, getdate(), 'M')
insert newPeople ( firstName, lastname, dob, sex)
                    values ( @GirlsName, @lastName, getdate(), 'F')
```

Inserting to the new table is amazingly fast because it's empty, and there are no indexes to slow down the insert rate. Now insert some data into the table — a few hundred thousand rows. Do this by running the new doNewBirths stored procedure. Changing the arguments will determine how many rows it inserts.

Here is a sample command line to insert 100,000 rows into the newpeople table. The two arguments for this procedure are @People int, which tells the procedure how many rows to insert, and @ReportInterval int, which tells the procedure how frequently to report insert stats. For 100,000 rows, we chose to report only every 10,000 rows:

```
sqlcmd -StracysLaptop -E -d people -Q"exec doBirths 100000, 10000"
```

You're now ready to move onto the next step of creating a clustered index to match the partition index:

```
-- create the index on the new table.
create clustered index cix_newPeople on newPeople(dob)
```

Creating the clustered index takes quite some time, but it doesn't affect your live system performance because it's not connected in any way to the live People table.

One more thing you need to do is create a check constraint on the new table to ensure that the data matches the partition function boundary you are just about to set up:

```
-- Before we do the switch,
-- create a check constraint on the source table
-- to enforce the integrity of the data in the partition
ALTER TABLE newPeople
ADD CONSTRAINT [CK_DOB_DateRange]
CHECK ([DOB] >= '7/11/2006');
GO
```

Now you can start making changes to the live partition to prepare it for the new set of data you want to load. The first step here is to alter the partition scheme to specify where the new partition is going to live. This has to be on the same filegroup as the new table you just filled up. In this case, this is as easy as everything is on Primary anyway. In a production system with multiple filegroups, this would be one of the empty filegroups available. For more details on using multiple filegroups, see the "Partitioning a Production System" section coming up shortly.

```
-- alter the partition scheme to ready a new empty partition
ALTER PARTITION SCHEME PeoplePS1
NEXT USED [PRIMARY];
GO
```

The next step is to create the new partition boundary in the partition function. This is done by using an ALTER PARTITION function statement. In this case, you have a RANGE RIGHT function, your new data is for 11 July 2006, and you want all the new data to be in the new partition, so using RANGE RIGHT, you specify the boundary as 11 July 2006:

```
-- Split the newest partition at 11 July 2006.
-- This is a RANGE RIGHT function,
-- so anything on 7/11 goes into the NEW partition,
-- anything BEFORE 7/11 goes into the OLD partition
-- The new partition this creates goes to the new partition
-- we prepared in the alter scheme above
ALTER PARTITION FUNCTION PeopleRangePF1()
SPLIT RANGE ('7/11/2006');
GO
```

The next step will switch the new data into the partition, but before doing that, check to see how many people you have in the newPeople table:

```
-- Check how many people we have in the newPeople table
select count (*) fron newPeople
-- 399996
```

Now you can apply the switch and move all those people into the new partition:

```
-- Now go switch in the data from the new table
ALTER TABLE newPeople
SWITCH      -- No partition here as we are switching in a NON partitioned table
TO People PARTITION 15;  -- but need to add the partition here !
GO
```

The switch ran very quickly, so you check how many people are in each table. First check to see how many people are now in the newPeople table:

```
select count (*) from newPeople
-- this table is now empty
```

As expected, the table is empty; and it is hoped that all 399,996 people are in the partition table in the new partition:

```
-- go check the partitions?
--  this will tell us how many entries there are in each partition?
select $partition.PeopleRangePF1(dob) [Partition Number], count(*) as total
from people
group by $partition.PeopleRangePF1(dob)
order by $partition.PeopleRangePF1(dob)

/*
Partition Number total
---------------- -----------
1                630366
2                1575914
3                1574769
4                1573157
5                1573374
6                1574617
```

```
7                   1575106
8                   1577206
9                   1578043
10                  1575668
11                  1576848
12                  788732
13                  157508
14                  59994
15                  399996
*/
-- We now have a 15th partition with all the new people in it
```

Querying the partition table, we now have a fifteenth partition with 399,996 people in it. As you can see, it was relatively easy to slide in a new partition.

Deleting Data from the Partition Table

After a new set of data that represents a new day, week, or month of data has been added to your table, you also need to go move out the old data, either to delete it or to archive it somewhere. The first step in this process is to create a new table for the data. This needs to be an empty table, and it needs to have the exact same structure as the partition table. In addition, it must be on the same filegroup as the partition you are going to remove:

```
-- Now go slide out the oldest partition.
-- Step one, we need a table to put the data into
create table oldPeople (
  [personID] [uniqueidentifier] NULL DEFAULT (newsequentialid()),
  [firstName] [varchar](80) NOT NULL,
  [lastName] [varchar](80) NOT NULL,
  [DOB] [datetime] NOT NULL,
  [DOD] [datetime] NULL,
  [sex] [char](1) NOT NULL
) on [PRIMARY]
-- Must be on the same filegroup as the source partition!
-- we need a clustered index on DOB to match the partition
create clustered index cix_oldPeople on oldPeople(dob)
go
```

Note that you don't need a check constraint on this table, as it's moving out of the partition, not into it.

Now that you have the table and clustered index to match the partition table and index, you can execute the switch to move out a set of data. This is done using the ALTER TABLE switch statement again, but note that now the syntax has changed a little; you have to specify partition numbers:

```
-- now go switch out the partition
ALTER TABLE People
SWITCH partition 1     -- which partition are we removing
TO OldPeople
-- No partition here as we are switching to a NON partitioned table
GO
```

That was remarkably easy, and amazingly fast. Now check how many rows are in each partition again:

```
-- Query the system meta data to see where the old data went to?

--  this will tell us how many entries there are in each partition?
select $partition.PeopleRangePF1(dob) [Partition Number], count(*) as total
from people
group by $partition.PeopleRangePF1(dob)
order by $partition.PeopleRangePF1(dob)

/*
Partition Number total
---------------- ----------
2                1575914
3                1574769
4                1573157
5                1573374
6                1574617
7                1575106
8                1577206
9                1578043
10               1575668
11               1576848
12               788732
13               157508
14               59994
15               399996
*/
-- Notice that partition 1 has gone!

-- lets see how many people are now in the oldPeople table?
select count (*) from oldPeople
-- 630366
```

You can see that partition 1 is no longer part of the partition table, and that the rows from that partition are now in the `oldPeople` table.

There is one more bit of tidying up you need to perform, and that's to alter the partition function to merge the old range that you no longer need. This is done using another ALTER PARTITION function statement, where you specify the old boundary that you no longer need:

```
-- next we can merge the first partition
ALTER PARTITION FUNCTION PeopleRangePF1()
MERGE RANGE ('01/01/1900');
GO
-- now go check the partition layout after the merge!

--  this will tell us how many entries there are in each partition?
select $partition.PeopleRangePF1(dob) [Partition Number], count(*) as total
from people
group by $partition.PeopleRangePF1(dob)
order by $partition.PeopleRangePF1(dob)

/*
```

```
Partition Number total
---------------- -----------
1                1575914
2                1574769
3                1573157
4                1573374
5                1574617
6                1575106
7                1577206
8                1578043
9                1575668
10               1576848
11               788732
12               157508
13               59994
14               399996

*/
-- Now we only have partitions 1-14 again
```

That was all pretty easy, but you aren't quite done yet. You have moved the old partition data out of the partition table but it's still on the same filegroup consuming fast, expensive disk resources. You want the data to be on the old, slow, cheap disks for archival, or in some location ready to be backed up and deleted.

To do this, you need to physically move the data from one filegroup to another. There are several ways you can do this, but the fastest and most efficient is to use a `select into`. This is pretty simple, but you do have to be a little careful about altering the default filegroup if anyone else might be creating objects in the database while you are doing your data movements. There are three steps you need to complete here.

1. Alter the default filegroup to be the archival filegroup.

2. Select into a new table.

3. Alter the default filegroup back.

Here is the code you can use to do this:

```
-- Once its slid out, we have to physically move the data
-- to a different filegroup for archival storage

-- to move it we need to do some MAGIC !!!

-- ***********************************************
-- *
-- *     --- WARNING ---
-- * WE MUST ENSURE no one else is creating new objects
-- * during this section !
-- * else they will end up on our slow disks
-- *
-- *
-- ***********************************************

-- Change the default filegroup to be slowDisks
```

```
-- This is so that thje select into creates the new table on slowDisks
ALTER DATABASE People MODIFY FILEGROUP [slowDisks] DEFAULT
GO

-- Move the data!
select * into archive2People
from oldPeople

-- alter the default filegroup back again!
ALTER DATABASE People MODIFY FILEGROUP [primary] DEFAULT
GO
```

Finally, query some system metadata to see where your new table is living. The following is the query you can use for this, with abbreviated results showing just the objects of interest:

```
-- Lets go check which filegroup all our objects are on
select object_name(i.object_id) as ObjectName, i.name as indexName, f.name as
filegroupName
from sys.indexes as i inner join sys.filegroups as f on i.data_space_id =
f.data_space_id
where i.object_id > 100

-- Returns
/*
ObjectName              IndexName               filegroupName
newPeople               cix_newPeople           PRIMARY
oldPeople               NULL                    PRIMARY
oldPeople               cix_oldPeople           slowDisks
archivePeople           NULL                    slowDisks
Person                  NULL                    PRIMARY
Person                  ix_HomePhone            PRIMARY
Person                  ix_dob_name             PRIMARY
Person                  ix_personid             PRIMARY
*/
```

Partitioning a Production System

The examples covered so far help to show how you can implement a sliding window scenario, but they gloss over some of the finer details that are going to be the key points on a production system. One of the main issues on a production system is that you will have multiple filegroups matched to different physical storage.

The only place this really changes any of what you've seen so far is when you're creating and altering the partition scheme. Rather than the example shown earlier, you would create a partition scheme using something like this:

```
CREATE PARTITION SCHEME [PeoplePS1]
AS PARTITION [PeopleRangePF1]
TO ([FileGroup1], [FileGroup2], [FileGroup3] );
GO
```

Here, each of your partitions would go to a different filegroup.

When you create filegroups, you need to make sure you have enough filegroups not just for the live table, but also for new data and for the old data before it's moved to archival storage or deleted. So you need filegroups for at least the number of live partitions, plus two more: one for the new data and one for the old data.

An alternative physical layout might have multiple partitions sharing the same filegroup. The exact details of laying out physical disks is beyond the scope of this chapter, but is touched on in Chapter 11.

Partitioning and DTA

DTA will provide partitioning recommendations if you ask it to. To do this you need to change the tuning options on the Tuning Options tab. Under the section titled Partitioning Strategy to Employ, change the default setting of No Partitioning to Full Partitioning. The other thing you need to do is determine what kind of queries to tune. It's no good using your INSERT , DELETE, or SWITCH queries, as DTA isn't really interested in them, so you have to tune the select statements that go against the nonpartitioned table. DTA isn't interested in INSERT, DELETE, or SWITCH statements because it can't improve their performance by adding indexes, so it ignores them and looks only at statements it can tune, i.e., SELECT statements.

If the table is big enough, and the queries would benefit from partitioning, DTA will provide scripts to create the partition function, the partition scheme, and the clustered index. Here is an example of a DTA partitioning recommendation we received from a different database. The underlying table has 57,000,000 rows, and uses 1.8GB of data space and 3.6GB of index space:

```
CREATE PARTITION FUNCTION [_dta_pf__2533](int) AS RANGE LEFT FOR VALUES (103863552,
196930103, 203421423, 246065168, 269171113, 269702979, 270375078, 273695583,
276447808, 280951053, 298459732, 298855583, 299375843, 299810346, 301474640)

CREATE PARTITION SCHEME [_dta_ps__8258] AS PARTITION [_dta_pf__2533] TO ([PRIMARY],
[PRIMARY], [PRIMARY], [PRIMARY], [PRIMARY], [PRIMARY], [PRIMARY], [PRIMARY],
[PRIMARY], [PRIMARY], [PRIMARY], [PRIMARY], [PRIMARY], [PRIMARY], [PRIMARY],
[PRIMARY])

CREATE NONCLUSTERED INDEX [_dta_index_myTable_6_741577680_23810504_K1_K2_K3] ON
[dbo].[myTable]
(
  [Col1] ASC,
  [Col2] ASC,
  [Col3] ASC
)WITH (SORT_IN_TEMPDB = OFF, DROP_EXISTING = OFF, IGNORE_DUP_KEY = OFF, ONLINE =
OFF) ON [_dta_ps__8258]([Colx])
```

Index Maintenance

A number of problems can occur with indexes over time as data changes in the underlying table. As rows are inserted, deleted, and updated, the distribution of data through the index can become unbalanced, with some pages becoming fully packed, resulting in additional results causing immediate page splits. Other pages can become very sparsely filled, causing many pages to be read to access a few rows of data. These problems can be easily overcome with some simple index maintenance.

The first thing you need to do is implement some monitoring to figure out when the indexes are getting to the stage where they need attention. The second step is figuring out which of the various options for index maintenance you should use to clean up the index.

Monitoring Index Fragmentation

In SQL Server 2000, we used DBCC showcontig to monitor index fragmentation. With SQL Server 2005, you now have a new function, sys.dm_db_index_physical_stats. The syntax for this function is detailed in full in BOL, so here's a look at running it with our People sample database:

```
use People
go

SELECT *
FROM sys.dm_db_index_physical_stats
  (
  DB_ID('People'),
  OBJECT_ID('People'),
  NULL,
  NULL ,
  'DETAILED'
  )
go
```

The results provide a lot of information, but there are just a few things you really want to focus on. In fact, to get the information you need on the level of fragmentation, you can use the following query:

```
SELECT index_id, index_level, avg_fragmentation_in_percent
FROM sys.dm_db_index_physical_stats
  (
  DB_ID('People'),
  OBJECT_ID('People'),
  NULL,
  NULL ,
  'DETAILED'
  )
go
```

What you are looking for is any level of index where the avg_fragmentation_in_percent is higher than 0, although low single digits are also acceptable. In the case of the People table, I dropped and recreated the table, created the indexes, and then loaded 200,000 rows. After executing these steps the results don't look so good, and they show a high level of index fragmentation:

```
index_id     index_level avg_fragmentation_in_percent
-----------  ----------- ----------------------------
1            0           98.6089375760737
1            1           96.4285714285714
1            2           0
6            0           1.38666666666667
6            1           57.1428571428571
6            2           0
7            0           98.3564458140729
```

```
7          1          100
7          2          0
8          0          99.1496598639456
8          1          98.4375
8          2          0
9          0          98.4857309260338
9          1          88.8888888888889
9          2          0
10         0          98.772504091653
10         1          40
10         2          0
```

You would probably want to try to clean the indexes up a bit.

Cleaning Up Indexes

Now that you know you have fragmented indexes, you have three options for cleaning them up. The first and most comprehensive is to drop and recreate the indexes. This is the most intrusive, as each index needs to be dropped and then recreated. When an index is dropped, it is not available for use. Moreover, the drop and create operations are atomic, so the table is locked while this is happening, and not available for use. The second option is to use the statement ALTER INDEX REORGANIZE, which is new for SQL Server 2005. This statement replaces DBCC INDEXDEFRAG. The third option is to use the other new statement ALTER INDEX REBUILD., which replaces DBCC DBREINDEX.

If you have the luxury and time to take the table offline, you should use the first option, and drop and recreate the indexes. If you need to keep the table online, and want a less intrusive option, you should use either of the ALTER INDEX options. Both ALTER INDEX options are online, allowing the table to remain available during the index maintenance operation. The more online of the two is ALTER INDEX REORGANIZE, but it doesn't do as comprehensive a job with the index. We'll run each option on the badly fragmented index and see how well it does.

We'll start with ALTER INDEX REORGANIZE. After running the command:

```
alter index all on people reorganize
```

the index fragmentation now looks like this:

```
index_id    index_level avg_fragmentation_in_percent
----------- ----------- ----------------------------
1           0           0.960960960960961
1           1           96.4285714285714
1           2           0
6           0           1.38740661686233
6           1           57.1428571428571
6           2           0
7           0           2.53968253968254
7           1           100
7           2           0
8           0           1.9639407598197
8           1           98.4375
8           2           0
```

```
9          0          2.031144211239
9          1          88.8888888888889
9          2          0
10         0          2.45464247598719
10         1          40
10         2          0
```

It made an improvement. You aren't back to the level you could be, but it was fast.

Now try the next option, ALTER INDEX REBUILD:

```
alter index all on people rebuild
```

After running this command, the indexes look like this:

```
index_id     index_level avg_fragmentation_in_percent
-----------  ----------- ----------------------------
1            0           0
1            1           11.7647058823529
1            2           0
6            0           0
6            1           0
6            2           0
7            0           0
7            1           0
7            2           0
8            0           0
8            1           12.5
8            2           0
9            0           0
9            1           0
9            2           0
10           0           0
10           1           0
10           2           0
```

It's pretty easy to see the large improvement in this over the results from REORGANIZE.

Finally, do the big one, and drop and recreate the indexes. After doing this, the indexes look like the following:

```
index_id     index_level avg_fragmentation_in_percent
-----------  ----------- ----------------------------
1            0           0
1            1           0
1            2           0
6            0           0
6            1           0
6            2           0
7            0           0
7            1           0
7            2           0
```

8	0	0
8	1	12.5
8	2	0
9	0	0
9	1	0
9	2	0
10	0	0
10	1	0
10	2	0

That's a quick look at index maintenance. What we haven't done is monitor the impact that the fragmentation might have had on queries, nor have we looked at many of the other options for index creation.

Database Tuning Advisor

It used to be that the DBA had to spend a lot of time reviewing the database design, learning about data distribution, finding and examining in detail the main queries, and then manually tuning indexes to try to find the best set of indexes to suit individual queries. With DTA this slow and laborious process is now no longer needed. You can use DTA to tune individual queries as they are being developed, and to tune whole workloads as they become available.

DTA does this either by analyzing individual queries from SQL Management Studio, or with a SQL Server Profiler Trace file. The workload should contain at least one example of each query called, but it doesn't need to contain repeated calls to the same procedure as you would expect to see in a trace from a production system. This is because DTA will only tune each unique query; it isn't going to look at the interaction of all the queries in the result set and provide a balanced set of indexes to suit a mix of INSERT, UPDATE, and DELETE statements. It will simply look at each query and provide recommendations to improve that query, so the DBA still has some work to do in deciding which indexes to implement to get the best compromise between insert, update, and delete performance.

Now we'll jump straight into using DTA to create some indexes for us.

Using DTA to Tune Individual Queries

Imagine a scenario in which a developer DBA is writing queries for a new database that has no queries and wants to create an initial set of indexes. You have to have a database with data in it, and that data has to be representative of the final data distribution. In the sample workload, you'll examine the index recommendations with three levels of data in the target tables. Here are the numbers of rows in each table where you'll run DTA for the insertpeople query.

	Insert	Update 1
People	0	1,000,000
BoysNames	100	100
GirlsNames	100	100
LastNames	2,000	2,000

Before starting to run DTA, you need to figure out how to determine the effectiveness of each of the DTA recommendations. DTA will give you its expectation of performance improvement, but you should check its effectiveness for yourself, so you need some way to measure before and after performance.

We've chosen to use three metrics for this. The first is the insert time for each row. To get this you can use a simple stored procedure that calls the `insert` stored procedure multiple times and reports how many rows it inserted and the insert rate at pre-determined intervals. The second metric is the output of the `statistics IO`. You can gather this data using SQL Server management Studio, by turning on the Query option for `Statistics IO`. The third metric is Statistics Time.

Before you start tuning, capture your starting metrics; and to ensure that you get consistent results, you also need to capture a cold time and several warm times, and then average the warm times.

One other thing you'll look at in this example is the wait time during query execution. You can only do this if you run the procedure in a tight loop, as unless the query is very slow running, you won't be able to capture the instantaneous results you need to see any waits; but by running in a tight loop, you can sample the wait stats repeatedly and stand a good chance of seeing what the query is waiting on.

The examples shown in the figures in this chapter were run on an Intel Centrino 1.73GHz laptop with 2GB of RAM, and a single 110GB disk that's been partitioned into 55GB as C: and 55GB as D:. For comparison of the results, we also repeated the tests on a desktop machine with dual 3GHz Intel processors with HT enabled. This machine has 4GB of RAM, a 40GB disk running the OS, and four 160GB SATA disks configured as a RAID 0 array (striped with a 128KB stripe size) connected to a four-port SATA controller on the PCI bus. The PCI bus here limits the disk throughput to around 100 MB/Sec for large sequential I/O.

Start off by capturing stats for the `insertpeople` stored procedure with an empty `people` table. To ensure that the server is in a cold state, use the following commands before each cold run to flush memory to disk, and make sure you get a full stored procedure compile cycle on the first run. This is much faster than restarting SQL Server every time, and gives good repeatable results:

```
dbcc dropcleanbuffers
dbcc freeproccache
```

Now run the stored procedure and see how fast it goes by using this script:

```
use People
go

truncate table people
go

dbcc dropcleanbuffers
dbcc freeproccache
go

set statistics time on
set statistics io on
go

-- Cold run
exec insertPeople
```

```
go

-- first warm run
exec insertPeople
go

-- second warm run
exec insertPeople
go

-- third warm run
exec insertPeople
go

set statistics time off
set statistics io off
go

-- we ran the SP to insert 2 people 4 times, so we should have 8 people in the DB
select count (*) from people
go
```

Following are the results of executing the procedure several times:

```
Cold Run

SQL Server parse and compile time:
   CPU time = 0 ms, elapsed time = 89 ms.

SQL Server Execution Times:
   CPU time = 0 ms,  elapsed time = 1 ms.
Table 'BoysNames'. Scan count 1, logical reads 1, physical reads 1, read-ahead
reads 0, lob logical reads 0, lob physical reads 0, lob read-ahead reads 0.

SQL Server Execution Times:
   CPU time = 0 ms,  elapsed time = 1 ms.
Table 'GirlsNames'. Scan count 1, logical reads 1, physical reads 1, read-ahead
reads 0, lob logical reads 0, lob physical reads 0, lob read-ahead reads 0.

SQL Server Execution Times:
   CPU time = 0 ms,  elapsed time = 1 ms.
Table 'lastNames'. Scan count 1, logical reads 8, physical reads 8, read-ahead
reads 0, lob logical reads 0, lob physical reads 0, lob read-ahead reads 0.

SQL Server Execution Times:
   CPU time = 0 ms,  elapsed time = 5 ms.

SQL Server Execution Times:
   CPU time = 0 ms,  elapsed time = 1 ms.
Table 'BoysNames'. Scan count 1, logical reads 1, physical reads 0, read-ahead
reads 0, lob logical reads 0, lob physical reads 0, lob read-ahead reads 0.

SQL Server Execution Times:
   CPU time = 0 ms,  elapsed time = 1 ms.
```

```
Table 'GirlsNames'. Scan count 1, logical reads 1, physical reads 0, read-ahead
reads 0, lob logical reads 0, lob physical reads 0, lob read-ahead reads 0.

SQL Server Execution Times:
   CPU time = 0 ms,  elapsed time = 1 ms.
Table 'lastNames'. Scan count 1, logical reads 8, physical reads 0, read-ahead
reads 0, lob logical reads 0, lob physical reads 0, lob read-ahead reads 0.

SQL Server Execution Times:
   CPU time = 0 ms,  elapsed time = 29 ms.

SQL Server Execution Times:
   CPU time = 0 ms,  elapsed time = 2 ms.
SQL Server Execution Times:
   CPU time = 0 ms,  elapsed time = 1 ms.
Table 'people'. Scan count 0, logical reads 1, physical reads 0, read-ahead reads
0, lob logical reads 0, lob physical reads 0, lob read-ahead reads 0.

SQL Server Execution Times:
   CPU time = 0 ms,  elapsed time = 91 ms.
Table 'people'. Scan count 0, logical reads 1, physical reads 0, read-ahead reads
0, lob logical reads 0, lob physical reads 0, lob read-ahead reads 0.

SQL Server Execution Times:
   CPU time = 0 ms,  elapsed time = 217 ms.

-- Warm Run times

SQL Server parse and compile time:
   CPU time = 0 ms, elapsed time = 1 ms.

SQL Server Execution Times:
   CPU time = 0 ms,  elapsed time = 1 ms.
Table 'BoysNames'. Scan count 1, logical reads 1, physical reads 0, read-ahead
reads 0, lob logical reads 0, lob physical reads 0, lob read-ahead reads 0.

SQL Server Execution Times:
   CPU time = 0 ms,  elapsed time = 1 ms.
Table 'GirlsNames'. Scan count 1, logical reads 1, physical reads 0, read-ahead
reads 0, lob logical reads 0, lob physical reads 0, lob read-ahead reads 0.

SQL Server Execution Times:
   CPU time = 0 ms,  elapsed time = 1 ms.
Table 'lastNames'. Scan count 1, logical reads 8, physical reads 0, read-ahead
reads 0, lob logical reads 0, lob physical reads 0, lob read-ahead reads 0.

SQL Server Execution Times:
   CPU time = 16 ms,  elapsed time = 1 ms.

SQL Server Execution Times:
   CPU time = 0 ms,  elapsed time = 1 ms.
Table 'BoysNames'. Scan count 1, logical reads 1, physical reads 0, read-ahead
reads 0, lob logical reads 0, lob physical reads 0, lob read-ahead reads 0.
```

```
SQL Server Execution Times:
    CPU time = 0 ms,   elapsed time = 1 ms.
Table 'GirlsNames'. Scan count 1, logical reads 1, physical reads 0, read-ahead
reads 0, lob logical reads 0, lob physical reads 0, lob read-ahead reads 0.

SQL Server Execution Times:
    CPU time = 0 ms,   elapsed time = 1 ms.
Table 'lastNames'. Scan count 1, logical reads 8, physical reads 0, read-ahead
reads 0, lob logical reads 0, lob physical reads 0, lob read-ahead reads 0.

SQL Server Execution Times:
    CPU time = 0 ms,   elapsed time = 31 ms.

SQL Server Execution Times:
    CPU time = 0 ms,   elapsed time = 1 ms.
Table 'people'. Scan count 0, logical reads 1, physical reads 0, read-ahead reads
0, lob logical reads 0, lob physical reads 0, lob read-ahead reads 0.

SQL Server Execution Times:
    CPU time = 0 ms,   elapsed time = 1 ms.
Table 'people'. Scan count 0, logical reads 1, physical reads 0, read-ahead reads
0, lob logical reads 0, lob physical reads 0, lob read-ahead reads 0.

SQL Server Execution Times:
    CPU time = 0 ms,   elapsed time = 2 ms.

SQL Server Execution Times:
    CPU time = 16 ms,   elapsed time = 36 ms.
```

This is some very useful information in this output. Looking at both the cold and warm run outputs, you can see that they are both pretty fast, with a cold run elapsed time of 217 mS and a warm run elapsed time of 36 mS.

Looking at the cold run stats and focusing on the number of physical reads, you can see that there were a total of ten physical reads: one to read the Boysnames table, one to read the Girlsnames table, and eight to read the lastnames table into memory.

The warm run stats show that there were no physical reads, only logical reads. The parse and compile time was also greatly reduced. This tells us that the query didn't need recompiling, which is good because it will save a lot of time each time it's called. The warm run stats also show that it's taking about 30 to 40 mS for each insert.

Given that we are only issuing 10 reads to execute the query, and that repeated calls don't invoke additional physical reads, it's going to be hard to improve performance by further reducing these already low numbers. It's also going to be hard to see any small time-based improvements when the time taken is already so short, at just 30-40 milliseconds.

To make it easier to observe small changes in performance, we are going to need to execute the queries hundreds or thousands of times, and then look at the overall stats for a very large number of executions. This will help highlight any small changes.

To do this, you need to put the script into a loop and run it thousands of times to determine whether that gives a better measurement. Use the following command-line statement:

```
sqlcmd -StracysLaptop -E -d people -Q"exec makepeople 10000, 500"
```

These are the results of the makePeople stored procedure:

```
Inserted 1000 people in 670mS at a rate of 1492.54 per Second
Inserted 1000 people in 720mS at a rate of 1388.89 per Second
Inserted 1000 people in 656mS at a rate of 1524.39 per Second
Inserted 1000 people in 686mS at a rate of 1457.73 per Second
Inserted 1000 people in 720mS at a rate of 1388.89 per Second
```

The inserts are going fast enough that you are getting between 1,400 and 1,500 inserts per second.

Now you should see what you are waiting on. To do that, modify the sqlcmd line as follows so it would run for considerably longer. Then you can query the sys.processes table to see what the wait types are for your query. Here is the modified cmd line:

```
sqlcmd -StracysLaptop -E -d people -Q"exec makepeople 10000, 500"
```

This is the query that will enable you to monitor what you are waiting on:

```
set nocount on
while 1 > 0
begin
   select spid, kpid, blocked, waittime, lastwaittype, waitresource
   from master..sysprocesses
   where program_name = 'SQLCMD'
   waitfor delay '00:00:00.05'
end
```

These are the results of the query (cleaned up to save space):

spid	kpid	blocked	waittime	lastwaittype
55	3336	0	0	WRITELOG
55	3336	0	0	WRITELOG
55	3336	0	0	WRITELOG
55	3336	0	0	WRITELOG

Not surprisingly, on such a simple insert on a very basic slow disk, most of the time is spent waiting on the log write. What the information here has told you is that most of the stats are meaningless except for the raw write rate that results from the makePeople stored procedure.

One final check before going onto DTA is to take a look at the output of showplan_text to see what the query plan looks like. You can then compare this with the query plan after applying any recommendations from DTA and see how it changes.

The output is too verbose to include here, but you can get it from this book's Web site at www.wrox.com. The key elements of interest are shown here:

```
|--Table Scan(OBJECT:([People].[dbo].[BoysNames]))
|--Table Scan(OBJECT:([People].[dbo].[GirlsNames]))
|--Table Scan(OBJECT:([People].[dbo].[lastNames]))
```

This shows that you are using a table scan to get the names from the lookup tables. In most cases this works just fine because the tables are so small (boysNames and girlsNames), but this isn't so optimal on lastNames, where the table has 2,000 rows and occupies seven or eight database pages.

Now see what DTA recommends for you. Running DTA against the sample query is simple. Open the script run insertpeople.sql in a new query window. Right-click the window and select Analyze Query in Database Engine Tuning Advisor, as shown in Figure 15-1.

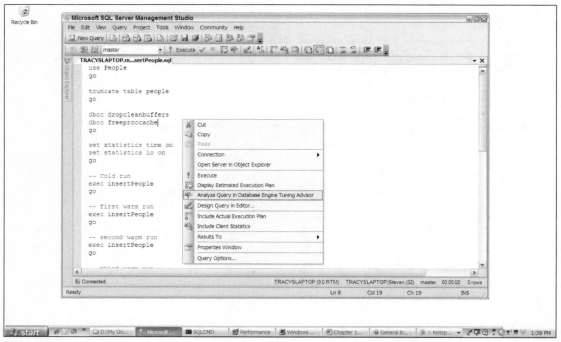

Figure 15-1

This brings up the Database Engine Tuning Advisor, shown in Figure 15-2.

There are two things you need to change before you click the Start Analysis button. First, change the database for workload analysis from master to people. Second, select which database you want to tune by selecting the people database. Now you are ready to start the analysis session by clicking the Start Analysis button. When you start the analysis session, DTA adds a new Progress tab and updates its analysis progress, as shown in Figure 15-3.

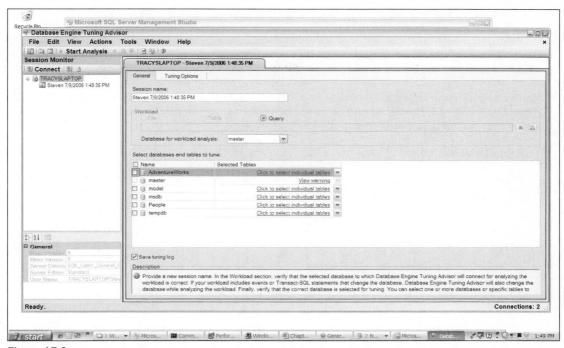

Figure 15-2

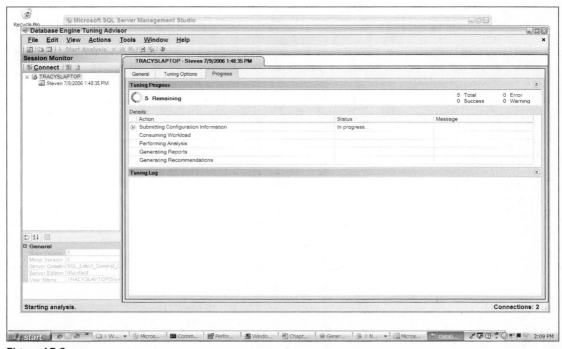

Figure 15-3

When the analysis is complete, DTA adds two more tabs: Recommendations and Reports.

For the insert query, DTA has recommended that you create a clustered index on the lastNames table. This will reduce the number of reads in the lastNmes table from 8 to 1 or 2 on each query. Percentage-wise, this is quite a large reduction.

Now you should implement the recommendation and check the performance difference. Start by looking at the stats time and I/O after adding the clustered index on LastNames. The following is abbreviated stats output, showing just the key areas that have changed:

```
-- COLD Run

Table 'lastNames'. Scan count 1, logical reads 9, physical reads 1, read-ahead
reads 7, lob logical reads 0, lob physical reads 0, lob read-ahead reads 0.


Table 'lastNames'. Scan count 0, logical reads 2, physical reads 0, read-ahead
reads 0, lob logical reads 0, lob physical reads 0, lob read-ahead reads 0.


SQL Server Execution Times:
   CPU time = 15 ms,   elapsed time = 590 ms.

-- Warm Run

Table 'lastNames'. Scan count 1, logical reads 9, physical reads 0, read-ahead
reads 0, lob logical reads 0, lob physical reads 0, lob read-ahead reads 0.

Table 'lastNames'. Scan count 0, logical reads 2, physical reads 0, read-ahead
reads 0, lob logical reads 0, lob physical reads 0, lob read-ahead reads 0.


SQL Server Execution Times:
   CPU time = 0 ms,   elapsed time = 4 ms.
```

There are two differences between these stats and the earlier pre-indexed stats. Now that you are using the clustered index on lastNames, the number of logical reads is reduced dramatically, from eight down to two. In addition, when the table is first read on the cold run, now it is being read in using a read ahead, which brings the whole table into memory much more quickly than if you use a regular table scan as you did before indexing.

Now take a look at the showplan_text output and confirm what you are observing in the I/O stats. Here is the relevant section from the plan output:

```
|--Clustered Index Scan(OBJECT:([People].[dbo].[lastNames].[cix_LastNames_ID]))
```

This shows that you are in fact using the newly added clustered index. Now see how much this affects the execution of the query (remember that before you were able to achieve 1,300–1,400 inserts per second):

```
Inserted 1000 people in 530mS at a rate of 1886.79 per Second
Inserted 1000 people in 606mS at a rate of 1650.17 per Second
Inserted 1000 people in 610mS at a rate of 1639.34 per Second
Inserted 1000 people in 533mS at a rate of 1876.17 per Second
```

This shows that the rate of insertion has increased to 1,600–1,900 per second. That's quite an improvement for adding a clustered index.

One final thing to check: What are you waiting on?

spid	kpid	blocked	waittime	lastwaittype
54	5804	0	0	WRITELOG
54	5804	0	0	WRITELOG
54	5804	0	0	WRITELOG
54	5804	0	0	WRITELOG

No surprises there: It's still the log that's limiting insert performance.

Indexes for Updates

Next you want to tune the update query. Start that by capturing some metrics around the query's performance. Before you do that, fill the table up a bit by writing a million rows to the `people` table. You need that many in order to get a full set of results for the `marriage` query, which pulls out the top 1,000 rows for a given date range.

Truncate the `people` table, run `makepeople` to fill it with 1,000,000 rows, truncate the `lastnames` table, and then fill it with 2,000 rows. After that, you can start capturing metrics around the raw query performance again. Here are the results of the cold run and three warm runs, edited to remove the many extra rows, and with some additional formatting for clarity:

```
Table '#boys'.
Scan count 0, logical reads 1003, physical reads 0, read-ahead reads 0, lob logical
reads 0, lob physical reads 0, lob read-ahead reads 0.

Table 'people'.
Scan count 1, logical reads 1824, physical reads 0, read-ahead reads 1904, lob
logical reads 0, lob physical reads 0, lob read-ahead reads 0.

SQL Server Execution Times:
   CPU time = 63 ms,  elapsed time = 1197 ms.

(1000 row(s) affected)
Table '#girls'.
Scan count 0, logical reads 1003, physical reads 0, read-ahead reads 0, lob logical
reads 0, lob physical reads 0, lob read-ahead reads 0.

Table 'people'.
Scan count 1, logical reads 1897, physical reads 0, read-ahead reads 64, lob
logical reads 0, lob physical reads 0, lob read-ahead reads 0.

SQL Server Execution Times:
   CPU time = 46 ms,  elapsed time = 866 ms.

(1000 row(s) affected)

SQL Server Execution Times:
   CPU time = 0 ms,  elapsed time = 1 ms.
Table '#boys'.
```

```
Scan count 1, logical reads 4, physical reads 0, read-ahead reads 0, lob logical
reads 0, lob physical reads 0, lob read-ahead reads 0.

SQL Server Execution Times:
   CPU time = 0 ms,  elapsed time = 1 ms.
Table '#girls'. Scan count 1, logical reads 4, physical reads 0, read-ahead reads
0, lob logical reads 0, lob physical reads 0, lob read-ahead reads 0.

SQL Server Execution Times:
   CPU time = 0 ms,  elapsed time = 1 ms.

Table 'people'.
Scan count 2, logical reads 32281, physical reads 0, read-ahead reads 14172, lob
logical reads 0, lob physical reads 0, lob read-ahead reads 0.

Table 'Worktable'.
Scan count 1, logical reads 5, physical reads 0, read-ahead reads 0, lob logical
reads 0, lob physical reads 0, lob read-ahead reads 0.

SQL Server Execution Times:
   CPU time = 813 ms,  elapsed time = 8350 ms.

(1 row(s) affected)

SQL Server Execution Times:
   CPU time = 0 ms,  elapsed time = 1 ms.

SQL Server Execution Times:
   CPU time = 0 ms,  elapsed time = 1 ms.

SQL Server Execution Times:
   CPU time = 922 ms,  elapsed time = 10464 ms.
```

This shows that the cold run took almost 10 seconds to complete.

The warm run looks like this:

```
SQL Server parse and compile time:
   CPU time = 0 ms, elapsed time = 1 ms.
SQL Server parse and compile time:
   CPU time = 0 ms, elapsed time = 1 ms.

Table '#boys'.
Scan count 0, logical reads 1003, physical reads 0, read-ahead reads 0, lob logical
reads 0, lob physical reads 0, lob read-ahead reads 0.

Table 'people'.
Scan count 1, logical reads 1895, physical reads 0, read-ahead reads 0, lob logical
reads 0, lob physical reads 0, lob read-ahead reads 0.

SQL Server Execution Times:
   CPU time = 47 ms,  elapsed time = 216 ms.
```

```
(1000 row(s) affected)
Table '#girls'.
Scan count 0, logical reads 1003, physical reads 0, read-ahead reads 0, lob logical
reads 0, lob physical reads 0, lob read-ahead reads 0.

Table 'people'.
Scan count 1, logical reads 1765, physical reads 0, read-ahead reads 0, lob logical
reads 0, lob physical reads 0, lob read-ahead reads 0.

SQL Server Execution Times:
   CPU time = 47 ms,  elapsed time = 46 ms.

(1000 row(s) affected)

SQL Server Execution Times:
   CPU time = 0 ms,  elapsed time = 1 ms.
Table '#boys'.
Scan count 1, logical reads 4, physical reads 0, read-ahead reads 0, lob logical
reads 0, lob physical reads 0, lob read-ahead reads 0.

SQL Server Execution Times:
   CPU time = 0 ms,  elapsed time = 3 ms.
Table '#girls'.
Scan count 1, logical reads 4, physical reads 0, read-ahead reads 0, lob logical
reads 0, lob physical reads 0, lob read-ahead reads 0.

SQL Server Execution Times:
   CPU time = 0 ms,  elapsed time = 1 ms.
Table 'people'.
Scan count 2, logical reads 32281, physical reads 0, read-ahead reads 0, lob
logical reads 0, lob physical reads 0, lob read-ahead reads 0.

Table 'Worktable'.
Scan count 1, logical reads 4, physical reads 0, read-ahead reads 0, lob logical
reads 0, lob physical reads 0, lob read-ahead reads 0.

SQL Server Execution Times:
   CPU time = 703 ms,  elapsed time = 713 ms.

(1 row(s) affected)

SQL Server Execution Times:
   CPU time = 15 ms,  elapsed time = 1 ms.

SQL Server Execution Times:
   CPU time = 812 ms,  elapsed time = 980 ms.
```

There was a significant improvement between the cold and warm run, down to the reduction in compilation time and the faster access, as the tables are now mostly loaded into memory. This is shown in the reduction in read ahead reads between the cold and warm runs.

This procedure is taking between 10 seconds for a cold run and 1 second for a warm run, so it should be much easier to see any improvement that the DTA can make. However, we'll still run it in a loop and see what the average update rate is over a longer period of executions.

This is the command to run:

```
sqlcmd -E -d people -Q"exec domarriages 100, 10"
```

These are the results :

```
Married 20 people in 15326mS at a rate of 1.30497 per Second
Married 20 people in 18610mS at a rate of 1.07469 per Second
Married 20 people in 15470mS at a rate of 1.29282 per Second
Married 20 people in 14610mS at a rate of 1.36893 per Second
Married 20 people in 14890mS at a rate of 1.34318 per Second
Married 20 people in 17076mS at a rate of 1.17123 per Second
```

The results show that the query is taking between 1 and 1.36 seconds to execute, so it should be relatively easy to see any performance improvement.

Before going on to run DTA, let's take a quick look at the wait types. Run the command again and run the monitoring code and capture the `waittypes` from `sysprocesses`. The output should look something like this:

spid	kpid	blocked	waittime	lastwaittype
52	4212	0	546	LOGMGR_RESERVE_APPEND
52	4212	0	0	SOS_SCHEDULER_YIELD

There was a pretty even split between these two wait types. SQL Server Books Online (SQL BOL) explains what each of the wait types means. Look these up either by searching on the wait type or by searching for `sys.dm_os_wait_stats`. The `LOGMGR_RESERVE_APPEND` occurs when you are waiting to see if truncating the log will give you enough space to write the current log record. In this case, the database was configured with the simple recovery model, and the log file is on a very slow disk, so you should expect to see a lot of log-related waits.

`SOS_SCHEDULER_YIELD` occurs when a task voluntarily yields the scheduler and has to wait for a new quantum. These are quite different from the wait types in the insert query, which is expected because the update has a very different characteristic than the insert.

Now see what DTA has to say about this workload. This time we'll show you how to run DTA against a workload. The next step here is to set up SQL Server Profiler to capture a trace file, which is covered in Chapter 13. The key things you need to remember when setting up SQL Serve profiler for this trace are twofold: use the tuning template, and ensure that the files are set to roll over, although the overall file size will be trivial.

Once Profiler is set up and the trace is running, execute the `marriage` stored procedure once, and then stop the trace, which saves the file. Now you have a workload trace file on disk, and you can start up DTA and use it to tune the workload. Launch DTA and connect to your SQL Server. If you have been following through the earlier sections, you will see the earlier trace sessions in the left pane of DTA, as shown in Figure 15-4.

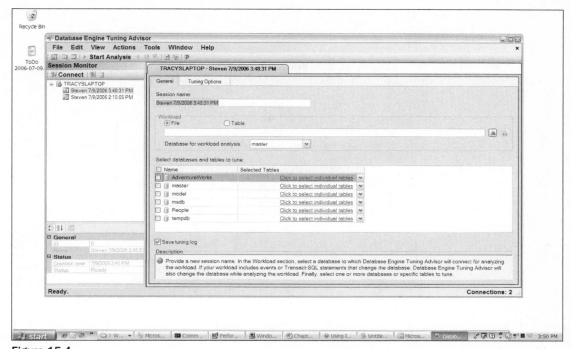

Figure 15-4

This is another part of DTA that is worth briefly mentioning. Each of your tuning sessions is saved, so you can go back and review what you asked DTA to tune, and the recommendations DTA came up with. However if you just use the default session names, as we have been doing, then the tuning session names don't really have a lot of meaning, and pretty soon it's difficult to know what each session was for. Therefore, we suggest that you come up with a naming scheme that makes sense to you. This will help you find the session you're looking for in the future.

After setting the database to be `People` in both the drop-down selection and the list of databases to tune, you need to tell DTA that you want to tune a file, and where the file is. Either type in the filename and full path, or use the Browse button to select the trace file you just created, as shown in Figure 15-5.

Now we can start the Analysis session again and see what results DTA has for us this time. You can see those results in Figure 15-6.

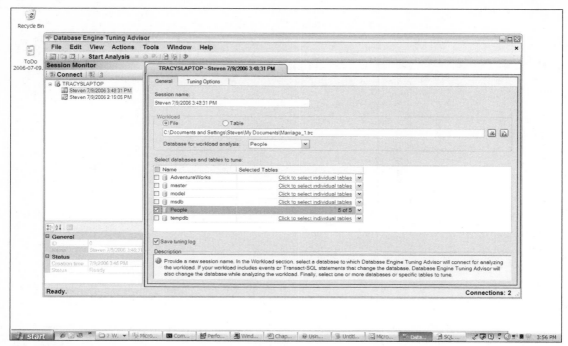

Figure 15-5

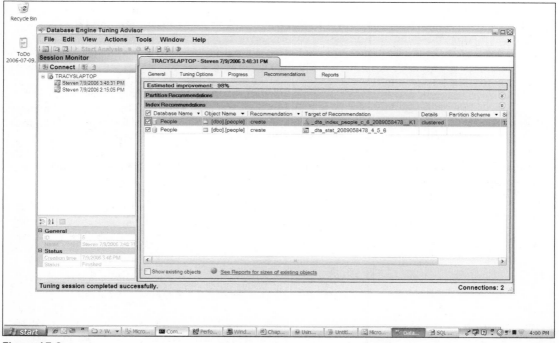

Figure 15-6

This time DTA has two recommendations, and reckons it can improve things by 98 percent. Take a closer look at what you can do with these recommendations. To do this, just scroll the recommendations window way over to the right to find the `Definition` column, If you hover over this a ToolTip pops up, telling you to click on the link to get a T-SQL script of the recommendations. Doing so will reveal a script like the one shown in Figure 15-7.

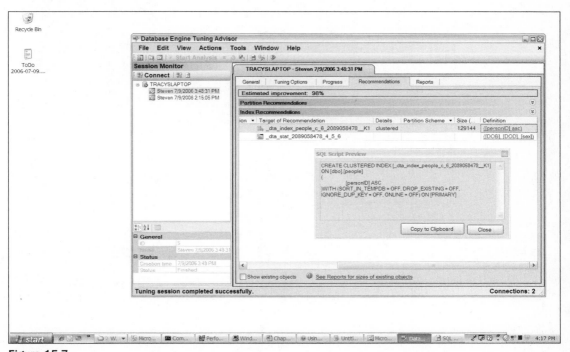

Figure 15-7

You can now copy this script either to the clipboard and from there into a file, or directly into SQL Server Management Studio to be executed. Alternately, after taking a look at the recommendations, you can have DTA run them for you by selecting Apply Recommendations from the Actions menu.

Before doing that, take a look at some of the other information in the Reports tab. This area of DTA holds a lot of useful information about what DTA did and why. In the simple case we have been working with here, most of the interesting information is on the Statement cost reports. Start with the first report in the list, shown in Figure 15-8.

This shows the various statements in the workload, and the estimated improvement that DTA expects to gain from the recommendation. In this case, all of the improvement comes from the `update` statement, which the Tuning report believes will be improved by 99.90 percent.

To apply the changes, simply let DTA make them. When you select Apply Recommendations, DTA asks whether you want to run the script now or schedule it for some time in the future. Choose to make the changes right away so you can see the immediate impact. While it's executing, DTA shows the status of the changes, as shown in Figure 15-9.

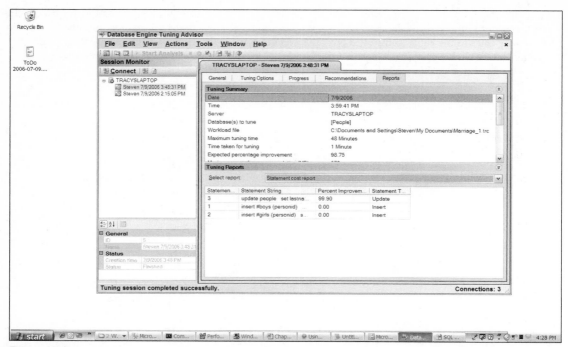

Figure 15-8

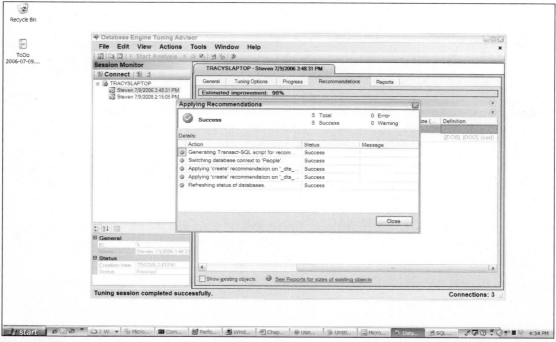

Figure 15-9

Now that it's done, go back and see how fast your queries are running. Start with the output of stats I/O and stats time. Running the same script again now gives you the following results.

This is the cold run:

```
SQL Server parse and compile time:
   CPU time = 0 ms, elapsed time = 1 ms.
SQL Server parse and compile time:
   CPU time = 0 ms, elapsed time = 63 ms.

Table '#boys'.
Scan count 0, logical reads 1003, physical reads 0, read-ahead reads 0, lob logical
reads 0, lob physical reads 0, lob read-ahead reads 0.

Table 'people'.
Scan count 1, logical reads 1759, physical reads 3, read-ahead reads 1974, lob
logical reads 0, lob physical reads 0, lob read-ahead reads 0.

SQL Server Execution Times:
   CPU time = 32 ms,  elapsed time = 851 ms.

(1000 row(s) affected)
Table '#girls'.
Scan count 0, logical reads 1003, physical reads 0, read-ahead reads 0, lob logical
reads 0, lob physical reads 0, lob read-ahead reads 0.

Table 'people'.
Scan count 1, logical reads 1794, physical reads 0, read-ahead reads 0, lob logical
reads 0, lob physical reads 0, lob read-ahead reads 0.

SQL Server Execution Times:
   CPU time = 46 ms,  elapsed time = 49 ms.

(1000 row(s) affected)

SQL Server Execution Times:
   CPU time = 0 ms,  elapsed time = 1 ms.
Table '#boys'.
Scan count 1, logical reads 4, physical reads 0, read-ahead reads 0, lob logical
reads 0, lob physical reads 0, lob read-ahead reads 0.

SQL Server Execution Times:
   CPU time = 0 ms,  elapsed time = 1 ms.
Table '#girls'.
Scan count 1, logical reads 4, physical reads 0, read-ahead reads 0, lob logical
reads 0, lob physical reads 0, lob read-ahead reads 0.

SQL Server Execution Times:
   CPU time = 0 ms,  elapsed time = 1 ms.
Table 'people'.
Scan count 2, logical reads 9, physical reads 0, read-ahead reads 0, lob logical
reads 0, lob physical reads 0, lob read-ahead reads 0.

Table 'Worktable'.
```

```
Scan count 1, logical reads 5, physical reads 0, read-ahead reads 0, lob logical
reads 0, lob physical reads 0, lob read-ahead reads 0.

SQL Server Execution Times:
   CPU time = 94 ms,  elapsed time = 1012 ms.
```

This is the result for the warm run:

```
SQL Server parse and compile time:
   CPU time = 0 ms, elapsed time = 1 ms.
SQL Server parse and compile time:
   CPU time = 0 ms, elapsed time = 1 ms.

Table '#boys'.
Scan count 0, logical reads 1003, physical reads 0, read-ahead reads 0, lob logical
reads 0, lob physical reads 0, lob read-ahead reads 0.

Table 'people'.
Scan count 1, logical reads 1793, physical reads 0, read-ahead reads 0, lob logical
reads 0, lob physical reads 0, lob read-ahead reads 0.

SQL Server Execution Times:
   CPU time = 32 ms,  elapsed time = 44 ms.

(1000 row(s) affected)
Table '#girls'.
Scan count 0, logical reads 1003, physical reads 0, read-ahead reads 0, lob logical
reads 0, lob physical reads 0, lob read-ahead reads 0.

Table 'people'.
Scan count 1, logical reads 1736, physical reads 0, read-ahead reads 0, lob logical
reads 0, lob physical reads 0, lob read-ahead reads 0.

SQL Server Execution Times:
   CPU time = 46 ms,  elapsed time = 447 ms.

(1000 row(s) affected)

SQL Server Execution Times:
   CPU time = 0 ms,  elapsed time = 1 ms.
Table '#boys'.
Scan count 1, logical reads 4, physical reads 0, read-ahead reads 0, lob logical
reads 0, lob physical reads 0, lob read-ahead reads 0.

SQL Server Execution Times:
   CPU time = 0 ms,  elapsed time = 1 ms.
Table '#girls'.
Scan count 1, logical reads 4, physical reads 0, read-ahead reads 0, lob logical
reads 0, lob physical reads 0, lob read-ahead reads 0.

SQL Server Execution Times:
   CPU time = 0 ms,  elapsed time = 1 ms.
```

```
Table 'people'.
Scan count 2, logical reads 9, physical reads 0, read-ahead reads 0, lob logical
reads 0, lob physical reads 0, lob read-ahead reads 0.

Table 'Worktable'.
Scan count 1, logical reads 4, physical reads 0, read-ahead reads 0, lob logical
reads 0, lob physical reads 0, lob read-ahead reads 0.

   CPU time = 78 ms,  elapsed time = 494 ms.
```

That has reduced the CPU time for the warm run from 812 mS to 78 mS, although the elapsed time only came down from around 1 sec to 500 mS. Now see how fast it runs in a tight loop:

```
Married 20 people in 9860mS at a rate of 2.0284 per Second
Married 20 people in 8890mS at a rate of 2.24972 per Second
Married 20 people in 9110mS at a rate of 2.19539 per Second
Married 20 people in 6936mS at a rate of 2.88351 per Second
Married 20 people in 5280mS at a rate of 3.78788 per Second
Married 20 people in 5376mS at a rate of 3.72024 per Second
```

That's pretty remarkable; you have gone from just over 1 update per second to 2–4 inserts per second.

Now check the waits again:

```
spid   kpid   blocked waittime           lastwaittype
58     4688   0       859                LOGMGR_RESERVE_APPEND
```

This time the waits are predominantly this one wait type.

Finally, take a quick look at the `showplan_text` output to see how the DTA recommendations are changing the query plan.

This is the showplan output for the update before applying the DTA recommendations:

```
       |--Table Update(OBJECT:([People].[dbo].[people]),
SET:([People].[dbo].[people].[lastName] = RaiseIfNull([Expr1016])))
            |--Table Spool
                |--Compute Scalar(DEFINE:([Expr1016]=[Expr1016]))
                    |--Nested Loops(Left Outer Join)
                        |--Top(ROWCOUNT est 0)
                        |    |--Table Scan(OBJECT:([People].[dbo].[people]),
WHERE:([People].[dbo].[people].[personID]=[@girlID]) ORDERED)
                        |--Assert(WHERE:(CASE WHEN [Expr1015]>(1) THEN (0) ELSE
NULL END))
                            |--Stream Aggregate(DEFINE:([Expr1015]=Count(*),
[Expr1016]=ANY([People].[dbo].[people].[lastName])))
                                |--Table
Scan(OBJECT:([People].[dbo].[people]),
WHERE:([People].[dbo].[people].[personID]=[@BoyID]))
```

You can clearly see that you are using a table scan to apply the update to `People`.

This is the showplan output after applying the DTA recommendations:

```
        |--Clustered Index
Update(OBJECT:([People].[dbo].[people].[_dta_index_people_c_6_2089058478__K1]),
SET:([People].[dbo].[people].[lastName] = RaiseIfNull([Expr1016])))
            |--Table Spool
                |--Compute Scalar(DEFINE:([Expr1016]=[Expr1016]))
                    |--Nested Loops(Left Outer Join)
                        |--Top(ROWCOUNT est 0)
                        |    |--Clustered Index
Seek(OBJECT:([People].[dbo].[people].[_dta_index_people_c_6_2089058478__K1]),
SEEK:([People].[dbo].[people].[personID]=[@girlID]) ORDERED FORWARD)
                            |--Assert(WHERE:(CASE WHEN [Expr1015]>(1) THEN (0) ELSE
NULL END))
                                |--Stream Aggregate(DEFINE:([Expr1015]=Count(*),
[Expr1016]=ANY([People].[dbo].[people].[lastName])))
                                    |--Clustered Index
Seek(OBJECT:([People].[dbo].[people].[_dta_index_people_c_6_2089058478__K1]),
SEEK:([People].[dbo].[people].[personID]=[@BoyID]) ORDERED FORWARD)
```

This starts with the clustered index tag, showing that you are now using the newly created clustered index to apply the update, and this is what's providing the big benefit.

Reassessing Inserts after Adding Update Indexes

Now go back and measure the impact the update indexes have had on the insert procedure. You haven't done anything else to the insert procedure, but the update procedure added a clustered index to People, so now the insert procedure will have to contend with the additional overhead of index maintenance, inserting new records, and splitting index pages. It's going to be interesting to see how much slower this makes the inserts, and how it changes what you are waiting on.

Start by looking at the stats time and I/O output:

```
-- COLD RUN
SQL Server parse and compile time:
   CPU time = 0 ms, elapsed time = 51 ms.

SQL Server Execution Times:
   CPU time = 0 ms,  elapsed time = 1 ms.
Table 'BoysNames'. Scan count 1, logical reads 1, physical reads 1, read-ahead
reads 0,
lob logical reads 0, lob physical reads 0, lob read-ahead reads 0.

SQL Server Execution Times:
   CPU time = 0 ms,  elapsed time = 21 ms.
Table 'GirlsNames'. Scan count 1, logical reads 1, physical reads 1, read-ahead
reads 0,
lob logical reads 0, lob physical reads 0, lob read-ahead reads 0.

SQL Server Execution Times:
   CPU time = 0 ms,  elapsed time = 1 ms.
Table 'lastNames'. Scan count 1, logical reads 9, physical reads 1, read-ahead
reads 7,
```

```
lob logical reads 0, lob physical reads 0, lob read-ahead reads 0.

SQL Server Execution Times:
   CPU time = 0 ms,  elapsed time = 2 ms.

SQL Server Execution Times:
   CPU time = 0 ms,  elapsed time = 1 ms.
Table 'BoysNames'. Scan count 1, logical reads 1, physical reads 0, read-ahead
reads 0,
lob logical reads 0, lob physical reads 0, lob read-ahead reads 0.

SQL Server Execution Times:
   CPU time = 0 ms,  elapsed time = 1 ms.
Table 'GirlsNames'. Scan count 1, logical reads 1, physical reads 0, read-ahead
reads 0,
lob logical reads 0, lob physical reads 0, lob read-ahead reads 0.

SQL Server Execution Times:
   CPU time = 0 ms,  elapsed time = 1 ms.
Table 'lastNames'. Scan count 0, logical reads 2, physical reads 0, read-ahead
reads 0,
lob logical reads 0, lob physical reads 0, lob read-ahead reads 0.

SQL Server Execution Times:
   CPU time = 0 ms,  elapsed time = 29 ms.
SQL Server parse and compile time:
   CPU time = 0 ms, elapsed time = 1 ms.


SQL Server Execution Times:
   CPU time = 0 ms,  elapsed time = 1 ms.
Table 'people'. Scan count 0, logical reads 3, physical reads 1, read-ahead reads
0, lob
logical reads 0, lob physical reads 0, lob read-ahead reads 0.

SQL Server Execution Times:
   CPU time = 0 ms,  elapsed time = 63 ms.
Table 'people'. Scan count 0, logical reads 3, physical reads 0, read-ahead reads
0, lob
logical reads 0, lob physical reads 0, lob read-ahead reads 0.

SQL Server Execution Times:
   CPU time = 0 ms,  elapsed time = 1 ms.

SQL Server Execution Times:
   CPU time = 0 ms,  elapsed time = 168 ms.

-- WARM RUN

SQL Server parse and compile time:
   CPU time = 0 ms, elapsed time = 1 ms.
SQL Server parse and compile time:
   CPU time = 0 ms, elapsed time = 1 ms.
```

```
SQL Server Execution Times:
   CPU time = 0 ms,   elapsed time = 1 ms.
Table 'BoysNames'. Scan count 1, logical reads 1, physical reads 0, read-ahead
reads 0, lob logical reads 0, lob physical reads 0, lob read-ahead reads 0.

SQL Server Execution Times:
   CPU time = 0 ms,  elapsed time = 1 ms.
Table 'GirlsNames'. Scan count 1, logical reads 1, physical reads 0, read-ahead
reads 0, lob logical reads 0, lob physical reads 0, lob read-ahead reads 0.

SQL Server Execution Times:
   CPU time = 0 ms,  elapsed time = 1 ms.
Table 'lastNames'. Scan count 1, logical reads 9, physical reads 0, read-ahead
reads 0, lob logical reads 0, lob physical reads 0, lob read-ahead reads 0.

SQL Server Execution Times:
   CPU time = 0 ms,  elapsed time = 1 ms.

SQL Server Execution Times:
   CPU time = 0 ms,  elapsed time = 1 ms.
Table 'BoysNames'. Scan count 1, logical reads 1, physical reads 0, read-ahead
reads 0, lob logical reads 0, lob physical reads 0, lob read-ahead reads 0.

SQL Server Execution Times:
   CPU time = 0 ms,  elapsed time = 1 ms.
Table 'GirlsNames'. Scan count 1, logical reads 1, physical reads 0, read-ahead
reads 0, lob logical reads 0, lob physical reads 0, lob read-ahead reads 0.

SQL Server Execution Times:
   CPU time = 0 ms,  elapsed time = 1 ms.
Table 'lastNames'. Scan count 0, logical reads 2, physical reads 0, read-ahead
reads 0, lob logical reads 0, lob physical reads 0, lob read-ahead reads 0.


SQL Server Execution Times:
   CPU time = 0 ms,  elapsed time = 1 ms.
Table 'people'. Scan count 0, logical reads 3, physical reads 0, read-ahead reads
0, lob logical reads 0, lob physical reads 0, lob read-ahead reads 0.

SQL Server Execution Times:
   CPU time = 0 ms,  elapsed time = 1 ms.
Table 'people'. Scan count 0, logical reads 3, physical reads 0, read-ahead reads
0, lob logical reads 0, lob physical reads 0, lob read-ahead reads 0.

SQL Server Execution Times:
   CPU time = 0 ms,  elapsed time = 3 ms.

SQL Server Execution Times:
   CPU time = 0 ms,  elapsed time = 33 ms.
```

On the cold run, you increased the number of logical reads from 1 to 3. Physical reads didn't change because the whole database is pretty well cached by now. This change is too small to see on a single run, so you'll need to run the query a few thousand times. Before you do that, take a look at the `showplan_text` output.

The only obvious change here is that you can see that you are now doing an insert into a clustered index table versus the heap you were inserting into before:

```
|--Clustered Index
Insert(OBJECT:([People].[dbo].[people].[_dta_index_people_c_6_2089058478__K1]),
SET:([People].[dbo].[people].[firstName] =
RaiseIfNull([@BoysName]),[People].[dbo].[people].[lastName] =
RaiseIfNull([@lastName]),[People].[dbo].[peop
```

Now see how this has changed the insert rate when you run `makePeople`. This is now reporting the following:

```
Inserted 10000 people in 5250mS at a rate of 1904.76 per Second
Inserted 10000 people in 5296mS at a rate of 1888.22 per Second
Inserted 10000 people in 5233mS at a rate of 1910.95 per Second
Inserted 10000 people in 5300mS at a rate of 1886.79 per Second
Inserted 10000 people in 5233mS at a rate of 1910.95 per Second
```

This shows that you haven't caused any impact on the insert rate, which remains at around 1,800 to 1,900 per second. This is more evidence that the limiting factor for this insert is the speed with which we can write to the log (not surprisingly, on a laptop system this is pretty slow). This can also be the case on a large enterprise server where the amount of log activity could be much higher, but the log files are on a slow disk or poorly configured disk array, which yet again limits ultimate insert performance.

The wait stats for the query show that you are still waiting on the `WriteLog`, so you haven't seen a change to the point where index maintenance started to be the bottleneck.

Too Many Indexes?

One final scenario we are going to look at is how DTA tells you when you have too many indexes. To make this obvious, we'll add a whole stack of other indexes to the four tables in this scenario, run DTA against the `insert` and `update` procedures, and see what it tells you about indexes you aren't using.

Here is the script to create some bad indexes to see what DTA will recommend:

```
-- Create Bad indexes
use people
go

create clustered index cix_boysnames on BoysNames ( ID, Name)
go
create index ix_boysnames_id on BoysNames (id)
go
```

```
create index ix_boysnames_name on BoysNames (name)
go

create clustered index cix_girlsnames on GirlsNames ( ID, Name)
go
create index ix_Girlsnames_id on GirlsNames (id)
go
create index ix_Girlsnames_name on GirlsNames (name)
go

create clustered index cix_LastNames on LastNames ( ID, Name)
go
create index ix_Lastnames_id on LastNames (id)
go
create index ix_Lastnames_name on LastNames (name)
go

create clustered index cix_people on people(firstname)
go
create index ix_people_id on people(personid)
go
create index ix_people_dob on people(dob)
go
create index ix_people_lastname on people(lastname)
go
create index ix_people_dod on people(dod)
go
create index ix_people_sex on people(sex)
go
```

Here are the results of running the query to makePeople:

```
Inserted 1000 people in 1203mS at a rate of 831.255 per Second
Inserted 1000 people in 750mS at a rate of 1333.33 per Second
Inserted 1000 people in 640mS at a rate of 1562.5 per Second
Inserted 1000 people in 673mS at a rate of 1485.88 per Second
Inserted 1000 people in 656mS at a rate of 1524.39 per Second
```

These results show that insert performance has dropped dramatically. The worst batch is at only 831 inserts per second. This is about half the best rate achieved, which was nearly 2,000 inserts per second. The wait stats show that you are still waiting on the log write, although you are clearly spending a lot more time in index maintenance, and in reading extra pages The stats I/O time indicates that you are incurring a few extra reads on the boysNames and girlsNames tables, but otherwise there isn't a great difference in the stats. The showplan indicates that there is an index scan on both boysNames and girlsNames, rather than the single-page table scan that was there before. This is what is accounting for the extra page reads:

```
|--Index Scan(OBJECT:([People].[dbo].[BoysNames].[ix_boysnames_name]))
|--Index Scan(OBJECT:([People].[dbo].[GirlsNames].[ix_Girlsnames_name]))
|--Index Scan(OBJECT:([People].[dbo].[lastNames].[ix_Lastnames_name]))
```

In addition, you are no longer using a useful clustered index on lastNames, but have to use the non-clustered index, which results in an extra page read required on every lastNames access. Overall the performance degradation isn't that great. On a system with a faster disk it might be considerably higher.

Now see what DTA has to say about all these extra indexes. You can use the trace file you captured earlier of the DoMarriage trace, but you'll have to change the DTA options. Open DTA and select the trace file you used earlier. Select the Tuning Options tab, and under the section titled "Physical Design Structures (PDS) to keep in database" change the default selection from Keep All Existing PDS to "Do Not Keep Any Existing PDS. You can have DTA advise you about additional indexes as well by keeping the same options selected under the PDS section, or you can have DTA just show you which indexes to remove. For now, ask DTA to examine the existing indexes and to recommend additional indexes if it finds any, as shown in Figure 15-10.

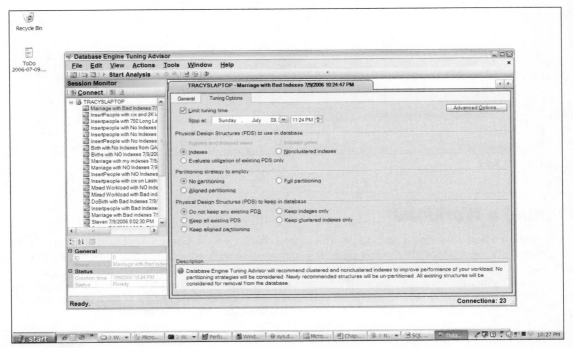

Figure 15-10

Now that you have done that, you can start the analysis session and see what results DTA provides. The results are shown in Figure 15-11.

DTA has easily found the bad indexes. It's recommending that you drop 12 of them, and in their place create two new indexes and two new statistics.

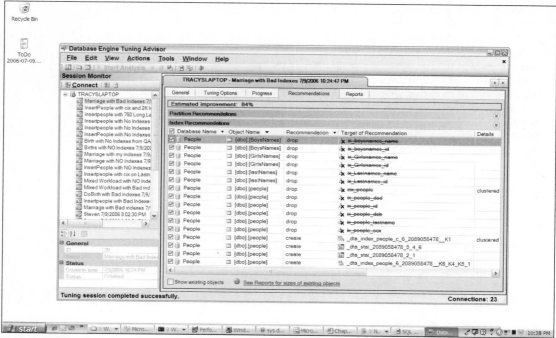

Figure 15-11

Tuning a Workload

Tuning a whole workload is just as easy. The biggest challenge with tuning a workload is when creating the trace file of the workload in the first place, as you must determine what to put into the trace file. In the sample scenario, there are only five different queries. Even if they are called in very different patterns, DTA doesn't really care about how frequently the statement is called — it's just looking for queries that it can tune. To create a workload file to tune, all you need to do is gather one example of each of your queries and pass that to DTA; in turn, it will provide recommendations for the whole workload.

To see how this works, start from the point where you have a workload trace file — in this case, named `workload.trc`. Open DTA and change the name of the session to represent what you are doing. Call this trace session **Mixed Workload with No indexes,** indicating that you are starting out with no indexes in the database.

Select the file that contains the trace file you previously created, and then select the tuning options you want. In this case, you are only interested in new indexes. After selecting the database to tune, start the analysis. In this sample scenario, DTA came back with the recommendations shown in Figure 15-12.

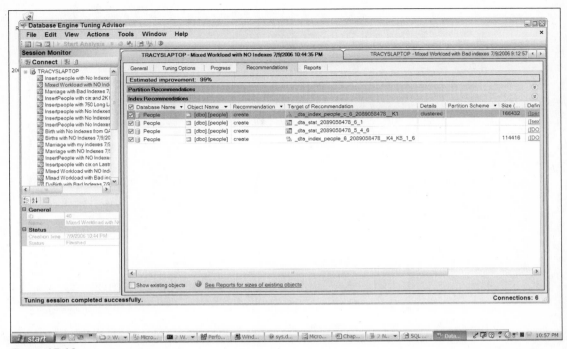

Figure 15-12

A note of caution when tuning a workload: DTA will make recommendations based on the cost estimates for each part of the workload. In a workload with a variety of queries, DTA will focus on the big gains, and may therefore miss recommendations for some of the smaller queries. Because of this, it's still worthwhile to tune individual queries after applying recommendations for the whole workload.

A good example of this can be seen when DTA didn't recommend indexes on the `lastNames` table when tuning the workload. When you tuned just the `insertPeople` procedure, DTA was able to see enough of an improvement to recommend indexes. Figure 15-13 shows the recommendations DTA comes up with for the `lastNames` table when tuning the `insertPeople` procedure.

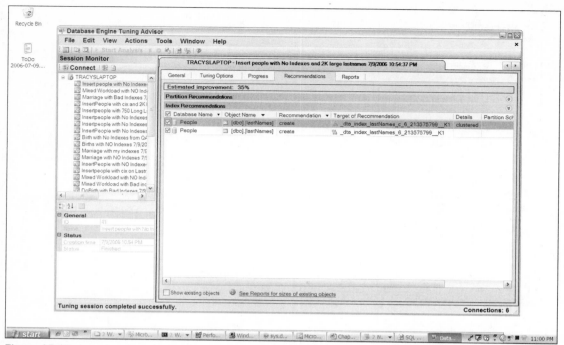

Figure 15-13

Summary

This chapter started by looking at all the new index-related features in SQL Server 2005. From there we examined the details of partitioning, looking at how to set up partitioning, and covering the three main scenarios for partitioning: creating a partition from an existing table, adding a new partition, and deleting an old partition. Next we took a look at index fragmentation and how the commands for this have changed since SQL Server 2000. Finally we looked at Database Tuning Advisor, including comprehensive coverage of the various options and how to asses the value of DTAs recommendations. In the next chapter we will be looking at replication.

16

Replication

Today's enterprise needs to distribute its data across many departments and geographically dispersed offices. SQL Server replication provides ways to distribute data and database objects among its SQL Server databases, databases from other vendors such as Oracle, and mobile devices such as Pocket PC and point-of-sale terminals. Along with log shipping, database mirroring, and clustering, replication provides functionalities that satisfy customers' needs in load balancing, high availability, and scaling.

In this chapter, we introduce you to the concept of replication, how to implement basic snapshot replication, and things to pay attention to when setting up transactional and merge replication. We also go over the newly introduced peer-to-peer replication in SQL Server 2005. Along the way, we go over some best practices.

Replication Overview

SQL Server replication closely resembles the magazine publishing industry, so we'll use that analogy to explain its overall architecture. Consider *National Geographic*. For each monthly issue, the publisher has to collect articles, photos, and interviews. These items then form a pool, from which the editors pick out items to be included in a monthly issue, called a *publication*. Once a monthly publication is printed, it is shipped out via various distribution channels to subscribers all over the world.

In SQL Server replication, similar terminology is used. The pool from which a publication is formed can be considered a database. Each piece selected for publication is an *article*; it can be a table, a stored procedure, or another database object. Like a magazine publisher, replication also needs a *distributor* to deliver publications, keep track of delivery status, and maintain a history of synchronization to maintain data consistency. Depending on the kind of replication model you choose, articles from a publication can be stored as files stored in a folder that both publisher and subscriber(s) have access to, or transactions within articles can be committed on subscribers synchronously or asynchronously. Regardless of how publications are delivered, replication always needs a distributor database to keep track of delivery status. Depending on the capacity of the publication server, the distributor database can be on the same server as the publisher or other dedicated or nondedicated servers.

Conceptually, however, there are differences between SQL Server replication and a magazine publishing business. For example, in some replication models, a subscriber or subscribers can update articles and have them propagated back to the publisher or other subscribers. In the peer-to-peer replication model, each participant of replication acts both as publisher and subscriber, so that changes made in different databases will be replicated back and forth between multiple servers.

There are quite a few enhancements in replication with the release of SQL Server 2005 (for example, replication of new data types such as `varchar(max)`, XML data types, and CLR objects, including assemblies). You can also replicate partitioned tables and full-text indexes. One significant improvement is that most ALTER DDL statements work without removing replication first.

Another significant enhancement in SQL Server 2005 is the introduction of peer-to-peer replication. This headless replication model provides a good alternative for load-balancing and high-availability scenarios.

Replication types

SQL Server 2005 has the basic replication types that existed in SQL Server 2000: snapshot replication, transactional replication, and merge replication. In addition, peer-to-peer replication was introduced in SQL Server 2005. Among those types, snapshot replication is the most basic.

Snapshot Replication

As its name implies, snapshot replication takes a snapshot of a publication and makes it available to subscribers. When the publication is applied on the subscribing database, the articles in the subscriber, such as tables, views, and stored procedures, will be dropped and recreated. Snapshot replication is best suited for fairly static data, when it is acceptable to have copies of data that is out of date between replication intervals, or when article size is small. For example, suppose you have lookup tables to maintain ZIP codes. Those tables can be good snapshot-replication candidates in most cases, because they are fairly static.

Transactional Replication

Transactional replication allows for faster data synchronization with less latency. When an environment is enabled for transactional replication, the subscriber should already have the initial snapshot applied. For subsequent changes applied to published articles, a log-reader process will record them and propagate those changes to the subscriber. Depending on how it is set up, this data synchronization can occur near real time, so it is useful for cases where you want incremental changes to happen at the subscriber quickly.

Merge Replication

Merge replication is usually used when there is no constant network connectivity among publishers and subscribers. It allows sites to work fairly autonomously and merge the changes to the data when they are together online again. Once again, it needs a snapshot to initialize the replication. When that is done, subsequent changes are tracked with triggers. When there are data conflicts during replication, they will be resolved by the rules set up earlier.

Replication Components

The SQL Server Agent plays a very important role in replication, as it did in SQL Server 2000. Publication creation, data distribution and merging, setting and checking status, and cleaning up replication history are all triggered by SQL Server Agent jobs.

In addition to SQL Server Agent, there are other agents specifically designed for replication, such as the Snapshot Agent, Distribution Agent, Merge Agent, Log Reader Agent, and Queue Reader Agent. These agents are all executables that will be called when you initiate jobs either directly from SQL Server Agent or from replication tools from Management Studio.

Implementing Replication

With so much terminology involved, replication can be confusing and misleading initially. In this section, you'll go through one exercise to set up snapshot replication. One added benefit of doing this is that various tools and wizards for replication setup were totally rewritten in SQL Server 2005. The gist is still the same, but it is nice to see the different user interface here.

You shouldn't have much trouble setting up snapshot replication. Transactional and merger replication is similar. We will review the major differences right after snapshot replication setup.

The Setup

We will use AdventureWorks as the publishing and subscribing database for this exercise. To make things easier, you'll create a new table for this purpose. For the purposes of the exercise, assume AdventureWorks is a car company that sells fuel-efficient hybrid cars in the U.S., China, and Sweden. You'll set up snapshot replication between database servers in the U.S. and China to refresh data. Furthermore, you can set up transactional replication between database servers in the U.S. and Sweden. The data can also be used to set up merge replication. Use the following script to create the table and insert some relevant data:

```
CREATE TABLE Sales.Cars
(ProdID INT PRIMARY KEY,
ProdDesc varchar(35),
Country varchar(7),
LastUpdate smalldatetime
)

INSERT INTO Sales.Cars (ProdID, ProdDesc, Country, LastUpdate)
VALUES ('1', 'ProEfficient Sedan', 'US', GetDate())

INSERT INTO Sales.Cars (ProdID, ProdDesc, Country, LastUpdate)
VALUES ('2', 'ProEfficient Van', 'US', GetDate())

INSERT INTO Sales.Cars (ProdID, ProdDesc, Country, LastUpdate)
VALUES ('3', 'JieNeng Crossover', 'China', GetDate())

INSERT INTO Sales.Cars (ProdID, ProdDesc, Country, LastUpdate)
VALUES ('4', 'JieNeng Utility', 'China', GetDate())
```

```
INSERT INTO Sales.Cars (ProdID, ProdDesc, Country, LastUpdate)
VALUES ('5', 'EuroEfficient Wagon', 'Sweden', GetDate())

INSERT INTO Sales.Cars (ProdID, ProdDesc, Country, LastUpdate)
VALUES ('6', 'EuroEfficient Pickup', 'Sweden', GetDate())
```

Replication can be implemented through both GUI wizard pages and scripting. If you are new to replication, we recommend that you go through the GUI and property pages through SQL Server Management Studio first. Best of all, Management Studio allows you to generate SQL scripts at the end of processes, which you can save to a file and edit for other deployment.

You must implement a distributor before you can create publications and subscribe to publications, so you'll create the distributor first. A distributor is needed for all types of replications.

Setting up Distribution

As we mentioned earlier, a distributor consists of a distribution database (where replication history, status, and other important information will be stored) and a shared folder (where data and articles can be stored, retrieved, and refreshed). In addition, you need to find out the domain name and account that will be used during the process to run various replication agents, such as the Snapshot Agent, Log Reader Agent, and Queue Reader Agent. That is not necessary, though, because you can choose to impersonate the SQL Server Agent account. That is good for testing and learning, but when you put things into production, a dedicated domain account is recommended for security reasons.

Here is a step-by-step process to follow:

1.   Using SQL Server Management Studio, connect to the distributor server. Expand the server in Object Explorer.

2.   Right-click Replication, and select Configure Distribution.

3.   You will see the Welcome screen; click Next. Then you will see the screen in Figure 16-1, where you will pick which server will be served as distributor.

4.   Click Next, and you will be asked to enter the snapshot folder. Since the snapshot folder will be accessed by subscribers, a network path is needed, which you'll enter in the next screen.

5.   Once you've picked the snapshot folder, you can then proceed with the distribution database on the next page of the wizard, as shown in Figure 16-2. From here, you can separate the data file and log file so they are on different hard-disk spindles for better performance.

6.   On the next page, you see a list of publishers that can use this server as its distributor. Check the boxes for the publishers you want to use.

7.   On the next page, before you let the wizard create the distribution for you, you'll see a screen where you can choose to have the wizard configure the distribution and also have it generate a script for you. Select to create a script file before you click Next.

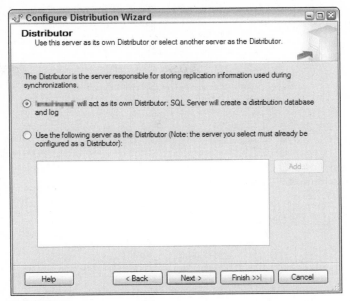

Figure 16-1

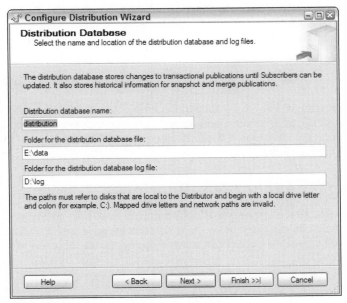

Figure 16-2

8. On the next page, you specify where and how you want the script file generated, as shown in Figure 16-3.

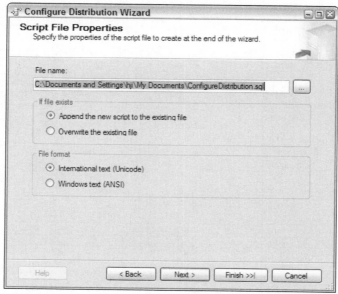

Figure 16-3

9. The last stage is the summary page before the wizard will go ahead.

10. Click Finish, and the process will begin. Afterward, you will see the finished report.

As you can see, setting up distributor is not a difficult task. A distribution database is created. In addition, as mentioned earlier, SQL Server Agent plays a very important role in setting up replication. If you expand the SQL Server Agent in Object Explorer, and open the Jobs folder, you'll see that a number of new jobs were created for the replication.

Implementing Snapshot Replication

By now, you know that all replication needs publication, distribution, and subscription. Now that you've set up the distribution, you can use that for the replication exercise later in this chapter. As with any replication, you need to create a publication before subscribers can subscribe to it, so that is what you'll do next.

Setting Up Snapshot Publication

Once again, we will use Management Studio to accomplish the setup, and you can elect to have everything scripted at the end of the process.

1. Within Management Studio, while connected to the server where publication database resides, expand the Replication folder. Right-click Local Publications and pick New Publication.

2. You will see the Publication Wizard welcome screen; click Next. On the next screen, you will be asked to pick a database for publication. Pick AdventureWorks as your database to create a publication, and click Next.

3. Next you will be presented with a screen to pick the publication type. In this case, pick Snapshot publication and click Next.

4. Next, you need to pick articles such as tables, views, and other database objects to be included in this publication, as shown in Figure 16-4.

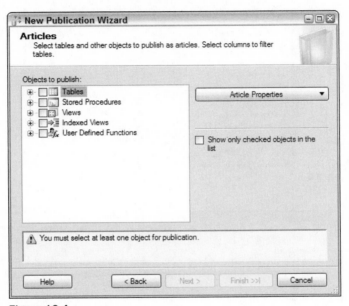

Figure 16-4

5. Pick the Cars table you created earlier for publication. Expand the Tables item; then select the Cars table and its children, as shown in Figure 16-5.

   You can see that the Cars table under the Sales schema is selected. Furthermore, if necessary, you can pick and choose columns of the table for publication by unchecking the box next to the column name. We will not use this feature here, but it can be useful in certain scenarios.

   Also note that you can set properties of articles that you choose to publish. These properties affect how the article will be published and some behaviors when it is synchronized with the subscriber. Again, don't change the default properties here, but they can be very useful.

6. On the next page, the wizard will give you an option to filter out rows. Click the Add button.

7. As we mentioned earlier, since we are trying to replicate data to the Chinese market, you need to filter the cars by country, as shown in Figure 16-6.

   After you click OK, the filter will be applied.

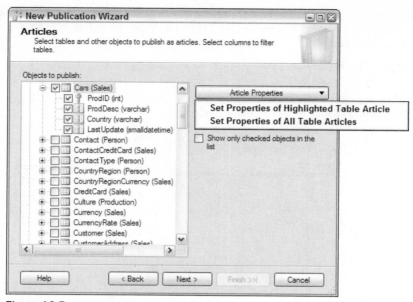

Figure 16-5

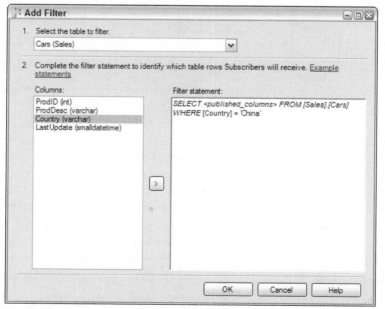

Figure 16-6

8. Next, you need to define when to run the Snapshot Agent. In this case, don't schedule it; you will invoke it manually by running SQL Server Agent job yourself.

9. As mentioned earlier, different replication models call for different agents to be run. For security purposes, you need to define the account under which the agents run, on the next screen. Click the Security Settings button to configure the account.

   It is convenient to have a dedicated domain account with a secure password that does not need to be changed very often for this purpose. However, if you don't have that access, you can choose to impersonate the SQL Server Agent account for this exercise. It is best to have a dedicated account, though, as shown in Figure 16-7.

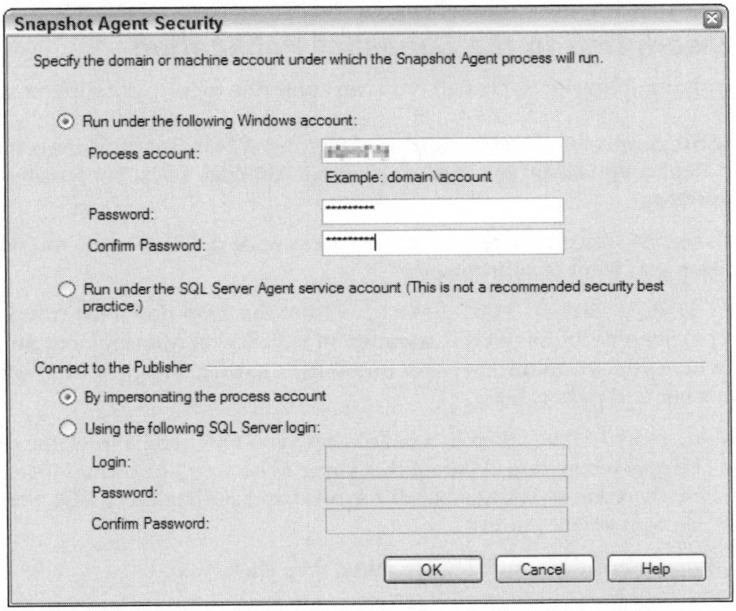

Figure 16-7

   Once the account is set, click OK to continue:

10. Now we are almost done with this publication. You can choose to generate a script file at this stage:

The rest of the process is pretty similar to the distributor creation documented earlier. Once you click Finish, the snapshot publication will be created. Again, you can use Object Explorer to see the publication and SQL Server jobs created during this process.

You will also notice that folders and files are created for this snapshot publication. The subfolders and files are created under the shared folder defined when the distributor was set up earlier. To verify that, you can go to the shared folder in Explorer and browse for files generated. Figure 16-8 can give you some ideas.

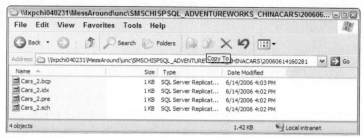

Figure 16-8

Setting up Subscription to the Snapshot Publication

Now that a snapshot publication is created, you can subscribe to it from a different server.

1. Once again, connect to the subscription server using SQL Server Management Studio, and expand Replication folder in Object Explorer. Right-click Local Subscription, and pick New Subscriptions.

2. You will see the welcome screen of subscription wizard. Click Next. You will need to choose the publication you want to subscribe to.

   Pick <Find SQL Server Publisher...> from the drop-down list. You will see the typical Connect to Server window that is common in SQL Server Management Studio. Connect to the server where you set up the snapshot publication earlier, and click Connect. You will then see the publisher and publication:

3. Click Next, and you'll be taken to a page where you will need to pick the distribution agent location. Here is where you decide if this going to be a pull or push delivery. Unlike SQL Server 2000, where there are separate wizards for push and pull delivery, SQL Server 2005 combines them in one convenient place.

   Make your subscription a pull subscription; then click Next.

4. In this page, you can set proper subscriber properties. Or if you want to add additional subscribers, you can do so on this page as well.

5. Click Next. Here you will see the familiar window of Agent security setting. This is similar to the step where we set up the domain account for Snapshot Agent. Click (...) to set up the security options, as shown in Figure 16-9.

   If you want to specify different domain account for Distribution Agent Security, you need to fill out account information on this screen. For the purpose of testing, you can set it up as shown in Figure 16-9. Click OK; then click Next

6. Now you need to set the synchronization schedule. Since this is just your first test example, make it simple and set it to run on demand. Click the drop-down and select Run on demand only.

7. In the exit page, you need to decide the initial synchronization. Check the box to select initialization, and in the drop-down, choose to initialize immediately:

8. The rest of steps are simple. The wizard will ask if you want to generate a script, present a report, and finish subscription creation.

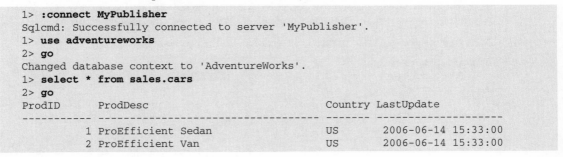

Figure 16-9

Verifying Snapshot Replication

So far, the setup is pretty simple. But how do you know it actually works? You can conduct some tests here to make sure it does indeed work properly.

1. First, connect to the publication server and verify the records there:

```
1> :connect MyPublisher
Sqlcmd: Successfully connected to server 'MyPublisher'.
1> use adventureworks
2> go
Changed database context to 'AdventureWorks'.
1> select * from sales.cars
2> go
ProdID      ProdDesc                              Country LastUpdate
----------- ------------------------------------- ------- --------------------
          1 ProEfficient Sedan                    US      2006-06-14 15:33:00
          2 ProEfficient Van                      US      2006-06-14 15:33:00
```

```
              3  JieNeng Crossover               China     2006-06-14 15:33:00
              4  JieNeng Utility                 China     2006-06-14 15:33:00
              5  EuroEfficient Wagon             Sweden    2006-06-14 15:33:00
              6  EuroEfficient Pickup            Sweden    2006-06-14 15:33:00

(6 rows affected)
```

2. Now connect to the subscription server. Since you've already initialized the subscription, you
    will only see cars for the Chinese market:

```
1> :connect MySubscriber
Sqlcmd: Successfully connected to server 'MySubscriber'.
1> use adventureworks
2> go
Changed database context to 'AdventureWorks'.
1> select * from sales.cars
2> go
ProdID       ProdDesc                                      Country LastUpdate
-----------  --------------------------------------------- ------- --------------------
              3  JieNeng Crossover               China     2006-06-14 15:33:00
              4  JieNeng Utility                 China     2006-06-14 15:33:00

(2 rows affected)
```

3. Now suppose you made some changes to cars for the Chinese market and upgraded JieNeng
    Crossover to JieNeng Crossover LE at the publication server:

```
1> :connect MyPublisher
Sqlcmd: Successfully connected to server 'MyPublisher'.
1> use adventureworks
2> go
Changed database context to 'AdventureWorks'.
1> update sales.cars set proddesc = 'JieNeng Crossover LE' where prodid = 3
2> go

(1 rows affected)
```

4. Since you've updated records at the publisher, you need to take a new snapshot by running the
    SQL Server Agent jobs. In the Object Explorer, expand the SQL Server Agent Jobs folder, right-
    click the "MYPUBLISHER-AdventureWorks-ChinaCars-1" job, and select Start Job from the
    context menu.

5. Since you implemented a pull subscription, we will need to go to the subscriber and run the job
    to refresh this snapshot. Open the Object Explorer on the subscriber, Expand the SQL Server
    Agent Jobs folder, right-click the job, and select Start Job from the context menu.

6. After this is done, check to make sure the data is indeed refreshed:

```
1> :connect MySubscriber
Sqlcmd: Successfully connected to server 'mySubscriber'.
1> use adventureworks
2> go
Changed database context to 'AdventureWorks'.
```

```
1> select * from sales.cars
2> go
ProdID       ProdDesc                                 Country LastUpdate
-----------  ---------------------------------------  ------- --------------------
          3 JieNeng Crossover LE                      China   2006-06-14 15:33:00
          4 JieNeng Utility                           China   2006-06-14 15:33:00

(2 rows affected)
```

Implementing Transactional and Merge Replication

Procedurally, setting up transactional and merge replication is very similar to the snapshot replication discussed earlier. We will not be discussing the detailed step-by-step instructions here. Instead, we will discuss some differences and things you need to pay attention to.

The typical transactional replication is not too different from snapshot replication. One major component added is the Log Reader Agent. This agent tracks all changes made to the article so it can be propagated to the subscriber. As a result, the load on distribution database is higher than snapshot replication, which means you need to keep a closer eye on it, especially the log file of the distribution database.

If you implement transactional publication with updateable subscription, subscriber changes can be refreshed back to the publisher. However, SQL Server will need to add one additional column in tables included in the publication to track changes. This column is called MSrepl_tran_version and is a unique identifier column. Therefore, if you have code like this:

insert into sales.cars values (9, 'English Car', 'UK', getdate())

This code will fail because it does not have a column list. As a result, the application of that code will need to be updated. To fix that, the column list that corresponds to the values in parenthesis must be given right after the table name.

For transactional replication with updatable subscription, a linked server is used among SQL Server publishing and subscribing databases. The linked server uses MS DTC (Distributed Transaction Coordinator) to coordinate transactions; therefore, MS DTC on the publisher must be enabled to accept remote connections.

For merge replication, all articles must have a unique identifier column with a unique index and the ROWGUIDCOL property. If they don't have it, SQL Server will add one for you. Just like transactional replication with updateable subscription, an insert statement without the column list will fail.

Additional agents will be used for transactional and merge replication, such as the Log Reader Agent and Queue Reader Agent. The agents will require a domain account to run under. The domain account can be their own or shared with other agents. How you choose to implement that depends on your company's security policy.

For merge replication, you can choose to synchronize data over https. That requires IIS (version 5.0 and version 6.0) that uses replisapi.dll.

Peer-to-Peer Replication

Peer-to-Peer is a type of transactional replication. Unlike the traditional replication types, it provides a headless topology, where there is no single publisher and one or more subscribers. In peer-to-peer replication, every participant is both a publisher and a subscriber. It is suited for cases where user applications need to read or modify data at any of the databases that participate in the setup. It provides an interesting alternative for load-balancing and high-availability scenarios. Note that this feature is only available in the Enterprise Edition of SQL Server 2005. Oracle calls this kind of replication "multimaster," whereas DB2 calls it "update anywhere."

There are a few things to keep in mind when evaluating and setting up peer-to-peer replication:

❑ It is designed for a small number of participating databases. A good rule-of-thumb number is less than 10. If you use more than that, you could encounter performance issues.

❑ Unlike merge replication, peer-to-peer replication does not handle conflict resolution.

❑ Peer-to-peer also does not support data filtering. That would defeat the purpose because everybody is an equal partner here for high availability and load balancing.

❑ Applications can scale out read operation across multiple databases. Databases are always online. Participating nodes can be added or removed for maintenance.

❑ As mentioned, peer-to-peer replication is only available in Enterprise Edition. However, for your testing purposes, it is available in Developer Edition of SQL Server 2005.

From an implementation standpoint, the process is very similar to the replication types discussed earlier. However, there are a few things that you need to pay attention to:

1. Before you start, the easiest approach is to start with one database, back it up, and restore it on all other participating databases. This way, you will start from a clean and consistent slate.

2. All replications need a distributor, so it needs to be ready before you start setting up peer-to-peer replication.

3. After the distributor is set, you need to create a publication just like a regular transactional replication publication. However, do not create the initial snapshot or schedule the Snapshot Agent at the Snapshot Agent screen. In addition, you need to make sure that the publication name is the same across all participating servers. Otherwise, peer-to-peer setup will fail.

4. After the publication is created, you need to modify a property before you have access to peer-to-peer replication setup. Expand your Object Explorer within Management Studio so the newly created publication is highlighted. Right-click it and pick Properties, as shown in Figure 16-10.

   Please note that there is no option for you to configure peer-to-peer in this context menu, as you can see from the preceding screenshot. That will change once you change the Subscription Options, which you will do next. After the property window opens, pick the Subscription Options page, shown in Figure 16-11.

   Set the "Allow peer-to-peer subscriptions" to True before setup can continue.

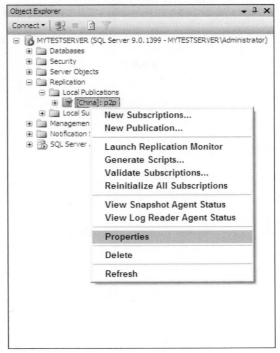

Figure 16-10

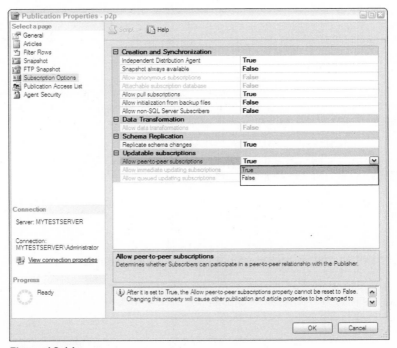

Figure 16-11

5.   After that is done, you can proceed with the rest of the setup by right-clicking the publication and selecting "Configure Peer-to-Peer Topology..." as you can see in Figure 16-12. Once again, you can only see this after the Subscription Options is modified. This feature is only available in SQL Server 2005 Enterprise Edition.

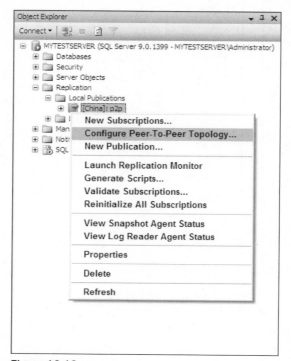

Figure 16-12

6.   Follow the rest of the steps. As mentioned earlier, most of the rest are pretty similar to typical replication setup. One difference is that this process will ask you to add Peers, instead of adding subscribers as you did with the other types of replication.

Replication Monitoring

As mentioned earlier, all SQL Server management tools are totally rewritten with SMO, SQL Server Management Objects. You can see that from all the setup screenshots discussed earlier. Replication tools are no exception. In SQL Server 2005, you can monitor your replication activities from a centralized location called Replication Monitor. You can invoke Replication Monitor from Management Studio. Expand a publishing server and right-click the Replication folder to launch it.

To look at subscription status, double-click any entry of the All Subscriptions tab to bring up a window where you can easily view reports and status of publication to distribution, distribution to subscription, and undistributed commands. It is a pretty user-friendly tool that provides a good overview of all your replication status.

One very nice feature introduced in SQL Server 2005 replication monitoring is Tracer Token, shown in Figure 16-13. You can think of tracer token as a dummy record that the replication monitor uses to gauge the performance of your replication model. It can give you a pretty good idea of latency among your publisher, distributor, and subscriber.

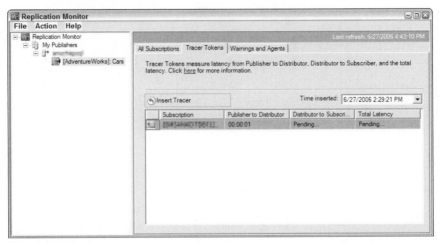

Figure 16-13

Summary

We've covered replication in this chapter. One thing we didn't talk about is Replication Management Objects (RMO). RMO is a managed code-programming model for SQL Server 2005 replication. All the steps and processes we have so far discussed can be programmed using RMO. However, because of the size limitations of this chapter, we will not be able to discuss it here. One good place to get started is to go through sample applications and code samples from Books Online.

Along with log shipping, database mirroring, and clustering, SQL Server 2005 provides many features to satisfy customer's needs in load balancing, high availability, disaster recovery, and scaling.

17

Database Mirroring

Database mirroring is a software solution for increasing the probability that the database will be available. Database mirroring is a brand new feature in SQL Server 2005. Maximizing the database availability is a top priority for most DBAs. It is hard to explain the pain a DBA goes through when a database goes down; you're unable to get it right back online, and at the same time you're answering pointed questions from your manager. Database mirroring will come to the rescue in certain scenarios, which we explain in this chapter. It will help you get the database back online with automatic or manual failover to your mirror database, adding another alternative to the SQL Server arsenal. In this chapter, we explain the database mirroring concepts, show you how to administer the mirrored database, and give you an example of how to implement database mirroring. We also discuss database snapshot, another brand new feature in SQL Server 2005, which you can use with database mirroring to read the mirrored databases.

Overview of Database Mirroring

Database mirroring is a high-availability solution at the database level, implemented on a per-database basis. To maximize database availability, you need to minimize planned as well as unplanned downtime. Planned downtime is very common, such as changes you have to apply to your production system, hardware upgrades, software upgrades (security patches and service packs), database configuration changes, or database storage upgrades. These all require your database or server to be unavailable for short periods of time if everything goes as planned. Unplanned downtime can be caused by hardware failures such as storage failure, by power outages, by human error, or by natural disasters, all of which can cause the production server or data center to be unavailable.

Database mirroring helps minimize both planned and unplanned downtime by:

- ❑ Providing ways to perform automatic or manual failover for mirrored databases

- ❑ Keeping the mirrored database up to date with the production database, either synchronously or asynchronously. You can set the operating modes for database mirroring, which we will discuss shortly.

❑   Allowing the mirrored database to be in a remote data center, to provide a foundation for disaster recovery

You cannot mirror the `master`, `msdb`, `tempdb`, *or* `model` *databases. You can mirror multiple databases in a SQL Server instance, though.*

Figure 17-1 illustrates a number of mirroring concepts, which we'll discuss in detail.

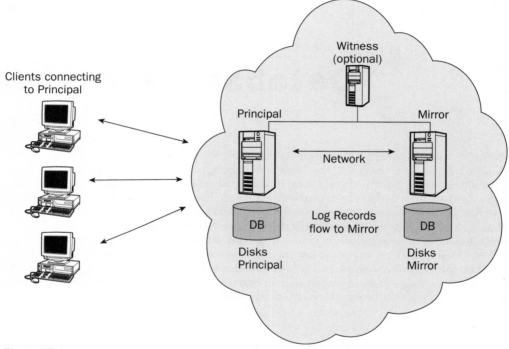

Figure 17-1

Database Mirroring involves two copies of a single database, residing on separate instances of SQL Server, usually on different computers. You can have separate instances of SQL Server 2005 on the same computer, but that would most likely not fit your high-availability requirements other than for testing purposes. At any given time, only one copy of the database is available to clients. This copy of the database is known as the *principal* database. The SQL Server that hosts this principal database is known as the *principal server*. Database mirroring works by transferring and applying the stream of database log records to the copy of the database. The copy of the database is known as the *mirror* database. The SQL Server that hosts this mirror database is known as the *mirror server*. The principal and mirror servers are each considered a *partner* in a database mirroring *session*. As you would guess, a given server may assume the role of principal for one database and the role of mirror for another database. Database mirroring applies every database modification (DML, DDL, and so on) on the principal database to the mirror database, including physical and logical database changes such as database files and indexes. We will discuss the *witness* server later.

Operating Modes of Database Mirroring

We mentioned that to keep the mirror database up to date, database mirroring transfers and applies the stream of database log records on the mirror database. It is important to understand which *operating mode* database mirroring is configured in. The following table outlines the operating modes of database mirroring.

Operating Mode	Transaction Safety	Transfer Mechanism	Quorum Required	Witness Server	Failover Type
High Performance	OFF	Asynchronous	No	N/A	Forced failover only (with possible data loss). This is a manual step.
High Safety WITHOUT automatic failover	FULL	Synchronous	Yes	No	Manual or forced
High Safety WITH automatic failover	FULL	Synchronous	Yes	Yes	Automatic or manual

There are three possible operating modes for a database mirroring session. The exact mode of the operation is based on the setting of transaction safety and whether the witness server is part of the mirroring session.

When you set up database mirroring, you have to decide whether you want the principal database and mirror database to be in sync all the time for full data safety or if you can live with some data loss in case of principal failure. You have two options: SAFETY FULL or SAFETY OFF. These options are part of the ALTER DATABASE statement when you set up database mirroring, as we'll explain later. As you know, in SQL Server, data changes are first recorded in the transaction log before any changes to the actual data pages are made. The transaction-log records are first placed in the database's log buffer in memory and then flushed to the log file on the disk (referred to as "hardening the transaction log") as soon as possible.

If you choose SAFETY FULL, you are setting up database mirroring in high-safety (also known as *synchronous mirroring*) mode. As the principal server hardens (flushes the log buffer to disk) log records of the principal database to disk, it also sends log buffers to the mirror. The principal then waits for a response from the mirror server. The mirror responds to a commit when it has hardened those same log records to the mirror's log. The commit is then reported to the client. Synchronous transfer guarantees that all transactions in the mirror database's transaction log will be synchronized with the principal database's transaction log, so the transactions are considered safely transferred. Figure 17-2 shows the sequence of events when SAFETY is set to FULL.

Keep in mind that it is guaranteed that you won't lose data and that both the principal and mirror will be in sync as long as the transaction is committed successfully. There is a little cost here because the transaction is not committed until it is hardened to the log on the mirror. There will be a slight increase in response time and reduction in transaction throughput because the principal has to wait for an acknowledgement from the mirror that the transaction is hardened to the mirror log. How much that delay might be depends on many factors like network latency, application architecture, disk throughput, and more. An application with lots of small transactions will experience more impact on response time than with long transactions, because transactions wait for acknowledgement from the mirror, and the wait time adds proportionately more to the response time of short transactions.

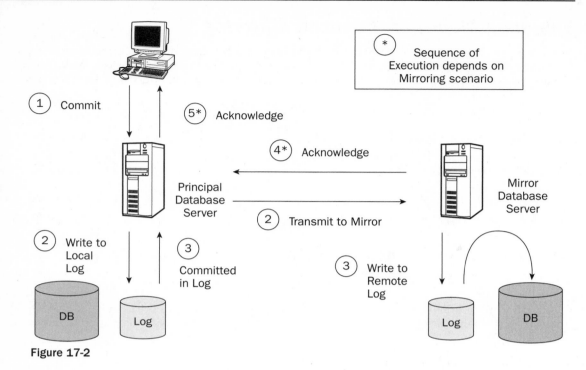

Figure 17-2

If you choose the SAFETY OFF, you are setting up database mirroring in high performance (also known as *asynchronous mirroring*) mode. In this mode, the log transfer process happens the same way as in synchronous mode, but the difference is that the principal does not wait for acknowledgement from the mirror that the log buffer is hardened to the disk on a commit. As soon as step 3 in Figure 17-2 occurs, the transaction is committed on the principal. The database is synchronized after the mirror server catches up to the principal server. Since the mirror server is busy keeping up with the principal server, if the principal suddenly fails, you may lose data. In this operating mode, there will be minimal impact on response time or transaction throughput, as this mode operates as if there is no mirroring.

We need to mention two important terms here. We will discuss these points additionally later in the chapter.

❑ **Send Queue:** While sending the log records from the principal to the mirror, if the log records can't be sent at the rate at which they are generated, a queue builds up at the principal. This is known as the *send queue*. The send queue does not use extra storage or memory. It exists entirely in the transaction log of the principal. It refers to the part of the log that has not yet been sent to the mirror.

❑ **Redo Queue:** While applying log records on the mirror, if the log records can't be applied at the rate at which they are received, a queue builds up at the mirror. This is known as the redo queue. Like the send queue, the redo queue does not use extra storage or memory. It exists entirely in the transaction log of the mirror. It refers to the part of the hardened log that remains to be applied to the mirror database to roll it forward.

Database Mirroring Example

Now that you understand transaction safety, you can look at an example to better understand the operating modes and other mirroring concepts. You will need to designate three SQL Server instances for this example: one principal server, one mirror server, and one witness server. You will set up high-safety mode with automatic failover with this example. This example assumes that all three SQL server instances are on the network and are running under some domain account, which is admin on the instance and has access to the other instances. You will need the AdventureWorks sample database that comes with SQL Server installation. Also, make sure that you have installed the SP1 on SQL Server 2005.

Preparing the Endpoints

We discuss endpoints in great detail in Chapter 8. You can refer to the "Transport Security" section in that chapter for details. For database-mirroring partners to connect to each other, they must trust each other. That is established by means of TCP endpoints. So on each partner, you have to create the endpoint using the T-SQL statement CREATE ENDPOINT and grant the connect permission on these endpoints using the GRANT CONNECT ON ENDPOINT statement. The endpoint concept is exactly the same as discussed in Chapter 8, so the rules are the same. The only difference is that instead of creating an endpoint for Service Broker, you are creating an endpoint for database mirroring here. The security rules are the same; you can either use the Windows authentication or certificates for authentication. In this example, you will use certificates so that you can learn how to use them for transport authentication. Windows authentication is very easy to establish, so we will leave that for you as an exercise.

First, you need to create the certificates on each partner. You can find all the scripts for this chapter on this book's Web page on www.wrox.com. Open the script CreateCertOnPrincipal.sql and connect to the principal server. The code looks like this:

```
USE MASTER
GO
IF NOT EXISTS(SELECT 1 FROM sys.symmetric_keys where name =
'##MS_DatabaseMasterKey##')
CREATE MASTER KEY ENCRYPTION BY PASSWORD = '23%&weq^yzYu2005!'
GO

IF NOT EXISTS (select 1 from sys.databases where
[is_master_key_encrypted_by_server] = 1)
ALTER MASTER KEY ADD ENCRYPTION BY SERVICE MASTER KEY
GO

IF NOT EXISTS (SELECT 1 FROM sys.certificates WHERE name = 'PrincipalServerCert')
CREATE  CERTIFICATE PrincipalServerCert
WITH SUBJECT = 'Principal Server Certificate'
GO

BACKUP CERTIFICATE PrincipalServerCert TO FILE = 'C:\PrincipalServerCert.cer'
```

For simplicity, we are using the certificates created by SQL Server, but there are other ways of creating and distributing certificates, which will work equally here. The BACKUP CERTIFICATE statement will back up the public key certificate for this private key.

Now create the endpoint on the principal server. Open the script `CreateEndPointOnPrincipal.sql` and connect to the principal server. Here's the code:

```
--Check If Mirroring endpoint exists
IF NOT EXISTS(SELECT * FROM sys.endpoints WHERE type = 4)
CREATE ENDPOINT DBMirrorEndPoint
STATE = STARTED AS TCP (LISTENER_PORT = 4040)
FOR DATABASE_MIRRORING ( AUTHENTICATION = CERTIFICATE PrincipalServerCert,
                         ENCRYPTION = REQUIRED
                         ,ROLE = ALL
                       )
```

In this code, you can see that you have created the endpoint `DBMirrorEndPoint`, and you have specified the `PrincipalServerCert` certificate to use for authentication. You also specified `ROLE = ALL`, which indicates that this server can either act as the principal, mirror, or witness server. If you want this server to act only as the witness, you can specify `WITNESS` as a parameter. You can also specify the `PARTNER` option, which indicates that the server can act as either the principal or the mirror but not the witness.

Now create the certificates on both the mirror and the witness. Open the script `CreateCertOnMirror.sql` and run it on the mirror server:

```
USE MASTER
GO
IF NOT EXISTS(SELECT 1 FROM sys.symmetric_keys where name =
'##MS_DatabaseMasterKey##')
CREATE MASTER KEY ENCRYPTION BY PASSWORD = '23%&weq^yzYu2005!'
GO

IF NOT EXISTS (select 1 from sys.databases where
[is_master_key_encrypted_by_server] = 1)
ALTER MASTER KEY ADD ENCRYPTION BY SERVICE MASTER KEY
GO

IF NOT EXISTS (SELECT 1 FROM sys.certificates WHERE name = 'MirrorServerCert')
CREATE  CERTIFICATE MirrorServerCert
WITH SUBJECT = 'Mirror Server Certificate'
GO

BACKUP CERTIFICATE MirrorServerCert TO FILE = 'C:\MirrorServerCert.cer'
```

Next, open the script `CreateEndPointOnMirror.sql` and run it on the mirror server:

```
--Check If Mirroring endpoint exists
IF NOT EXISTS(SELECT * FROM sys.endpoints WHERE type = 4)
CREATE ENDPOINT DBMirrorEndPoint
STATE=STARTED AS TCP (LISTENER_PORT = 4040)
FOR DATABASE_MIRRORING ( AUTHENTICATION = CERTIFICATE MirrorServerCert,
                         ENCRYPTION = REQUIRED
                         ,ROLE = ALL
                       )
```

Open the script `CreateCertOnWitness.sql` and run it on the witness server:

```
USE MASTER
GO
IF NOT EXISTS(SELECT 1 FROM sys.symmetric_keys where name =
'##MS_DatabaseMasterKey##')
CREATE MASTER KEY ENCRYPTION BY PASSWORD = '23%&weq^yzYu2005!'
GO

IF NOT EXISTS (select 1 from sys.databases where
[is_master_key_encrypted_by_server] = 1)
ALTER MASTER KEY ADD ENCRYPTION BY SERVICE MASTER KEY
GO

IF NOT EXISTS (SELECT 1 FROM sys.certificates WHERE name = 'WitnessServerCert')
CREATE  CERTIFICATE WitnessServerCert
WITH SUBJECT = 'Witness Server Certificate'
GO

BACKUP CERTIFICATE WitnessServerCert TO FILE = 'C:\WitnessServerCert.cer'
```

And finally, open the script `CreateEndPointOnWitness.sql` and run it on the witness server:

```
--Check If Mirroring endpoint exists
IF NOT EXISTS(SELECT * FROM sys.endpoints WHERE type = 4)
CREATE ENDPOINT DBMirrorEndPoint
STATE=STARTED AS TCP (LISTENER_PORT = 4040)
FOR DATABASE_MIRRORING ( AUTHENTICATION = CERTIFICATE WitnessServerCert, ENCRYPTION
= REQUIRED
                         ,ROLE = ALL
                         )
```

Since all the partners can talk to each other, each partner needs permission to connect to the others. To do that, you have to create logins on each server and associate the logins with certificates from the other two servers and grant connect permission to that user on the endpoint.

First, you have to copy certificates we have created in the previous scripts with the BACKUP CERTIFICATE command to the other two servers. For example, copy the certificate `PrincipalServerCert.cer` on the principal from the C: drive to both the witness and mirror servers, on some drive. In this example, we assume that they are copied on the C: drive.

Open the script `Principal_CreateLoginAndGrant.sql` and run it on the principal server:

```
USE MASTER
GO

--For Mirror server to connect
IF NOT EXISTS(SELECT 1 FROM sys.syslogins WHERE name = 'MirrorServerUser')
CREATE LOGIN MirrorServerUser WITH PASSWORD = '32sdgsgy^%$!'

IF NOT EXISTS(SELECT 1 FROM sys.sysusers WHERE name = 'MirrorServerUser')
CREATE USER MirrorServerUser;
```

```
IF NOT EXISTS(SELECT 1 FROM sys.certificates WHERE name = 'MirrorDBCertPub')
CREATE CERTIFICATE MirrorDBCertPub  AUTHORIZATION MirrorServerUser
FROM FILE = 'C:\MirrorServerCert.cer'

GRANT CONNECT ON ENDPOINT::DBMirrorEndPoint TO MirrorServerUser
GO


--For Witness server to connect
IF NOT EXISTS(SELECT 1 FROM sys.syslogins WHERE name = 'WitnessServerUser')
CREATE LOGIN WitnessServerUser WITH PASSWORD = '32sdgsgy^%$!'

IF NOT EXISTS(SELECT 1 FROM sys.sysusers WHERE name = 'WitnessServerUser')
CREATE USER WitnessServerUser;

IF NOT EXISTS(SELECT 1 FROM sys.certificates WHERE name = 'WitnessDBCertPub')
CREATE CERTIFICATE WitnessDBCertPub  AUTHORIZATION WitnessServerUser
FROM FILE = 'C:\WitnessServerCert.cer'

GRANT CONNECT ON ENDPOINT::DBMirrorEndPoint TO WitnessServerUser
GO
```

This script creates two users on the principal server: `MirrorServerUser` and `WitnessServerUser`. These users are mapped to the certificates from the mirror and the witness. After that, you granted connect permission on the endpoint. So now the mirror and the witness server have permission to connect to the endpoint on the principal server. You have to perform the same steps on the mirror server and witness server also. Open `Mirror_CreateLoginAndGrant.sql` and run it on the mirror server. Then open `Witness_CreateLoginAndGrant.sql` and run it on the witness server.

Now you have configured the endpoints on each server, using certificates. If you want to use the Windows authentication, the steps to configure the endpoints are bit easier than using certificates. All you have to do is the following on each server. This example is for the principal:

```
IF NOT EXISTS(SELECT * FROM sys.endpoints WHERE type = 4)
CREATE ENDPOINT DBMirrorEndPoint
STATE = STARTED AS TCP (LISTENER_PORT = 4040)
FOR DATABASE_MIRRORING ( AUTHENTICATION = WINDOWS, ROLE = ALL)

GRANT CONNECT ON ENDPOINT::DBMirrorEndPoint TO
[MyDomain\MirrorServerServiceAccount]
GO

GRANT CONNECT ON ENDPOINT::DBMirrorEndPoint TO
[MyDomain\WitnessServerServiceAccount]
GO
```

Of course, you have to change the logins appropriately. In Windows authentication mode, each server will use the service account under which it is running to connect to the other partners. So you have to grant connect permission on the endpoint to the service account of SQL Server. You can use SQL Server Management Studio to configure the endpoint using Windows authentication. Right-click the database you want to mirror and choose Tasks⇨Mirror. A wizard will start. Click the Configure Security button, which will take you through the steps to configure the endpoint for database mirroring. The wizard will try to use 5022 as the default TCP port for database mirroring. You can change it if you want to.

You will just need one mirroring endpoint per server; it doesn't matter how many databases you mirror. Make sure to use a port that is not used by other endpoints. You can specify any open port number between 1024 and 32767.

Do not reconfigure an in-use database mirroring endpoint (using ALTER ENDPOINT*). The server instances use each other's endpoints to learn the state of the other systems. If the endpoint is reconfigured, it might restart, which can appear to be an error to the other server instances. This is particularly important in high-safety mode with automatic failover, in which reconfiguring the endpoint on a partner could cause a failover to occur.*

Preparing the Database for Mirroring

Before you can set up the mirror, you'll need a database to work with. Open the CreateDatabase.sql script. Connect to your designated principal server. The code is here:

```
IF NOT EXISTS(SELECT 1 FROM sys.sysdatabases WHERE name = 'TestMirroring')
CREATE DATABASE TestMirroring

--Although when you create the database it is in full recovery mode
--i am doing it here as a reminder that you will need to set the
--recovery model to FULL recovery in order to establish mirror the database.
ALTER DATABASE TestMirroring SET RECOVERY FULL
```

This script will create database called TestMirroring for the example here. This is the database we would like to mirror. Connect to your designated principal server and run the script.

Now open BackupDatabase.sql. Connect to principal server. Here is the code:

```
--Take a full database backup.
BACKUP DATABASE [TestMirroring] TO  DISK = N'D:\Backup\TestMirroring.bak'
WITH FORMAT, INIT, NAME = N'TestMirroring-Full Database Backup',STATS = 10
GO
```

Using this script, back up TestMirroring. You will have to do a full database backup. You will now have to restore this database on your designated mirror server with the NORECOVERY option in the RESTORE DATABASE statement. We assume in the following script that the backup of the principal database exists in the D:\backup folder on the mirror server.

Open RestoreDatabase.sql and connect to the designated mirror server. Here is the code:

```
--If the path of the mirror database differs from
--the path of the principal database (for instance, their drive letters differ),
--creating the mirror database requires that the restore operation
--include a MOVE clause. See BOL for details on MOVE option.

RESTORE DATABASE [TestMirroring]
FROM DISK = 'D:\Backup\TestMirroring.bak'
WITH
 NORECOVERY
,MOVE N'TestMirroring' TO N'D:\Backup\TestMirroring.mdf'
,MOVE N'TestMirroring_log' TO N'D:\Backup\TestMirroring_log.LDF'
```

This code will restore the database `TestMirroring` in `NORECOVERY` mode on your mirror server. The database must be restored with the `NORECOVERY` option. Now we have a database ready to be mirrored, but you'll need to understand what it takes to do initial synchronization between the principal and mirror in real life.

> *To establish the mirroring session, the database name must be the same on both principal and mirror. Also, before you back up the principal, make sure that the database is in* `FULL` *recovery model.*

Initial Synchronization between Principal and Mirror

You have just backed up and restored the `TestMirroring` database for mirroring. Of course, mirroring the `TestMirroring` size database is not a real-life scenario by any means. In real life, you may want to mirror a live database with hundreds of thousands of MB. So depending upon the database size and also the distance between the servers, it may take a long time to copy and restore the database on the mirror. During this time, the principal database may have produced many transaction logs. Before you set up mirroring, you must copy and restore all these transaction logs with the `NORECOVERY` option on the mirror server. If you do not want to bother copying and restoring these transaction logs on the mirror, you can suspend the transaction-log backups (if you have a SQL job to do backup transaction logs, you can disable that job) until the database on the mirror is restored and the database mirroring session is established (you will learn that very soon). After the database mirroring session is established, you can resume the transaction-log backup on the principal again. It is very important to understand that in this approach, since you have stopped the transaction-log backups, the transaction-log file will grow, so make sure you have enough disk space for log-file growth.

In order for the database mirroring session to be established, both databases (principal and mirror) must be in sync. So at some point you have to stop the transaction-log backup on your principal. You have to decide when you want to do it: before backing up the full database and restoring on the mirror server or after backing up the full database. In the first case, you have to plan for transaction-file growth, and in the second case, you have to copy and restore all the transactions logs on the mirror before you establish the mirroring session.

Our suggestion is that if you are mirroring a very large database, it is going to take a long time to back up and restore it on the mirror server. So plan mirroring installation during low-activity periods on your system. Increase the time between each transaction-log backup so that you have a smaller number of logs to copy and restore on the mirror. If you have very minimal database activities, you can stop taking transaction-log backups on the principal, back up the database on the principal, restore on the mirror, establish the mirroring session, and then restart the transaction-log backup job on the principal.

Establishing the Mirroring Session

Now you'll create some database activities in the `TestMirroring` database before you establish the mirroring session, so you will understand practically what we have just discussed.

Open the script `InsertData.sql` and connect to principal server. This script creates a table in the `TestMirroring` database and inserts data into that table from the `AdventureWorks.person.address` table.

Open `BackupLogPrincipal.sql`, connect to the principal, and run it:

```
USE MASTER
GO
BACKUP LOG TestMirroring TO DISK = 'd:\BACKUP\TestMirroring1.trn'
```

That will back up the log of `TestMirroring`. Now the `TestMirroring` databases on the principal and the mirror are *not* in sync. See what happens if you try to establish the mirroring session between these databases.

Open the script `SetupMirrorServer.sql` and connect to the mirror server. The code is here:

```
USE MASTER
GO
ALTER DATABASE TestMirroring
SET PARTNER = 'TCP://MyPrincipalServer:4040'
```

Run this script. This will run successfully. Now open the script `SetupPrincipalServer.sql` and connect to the principal server. See the following code:

```
USE MASTER
GO
ALTER DATABASE TestMirroring
SET PARTNER = 'TCP://MyMirrorServer:4040'
```

This script will fail on the principal with following message:

```
Msg 1412, Level 16, State 0, Line 1
The remote copy of database "TestMirroring" has not been rolled forward to a point
in time that is encompassed in the local copy of the database log.
```

This shows that the database on the mirror is not rolled forward enough to establish the mirroring session. So now you have to restore the log you backed up on the principal to the mirror server with `NORECOVERY` mode to sync the mirror with the principal. Open the script `RestoreLogOnMirror.sql` and connect to the mirror server. Here is the code:

```
USE MASTER
GO
RESTORE LOG TestMirroring
FROM DISK = 'D:\BACKUP\TestMirroring1.trn'
WITH NORECOVERY
```

This script assumes that you have copied the log in `D:\Backup` folder on the mirror server. If you put the log somewhere else, substitute that folder location. Run the script. Now the principal and mirror databases are in sync.

Open `SetupMirrorServer.sql` again, and run it on the mirror server. Then open `SetupPrincipal Server.sql`, and run it on principal server. It should succeed now. You have just established the mirroring session.

Note that the order in which you execute these scripts is important:

1. Connect to the mirror server and run `SetupMirrorServer.sql`.

2. Connect to the principal server and run `SetupPrincipalServer.sql`.

When you establish the mirroring session, the transaction safety is set to `FULL` by default. So the mirroring session is always established in high-safety operating mode *without* automatic failover.

When you run the `SetupPrincipalServer.sql` or `SetupMirrorServer.sql`, you may get the following type of error:

```
2006-05-27 17:53:16.630 spid15s     Database mirroring connection error 4 'An
error occurred while receiving data: '64(The specified network name is no longer
available.)'.' for 'TCP://MyMirrorServer:4040'. 2006-05-27 17:55:13.710 spid15s
Error: 1443, Severity: 16, State: 2.
```

It may be possible that the firewall on the mirror or principal server is blocking the connection on the port specified.

High-Safety Operating Mode with Automatic Failover

You have established the mirroring session in high-safety operating mode *without* automatic failover. Now you want to change it to *with* automatic failover. This means that if the principal database (or the server hosting it) fails, the database mirroring will failover to the mirror server, and the mirror server will now assume the principal role and serve the database. But you need a third server, the witness for automatic failover to the mirror. The witness just sits there as a third-party and is used by the mirror to verify that the principal is really down, giving a "2 out of 3" agreements for automatic failover. No user action is necessary to failover to the mirror *if* a witness server is present.

Witness Server

If you choose the `SAFETY FULL` option, you have an option to set up a witness server, as shown in Figure 17-1. (We'll discuss how to set up a witness server soon.) The presence of the witness server in high-safety mode determines whether you can perform automatic failover or not when the principal database fails. Note that automatic failover will happen when following conditions are met:

❑   Witness and mirror are both connected to principal when the principal is failing (going away).

❑   Safety is set to `FULL`.

❑   Mirroring state is synchronized.

You must have a separate instance of SQL Server other than the principal and mirror servers to fully take advantage of database mirroring with automatic failover. You can also use the same witness server to participate in multiple, concurrent database mirroring sessions.

Now you'll establish the witness server in your example. Open the `SetupWitnessServer.sql` and connect to either the principal or mirror server. The code is here:

```
USE MASTER
GO
ALTER DATABASE TestMirroring
SET WITNESS = 'TCP://MyWitnessServer:4040'
```

Yes, you must connect to either the principal or the mirror to run this script. When you run the script, both the principal and mirror servers must be up and running. Run the script. You have now a witness server established, which will provide automatic failover support.

The witness server is optional in database mirroring unless you want automatic failover.

The Quorum

You have seen how to set up the witness server. When you set up the witness server, a *quorum* is required to make the database available. A quorum is a relationship between two or more connected server instances in a database mirroring session.

Three types of quorums are possible:

❑   A Full quorum, where both partners and witness are connected

❑   A partner-to-partner quorum, when both partners are connected

❑   A witness-to-partner quorum, where a witness and one of the partners are connected

A database that thinks it is the principal in its DBM session must have at least a partial quorum to serve the database. We will talk more about quorum later in the chapter.

High-Safety Operating Mode *without Automatic Failover*

High safety without automatic failover is the default operating mode set when you establish database mirroring. In this operating mode, a witness is not set up, so automatic failover is not possible. Since the witness server is not present in this operating mode, the principal doesn't need to form a quorum to serve the database. If the principal loses its quorum with the mirror, it will still keep serving the database.

High-Performance Operating Mode

By default, the SAFETY is ON when you establish the mirroring session, so to activate the high-performance operating mode, you have to turn the safety OFF. You set the SAFETY to OFF using ALTER DATABASE TestMirroring SET PARTNER SAFETY OFF.

There will be minimal impact on transaction throughput and response time in this mode. The log transfer to mirror works the same way as in high-safety mode, but since the principal doesn't wait for hardening the log to disk on the mirror, there is a possibility that if the principal goes down unexpectedly, you may lose data.

You can configure the witness server in high-performance mode, but since you cannot do automatic failover in this mode, the witness will not provide any benefits. So you should not define a witness when you configure database mirroring in high-performance mode. You can remove the witness server by running the following command if you want to change the operating mode to high performance with no witness:

```
USE Master
ALTER DATABASE TestMirroring SET WITNESS = OFF
```

If you configure the witness server in a high-performance mode session, the enforcement of quorum means that:

❑   If the mirror server is lost, the principal must be connected to the witness. Otherwise, the principal server takes its database offline until either the witness or mirror server rejoins the session.

❑   If the principal server is lost, forcing service to the mirror requires that the mirror server be connected to the witness.

The only way you can failover to the mirror in this mode is by running the following command on the mirror when the principal server is disconnected from the mirroring session. This is called forced failover. See the table presented earlier in this chapter for the different failover types. We will discuss this further later in the chapter.

```
USE MASTER
ALTER DATABASE <db_name> SET PARTNER FORCE_SERVICE_ALLOW_DATA_LOSS
```

The forced failover causes an immediate recovery of the mirror database. Because of that, it may you lose data. This mode is best used for transferring data over long distances (for disaster recovery to a remote site) or for mirroring an active database where some potential data loss is acceptable. For example, you can use high-performance mode for mirroring your warehouse. Then you can use a database snapshot (we will discuss that later in this chapter) to create a snapshot on the mirror server to create a reporting environment off of the mirrored warehouse.

Database Mirroring and SQL Server 2005 Editions

Now that you understand the operating modes of database mirroring, the following table summarizes which features of database mirroring are available in which SQL Server 2005 editions.

Database Mirroring Feature	Enterprise Edition	Developer Edition	Standard Edition	Workgroup Edition	SQL Express
Partner (Principal or Mirror)	✓	✓	✓		
Witness	✓	✓	✓	✓	✓
Safety = FULL	✓	✓	✓		
Safety = OFF	✓	✓			
Available during UNDO after failover	✓	✓	✓		
Parallel REDO	✓	✓			

The Workgroup and SQL Express editions can only be used as a witness server in mirroring session. Some other features mentioned later in this chapter required either the Enterprise or Developer edition. If you want to use high-performance operating mode, you will need the Enterprise or Developer edition.

SQL Server may use multiple threads to roll forward the log in the redo queue on the mirror database. This is called *parallel redo*. This feature is only available in the Enterprise or Developer edition. Also, if the mirror server has fewer than five CPUs, SQL Server will only use a single thread for redo. Parallel redo is also optimized by using one thread per four CPUs.

Database Mirroring Catalog Views

In the example so far, you have set up the mirroring session but don't yet know how to get information about the mirroring configuration. So before we move further with failover scenarios and other topics, we'll discuss how you can find out that information. The following are the catalog views you can use to get information about database mirroring. It would be redundant to mention each and every column in database mirroring catalog views here, because Books Online has described them well. Our goal here is to show you when and how you should use these views.

sys.database_mirroring

The most important view to monitor mirroring state, safety level, and witness status (when present) is sys.database_mirroring. See the following query, which you can execute on either partner (principal or mirror), and you will get the same results.

```
SELECT
 DB_NAME(database_id) AS DatabaseName
,mirroring_role_desc
,mirroring_safety_level_desc
,mirroring_state_desc
,mirroring_safety_sequence
,mirroring_role_sequence
,mirroring_partner_instance
,mirroring_witness_name
,mirroring_witness_state_desc
,mirroring_failover_lsn
,mirroring_connection_timeout
,mirroring_redo_queue
FROM sys.database_mirroring
WHERE mirroring_guid IS NOT NULL
```

You will use this query often once you establish the mirroring session. If you run this query after you establish the mirroring session in the example scenario, you will see output something like the following. We have put the result in a table for ease of reading. Of course, some values will be different based on your server names and so on.

Metadata column in Select list above	Principal values: MyPrincipalServer	Mirror values: MyMirrorServer
DatabaseName	TestMirroring	TestMirroring
mirroring_role_desc	PRINCIPAL	MIRROR
mirroring_safety_level_desc	FULL	FULL
mirroring_state_desc	SYNCHRONIZED	SYNCHRONIZED
mirroring_safety_sequence	2	2
mirroring_role_sequence	3	3
mirroring_partner_instance	TCP://MyMirrorServer.corp.mycompany.com:4040	TCP://MyPrincipalServer.corp.mycompany.com:4040
mirroring_witness_name	TCP://WitServer.corp.mycompany.com:4040	TCP://WitServer.corp.mycompany.com:4040
mirroring_witness_state_desc	CONNECTED	CONNECTED

Table continued on following page

Metadata column in Select list above	Principal values: MyPrincipalServer	Mirror values: MyMirrorServer
mirroring_failover_lsn	38000000011500001	38000000011500001
mirroring_connection_timeout	10	10
mirroring_redo_queue	NULL	NULL

Some values in the preceding table are self-explanatory, but others are not. The column `mirroring_safety_sequence` gives the count of how many times the safety has changed (from FULL to OFF and back) since the mirroring session was established. The column `mirroring_role_sequence` gives the count of how many times failover has happened since the mirroring session was established.

The column `mirroring_failover_lsn` gives the log sequence number of the latest transaction that is guaranteed to be hardened to the disk on both partners. In this case, because there is very little database activity, both these numbers are the same, if you use the `InsertData.sql` script in a WHILE loop (if you change the script, make sure not to use an infinite loop!).

The `mirroring_connection_timeout` column gives the mirroring connection time out in seconds. This is the number of seconds to wait for a reply from a partner or witness before considering them unavailable. The default time-out value is 10 seconds. If it is null, the database is inaccessible or is not mirrored.

The `mirroring_redo_queue` is not yet implemented in this release.

sys.database_mirroring_witnesses

If you have a witness established for your mirroring session, you can get some information from the catalog view `sys.database_mirroring_witnesses`:

```
SELECT * FROM sys.database_mirroring_witnesses
```

You can execute this query on the witness server to list the corresponding principal and mirror server names, database name, and safety level for all the mirroring sessions for which this server is a witness. You can get multiple rows with this query if the same server is acting as a witness for more than one mirroring session. This view will also give you information about how many times failover has happened between mirroring partners since the mirroring session was established in the `role_sequence_number` column. You can also get the information on whether database mirroring is suspended or not using the `is_suspended` column. If this column is 1, mirroring is currently suspended.

sys.database_mirroring_endpoints

You can use the following query to get important information about database mirroring endpoints such as port number, whether encryption is enabled or not, authentication type, and endpoint state:

```
SELECT
  dme.name AS EndPointName
  ,dme.protocol_desc
  ,dme.type_desc AS EndPointType
```

```
,dme.role_desc AS MirroringRole
,dme.state_desc AS EndPointStatus
,te.port AS PortUsed
,CASE WHEN dme.is_encryption_enabled = 1
      THEN 'Yes'
      ELSE 'No'
 END AS Is_Encryption_Enabled
,dme.encryption_algorithm_desc
,dme.connection_auth_desc
FROM sys.database_mirroring_endpoints dme
JOIN sys.tcp_endpoints te
  ON dme.endpoint_id = te.endpoint_id
```

This query uses the `sys.tcp_endpoints` view because the port information is not available in the catalog view `sys.database_mirroring_endpoints`.

Database Mirroring Role Change

In the example so far, you have learned how to establish the database mirroring session. You must have noticed that if you try to query the `TestMirroring` database on your mirror server, you will get an error like this:

```
Msg 954, Level 14, State 1, Line 1
The database "TestMirroring" cannot be opened. It is acting as a mirror database.
```

You cannot access the mirrored database. So how do you switch the roles of the mirroring partners? There are three ways you can failover to the mirror server as described in the table earlier in this chapter. The failover types depend on which transaction safety is used (`FULL` or `OFF`) and whether a witness server is present or not.

Automatic Failover

Automatic failover is a database mirroring feature in high-availability mode (`SAFETY FULL` with a witness present). When a failure occurs on the principal, automatic failover is initiated. Since you have set up database mirroring in high-availability mode with a witness server, you can do automatic failover. The following are the events that happen in an automatic failover scenario.

1. **Failure occurs:** The principal database becomes unavailable. This could be the result of a power failure, hardware failure, storage failure, or some other reason.

2. **The Failure is detected:** The failure is detected by the mirror and the witness. Note that both partners and witness continually ping each other for their presence. Of course, it is not just a simple ping and involves more than just a ping, like whether the SQL Server is available, whether the principal database is available, and so on. There is a timeout specified for the ping, which is set to 10 seconds by default when you set up the database mirroring session. You can change the timeout by using following command: `ALTER DATABASE <db_name> SET PARTNER TIMEOUT <value_in_seconds>`. If the principal does not respond to the ping message within the timeout period, it is considered to be down, and failure is detected. You should leave the default setting for timeout to 10 seconds, or at least do not change it to less than 10 seconds, because under heavy load and sporadic network conditions, false failures may occur and your database will start failing over back and forth.

3. **A complete redo is performed on the mirror:** The mirror database has been in the restoring state until now. The mirror is continuously redoing the log (rolling it forward to the database) until now. When failure is detected, the mirror needs to recover the database. In order to do that, the mirror needs to redo the remaining log entries in the redo queue.

4. **Fail over decision:** The mirror now contacts the witness server and decides whether the database should now failover to the mirror or not. Note here that in the high-safety mode with automatic failover, the witness must be present for automatic failover. The decision takes about 1 second, so if the principal comes back up before Step 3 is complete, that failover is terminated.

5. **The Mirror becomes the principal:** After both the witness and the mirror have agreed on the failover decision, the database is recovered completely. The redo happens while the failover decision is being made. The mirror's role is switched to principal, recovery is run (this involves setting up various database states and rolling back any in-flight system transactions and starting up rollback of user transactions); then the database is made available. Undo of the user transactions continues in parallel (and holds some locks) until it is completed. The database is now served to the clients and normal operations are performed.

6. **Undo:** There may be uncommitted transactions (the transactions shipped to the mirror while the principal was available but not committed before principal went down) in the transaction log of the new principal, which are now rolled back.

Normally, the time taken to failover in this operating mode is very small, usually seconds, but that mostly depends on the redo phase. If the mirror is already caught up with the principal before the principal has gone down, the redo phase will not introduce time lag. The time to apply the redo records depends on the redo queue length and the redo rate on the mirror. Note that the failover will not happen if the `mirroring_state` is not synchronized. There are some performance counters available, which we will study in the "Performance Monitoring Database Mirroring" section, later in this chapter. From these counters, you can estimate the time it will take to apply the log in the redo queue on the mirror.

To measure the actual time, you can use the profiler or trace an event. See Chapter 13 to learn more about running traces and using the profiler. Let's use the profiler here to measure the actual time it takes to failover. Open SQL Profiler, connect to the mirror server, and select the event Database Mirroring State Change under the Database events group. Run the trace. Two columns in the trace are of interest: `TextData` and `StartTime`. `TextData` provides the description of the database mirroring state change event. `StartTime` represents the timestamp at which the event took place. Start the profiler. Now stop the SQL Server service on your principal server. Soon, automatic failover will happen. Profiler will trace the events, as shown in Figure 17-3.

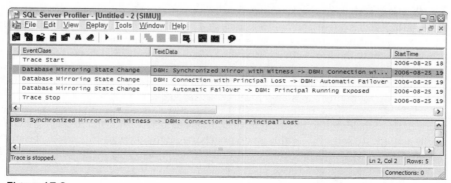

Figure 17-3

Figure 17-3 shows that the event Synchronized Mirror with witness is to contact the witness server that principal is lost, which is step 4 event in Figure 17-2. Then the mirror failed over and is running exposed, which means that the partner is lost. You will also see a message similar to the following in the mirror server error log.

```
The mirrored database "TestMirroring" is changing roles from "MIRROR" to
"PRINCIPAL" due to Auto Failover.
```

You will also notice in the `StartTime` column that the actual failover time for this automatic failover was about six seconds.

The length of the failover depends upon the type of failure and the load on the database. Under load, it takes longer to failover than in a no-load condition. Also, a manual failover takes a little more time compared to automatic failover. You will see messages similar to the following in the SQL ErrorLog.

```
The mirrored database "TestMirroring" is changing roles from "MIRROR" to
"PRINCIPAL" due to Failover from partner.
Starting up database 'TestMirroring'.
Analysis of database 'TestMirroring' (9) is 81% complete (approximately 0 seconds
remain).
Analysis of database 'TestMirroring' (9) is 100% complete (approximately 0 seconds
remain).
Recovery of database 'TestMirroring' (9) is 0% complete (approximately 30 seconds
remain). Phase 2 of 3.
Recovery of database 'TestMirroring' (9) is 16% complete (approximately 17 seconds
remain). Phase 2 of 3.
13 transactions rolled forward in database 'TestMirroring' (9).
Recovery of database 'TestMirroring' (9) is 16% complete (approximately 17 seconds
remain). Phase 3 of 3.
Recovery of database 'TestMirroring' (9) is 100% complete (approximately 0 seconds
remain). Phase 3 of 3.
```

The additional steps during analysis and recovery of the database cause the manual failover to take longer.

When the failover happens, the clients need to be redirected to the new principal server. We will discuss that in the section "Preparing Mirror Server for Failover," along with other things you have to do on the mirror server to prepare it for failover and take the load.

Manual Failover

In a manual failover, you are making a decision to switch the roles of the partners. The current mirror server will become the new principal, and the current principal becomes the new mirror. For manual failover, the `SAFETY` must be set to `FULL`. It doesn't matter whether you have the witness set up or not. You can use following command for manual failover:

```
ALTER DATABASE TestMirroring SET PARTNER FAILOVER
```

You have to run this command on the principal server in order to successfully failover. Also, the `mirroring_state` must be synchronized in order for successful failover. If it is not synchronized, you will get the following message when you try to execute the failover command on the principal:

```
Msg 1422, Level 16, State 2, Line 1
The mirror server instance is not caught up to the recent changes to database
"TestMirroring". Unable to fail over.
```

Now try a manual failover using your example server. Open the `DatabaseMirroringCommands.sql` script. When you did automatic failover earlier, we asked you to stop the original principal SQL Service. Make sure to start that service back up before the manual failover, because both the mirror and principal must be up and running for this step.

If you want to see what's happening behind the scenes, you can start SQL Profiler, connect it to the mirror server, and select the event Database Mirroring State Change under the Database event group. Run the trace. Two columns in the trace are of interest: `TextData` and `StartTime`. Also, you can start another instance of profiler and connect to the principal.

Now connect to your principal server and run the command `ALTER DATABASE TestMirroring SET PARTNER FAILOVER`. You can also use SQL Server Management Studio to do a manual failover as follows: Right-click the principal database and select Tasks➪Mirror➪Failover. That will pop up a dialog box for confirmation, where you should click OK.

You can use manual failover for planned downtime. We will talk about this in the section "Preparing the Mirror Server for Failover."

Forced Service Failover

For forced service failover, you need to run the following command on the mirror server. You should rarely use this command, since you may lose data.

```
ALTER DATABASE TestMirroring SET PARTNER FORCE_SERVICE_ALLOW_DATA_LOSS
```

When you run this command, the mirror should not be able to connect to principal; otherwise, you will not be able to failover. If your principal is up and running and if the mirror can connect to it when you try to run the command, you will get the following error message:

```
Msg 1455, Level 16, State 2, Line 1
The database mirroring service cannot be forced for database "TestMirroring"
because the database is not in the correct state to become the principal database.
```

Now try this exercise using your example server. Since you have set up the database mirroring in full-safety mode with automatic failover, you first need to remove it. Open the `DatabaseMirroringCommands.sql` script. Run the following command on either the principal or the mirror:

```
ALTER DATABASE TestMirroring SET WITNESS OFF
```

Then run the following command on the principal:

```
ALTER DATABASE TestMirroring SET SAFETY OFF
```

Now the database `TestMirroring` is set with `SAFETY OFF` and no witness. Now you can force a service failover. You'll have to simulate the scenario where mirror cannot form a quorum (cannot connect) with principal. To achieve that, stop the SQL Server service on the principal. Now run the following command on the mirror server:

```
ALTER DATABASE TestMirroring SET PARTNER FORCE_SERVICE_ALLOW_DATA_LOSS
```

This command now will force the `TestMirroring` database on the mirror server to recover and make it online. The `mirroring_state` (`sys.database_mirroring`) does not matter (synchronized or not) in this case, because it is a forced failover, and that is why you may lose data in this scenario.

Now see what happens if you bring the original principal server (the one where you stopped SQL Server service) back online. After you bring the server online, the mirroring session will be suspended. You can use the `query sys.database_mirroring` view in the `MirroringCatalogView.sql` script to view the mirroring state by connecting on either the principal or the mirror. You can resume the mirroring session by running the following from the `DatabaseMirroringCommands.sql` script on either the principal or the mirror.

```
ALTER DATABASE TestMirroring SET PARTNER RESUME
```

Database Availability Scenarios

So far we have talked about database mirroring operating modes and how to failover in different operating modes. In this section, we talk about what happens to the database availability to clients when the server is lost. The server might be lost not just because the power is off but because of a communication link failure or some other reason; the point is that the other server in the mirroring session cannot communicate. Several different scenarios exist. To keep matters clear, we will use three server names for this section: ServerA (principal), ServerB (mirror) and ServerC (witness).

Principal is Lost

If the principal server is lost, the failover scenario depends on the transaction safety (FULL or OFF) and whether a witness is present or not.

Scenario 1: Safety FULL with a Witness

We have discussed this scenario in the automatic failover section. In this scenario, the mirror forms a quorum with the witness because the principal is lost. Automatic failover will happen (of course, some conditions must be met as we mentioned earlier for automatic failover to happen), the mirror becomes the new principal server, and the database will be available on the new principal.

In this situation, before the failure, ServerA was the principal, ServerB was the mirror, and ServerC was the witness. ServerA now fails. After failover, ServerB becomes the principal and will serve the database. However, because there is no mirror server after failover (because ServerA is down), ServerB is running exposed, and the mirroring state is DISCONNECTED. If ServerA becomes operational, it will automatically assume the roll of the mirror, except for the fact that the session will be suspended until the admin issues a resume.

If SAFETY is full and you have configured a witness, in order to make database service available, at least two servers should be available to form a quorum. In this scenario, if ServerA fails, ServerB becomes the principal, and it will serve the database. But now if ServerC (witness) goes down, ServerB will not be able to serve the database.

Scenario 2: Safety FULL without a Witness

In this operating mode, safety is high, but automatic failover is not possible. So if the principal fails, the database service is unavailable to the clients. You need to manually perform several steps to make the database service available again. You can force service to make the database available.

In this situation, before the failure, ServerA was the principal, ServerB was the mirror, and there was no witness. ServerA is now lost, so the database is unavailable to clients. In order to make the database available, you need to execute the following commands on the mirror.

```
ALTER DATABASE <database name>SET PARTNER OFF
RESTORE DATABASE <database name> WITH RECOVERY
```

These commands will bring the database on ServerB online, and the database server will be available again. When ServerA becomes available, you have to reestablish the mirroring session.

There is another option here, where you do not have to reestablish the mirroring session. Run the following command on ServerB (which is still the mirror after ServerA becomes unavailable).

```
ALTER DATABASE TestMirroring SET PARTNER FORCE_SERVICE_ALLOW_DATA_LOSS
```

That will bring the database online on ServerB, which becomes the principal server. When ServerA comes online, it will automatically assume the role of the mirror. However, the mirroring session will be suspended, meaning no logs will move from ServerB to ServerA. You can resume the mirroring session (start moving logs from ServerB to ServerA) by running the following command.

```
ALTER DATABASE TestMirroring SET PARTNER RESUME
```

When your database is really huge (hundreds of GBs), it is a real pain to backup and restore to reestablish the mirroring session.

Whether you choose to break the mirroring session or force service, you will lose the transactions that haven't yet made it to the mirror at the time of failure.

Scenario 3: SAFETY OFF

When SAFETY is OFF, the witness doesn't add any value, so we recommend that you do not configure a witness in that case. If the principal server is lost in this scenario, the database service becomes unavailable. You have to force the service to make the database service available again.

In this scenario, before the failure, ServerA was the principal and ServerB was the mirror. ServerA now fails, so the database service is not available to clients. You can failover to ServerB using the following command.

```
ALTER DATABASE TestMirroring SET PARTNER FORCE_SERVICE_ALLOW_DATA_LOSS
```

However, the SAFETY is OFF, so it is possible that there were transactions that didn't make it to the mirror at the time of the failure of the principal. These transactions will be lost. Therefore, manual failover with safety off involves acknowledging the possibility of data loss. When ServerA becomes operational again, it will automatically assume the role of the mirror, but the mirroring session will be suspended. You can resume the mirroring session again by running the following command:

```
ALTER DATABASE TestMirroring SET PARTNER RESUME
```

Mirror is Lost

If mirror fails, the principal will continue functioning, so the database service is still available to the clients. The mirroring state will be DISCONNECTED, and the principal is running exposed in this case. You can use the sys.database_mirroring view to find the mirroring state on the principal server.

When the mirror goes down, you have to be a little careful, and you have to take steps to make sure that the principal serves the database without any issue. When the mirror goes down, the mirroring state will be changed to DISCONNECTED, and as long as the state is DISCONNECTED, the transaction-log space cannot be reused even if you back up the transaction log. If your log files keep growing and reach their maximum size limit, or your disk runs out of space, the complete database comes to a halt.

You have some options here:

❏ Make sure you have plenty of disk space for the transaction log to grow on the principal and make sure to bring back the mirror before you run out of space.

❏ Break the database mirroring session using the command ALTER DATABASE TestMirroring SET PARTNER OFF. The problem here is that when your mirror server becomes operational, you will have to reestablish the mirroring session by a backup and restore of the database on principal and performing other steps as we have mentioned in the example. If your database is huge, the backup and restore step could be very painful and can take a long time, so consider the following step.

❏ Break the database mirroring session using the command ALTER DATABASE TestMirroring SET PARTNER OFF. Make a note of the time when the mirror went down. Make sure your job that backs up the transaction log is running on the principal. When the mirror comes back up online, apply all the transaction logs on the mirror database. The first transaction log you would apply is the one you backed up after the mirror went down. Make sure to apply the transaction log on the mirror database with the NORECOVERY option. That way, you do not have to back up the whole database and restore it on the mirror. Of course, you have to perform other steps to reestablish the mirroring session because the session was broken.

Witness Is Lost

If witness is lost, the database mirroring session will continue functioning without interruption. The database will be available. Automatic failover will not happen. When witness comes back online, it will automatically join the mirroring session, of course, as witness. With safety set to FULL, if the witness is lost, and then the mirror or the principal is lost, the database service will be unavailable to the clients.

Mirror and Witness Are Lost

Assume that you have configured the mirroring session with a witness. If the mirror server is unavailable, the principal will still make the database service available, but it is running exposed. If the witness is also lost, the principal becomes isolated and cannot service the clients. Even though the principal database is running, it is not available to the clients. If you try to access the database, you will get the following message:

```
Msg 955, Level 14, State 1, Line 1
Database <db_name> is enabled for Database Mirroring, but neither the partner nor
witness server instances are available: the database cannot be opened.
```

If both the mirror and witness are lost, the only way you can bring the database service online to clients is by breaking the mirroring session, by running the following command on the principal:

```
ALTER DATABASE <database name> SET PARTNER OFF
```

Once the mirror becomes available, you can reestablish the mirroring session. To reestablish the mirroring session, you may have to back up and restore the database on the mirror, but if you want to avoid that step, refer to the third option in the "Mirror Is Lost" section. Once the witness becomes available, you can join in the witness as well, but you have to establish the mirroring session with the mirror before the witness can join in, as you have seen.

Monitoring Database Mirroring

There are different ways to monitor database mirroring, based on what information you are looking for. For basic information about the database mirroring state, safety level, and witness status, you can use catalog views. You can refer to the "Database Mirroring Catalog Views" section for more details about catalog views. To monitor the performance of database mirroring, SQL Server provides a set of System Monitor performance objects. There is also a GUI "Database Mirroring Monitor" available with SQL Server Management Studio, which you can access if your database is mirrored. We will discuss the key System Monitor counters and then the GUI in this section.

Monitoring Using System Monitor

The object SQL Server: Database Mirroring has plenty of counters to monitor database mirroring performance. You can use these counters to monitor the database mirroring activities on each partner and also the traffic between them. See Figure 17-4. You can use these counters for each database instance, so if you are mirroring more than one database on a server, select the database you want to monitor from the list box. Below are the key counters.

Figure 17-4

Counters for the Principal

The following counters can be used on the principal server:

- **Log Bytes Sent/Sec:** This counter will tell you the rate at which the principal is sending transaction-log data to the mirror.

- **Log Send Queue KB:** The total kilobytes of the log that have not been sent to the mirror server yet. As the transaction-log data is sent from the principal to the mirror, the Log Send Queue will be depleted and will grow as new transactions are recorded into the log buffer on the principal.

- **Transaction Delay:** The delay (in milliseconds) in waiting for commit acknowledgement from the mirror. This counter reports the total delay for all the transactions in process at the time. You can determine the average delay per transaction by dividing this counter by the Transactions/sec counter. In high-performance mode, this counter will always be zero. Make sure to choose the database instance you are interested in for this counter.

  Do a simple exercise using the `InsertData.sql` script from earlier to get a feel for how this counter tells you the delay in transaction. Start the Performance Monitor and add this counter on your principal. Run the script. Note the average for this counter. It will show some value greater than 0. Then run the command `ALTER DATABASE TestMirroring SET SAFETY OFF` on the principal. This will put database mirroring in high-Performance mode. Now run the script again. You will notice that the counter would reflect 0.

- **Transaction/Sec:** You will find this counter in the `Database` object. This counter measures database throughput and shows many transactions are processed in a second. This counter gives you an idea of how fast the log file will grow if your mirror is down, the mirror state is `DISCONNECTED`, and you need to expand the log file. Make sure to choose the database instance you are interested in for this counter.

- **Log Bytes Flushed/Sec:** This counter is under the `Database` object. This counter tells you how many bytes are written to disk (log hardening) per second on the principal. This is the log-generation rate of your application. These are also the bytes sent to the mirror at the time it is flushed to the disk on the principal. In normal operating conditions, the Log Bytes Flushed/Sec and Log Bytes Sent/Sec counters would show same number. If you look at Figure 17-2, the activity labeled 2 happens at the same time, and that is exactly what the Performance Monitor tells you.

Counters for Mirror

The following counters can be used on the mirror server:

- **Redo Bytes/Sec:** This counter tells you the rate at which log bytes are rolled forward (replayed) to the data pages per second from the redo queue.

- **Redo Queue KB:** This counter shows the total KB of the transaction log still to be applied to the mirror database (rolled forward). You will see later how to calculate the estimated time the mirror will take to redo the logs using this counter and the Redo Bytes/Sec counter. The failover time will depend on how big this queue is and how fast the mirror can empty this queue.

- **Log Bytes Received/Sec:** This counter will tell you the rate at which log bytes are received from the principal. If the mirror can keep up with principal to minimize the failover time, ideally the Log Bytes Received/Sec and Redo Bytes/Sec counter will show the same *average* value, which means that the Redo Queue KB is zero. Whatever bytes the principal has sent are immediately rolled forward to the data pages on the mirror and there is no redo left, so the mirror is ready to failover right now.

From a DBA standpoint, we would like to know approximately how far the mirror is behind the principal and once mirror catches up how long would it take to redo the transaction log so that it can failover. There is some calculation required, which we can tell you about, but also, there is the Database Mirroring Monitor tool, which ships with SQL Server and can give you all this information readily. We will look at that tool in a moment. First, we'll describe the calculations, so you know how they are calculated in the tool.

To calculate the estimated time for mirror to catch up (in seconds) with principal, you can use the Log Send Queue counter from the principal and the Log Bytes Received/Sec counter on the mirror. You can also use Log Bytes Send/Sec counter on the principal instead of Log Bytes Received/Sec on the mirror. Use the average value. The following is the calculation:

```
Estimated time to catch up (in seconds) = (Log Send Queue)/ (Log Bytes Received
/sec)
```

To calculate the estimated time for the mirror to replay the transaction log (redo) in order to get ready for failover, you can use the Redo Queue KB counter (this counter gives you KB value, so convert it to Bytes) and the Redo Bytes/Sec counter on mirror. Use the average value. The following is the calculation:

```
Estimated time to redo (in seconds) = (Redo Queue)/ (Redo Bytes/sec)
```

Monitoring Using Database Mirroring Monitor

The database mirroring development team in SQL Server came up with this really nice tool to monitor the database mirroring activities that will make the DBA's life very easy. You can access this tool by running `sqlmonitor.exe` from the command prompt and then selecting Go⇨Database Mirroring Monitor, or you can right-click any user database in Object Explorer in SQL Management Studio on any registered SQL Server 2005 machine and select Tasks⇨Launch Database Mirroring Monitor. The Database Mirroring Monitor is shown in Figure 17-5.

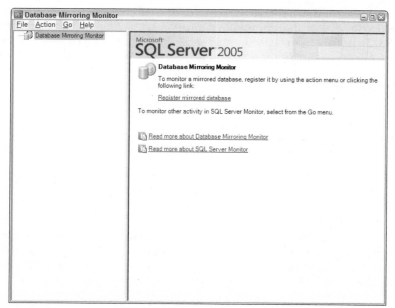

Figure 17-5

You can monitor all your mirroring sessions here. You have to register the mirrored database in this tool before you can use it. You can do that by clicking Action⇨Register Mirrored Database, and then just follow the wizard. You can give the wizard either the principal server name or the mirror server name, and it will figure out the other. Figure 17-6 shows the Database Mirroring Monitor with a registered mirrored database.

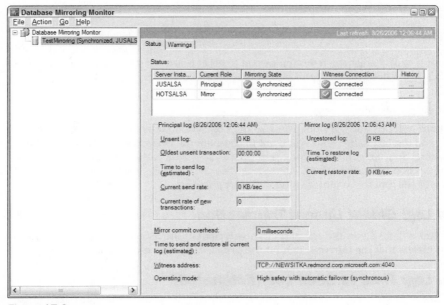

Figure 17-6

You can monitor the key counters we mentioned in the previous section using this GUI. You can also set alerts for these counters to get an e-mail or take an action if they exceed a set threshold, which you will see later.

If you set up mirroring using the SQL Management Studio, it creates the SQL job called Database Mirroring Monitor Job, which runs every one minute by default to refresh these counters. This data is stored in the `msdb.dbo.dbm_monitor_data` table. You can change the job schedule if you want to. If you set up database mirroring using the scripts we provided, you can create the SQL job using the following command to refresh the counters:

```
sp_dbmmonitoraddmonitoring [ update_period ]
```

The [`update_period`] by default is one minute. You can specify a value between 1 and 120, in minutes. If you do not create this job, you just have to press F5 when you are on the Database Mirroring Monitor screen. It will call the `sp_dbmmonitorresults` stored procedure to refresh the data (adding a row for new readings) in the `msdb.dbo.dbm_monitor_data` table. Actually, `sp_dbmmonitorresults` calls another stored procedure in the `msdb` database called `sp_dbmmonitorupdate` to update the status table and calculate the performance matrix displayed in the UI. If you hit F5 more than once in 15 seconds, it will not refresh the data in the table.

Take a look at the Status screen details in Figure 17-6. The status area where the server instance names, their current role, mirroring state, and witness connection status (if there is a witness) comes from the catalog view sys.database_mirroring. If you click the History button, it will give you the history of the mirroring status and other performance counters based on how far you want to go. The mirroring status and performance history is kept for seven days (168 hrs) by default in the msdb.dbo.dbm_monitor_data table. If you want to change the retention period, you can use the sp_dbmmonitor changealert stored procedure, like this:

```
EXEC sp_dbmmonitorchangealert TestMirroring, 5, 8, 1
```

This example will change the retention period to eight hours for the TestMirroring database. You can refer to BOL for a description of this stored procedure.

Principal Log: Unsent Log

This counter will provide the same value as the Log Send Queue KB counter on the principal. Unsent Log will read the last value, so if you want to compare the Performance Monitor and this counter, look at the last value. You can run the script InsertData.sql from earlier in the chapter after suspending the mirroring session using the ALTER DATABASE TestMirroring SET PARTNER SUSPEND command, and you will see that this counter value will start going up.

Principal Log: Oldest Unsent Transaction

This counter will give you the age in hh:mm:ss format of the oldest unsent transaction sitting in the Send Queue. It means that the mirror is behind the principal by that much time.

Principal Log: Time to Send Log (Estimated)

This counter will give you the estimated time the principal instance requires to send the log to that is currently in the Send Queue to the mirror server. Because the rate of the incoming transaction can change, this counter can only give you an estimate. This counter will give you a rough estimate of the time it will require to manually failover. If you suspend the mirroring, you will notice that this counter will show a value of "Infinite," which means that since you are not sending any transaction logs to the mirror, the mirror will never catch up.

Principal Log: Current Send Rate

This counter gives you the rate at which the transaction log is sent to the mirror in KB/Sec. This is the same as the Performance Monitor counter Log Bytes Sent/Sec. The counter Current Send Rate gives you the value in KB, whereas the counter Log Bytes Sent/Sec gives the value in bytes. When Time to Send Log is infinite, this counter will show a value of 0 KB/Sec because no log is being sent to the mirror.

Principal Log: Current Rate of New Transaction

This counter gives you the rate at which new transactions are coming in per second. This is same as the Transaction/sec counter in Database objects.

Mirror Log: Unrestored Log

This counter is for mirror server and will give you the amount of log in KB sitting in the Redo Queue yet to be restored. This is the same as the Redo Queue KB counter for the mirror server. If this counter is 0, the mirror is keeping up with the principal and can failover right away, if necessary.

Mirror Log: Time to Restore Log

This counter gives you an estimate, in minutes, of how long the mirror will take to replay the transaction sitting in the Redo Queue. We have done this calculation above. This is the estimate time that the mirror will require before failover.

Mirror Log: Current Restore Rate

This counter gives the rate at which the transaction log is restored into the mirror database in KB/Sec.

Mirror Committed Overhead

This counter measures the delay (in milliseconds) in waiting for a commit acknowledgement from the mirror. This counter is the same as the Transaction Delay on the principal. This counter is relevant only in high-safety mode. For high-performance mode, this counter will be zero because the principal does not wait for the mirror to harden the log to disk.

Time to send and restore all current Log (Estimated)

This counter measures the time needed to send and restore all of the logs that have been committed at the principal as of the current time. This time may be less than the sum of the values of the Time to send log (estimated) and Time to restore log (estimated) fields, because sending and restoring can operate in parallel. This estimate does predict the time required to send and restore new transactions committed at the principal while working through backlogs in the Send Queue.

Witness Address

This field shows you the fully qualified domain name of the witness with the port number assigned for that endpoint.

Operating Mode

This field shows the operating mode of the database mirroring session, one of the following:

- ❑ High performance (asynchronous)
- ❑ High safety without automatic failover (synchronous)
- ❑ High safety with automatic failover (synchronous)

Setting Threshold on Counters and Sending Alerts

You can set the warning for different mirroring thresholds so you will receive alerts based on the threshold you have set. Figure 17-7 shows the Warnings tab.

There are different warnings for which you can set the thresholds. You can set the alert using SQL Server Management Studio for this event. To learn how to set Alerts, refer to Chapter 5. We will give you a quick summary of how to set the alerts here. Start by clicking the Set Thresholds button to open the window shown in Figure 17-8.

You can see that you can set the threshold for counters on both the principal and mirror servers individually so that you can either keep the threshold the same or different based on your needs. For this example, select the checkbox for the first warning, "Warn if the unsent log exceeds the threshold," and set the threshold value to 100 KB, just for the principal server.

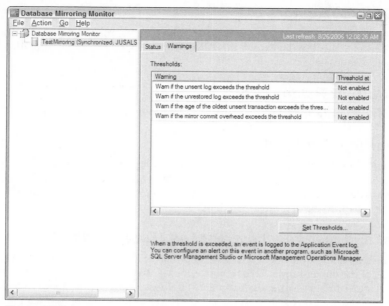

Figure 17-7

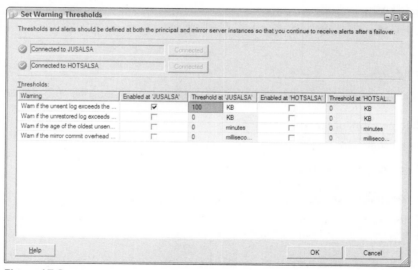

Figure 17-8

Now under Alert folder in SQL Server Agent in SQL Management Studio, add a new alert. You will see a screen similar to the one shown in Figure 17-9. Type the name for your alert. Select the database name for which you need this alert, in this case, TestMirroring. Now SQL Server will raise the error when the threshold you set is exceeded. The error number is 32042, so type that error number. You can refer to the section "Using Warning Thresholds and Alerts on Mirroring Performance Metrics" in Books Online to get the error numbers for other events. Now click the Response on left pane and fill out the information of the operator who will receive the alert when the threshold is exceeded. That's it. You can test this alert by suspending the database mirroring using the `ALTER DATABASE TestMirroring SET PARTNER SUSPEND` on the principal. The log will not be sent to the mirror and the Unsent Log counter will start increasing. Once it reaches the threshold of 100KB, you should get the alert. We will look at an example of how to set up the database mirroring event change (suspended, synchronizing, synchronized) and send a notification later in the section titled "Mirroring Event Listener Example."

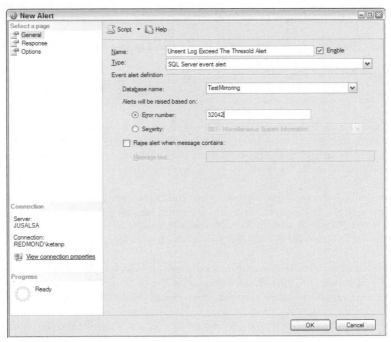

Figure 17-9

Monitoring using SQL Profiler

SQL Server 2005 Profiler contains one event class for database mirroring, the Database: Database Mirroring State Change event. This event will record all the database mirroring state changes (suspended, synchronizing, synchronized, and so on) that happen on the server.

Troubleshooting Database Mirroring

The two areas where you get errors with mirroring are during setup and at runtime. We'll discuss each of these separately.

Troubleshooting Setup Errors

You may get the following error while setting up database mirroring:

```
2006-05-27 17:53:16.630 spid15s      Database mirroring connection error 4 'An
error occurred while receiving data: '64(The specified network name is no longer
available.)'.' for 'TCP://MyMirrorServer:4040'. 2006-05-27 17:55:13.710 spid15s
Error: 1443, Severity: 16, State: 2.
```

It may be possible that the firewall on mirror or principal server is blocking the connection on the port specified. Make sure that the firewall is not blocking communication on that port.

You may get the following error while setting up database mirroring on the principal:

```
Msg 1412, Level 16, State 0, Line 1
The remote copy of database "TestMirroring" has not been rolled forward to a point
in time that is encompassed in the local copy of the database log.
```

This indicates that the database on mirror is not rolled forward enough to establish the mirroring session. You may have backed up some transaction logs while backing up and restoring the database, so you have to restore these logs to the mirror server with the NORECOVERY option to sync the mirror with the principal. See the RestoreLogOnMirror.sql script for an example.

Make sure that the SQL Server Windows service accounts on each server are trusted and that the user account under which the SQL Server instance is running has the necessary connect permissions. If the servers are on nontrusted domains, make sure the certificates are correct. You can refer to the "Database Mirroring Endpoint" section for details regarding how to configure the certificates.

Make sure the endpoint status is started on all partners and the witness. You can use the Mirroring CatalogView.sql script, which we have provided in the code for this chapter. Look for the EndPointStatus column and make sure that the value is STARTED.

Make sure that you are not using a port used by other process. The port number must be unique per server, not per SQL Server instance. You can use any port number between 1024 and 32767. You can use the MirroringCatalogView.sql script to view the port information under the PortUsed column.

Make sure that the encryption settings for the endpoints are compatible on the principal, mirror, and witness. You can check the encryption setting using MirroringCatalogView.sql. Look for the script that selects from the catalog view sys.database_mirroring_endpoints, and check for the IS_ENCRYPTION_ENABLED column. This column has a value of either 0 or 1. A value of 0 means encryption is DISABLED for the endpoint, and a value of 1 means encryption is either REQUIRED or SUPPORTED.

Make sure that you have identified the correct fully qualified names of the partners and witness (if any) in the ALTER DATABASE command.

Troubleshooting Runtime Errors

If your database mirroring setup is done correctly and you get errors after that, the first thing you want to look at is the sys.database_mirroring catalog view. Check the status of the mirroring state. If it is SUSPENDED, check the SQL ErrorLog for more details. You may have added a data file or log file on the principal, and you do not have the exact same path on the mirror, which will cause a Redo error to occur on the mirror, and the database session will be suspended. You will see an error similar to the following in the mirror server error log:

```
Error: 5123, Severity: 16, State: 1.
CREATE FILE encountered operating system error 3(The system cannot find the path
specified.) while attempting to open or create the physical file
'D:\t\TestMirroring_1.ndf'.
```

If that is the case, create the folder on the mirror and then resume the mirroring session using the following command:

```
ALTER DATABASE TestMirroring SET PARTNER RESUME
```

If you have added the file and you do not have that drive on the mirror, you have to delete that file from the principal. You may have to empty the file before you delete it, if pages are allocated on the file. Then resume the mirroring session again.

If you cannot connect to the principal database even though your server is online, it is most likely because safety is set to FULL, and the principal server cannot form a quorum because both the witness and mirror are lost. This can happen, for example, if your system is in high-safety mode with witness, and the mirror has become disconnected from the old principal, followed by the witness. You force the mirror server to recover, using the following command on the mirror:

```
ALTER DATABASE TestMirroring SET PARTNER FORCE_SERVICE_ALLOW_DATA_LOSS
```

After that, since again both the old principal and the witness are not available, the new principal cannot serve the database, so turn the SAFETY to OFF using the ALTER DATABASE <db_name> SET PARTNER SAFETY OFF command.

Check to make sure there is sufficient disk space on the mirror for both redo (free space on the data drives) and log hardening (free space on the log drive).

Preparing the Mirror server for Failover

When you set up mirroring, your intentions are clear that in the event of failover, the mirror takes on the full load. In order for the mirror to be fully functional as a principal, you have to do some configurations on the mirror server. Please note that database mirroring is a database-to-database failover solution only. The entire SQL Server instance is *not* mirrored. If you want to implement full instance failover, you have to consider failover clustering. We will compare different high-availability technologies in the section "Database Mirroring and other High Availability Solutions."

Hardware, Software, and Server Configuration

Your mirror server hardware should be identical (CPU, memory, storage, and network capacity) to that of the principal if you want your mirror server to handle the same load as your principal. You may argue that if your principal is a 16-way, 64-bit server with 32GB RAM, having an identical hardware for mirror is a costly solution if your principal is not going down often. You may feel that such expensive hardware is sitting idle. If your application is not that critical, you may want to have a smaller server for just failover and take the load for some time, but I would argue that if the application is not that critical, you do not have such extensive hardware on the primary either. Also with such huge hardware, the process on the server must be very heavy. So if you failover, your mirror should be able to handle that load even it is for some time. You have to determine the business cost versus hardware cost and make the decision. Also, you can use your mirror server for noncritical work so that while it is just a mirror, it can be used for some other process. Of course, you have to plan that out properly to make proper use of your mirror server.

Make sure that you have the same OS version, service packs, and patches on both servers. Of course, during a rolling upgrade (we will discuss that in the "Preparing for Planned Downtime" section), service packs and patch levels can be different temporarily.

Make sure you have same edition of SQL Server on both partners. If you are using a witness, you don't have to have the same edition. You can use a smaller server for the witness because it doesn't carry any load at all. Of course, the availability of the witness server is critical for automatic failover. You can refer to the table in the section "Database Mirroring and SQL Server 2005 Editions" for more details on which edition supports which database mirroring features.

Make sure you have an identical directory structure for the SQL Server install and database files on both the partners. If you add a database file to a volume/directory and that volume/directory does not exist on mirror, the mirroring session will be suspended right away.

Make sure that all the SQL Server configurations are also identical (`tempdb` size, trace flags, startup parameters, memory settings, degree of parallelism) for both principal and mirror.

Logins and their permissions are very important. All SQL Server logins on the principal must also be present on the mirror server; otherwise, your application will not be able to work in the event of failover. You can use SQL Server Integration Service, which has a "Transfer logins" task to copy logins and passwords from one server to another. You will still need to set the database permission for these logins. If you transfer these logins to a different domain, you have to match the SID also.

There are many other objects that may exist and are needed for that application on the principal. You have to transfer all these objects to the mirror server (for example, SQL jobs, SQL Server Integration Services packages, linked server definitions, maintenance plans, supported databases, SQL Mail or Database mail settings, and DTC settings).

If you are using SQL Server authentication, you have to resolve the logins on the new principal server after failover. You can use the `sp_change_users_login` stored procedure to resolve these logins. Note that `sp_change_users_login` cannot be used with a SQL Server login created from a Windows principal.

Make sure to have a process in place so that when you make any changes to any configuration on the principal, you repeat or transfer the changes on the mirror server.

Once you set up your mirror, failover the database and let your application run for some time on the new principal, because that is the only way you can make sure that all the settings are correct. Try to schedule this task during less busy hours and make sure you do the proper communication on your test.

Database Availability During Planned Downtime

There are two ways you can configure the mirroring session as far as transaction safety is concerned: SAFETY FULL and SAFETY OFF. We'll look at steps for both these options and see how to use the "rolling upgrade" technique to perform a software and hardware upgrade while keeping the database up for applications.

SAFETY FULL

Assuming that you have configured the mirroring session with safety full, if you have to perform software and hardware upgrades, perform these steps in order.

1. Perform the hardware and software changes on the mirror server first. If you have to restart the SQL Server or the server itself, you can do so. As soon as the server comes back up again, mirroring sessions will be established automatically and the mirror will start synchronizing with the principal. Note that the principal is exposed for the duration that the mirror database is down, so if you have a witness configured, make sure that it is available during this time, or the principal will be running isolated and will not be able to serve the database, because it cannot form the quorum.

2. Once the mirror is synchronized with the principal, you can now failover using the ALTER DATABASE <db_name> SET PARTNER FAILOVER command. The application will not connect to the new principal. We will talk about application redirection when database is mirrored in the "Client Redirection" section later. Open and in-flight transactions during failover will be rolled back. If that is not tolerable for your application, you can stop the application for the brief moment of failover and restart the application after failover succeeds. Now perform the hardware or software upgrade on your old principal server. After you are done with upgrades and the database becomes available on the old principal, it will assume the role of mirror, the database mirroring session will be established automatically, and it will start synchronizing.

3. If you have a witness set up, perform the hardware or software upgrade on that server.

4. Your old principal is currently acting as a mirror. You can fail back to your old principal because all your upgrades are done. If you have the same hardware on the new principal, leave it as is so that you don't have to stop the application for a brief moment. But if your hardware is not identical, you should consider switching back to your original principal.

SAFETY OFF

If you have configured the database mirroring with SAFETY OFF, you can still use the "rolling upgrade" technique by following these steps:

1. Perform the hardware and software changes on the mirror first. See more details in the "SAFETY FULL" section.

2. Change the SAFETY to FULL using the ALTER DATABASE <db_name> SET SAFETY FULL command. You have to run this on the principal server. Plan this activity during off-peak hours so that your mirror server will not take too much time to get synchronized.

3. Once the mirror is synchronized, you can perform the failover to the mirror.

4. Perform the hardware and software upgrade on the old principal. Once the old principal comes back up, it will assume the mirror role and start synchronizing with the new principal.

5. Once synchronized, you can fail back to your original principal.

If you are using mirroring just for making a redundant copy of your database, you may not want to failover for planned downtime, because you may not have done all the other settings properly on mirror as mentioned in the "Hardware, Software, and Server Configuration" section. In that case, you have to take the principal down for upgrade, and the database service will not be available.

SQL Job Configuration on the Mirror

For identical configuration on both the principal and mirror servers, you also have to copy SQL jobs on your mirror server as we mentioned earlier. When the database is the mirror, you do not want these SQL jobs to run. You have some options on how to do that:

❑ Disable these jobs and enable them manually when the database becomes the principal. As a DBA, you do not want to baby-sit these jobs, so this is not a good option.

❑ Have some logic in the SQL job steps that checks for the database mirroring state and run the next step only if the database mirroring state is principal.

❑ Listen for the database mirroring change event when the database becomes principal and execute a SQL job that will enable all the SQL jobs you want to run. Stop or disable these jobs again when the event is fired, indicating that the database state has changed to mirror. We will discuss how to listen to these database mirroring state change events in the "Mirroring Event Listener Setup" section later.

Database TRUSTWORTHY Bit on the Mirror

If you restore the database, the TRUSTWORTHY bit is set to 0 automatically. So when you set up database mirroring, this bit will be set to 0 as soon as you restore your database on your mirror server. If your application requires this bit to be 1, in case of failover, your application will fail because this bit is set to 0 on the mirror, which is now the new principal. To avoid this, when you set up the database mirroring, once it is set up correctly, failover to the mirror and set this bit to 1 using ALTER DATABASE <db_name> SET TRUSTWORTHY ON. Then optionally fail back to your original principal.

Client Redirection to the Mirror

In SQL Server 2005, if you connect to a database that is being mirrored with ADO.NET or the SQL Native Client, your application can take advantage of the drivers' ability to automatically redirect connections when a database mirroring failover occurs. You must specify the initial principal server and database in the connection string and optionally the failover partner server. There are many ways to write the connection string, but here is one example, specifying server A as the principal, server B as the mirror, and AdventureWorks as the database name:

```
"Data Source=A;Failover Partner=B;Initial Catalog=AdventureWorks;Integrated
Security=True;"
```

The failover partner in the connection string is used as an alternate server name if the connection to the initial principal server fails. If the connection to the initial principal server succeeds, the failover partner name will not be used, but the driver will store the failover partner name that it retrieves from the principal server on the client-side cache.

Assume a client is successfully connected to the principal, and a database mirroring failover (automatic, manual, or forced) occurs. The next time the application attempts to use the connection, the ADO.NET or SQL Native Client driver will detect that the connection to the old principal has failed and will automatically retry connecting to the new principal as specified in the failover partner name. If successful, and there is a new mirror server specified for the database mirroring session by the new principal, the driver will retrieve the new partner failover server name and place it in its client cache. If the client cannot connect to the alternate server, the driver will try each server alternately until the login timeout period is reached.

The great advantage of using the database mirroring support built into ADO.NET and the SQL Native Client driver is that you do not need to recode the application, or place special codes in the application, to handle a database mirroring failover.

If you do not use the ADO.NET or SQL Native Client automatic redirection, you can use other techniques that will enable your application to failover. For example, you could use Network Load Balancing (NLB) to manually redirect connections from one server to another, while the client just connects to a virtual server name. Of course, in NLB you have to configure to make sure that the entire load is diverted to the principal and not actually doing NLB, because at a given point only the principal database is available. Also, you will have to listen to the mirroring state change event to change the NLB configuration to divert the load to a particular server. You might also write your own redirection code and retry logic.

Mirroring Multiple Databases

You can mirror multiple databases on the same server, as we have discussed. You can either use the same server for a mirror partner, or you can use a different mirror server for each database. I would recommend that you use the same mirror server for mirroring multiple databases from a principal server. That way, the maintenance is less, and the system has less complexity; otherwise, you will have to perform all the steps we mentioned in the "Hardware, Software, and Server Configuration" section on each mirror server.

If you want to use the database mirroring feature, especially with high-safety and automatic failover, you have to be careful when you design your application. Consider a scenario where your application is using two databases, DB1 and DB2, on a server called ServerA. Now you have set up database mirroring for both these databases to your mirror server ServerB with automatic failover. Suppose a failover occurs with only DB1 (perhaps because of a disk failure on the disk where DB1 resides or a sporadic network issue that could cause the mirroring session of one database to time out), and because of the automatic failover, the database will failover to the mirror ServerB. So ServerB will be the principal for database DB1, and ServerA is the principal for database DB2. Where would your application connect? Even though both databases are available, your application would not function correctly. This could also happen if you manually failover the one database and not the other.

So an application that relies on multiple databases is not a good candidate for a high-safety with automatic failover scenario. You can probably have high-safety mode *without* automatic failover and have an alert when mirroring state changes so that you can manually failover all the databases or have a SQL job that does that for you.

Also remember that you cannot mirror a system database. Also, make sure that you do not mirror too many databases on a single server, or it may affect server and application performance. You should not mirror more than 10 databases at a time on an instance. Use Performance Monitor counters and the Database Mirroring Monitoring tool to see how your servers are performing.

Database Mirroring and Other High-Availability Solutions

Database mirroring is another weapon in the arsenal of SQL Server high-availability solutions. There are at least four high-availability solutions that SQL Server 2005 provides. Of course, each solution has some overlaps with the others, and each has some advantages and disadvantages. The following is the list of these technologies.

- ❑ **Failover clustering:** This is a typical solution for high availability, with a two-node Windows failover cluster with one SQL Server instance. Clustering is discussed in more detail in Chapter 20.

- ❑ **Database mirroring:** For this discussion, we will consider the high-safety mode with witness.

- ❑ **Log shipping:** SQL Server built-in log shipping. Log shipping is discussed in detail in Chapter 19.

- ❑ **Transactional replication:** For comparison purposes, we'll consider a separate distribution server with a single subscriber server as a standby if the publisher fails.

We will compare database mirroring with these other technologies here.

Database Mirroring and Clustering

Obviously, the most distinct difference between database mirroring and a cluster solution is the level at which each provides redundancy. Database mirroring provides protection at database level, as we have seen, whereas a cluster solution provides protection at the server-instance level.

As we discuss in the "Mirroring Multiple Databases" section, if your application requires multiple database access, clustering is a better solution. If you need to provide availability of one database at a time, mirroring is better solution and has many advantages (for example, ease of configuration) compared to clustering.

Unlike clustering, database mirroring does not require proprietary hardware and does not have a potential failure point with shared storage. Database mirroring brings the standby database into service much faster than any other high-availability technology and works well with new capabilities in ADO.NET and SQL Native Access Client for client-side failover.

Another important difference is that in database mirroring, the principal and mirror servers are separate SQL Server instances with distinct names, whereas a SQL Server instance on a cluster gets one virtual server name and IP address that remains the same no matter what node of the cluster is hosting the instance.

You cannot use database mirroring within a cluster, although you can consider using database mirroring as a method for creating a hot standby for a cluster instance database. If you do, be aware that because a cluster failover is longer than the timeout value on database mirroring, a high-availability mode mirroring session will react to a cluster failover as a failure of the principal server. It would then put the cluster node into a mirroring state. You can increase the database mirroring timeout value by using following command:

```
ALTER DATABASE <db_name> SET PARTNER TIMOUT <interger_value_in_seconds>
```

Database Mirroring and Transactional Replication

The common process between database mirroring and transactional replication is reading the log on the originating server. Although the synchronization mechanism is different, database mirroring directly initiates IO to the log file to transfer the log.

Transactional replication can be used with more than one subscriber, while database mirroring is a one-database-to-one-database solution. You can read near real time data on the subscriber database, while you cannot read data on mirrored databases, unless you create database a snapshot, where you can read static data as of the create time of the snapshot.

Database Mirroring and Log Shipping

Database mirroring and log shipping both rely on moving the log and restoring it. In database mirroring, the mirror database is constantly in a recovering state, and that's why you cannot query the mirrored database. In log shipping, the database is in standby mode, so you can query the database if the log is not being restored at that time. Also, log shipping supports the bulk-logged recovery model, while mirroring does not.

If your application relies on multiple databases for its operation, you may want to consider log shipping for failover. Although sometimes it is little bit tedious to set up log shipping going the other way once a failover has occurred, mirroring is easy in that aspect.

You can use log shipping and mirroring together. You can use log shipping to ship the log to a remote site for disaster recovery and have a database-mirroring, high-availability configuration in house.

In the high-performance mode, there is a potential for data loss if the principal fails and the mirror is recovered using a forced service recovery. If you are log shipping the old principal, and if the transaction-log file of the old principal is undamaged, you can make a "tail of the log" backup of the principal to get the last set of log records from the transaction log. If the standby log-shipping database has had every other transaction-log backup applied to it, you can then apply the tail of the log backup to the standby server and not lose any of the old principal's data. You can then compare the data in the log-shipping standby server with the remote database and potentially copy missing data to the remote server.

Mirroring Event Listener Setup

In this section, we provide steps you can use to take some action when the database mirroring session changes state (for example, from disconnected to synchronizing or from synchronized to suspended). You can perform the following steps to configure an alert for mirroring state change events and take some action on these events.

Right-click the Alert folder under SQL Server Agent in SQL Server Management Studio and select New Alert. You'll see the window shown in Figure 17-10.

Type the name of the event and select the event type as "WMI event alert" from the drop-down box. The namespace will be automatically filled out for you. In the query field, type the following query:

```
SELECT * FROM DATABASE_MIRRORING_STATE_CHANGE
```

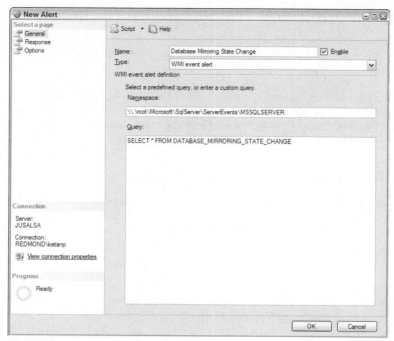

Figure 17-10

In this example, the alert will be fired for all the database mirroring state change events for all the databases mirrored on this server. If you want to be alerted on a specific database mirroring state change events for a specific database, you can add a WHERE clause to the SELECT statement, as show here:

```
SELECT * FROM DATABASE_MIRRORING_STATE_CHANGE WHERE State = 8 AND Database =
'TestMirroring'
```

This statement will only listen for the "automatic failover" state change (state = 8) for the TestMirroring database. The following table lists all the database mirroring state change events so that you can use this table to build the WHERE clause to listen to specific events.

State	Name	Description
0	Null Notification	This state occurs briefly when a mirroring session is started.
1	Synchronized Principal with Witness	This state occurs on the principal when the principal and mirror are connected and synchronized and the principal and witness are connected. For a mirroring configuration with a witness, this is the normal operating state.
2	Synchronized Principal without Witness	This state occurs on the principal when the principal and mirror are connected and synchronized but the principal does not have a connection to the witness. For a mirroring configuration without a witness, this is the normal operating state.

State	Name	Description
3	Synchronized Mirror with Witness	This state occurs on the mirror when the principal and mirror are connected and synchronized and the mirror and witness are connected. For a mirroring configuration with a witness, this is the normal operating state.
4	Synchronized Mirror without Witness	This state occurs on the mirror when the principal and mirror are connected and synchronized but the mirror does not have a connection to the witness. For a mirroring configuration without a witness, this is the normal operating state.
5	Connection with Principal Lost	This state occurs on the mirror server instance when it cannot connect to the principal.
6	Connection with Mirror Lost	This state occurs on the principal server instance when it cannot connect to the mirror.
7	Manual Failover	This state occurs on the principal server instance when the user fails over manually from the principal or on the mirror server instance when a force service is executed at the mirror.
8	Automatic Failover	This state occurs on the mirror server instance when the operating mode is high safety with automatic failover (synchronous) and the mirror and witness server instances cannot connect to the principal server instance.
9	Mirroring Suspended	This state occurs on either partner instance when the user suspends (pauses) the mirroring session, or when the mirror server instance encounters an error. It also occurs on the mirror server instance following a force service command. When the mirror comes online as the principal, mirroring is automatically suspended.
10	No Quorum	If a witness is configured, this state occurs on the principal or mirror server instance when it cannot connect to its partner or to the witness server instance.
11	Synchronizing Mirror	This state occurs on the mirror server instance when there is a backlog of unsent log. The status of the session is Synchronizing.
12	Principal Running Exposed	This state occurs on the principal server instance when the operating mode is high safety (synchronous) and the principal cannot connect to the mirror server instance.
13	Synchronizing Principal	This state occurs on the principal server instance when there is a backlog of unsent log. The status of the session is Synchronizing.

Now select the Response page, shown in Figure 17-11. In this page you will be able to fill out what you want SQL Server to do if the event happens. In Figure 17-11, you want to execute the SQL job "TestEventChange" when database mirroring state change event happens and notify me via e-mail and also page me. You can also go to the Options page, where you can specify an additional message. Click OK. You are now all set to receive the alert when database mirroring process changes its state.

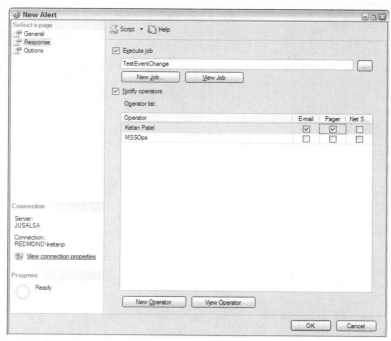

Figure 17-11

In the SQL job, you can actually add the following script to store the history of database mirroring state change events in a table. You should create this table first in some other database, such as `msdb`.

```
CREATE TABLE dbo.MirroringStateChanges
(
 EventTime varchar(max) NULL
,EventDescription varchar(max) NULL
,NewState int NULL
,DatabaseName varchar(max) NULL
)
```

Add the following script as a job step to insert into this table.

```
INSERT INTO dbo.MirroringStateChanges
(
 [EventTime]
,[EventDescription]
,[NewState]
,[DatabaseName]
)
VALUES
```

```
(
 $(ESCAPE_NONE(WMI(StartTime)))
,$(ESCAPE_NONE(WMI(TextData)))
,$(ESCAPE_NONE(WMI(State)))
,$(ESCAPE_NONE(WMI(DatabaseName)))
 )
```

You can change the database mirroring state using the ALTER DATABASE command to test this alert. Also, the database mirroring event change is logged to Event Viewer under Application events, something like the following:

```
The mirrored database "TestMirroring" is changing roles from "MIRROR" to
"PRINCIPAL" due to Failover from partner
```

Database Snapshots

As you have probably figured out, the mirror database is in NORECOVERY mode, so you cannot read the mirror database. You will want to read data from the mirror database for some reason, however.

SQL Server 2005 (Enterprise Edition and Developer Edition) has a new feature called Database Snapshots. A database snapshot is a read-only, static view of a database (the source database). This feature will come handy to read the mirror database. Multiple snapshots can exist on a source database and always reside on the same server instance as the database. Each database snapshot is transactionally consistent with the source database as of the moment of the snapshot's creation. A snapshot persists until it is explicitly dropped by the database owner.

Using this feature, you can create a snapshot on the mirror database. You can read the snapshot database as you would read any other database. The database snapshot operates at data-page level. Before a page of the source database is modified for the first time, the original page is copied from the source database to the snapshot. This process is called a *copy-on-write* operation. The snapshot stores the original page, preserving the data records as they existed when the snapshot was created. Subsequent updates to records in a modified page on the source database do not affect the contents of the snapshot. In this way, the snapshot preserves the original pages for all data records that have ever been modified since the snapshot was taken. Even if you change the source database, the snapshot will still have the same data from the time when it was created. (See the topic "Using Database Snapshots with Database Mirroring" in SQL Server Books Online for more information.)

The following is an example of how to create a snapshot on the TestMirroring database:

```
CREATE DATABASE TestMirroring_Snapshot ON
( NAME = TestMirroring_Data1, FILENAME = C:\Test\Test_Mirroring_snapshot_Data1.SS')
AS SNAPSHOT OF TestMirroring
GO
```

Since new data changes will be continuous on the mirror database, if you want to read the changed data in the snapshot after you have created it, you will need to drop the snapshot and recreate it again. You can drop the snapshot in the same manner as you would drop a database:

```
DROP DATABASE TestMirroring_Snapshot
```

Taking a database snapshot will have some performance impact on the mirror server, so please evaluate the impact if you want to create many snapshots on multiple databases on a server. Most important, from a DBM perspective, having too many snapshots on a mirror database can slow down the redo and cause the database to fall more and more behind the principal, potentially creating huge failover times. Also, prepare an area of disk space as big as the size of the source database, because as data changes on the source database, the snapshot will start copying original pages to snapshot files, and it will start growing. Replication is a great reporting solution, so you can consider that also.

Summary

Database mirroring provides a database redundancy solution using the log-transfer mechanism. The log records are sent to mirror log as soon as log buffer is written to the disk on the principal. Mirroring can be configured in either high-performance mode or high-safety mode. In high-safety mode, if the principal fails, the mirror server will automatically become a new principal and recover its database. Understanding the application behavior in terms of log-generation rate, number of concurrent connections, and size of transactions is important in achieving the best performance. The network plays a very important role in a database mirroring environment. When used with a high-bandwidth and low-latency network, database mirroring can provide a reliable, high-availability solution against planned and unplanned downtime. In Chapter 18, we look at the backup and recovery options SQL server provides in detail.

18

Backup and Recovery

Data is a very important asset for an organization to maintain information about their customers, inventory, purchases, financials and products. Over the course of many years, organizations amass information to improve daily customer experience, as well as to leverage this information to support strategic decisions. Downtime is unacceptable and can be costly for the organization; for example, a stock brokerage house cannot take stock orders or an airline cannot sell tickets without their databases. Every hour the database is down can add up to millions of dollars of business opportunity lost. To keep their business activities going, organizations deploy high-availability solutions as failover clustering, data mirroring, and log shipping so that when a database server fails, they can continue to run their business on a standby database server. All of these topics are covered in other chapters in this book. Additionally, a SAN system is protected by fault-tolerant disk arrays. In addition, to protect from a local disaster, businesses normally have a disaster recovery plan to handle a situation where the site where the organization does its business is down and needs to quickly redeploy the data center to continue to serve customers.

While a high-availability solution tries to keep the business data online, a database backup plan is crucial to protect the business data asset. If there is a data-error problem and the database is unrecoverable, the DBA can use the database backup to recover the database to a consistent state. Moreover, the database backup strategy will try to reduce the amount of data loss in case of an error problem encountered during the course of the daily database activities. In this chapter, we first present an overview of backup and restore. Then we walk you through planning and developing a backup plan, managing backups, and performing restores. We also discuss data archiving and disaster recovery planning.

Types of Failure

Different failures can bring down your database. Anything from a user error to a natural disaster could take your database offline. Your backup and recovery plan needs to account for all of these failures.

Hardware Failure

Nowadays, hardware is fairly reliable. However, components can still fail, including the CPU, memory, bus, network card, disk drives, and controllers. A database system on a high-availability solution can mitigate a hardware failure so that if one database server fails, SQL Server will failover to the standby database server that includes fault-tolerant disk arrays and perhaps using redundant IO controllers. All of this will help keep the database online. However, what high-availability solutions cannot protect is when a faulty controller or a disk causes IO failures and corrupts the data.

> *Use SQLIOStress to help identify the optimal disk configuration or troubleshoot IO faults. Download from http://support.microsoft.com/default.aspx?scid=kb;en-us;231619.*

User Error

A common user error is not including a restrictive WHERE clause during an update or delete operation and modifying more rows than expected. As a preventive measure, users should start data modifications inside a BEGIN TRANSACTION, and then the user can verify that the correct numbers of rows were updated before executing a COMMIT TRANSACTION. If the data modification was not performed inside a transaction, the data will be permanently changed and the user would have no capability to undo the changes. Then, to recover the data, a DBA will need to restore from backup. One option in the case of user error is to use a log explorer utility to read the transaction log and undo the data changes.

Application Failure

The user application may contain a bug that causes unwanted data modifications. To prevent it, the application should go through a strict QA process to uncover any such bugs. However, there is no guarantee that an undetected bug may not cause unwanted data modifications in the future. Once the bug is detected and corrected, the DBA may need to recover the database from backup or possibly using a log explorer utility. The scenario is to identify the time that the problem occurred and to recover to that point in time.

Software Failure

The operating system can fail, as can the relational database system. A software driver may be faulty and causing data corruption; for example, the IO hardware controller may be functioning correctly, but the software driver may not be. One preventive measure is to maintain the system current with service packs and patches, including security patches. The DBA may choose any of the following patch-management solutions: Automatic updates from Microsoft Update, Windows Server Update Services, SMS, or a partner solution to keep the servers updated. Unfortunately, some of these updates may require a reboot either to SQL Server or to the Windows OS that will cause some planned downtime. But planned downtime can be mitigated by a high-availability solution to fail over to the standby database server. Choose a maintenance time window when there is lowest user activity; identify the patches that require a reboot ahead of time and apply them at one time whenever possible, so as to require only a single reboot. Record each software driver version and check the vendor Web site for the most current updates. Additionally, the driver must be approved for the computer hardware and the Windows version. Having a supported and updated driver version can make a significant performance difference to the hardware device.

Too Much Privilege

Oftentimes, applications are using SQL Server logins that have more privilege than necessary. That is, instead of restricting security to just what the application needs, it is faster and easier to just grant DBO or SA security. Then the application using this privilege may delete data from the wrong table, either as a result of a bug or by a user accidentally using a freeform query window. To reduce this risk, to give application users only the database permissions to do their work, limit access to freeform SQL tools, and restrict SA and DBO permissions only to users who need it and have the experience to know how to use it.

Local Disasters

An unexpected disaster can devastate an area where the data center may become inoperable or completely destroyed. You'll need to relocate the data center, and that is where the disaster planning comes into effect: to quickly bring up the new data center and reopen for business. Depending on the disaster, there can be data loss where the location is inaccessible, and you may be unable to extract the last few data records. To reduce the exposure from a local disaster, an organization may set up a disaster recovery site by means of data mirroring, a geographically dispersed failover cluster, log shipping, or SAN replication.

Overview of Backup and Restore

Before you can effectively formulate a backup and restore plan, you'll need to know how backup and recovery works on a mechanical level. SQL Server 2005 has several different backup and recovery processes that you can use, depending on the needs of your organization. In this section, we examine how backup and recovery work and help you choose the best plan for your needs.

How Backup Works

Database backup is a procedure that safeguards your organization's investment to reduce the amount of data loss. A database backup is the process of making a point-in-time copy of the data and transaction log into an image on either disks or tapes. SQL Server 2005 implements versatile backup processes that can be used separately or together to produce the optimal backup strategy required by an organization. Moreover, SQL Server 2005 can perform the database backup while it is online and available to users. Additionally, it supports up to 64 concurrent backup devices. The following types of backup are available:

- ❑ A *full backup* is an image copy of all data in the database including the transaction log. Using this backup type, you can restore the database to the point in time when the backup was taken. It is the most basic of the backups, where all of the database files are combined into the image. Therefore, in a restore, all of the database files are restored without any other dependencies, and the database is available.

- ❑ A *partial backup* is an image copy of the primary and read/write filegroups. Read-only filegroups can optionally be included in the backup copy. It allows more flexibility to speed backups by providing better manageability for a larger database where large read-only filegroups can be backed up once after been set up as read-only. For example, a large database may have archival data that does not change, so there is no need to back it up every time, reducing the amount of data to back up.

❑ A *file backup* is an image copy of files or filegroups of a database. This method is typically used for very large databases where it is not feasible to do a full database backup. A transaction log backup is needed with this backup type if the backup includes read/write files or filegroups. The challenge is maintaining the files, filegroups, and transaction-log backups, because larger databases have many files and filegroups. Additionally, it requires more steps to restore the database.

❑ A *differential backup* is an image copy of all the data that has changed since the last full backup. The SQL Server 2005 backup process identifies each changed extant and backs it up. Restoring from a differential backup requires the full base backup. Each differential is always based on the full backup, not on a previous differential. If the database is very volatile, the differential backup may approach the size of the full backup and may be as slow as SQL Server needs to identify each changed extant.

❑ A *full differential backup* is a copy of all extants modified for the complete database since the last full backup. Restoring requires the full database backup. Typically, this type of backup is used in combination with the full database backup, where a full backup may be taken every weekend and full differential backups every weekday.

❑ A *partial differential backup* is a copy of all extents modified since the last partial backup. To restore requires the partial backup.

❑ A *file differential backup* is a copy of the file or filegroup of all extants modified since the last file or filegroup backup. A transaction-log backup is required after this backup for read/write files or filegroups. Moreover, after the restore, you need to restore the transaction log as well. Choosing to use the file backup and file differential backup methods will increase the complexity of the restore procedures. Furthermore, it may take longer to restore the complete database.

The Transaction Log on SQL Server 2005 is a main component for a transactional relational database system that maintains the ACID properties for transactions, which are: atomicity, consistency, isolation, and durability. SQL Server 2005 and earlier versions implement the write ahead logging (WAL) protocol, which means that the transaction-log records are written to a stable media prior to the data is written to disk and before SQL Server 2005 sends an acknowledgment that the data has been permanently committed. A stable media is usually a physical disk drive but can be any device that guarantees that on restart the data will not been lost. On a Storage Area Network (SAN), which may have a built-in cache, instead of writing the transaction log directly to physical disk drives, in a power failure, the SAN must certify that it implements a battery backup to provide ample time to write all cached IO to physical disk drives before it powers down. Additionally, SAN vendors often mirror their built-in cache for redundancy. The transactional relational database system expects that the data is available on restart, and, if not, it will identify that the database as corrupted because it cannot determine the data consistency of the database.

In addition, when a data modification occurs, SQL Server 2005 generates a new log sequence number (LSN) used on restart to identify the consistency of the data while performing database recovery. Additionally, the LSN is used when restoring the transaction log; SQL Server 2005 uses it to determine the sequences of each transaction log restored. If, for example, a transaction-log backup is not available, that is known as a *broken log chain* and will prevent a transaction-log recovery past that point. Backing up the transaction log to point-in-time recovery is a critical part of a backup strategy. There are three transaction-log backup types that a DBA can perform:

❑ A *pure transaction-log backup* is when there have not been any bulk-logged operations performed on the database. That is, every data modification performed is represented in the transaction log. The database recovery model can be in Full or in Bulk-Logged mode, provided that no bulk-logged operation has been performed. This is the most common transaction-log backup type, as it best protects the data and provides the capability to recover to a point in time.

❑ A *bulk transaction-log backup* is when Bulk-Logged operations have been performed in the database, and therefore point in time recovery is not allowed. To improve performance on bulk operations, that is, to reduce transaction logging, the database can be set in the Bulk-Logged recovery model where only the allocation pages are logged, not the actual data modifications in the transaction log. During a transaction-log backup, SQL Server will extract and include the bulk-logged data inside the transaction-log backup to allow recoverability.

❑ A *tail transaction-log backup* is a transaction backup when the database has been damaged. For example, if the data files are not accessible but the transaction log files are, you may back up the transaction log to capture the last database modifications. During restore, the tail transaction log can be used to restore the database up to the point of database failure. This cannot be performed if the database is in the Bulk-Logged recovery model and bulk operations have been performed, because the transaction-log backup would need to retrieve the data modifications for the bulk operations from the data files that are not accessible.

Another available backup option is to detach the database or shut down SQL Server and use the OS to copy the database files to a backup device. To backup the database files, you would detach the database like this:

```
EXEC MASTER.dbo.sp_detach_db @dbname = N'AdventureWorks',
@keepfulltextindexfile=N'TRUE'
```

To restore, you would attach the database files like this:

```
EXEC MASTER.dbo.sp_attach_db @dbname = N'AdventureWorks',   @filename1 =
N'F:\MSSQL\Data\AdventureWorks_Data.mdf',   @filename2 =
N'F:\MSSQL\Data\AdventureWorks_log.ldf' ;
```

How Restore Works

Restore is the ability to recover the database in case of a failure and is a major function of a transactional relational database system. To *recover* the database is to produce a consistent, stable, and accurate copy of the database to a certain point in time. When a DBA restores a database, three restore phases must happen.

In the *copy phase*, the database image is created and initialized on disk, and then the full backup is copied. That can be followed by any differential and transaction-log backups.

After all the full backup has been applied, and any differential and transaction logs have been restored, the DBA performs a *redo phase* where all committed transaction records that were in the transaction log but not in the data are applied. The WAL protocol guarantees that the transaction records that were committed have been written to the transaction-log stable media. Then, during the redo, SQL Server evaluates the transaction-log records and applies the data modifications to the data of the database. The duration of the redo phase depends on how many data modifications SQL Server 2005 had performed, which depends on what SQL Server was doing at the time of the failure, and also the recovery interval setting. For example, if SQL Server 2005 just finished updating 10-million rows from a table and committed the transaction but was unexpectedly shut down right after, during recovery it would have to redo those data modifications to the data. The SQL Server 2005 recovery interval setting influences the recovery time by how many dirty pages will be kept in memory before the checkpoint process must write them to stable media. By default, the recovery interval is set to 0, which means that SQL Server will keep less than a minute of work. With that setting, during recovery, there is minimal redo work before the database becomes available for users. The higher the recovery interval value, the longer the recovery may take.

After the redo phase is the *undo phase*, where any transaction-log records that did not complete are rolled back. Depending on the amount of work and the length of the transactions at the time before shutdown, this phase can take some time. For example, if the DBA was in the middle of deleting 10-million rows, SQL Server 2005 is required to roll back all those rows during recovery. SQL Server 2005 does make the database available to users while in the undo phase, but users should expect some performance impact while in the redo phase.

Recovery Models

Understanding the recovery models is essential to developing an effective backup strategy. The recovery model determines how the transaction log is managed by SQL Server 2005 which in turn determines the recovery options, such as the backup types that can be performed on the database and the data loss exposure.

In the full recovery model, the transaction log records all data modifications, makes available all database recovery options, and implements the highest data protection but uses the most transaction-log space. This recovery model can be used with all database backup operations, has the capability of point-in-time recovery, allows backing up the tail transaction log, and the transaction log is accessible. If the full database backup occurred at 1:00 p.m., a transaction-log backup occurs at 1:30 p.m., and the physical drives containing the data files fail at 2:00 p.m. You will be able to recover up to 2:00 p.m. by performing a tail transaction-log backup. As a result, no data will have been lost. Most OLTP production systems and mission-critical applications that require minimal data loss should be using this recovery model.

The Bulk-Logged recovery model performs minimal logging for certain database operations such as bulk import operations like BCP, Bulk Insert, SELECT INTO, CREATE INDEX, ALTER INDEX REBUILD, and DBCC DBREINDEX. Instead of logging every modification for these database operations, it logs the extant allocations. As a result, these operations will execute faster, as they are minimally logged, but it presents possible data-loss risks for recovery. A transaction-log backup is allowed, and if no bulk-logged operations have been performed, the transaction log contains all data modifications exactly like the Full recovery model. If bulk-logged operations have been performed, the transaction-log backup will contain the data that was not logged. Additionally, after a bulk-logged operation, point-in-time recovery using transaction-log backup is disallowed.

Consider the same case scenario. A bulk-logged database operation has been performed. The full database backup occurred at 1:00 p.m., a transaction log backup occurs at 1:30 p.m. and then the physical drives containing the data files fail at 2:00 p.m. You would not be able to recover up 2:00 p.m., because the transaction-log backup would need to access the data files to retrieve the data modifications performed during the bulk-logged operations. As a result, data will be lost and you can only recover up to 1:30 p.m.

The data loss in this scenario can be minimized with some bulk-logged database operations by implementing shorter transactions and performing transaction-log backups during the bulk-logged operations.

Oftentimes, this recovery model is used when the DBA is performing bulk-logged operations and then switches back to full after the bulk-logged operation completes to improve the performance for bulk operations. Additionally, this model is commonly used in an `OLAP` or `Report` database where there are nightly bulk data loads. A backup is taken, and afterward no data is modified during the day, where if the data is lost because of a failure, it can be restored from backup.

The simple recovery model implements minimal logging, just like the bulk-logged recovery model, except that it keeps the transaction-log records until the next checkpoint process that writes the dirty data pages into physical disks. Then the checkpoint process truncates the transaction log. Transaction-log backups are not allowed; therefore, point-in-time recovery is not available. Typically, this recovery model is used for development or test servers, where data loss is acceptable and data can be reloaded. Moreover, this model may be used by an `OLAP` and `Reporting` database where there may be only a nightly data load and then a full or differential backup is performed. With this model, if the database were to fail during the data load, you would have to start from the beginning, unless a full or differential backup was taken during the process. Furthermore, if a DBA switches from one of the other recovery models to this one, the transaction-log continuity will be broken, as it will truncate the transaction log. A full or differential backup should be taken. In addition, during the time that the database is in this recovery model, the database is more exposed to potential data loss.

Transactional replication, log shipping, or data mirroring is not allowed in the simple recovery model, as there is no transaction log.

Choosing a Model

The recovery model you choose depends on the amount of acceptable data loss, the database's read and write daily activities, and how critical that database is to the daily business of your organization.

Choose the full recovery model for a mission-critical database to keep data loss to a minimum, because it is fully logged, and in case of damaged data files, the tail transaction log can be backed up and used to restore the database to a point in time. Therefore, OLTP production systems usually use the full recovery model, except when the database is modified nightly, as is sometimes the case with `OLAP` or `Reporting` databases.

You can use the bulk-logged recovery model to increase bulk operations' performance because it does minimal logging. For example, you could do a nightly bulk operation and then switch back to full recovery. The bulk-logged model will fully log, as is the case with the full recovery model, except for the bulk operations. Therefore, you could use bulk-logged recovery as a permanent recovery model, except it poses a data risk. As long as there are no bulk-data operations, the DBA can back up the transaction log, but oftentimes unknown to the DBA, the tail transaction-log backup recovery may no longer be available if a bulk operation has been performed. To protect from someone doing bulk operations without a database backup and to reduce that data risk, you should switch to bulk-logged only when a bulk operation needs to be performed. Bulk-logged can be a permanent recovery model in an `OLAP` or `Report` database where there is no daily modification activity, as there is a result limited data loss risk if the databases are backed up right after any nightly data load. There is no chance of data loss throughout the day, as nothing would have changed. Also, some data loss may be acceptable, as the `OLAP` and `Reporting` databases can be reloaded from the OLTP data source whenever needed.

Simple recovery model acts like the bulk-logged model, except that it does not save the transaction log; instead, the checkpoint process truncates it. Therefore, no one has to maintain the transaction log. This recovery model is commonly used for development, read-only, and test systems where transaction-log backups are not required. If there is data loss, a new copy of the data can be reloaded from the OLTP data source. If the DBA switches to this recovery model from one of the others, the transaction-log continuity is broken, because there is no way to back up the transaction log. In this recovery model, there is no point-in-time recovery, because the DBA cannot back up the transaction log. Therefore, any restore would be from the previous full and any differential backups.

Switching Recovery Models

SQL Server 2005 allows complete flexibility to switch among the recovery models. However, be aware of the limitations when switching among them, as switching can result in data loss during recovery. The following list outlines the limitations of switching recovery models.

❑ **Switching from full to bulk-logged:** Because bulk-logged database operations may be performed, a transaction-log backup is recommended at a minimum, so that the DBA can recover to this last transaction log if the tail transaction log is not available. To change to this recovery model, use this command:

```
ALTER DATABASE < db_name> SET RECOVERY MODEL BULK_LOGGED
```

❑ **Switching from full to simple:** Because the transaction-log continuity will be broken by this recovery model, a transaction-log backup is recommended, at minimum, before the switch. After the recovery model switch, transaction-log backups and point-in-time recovery are disallowed. To change to this recovery model, use this command:

```
ALTER DATABASE < db_name> SET RECOVERY MODEL SIMPLE
```

❑ **Switching from bulk-logged to full:** Because bulk-logged database operations may have been performed, and to minimize potential data loss if the tail transaction log is not accessible, a transaction-log backup is recommended after the switch. To change to this recovery model, use this command:

```
ALTER DATABASE < db_name> SET RECOVERY MODEL FULL
```

❑ **Switching from bulk-logged to simple:** Because in this recovery model there is a greater chance of data loss in case of a database failure, at a minimum a transaction-log backup is highly recommended before the switch. To change to this recovery model, use this command:

```
ALTER DATABASE < db_name> SET RECOVERY MODEL SIMPLE
```

❑ **Switching from simple to full:** To allow the full recovery model to start to apply transaction-log backups, a full, differential, file, filegroup backup is required after the switch. To change to this recovery model, use this command:

```
ALTER DATABASE < db_name> SET RECOVERY MODEL FULL
```

❑ **Switching from simple to bulk-logged:** Supported. To allow the bulk-logged recovery model to start to apply transaction-log backups, a full, differential, file, or filegroup backup is required after the switch. To change to this recovery model, use this command:

```
ALTER DATABASE < db_name> SET RECOVERY MODEL BULK_LOGGED
```

The recovery model is configured for each database. You can also switch the recovery model from the SQL Server Management Studio by opening the Database Properties and choosing Options, as shown in Figure 18-1.

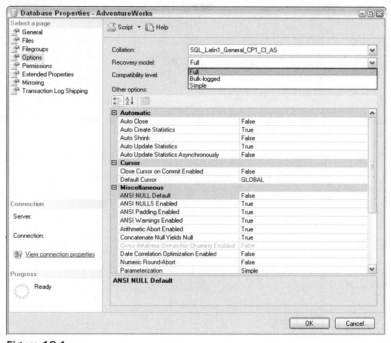

Figure 18-1

Verifying the Backup Images

With any backup solution, a critical operation is to verify the backup images that they will restore. Oftentimes, a DBA may be meticulously doing backups, but along the way, the database becomes corrupted and every backup from that point on is not useable. Plan on doing periodic restores to verify recoverability. Additionally, perform database consistency checks to validate the database structures. Use the RESTORE VERIFYONLY T-SQL command to perform validation checks on the backup image. It does not restore the backup, but will perform validation checks, including:

❏ Backup set is readable

❏ Page ID

❏ If the backup was created WITH CHECKSUMS, will validate it

❏ Check destination devices for sufficient space

However, the RESTORE VERIFYONLY command will not completely guarantee that the backup is restorable. That is why you need a policy to randomly restore a backup to a test server. RESTORE VERIFYONLY simply provides another level of validation. Here's the syntax:

```
RESTORE VERIFYONLY FROM <backup_device_name>
```

An example resulting message is the following:

```
The backup set on file 1 is valid.
```

For higher reliability to protect from a malfunctioning backup device that may make the whole backup unrecoverable, use mirroring of backup sets for redundancy. They can be either disk or tape and have the following restrictions:

❑   Backup devices must be identical.

❑   To create a new or extend a backup, the mirror backup set must be intact. If one is not present, the media backup set cannot be used.

❑   To restore from a media backup set, only one of the mirror devices must be present.

❑   If one mirror of the media backup set is damaged, no additional mirroring can performed on that media backup set.

For example, to use backup device mirroring on the AdventureWorks database:

```
BACKUP DATABASE AdventureWorks
TO TAPE = '\\.\tape0', TAPE = '\\.\tape1'
MIRROR TO TAPE = '\\.\tape2', TAPE = '\\.\tape3'
WITH FORMAT, MEDIANAME = 'AdventureWorksSet1'
```

Backup History Tables

SQL Server 2005 maintains the backup history for the server in the MSDB database in a group of tables from which it can identify the backup available for a database. In the Restore dialog box, SQL Server will present the restores available for the database. The tables are the follows:

❑   Backupfile: A row for each data or log file backed up

❑   Backupfilegroup: A row for each filegroup in a backup set

❑   Backupmediafamily: A row for each media family

❑   Backupmediaset: A row for each backup media set

❑   Backupset: A row for each backup set

A media set is an ordered collection of all tapes or disks from all devices that took part in the backup. A media family is a collection of all backup media on a single device that took part in the backup. A media backup is a tape or disk device used for backup.

The following three backup information statements return information from the history backup tables:

❑   RESTORE FILISTONLY: Returns a list of database and log files in a backup set from the backup file table:

```
RESTORE  FILELISTONLY  FROM AdventureWorks_Backup
```

❑ RESTORE HEADERONLY: Returns all the backup header information for all the backup sets in a device from the `backupset` table:

```
RESTORE  HEADERONLY FROM AdventureWorks_Backup
```

❑ RESTORE LABELONLY: Returns information about the backup media of a backup device from the `backupmediaset` table:

```
RESTORE LABELONLY FROM AdventureWorks_Backup
```

Permissions required for backup and restore

SQL Server provides granular permission for both backup and restoring a database. A Windows or SQL Server authenticated user or group can be given permission to perform the backup and restore operations. To have permission to back up a database, a user must have at minimum the following permissions:

❑ Server role: none

❑ DB role: db_backupoperator

To restore a database, a user must have at minimum the following permissions:

❑ Server role: dbcreater

❑ DB role: db_owner

Backup System Databases

SQL Server 2005 system databases are critical to the operation of each SQL Server instance. These databases are not often modified, but they contain important information that needs to be backed up. After creating a new SQL Server 2005 instance, develop a backup plan to perform a full backup of the system databases, except for tempdb. SQL Server 2005 recreates tempdb every time it is restarted, as it does not contain any data to recover.

Master

The master database contains the login information, metadata about each database for the SQL instance. Moreover, it contains SQL Server configuration information. For example, the database is altered every time you:

❑ Add, remove, or modify a database level setting

❑ Add or delete a user database

❑ Add or remove a file or filegroup in a user database

❑ Add, remove, or modify a login's security

❑ Modify a SQL Server 2005 server-wide configuration

❑ Add or remove a logical backup device

❑ Configure distributed queries or remote procedure calls (RPC).

❑ Add, modify, or remove a linked server or remote login

601

Although these modifications occur infrequently, when they do, consider doing a full database backup. If a backup is not performed, you stand to lose the modifications if a previous backup of the master is restored. Moreover, as a precautionary measure, before and after any service pack or hotfix, perform a new backup of the master database.

MSDB

The msdb database contains SQL jobs, backup jobs, schedule, operators, backup, and restore history and can contain Integration Services packages and others. If you create a new job or add a new Integration Services package and msdb were to fail, the previous backup would not contain these new jobs and would need to be recreated.

Tempdb

Tempdb cannot be backed up. As it is recreated every time SQL Server 2005 is restarted, there is no data in it that needs to be recovered.

Model

Typically, the model database changes even less frequently than the other system databases. Model is the template database used when a new database is created. If you want a certain database object to be present in every new database, like a stored procedure or table, place it in Model. In these cases, it should be backed up or any Model modifications will be lost and need to be recreated, if not backed up.

Full-text Backup

Full-text search performs fast querying of unstructured data using keywords based on the linguistic verse in a particular language. It is primarily used to search char, varchar, and nvarchar fields. Prior to querying, the full-text index must be created by a population or crawl process, during which full-text search performs a breakdown of the keywords and stores them in the full-text index. Each full-text index is then stored in a full-text catalog. Then a catalog is stored in a filegroup. The full-text indexing and querying is performed by the Microsoft full-text engine SQL Server (MSFTESQL). Unlike previous versions of SQL Server, in SQL Server 2005 a full backup will include the full-text files. Additionally during the backup, the full-text catalog can be queried, but all modification operations are suspended until the backup completes, where they are held by the notification log. In addition to the full database backup and database differential backup, SQL 2005 provides more granular backup functionality where a full-text file or filegroup can be backed up.

For an example of a full-text file backup:

```
BACKUP DATABASE Adventureworks  FILE = 'FulltextFI' TO Adventureworks_FT
```

For an example of a full-text filegroup backup:

```
BACKUP DATABASE Adventureworks  FILEGROUP = 'FulltextFG' TO Adventureworks_FT
```

Planning for Recovery

To mitigate the risk and extent of data loss, one of the DBA's most important tasks is database backup and planning for recovery. You need to develop a backup plan that will minimize the data loss and is able to be implemented within the maintenance time window allowed. You need to choose the best SQL Server backup capabilities that will achieve the preferred backup plan that meets the business continuity and data loss requirements. Also, you must set up the backup procedure and monitor it every day to ensure that it is working successfully. You must validate that the database backup will restore properly. An organization may be current with their backups and may think that they have the backups to restore their database, only to find that the database was corrupted and some of the recent database backups will not restore. Cases like these can go undiscovered for months until someone needs to restore a database and finds out that it is not recoverable. To reduce this risk, you should run the database-consistency checks against each database and design a process to test the recoverability of the database backup. Additionally, the database backups should be sent offsite to protect them in case of a local disaster, but keep local copies of recent backups, if you need to perform a quick restore. Another critical task is disaster recovery planning. If the organization data center were to be completely destroyed, you should be able to quickly deploy a new data center with minimum data loss and minimum business disruptions. Disaster recovery planning is not complete until a team periodically simulates a data center failure and proceeds through the test drill to deploy a new data center.

Recovery Requirements

Any backup planning should start with the end goal in mind: the recoverability requirements. Categorize each database server and database with respect to the recovery requirements. Some database servers are mission critical; they keep the business activity going, and when they are down the business will incur a financial loss. Other servers may have decision support or reporting functions that are less critical. Before you can begin to plan, you have to know what items the plan should include.

Determine the availability requirements for each database. How critical is it to maintain the business daily activity, and what is the financial loss if this database is not available? Can the business continue to operate if the database is down, and how long can the business afford to have it down? Also, what part of the database must be online? You can consider a piecemeal restore to reduce your restore time, especially on larger databases where the restore can take a long time. Determine what parts of the database must be available, and arrange the data into filegroups so that you can recover the most critical filegroups first. Archived data or reporting data is less critical and can be recovered last.

For each database, consider the financial loss during downtime that the business will incur, as that may determine the database recovery priority. Additionally, the organization may allocate newer, redundant hardware and RAID array with a high-availability solution to mitigate downtime. The organization may also consider faster and more backup devices to quickly restore the database.

When you ask how much data the organization can afford to lose, oftentimes, the answer is none. Zero data loss can be achieved but at a very high cost in hardware, infrastructure, and processes that would need to be implemented. It is more feasible to identify which data-loss scenarios to protect from and plan for those risks. There may be scenarios that are less likely to happen and some data-loss risk may be acceptable, as protecting from every possible event will drive up the total cost of ownership. Furthermore, identify the databases that are most critical to reduce data loss and plan the processes around those databases.

Determine how easy or difficult it would be to recreate lost data for each database. For certain databases, data can be easily recreated by either extracting data from another system or from flat-file data loads. Typically, decision-support databases use ETL tools to extract data; for example, if some unrecoverable data loss had occurred, the ETL tool can be executed to reload the data.

What is the acceptable downtime in a media failure, such as a failed disk drive? As disk technology keeps becoming less expensive, most organizations will deploy databases on a fault-tolerant disk array that will reduce the exposure of one of the disk drive failing, causing the database to become unavailable. For example, on a RAID 5 set, a loss of a single drive will cause a noticeable performance slowdown. Also if a second drive in the same RAID 5 were to fail, the data would be lost. To mitigate this risk, have spare drives in the disk array system, and get a service-level agreement from the hardware provider to deliver and install the drives. Another scenario to consider that often happens is a department inside the organization deploying a database in a less than ideal hardware environment. With time, the database becomes mission critical to that department, but it lives under the DBA's radar with no accountability. The DBA should attempt to identify all database sources within the organization and develop a recovery plan.

Consider the size of each database. If an organization has databases that are terabytes in size, the restore time will be considerably longer. You may need additional strategies, such as a piecemeal restore. Also, determine if the database has any external dependencies with other databases that require that both databases be restored for users to be able to perform their daily activity. Find out if there are there any linked servers, external applications, or mainframe connectivity that this database has dependencies with.

Make a list of local disasters that can happen in the area and plan how to react to each. In case of a local disaster (for example, a server lost in a fire), what is the acceptable downtime? Prioritize the databases starting with the most critical and identify the available hardware that can be allocated for redeployment and where it is located.

Identify the staff required for backup, restore, and disaster recovery. They need to understand the disaster recovery procedures and where they fit in these procedures. Record what times each staff member will be available, their contact numbers, the chain of communication, and the responsibility of each member. Determine the chain of command, and find out, if the lead is unavailable, if the backup members have the expertise to carry on the duties for backup, restore, and disaster recovery. Find out the expertise of the staff and what additional training will they need to support the environment. Identify any training classes that may be beneficial.

Finally, document any information about store SQL jobs, linked servers, and logins that may be needed when the database is restored onto another database server.

Data Usage Patterns

Part of your recovery plan should include analyzing how your data is used in a typical scenario. Determine for each database how often the data is modified. You'll require different backup strategies for a database that may have a data load once a day than for others that may be read-only or some that change every minute. Separate the tables that get modified from read-only tables. Each type can be placed on different filegroups and a backup plan developed around it.

Identify the usage pattern of the databases during the day to determine the backup strategy to use. For example, during high activity, a DBA may schedule more frequent differential or transaction-log backups, while full backups may be performed during off-peak hours.

Determine the disk space used by the transaction log during peak times and its performance. For example, during peak times, the transaction log may fill the available disk drive allocated to it. Moreover, during peak time, the number of disks allocated for the transaction log may not be adequate to sustain the database performance. The database recovery model setting will affect both disk space and performance.

For a database in the full recovery model, consider switching to bulk-logged mode during bulk operations to improve performance, as that will do minimal transaction logging. Prior to the start of the bulk operations, you should at minimum perform a transactional or differential backup to protect from the risk of a data-drive failure when the tail transaction log may not be accessible.

Maintenance Time Window

Oftentimes, the backup strategy is dictated by the maintenance time window available to perform database defragmentation, backups, statistics updates, and other maintenance activities. To keep enhancing the customer experience, organizations are demanding more timely information and giving customers greater access to information, and customers are more dependant on having this information. This creates a challenge to create the best customer experience, mitigate the risk of data loss, and enable quick restores if the database system fails.

The task of the DBA is to find the best backup strategy to meet the organization's business requirements. Usually, the maintenance time window is limited. SQL Server 2005 implements various backup options that can be used in combination to meet these requirements. Some of the challenges you have to face when you design a backup strategy are:

❑ Available backup time may be limited in a mission-critical, highly available database. Oftentimes, organizations have service-level agreements and must finish their maintenance by certain times of the next morning when users are back on the system. If the backup takes longer, it may make other database activities start later and not finish by the time users log in to the system, costing the organization opportunity loss.

❑ There may be a large number of databases to back up during the maintenance time window. However, you can try to optimize your time for all available backup media by performing concurrent backups within the capacity of the database server.

❑ As the database keeps growing, it will put pressure on the maintenance window. Additional backup devices, higher- performance database servers, and faster IO may be needed to relieve the pressure. Sometimes the maintenance time window can be increased, but oftentimes it cannot. You may need to consider a SAN copy solution to speed the backup process.

❑ Other database activities are likely performed on all of the databases in the database server (for example, database-consistency checking, defragmentation, update statistics, and perhaps data loads). As the database grows, these other activities may take longer to perform, too.

❑ Software updates, security patches, service packs, and database structure updates may need to fit within this maintenance time window.

❑ Full text catalogs may need to be processed.

❑ As more organizations see the benefit of decision-support systems such as SQL Server Analysis Services, the analysis services database may need to be processed during this time.

As a result, the solution will need to address and balance among the following goals:

❑ A backup strategy that can be accomplished within the allocated maintenance time window

❑ A restore strategy based on the backup strategy that will require the minimum number of steps and complexity to recovery the databases

❑   Minimal to no data loss

❑   The backup strategy that is least expensive to maintain and manage

To meet these requirements, a small database can use a full database backup every night. However, as the database becomes larger, that may not be possible. A good next step is to perform a full database backup on the weekend and nightly full differential backups. As the database becomes larger, consider moving read-only and read/write data to different filegroups, then using full partial backups during the weekend and partial differential during the night. As the database continues to grow, consider an individual file nightly backup. A file backup solution is more difficult to maintain, and another preferred solution for these larger database may be a SAN copy operation. It is a more expensive solution, but for these larger databases, it can better meet the backup and restore requirements with the fewest steps and highest availability.

Also consider how the database is to be used. If the database is mission critical, apply redundancy around the hardware; for example, a failover cluster solution with fault-tolerant disk drives. Additionally, identify the data loss that the organization can afford and plan to back up the transaction log to meet the time requirement. Plan to use the full recovery model as at that point, so that if the data files are lost, the tail transaction log may be accessible to restore to that same point in time.

The other important component is the number of steps required to restore the database and the amount of time required. The more steps required, the higher the probability that something may not work or one of the backup images may be unavailable. When a database failure occurs, the goal is to restore it as fast as possible.

Other High-Availability Solutions

When your database has been deployed in a high-availability solution such as failover clustering, log shipping, or data mirroring, it may require additional backup considerations.

❑   In log shipping, the transaction log is backed up by the log-shipping process. No other transaction-log backup should be permitted, as that will break the log chain and will prevent any additional transaction log restores on the standby server. If that occurs, you would need to reconfigure log shipping.

❑   In data mirroring, if the mirror server is down, the principal server transaction log queues all modifications to be sent to the mirror in the transaction log. The transaction log cannot be truncated past the point where it has not sent data modifications to the mirror server.

❑   A failover cluster is a single database, so there are no special considerations. However, if the failover cluster is integrated with log shipping or data mirroring, the transaction-log limitations that we already mentioned apply.

❑   In transaction replication, if the subscriber is down, the transaction log cannot be truncated past the point where it has not replicated those data modifications to the subscriber server.

Developing and Executing a Backup Plan

SQL Server 2005 provides two methods for planning and executing backups. You can either use the graphical interface of Management Studio or the T-SQL backup commands. We'll cover both of these methods here, starting with Management Studio.

SQL Server 2005 Management Studio

SQL Server 2005 Management Studio exposes backup management capabilities for a DBA to either develop a scheduled maintenance plan or directly perform a backup. Before you start, decide the destination for the backup image. It can be a backup location such as a directory path with a filename or a backup device.

If you're using a backup device, first you'll need to create a logical device that defines where SQL Server will copy the backup image. From SQL Server 2005 Management Studio, go to Server Objects, choose Backup Devices, and then New Backup Device. You'll see the dialog box shown in Figure 18-2. There are two destination choices.

- ❏ **Tape:** Requires that a local tape drive be present on the database server
- ❏ **File:** Requires a valid disk destination

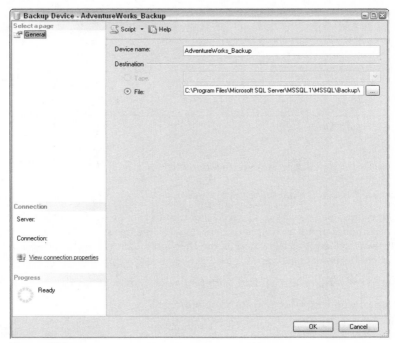

Figure 18-2

To perform database backup from SQL Server 2005 Management Studio, select the database you want to back up, right-click, and choose Tasks⇨Backup. The Backup Database dialog box appears, as shown in Figure 18-3.

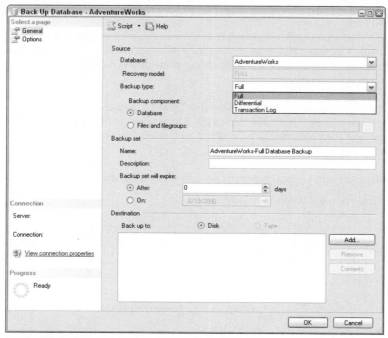

Figure 18-3

In the Source area of this dialog, configure the following:

❑ **Database:** Choose the database to back up.

❑ **Recovery model:** This value is grayed out, as it cannot be changed. Notice that this is in full recovery model. If it was simple recovery model, the transaction log could not be backed up, as the transaction log is truncated by the checkpoint process and files, and filegroups backups would not be available, except for read-only files or filegroups.

❑ **Backup type:** Choose among Full, Differential, or Transaction Log.

❑ **Backup component:** Choose from these options:

❑ **Database:** Choose to backup the database.

❑ **Files and filegroups:** Choose to backup files or filegroups. This option will present a dialog box where you can choose one or more files or filegroups.

In the Backup set area of this dialog, configure the following:

❑ **Name:** Give the backup set a name for easier identification. This name will distinguish the backup from others in the backup device.

❑ **Description:** Provide an optional description for this media set.

❏ **Backup set will expire:** Configure these options based on you're business's retention policy; this protects from SQL Server's backup process overwriting the backup set.

    ❏ **After:** Determines the number of days, from 0 to 99,999, after which the set can be overwritten. Zero is the default, which means the set never expires. You can change the server-wide default by choosing SQL Server Properties⇨Database Settings. Change the Default backup media retention (in days).

    ❏ **On:** Specify a date on which the backup set will expire.

SQL Server 2005 supports up to 64 backup devices. In the Destination area of this dialog, configure the following:

❏ **Disk:** Specify a full valid destination path with filename or a disk backup device.

❏ **Tape:** Specify a tape drive or a tape backup device. The tape drive must be local to the database server.

Clicking the Contents button shows the media set or media family of the device selected.

While in the Back Up Database dialog box, select Options to see the dialog box shown in Figure 18-4.

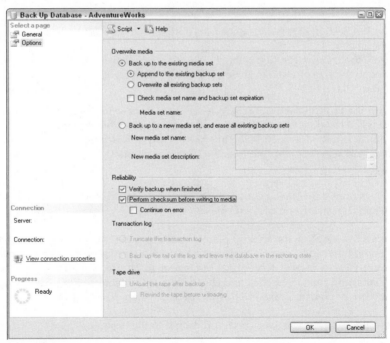

Figure 18-4

In the Overwrite media section, you can choose to back up to the existing media set, in which case, you have to configure these options:

❑ **Append to the existing backup set:** Preserves the existing backups by appending to that media set. It is the default.

❑ **Overwrite all existing backup sets:** Erases all the existing backups and replaces them with the current backup. It will overwrite all existing backup sets unless the "Check media set name and backup set expiration" box has been checked.

Or you can choose to back up to a new media set and erase all existing backup sets, which erases all backups in the media and begins a media set, according to your specifications.

The Reliability section of this dialog has two checkboxes that are both good recommended practices, as a backup is of no value if it is not recoverable.

❑ **Verify backup when finished:** After the backup finishes, SQL Server checks that all volumes are readable.

❑ **Perform checksum before writing to media:** SQL Server does a checksum prior to writing to media, which can be used during recovery to determine that the backup was not tampered with. However, there is a performance penalty with this operation.

The Transaction Log section of this dialog contains options that only apply during transaction log backups.

❑ **Truncate the transaction log:** During normal transaction-log backups, it is common practice to manage the size of the transaction log and to truncate it after it has been backed up to a backup media.

❑ **Back up the tail transaction log and leave the database in the restoring state:** This option is useful when the data files of the database are not accessible (for example, if the physical drives have failed but the transaction log in separate physical drives is still accessible). As a result, during database recovery, apply this as the last transaction-log backup to recover right to the point of failure.

The Tape Drive section of the dialog contains tape drive instructions to rewind and unload the tape. Then click OK and the backup process executes.

A better approach to executing the backup plan is to develop maintenance plans for each database, schedule them, and have SQL Server e-mail you a backup history report. To create maintenance plans for one or more databases, from SQL Server 2005 Management Studio, choose the Management folder, then Maintenance Plans, and then right-click and choose New Maintenance Plan. Then you'll be asked to name the maintenance plan and taken to the maintenance plan design screen.

1. Choose the Back Up Database Task and drag it to the designer.

2. Right-click on the Back Up Database Task to open the Properties, which are shown in Figure 18-5.

3. In the Connection field, choose local server connection, or, if this maintenance plan is to back up databases on another server, choose New Connection and provide the connection information.

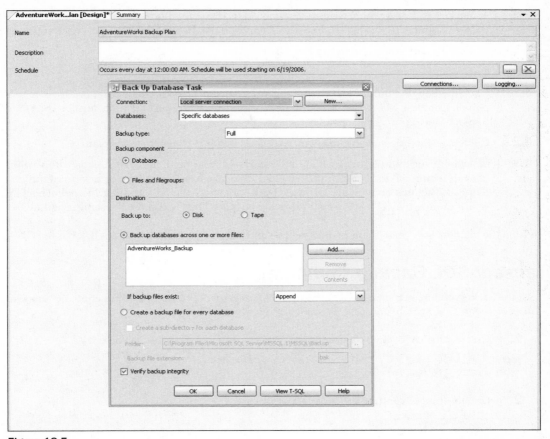

Figure 18-5

4. In the Databases field, choose one or more databases. You can choose more than one database if they have identical backup requirements.

5. In the Backup Component field, choose either Database or Files and Filegroups backup. If you choose Files and Filegroups, you'll need to choose which Files or Filegroups to backup.

6. In the Destination field, choose either disk or tape. Click the Add button to configure the backup location. For disk, provide the full path to the filename or the disk backup device. For tape, provide the tape location or the tape backup device. Additionally, you can use more than one file or backup device. If more than one is chosen, all the databases will be backed up across them, up to the 64 backup devices that SQL Server supports

7. On the If backup files exist field, select whether to append to the existing backup file or to overwrite; the default is Append.

8. To backup to a disk where each database is on its own file, choose Create a backup file for every database option. You can also choose to place each database backup in its own subdirectory.

9. Click the Verify backup integrity checkbox as a recommended practice.

10. Click OK.

11. Click the Logging button and choose how to receive the backup history report. If you choose e-mail, Database Mail must be configured. Moreover, an Agent Operator must be configured to e-mail the report. Then click OK.

12. Click the Schedule button and set up the schedule for this maintenance plan.

13. You can include additional back up database tasks for other database backups with various backup requirements. For example, one Back Up Database Task may be performing full database backups on several databases, but another may be performing differential backups, while another may be performing filegroup backup. They will share the same schedule.

When the maintenance plan is complete, it will be automatically scheduled as a SQL job into SQL Agent.

Transact-SQL Backup Command

All the backup commands using SQL Server 2005 Management Studio and all functionality are available directly using T-SQL. Here are some examples of the syntax:

1. Create a logical backup device for the AdventureWorks database backup:

```
EXEC sp_addumpdevice 'disk', 'AdventureWorksBackup',
'F:\BACKUP\AdventureWorks.bak';
```

2. Create a full AdventureWorks database backup:

```
BACKUP DATABASE AdventureWorks TO AdventureWorksBackup;
```

3. Create a full differential backup:

```
BACKUP DATABASE AdventureWorks TO AdventureWorksBackup    WITH DIFFERENTIAL;
```

4. Create a tail transaction-log backup, during a database failure when the data files are not accessible but the transaction log is.

```
BACKUP LOG AdventureWorks TO tailLogBackup WITH NORECOVERY;
```

Managing Backups

Managing your backups is another important DBA task. The better your maintenance procedure, the faster and more error-free the backups will be identified and quickly restored. Meticulously running backups does little good if the backups cannot be identified or, worse, were lost or overwritten. The following are some tips to help your backup management program:

❑ Descriptively label all the backups to prevent overwriting or misplacing a backup.

❑ Set up a retention policy to prevent a tape or disk backup from being overwritten. These may be dictated by corporate policy, government regulations, cost, space, or logistics.

❑ Tapes can go bad, so set up a reuse policy. Define how many times to reuse a tape before throwing it away. There is an additional tape cost, but a worn tape can stop a successful restore.

❑ Set up a storage location where the backups can easily be organized, located, and accessible. For example, if you're not available, someone else needs to perform the restore and will need to get to the location and correctly identify the backups. You should also keep a copy of the backups stored offsite in a location where they will be protected from a local disaster. This offsite location should allow 24-hour access in case you need access to a backup. Moreover, keep a copy of the more recent backups at your location in case they are quickly needed for a restore.

❑ The backup storage location should be secured where unauthorized individuals would not have access to sensitive data. Moreover, password-protect the backup. Furthermore, for the most sensitive data, use SQL Server 2005 column-level encryption.

❑ Set up a logistical procedure to promptly move a copy of each backup to the offsite location to prevent it from being destroyed in a disaster.

Backup and Restore Performance

As we have said, SQL Server 2005 supports 64 backup devices. It will use multiple backup devices in parallel to back up and restore for faster throughput. The backup device should be on a different controller from the database for better throughput. For disk devices, consider the RAID level used for fault tolerance and performance. Work with the SAN or disk array vendor to get their recommendations for the solution. Moreover, use a combination of full, differential, and transaction-log backups to improve performance.

Additionally, some of the largest database systems may use SAN Snapshot Disk technology supported by many SAN vendors for faster backup and restore (see Figure 18-6). It is configured as a three-way mirror where the business continuity volume (BCV) is data synchronized and then split from the mirror set. The disadvantage of this solution is the cost of the SAN hardware and software to implement it. The advantages of this solution are:

❑ Nearly instant and low-impact backups as the disk split occurs instantaneously.

❑ Nearly instant database restore. In a restore, the BCV can be reintroduced and attached to SQL Server for instant restore while it is data synchronizing the others in the mirror set.

❑ Keeps system online and available almost continuously with minimal impact to SQL Server as the data synchronization occurs on the SAN level.

❑ Allows you to mount the BCV disks on another SQL Server to perform conventional backups and consistency checks.

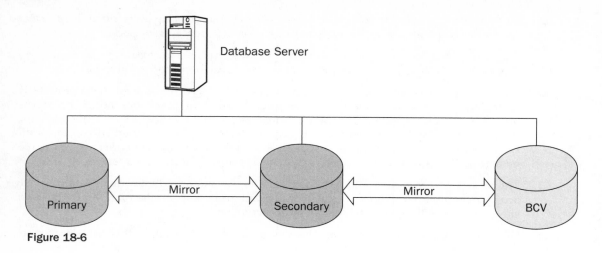

Figure 18-6

Performing Recovery

In this section, we discuss the various methods of recovery, through Management Studio and through T-SQL. We also discuss how to restore the system databases.

Restore Process

A DBA task is to ensure that backups are consistently taken and to validate that they will restore. Each backup sequence is labeled and stored to allow quick identification to restore a database.

Instant File Initialization

Previous versions of SQL Server required file initialization by filling the files with zeros to overwrite any existing data inside the file for the following SQL Server operations: create a database; add files, logs, or data to an existing database; increase the size of an existing file; restore a database or filegroup. As a result, for a large database, file initialization would take a significant time. In SQL Server 2005, however, data files can use instant file initialization provided that the SQL Server service account is assigned to the Windows SE_MANAGE_VOLUME_NAME permission, which can be done by assigning the account to the Perform Volume Maintenance Tasks security policy.

> *The instant file initialization works only on Windows XP and Windows 2003. Additionally, the transaction-log file cannot be instant-file initialized.*

Full Database Restore

A full restore contains the complete backup image of all the data in all files and enough of the transaction log to allow a consistent restore of committed transaction and uncommitted transaction. A full restore can be the base restore for differential and transaction-log restores to bring the database to a certain point in time. During the full restore, choose whether you want to overwrite the current database, if the database should be left in operation mode, or to allow additional restores like differential backups or transaction logs. You also need to choose "with move" if the database files are to be moved to a different directory location or filename. Then perform the full database restore followed by all differential and transaction-log backups. The advantage of this process is that it will recover the database in fewer steps and be online for user access. However, it is slow; there needs to be a maintenance window to perform it.

A full differential restore image contains all extants that have been modified since the last full backup. Typically, it is smaller and faster than a full backup image, provided there is not a high turnover of modification activity. A differential restore is commonly used to augment the full restore. During the restore, the full backup is restored, the database is left in norecovery mode, and the differential restore is performed.

Partial database Restore

A partial restore image contains the primary filegroup, all the read/write filegroups, and any read-only filegroups specified. A filegroup is read-only if it was changed to read-only prior to its last backup. A partial restore of a read-only database contains only the primary filegroup. This kind of backup is typically used when a database has read-only filegroups and, more important, large read-only filegroups that can be backed up to save disk space.

A partial differential backup image contains changes in the primary filegroup and any changes to read/write filegroups. To restore a partial differential, requires a partial backup image.

Transaction-Log Restore

As we've mentioned, a mission-critical database reduces data-loss exposure by performing periodic transaction log backups. The transaction-log restore requires a full database backup as its base or the files or filegroups backups. Then apply the differential restores, and then apply all transaction-log backups in sequence, with the oldest first to bring the database to a point in time either by completing all the transaction-log restores or stopping at a specific point. For example, you can restore the database to a point before a certain error by using one of the following transaction-log restore options:

- ❏ With Stopat: Stop the transaction restore at the specify time.
- ❏ With Stopatmark: Stop the transaction-log restore at the marked transaction.
- ❏ With Stopbeforemark: Stop the transaction-log restore before the marked transaction.

You can insert a transaction-log mark in the transaction log by using the WITH MARK option with the BEGIN TRANSACTION command. During each mark, a row is inserted into the logmarkhistory table in msdb after the commit completes.

An example of a transaction-log restore sequence may be as follows:

1. Restore the full database with NORECOVERY.
2. Restore any differential backups with NORECOVERY.
3. Restore each transaction log with NORECOVERY. You can use the STOP clause to restore the database to a point in time.
4. If you have the tail transaction log, restore it. Then set the database to RECOVERY.

After the database is recovered, no additional restores can be performed without starting over.

File/Filegroup Restore

An example of restoring a database in piecemeal by filegroup is below, starting with the `Primary` filegroup.

```
RESTORE DATABASE AdventureWorks FILEGROUP='PRIMARY' FROM AdventureWorks_Backup
WITH PARTIAL, NORECOVERY;
RESTORE DATABASE AdventureWorks FILEGROUP=' AdventureWorks2 ' FROM
AdventureWorks_Backup  WITH NORECOVERY;
RESTORE LOG AdventureWorks FROM AdventureWorks_Backup WITH NORECOVERY;
RESTORE LOG AdventureWorks FROM AdventureWorks_Backup WITH NORECOVERY;
RESTORE LOG AdventureWorks FROM AdventureWorks_Backup WITH NORECOVERY;
RESTORE LOG AdventureWorks FROM TailLogBackup WITH RECOVERY;
```

The Filegroup `AdventureWorks3`, which is read/write, is recovered next.

```
RESTORE DATABASE AdventureWorks FILEGROUP=' AdventureWorks3' FROM
AdventureWorks_Backup WITH NORECOVERY;
RESTORE LOG AdventureWorks FROM AdventureWorks_Backup WITH NORECOVERY;
RESTORE LOG AdventureWorks FROM AdventureWorks_Backup WITH NORECOVERY;
RESTORE LOG AdventureWorks FROM TailLogBackup2 WITH RECOVERY;
```

The Filegroup `AdventureWorks4`, which is read-only, is restored last and does not require transaction logs, as it is read-only.

```
RESTORE DATABASE AdventureWorks FILEGROUP=' AdventureWorks4 ' FROM
AdventureWorks_Backup WITH RECOVERY;
```

Files and filegroups backups require that the recovery model is either full or bulk-logged to allow transaction-log backups, unless the database is read-only.

Database Snapshot Restore

SQL Server 2005 supports database snapshots where a read-only, point-in-time copy of the database can be taken. The snapshot file, when taken, contains no data, because it uses the "copy on first write" technology. As the database is modified, the first time a value is modified, the old value is placed in the snapshot file. Usually, the database snapshot is used for point-in-time reporting, but it can be used for database recovery if a database snapshot is available and the user or application modifies some data by mistake. A restore from snapshot will return the database to the point in time that the snapshot was taken.

To create a database snapshot, use this syntax:

```
CREATE DATABASE AdventureWorks_dbss9AM ON ( NAME = AdventureWorks_Data, FILENAME =
'F:\MSSQL\Data\AdventureWorks_data_9AM.ss' )  AS SNAPSHOT OF AdventureWorks;
```

To restore from a snaphot, use this syntax:

```
USE MASTER
RESTORE DATABASE AdventureWorks FROM DATABASE_SNAPSHOT = 'AdventureWorks_dbss9AM';
```

Full-Text Restore

During a full or differential database restore, the full-text database is restored along with the database. Additionally, the filegroup or file of full-text can be restored independently of the database.

To restore a full-text file, use this syntax:

```
RESTORE DATABASE AdventureWorks FILE = ' FulltextFI'  FROM Adventureworks_FT
```

To restore a full-text filegroup, use this syntax:

```
RESTORE DATABASE AdventureWorks FILEGROUP = ' FulltextFG'  FROM Adventureworks_FT
```

History Tables Restore

The `msdb` database maintains restore metadata tables. These will be restored as part of `msdb` database restore.

❑   `restorefile`: Contains one row for each restored file, including files restored indirectly by filegroup name

❑   `restorefilegroup`: Contains one row for each restored filegroup

❑   `restorehistory`: Contains one row for each restore operation

SQL Server Management Studio Restore

To restore a database from SQL Server 2005 Management Studio, choose the Database folder, right-click the database of your choice, and choose Tasks⇨Restore. The Restore Database dialog box exposes the restore capability, shown Figure 18-7.

In addition to database restore, there are files and filegroups and transaction log restores available from the same restore menu.

In the Restore Database dialog, in the Destination for Restore area, select these options:

❑   **To Database:** Choose the name of an existing database or type the database name

❑   **To a point in time:** For a transaction log restore, choosing a stop time for the restoration is equivalent to the STOPAT in the Restore Log command. A point in time is commonly used when a database is been restored because of a user or application data modification error and you have identified the time when the error occurred. Therefore, you want to stop the restoration before the error. This option is not possible for the Simple recovery model, because the transaction log is truncated.

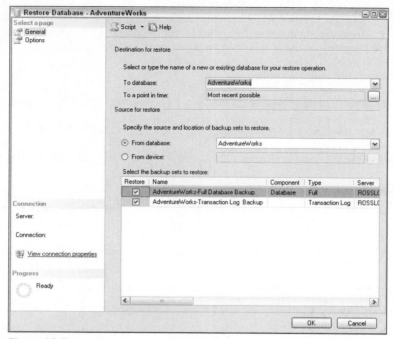

Figure 18-7

In the Source for restore area of this dialog, configure these options:

❑ **From database:** The name of the database to restore; this information is retrieved from the backup history tables in msdb.

❑ **From device:** Choose either the backup device or backup filename to restore from. This may be used when restoring a database onto another SQL Server 2005 instance, and there is no restore data in the backup tables in msdb.

Then select the backup sets to restore from the list at the bottom of the dialog. When selecting the restore source, it populates this field with the backup sets available for the database. Moreover, it provides an option to choose which backup sets to restore.

While in the Restore Database dialog box, select Options, and you'll be taken to the dialog shown in Figure 18-8.

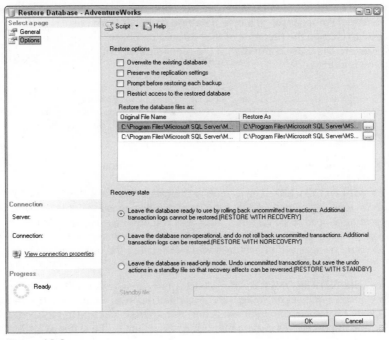

Figure 18-8

In the Restore Options section of this dialog, configure the following options:

❑ **Overwrite the existing database:** This checkbox is used when there is an existing database in the SQL Server instance. Checking this box this will overwrite the existing database; this is equivalent to the REPLACE option in the Restore Database command.

❑ **Preserve the replication settings:** Use this checkbox when you're restoring a publisher database; it's equivalent to the PRESERVE_REPLICATION option in the Restore Database command.

❑ **Prompt before restoring each backup:** Use this checkbox when you're swapping tapes that contain backup sets.

❑ **Restrict access to the restored database:** Use this checkbox when you need to perform additional database operations or validation before allowing users to access the database. This option limits database access to members of db_owner, dbcreator, or sysadmin and is equivalent to the RESTRICTED_USER option in the Restore Database command.

❑ **Restore the database files as:** Here you can choose to restore the database in another directory and filename. For example, if a new database copy has been created in the same directory, you will need to change the filename of the restored database. This is equivalent to the MOVE option in the Restore Database command. If the filenames are not changed, SQL Server will generate the following error.

```
Restore failed for Server 'Server1'.
(Microsoft.SqlServer.Smo)System.Data.SqlClient.SqlError: The file 'C:\Program
Files\Microsoft SQL Server\MSSQL.1\MSSQL\Data\AdventureWorks_Data.mdf' cannot be
overwritten.  It is being used by database 'AdventureWorks'.
(Microsoft.SqlServer.Smo)
```

In the Restore State section of this dialog, select one of these options:

❑ **Restore with RECOVERY:** The default setting recovers the database, which means that no more backup images can be restored and the database becomes available to users. If additional backup images need to be restored, such as a full database restore, followed by several transaction logs, the recovery should be performed after the last step, because after recovery, no additional backup images can be restored without starting the restore over. This is equivalent to the WITH RECOVERY option in Restore Database command.

❑ **Restore with NORECOVERY:** After a backup image is restored, the database is not recovered, to allow additional backup images to be applied, such as a database differential or a transaction log backup. Moreover, the database is not user accessible while in NoRecovery. Also, this state is used on the mirror server in data mirroring and is one of the states available on the secondary server in log shipping. This is equivalent to the WITH NORECOVERY option in the Restore Database command.

❑ **Leave the database in read-only mode:** After a backup image has been restored, the database is left in a state where it will allow additional backup images to be restored while allowing read-only user access. In this state, for the database to maintain data consistency, the undo, uncommitted transactions are saved in the standby file to allow proceeding backup images to commit them. Perhaps you're planning on applying additional backup images and may want to validate the data before each restore. Oftentimes, this option is used on the secondary server in log shipping to allow users access for reporting. This is equivalent to the WITH STANDBY option in the Restore Database command.

T-SQL Restore Command

All the restore commands using SQL Server 2005 Management Studio and all functionality are available directly from T-SQL. For example, to conduct a simple restore of a full database backup, use this syntax:

```
RESTORE DATABASE [AdventureWorks] FROM  DISK = 'F:\MSSQL\Backup\AdventureWorks.bak'
```

The following is a more complex example of a database restore using a full database, differential, and then transaction-log restores, including the STOPAT option, to allow the DBA to stop the restore at a point in time before a data modification that caused an error. As a good practice, the STOPAT option has been placed in all the transaction-log backups. If the stop date is in the previous transaction-log backup, it would stop there. Otherwise, if the stop date has been passed over, the restore process would have to be started again.

```
--Restore the full database backup
RESTORE DATABASE AdventureWorks FROM AdventureWorksBackup
    WITH NORECOVERY;
--Restore the differential database backup
RESTORE DATABASE AdventureWorks FROM AdventureWorksBackup
    WITH NORECOVERY;
-- Restore the transaction logs with a STOPAT to restore to a point in time.
RESTORE LOG AdventureWorks
    FROM AdventureWorksLog1
    WITH NORECOVERY, STOPAT = 'Apr 20, 2006 12:00 AM';
RESTORE LOG AdventureWorks
    FROM AdventureWorksLog2
    WITH RECOVERY, STOPAT = 'Apr 20, 2006 12:00 AM' ;
```

Restoring System Databases

The cause of the master database failure will determine the procedure that may be followed to recover it. For a failure where a new SQL Server 2005 instance must be installed, if you have a copy of the most recent master full database backup, follow these steps:

1. Install the new SQL Sever 2005 instance.

2. Start the SQL Server 2005 instance.

3. Install Service Packs and hotfixes.

4. Stop the SQL Server agent; if you do not, it may take the only single-user connection. Additionally, shut down any other services that may be accessing the SQL Server instance as that may take the only connection.

5. Start the SQL Server 2005 instance in single-user mode. There are several ways to set SQL Server 2005 to single user mode: by using SQL Server Configuration Manager, executing the SQL Server binary from the command line, or, from Windows Services, locating the SQL Server service. In all cases, add the −m startup parameter to set SQL Server 2005 to single user mode; then restart. The recommended approach is to go to SQL Server Configuration Manager, under SQL Server 2005 Services, and locate the SQL Server instance. Stop that SQL service; on the Advanced tab, add the −m startup parameter to the service, and restart the SQL service, as shown in Figure 18-9.

6. Use SQLCMD or an administration tool to log on to the SQL Server 2005 instance with a system administrator account. Restore the master database by executing the following command:

```
RESTORE DATABASE [MASTER] FROM  DISK = N'C:\Program Files\Microsoft SQL
Server\MSSQL.1\MSSQL\Backup\master.bak'
```

If SQL Server will not start because the master database is corrupted and a current master backup is not available, the master database would have to be rebuilt. Execute the SQL Server 2005 Setup.exe to repair the system databases.

The rebuildm.exe application, available in SQL Server 2000, is discontinued.

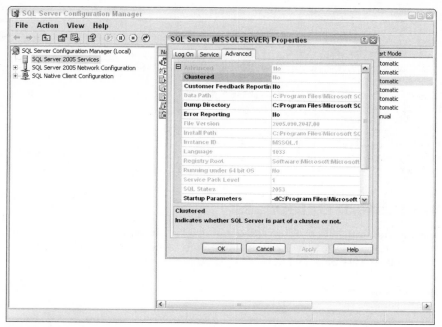

Figure 18-9

After the rebuild and SQL Server 2005 starts, if a current copy of the master database backup is available, set the SQL Server 2005 instance in single-user mode and restore it, according to the previous instructions. If a current master database backup is not available, any modifications to the master database (for example, login security, endpoints, or linked server) will be lost and need to be redeployed.

Additionally, setup.exe creates a new msdb and model during the system database rebuild. If a current copy of model and msdb are available, restore them. If not, all modifications performed to model and msdb will need to be redeployed.

The syntax to rebuild the master database is as follows:

```
start /wait setup.exe /qn INSTANCENAME=<InstanceName> REINSTALL=SQL_Engine
   REBUILDDATABASE=1 SAPWD=<NewStrongPassword>
```

Then attach the user databases.

If only the model or msdb databases are damaged, you can restore them from a current backup. If a backup is not available, you'll have to execute Setup.exe, which recreates all the system databases. Typically, model and msdb reside in the same disk system with master, and if there were a disk-array failure, most likely, all three would be lost. To mitigate disk failure, consider using a RAID array where master, model and msdb reside. Tempdb does not need to be restored, as it is automatically recreated by SQL Server at startup. Tempdb is a critical database and is a single point of failure for the SQL Server instance and should be deployed on a fault-tolerant disk array.

Archiving Data

Archiving a large amount of data from very large tables can be challenging. For example, if you select millions of rows from a billon-row table, copy them, and then delete them from that table, that will be a long-running delete process that may escalate to a table lock and reduce concurrency, which will not be acceptable, unless no one will be using the table. A commonly used procedure is to periodically delete a small number of rows to improve table concurrency, as the smaller number of rows may take page locks and may use an index for faster access and complete faster.

An efficient procedure to archive large amounts of data is to use a sliding time window table partitioning scheme. There are two approaches to this solution: using SQL Server 2005 data partitioning or using a partition view.

SQL Server 2005 table partitioning

A new feature of SQL Server 2005 is table partitioning, where a table can be carved into 1000 pieces, where each can reside on its own filegroup, and then the partition can be independently backed up. With table partitioning, a new empty partition is created when the next monthly data becomes available. Then the oldest partition can be switched out into a table and moved to an archive without table locking or reducing concurrency, because switching out a partition is only a schema change and occurs very quickly. The basic steps to create a table partition are:

1. Create a partition function that describes how the data is to be partitioned.

2. Create a partition schema that maps the pieces to the filegroups.

3. Create one or more tables using the partition scheme.

The following is an example of creating a partition table using a monthly sliding window.

```
--Create partition function
CREATE PARTITION FUNCTION [OrderDateRangePFN](datetime)
AS RANGE RIGHT
FOR VALUES (N'2005-01-01 00:00:00', N'2005-02-01 00:00:00', N'2005-03-01 00:00:00',
N'2005-04-01 00:00:00');
--Create partition scheme
CREATE PARTITION SCHEME [OrderDatePScheme]
AS PARTITION [OrderDateRangePFN]
TO ([filegroup1], [filegroup2], [filegroup3], [filegroup4], [filegroup5]);
--Create partitioned table SalesOrderHeader
CREATE TABLE [dbo].[SalesOrderHeader](
  [SalesOrderID] [int] NULL,
  [RevisionNumber] [tinyint] NOT NULL,
  [OrderDate] [datetime] NOT NULL,
  [DueDate] [datetime] NOT NULL,
  [ShipDate] [datetime] NULL,
  [Status] [tinyint] NOT NULL
) ON [OrderDatePScheme]([OrderDate]);
```

Partition View

This technique has been around since earlier versions of SQL Server, using a partition view to group independent, identical tables together (for example, a new table for each month). Here is the procedure:

1. Create individual, identical tables with a check constraint to limit the data that can reside on each.

2. Create a view to union all of these tables together.

3. Load the data through the partition view. SQL Server evaluates the table constraint to insert the data in the correct table.

4. Before the next date period, create a new table with the date period constraint and include it as part of the view definition. Then load the current data through the view.

5. To archive, remove the oldest table from the view definition and then archive it. Each table can be placed on its own filegroup and can be backed up individually.

This technique does not have the 1000-partition limitation but requires more manageability, as each table is independent and managed.

Disaster Recovery Planning

Disaster recovery requires considerable planning. For example, a local disaster can cause severe financial loss to the organization. To reduce this, the organization must be able to quickly execute the disaster recovery (DR) plan to bring its systems online. It requires a robust disaster recovery plan and periodic DR drills to ensure that everything will work as planned. Oftentimes, organizations have well-intended disaster recovery plans, but they have never tested these plans for readiness; in a real disaster, the plan does not go smoothly. DR planning is based on the specific organization business requirements. However, here are some general areas that will need to be addressed to put this plan into action.

Use project management software, such as Microsoft Project, where people, resources, hardware, software, and tasks and their completion can be input to provide a systematic approach to managing the tasks, resources, and critical paths. Then develop a checklist of detailed steps for recovery.

Disaster recovery solutions with Windows failover cluster are commonly used to provide hardware redundancy within the data center site and can be configured across data centers by use of a more expensive SAN solution to deploy a geographical dispersed Windows failover cluster. Moreover, log shipping and data mirroring can both be inexpensively deployed as disaster recovery solutions. Another solution is SAN replication to maintain a copy of the data in the remote location. Certain organizations have a standby disaster recovery solution available to take over all operations or, at the very least, the mission-critical operations. A few of these organizations failover to the disaster recovery site periodically to validate that their plan will work in a real disaster. Others may not have a disaster recovery plan but an agreement with another organization that offers disaster recovery.

You'll need hardware at the remote site, and if it is not already available, you need to have a plan to acquire the hardware required to bring the organization online quickly. Document the current hardware that will be needed. For computers, consider the number of CPUs and speed, hyperthreading, dual-core,

64-bit, local disk drive capacity, RAID level, and the amount of physical memory required. Preferably, try to acquire the exact hardware to minimize surprises. For the SAN or disk arrays, consider the disk space requirements, LUNs required, RAID level, and the SAN cache. For the network, acquire a similar network infrastructure to maintain the same performance. Some questions to ask:

- ❏ How quickly can these computers be made available? Who will deliver or pick up the hardware?

- ❏ Will the computers be preconfigured, or will the DR team need to configure them? Who will provide the expertise, and what is the availability for that staff resource?

- ❏ Will the SAN be preconfigured with the LUNs and RAID levels, or will the DR team need to configure? Who will provide the expertise, and what is the availability for that staff resource.

- ❏ Who will acquire the network equipment, and who will have the expertise to set it up and configure it?

- ❏ Will the DR site have Internet access, to download service packs, hotfixes, and for e-mail?

Make a detailed list of all software required, any hotfixes and service packs. Take an inventory of how each is going to be available to the DR team. Make sure that the software is at the required version level and that licensing keys are available and valid. Determine who is responsible to make available the software and the contact information that staff member. If the software is in a certain location, know who has the physical keys and what access they have. In this scenario, 24×7 access is required.

You need to have a current list of staff resources to be contacted in the event of a disaster that is current and periodically updated. Know who is responsible to maintain this list and where will it be found during a disaster. You also need to be sure of the chain of command and who is onsite and offsite.

Who will be onsite to execute? Create a detailed plan of the roles required and who is to fill those roles. Additionally, make sure there is a backup resource in case a staff resource is missing. How will the staff get to the DR site? Determine how many are needed in each role and who will be the overall project manager or lead to escalate any issues. Who will have the passwords? What logins are required to make the systems available for business?

The DR site must be accessible 24×7 and conveniently located. As larger DR deployment can take days to execute, the site should have beds for staff to take naps and easy access to food and transportation. Identify who has the key to access the remote site; if that person is not available, who is their replacement? Can resources remotely access the site if they must work from a remote location, and what is required to have remote access turned on? Are the backups for all the databases available at the DR site, or who is responsible to bring them there? If that staff resource is unavailable, who is their replacement?

To make sure that the DR plan will work during a real disaster and reduce loss, as a best practice, periodically simulate a disaster drill and put the DR planning in action to identify if there are any steps that were not taken into account, how quickly the organization can be expected to be online again, and areas that can be streamlined to speed the process. Most important is to ensure that the plan will execute as expected, smoothly and quickly. To get the most effect from this simulated scenario, everyone should approach it as if it was a real disaster and take exactly all actions as planned.

Summary

Backup and recovery are the last defenses to recover an organization data asset when everything else fails. The backup and restore functionality must be able to guarantee that many years of customer information, buying patterns, financial data, and inventory can be recovered. SQL Server 2005 is a scalable and highly available RDBMS solution supporting some of the largest databases with the highest number of concurrent users running mission-critical applications. These key backup and restore functionalities ensure that it can support a larger database with less manageability.

19

SQL Server 2005 Log Shipping

Log shipping is a technique that became available several releases ago. In log shipping, the database transaction log from one SQL Server is backed up and restored onto a secondary SQL Server, where it is often deployed for high-availability, reporting, and disaster-recovery scenarios. SQL Server 2005 log shipping has been enhanced to continue to deliver business continuity and to be one of the high-availability solutions to maintain a warm standby server for failover. For many years, organizations have depended on log shipping for their business continuity, as it is a low-cost, efficient, and simple solution to deploy. It takes advantage of the transaction-log backup and restore functionalities of SQL Server. The two log-shipping SQL Servers can be located next to each other for high availability or across a distance for disaster recovery. The only distance requirement for the two SQL Servers is that they share connectivity to enable the standby SQL Server to copy the transaction log and restore it. In this chapter, you learn about log-shipping architecture and deployment scenarios. We discuss how to configure log shipping and the various scenarios for switching roles between the primary and standby servers. We also tell you how to troubleshoot your log-shipping setup and how to integrate log shipping with other high-availability solutions.

Log Shipping Deployment Scenarios

In this section, we discuss different scenarios where log shipping is deployed: as a warm standby server to maintain a backup database copy in the same physical location to protect from a primary server failure; as a disaster recovery solution where the two servers are distantly located in case the local area where the primary server resides suffers from a disaster; or as a reporting solution where the standby server is used to satisfy the reporting needs.

Log Shipping as a Warm Standby Server

A common log-shipping scenario is as a warm standby server where the log-shipping server is located in proximity to the primary server. If the primary server goes down for planned or unplanned downtime, the standby server will take over and maintain business continuity. Then, the DBA may choose to fail-back when the primary server becomes available. Oftentimes, log shipping is used instead of Windows failover clustering, as it is a less expensive solution; for example, clustering requires a shared disk system that an organization may not own. Additionally, clustering requires Windows failover-cluster compatible hardware that appears in the Hardware Compatibility List. Log shipping does not have such hardware requirements, so an organization may already own hardware that is not failover-cluster compatible that it can use for log shipping.

Moreover, in log shipping, the primary and secondary server's databases are physically separated in certain cases where one database may become corrupted and the other may not. Windows failover clustering uses is one shared disk system with one database, which could become corrupted. It is simple to configure a warm standby server with log shipping, because it uses the dependable transaction log backup, operating system copy file, and transaction log restore. In most warm standby scenarios, the OPERATOR should configure the log-shipping jobs to execute at a shorter interval to maintain the standby server closely in sync with the primary server, to reduce the amount of time to switch roles, and to reduce data loss. Additionally, to further limit data loss, if the active portion of the primary server's transaction log is available, the standby server would be restored to the point in time of the failed primary server. However, in some situations, the active portion of the transaction log may not be available, or some transaction log files that were in transit may not have made it to the secondary, causing some data loss. In a typical role-switch scenario, the OPERATOR would recover all in-transit transaction logs and the active portion of the transaction log before recovering the standby server. Users would also need to be redirected, because log shipping, unlike Windows failover clustering, has no automatic user redirect.

Log Shipping as a Disaster Recovery Solution

An organization may have a local high-availability solution, perhaps around Windows failover clustering, but then deploy log shipping to a standby server at a remote location to protect from a power grid failure or local disaster. The challenges with this scenario are that the network bandwidth must have the capacity to support log shipping large log files to the remote location. Moreover, there is a potential that in a disaster some of the files may be in transit and may not make it to the standby server. Even if the bandwidth supports log shipping comfortably, there is a possibility that during a disaster the bandwidth may be constrained by other activity that will slow down the file transfers. Therefore, there is a possibility of data loss. For mission-critical applications where you want to minimize any data loss, you may need to choose another solution.

Even in the best scenario, because of the transaction-log granularity instead of at each individual committed transaction, there is a greater possibility that the active partition of the log from the primary server will not be accessible. You may need to accept a greater amount of data loss, or the backup folder may no longer be accessible and any transaction logs there will be lost. If the transaction log files in the backup folder or the active transaction log are not accessible, as in a disaster where the primary server can be restarted because of a power grid failure, for example, you may be able to stitch the primary server's active transaction log and transaction log files together by using a third-party transaction log analyzer to identify transactions that did not make it across and manually apply them. The transaction log files backed up by the backup job should be archived to provide point-in-time recovery of the primary (if, for example, a user error modifies some data that needs to be recovered). Moreover, archiving the transaction logs along with a full database backup will offer another disaster recovery option, when needed. To control when the transaction log files are deleted so that the OS backup program can back up these files on its own schedule, set the "Delete files older than" to a time period great than that of the OS backup program schedule. This option is found in the Transaction Log Backup Settings. For example, if the OS backup is scheduled to run every night, set the "Delete files older than" to at least keep the files there until the OS backup completes.

Log Shipping as a Report Database Solution

In certain scenarios, it may be feasible to use the standby server's database for production reporting provided that the database recovery mode is in standby. However, there are several inherent disadvantages to using this server for reporting. The restore process needs exclusive access to the database while restoring; if users are running reports, the restore process will fail to restore and the job will wait for the next restore interval to try again. Log Shipping Alerts may trigger, sending an alert that the standby server has fallen behind. Moreover, at the time of role-switching, there may be transaction logs that have not been applied because reporting prevented it, which would increase the role-switching time as these transaction logs are applied. However, log shipping can be configured to disconnect users that are in the database to restore the transaction logs, but longer-running reports may be kept from completing in that case. To improve the chances that the report will run to completion, the restore job interval would have to be longer, which makes the standby server fall further behind. Additionally, the data for the reports will not be current. Moreover, the secondary server's database schema cannot be optimized for reporting, because it is read-only. For example, if particular indices are beneficial to the report database, the indices need to be created in the primary server's database, which may suffer from having the additional indices. Therefore, using log shipping for reporting has several challenges and does not make a good reporting solution for some environments. For occasional reporting, provided the organization can live with these challenges, you can certainly use log shipping for reporting. A better report solution may be transaction replication, which provides concurrency, granularity, and near real-time synchronization with the added flexibility to modify the database schema.

Log-Shipping Architecture

The basic log-shipping architecture is shown in Figure 19-1. The architecture requires three servers: A primary server, a secondary server (also known as the standby server), and an optional monitor server.

Primary Server

The primary server is the production server that users connect to do work, and it holds the SQL Server 2005 instance that needs to be protected in case of hardware failure, software error, natural disaster, or user-induced errors. In log shipping, the primary server is configured to execute a SQL Agent job to back up the transaction log to a file. For log shipping to function, the server must be using the database recovery models of either Bulk Logged or Full. (See the Database Properties using SQL Server 2005 Management Studio.)

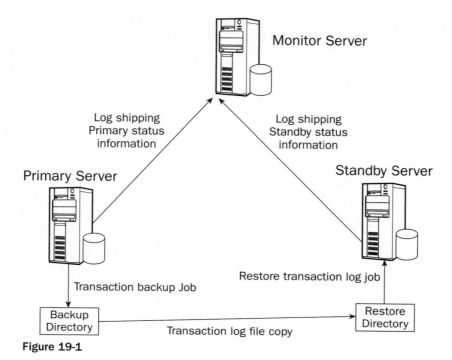

Figure 19-1

Secondary Server

The secondary server is the standby SQL Server 2005 instance that maintains a copy of the primary server database for high availability. The secondary server uses the SQL Agent to copy the transaction-log file from the backup folder where it was placed by the primary server's transaction-log backup to restore it. The secondary server is configured with two SQL Agent jobs: one to copy the transaction-log file from the backup folder and the other to restore the transaction log. For log shipping to function, it must be using the database recovery models of either Bulk Logged or Full. This server should have similar performance specifications to those of the primary server, to maintain consistent user experience during failover.

Monitor Server

Having a monitor server as part of log shipping is optional but is recommended. The monitor server should be a different physical server to prevent it from becoming a single point of failure from the primary or standby server. When the monitor server participates in log shipping, it manages the jobs that produce monitoring information, such as the last time the transaction log was backed up on the primary server, the last transaction log that was restored on the standby server, and the time deltas between the processes. The monitor server will also send alerts to page or e-mail the operator when log-shipping thresholds are crossed. A single Monitor Server can monitor multiple log-shipping environments. Without a monitor server, the primary and standby servers assume the monitoring duties.

Log Shipping Process

Log Shipping uses SQL Agent on the participating servers to execute the processes that maintain a warm standby server. Three main processes drive log shipping:

1. Back up the transaction log on the primary server. A SQL Agent job on the primary server backs up the transaction log at a user-configurable time interval to a file in a backup folder. By default, the filename is timestamped to provide uniqueness: for example, `databasename_yyyymmd dhms.trn`. The backup job by default is named `LSBackup_databasename`, and it executes an operating system command to backup the transaction log:

```
"C:\Program Files\Microsoft SQL Server\90\Tools\Binn\sqllogship.exe"
-Backup 0E5D9AA6-D054-45C9-9C6B-33301DD934E2 -server SQLServer1
```

2. Copy the transaction log to the standby server. A SQL Agent job on the standby server uses UNC or shared drive to access the backup folder on the primary server to copy the transaction-log file to a local folder on the standby server. The copy job by default is named `LSCopy_servername_databasename`, and it executes an operating system command to copy the transaction-log file:

```
"C:\Program Files\Microsoft SQL Server\90\Tools\Binn\sqllogship.exe"
-Copy F2305BFA-B9E3- 4B1C-885D-3069D0D11998 -server SQLServer2
```

3. Restore the transaction log on standby server. A SQL Agent job on the standby server restores the transaction log on the standby server. To restore the transaction log, the database must be in either Standby or NoRecovery mode. The restore job by default is named `LSRestore_server name_databasename`, and it executes an operating system command to copy the transaction-log file:

```
"C:\Program Files\Microsoft SQL Server\90\Tools\Binn\sqllogship.exe"
-Restore F2305BFA-B9E3-4B1C-885D-3069D0D11998 -server SQLServer2
```

Most of the log-shipping objects can be found in MSDB. For more information, see the SQL Server 2005 Books Online.

System Requirements

The servers that participate in log shipping must meet the minimum SQL Server 2005 hardware requirements; see the Microsoft SQL Server 2005 Books Online. Additionally, certain hardware infrastructure requirements are necessary to deploy log shipping.

Network

The log shipping SQL Servers must be networked such that the primary server has access to the backup folder, and the standby server has access to copy the transaction-log files from the backup folder and into its local folder. Also, the monitor server must be able to connect to both the primary and standby servers. To improve copying the transaction-log file in a very active log-shipping environment, place the participating servers on their own network segment and different network cards. Log shipping will function with any feasible network speed, but on a slow network the transaction-log file transfer will take longer, and the standby server will likely be further behind with the primary server.

Identical Capacity Servers

The primary and standby servers should have identical performance capacity, so that in a failover the standby server can take over and provide the same level of performance and user experience. Additionally, some organizations have service-level agreements (SLA) to meet.

Storage

To mitigate the risk of storage failure becoming a single point of failure, the primary and standby servers should not share the same disk system. Unlike a Windows failover cluster that requires a shared-disk infrastructure, log shipping has no such requirements. In a disaster recovery scenario configuration, the primary and standby servers would be located at a distance from each other and would be unlikely to share the same disk system. Moreover, when identifying the performance specification for the disk systems, consider the log-shipping IO activities.

Monitor Server

The monitor server should be on separate hardware from the primary or standby servers to prevent a failure to bring down the monitor server and lose monitoring capabilities. The monitor server incurs low activity as part of log shipping and may be deployed on another production server. Additionally, a single monitor server can monitor more than one log-shipping environment.

Software

The supported SQL Server editions for log shipping are the following:

- ❏   SQL Server 2005 Enterprise Edition
- ❏   SQL Server 2005 Standard Edition
- ❏   SQL Server 2005 Workgroup Edition

Also, the log-shipping servers should have identical case-sensitivity settings, and the log-shipping databases must use either full or bulk-logged recovery models.

Deploying Log Shipping

Before you can begin the log-shipping deployment process, you need to do some initial configuration. Then you have a choice of how you want to deploy: using the SQL Server 2005 Management Studio or using T-SQL scripts. Typically, a DBA will use the SQL Server 2005 Management Studio to configure log shipping and then generate SQL scripts for future redeployment. We'll cover both procedures here.

Initial Configuration

To configure your network for log shipping, first create a backup folder that the primary server can access that is network shared and accessible by the standby server. For example, you could use the folder c:\primaryBackupLog, which is also accessible by a UNC path:

`\\primaryserver\primaryBackupLog`. The primary server's SQL Agent account must have read and write permission to the folder, and the standby server's SQL Agent account or the proxy account executing the job should have read permission to this folder.

Next, create a destination folder on the standby server such as `c:\secondaryBackupDest`. The standby server's SQL Agent account or the proxy account executing the job must have read and write permission to this folder.

The recovery model for the log-shipped database must be set to either Full or Bulk_logged. There are two ways to set the recovery model: with Management Studio or with a T-SQL command. Using Management Studio, open the database properties and select Options. From the Recovery Model drop-down, choose the recovery model, as shown in Figure 19-2.

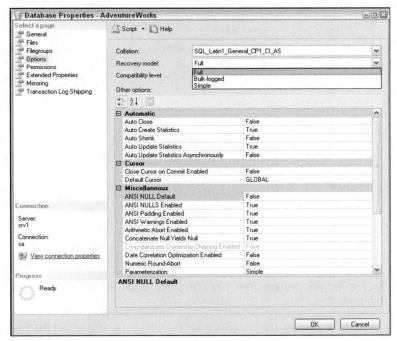

Figure 19-2

To use T-SQL, open a SQL query window and use the `ALTER DATABASE` command to change the recovery model. For example, to change the `AdventureWorks` database to full, use this T-SQL:

```
USE master;
GO
ALTER DATABASE AdventureWorks
SET RECOVERY FULL;
GO
```

Deploying with Management Studio

To deploy log shipping with Management Studio, start by opening the database to be configured and select the database properties; then select Transactional Log Shipping. Click the checkbox that reads "Enable this as a primary database in a log shipping configuration," as shown in Figure 19-3.

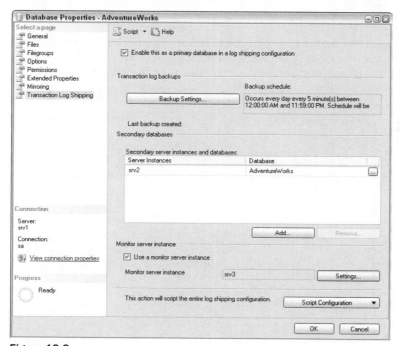

Figure 19-3

Then click the Backup Settings button, and you'll be taken to the Transaction Log Backup Settings dialog, as shown in Figure 19-4.

On this page, you need to provide the network path to the backup folder and the local path if the folder is local to the primary server. If the folder is local to the primary server, log shipping will use the local path. Remember that the SQL Server service and the SQL Agent account or its proxy running the backup job must have read and write permission to this folder. Whenever possible, have this folder should reside on a fault-tolerant disk system so that if a drive is lost, all the transaction log files are not lost.

Transaction-log backup files that have been applied and are older than the value in the "Delete files older than" field are deleted to control the folder size containing older transaction backup log files. However, for an additional level of protection, if the business requires point-in-time recovery, leave the files there until the OS backup program backups them up to another storage device, provided that a full database backup is also available to apply these transaction logs. The default setting is 72 hours.

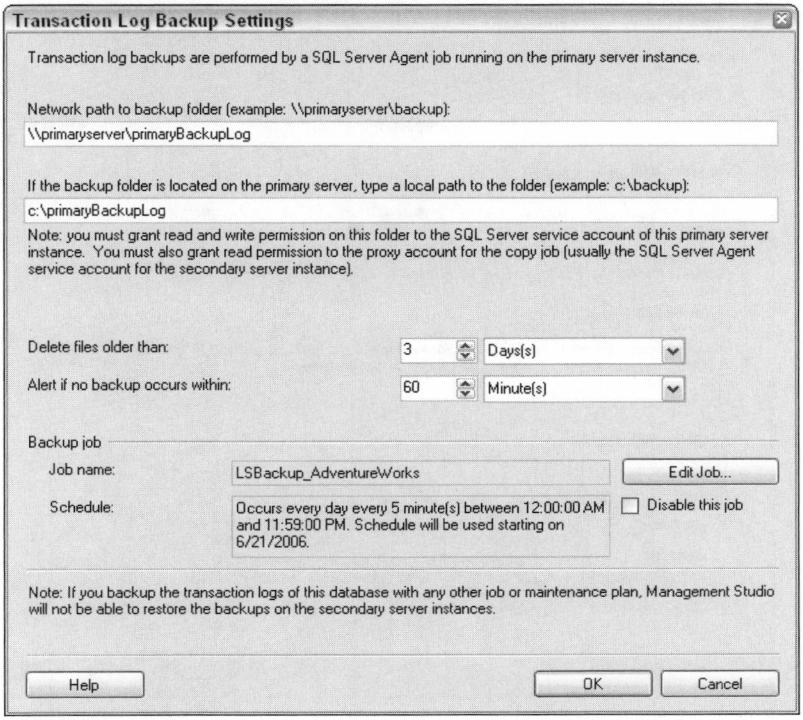

Transaction Log Backup Settings

Transaction log backups are performed by a SQL Server Agent job running on the primary server instance.

Network path to backup folder (example: \\primaryserver\backup):

\\primaryserver\primaryBackupLog

If the backup folder is located on the primary server, type a local path to the folder (example: c:\backup):

c:\primaryBackupLog

Note: you must grant read and write permission on this folder to the SQL Server service account of this primary server instance. You must also grant read permission to the proxy account for the copy job (usually the SQL Server Agent service account for the secondary server instance).

Delete files older than: 3 ☒ Days(s) ☒

Alert if no backup occurs within: 60 ☒ Minute(s) ☒

Backup job

Job name: LSBackup_AdventureWorks   [Edit Job...]

Schedule: Occurs every day every 5 minute(s) between 12:00:00 AM and 11:59:00 PM. Schedule will be used starting on 6/21/2006.   ☐ Disable this job

Note: If you backup the transaction logs of this database with any other job or maintenance plan, Management Studio will not be able to restore the backups on the secondary server instances.

[Help]   [OK]   [Cancel]

Figure 19-4

For the "Alert if no backup occurs within" field, the value you choose should be based on the business requirements. For example, how much data your organization can stand to lose determines the transaction backup interval setting or how critical the data is. Additionally, the alert time depends on the transaction backup interval setting. For example if the business requires a highly available standby server where the transaction log is backed up every couple of minutes, this setting should be configured to send an alert if the job fails to run within that interval. The default setting is one hour.

Click the Schedule button and set up a schedule for the transaction-log backup job. The important setting is the "Occurs every" field, which defaults to 15 minutes. This setting can be configured down to once every minute for higher availability. However, the time interval should be appropriately set to allow the previous transaction-log backup job to complete. This value helps determine how in sync the primary and standby servers are. When you're done here, click OK on the Job Schedule Properties page; then click OK on the Transaction Log Backup Settings to return to the database properties page for Transaction Log Shipping.

Click Add to set up a secondary (standby) server, as shown in Figure 19-5.

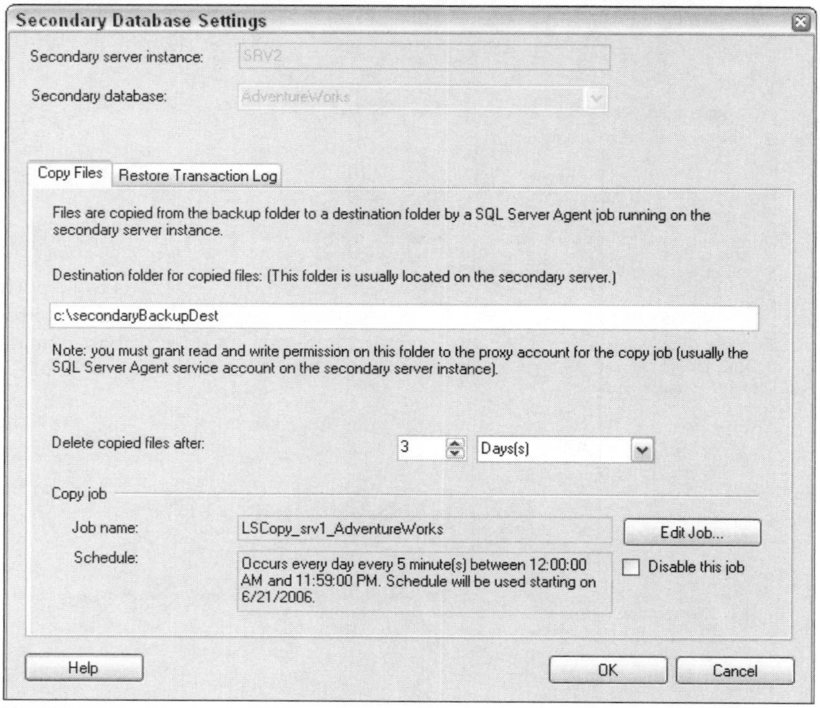

Figure 19-5

On the Secondary Database Settings page, click Connect and choose the Secondary Server instance. Then choose an existing database or a new database name. On the Initialize Secondary Database tab, there are three options to choose from for the secondary database.

- ❑ **Perform a new database backup and create a new secondary database using the database backup.** The Restore Options allows you to set the database folder locations for the data and the log files. If this is not set, the default database locations are used.

- ❑ **Restore from a previous database backup file, and provide a database backup file.** The Restore Options allows you to set database folder locations for the data and the log files. If this is not set, the location at database backup is taken as the default and will fail if the path is no longer available.

- ❑ **Secondary database already initialized.** This option means that the database has already been created. The transaction logs preceding the database restore must be available to enable log shipping to work. For example, the log sequence number (LSN) must match between the primary server and the secondary server databases. Additionally, the secondary database must be in either NoRecovery or Standby mode to allow additional transaction-log files to be applied.

On the Copy Files tab, choose the Destination folder for copied files directory (for example, c:\secondaryBackupDest). The SQL Agent account or the proxy executing the copy job must have read and write permissions to this folder. The "Delete copied files after" option controls the folder size after the transaction log is restored on the secondary server's database. Any files older than the specified time are deleted. The default is 72 hours.

Click the Schedule button to set up a schedule for the transaction-log-file copy job. The important setting is the "Occurs every" field, which defaults to 15 minutes. Click OK when you're done to return to the Secondary Database Setting page.

Click the Restore Transaction Log tab. You have two options for the "On Database state when restoring backups" field:

- ❑ **No recovery mode:** The secondary database is left in NORECOVERY mode, which allows the server to restore additional transactional-log backups but doesn't allow user access.

- ❑ **Standby mode:** The secondary database allows read-only operations to be performed in the database, such as reporting. However, as mentioned previously, the restore process needs exclusive access to the secondary database; if users are accessing the database, the restore process cannot complete.

For the "Delay restoring backups at least" setting, the default is 0 minutes. Typically, you would change this setting if your organization wants to keep the secondary database around in case of a primary database's data corruption. This delay may prevent the secondary database from restoring the corrupted transaction-log file.

The "Alert if no restore occurs within" setting defaults to 45 minutes and should be set to the tolerance level of the business. An alert can be a symptom of a serious error on the secondary database that will prevent it from accepting additional transaction-log restores. Look in the history of the restore job; the default name is LS_Restore_ServerName_DatabaseName and is found under SQL Agent jobs on the secondary server. Additionally, look in the Windows Event Viewer for any additional information. Furthermore, the OPERATOR may copy and paste the restore job command into a SQL command window, which provides additional error information to help diagnose the problem.

Click OK on the Secondary Database Settings page when you're done. To add another secondary server instance, click Add and follow the same steps to add another secondary server.

To add a monitor server, from the Transaction Log Shipping page of the primary database properties, click "Use a monitor server instance." Then click Settings. A separate monitor instance from either the primary or secondary server is recommended so that a failure of the primary or secondary server won't bring down the monitor server.

On the Log Shipping Monitor Setting page, Click Connect, and choose a monitor server instance for this log-shipping environment. The account must have sysadmin role permission on the secondary server. In the "By impersonating the proxy account of the job or Using the following SQL Server login" field, choose how the backup; copy and restore jobs connect to this server instance to update MSDB job history information. For integrated security, the jobs should connect by impersonating the proxy account of the SQL Server Agent running the jobs or by SQL Server login.

The "Delete history after" field controls the amount of history data held in MSDB and defaults to 96 hours. How long to hold history depends on your business-retention requirements and the disk space you have available. The default value will be fine for most deployments unless you're planning to perform data analysis over time; then you should change the default.

When you're done, click OK on the Log Shipping Monitor Settings page. Then click OK on the Database Properties to finish setting up the Log Shipping Configuration.

Deploying with T-SQL commands

Another deployment option is to use the actual T-SQL commands to configure log shipping. Even if you choose to use the SQL Server Management Studio to configure log shipping, you should save the generated command script to allow you to quickly reconfigure the server to expedite a disaster recovery scenario while avoiding any user-induced errors. The following T-SQL commands are equivalent to the steps you took in SQL Server Management Studio.

On the primary server, execute the following stored procedures in the MSDB:

- ❑ `master.dbo.sp_add_log_shipping_primary_database` — Configures the primary database for a log-shipping configuration; this configures the log-shipping backup job.

- ❑ `msdb.dbo.sp_add_schedule` — Creates a schedule for the log-shipping configuration

- ❑ `msdb.dbo.sp_attach_schedule` — Links the log-shipping job to the schedule

- ❑ `msdb.dbo.sp_update_job` — Enables the transaction-log backup job

- ❑ `master.dbo.sp_add_log_shipping_alert_job` — Creates the alert job and adds the job ID in the `log_shipping_monitor_alert` table. The alert job is enabled then.

On the secondary server, execute the following stored procedures:

- ❑ `master.dbo.sp_add_log_shipping_secondary_primary` — Sets up the primary information, adds local and remote monitor links, and creates copy and restore jobs on the secondary server for the specified primary database.

- ❑ `msdb.dbo.sp_add_schedule` — Sets the schedule for the copy job

- ❑ `msdb.dbo.sp_attach_schedule` — Links the copy job to the schedule

- ❑ `master.dbo.sp_add_log_shipping_secondary_database` — Sets up secondary databases for log shipping

- ❑ `msdb.dbo.sp_update_job` — Enables the copy job

- ❑ `msdb.dbo.sp_update_job` — Enables the transaction-log restore job

Back on the primary server, execute this stored procedure in the MSDB:

- ❑ `master.dbo.sp_add_log_shipping_primary_secondary` — Adds an entry for a secondary database on the primary server

Monitoring and Troubleshooting

Log shipping has monitoring capabilities to identify the progress of the backup, copy, and restore jobs. For example, if a job has not made any progress, that can be an indication that something is wrong and needs further analysis. If one of the jobs has failed, you can go to the SQL Agent job history and the Windows Event Viewer to identify the error message and correct it. Also, monitoring helps to determine if the backup, copy, or restore jobs are out of sync with the standby server. There are two approaches to monitoring the log-shipping process: using the Transaction Log Shipping Status report or executing the `master.dbo.sp_help_log_shipping_monitor` stored procedure. Either method can help you determine if the standby server is out of sync with the primary server and what is the time delta between the two. You can also determine which jobs are not making any progress and the last transaction-log backup, copy and, restore filename processed on the standby server.

Additionally, log shipping alerts jobs that check if a preset threshold has been exceeded by executing the `sys.sp_check_log_shipping_monitor_alert` stored procedure. If the threshold has been exceeded, the stored procedure raises an alert. You can choose to modify the log-shipping alert jobs to capture and notify you using SQL Agent.

Along with log shipping, if a monitor server is deployed, there will be one alert on the monitor server that manages the transaction-log backup, copy file, and restore transaction log. If not, the primary server will manage the alert job for the transaction-log backup, and the secondary server will manage the alert job for the copy file and restore transaction log. If the monitoring server is present, the primary and secondary servers will not deploy alert jobs.

The following is an example error if the transaction-log backup process has exceeded the preset threshold of 30 minutes:

```
Executed as user: NT AUTHORITY\SYSTEM. The log shipping primary database
SQLServer1.AdventureWorks has backup threshold of 30 minutes and has not performed
a backup log operation for 60 minutes. Check agent log and log shipping monitor
information. [SQLSTATE 42000](Error 14420).  The step failed.
```

The following is an example error if the restore transaction-log process has exceeded the preset threshold of 30 minutes:

```
Executed as user: NT AUTHORITY\SYSTEM. The log shipping secondary database
SQLServer2.AdventureWorks has restore threshold of 30 minutes and is out of sync.
No restore was performed for 60 minutes. Restored latency is 15 minutes. Check
agent log and log shipping monitor information. [SQLSTATE 42000] (Error 14421).
The step failed.
```

As an example, you can set up an alert so that when error 14420 or 14221 is raised, SQL Agent sends an alert to the operator.

Monitoring with Management Studio

The Transaction Log Shipping Status report displays monitoring information from the Management Studio. The report executes the `sp_help_log_shipping_monitor` stored procedure. When executed on the primary server, it reports on the transaction-log backup details; when executed on the secondary server, it reports on the copy and transaction-log restore details. When the monitor server is configured, the report executed from the monitor server will produce a consolidated report of the transaction-log backup, copy, and transaction-log restore details in one report. To access the Transaction Log Shipping Status report:

1. Connect to the primary, secondary, or monitor server. The monitor server is the most useful choice, because it has the consolidated log-shipping detail data.

2. If the Object Explorer is not visible, select the View⇨Object Explorer.

3. Choose the server node in the Object Explorer.

4. If the Summary page is not displayed, select the View⇨Summary.

5. In the Summary page, select the Reports button and click the Transaction Log Shipping Status.

Figure 19-6 shows an example of the Transaction Log Shipping Status report executed from the monitor server, showing the details for all log-shipping activities with no alerts.

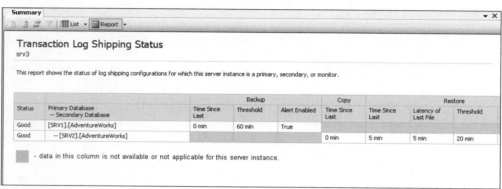

Figure 19-6

Figure 19-7 shows an example of the Transaction Log Shipping Status report executed from the monitor server, showing the details for all log-shipping activities with alerts.

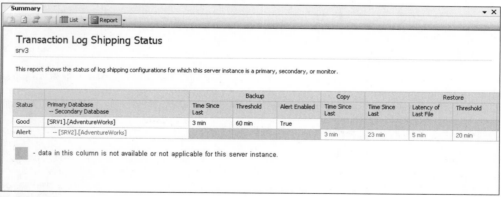

Figure 19-7

Monitoring with Stored Procedures

Executing the `sp_help_log_shipping_monitor` stored procedure in the `master` database from a SQL query window will produce log-shipping status details, similar to the Transaction Log Shipping Status report. If you execute it from the primary server, it will return detailed information on the transaction-log backup job. If you execute it from the secondary server, it will return information on the copy and transaction-log restore jobs. If it is executed from the monitor server, it will return a consolidated detail result of the transaction-log backup, copy, and transaction-log restore, as the monitor server has visibility to all log-shipping processes.

For additional log-shipping operational and troubleshooting detail information, the log-shipping tables can be queried using the log-shipping stored procedures mostly found in the MDDB database. For more information see, the SQL Server 2005 Books Online.

Troubleshooting Approach

As we've mentioned, log shipping consists of three basic operations: Back up the transaction log, copy the file, and restore the transaction log. Troubleshooting this process is simply a matter of identifying which operation is not functioning. You can use the log-shipping monitoring capabilities to identify where the problem is. For example, if the restore transaction-log file is showing that no new files have been restored in the last 60 minutes, you need to look at the secondary server first.

Look at the log-shipping job history under the SQL Agent and the Windows Event Viewer to determine the actual error message. For example, if the copy file job is failing, it may be that the network is down. If the restore transaction-log job is failing, it may be that the server is unavailable or that users are using the database if the database is in standby mode.

Moreover, beware that if the database recovery model is changed to Simple, it will break log shipping because the transaction log is truncated instead of backed up. At that point, you would need to reconfigure log shipping. If you have saved the log-shipping configuration scripts, the reconfiguration should be fairly simple. Additionally, there should not be any other transaction-log backup operation outside of log shipping, because that will break log shipping, since then the log chain will not match on the standby server.

Managing Changing Roles

A high-availability solution must allow smooth role switching between the current primary and secondary servers for business continuity. To accomplish this goal, log shipping requires that certain dependencies are available on the secondary server, because the scope of log shipping is at the database level. Any object outside of the log-shipped database will not be maintained by log shipping. For example, SQL Server logins are contained in the `master` database, and SQL jobs are contained in `msdb`. Therefore, these dependencies and others need to be systematically maintained by other procedures to allow users to connect to the secondary server after it becomes the new primary server. Furthermore, a process will need to be developed to redirect the application to the new primary server.

Synchronizing Dependencies

Log shipping applies changes that occur inside the log-shipping database but does not maintain any outside dependencies. Moreover, log shipping cannot be used to ship system databases. Newly added logins, new database users, jobs, and other dependencies that live in other databases are not synchronized by log shipping. In a failover scenario, when users attempt to login to the secondary server's database, they will not have a login there. Moreover, any jobs configured on the primary server will not be present either. Additionally, if the primary server uses linked servers to access a remote SQL Server,

641

the database operations would fail because they would not be able to find the linked server. Therefore, you need to identify the outside dependencies that the log-shipping database uses and develop a plan to make these resources available during the failover. Below are common log-shipping dependencies and solutions to those.

Login and Database Users

Because SQL Server logins and new database users are created on the primary server and its database, you need to develop a process to synchronize these users with the secondary server and database to prevent login-access issues in a failover scenario. This synchronization process works best if you set it up as a SQL job that runs at certain scheduled intervals. In a planned failover, you should run these SQL jobs before failover to update the secondary server with the current access information. Here are the steps:

1. To develop an Integration Services to Transfer logins, open SQL Server Business Intelligence Development Studio and Start a new Integration Services project.

2. In the Solution Explorer, name the project SSIS Transfer Logins, and rename the SSIS Package to Transfer Logins.

3. Click on the Toolbox and drag the Transfer Logins Task into the package.

4. Right-click the Transfer Logins Task and choose Edit.

5. Click Logins. You'll see the window shown in Figure 19-8.

6. For `SourceConnection`, enter a new connection to the primary server.

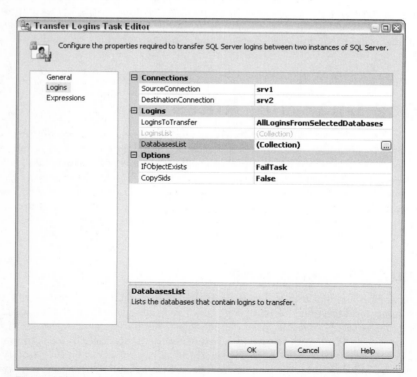

Figure 19-8

7. For `DestinationConnection`, enter a new connection for the secondary server.

8. For `LoginsToTransfer`, choose `AllLoginsFromSelectedDatabases`.

9. For `DatabasesList`, choose the log-shipping database.

10. In the Options section, in the `IfObjectExists` entry, choose what to do if the login exists, such as `FailTask`, `Override`, or `Dkip`. If the secondary server is hosting other databases, you may encounter duplicate logins.

11. Save the package, and choose Build⇨Build SSIS Transfer Logins to compile the package.

12. From Microsoft SQL Server 2005 Management Studio, connect to the Integration Services of the primary server.

13. Under the Stored Packages, choose MSDB, right-click, and choose Import Package.

The next step is to create a new SQL Job on the Primary Server and rename it "Sync Secondary Server Access Information." This job will synchronize the logins from the primary to the secondary servers and will include executing the new SSIS Transfer Logins package.

1. Create a step named BCP Syslogins with these characteristics:

   ❑ Type: Operating system

   ❑ Run As: SQL Agent Service (the account will need sysadmin permission to execute this command and will need to have read/write permission on the folder that it will copy the file from)

   ❑ Command: `BCP Master.sys.syslogins out c:\login1\syslogins.dat /N /S <Server_Name> -T`

2. Create a step named Copy Syslogins with these characteristics:

   ❑ Type: Operating system

   ❑ Run As: SQL Agent Service (the account will need to have read access to the source folder and read/write access to the destination folder)

   ❑ Command: `COPY c:\login1\syslogins.dat \\SecondaryServer\login2`

3. Create a step named Transfer Logins Task with these characteristics:

   ❑ Type: Operating system

   ❑ Run As: SQL Agent Service (the account will need sysadmin permission to execute this command)

   ❑ Command: `DTEXEC /sq <Package_Name> /ser <Server_Name>`

Next, create a new SQL Agent job on the secondary server called "Resolve Logins Job." This job resolves the logins on the secondary server once the secondary database has been recovered. The SQL Server Agent service account or a proxy account must have the sysadmin role to run this job.

1. Create a step named Resolve Logins with these characteristics:

   ❑ Type: Transact-SQL script (T-SQL)

   ❑ Command: `EXEC sp_resolve_logins @dest_db = '<Database_Name>', @dest_path = 'c:\login2\', @filename = 'syslogins.dat';`

SQL Agent Jobs

The Integration Services Transfer Jobs Task can be used to synchronize jobs from the primary to the secondary server. Create a package using SQL Server Business Intelligence Studio, and choose the Transfer Jobs Task. Provide the connection information and the jobs to transfer. Then compile and import a package into SQL Server 2005 or execute it as an SSIS filesystem. However, it is better to develop a SQL Agent job to periodically synchronize the secondary server.

Other Database Dependencies

Make a list of all dependencies that the log-shipping database depends on. These can be linked servers, another database, CLR procedures, database mail, and others. Develop a plan to synchronize these to the secondary server.

Switching Roles from the Primary to Secondary Servers

There are two potential types of role changes: planned and unplanned failover. A planned failover is most likely when the DBA needs to perform some type of maintenance, usually scheduled at a time of low business activity or during a maintenance window, and switches roles to apply a service pack on the primary server, for example. An unplanned failover is when in an unfortunate period the primary server becomes unavailable and for business continuity the DBA switches roles.

Planned Failover

For a planned failover, find a time when the primary server is less active. It is likely that the secondary server will not have had restored all of the transaction logs from the primary server, and there will be transaction log being copied across by the SQL Agent job that the restore SQL Agent job has not completed. Additionally, the active transaction log may contain records that have not been backed up. To bring the secondary server completely in synchronization, the active transaction log must be restored on the secondary server. The steps to accomplish it are:

1. Stop and disable the primary server transaction log backup job.

2. Manually copy all transaction-log backups that have not been copied from the primary server backup folder to the secondary server folder. Then restore each transaction log in sequence to the secondary server. A different option is to execute the log-shipping copy and restore jobs to restore the remainder of the transaction logs. Then use the log-shipping monitoring tool or report to verify that the entire set of transaction-log backups have been copied and restored on the secondary server.

3. Stop and disable the secondary server's copy and restore jobs.

4. Execute the Sync Secondary Server Access Information job and then disable it.

5. Back up the active transaction log from the primary to the secondary server with `NoRecovery`:

```
USE MASTER;
BACKUP LOG <Database_Name> TO DISK = 'C:\PrimaryBackupDir\<Database_Name>.trn'
WITH NORECOVERY;
```

This accomplishes two goals:

❑ Backs up the active transaction log from the primary server and restores it to the secondary server to synchronize the secondary database

❑   Changes the old primary server database to `NoRecovery` mode to allow transaction logs from the new primary server to be applied without initializing the database by a restore, as the log chain would not have been broken

6.   On the secondary server, restore the active transaction log and then recover the database:

```
RESTORE LOG <Database_Name>   FROM DISK = 'c:\secondarydirectory\Database_name.trn'
WITH RECOVERY
```

7.   If the active transaction log is not accessible, the database can be recovered without it:

```
RESTORE DATABASE <Database_Name>   WITH RECOVERY;
```

8.   On the new primary server, execute the Resolve Logins job to synchronize the logins. The secondary server's database becomes the primary server's database and will start to accept data modifications.

9.   Redirect all applications to the new primary server.

10.   Configure log shipping from the new primary server to the secondary server. The secondary server (the former primary server) is already in `NORECOVERY` mode. During log-shipping configuration, in the Secondary Database Settings dialog box, choose "No, the secondary database is initialized."

11.   When you finish configuring log shipping, the new primary server will be executing the transaction-log backup job, and the secondary server will be copying and restoring the transaction-log files. Set up and enable all SQL jobs that were synchronizing from the old primary server (for example, to synchronize the logins and database users to the old primary server).

Unplanned Role Change

If the primary server is unavailable, some data loss is probable. For example, the active transaction log may not be accessible, or the last transaction-log backup may not be reachable. Therefore, you will have to verify that the last copy and restore transaction logs have been restored by using the log-shipping monitoring and reporting functions. If the active transaction-log backup is accessible, it should be restored to bring the standby server in synchronization with the primary server up to the point of failure. Then restore the secondary database with `RECOVERY`.

After assessing the damage and fixing the old primary server, you will most likely need to reconfigure log-shipping configuration because the active transaction log may not have been accessible, or the log chain may have been broken. When you configure log shipping, in the Secondary Database Settings dialog box choose either to restore from a previous database backup or generate a new database backup to restore. You may choose to switch roles to promote the original primary server.

Switching Between Primary and Secondary Roles

After performing the steps in switching the primary and secondary roles in a planned role change where the Log Shipping jobs have been deployed to both primary and secondary servers, you can switch between primary and secondary Servers by:

1.   Stopping and disabling the primary server's transaction-log backup job

2.   Verifying that all the transaction-log backups have been copied and restored, either manually or by executing the SQL jobs to do that

3. Executing the Sync logins job

4. Stopping and disabling the transaction-log copy and restore jobs on the secondary server

5. Backing up the active transaction log on the primary server with NORECOVERY

6. Restoring the active transaction-log backup on the secondary server

7. Restoring the secondary server's database with RECOVERY

8. Executing the Resolve Logins job

9. Enabling the transaction-log backup on the new primary server to log-ship to the secondary server

10. Enabling the secondary server transaction-log copy and restore jobs

11. Enabling synchronization of the logins and database users

12. Enabling any other SQL jobs

Redirecting Clients to Connect to the Secondary Server

Log shipping does not provide any client-redirect capability. After switching roles, the client connections will need to be redirected to the secondary server with minimal disruptions to users. The approach you choose may depend on the infrastructure and who controls it. Additionally, the number of clients that need to be redirected, the required availability of the application, such as a service level agreement (SLA), and the application activity may all play a factor in the decision. At minimum, users will experience a brief interruption as the client applications get redirected. The following sections discuss a few common approaches to redirecting client connections to the secondary server.

Application Coding

The application can be developed as failover-aware with the capability to connect to the secondary server with either automatic retry or by manually changing the server name. The application logic would connect to the primary server first, but if it is unavailable, and after the retry logic has run unsuccessfully, the application can attempt to connect to the secondary server after it has been promoted to a primary server. After the secondary database has been recovered, however, it may not necessarily be ready to serve user requests. For example, you may need to run several tasks or jobs first, such as running the Resolve Logins task. After database recovery, the database may need to be put into single-user mode to prevent other users from connecting while you perform tasks or jobs. Therefore, the application logic must be able to handle this situation where the primary server is no longer available and the secondary server is not yet accessible. The application will provide an option to connect to the primary or secondary server as controlled by users. With the manual method, a procedure will need to be in place to tell users when the new primary server is available and that they can connect.

Network Load Balancing

Use a network load balancing solution, either Windows Network Load Balancing (NLB) or a hardware solution where the application connects using the load balancing network name or IP address and the load balancing solution directs the application to the database server. Therefore, in a failover scenario, the application will continue to connect to the network load balancing network name or IP address, while the load balancer will be updated manually or by script with the new primary server network name and IP address. Then clients will be redirected. NLB is included with certain versions of Microsoft Windows. Configuration is straightforward, and it acts as the cross-reference to direct applications to the current primary server.

Domain Name Service (DNS)

DNS provides name-to-IP address resolution and can be used to redirect clients to the new primary server. If you have access to the DNS server, you can modify the IP address to redirect client applications after a failover, either by script or by using the Windows DNS management tool. DNS acts as a cross-reference for the client application, because they will continue to connect to the same name, but the DNS modification will redirect the database request to the new primary server.

SQL Client Aliasing

This method may be less favorable if there are many client applications that connect directly to the database server, because aliasing would have to be applied at each client computer, which may not be feasible. It is more feasible if the client applications connect to a Web or application server that then connects to the database server. Then the SQL Client alias would have to be applied on the Web or application server, and all the clients would be redirected to the new primary server. To configure aliasing, go to the SQL Server Configuration Manager, under the SQL Native Client Configuration.

Database Backup Plan

A full database backup copies all the data and the transaction log to a backup device, which is usually a tape or disk drive. It is used in case of an unrecoverable failure, so that the database can be restored to that point in time. Additionally, a full database restore is required as a starting point for differential or transaction-log restores. The backup should stored offsite so that the database is not lost in the event of a disaster.

A differential database backup copies all modified extents in the database since the last full database backup. An *extent* is a unit of space allocation that consists of eight database pages that SQL Server uses to allocate space for database objects. Differential database backups are smaller than the full database backup, except in certain scenarios where the database is very active and every extent is modified since the last full backup. In terms of restoring from a differential database backup, a full database backup is required prior to the differential backup.

Full or differential database backup operations will not break log shipping, provided no transaction-log operations are performed that change it. There are several considerations to backup operations with log shipping, however:

❑ The database backup process and transaction-log backup cannot be run concurrently. Therefore, in a large, active database where the database backup can take some time, the transaction log may grow and the secondary server go out of sync, as it is not receiving the transaction-log restores in the same timely manner until the database backup completes.

❑ Another transaction-log backup cannot be performed in addition to log shipping, because that will break the log chain for the log-shipping process. SQL Server will not prevent an operator from creating additional transaction-log backup jobs on a log-shipping database.

❑ A transaction log backup that truncates the transaction log will break the log chain, and log shipping will stop functioning.

❑ If the database is changed to the simple recovery model, the transaction log will be truncated by SQL Server and log shipping will stop functioning.

Integrating Log Shipping with other High Availability Solutions

Log shipping can be deployed along with other Microsoft high-availability solutions (for example, in a Windows failover cluster, where it maintains a remote disaster recovery site if the local Windows failover cluster becomes unavailable). Moreover, it can be deployed with data mirroring to maintain a remote site if the data-mirroring pair becomes unavailable. Furthermore, log shipping can be deployed with replication to maintain a highly available replication publisher.

SQL Server 2005 Data Mirroring

Log shipping can be integrated with a SQL Server 2005 data mirroring solution. For example, an organization may deploy local data mirroring and log shipping from the principal server to a remote location. This would be applicable because data mirroring cannot have more than two partners; therefore, if an organization wants to protect its data investment by having a local data mirroring for high availability but require a business-continuity plan for disaster recovery, you can deploy log shipping from the primary server to a remote secondary server. However, during a data-mirroring role switch, log shipping will not automatically switch roles, and manual steps must be taken to allow the former mirror, which is now the principal, to start to log ship its transaction log to the secondary server by deploying log shipping from the new principal server.

Windows Failover Clustering

Log shipping can be deployed to ship a database from inside a Windows failover SQL cluster to a remote location for disaster recovery. For example, in a local disaster where the Windows failover cluster is not available, log shipping will offer business continuity at the remote location. Unless an organization is deploying a geographically dispersed Windows failover cluster, the cluster nodes are located near each other and can be both down in a local disaster. For best results in a cluster environment, the backup folder should be setup as a cluster resource and should be in the same cluster group with the SQL Server that contains the log-shipping database, so that in a cluster-failover scenario, the backup folder will failover with the log-shipping SQL Server to be accessible by the other Windows failover cluster node. Additionally, any configuration and data files in that Windows failover cluster that the other cluster node will need to access should be set up as a cluster resource included in the log-shipping SQL Server cluster group. For example, if you choose to execute the SSIS Transfer Logins Task package from a file instead of storing it in SQL Server, that folder should be included as a cluster resource to make it available to all cluster nodes. A folder can be set up as a cluster resource by first creating it. Then, using the cluster administrator, create a new resource and choose Shared Folder. Make sure that it is placed in the same group with the SQL Server that contains the log-shipping database. Inside the Windows failover cluster, the SQL Server can be made to depend on the folder. For example, if the folder is not yet online, SQL Server will wait for that resource. The decision to make something a dependency is based on whether the resource must be available before SQL Server starts. For example, if the backup folder for the transaction-log files is not available, should SQL Server wait? Probably not, because it is more critical that the database is up and serving users than if the transaction-log backup is down.

SQL Server 2005 Replication

In a replication topology where the SQL Server 2005 publisher is the data consolidator, it is a single point of failure. All of the subscribers connect to the publisher to receive data updates. If the publisher fails, replication would stop until the publisher can be brought online again. Oftentimes, log shipping has been used as a high-availability solution to protect the publisher from becoming a single point of failure. In this configuration, the primary server is the publisher who log ships its transaction log to a secondary server. Additionally, in order for replication to continue to work after the role switch, the primary and secondary servers configurations must be identical. Also, for transactional replication, to prevent the subscribers from having data that has not been shipped to the secondary server, the primary server should be configured with backup, where a transaction is not replicated to the subscribers until a transaction-log backup has been performed. This does produce a latency penalty where the subscribers are not quite real time, as replication needs to wait for log shipping. This latency can be reduced by decreasing the interval to perform the transaction-log backup. Without sync with backup, there is a possibility that the subscriber's data may not match with the publisher during a log-shipping role switch and data loss may occur. In merge replication, after the role switch, the merge publisher may be able to synchronize any changes lost during the role switch by merge replicating with each subscriber. A more common high-availability solution to prevent a single point of failure for the publisher is to configure a Windows failover cluster so that in case of a failure, replication fails over to the other cluster node. Log shipping is supported by transactional and merge replication.

Removing Log Shipping

Before deleting the log-shipping database, remove log shipping from it. When you remove log shipping, all schedules, jobs, history, and error information will be deleted. Again, there are two ways to remove log shipping: with Management Studio and with T-SQL. You may want to script the log-shipping configuration before deleting to quickly redeploy log shipping in the future.

Removing Log Shipping with Management Studio

To use Management Studio to remove log shipping, follow these steps:

1. Choose the primary database properties.

2. Under Select a page, choose Transaction Log Shipping.

3. Clear the checkbox marked "Enable this as a primary database in a log shipping configuration," and click OK

4. You can also choose to remove a secondary server from the primary server's Database Properties. Under secondary databases, choose the secondary server instance and click Remove.

5. To remove a monitor server instance, uncheck the Use a monitor server instance checkbox.

Removing Log Shipping with T-SQL Commands

To remove log shipping with T-SQL, issue this command on the primary server:

```
   Use Master;
sp_delete_log_shipping_primary_secondary  @primary_database, @secondary_server,
@secondary_database;
```

This command deletes secondary information on the primary server from the `Msdb.dbo.log_shipping_primary_secondaries` table:.

On the secondary server, issue this command:

```
Use Master;
sp_delete_log_shipping_secondary_database @secondary_database;
```

This command deletes the secondary information on the secondary server and its jobs by executing the `sys.sp_delete_log_shipping_secondary_database_internal` stored procedure:

Back on the primary server, issue this command:

```
Use Master;
sp_delete_log_shipping_primary_database @database;
```

This command deletes the log-shipping information from the primary server and its jobs, removes monitor info and the monitor, and deletes the `msdb.dbo.log_shipping_primary_databases` table:

Then, if desirable, you can delete the secondary database.

Log-Shipping Performance

On the primary server, to continue to meet performance requirements while concurrent users are accessing the log-shipping system, consider placing the log-shipping backup directory on a separate disk drive from the database. As part of ongoing administration, monitor the I/O performance counters for any bottlenecks (for example, average queue length higher than two for each physical drive). Do database administration activities such as index defragmentation at a time of lower activity, because depending on the level of fragmentation, the transaction-log file will be larger and take longer to backup and can affect users. To keep the secondary server closer in sync with the primary server, maintain shorter transactions.

To ensure fast recovery in a role switch, the secondary server should have identical capacity to the primary server. It will be more able to keep in sync with the primary server. Additionally, in a role switch, the secondary server will be able to provide the same performance experience that users expect. Similarly, separate the file copy directory from the database, and, as part of ongoing administration, monitor I/O performance counters. Furthermore, monitor network bandwidth, and ensure that there is capacity to move the transaction-log file in a timely manner.

Upgrading to SQL Server 2005 Log Shipping

SQL Server 2000 log shipping cannot be directly upgraded to SQL Server 2005. The log-shipping procedures have changed; therefore, when upgrading a SQL Server 2000 instance, the log-shipping process stops functioning. There are three common approaches to upgrading log shipping.

Minimum Downtime Approach

The minimum downtime approach requires that the secondary server be upgraded in place using the setup program to SQL Server 2005 first. This will not break log shipping, because SQL Server 2000 transaction logs can be applied to SQL Server 2005. Afterward, a planned failover takes place where the role-switch procedures are followed and users are redirected to the secondary server that has been promoted. After the role switch and after the users are redirected, stop and disable the log shipping jobs. The newly upgraded SQL Server 2005 primary server cannot log-ship to the old primary server running SQL Server 2000. Complete an in-place upgrade on the old primary server using the SQL Server 2005 setup program and leave it as the secondary server. Configure SQL Server 2005 log shipping from the new primary server to the secondary server using the same log-shipping shared folders used by SQL Server 2000. Additionally, in the Secondary Database Settings, on the Initialize Secondary Database page, choose "No, the Secondary database is initialized." SQL Server 2005 log shipping will then start shipping the transaction log. If you prefer, switch the roles back to the original primary server.

With Downtime Approach

With the downtime approach, the primary and secondary servers will not be available during the upgrade, as both are upgraded in place using the setup program. Use this method if you have allocated downtime to upgrade the SQL Server 2000 servers. Verify that the secondary server is in synch with the primary server by applying all the transaction-log backups and the active transaction log from the primary server. Stop and disable the log-shipping jobs; then do an in-place upgrade on the primary and secondary servers concurrently. Configure SQL Server 2005 log shipping using the same shared folders. Additionally, in the Secondary Database Settings, on the Initialize Secondary Database page, choose "No, the Secondary database is initialized." SQL Server 2005 log shipping will start shipping the transaction log without having to take a database backup and restore on the secondary server.

Deploy Log Shipping Approach

The deploy log shipping approach is more feasible when the log-shipping databases are small and can quickly be backed up, copied, and restored on the secondary server. It is similar to the with-downtime approach. But instead of verifying and waiting for the synchronizing of the secondary database, after the upgrade and during the SQL Server 2005 log-shipping configuration, you can choose "Yes, generate a full backup of the primary database" on the Initialize Secondary Database page. The log-shipping process will perform a database backup on the primary server and restore the backup onto the secondary server to start the log shipping.

Removing SQL Server 2000 Log-Shipping Tables and Jobs

After upgrading to SQL Server 2005 log shipping, the SQL Server 2000 log-shipping tables and SQL jobs can be deleted. The following SQL Server 2000 log-shipping tables can be deleted.

- ❏ `log_shipping_databases`
- ❏ `log_shipping_monitor`
- ❏ `log_shipping_plan_databases`
- ❏ `log_shipping_plan_history`

- ❏ `log_shipping_plans`
- ❏ `log_shipping_primaries`
- ❏ `log_shipping_secondaries`

Summary

Log shipping is a simple, inexpensive, dependable SQL Server high-availability solution with a long track record. As a disaster recovery solution, it has been deployed to maintain a standby server over a distance for business continuity to protect from a local disaster, power-grid failure, and network outages. Log shipping can ship the log anywhere in the world. Its only limitation is the network bandwidth capacity to transfer the transaction log file in a timely manner. It can be combined with a reporting solution when an organization requires point-in-time reporting rather than real time. Moreover, it has been deployed as an alternative to Windows failover clustering to provide a local, high-availability solution, where it is less expensive to implement, as it does not require a shared disk system. The challenge for deploying log shipping is that it does not provide any automatic client redirect; therefore, an operator needs to have an approach for it. In addition, the role switch requires some user intervention to ensure that all of the transaction logs have been restored to the standby server. Switching the roles back also requires some manual intervention. Another challenge is that log shipping is at the user database level and does not copy new logins, database users, SQL jobs, Integration Services, or DTS packages from the primary server. But using Integration Services' Tasks and SQL Agent jobs, it can be accomplished.

Many organizations have used log shipping very successfully by scripting all the processes such as role switching, login synchronization, and client redirects and are quickly able to fail over with minimal manual downtime. Furthermore, as log shipping involves two or more physical separate servers that do not have any shared components like a Windows failover cluster, you can achieve patch-management independence where one server is patched, the roles are switched, and then the other is patched. Data mirroring is a new high-availability technology that may eventually replace log shipping. However, log shipping is a time-tested, high-availability solution that many large, strategic customers with mission-critical applications depend on every day to provide local disaster recovery.

20

Clustering SQL Server 2005

Most DBAs don't think of their job as an adventure, but after installing their first SQL Server 2005 cluster, they may think again. Unlike most aspects of the DBA's job, installing, configuring, and administrating a SQL Server 2005 cluster is really an adventure, often fraught with excitement and danger lurking in the most unexpected places. And like most adventure stories, the outcome is uncertain.

Are we telling you that you can't just follow a bunch of steps and get clustering going for my company? Actually, you can, but the problem is that literally hundreds of steps must be executed correctly and in the right order. For most DBAs, this is a challenge. Many of the DBAs we know aren't crazy about reading instructions and following detailed steps. They prefer shooting from the hip, installing software without any forethought and working out problems as they find them. But with clustering, this approach won't work.

Let me rephrase this for emphasis: If you want to have a successful SQL Server 2005 cluster, you must spend many hours on the following tasks:

- ❏ Studying all aspects of clustering and mastering all of its intricacies
- ❏ Researching hardware and software configurations to identify what will work best for your organization
- ❏ Planning each and every step in the greatest detail
- ❏ Configuring hardware
- ❏ Configuring the operating system
- ❏ Configuring SQL Server 2005
- ❏ Testing
- ❏ Documenting
- ❏ Administering and troubleshooting the production SQL Server 2005 cluster

If all of this hard work and attention to detail doesn't scare you away, you are ready to read this chapter as your first step toward your adventure.

What if you are one of those DBAs who like to shoot from the hip? If you want to keep your job and become a professional DBA, you will have to learn to change your work habits (at least for clustering). This is not easy, but it's not optional if you want to install, configure, and administer a successful SQL Server 2005 cluster. Fortunately, this chapter will provide you the foundation you need to get started.

This chapter provides the tried and true information you need to successfully install, configure, and administer a SQL Server 2005 cluster installation. You will learn how clustering works and whether it's the right solution for your organization. You'll learn how to choose between upgrading an old cluster and building a new one. We'll tell you how to plan for clustering, including hardware and the OS. We'll walk you through the steps for installing a SQL Server cluster. Finally, we'll tell you how to maintain and troubleshoot an operating SQL Server cluster.

Clustering and Your Organization

Many DBAs seem to have difficulty understanding exactly what clustering is. What do we (and Microsoft) mean when we refer to SQL Server 2005 clustering? Here's a good working definition:

Microsoft SQL Server 2005 clustering is a high-availability option designed to increase the uptime of SQL Server 2005 instances. A SQL Server 2005 cluster includes two or more physical servers (called *nodes*) identically configured. One is designated as the *active node*, where a SQL Server 2005 instance is running in production, and the other is an *inactive node*, where SQL Server is installed but not running. If the SQL Server 2005 instance on the active node fails, the inactive node will become the active node and continue SQL Server 2005 production with minimal downtime.

This definition is straightforward and to the point, but it has a lot of implications that are not so clear, and this is where many clustering misunderstandings arise. One of the best ways to more fully understand what clustering can and cannot do is to drill down into the details.

What Clustering Can Do

The benefits of using SQL Server 2005 clustering are very specific. Clustering is designed to boost the availability of physical server hardware, the operating system, and the SQL Server services. When any of these aspects fail, it causes an instance of SQL Server 2005 to fail. If any of these three fail, another server in a cluster can automatically be assigned the task of taking over the failed SQL Server 2005 instance, reducing downtime.

The use of clusters can help reduce downtime when you're performing maintenance on cluster nodes. For example, if you need to change out hardware on a physical server or add a new service pack to the operating system, you can do so one node at a time. First, you would upgrade the node that is not running an active SQL Server 2005 instance. Next, you would manually failover from the production node to the now upgraded node, making it the active node. Then you would upgrade the currently inactive node. Once it is upgraded, you would fail back to the original node. This cluster feature helps to reduce the overall downtime caused by upgrades.

What Clustering Cannot Do

The list of what clustering cannot do is much longer than the list of what it can do. This list is long because of the many myths of clustering. Clustering is just one part of many required parts to ensure high availability. In many ways, it is not even the most important part; it is just one of the many pieces of the puzzle. Other aspects of high availability, such as the power supply, are actually much more important. Without power, the most expensive cluster hardware in the world won't work. If all of the pieces of the puzzle are not in place, spending a lot of money on clustering may not be a good investment. We'll talk about this more later.

Clustering does not guarantee a complete absence of downtime. Some DBAs believe that a cluster will reduce downtime to zero. This is not the case. It can help reduce downtime but not eliminate it. Clustering is also not designed to protect data. This is a great surprise to many DBAs. Data must be protected using other options, such as backups, log shipping, or disk mirroring.

Clustering is not designed for load balancing, either. Many DBAs, especially those who work for large commercial Web sites, think that clustering provides load balancing between the nodes of a cluster. This is not the case. Clustering only helps boost the uptime of SQL Server 2005 instances. If you need load balancing, you must look for a different solution.

Clustering requires expensive hardware and software. It requires certified hardware and the Enterprise or Data Center versions of the operating system and SQL Server 2005. Many organizations cannot cost-justify this expense. Clustering is designed to work within the confines of a data center, not over geographic distances. Because of this, clustering is not a good solution if you want to failover to another data center located far from your production data center.

Clustering requires more highly trained DBAs. As you will quickly become aware as you read this chapter, SQL Server 2005 clustering is not for beginning DBAs. DBAs with clustering experience command greater salaries.

Although SQL Server 2005 is cluster-aware, not all front-end applications that use SQL Server 2005 as the backend are cluster-aware. For example, even if the failover of a SQL Server 2005 instance is relatively seamless, a front-end application may or may not be so smart. There are many applications that require users to exit and then restart the front-end application after a SQL Server 2005 instance failover.

Choosing SQL Server 2005 Clustering for the Right Reasons

When it comes right down to it, the only justification for a SQL Server 2005 cluster is to boost the high availability of SQL Server instances, but this justification only makes sense if the following are true:

- ❏ The cost (and pain) of being down is more than the cost of purchasing the cluster hardware and software and maintaining it over time.

- ❏ You have in place the ability to protect your data. Remember, clusters don't protect data.

- ❏ You don't need to be able to failover to a geographically separate data center, unless you have a Microsoft certified third-party hardware and software solution. SQL Server 2005, out of the box, does not support geographically dispersed clustering.

❑   You have in place all the necessary pieces required to support a highly available server environment, such as backup power and so on.

❑   You have DBAs on staff qualified to install, configure, and administer a SQL Server 2005 cluster.

If all of these things are true, your organization has all the right reasons for installing a SQL Server 2005 cluster, and you should proceed. But if all of these pieces are not in place, and you are not willing to put them into place, you are most likely wasting your time and money with a SQL Server 2005 cluster and would probably be better off with an alternative, high-availability option, such as one of those discussed next.

Alternatives to Clustering

SQL Server 2005 clustering is just one of many options available to help ensure the high availability of your SQL Server 2005 instances. In this section, we take a brief look at alternatives to clustering. We start with the least expensive and easy to implement options and then take a look at the more expensive and harder-to-implement options.

Warm Backup Server

A warm backup refers to having a spare physical server available that you can use as your SQL Server 2005 server should your production server fail. Generally speaking, this server will not have SQL Server 2005 installed or any database backups installed on it. This means that it will take time to install SQL Server 2005, restoring the databases, and repointing applications to the new server before you are up and running again. It also means that you may lose some of your data if you cannot recover the transaction logs from the failed production server and you only have your most recent database backups to restore from.

If being down awhile or possibly losing data are not big issues, having a warm backup server is the least expensive way to ensure that your organization stays in business should your production SQL Server 2005 server fail.

Hot Backup Server

The major difference between a warm backup server and a hot backup server is that your spare server will have SQL Server 2005 preinstalled on it and a copy of the most recent database backups on it. This means that you save a lot of installation and configuration time, getting back into production sooner than having a warm backup server. You will still need to repoint your database applications, and you may lose some of your data should you not be able to recover the transaction logs from the failed server.

Log Shipping

Log shipping is one step beyond what a hot backup server can provide. In a log-shipping scenario, you have two SQL Servers, like with the hot backup server. This includes the production server and a spare. The spare will also have SQL Server 2005 installed. The major difference between a hot backup server and log shipping is that log shipping adds the ability not only to send database backups from the production server to the spare server automatically; it also can send database transaction logs and automatically restore them. This means that there is less manual work than with a hot backup server and that there is less chance for data loss, as the most data you might lose would be the equivalent of one transaction log. For example, if you create transaction logs every 15 minutes, in the worst case, you would only lose 15 minutes of data. Log shipping is covered in detail in Chapter 19.

Replication

Many experts include SQL Server 2005 replication as a means of increasing high availability, but we are not of this camp. Although replication is great for moving data from one SQL Server to one or more SQL Servers, it is a lousy high-availability option. It is much too complex and limited in its ability to easily replicate entire databases to be worth the effort of spending any time trying to make it work in failover scenarios. Replication is covered in more detail in Chapter 16.

Database Mirroring

Database mirroring is new to SQL Server 2005 and in many ways is a very good alternative to SQL Server 2005 clustering. Like clustering, database mirroring can be used to automatically failover a failed instance of SQL Server 2005 to a spare server, on a database-by-database basis. But the biggest difference between clustering and database mirroring is that data is actually protected, not just the SQL Server 2005 instance. In addition, database mirroring can be done over long distances, does not require specially certified hardware, is less expensive than clustering, requires less knowledge to set up and manage, and is fully automatic, like clustering. In many cases, database mirroring is a much better choice than clustering for high availability. Database mirroring is covered in detail in Chapter 17.

Third-Party Clustering Solutions

Microsoft is not the only company that offers a clustering solution for SQL Server 2005. Several third-party companies offer solutions. In general, these options are just as expensive and complex as Microsoft's clustering option, offering few, if any, benefits over what Microsoft offers.

What to Do?

While we hope that this brief run-down has helped you clarify your options, it is not enough information for you to make a good decision. If the best solution is not self-evident, you will need to spend a lot of time researching the preceding options before you can really determine what is best for your organization.

Clustering: The Big Picture

In this section we take a brief look at how clustering works, along with clustering configuration options. I will also be introducing some terminology that you need to be familiar with.

How Clustering Works

Clustering is a complex technology with lots of messy details. To keep from scaring you too much too soon, we'll take a look at the big picture of how clustering works. In this section, we take a look at active and passive nodes, the shared disk array, the quorum, public and private networks, and the virtual server. Finally, we explain how a failover works.

Active vs. Passive Nodes

Although a SQL Server 2005 cluster can support up to eight nodes, clustering actually only occurs between two nodes at a time. This is because a single SQL Server 2005 instance can only run on a single node at a time, and should a failover occur, the failed instance can only failover to another individual node. This adds up to two nodes. Clusters of three or more nodes are only used where you need to cluster multiple instances of SQL Server 2005. We'll discuss larger clusters later in this chapter.

In a two-node SQL Server 2005 cluster, one of the physical server nodes is referred to as the *active* node, and the second one is referred to as the *passive* node. It doesn't matter which of the physical servers in a cluster is designated as the active or the passive, but it is easier from an administrative point of view to go ahead and assign one node as the active and the other as the passive. This way, you won't get confused which physical server is performing which role at the current time.

When we refer to an active node, we mean that this particular node is currently running an active instance of SQL Server 2005 and that it is accessing the instance's databases, which are located on a shared data array.

When we refer to a passive node, we mean that this particular node is not currently in production and is not accessing the instance's databases. When the passive node is not in production, it is in a state of readiness, so that if the active node fails, and a failover occurs, it can automatically go into production and begin accessing the instance's databases located on the shared disk array. In this case, the passive node then becomes the active node, and the formerly active node becomes the passive node (or the failed node, if a failure occurs that prevents it from operating).

Later in this chapter, we will take a look two different types of SQL Server 2005 cluster configurations: one called active/passive and one called active/active.

Shared Disk Array

Unlike nonclustered SQL Server 2005 instances, which usually store their databases on local disk storage, clustered SQL Server 2005 instances store data on a shared disk array. By *shared*, we mean that both nodes of the cluster are physically connected to the disk array but that only the active node can access the instance's databases. There is never a case where both nodes of a cluster are accessing an instance's databases at the same time. This is to ensure the integrity of the databases.

Generally speaking, a shared disk array is a SCSI- or fiber-connected RAID 5 or RAID 10 disk array housed in a stand-alone unit, or it might be a SAN. This shared array must have at least two logical partitions. One partition is used for storing the clustered instance's SQL Server databases, and the other is used for the quorum.

The Quorum

When both nodes of a cluster are up and running, participating in their relevant roles (active and passive), they communicate with each other over the network. For example, if you change a configuration setting on the active node, this configuration change is automatically sent to the passive node and the same change is made. This generally occurs very quickly and ensures that both nodes are synchronized.

As you might imagine, though, it is possible that you could make a change on the active node, but before the change is sent over the network and the same change made on the passive node (which will become the active node after the failover), the active nodes fails, and the change never gets to the passive node. Depending on the nature of the change, this could cause problems, even causing both nodes of the cluster to fail.

To prevent this from happening, a SQL Server 2005 cluster uses a *quorum*. A quorum is essentially a log file, similar in concept to database logs. Its purpose is to record any change made on the active node, and should any change recorded here not get to the passive node because the active node has failed and cannot send the change to the passive node over the network, the passive node, when it becomes the active node, can read the quorum file and find out what the change was and then make the change before it becomes the new active node.

In order for this to work, the quorum file must reside on the *quorum drive*. A quorum drive is a logical drive on the shared array devoted to the function of storing the quorum.

Public and Private Networks

Each node of a cluster must have at least two network cards. One network card will be connected to the public network and the other to a private network.

The public network is the network that the SQL Server 2005 clients are attached to, and this is how they communicate to a clustered SQL Server 2005 instance.

The private network is used solely for communications between the nodes of the cluster. It is used mainly for the *heartbeat signal*. In a cluster, the active node puts out a heartbeat signal, which tells the other nodes in the cluster that it is working. Should the heartbeat signal stop, a passive node in the cluster becomes aware that the active node has failed and that it should at this time initiate a failover so that it can become the active node and take control over the SQL Server 2005 instance.

The Virtual Server

One of the biggest mysteries of clustering is how do clients know when and how to switch communicating from a failed cluster node to the new active node? And the answer may be a surprise. They don't. That's right; SQL Server 2005 clients don't need to know anything about specific nodes of a cluster (such as the NETBIOS name or IP address of individual cluster nodes). This is because each clustered SQL Server 2005 instance is given a virtual name and IP address, which clients use to connect to the cluster. In other words, clients don't connect to a node's specific name or IP address but instead connect to a virtual name and IP address that stays the same no matter what node in a cluster is active.

When you create a cluster, one of the steps is to create a virtual cluster name and IP address. This name and IP address is used by the active node to communicate with clients. Should a failover occur, the new active node uses this same virtual name and IP address to communicate with clients. This way, clients only need to know the virtual name or IP address of the clustered instance of SQL Server, and a failover between nodes doesn't change this. At worst, when a failover occurs, there may be an interruption of service from the client to the clustered SQL Server 2005 instance, but once the failover has occurred, the client can once again reconnect to the instance using the same virtual name or IP address.

How a Failover Works

Although there can be many different causes of a failover, we'll look at the case where the power stops for the active node of a cluster and the passive node has to take over. This will provide a general overview of how a failover occurs.

Assume that a single SQL Server 2005 instance is running on the active node of a cluster and that a passive node is ready to take over when needed. At this time, the active node is communicating with both the database and the quorum on the shared array. Because only a single node at a time can be communicating with the shared array, the passive node is not communicating with the database or the quorum. In addition, the active node is sending out heartbeat signals over the private network, and the passive node is monitoring them to see if they stop. Clients are also interacting with the active node via the virtual name and IP address, running production transactions.

Now, for whatever reason, the passive node stops working because it no longer is receiving any electricity. The passive node, which is monitoring the heartbeats from the active node, now notices that it is not receiving the heartbeat signals. After a predetermined delay, the passive node assumes that the active node has failed and it initiates a failover. As part of the failover process, the passive node (now the active node) takes over control of the shared array and reads the quorum, looking for any unsynchronized configuration changes. It also takes over control of the virtual server name and IP address. In addition, as the node takes over the databases, it has to do a SQL Server startup, using the databases, just as if it is starting from a shutdown, going through a database recovery. The time this takes depends on many factors, including the speed of the system and the number of transactions that might have to be rolled forward or back during the database recovery process. Once the recovery process is complete, the new active nodes announces itself on the network with the virtual name and IP address, which allows the clients to reconnect and begin using the SQL Server 2005 instance with minimal interruption.

Clustering Options?

Up to this point, we have been talking about simple two-node clusters running a single instance of SQL Server 2005. In fact, this is only one of many options you have when clustering SQL Server 2005. In this section, we take a look at these options.

Active/Passive vs. Active/Active

In the examples so far, we have been describing what is called an active/passive cluster. This is a two-node cluster where there is only one active instance of SQL Server 2005. Should the active node fail, the passive node will take over the single instance of SQL Server 2005.

In order to save hardware costs, some organizations like to configure what is called an active/active cluster. This is also a two-node cluster, but instead of only a single instance of SQL Server 2005 running, there are two instances, one on each physical node of the cluster. In this case, should one instance of SQL Server 2005 fail, the other active node will take over, which means the remaining node must run two instances of SQL Server 2005 instead of one.

The advantage of an active/active cluster is that you make better use of the available hardware. Both nodes of the cluster are in use instead of just one, like in an active/passive cluster. The disadvantage is that when a failover occurs, then both SQL Server 2005 instances are running on a single server, which can hurt the performance of both instances. To help overcome this problem, both of the physical servers can be oversized in order to better be able to meet the needs of both instances should a failover occur. In addition, if you have an active/active cluster running two instances of SQL Server 2005, each instance will need its own logical disk on the shared array. Logical disks cannot be shared among instances of SQL Server 2005.

If you have the need for two SQL Server 2005 clustered instances, you have three choices:

❏ Two active/passive clusters

❏ One active/active cluster

❏ One 3-node cluster (more on this shortly)

Which should you choose? If you want to be conservative, chose two active/passive clusters because they are easier to administer and provide more redundant hardware, and also they won't cause any application slowdown should a failover occur.

If you want to save hardware costs and don't mind potential application slowdowns and the added complexity of this option, use an active/active cluster.

If you think that you will be adding more clustered SQL Server 2005 instances in the future, and don't mind the complexity of large clusters, consider a multinode cluster.

Multinodes Clusters

The number of nodes supported for SQL Server 2005 clustering depends on which version of the software you purchase, along with which version of the operating system you intend on using.

Purchase the Right Software

One of the reasons it is very important to research your clustering needs is because they directly affect what software you need, along with licensing costs. Here are your options:

- ❑ Windows Server 2003 Enterprise Edition (32-bit or 64-bit) and SQL Server 2005 Standard Edition (32-bit or 64-bit). Supports up to 2-node clustering

- ❑ Windows Server 2003 Enterprise Edition (32-bit or 64-bit) and SQL Server 2005 Enterprise Edition (32-bit or 64-bit). Supports up to 8-node clustering

- ❑ Windows Server 2003 Datacenter Edition (32-bit or 64-bit) and SQL Server 2005 Enterprise Edition (32-bit or 64-bit). Supports up to 8-node clustering

If you need only a two-node cluster, you can save a lot of money by purchasing Windows Server 2003 Enterprise Edition and SQL Server 2005 Standard Edition. If you want more than two clustered nodes, your licensing costs will escalate quickly.

What about Windows 2000 Server, can you cluster SQL Server 2005 with it? Yes you can, if you want. But given the increased stability of clustering in Windows 2003 over Windows 2000, we recommend using Windows 2003.

Number of Nodes to Use?

Like most things in clustering, there are no clear-cut answers to how many nodes should your cluster use. Before we try to offer some advice in this area, let's first discuss how multinode clustering works.

As we have already discussed, in a two-node cluster, an instance of SQL Server 2005 runs on the active node, while the passive node is currently not running SQL Server 2005, but is ready to do so when a failover occurs. This same principle applies to multinode clusters.

For example, let's say that you have a three-node cluster. In this case, two of the nodes would be active, running their own individual instances of SQL Server 2005, and the third physical node would act as a passive node for the other two active nodes. If either of the two active nodes failed, the passive node would take over after a failover.

Let's look at the other extreme, an eight-node cluster. In this case, you could have seven active nodes and one passive. Should any of the seven active nodes fail, then the passive node would take over after a failover.

The advantage of larger nodes is that less hardware is used for failover needs. For example, in a two-node cluster, 50 percent of your hardware is used for redundancy. But if you are using an eight-node cluster, only 12.5 percent of your cluster hardware is used for redundancy.

On the downside, using only one passive node in a multiple-node cluster makes the assumption that no more than one of the active nodes will fail at the same time. Or if they do, the failed over nodes will run slowly on the single node. On the other hand, if you want, a multinode cluster can have more than one passive node. For example, you could have six active nodes and two passive nodes. Besides these risks, multinode clusters are more complex to manage than two-node clusters, on top of being very expensive in hardware and software licensing costs.

So how many nodes should your cluster have? It depends on your needs (how many SQL Server 2005 instances do you need to cluster?) along with your budget, your in-house expertise, and your aversion to complexity. Some companies have many different SQL Server instances they need to cluster, but choose to use multiple two-node active/passive clusters instead of a single multinode cluster. In many cases, it is best just to keep things as simple as possible.

Clustering Multiple Instances of SQL Server on the Same Server

Up to this point, we have made the assumption that a single instance of SQL Server 2005 will run on a single physical server, but this is not a requirement. In fact, SQL Server 2005 Enterprise Edition can run up to 50 instances on a single clustered physical server, and SQL Server 2005 Standard Edition up to 16 instances. But is this a good idea? Not in the world we live in.

The purpose of clustering is to boost high availability; it is not to save money. Adding multiple instances to a cluster adds complexity, and complexity reduces high availability. Cluster multiple instances of SQL Server 2005 on the same physical node at your own risk.

Upgrading SQL Server Clustering

If your organization is like most, it probably already has some older version SQL Server clusters in production. If so, you will have to make a choice about how to upgrade them to SQL Server 2005. Your available options include:

❑   Don't upgrade.

❑   Perform an in-place SQL Server 2005 upgrade.

❑   Rebuild your cluster from scratch, and then install SQL Server 2005 clustering.

We'll look at all of these options in this section.

Don't Upgrade

This is an easy decision. Not upgrading is simple and doesn't cost anything. Just because a new version of SQL Server comes out doesn't automatically mean you have to upgrade. If your current SQL Server cluster is running fine, why change it? You are just asking for potential new problems where you have none now, and you will have new costs.

On the other hand, if your current SQL Server cluster is not fine, you have the perfect reason to upgrade. SQL Server 2005 offers many new benefits and they may solve the problems your current cluster is experiencing. But don't automatically assume this is the case. Before you upgrade, do the research to determine if the new features of SQL Server 2005 will actually resolve your problems. If not, sticking with what you know may be the best choice.

Upgrading Your SQL Server 2005 Cluster In-Place

If you decide to upgrade, your next step is to decide whether you want to upgrade in-place or start over from scratch with a fresh install. In this section, we take a look at how you upgrade in-place.

Before we begin talking about how to upgrade a current cluster to a SQL Server 2005 cluster, we first need to discuss what operating system you are currently running. If you are on Windows Server 2003 with the latest service pack, you are in good shape and upgrading to SQL Server 2005 in-place should not be a problem. But if you are not running Windows 2003 Server, then you should seriously consider rebuilding your server nodes so that they are running at the latest operating system level.

The logic behind this is that if you are going to all the trouble to upgrade to SQL Server 2005, you should be running on the latest operating system platform, otherwise, you are not taking advantage of the latest technology and the benefits they bring to high availability. So if you are still running Windows Server 2000 (or earlier), I strongly recommend that you don't upgrade in place. And don't even think about upgrading the operating system in place, then upgrading to SQL Server 2005 in place. You are just asking for trouble.

You can upgrade from a SQL Server 7.0 or SQL Server 2000 cluster to SQL Server 2005. If you are running SQL Server 6.5, you are out of luck.

Assuming you are running Windows Server 2003, these are the major steps to performing an upgrade from your current version of SQL Server to SQL Server 2005.

1. Ensure that your current SQL Server cluster is running 100 percent correctly. If there are any problems with the current cluster, do not perform an in-place upgrade. It will most likely fail.

2. Review the preparation steps found later in this chapter, and follow them closely.

3. Run the free Microsoft ClusPrep utility. It will help you determine if you can perform a successful upgrade. Download this tool from Microsoft's Web site.

4. Run the SQL Server 2005 Upgrade Advisor to identify any potential issues that should be corrected before the upgrade begins.

5. Assuming all of the previous steps are successful, you can then perform the upgrade by running the SQL Server 2005 Installation Wizard and follow its instructions. The Installation Wizard will recognize your current SQL Server cluster installation and will guide you through the upgrade.

6. Once the upgrade is complete, you will want to test the upgrade extensively before releasing it to production.

Even if you will be performing an upgrade, you will want to read this entire chapter in order to familiarize yourself with SQL Server 2005 clustering.

Rebuilding Your Cluster from Scratch

Instead of upgrading in place, it is often a good idea to rebuild your cluster from scratch. This is especially true if any one of the following conditions exist:

❑ You need to upgrade your current hardware (it is either old or underpowered).

❑ You need to upgrade the operating system.

❑ The current cluster installation is unstable.

❑ You have disdain for upgrading software in-place and prefer a fresh install.

If you do decide to upgrade from scratch, you have to decide whether you will be installing onto new hardware or will be using your old hardware.

If you install on new hardware, you have the convenience of building the cluster, and testing it, at your own pace, while the current cluster is still in production. This helps to ensure that you have done an outstanding job and at the same relieves some of the stress that you will experience if you have to reuse your old hardware and then rebuild the cluster during a brief and intense rebuild.

If you don't have the luxury of new hardware, and have to use your old hardware, you will have to identify a good time so that your system can be down while the rebuild occurs. This could range from a 4 to a 12 hour period, depending on your particular circumstances. Besides the time your cluster will be down, there is also the added risk of unexpected problems. For example, you might make an installation mistake halfway through the upgrade and have to start over. Because of the uncertainty involved, you should first estimate how much time you thing the upgrade will take under good circumstances, and then double this time as the size of your requested window of downtime. This way, your users will be prepared for the worst.

Whether you upgrade using new hardware or old hardware, there are two additional issues you will have to consider. Will you reuse your current virtual server name and IP address or select new ones? And how will you move your data from the old cluster to the new cluster? Let's look at each of these issues, one at a time.

The clients that access your current SQL Server cluster do so using a cluster's virtual name and IP address. If you want the clients to continue using the same virtual name and IP address, you will need to reuse the old virtual name and IP address in the new cluster. This is the most common approach because it is generally easier to change a single virtual name and IP address than reconfiguring dozens, if not hundreds, of clients who access the cluster.

If you are upgrading using old hardware, reusing the former virtual name and IP address is not an issue because the old cluster is brought down, then the new one back up, so there is never a case where the virtual name and IP address could be on two clusters at the same time (which won't work).

If you upgrade by using new hardware, you will need to assign a virtual name and IP address for testing, but you won't be able to use the old ones because they are currently in use. In this case, you will need to use a temporary virtual name and IP address for testing, and when you are ready for the actual changeover from the old to the new cluster, you will need to follow these general steps:

1. Secure your data

2. Remove SQL Server clustering from the old cluster or turn off the old cluster.

3. On the new cluster, remove SQL Server 2005 clustering, and then reinstall it using the virtual name and IP address of the old cluster.

4. Restore the data.

Uninstalling SQL Server 2005 clustering and then reinstalling it with the old virtual name and IP address is a pain but doesn't take a long time. Besides, this is the only way to change the virtual name or IP address of a SQL Server 2005 cluster install.

Now, how do you move the data from the old cluster to the new? This depends somewhat on whether or not you are using old hardware or new hardware.

If you use old hardware, all you really have to do is to back up the system and user databases and then detach the user databases. Rebuild the cluster without deleting the backups or detached databases. When the cluster is rebuilt, restore the system databases and reattach the detached databases. This of course assumes that the databases will remain in their current location. If you need to move the databases, then you need to follow the next option.

If you are moving to new hardware, or will be moving the location of the databases on old hardware, you would first do full backups of the system and user databases, and then detach the user databases. Next, move these to the new server, or new location. Then when the cluster is rebuilt, restore the system databases and reattach the user databases.

Because of space limitations, these steps don't include all the gory details, such as what happens if the drive letter changes, and so on. The key to success is to plan all of these steps and, if possible, perform a trial run before you do an actual cutover.

Backout Plan

No matter how you decide to upgrade to SQL Server 2005 clustering, you need to have a backout plan. Essentially, a backout plan is what you do if your upgrade fails. We can't tell you exactly what to do for a backout plan, because we don't know your particular circumstances. But we do know that you need a backout plan if the upgrade fails. So as you are planning your upgrade, consider how the plan could fail, and come up with options to get you back in business should things not go well. Your job could depend on how good your backout plan is.

Which Upgrade Option is Best?

Speaking from personal experience, we always prefer to upgrade by rebuilding clusters from scratch on new hardware. This is the easiest, fastest, least risky, and least stressful way. Unfortunately, you may not have this option for whatever reasons management gives you. In this case, you will have to work with what you have been given. The key to a successful upgrade is lots of detailed planning, and as much testing as possible, and of course, having a great backout plan.

Getting Prepared for Clustering

When it comes to SQL Server 2005 clustering, the devil is in the details. If you are not familiar with this phrase, you will be by the time you complete your first SQL Server 2005 clustering installation. If you take the time to ensure that every step is done correctly and in the right order, your cluster installation will be smooth and relatively quick. But if you don't like to read instructions, instead preferring the trial and error approach to computer administration, then expect to face a lot of frustration and a lot of time installing and reinstalling your SQL Server 2005 cluster, as not paying attention to the details will bite you over and over again.

The best way, we have found, to ensure a smooth cluster installation is to create a very detailed, step-by-step plan for the installation, down to the screen level. Yes, this is boring and tedious, but doing so will force you to think through every option and how it will affect your installation and your organization (once it is in production). In addition, such a plan will come in handy the next time you build a cluster, and will also be great documentation for your disaster recovery plan. You do have a disaster recovery plan, don't you?

Preparing the Infrastructure

Before you even begin building a SQL Server 2005 cluster, you must ensure that your network infrastructure is in place. Here's a checklist of everything required before you begin installing a SQL Server 2005 cluster. In many cases, these items are the responsibility of others on your IT staff, but it is your responsibility to ensure that all of these are in place before you begin building your SQL Server 2005 cluster.

❑ Your network must have at least one Active Directory server and ideally two for redundancy.

❑ Your network must have at least one DNS server and ideally two for redundancy.

❑ Your network must have available switch ports for the public network cards used by the nodes of the cluster. Be sure they are manually set to match the manually set network card settings used in the nodes of the cluster. In addition, all the nodes of a cluster must be on the same subnet.

❑ You will need to secure IP addresses for all the public network cards.

❑ You must decide how you will configure the private heartbeat network. Will you use a direct network card to network card connection, or use a hub or switch?

❑ You will need to secure IP addresses for the private network cards. Generally, use a private network subnet such as 10.0.0.0 – 10.255.255.255, 172.16.0.0 – 172.31.255.255, or 192.168.0.0 – 192.168.255.255. Remember, this is a private network seen only by the nodes of the cluster.

❑ Ensure that you have proper electrical power for the new cluster servers and shared array (assuming they are being newly added to your data center).

❑ Ensure that there is battery backup power available for all the nodes in your cluster and your shared array.

❑ If you don't already have one, create a SQL Server service account to be used by the SQL Server services running on the cluster. This must be a domain account, with the password set to never expire.

❑ If you don't already have one, create a cluster service account to be used by the Windows Clustering service. This must be a domain account, with the password set to never expire.

❑   Create three global groups, one each for the SQL Server Service, the SQL Server Agent Service, and the SQL Text Service. You will need these when you install SQL Server 2005 on a cluster.

❑   Determine a name for your virtual cluster (Clustering Services) and secure a virtual IP address for it.

❑   Determine a name for your virtual SQL Server 2005 cluster and secure a virtual IP address for it.

❑   If you are using a Smart UPS for any node of the cluster, remove it before installing Cluster Services; then re-add it.

❑   If your server nodes have AMP/ACPI power saving features, turn them off. This includes network cards, drives, and other components. Their activation can cause a failover.

We will talk more about most of these as we go over the installation process. I have included this list here so that you understand that these are steps you need to take before actually beginning a cluster install.

Preparing the Hardware

Based on our experience building clusters, the hardware presents the thorniest problems, often taking the most time to research and configure. Part of the reason for this is that there are many hardware options, some of which work, and others that don't. Unfortunately, there is no complete resource you can use to help you sort through this. Each vendor offers different hardware, and the available hardware is always changing, along with new and updated hardware drivers, making this entire subject a moving target with no easy answers. In spite of all this, here is what you need to know to get started on selecting the proper hardware for your SQL Server 2005 cluster.

Finding Your Way Through the Hardware Jungle

Essentially, here's the hardware you need for a SQL Server cluster. To keep things simple, we will only be referring to a two-node active/passive cluster, although these same recommendations apply to multinode clusters. The following are my personal minimum recommendations. If you check out Microsoft's minimum hardware requirements for a SQL Server 2005 cluster, they will be somewhat less. Also, I highly suggest that each node in your cluster be identical. This can save lots of installation and administrative headaches.

The specifications for the Server Nodes should be the following:

❑   Dual CPUs, 2 GHz or higher, 2MB L2 Cache (32-bit or 64-bit)

❑   1GB or more RAM

❑   Local mirrored SCSI drive (C:), 9GB or larger

❑   SCSI DVD drive

❑   SCSI connection for local SCSI drive and DVD drive

❑   SCSI or Fiber connection to shared array or SAN

❑   Redundant power supplies

❑   Private network card

❑   Public network card

❑   Mouse, keyboard, and monitor (can be shared)

The Shared Array should have a SCSI-attached RAID 5 or RAID 10 array with appropriate high-speed SCSI connection. With Microsoft Clustering, SCSI is only supported if you have a 2-node cluster. If you want to cluster more than two nodes, you must use a fiber-attached disk array or SAN. Or you may have a fiber-attached RAID 5 or RAID 10 array with appropriate high-speed connection. Or you may use a fiber-attached SAN storage array with appropriate high-speed connection (generally a fiber switch).

Because this chapter is on SQL Server 2005 clustering, not hardware, we won't spend much time on hardware specifics. If you are new to clustering, I would suggest you contact your hardware vendor for specific hardware recommendations. Keep in mind that you will be running SQL Server 2005 on this cluster, so ensure that whatever hardware you select meets the needs of your predicted production load.

The Hardware Compatibility List

Whether you select your own hardware or get recommendations from a vendor, it is highly critical that the hardware selected is listed in the Cluster Solutions section of the Microsoft Hardware Compatibility List (HCL), which can be found at `http://www.microsoft.com/whdc/hcl/default.mspx`.

As you probably already know, Microsoft lists all of the hardware in the HCL that is certified to run their products. If you are not building a cluster, you can pick and choose almost any combination of certified hardware from multiple vendors and know that it will work with Windows 2003 Server. This is not the case with clustering. If you look at the Cluster Solutions in the HCL, you will notice that entire systems, not individual components, have to be certified. In other words, you can't just pick and choose individually certified components and know that they will work. Instead, you must select from approved cluster systems, which include the nodes and the shared array. In some ways, this reduces the variety of hardware you can choose from. On the other hand, by only selecting approved cluster systems, you can be assured the hardware will work in your cluster. And assuming you need another reason to select only an approved cluster system, Microsoft will not support a cluster that does not run on an approved system.

In most cases, you will find your preferred hardware as an approved system. But, as you can imagine, the HCL is always a little behind, and newly released systems may not be on the list yet. So what do you do if the system you want is not currently on the HCL? Do you select an older, but tested and approved system, or do you take a risk and purchase a system that has not yet been tested and officially approved? This is a tough call. But what we have done in the past when confronted by this situation is to require the vendor to certify, on their own, that the hardware will become certified by Microsoft at some time in the future, and if the hardware is not approved (as promised) that the vendor has to correct the problem by replacing unapproved hardware with approved hardware at their cost. We have done this several times and it has worked out fine so far.

Preparing the Hardware

As a DBA, you may or may not be the one who installs the hardware. In any case, here are the general steps most people follow when building cluster hardware:

1. Install and configure the hardware for each node in the cluster as if they will be running as stand-alone servers. This includes installing the latest approved drivers.

2. Once the hardware is installed, install the operating system and latest service pack, along with any additional required drivers.

3. Connect the node to the public network. To make things easy, name the network used for public connections as "network."

4. Install the private heartbeat network. To make things easy, name the private heartbeat network "private."

5. Install and configure the shared array or SAN.

6. Install and configure the SCSI or fiber cards in each of the nodes and install the latest drivers.

7. One at a time, connect each node to the shared array or SAN following the instructions for your specific hardware. It is critical that you do this one node at a time. By this, we mean that only one node at a time should be physically on and connected to the shared array or SAN and configured. Once that node is configured, turn it off and turn the next node on and configure it, and so on, one node at a time. If you do not following this procedure, you risk corrupting the disk configuration on your nodes, requiring you to start over again.

8. After connecting each node to the shared array or SAN, you will need to use Disk Administrator to configure and format the drives on the shared array. You will need at least two logical drives on the shared array. One will be for storing your SQL Server databases, and the other one will be for the Quorum drive. The data drive must be big enough to store all the required data, and the Quorum drive must be at least 500MB (which is the smallest size that an NTFS volume can efficiently operate). When configuring the shared drives using Disk Administrator, it is required that each node of the cluster use the same drive letter when referring to the drives on the shared array or SAN. For example, you might want to assign your data drive as drive "F:" on all the nodes, and assign the Quorum drive letter "Q:" on all the nodes.

9. Once all of the hardware is put together, it is critical that it be functioning properly. This means that you need to test, test, and test again, ensuring that there are no problems before you begin installing clustering services. While you may be able to do some diagnostic hardware testing before you install the operating system, you will have to wait until after installing the operating system before you can fully test the hardware.

Once all of the hardware has been configured and tested, you are ready to install Windows 2003 Clustering, which is our next topic.

Clustering Windows Server 2003

Before you can install SQL Server 2005 clustering, you must first install Windows Server 2003 clustering services. Once it is successfully installed and tested, then you can install SQL Server 2005 clustering. In this section, we take a step-by-step approach to installing and configuring Windows 2003 clustering.

Before Installing Windows 2003 Clustering

Before you install Windows 2003 clustering, you need to perform a series of important steps. This is especially important if you didn't build the cluster nodes, as you want to ensure everything is working correctly before you begin the actual cluster installation. Once they are complete, then you can install Windows 2003 clustering. Here are the steps you must take:

1. Double check to ensure that all the nodes are working properly and are configured identically (hardware, software, and drivers).

2. Check to see that each node can see the data and Quorum drives on the shared array or SAN. Remember, only one node can be on a time until Windows 2003 clustering is installed.

3. Verify that none of the nodes have been configured as a Domain Controller.

4. Check to verify that all drives are NTFS and are not compressed.

5. Ensure that the public and private networks are properly installed and configured.

6. Ping each node in the public and private networks to ensure that you have good network connections. Also, ping the Domain Controller and DNS server to verify that they are available.

7. Verify that you have disabled NetBIOS for all private network cards.

8. Verify that there are no network shares on any of the shared drives.

9. If you intend to use SQL Server encryption, install the server certificate with the fully qualified DNS name of the virtual server on all nodes in the cluster.

10. Check all of the error logs to ensure there are no nasty surprises. If there are, resolve them before proceeding with the cluster installation.

11. Add the SQL Server and Clustering service accounts to the Local Administrators group of all the nodes in the cluster.

12. Check to verify that no anti-virus software has been installed on the nodes. Anti-virus software can reduce the availability of clusters and must not be installed on them. If you want to check for possible viruses on a cluster, you can always install the software on a non-node and then run scans on the cluster nodes remotely.

13. Check to verify that the Windows Cryptographic Service Provider is enabled on each of the nodes.

14. Check to verify that the Windows Task Scheduler service is running on each of the nodes.

15. If you intend to run SQL Server 2005 Reporting Services, you must then install IIS 6.0 and ASP.NET 2.0 on each node of the cluster.

These are a lot of things you must check, but each of these is important. If skipped, any one of these steps could prevent your cluster from installing or working properly.

Installing Windows Server 2003 Clustering

Now that all of your nodes and shared array or SAN is ready, you are ready to install Windows 2003 clustering. In this section, we take a look at the process, from beginning to end.

To begin, you must start the Microsoft Windows 2003 Clustering Wizard from one of the nodes. While it doesn't make any difference to the software which physical node is used to begin the installation, we generally select one of the physical nodes to be the primary (active) node, and start working there. This way, you won't potentially get confused when installing the software.

If you are using a SCSI shared array, and for many SAN shared arrays, you will want to be sure that the second physical node of your cluster is turned off when you install cluster services on the first physical node. This is because Windows 2003 doesn't know how to deal with a shared disk until cluster services is installed. Once you have installed cluster services on the first physical node, you can then turn on the second physical node, boot it, and then proceed with installing cluster services on the second node.

Installing the First Cluster Node

To begin your installation of SQL Server 2003 Clustering, open Cluster Administrator. If this is the first cluster, you will be presented with the dialog shown in Figure 20-1.

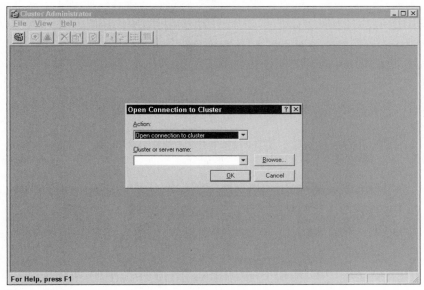

Figure 20-1

From the Action drop-down box, select Create New Cluster and click OK. This brings up the New Server Cluster Wizard.

Click Next to begin the Wizard.

The next steps seem easy because of the nature of the Wizard, but if you choose the wrong options, they can have negative consequences down the line. Because of this, it is important that you carefully think through each of your responses. Ideally, you already have made these choices during your planning stage.

The first choice you must make is the domain the cluster will be in, as shown in Figure 20-2. If you have a single domain, this is an easy choice. If you have more than one domain, select the domain that all of your cluster nodes reside in.

The second choice is the name you will assign the virtual cluster, as shown in Figure 20-3. This is the name of the virtual cluster, not the name of the virtual SQL Server. About the only time you will use this name is when you connect to the cluster with Cluster Administrator. SQL Server 2005 clients will not connect to the cluster using this virtual name. Once you enter the information, click Next to proceed.

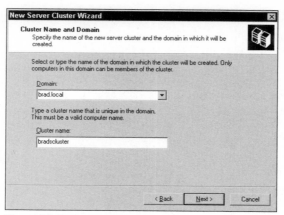

Figure 20-2

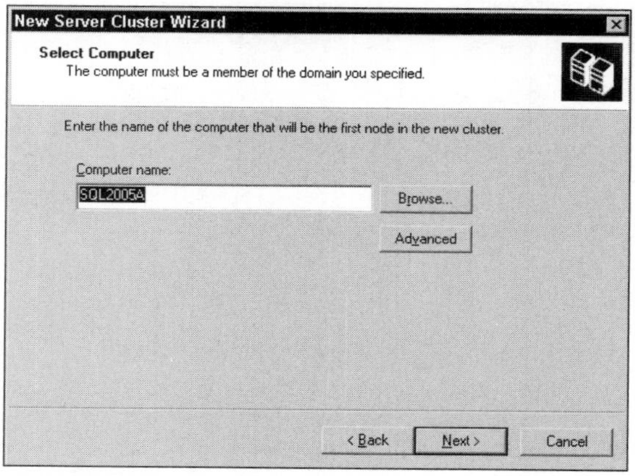

Figure 20-3

Now you have to tell the Wizard the physical name of the node you want to install clustering on. Assuming that you are running the Cluster Wizard on the primary node of your cluster, the computer name you see in Figure 20-3 will be the name of the physical node you are installing on. If you are installing from one node but want to install clustering on a different node, you can, but it just gets confusing if you do. It is much easier to install on the same node.

Notice the Advanced button in Figure 20-3. If you click it, you see a window that looks like Figure 20-4.

The Advanced Configuration Option screen allows you to choose between a Typical and an Advanced Configuration. In almost all cases, the Typical configuration will work fine, and that is the option we use during this example. The Advanced configuration option is only needed for complex SAN configuration, and is beyond the scope of this book.

So click Cancel and the original screen returns, as shown in Figure 20-3. Enter the correct physical node, if need be, and click Next.

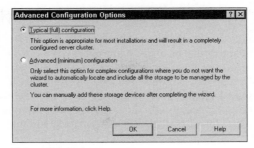

Figure 20-4

This next step is very important. What the Cluster Wizard does is to verify that everything is in place before it begins the actual installation of the cluster service on the node. As you can see in Figure 20-5, the Wizard goes through many steps, and if you did all of your preparation correctly, when the testing is done, you will see a green bar under Tasks Completed, and you will be ready to proceed. But if you have not done all the preliminary steps properly, you may see a yellow or red icons next to one or more of the many tested steps, and a green or red bar under Tasks Completed.

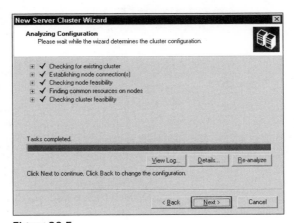

Figure 20-5

Ideally, you will want to see a screen like Figure 20-6, with a green bar and no yellow icons next to the test steps. In some cases, you may see yellow warning icons next to one or more of the test steps, but still see a green bar at the bottom. While the green bar indicates that you can proceed, it does not mean that the cluster will complete successfully or be configured like you want it to be. If you see any yellow warning icons, you can drill down into them and see exactly what the warning is. Read each warning very carefully. If the warning is something unimportant to you, it can be ignored. But in most cases, the yellow warnings need to be addressed. This may mean you have to abort the cluster service installation at this time, fix the problem, and install it after you correct the problem.

If you get any red warning icons next to any of the test steps, then you will also get a red bar at the bottom, which means that you have a major problem that needs to be corrected before you can proceed any farther. Drill down to see the message and act accordingly. Most likely, you will have to abort the installation, fix the issue, and then try installation again.

Assuming that the installation is green and you are ready to proceed, click Next.

The next step is to enter the IP address of our virtual cluster. This is the IP address for the cluster, not the virtual SQL Server. The IP address must be on the same subnet as all of the nodes in the cluster. Click Next.

In the Cluster Service Account screen, shown in Figure 20-6, you enter the name of the domain account you want to use as the cluster service account. You will also enter the account's password and the name of the domain where the account was created. This account should have already been created in your domain and added to all of the cluster nodes in the Local Administrators Group. Click Next.

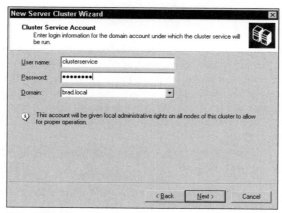

Figure 20-6

The next Cluster Wizard screen is the Proposed Cluster Configuration, shown in Figure 20-7. But before you click Next, be sure to click on the Quorum button and check which drive the Cluster Wizard has selected for the Quorum. In this case, Drive Q: has been chosen, which is correct. Most of the time, the Cluster Wizard will select the correct drive for the Quorum, but not always. This is why it is important to check this screen to see if the correct drive was chosen. Because we named by Quorum drive Q:, it is very easy to determine that the correct drive was chosen by the Cluster Administrator. That is why we earlier suggested that you name the Quorum drive Q:.

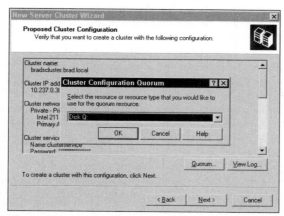

Figure 20-7

Assuming everything is OK, click OK to accept the Quorum drive, and then click Next. At this time the Cluster Wizard will reanalyze the cluster, again looking for any potential problems. If none are found, click Next; then click Finish to complete the installation of SQL Server 2003 clustering on the first node.

Installing the Second Node of Your Cluster

Once you have installed the first node of your cluster, it is time to install the second node. Like the first node, the second node is installed from Cluster Administrator. Because the cluster already exists, you are just adding the second node to the currently existing cluster. You can install the second node from either the first node or the second node. We suggest you do it from the second node so that you don't get confused.

To install the second node, bring up Cluster Administrator. If you are doing this from the second node, you will get the same screen as you saw when you installed the first node (See Figure 20-1). From here, select Add Nodes to Cluster. This brings up the Add Nodes Wizard, which is very similar to the previous Create Cluster Wizard you just ran, except it has fewer options.

As the Wizard proceeds, you will enter the name of the physical node to add to the current cluster, after which a series of tests will be automatically run to verify that the node is ready to be clustered. As before, if you run into any problems — yellow or red warnings — you should correct them first before continuing. Once all problems have been corrected, you are then asked to enter the password for the cluster service account (to prove that you have permission to add a node to the cluster) and the node is added to the cluster.

Verifying the Nodes with Cluster Administrator

Once you have successfully installed the two nodes of your cluster, it is a good idea to view the nodes from Cluster Administrator. When you bring up Cluster Administrator for the first time after creating a cluster, you may have to tell Cluster Administrator to Open a Connection to Cluster, and type in the name of the virtual cluster you just created. Once you have done this, the next time you Open Cluster Administrator, it will automatically open this cluster for you by default.

After opening up Cluster Administrator, you will see a screen very similar to Figure 20-8.

Notice that two resource groups have been created for you: Cluster Group and Group 0. The Cluster Group includes three cluster resources: the Cluster IP Address, the Cluster Name, and the Quorum drive. These were all automatically created for you by the Cluster Wizard. We will talk more about Group 0 a little later.

When you look next to each cluster resource, the State for each resource should be online. If not, your cluster may have a problem that needs fixing. As a quick troubleshooting technique, if any of the resources are not online, right-click the resource and choose Bring Online. In some cases, this will bring the resource online and you will not experience any more problems. But if this does not work, you need to begin troubleshooting your cluster.

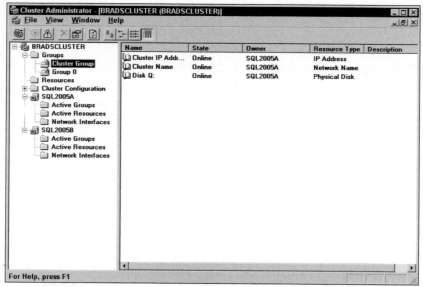

Figure 20-8

Also, next to each resource is listed the Owner of the resource. All the resources in a resource group will always have the same owner. Essentially, the owner is the physical node where the cluster resources are currently running. In Figure 20-8, the physical node they are running on is SQL2005A, which is the first node in the two-node cluster. If a failover occurs, all of the resources in the resource group will then change to the other node in your cluster.

Configuring Windows Server 2003 for Clustering

Before you install SQL Server clustering, there is one small step you need to perform, and that is to prepare a resource group for the SQL Server resources that will be created when SQL Server is installed.

Most likely, when you created the cluster, as above, you will see a Resource Group named Group 0. This resource group was created when the cluster was created, and it most likely includes the shared resource for your SQL Server databases to use. See figure 20-9.

In the example, Disk F:, the shared array for SQL Server, is in Group 0. If you like, you can leave the resource group by this name, but it is not very informative. I suggest that you rename Group 0 to SQL Server Group. You can do this by right-clicking on Group 0 and selecting Rename.

In some cases, the Cluster Wizard may put the SQL Server shared disk array in the Cluster Group resource group and not create a Group 0. If this is the case, you will need to create a new resource group and then move the SQL Server shared disk array from the Cluster Group to the newly created SQL Server Resource group.

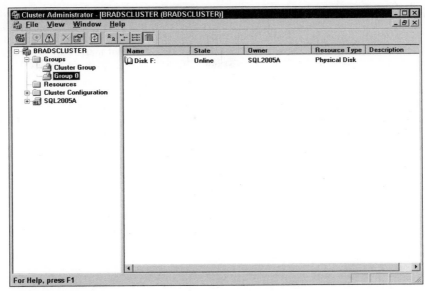

Figure 20-9

Here's how you create a new resource group using Cluster Administrator:

1. Start Cluster Administrator.

2. Select File⇨New⇨Group. This starts the New Group Wizard.

3. For the Name of the group, enter "SQL Server Group." Optionally, you can also enter a description of this group. Click Next.

4. Now, you must select which nodes of your cluster will be running SQL Server. This, of course, will be all of your nodes. The nodes are listed on the left side of the Wizard. Control-Click each of the nodes on the left and then select Add. This will move the selected nodes from the left side of the Wizard to the right side. Click Finish.

The new SQL Server Group resource group has now been created.

Now that the group has been created, it must be brought online. From Cluster Administrator, right-click the SQL Server resource group (it will have a red dot next to it) and select Bring Online. The red dot next to the resource group name goes away, and the SQL Server Group resource group is now online and ready for use.

Now, your next step is to move any disk resources from the Cluster Group (except the Quorum drive) to the SQL Server Group. This is a simple matter of dragging and dropping the disk resources from the Cluster Group to the SQL Server Group. Once you have done this, you are ready for the next step.

Test, Test, and Test Again

Once you have installed Windows 2003 clustering on your nodes, you need to thoroughly test the installation before beginning the SQL Server 2005 cluster install. If you don't, and problems arise later with Windows 2003 clustering, you may have to remove SQL Server 2005 clustering to fix it, so you might as well identify any potential problems and resolve them now.

The following are a series of tests you can perform to verify that your Windows 2003 cluster is working properly or not. After you perform each test, verify if you get the expected results (a successful failover), and also be sure you check the Windows event log files for any possible problems. If you find a problem during one test, resolve it before proceeding to the next test. Once you have performed all of these tests successfully, you are ready to continue with the cluster installation.

Preparing for the Tests

Before you begin, identify a workstation that has Cluster Administrator on it, and use this copy of Cluster Administrator for interacting with your cluster during testing. You will get a better test using a remote copy of Cluster Administrator than trying to use a copy running on one of the cluster nodes.

Move Groups Between Nodes

The easiest test to perform is to use Cluster Administrator to manually move the Cluster Group and SQL Server resource groups from the active node to a passive node, and then back again. To do this, right-click the Cluster Group and then select Move Group. Once the group has been successfully moved from the active node to a passive node, use the same procedure above to move the group back to the original node. The moves should be fairly quick and uneventful. Use Cluster Administrator to watch the failover and failback, and check the Event Logs for possible problems. After moving the groups, all of the resources in each group should be in the online state. If not, you have a problem that needs to be identified and corrected.

Manually Initiate a Failover in Cluster Administrator

This test is also performed from Cluster Administrator. Select any of the resources found in Cluster Group resource group (not the cluster group itself), right-click on it, and select Initiate Failure. Because the cluster service always tries to recover up to three times from a failure, if it can, you will have to select this option four times before a test failover is initiated. Watch the failover from Cluster Administrator. After the failover, fail back using the same procedure, again watching the activity from Cluster Administrator. Check the Event Logs for possible problems. After this test, all of the resources in each group should be in the online state. If not, you have a problem that needs to be identified and corrected.

Manually Failover Nodes by Turning Them Off

This time, you will only use Cluster Administrator to watch the failover activity, not to initiate it. First, turn off the active node by turning it off hard. Once this happens, watch the failover in Cluster Administrator. Once the failover occurs, turn the former active node on and wait until it fully boots. Then turn off the now current active node by turning it off hard. And again, watch the failover in Cluster Administrator. After the failover occurs, bring the off node back on. Check the Event Logs for possible problems. After this test, all of the resources in each group should be in the online state. If not, you have a problem that needs to be identified and corrected.

Manually Failover Nodes by Breaking the Public Network Connections

In this test, you will see what happens if network connectivity fails. First, both nodes being tested should be on. Second, unplug the public network connection from the active node. This will cause a failover to a passive node, which you can watch in Cluster Administrator. Third, replug the public network connection back into the server. Fourth, unplug the public network connection from the now active node. This will cause a failover to the current passive node, which you can watch in Cluster Administrator. Once the testing is complete, replug the network connection into the server. Check the Event Logs for possible problems. After this test, all of the resources in each group should be in the online state. If not, you have a problem that needs to be identified and corrected.

Manually Failover Nodes by Breaking the Shared Array Connection

This test is always exciting, as it is the test that is most apt to identify potential problems. First, from the active node, remove the shared array connection. This will cause a failover which you can watch in Cluster Administrator. Second, reconnect the broken connection. Second, from the now active node, remove the shared array connection. Watch the failover in Cluster Administrator. When done, reconnect the broken connection. Check the Event Logs for possible problems. After this test, all of the resources in each group should be in the online state. If not, you have a problem that needs to be identified and corrected.

If you identify any problems, check the troubleshooting section found later in this chapter. As we mentioned before, if any particular test produces unexpected problems, such as failover not working or errors are found in the Event Logs, identify and resolve them now before proceeding with the next test. Once you have resolved any problems, be sure to repeat the test that originally indicated the problem in order to verify that it has been fixed.

Configuring the Microsoft Distributed Transaction Coordinator

While not required, it is recommended that you install the Microsoft Distributed Transaction Coordinator (MS DTC) on each of the cluster nodes before installing SQL Server 2005 clustering. This is because SQL Server 2005 requires this service o perform some functions, including running distributed queries, two-phase commit transaction, and some aspects of replication. MS DTC must be installed after installing Windows 2003 clustering but before installing SQL Server 2005 clustering.

While you can set up MS DTC for clustering from the command line, it is much easier to use Cluster Administrator, as described here. This is because this procedure automatically configures MS DTC on all of the cluster nodes at the same time. Take your time to ensure that you do it right the first time.

1. Start Cluster Administrator.

2. Right-click the Cluster Group resource group, select New⇨Resource. This starts the new Resource Wizard.

3. In the first screen of the Resource Wizard, enter the name of the resource you are creating, which would be "MSDTC Resource." If you like, you can also enter an optional description of this resource. Under Resource Type, select Distributed Transaction Coordinator. Under Group, Cluster Group should already be displayed. Click Next.

4. In the Possible Owners screen, you will see that all of the nodes of the cluster are listed under Possible Owners. This is correct and should not be changed. Click Next.

5. In the Dependencies screen, press and hold the CTRL key on the quorum disk resource and the Cluster Name, then click Add. Then click finish.

At this time, the MSDTC Resource is created. Now that the resource has been created, you must bring it online. From Cluster Administrator, right-click on the MSDTC Resource (it will have a red dot next to it) and select Bring Online. The red dot next to the resource name goes away, and the MSDTC Resource is now online and ready for use. If the new resource won't come online, delete it and try again.

Clustering SQL Server 2005

Believe it or not, the procedure to install a SQL Server 2005 instance onto a cluster is one of the easiest parts of getting your SQL Server 2005 cluster up and running. The SQL Server 2005 setup program is used for the install, and it does the hard work for you. All you have to do is make a few (but critically important) decisions, and then sit back and watch the installation take place. In fact, the setup program even goes to the trouble to verify that your nodes are all properly configured, and if not, will suggest how to fix any problems before the installation begins.

When the installation process does begin, the setup program recognizes all the nodes, and once you give it the go-ahead to install on each one, it does, all automatically. SQL Server 2005 binaries are installed on the local drive of each node, and the system databases are stored on the shared array you designate.

In the next section are the step-by-step instructions for installing a SQL Server 2005 instance in a cluster. The assumption for this example is that you will be installing this instance in a two-node active/passive cluster. Even if you will be installing a two-node active/active or a multinode cluster, the steps in this section are virtually the same. The only real difference is that you will have to run SQL Server 2005 setup for every instance you want to install on the cluster, and you will have to specify a different logical drive on the shared array.

Clustering SQL Server

To begin installing your SQL Server 2000 cluster, you will either need the installation CD or DVD. You can either install it directly from the media, or you can copy the install files from the media to the current active node of the cluster, and run the setup program from there.

To begin the installation, run Setup.exe, and after an introductory screen, you will get the first install screen, shown in Figure 20-10.

This screen is used to list what prerequisites need to be installed before SQL Server 2005 can be installed. The number of components may vary from the Figure 20-12, depending on what you have already installed on your nodes. What is interesting to note here is that these prerequisite components will only be installed immediately on the active node, and they will be installed on the passive node later during the installation process. This is done automatically and you don't have to worry about it.

Figure 20-10

Click Install to install these components, and when they are installed, you will get a screen telling you that they were installed successfully, and you can click Next to proceed. On occasion, we have seen these components fail to install correctly. If this happens to you, you will have to troubleshoot the installation. Generally speaking, try rebooting both nodes of the cluster and try installing them again. This often fixes whatever caused the first try to fail.

Once the prerequisite components have been successfully installed, the SQL Server Installation Wizard launches. Click Next to proceed. The next step is for the SQL Server Installation Wizard to perform a System Configuration Check, shown in Figure 20-11. This is very similar to the check that was performed with clustering services was set up when you installed Windows Clustering. As before, ideally you want all checks to be successful, with a green icon. If you get any yellow warning or red error icons, you need to find out what the problem is, and correct it before proceeding. In some cases, yellow warning icons can be ignored, but red error icons cannot. If you have any yellow or red icons, you may have to abort the setup process, fix the problem, and then restart the setup process. Assuming all is well, click Next to proceed.

Figure 20-11

The next screen is the Registration screen where you enter your company name and license key, if applicable.

Next, you must select the SQL Server 2005 components to install. See Figure 20-12.

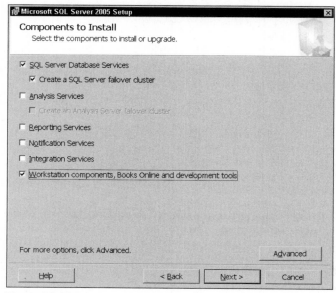

Figure 20-12

We won't go into a lot of detail on this screen, because this same material is covered in Chapter 2. We do want to point out the options Create a SQL Server failover cluster and Create an Analysis Server failover cluster (currently grayed out). Since you are creating a SQL Server 2005 cluster, you must select the Create a SQL Server failover cluster. And if you are going to install Analysis Services (we are not in this example) then you must select Create an Analysis Server failover cluster. Once you have selected all the components you need to include, click Next.

As with any install of SQL Server 2005, the next step is to select the name of the instance to be installed, as shown in Figure 20-13. You can choose between a default instance and a named instance. Click Next to proceed.

Now, here is a very important step, shown in Figure 20-14. This is when you enter the name of the virtual SQL Server 2005 instance you are currently installing. This is the name that clients will use to connect to this instance. Ideally, you have already selected what name to use that makes the most sense to your organization. Click Next to proceed. If you ever need to change this virtual name, you will have to install and then reinstall SQL Server 2005 clustering.

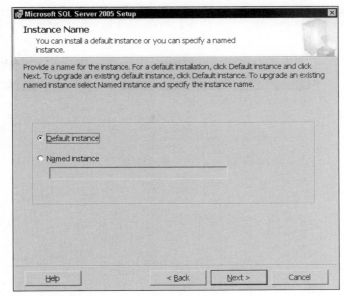

Figure 20-13

Figure 20-14

The next step is also a very important screen, shown in Figure 20-15. This is where you enter the virtual IP address for this instance of SQL Server 2005. Like the cluster virtual name, it is used by clients to connect to this instance of SQL Server 2005. The IP address must belong to the same subnet as the IP addresses used by all of the nodes.

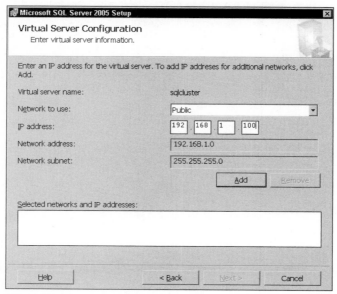

Figure 20-15

In addition, in this screen you must select the network to be used for the public network (the network used by the clients to connect to this instance of SQL Server 2005). All of the available networks will be available from the drop-down box next to Network to use. If you had previously taken our advice to name the public and private networks, Public and Private, respectively, it will be very easy for you to select the correct network, as we have above.

Once you have entered the IP address and selected the public network, click Add, so that the information you just selected is in the Selected networks and IP addresses box; then click Next.

In the Cluster Group Selection screen, shown in Figure 20-16, select the SQL Server Group as the group where you want to create the SQL Server resources. In addition, be sure that the Data files will be created on the correct logical drive of the shared array using the folder name you choose. Select Next to proceed.

In the Cluster Node Configuration screen, shown in Figure 20-17, you get to specify which nodes you want to install this instance of SQL Server on. Because our example is for only two nodes, the default setting works for us. Notice that under Required node is SQL2005A, which is the name of the physical node where we are running the setup program. And under Selected nodes is SQL2005B, the second physical node in your two-node cluster. Select Next to proceed.

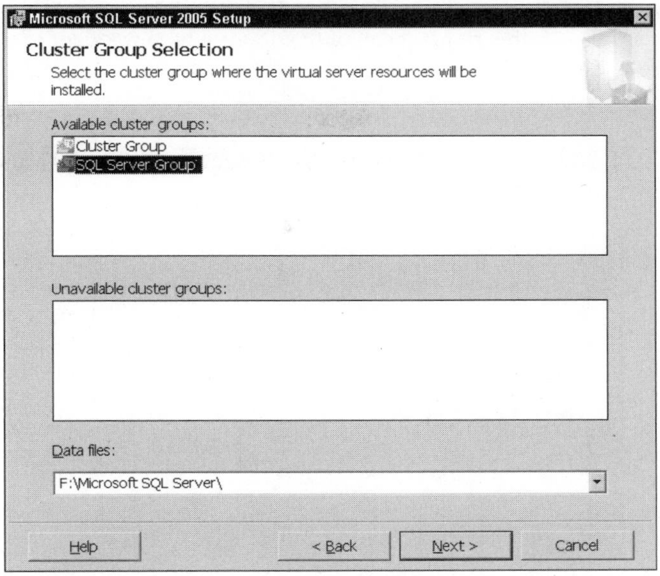

Figure 20-16

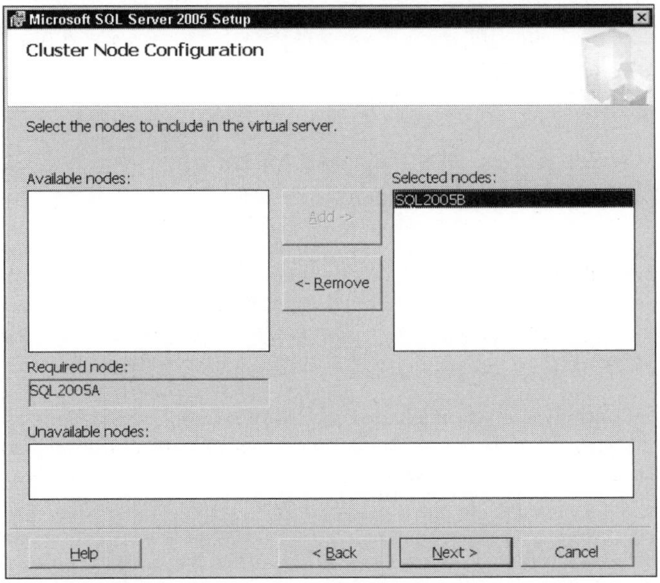

Figure 20-17

In the Remote Account Information screen, shown in Figure 20-18, you must select an account (with password) that has administrative rights on all of the nodes where we want to install this instance of SQL Server 2005. This can be any domain account that is an administrator of all the nodes. Select Next to proceed.

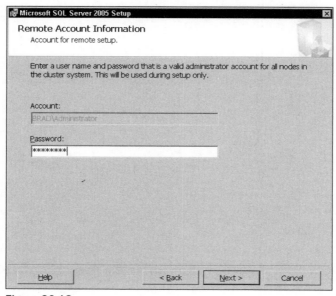

Figure 20-18

The Service Account screen is identical to the screen you see when you install SQL Server 2005 on a non-cluster, and it is configured the same. Click Next to proceed.

In the Domain Groups for Clustered Services screen, shown in Figure 20-19, you must select pre-existing global domain groups that are used to contain the startup account for each clustered service. You can choose to add all three services to the same global domain group, or to create separate global domain groups, one for each service, as has been done above. Once you have selected appropriate domain groups, click Next to proceed.

The next four screens of the Installation Wizard, not shown here, are the same as for any other installation of SQL Server 2005, and are discussed booking Chapter 2. After you have completed these screens, the installation of this instance of SQL Server 2005 begins, and you see the Setup Progress screen, shown in Figure 20-20.

The installation process will take some time as it is installing the binaries on both nodes of the cluster and installing the system data files on the shared array. The Setup Progress Screen shows the status of the first node's install. If you want to see the status of the second node's install, you can change the drop-down box next to Node to the second node and watch its progress.

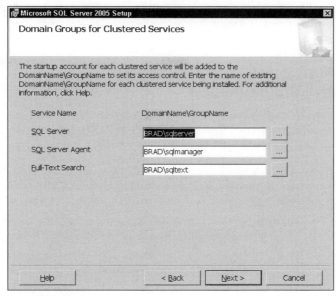

Figure 20-19

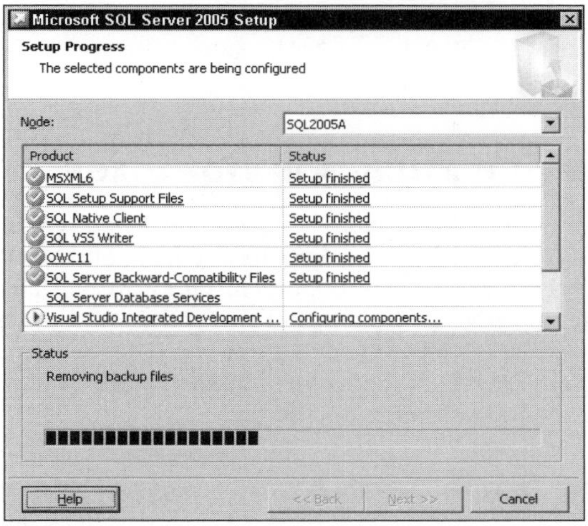

Figure 20-20

As the installation proceeds, you will want to see all green icons next to each installation step. If any step should fail, then the entire installation process will need to be rolled back, any problems fixed, and SQL Server 2005 installed fresh. In most cases, canceling a bad installation will uninstall what has already been installed, but not always. Sometimes, if the installation breaks; it just dies and a rollback of what has been done so far will not occur. If this is the case you can either choose to reinstall on top of the existing bad install (which often does not work), manually uninstall the failed installation (check Microsoft's Web site for assistance in this area), or rebuild your cluster from scratch (starting with the operating system).

It the install was a success, you will see a final screen, where you can click Finish.

Clustering Analysis Services

SQL Server 2005 Analysis Services can be clustered just like SQL Server 2005, and in fact, is installed using the same setup program used to install SQL Server 2005. The following are some points to keep in mind if you decide to cluster SQL Server 2005 Analysis Services.

❑ SQL Server 2005 Analysis Services can be installed by itself or with SQL Server 2005. Because some of the features of Analysis Services require components of the SQL Server 2005 database engine, it is generally a good idea to install both of them in your cluster.

❑ SQL Server 2005 Analysis Services is installed using the same setup program as SQL Server 2005. When running the setup program, you select, or not select, Analysis Services to be installed in the Components to Install screen.

❑ Because SQL Server 2005 Analysis Services needs to store program files, data files, and shared files, you will have to specify the location of your shared array, where they will reside. These files must reside on a shared array if you want Analysis Services to run after a failover. To specify the location of the shared array, you must select the Advanced button from the Components to Install screen in the setup wizard.

Other than these points, installing SQL Server 2005 Analysis Services in a cluster is virtually identically to installing SQL Server 2005 in a cluster.

Installing the Service Pack and Hot Fixes

Once you have installed SQL Server 2005 clustering, your next step is to install the latest SQL Server 2005 service pack and hot fixes, which can be downloaded from Microsoft's Web site. Installing a service pack or hot fix is fairly straightforward because it is cluster-aware. Once the service pack or hot fix setup program is started, it detects that you have a cluster and will upgrade all nodes simultaneously. Once setup is complete, you may need to reboot your servers and failover the nodes. Generally, once you have run the service pack, you should reboot the active node first. Once it has rebooted, you reboot the passive node. This way, failover and failback is automatic.

Checking the SQL Server 2005 Installation From Cluster Administrator

Once an instance of SQL Server 2005 clustering is installed, you can view its cluster resources by going to Cluster Administrator and opening up the SQL Server Group resource.

Figure 20-21 shows the cluster resources for the SQL Server 2005 cluster you just built. You can see all of the names of the resources, their state, and which node the resources are running on. As we have already mentioned, Cluster Administrator is a great tool for seeing if all the resources are up and running and which node is the current active node.

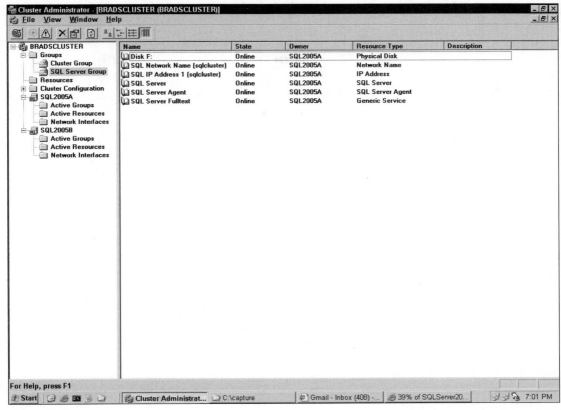

Figure 20-21

Here is a brief run-down on each of the SQL Server 2005 cluster resources:

❑ Disk F: This is the shared disk array where the SQL Server data files and logs are stored.

❑ SQL Network Name (sqlcluster): This is the virtual SQL Server name used by clients to connect to this clustered instance of SQL Server 2005. The name "sqlcluster" is the name we have assigned this cluster instance, and will not be the same as your cluster, unless you name yours the same as ours.

❑ SQL IP Address (sqlcluster): This is the virtual SQL Server IP address used by clients to connect to this clustered instance of SQL Server 2005. Again, the name "sqlcluster" is the name of the virtual server, and is the one we have used for this cluster. Your name will most likely be different.

❑ SQL Server: This is the SQL Server service.

❑ SQL Server Agent: This is the SQL Server Agent service.

❑ SQL Server Fulltext: This is the SQL Server Fulltext service. Even though you may not use this service, it is automatically installed as a cluster resource.

Installing Clustering on Multiple Nodes

When we talk about installing SQL Server 2005 clustering on multiple nodes, we are referring to two different scenarios. They include:

❑ A 2-node active/active cluster, where you are running a single instance of SQL Server 2005 on each node. If one of the two active nodes should fail, the failed active instance would fail over to the other active node, with the end result that you are running two active instances of SQL Server 2005 on the same physical node.

❑ A 3-node to 8-node SQL Server 2005 cluster, where one of the nodes is designated as a passive node for failover purposes, and the rest are active nodes, with each one running a single instance of SQL Server 2005. If any of the active nodes fails, the failover would go to the designated passive node to run on.

Installing multiple instances of SQL Server in a cluster is virtually identical to installing a SQL Server 2005 cluster as we described. In general, here is what you need to know about installing multiple instances of SQL Server 2005 in a cluster:

❑ All of the nodes in the cluster should have identical hardware, software, and be configured identically.

❑ You will need a hub or switch for the private network connection among the nodes.

❑ You will need a separate shared drive for each instance of SQL Server 2005 installed. These are besides the shared drive required for the quorum. You will only need one quorum drive for your cluster.

❑ You will need distinct virtual names and IP addresses for each SQL Server 2005 instance.

❑ Each SQL Server 2005 instance must be in its own distinct resource group in the cluster.

❑ You will need to run SQL Server 2005 Setup for each separate instance of SQL Server 2005 you want in the cluster.

❑ You will need to configure each active node, should a failover occur, to failover to the designated passive node.

Because running more than a single instance of SQL Server 2005 on a cluster is complex, we highly recommend that you build this cluster from scratch, and test it thoroughly before putting it into production.

Test, Test, and Test Again

Once you have installed SQL Server 2005 clustering on your nodes, you need to thoroughly test the installation, just as you did after first installing Windows 2003 clustering. But not only do you want to test SQL Server 2005 clustering; you also want to test how your clients "react" to failovers. Because of this, the following testing section is very similar to the one you previously read but has been modified to meet the more complex needs of the additional client testing you need to do.

The following are a series of tests you can perform to verify that your SQL Server 2005 cluster, and their clients, works properly during failover situations. After you perform each test, verify if you get the expected results (a successful failover), and also be sure you check the Windows log files for any possible problems. If you find a problem during one test, resolve it before proceeding to the next test.

Preparing for the Testing

As with your previous cluster testing, identify a workstation that has Cluster Administrator on it, and use this copy of Cluster Administrator for interacting with your cluster during testing.

Now for the hard part. Essentially, you need to test how each client that will be accessing your SQL Server 2005 cluster. In other words, you want to test to see what will happen to each client should a failover occur. Some client software deals with clustering failovers automatically, while others choke and die. The only way to know for sure is to test them.

To test them, you must first identify all the client applications, which might be one product, or a dozen products. Each of these products will have to be configured to access the virtual server name (and IP address) on the new SQL Server instance. In addition, for the clients to work, you will have to have the appropriate databases restored or installed on the new cluster. Yes, this is a lot of work. But this is necessary if you want a highly available clustering solution you can count on.

Once you have at least one copy of each of your client applications connected to the SQL Server 2005 instance, you are ready for testing. Keep in mind that, while testing, you are testing multiple things, including the Windows 2003 cluster, the SQL Server 2005 cluster, and the client applications.

Move Groups Between Nodes

The easiest test to perform is to use Cluster Administrator to manually move the cluster and SQL Server resource groups from the active node to a passive node, and then back again. To do this, right-click on a resource group and then select Move Group. This will initiate the move of the resources groups from your active node to the designated passive node.

Once this happens, check Cluster Administrator and each of the client applications. Each should continue to operate as if no failover had occurred. Cluster Administrator should pass this test easily. The clients are another story. You will need to check each client to see if they continue to work as before. If not, you need to determine why not, which is not always easy. Most clients that stop working after a failover will reconnect if you exit and restart the client.

Once the group has been successfully moved from the active node to a passive node, then use the same procedure above to move the group back to the original node. And as before, check Cluster Administrator, the clients, and the Event Logs to see if there were any problems. If you have Cluster Service or SQL Server 2005 problems due to the test failover, you need to resolve them now before proceeding. If you have a client problem, you can continue with your testing and try to resolve them later. In most cases, if a client fails this first test, it will fail all of the tests.

Manually Initiate a Failover in Cluster Administrator

This test is also performed from Cluster Administrator. Select any of the resources found in SQL Server Group resource group (not the group itself), right-click it, and select Initiate Failure. Because the cluster service always tries to recover up to three times from a failover, if it can, you will have to select this option four times before a test failover is initiated.

As before, after the first failover, check for any problems; then failback using the same procedure; then check again for problems.

Manually Fail Over Nodes by Turning Them Off

Turn off the active node. Once this happens, watch the failover in Cluster Administrator and the clients. As before, check for any problems. Next, turn on the node and wait until it boots back up successfully. Then turn off the now current active node by turning it off hard. And again, watch the failover in Cluster Administrator and the clients, and check for problems. Turn the node back on when done.

Manually Fail Over Nodes by Breaking the Public Network Connections

Unplug the public network connection from the active node. This will cause a failover to a passive node, which you can watch in Cluster Administrator and the clients. Check for any problems. Now plug the public network connection back into the server, and unplug the public network connection from the now active node. This will cause a failover to the current passive node, which you can watch in Cluster Administrator. And again, watch the failover in Cluster Administrator and the clients, and check for problems. Once the testing is complete, plug the network connection back into the server.

Manually Fail Over Nodes by Breaking the Shared Array Connection

From the active node, remove the shared array connection. This will cause a failover that you can watch in Cluster Administrator and applications. Check for any problems. Next, reconnect the broken connection from the now active node, remove the shared array connection. Watch the failover in Cluster Administrator. And again, watch the failover in Cluster Administrator and the clients, and check for problems. When done, reconnect the broken connection.

If you pass all of these tests the first time, it would almost be a miracle. But miracles do happen. If you run into problems, you have to figure them out before continuing.

Maintaining the Cluster

Once you have your SQL Server 2005 cluster up and running (and tested) you are ready to put it into production. This may involve creating new databases, moving databases from older servers to this one, setting up jobs, and so on. In most cases, managing SQL Server 2005 on a cluster is the same as managing it on a non-cluster. The key thing to keep in mind is that whenever you access your cluster with any of your SQL Server 2005 administrative tools, such as Management Studio, you will be accessing it using its virtual name and IP address, but if you are using any of the operating system tools, such as System Monitor, you will need to point these directly to the node in question (which is usually the active node).

In most cases, as a DBA, you probably will be administering SQL Server 2005 using Management Studio, but sometimes you will need to access the individual nodes of the cluster. If you have easy access to the cluster, you can always log on locally. Or if you prefer remote administration, you can use Terminal Services to access the nodes.

When a DBA first begins to administer their first cluster, they get a little confused where SQL Server 2005 is actually running. Keep in mind that a clustered instance of SQL Server 2005 (even in a multinode cluster) only consists of two nodes: the active and passive nodes. At any one time, an instance of SQL Server 2005 is only running on the active node, not the passive node. So when you need to look at the nodes directly, generally you will want to look at the active node. If you don't know which node is currently active, you can find out by using Cluster Administrator.

When you log into the active node (or connect to it remotely using Terminal Services), and then bring up Windows Explorer (a routine task), you will be able to see the SQL Server data drives and the quorum drive. But if you log onto the passive node, you will not be able to see the SQL Server data drives or the quorum drive. This is because drives can only be accessed from a single node at a time. On the other hand, if you check the Event Logs on either the active or passive nodes, you will see that they are virtually identical, with events from both nodes being displayed. Event logs are replicated between the active and passive nodes.

If you access your cluster through Terminal Services, be aware of a couple of odd behaviors. For example, if you use Terminal Services to connect to the cluster using the virtual cluster name and IP address, you will be connecting to the active node, just as if you used Terminal Services to connect to the active node directly (using its virtual name and IP address). But if a failover should occur and you are using Terminal Services to access the cluster using the virtual cluster name and IP address, Terminal Services will get a little confused, especially if you are using Windows Explorer. For example, you may discover that your data and quorum drives no longer appear to be accessible, even though they really are. To resolve this problem, log out of Terminal Services and reconnect after a failover; then things will appear as they should.

Learn to Love Cluster Administrator

While you won't need to use Cluster Administrator a lot, you still need to become very familiar with it as the DBA of a SQL Server 2005 cluster. You'll mostly use it when you need to perform some maintenance on your cluster and you need to manually fail over the cluster from one node to another, or to troubleshoot and fix problems.

You should keep close tabs on the resource groups so that you can find out which nodes the resource groups are currently running on, along with their current status. Sometimes, failovers occur so quickly that you are not aware that one has even occurred. By checking the current Owner of the resources, you can easily and quickly tell which node the resources are running on. The active node is the node where the resources are currently running. If you don't want to have to be checking the Cluster Administrator all the time to see if a failover has occurred, you always have the option of setting up a SQL Server 2005 alert, so you can keep abreast of what is happening on you cluster.

Once your cluster is up and running, be sure you take the time to familiarize yourself with Cluster Administrator.

Doing the Routine

The day-to-day activities of managing a SQL Server 2005 cluster are not much different than that of a non-clustered instance of SQL Server 2005. In addition to the routine you follow for all of you SQL Servers, here are some steps you can do in addition for you clusters.

Checking the Cluster

Each morning, start up Cluster Administrator to verify that the active node has not changed (due to a failover) and also review the status of each of the resources. It is uncommon to ever find a problem this way, but when does occur that shows here, you want to address it immediately.

Reviewing Logs

Because of the complexity of clusters, you should review all of the operating system Event Logs every day, looking for any potential issues. One of the most common we have found over the years administering SQL Server clusters are shared disk-related errors, which can indicate a configuration problem, software driver problem, or hardware problem, all of which need to be corrected as soon as possible.

We want to remind you one last time that SQL Server clusters do not protect your data on the shared array. You must still back up your data.

Dealing with Cluster Failovers

SQL Sever 2005 instance failovers can occur for many different reasons. When one does occur, you need to identify what happened and why. This way, you can fix whatever caused the problem so it won't happen again.

In some cases after a failover, you can just fail back and everything will be fine. In the other extreme, you may have to replace a failed node. Here's what you must do if you have a failover that requires you to replace a failed node. In this example, we are assuming this is a two-node active/passive cluster and that the failed node won't even turn on.

In this scenario, you can continue to run on the now active node until you can secure some downtime to replace the failed node. Unfortunately, to fix a "broken" node, SQL Server 2005 must be downed for a while as it is fixed.

Removing the Failed Node

Because there is only one node currently active in your cluster, you must perform all of these steps from the single, active node.

1. Back up all of your data. You will want a copy of all your data somewhere else, like tape, or on another array. In addition, SQL Server 2005 will be down during this process, so be sure that you are doing this doing an approved downtime.

2. In Control Panel, select Add or Remove Programs, select SQL Server, and then click Change.

3. On the Component Selection screen which appears, select the components you want to remove from the selected SQL Server instance, and click Next to proceed.

4. The System Configuration Checker begins and scans your current configuration. When it is done, click Next.

5. On the Change or Remove Instance screen, click Maintain the Virtual Server.

6. The Cluster Node Configuration screen appears. To remove the failed node, select the node from the Selected Nodes list, and then click Remove. Then click Next; and on the final screen, click Update. This will begin the removal of the SQL Server 2005 instance from the failed node, but leaving it running on the good node. You perform this step even though the failed node is not accessible.

7. Now, you must evict the failed node from cluster services. To do this, start Cluster Administrator on the active node.

8. Right-click the failed node displayed in Cluster Administrator, and then click Evict Node. This will remove the failed node from the cluster.

At this point, the failed node has been removed and you have a one-node cluster that is still fully functioning as a SQL Server 2005 instance. If desired, clients can connect using the virtual SQL Server 2005 cluster name and do work.

Re-Adding the New Node

At some point, you will need to rebuild the hardware and operating system on the failed node so that it is again identical to the good node. Once the hardware and operating system is ready, the next step is re-add the new node to the cluster, then add SQL Server 2005 back to the node.

1. From the new node, use Cluster Administrator to add the new node to the cluster. Follow the same steps you used to add the second node to your cluster when you first built the cluster.

2. From the old node, in Control Panel, select Add or Remove Programs, select SQL Server, and then click Change.

3. On the Component Selection screen that appears, select the components you want to add to the selected SQL Server instance, and click Next to proceed.

4. The System Configuration Checker begins and scans your current configuration. Assuming there are no problems with the configuration, click Next.

5. On the Change or Remove Instance screen, click Maintain the Virtual Server.

6. The Cluster Node Configuration screen appears. To add the new node, select the node from the Available Nodes list, and then click Add. Then click Next, and on the final screen, click Update. This will add the SQL Server 2005 instance to the new node, installing the software on it similarly to how it did when the cluster was first built.

7. Once the new node has been added, thoroughly test it before putting it back into production.

What Happens if My Disk Array Dies?

As you know by now, a cluster does not protect your data, only the cluster nodes themselves. So what happens if the shared array stops working? How do you recover? In most cases, if your shared array fails, you will have to remove SQL Server clustering and clustering services from the two nodes, fix or replace the shared array, then reinstall clustering services and SQL Server 2005 clustering. And last of all, restore your databases.

Installing Patches and Service Packs

Installing operating system patches and service packs, and SQL Server 2005 service packs and hot fixes, have become part of the routine for DBAs. Even though we have come to hate installing them, we can't forget that each new release helps to make our platform more secure and stable. The following is some advice on installing this despised but important code.

Operating System Patches and Service Packs

Upon release, don't immediately install a new patch or service pack until you have had the opportunity to get feedback from the user community on potential problems. If you have a test cluster, upgrade it first to see how your software "reacts" to the new software. You don't necessarily need to install each monthly patch every month. Instead, save them up and do them once a quarter. This helps to reduce downtime. On the other hand, if your organization's security policies require that monthly patches be put on, then do so.

Patches and service packs are normally installed one node at a time. If this is the case, first install the patch or service pack on the designated passive node of the cluster. If all goes well, then fail over from the active to the passive node and install the patch or service pack on the former active node, then fail back. If you have more than two nodes, then rotate through all of the active nodes one at a time as each one successfully completes. You should do this during a low activity time to minimize user disruptions as the failovers occur.

SQL Server 2005 Service Packs and Hot Fixes

Upon release of a new service pack or hot fixes, be sure you test them thoroughly on a test system (with your current applications), before upgrading your clusters. While a test SQL Server cluster is ideal for testing, testing a service pack or hot fix on a non-clustered SQL Server (with your applications) is also a fairly good test.

SQL Server 2005 service packs and hot fixes are cluster-aware and will automatically update all nodes of a cluster at the same time. This makes installation easy, but will require some scheduled downtime as you may need to reboot the servers and fail them over after the installation.

Test, Test, and Test Regularly

By now, you are probably getting a little tired of us talking about testing, but it is important to the continuing successful administration of a SQL Server 2005 cluster that you test it regularly, just as it was when you first installed the cluster. Essentially, there are two times when you want to test an existing SQL Server 2005 cluster:

❏ Whenever you make any changes to the cluster, including hardware, software, or configuration.

❏ On a periodic basis, such as once a quarter, just to test if everything is still working.

When you do test, you should follow the test plan described earlier in this chapter you used after you built the cluster. This way, you can be sure that all aspects of your cluster work properly.

Like most things, you don't have to be an ogre about testing; your ongoing testing procedure can vary based on the circumstances. For example, if you make simple a configuration change in Cluster Administrator and you know exactly what you did and why, then testing right after the change is probably not mandatory, and testing can take place the next time you perform a bigger change, or wait until your regular, quarterly test. In addition, if you have just tested your cluster two weeks before a scheduled quarterly test, you can probably skip the quarterly this test time. The key thing is to remember to test regularly.

Troubleshooting Cluster Problems

Troubleshooting cluster-related issues is not for the faint of heart or for the beginner. It requires a lot of fortitude, persistence, experience, and a support contract with Microsoft Technical Support. The problem is that clustering is very complex and involves your node hardware, shared array, hardware drivers, operating system, clustering services, and SQL Server 2005. Any problem you are having could be caused by any one of them, and identifying the exact cause of a problem is often difficult.

Another reason cluster troubleshooting is difficult is because the feedback you get, in the form of messages or logs, is not always accurate or complete, assuming you get any feedback at all. And when you do get feedback, the resources to identify and remedy problems are minimal.

Because of all of this, if you have a cluster, you should plan on purchasing Microsoft Technical Support for your cluster. This is a very good investment, and one that will pay for itself. We have used Microsoft Technical Support many times, and in most cases, they have been able to help. You don't need to automatically call support as soon as you have a problem; you should always try to identify and resolve problems if you can. But at some point, especially if your cluster is down and you need help getting it back up, you need to be able to recognize when you can't resolve the problem by yourself and when you need help from Microsoft.

In this section we have included some general advice to get you started on how to identify and resolve cluster-related problems.

How to Approach Clustering Troubleshooting

As we discussed how to install clustering in this chapter, we have emphasized over and over the importance of performing a task, testing, and if everything is working OK, then proceed with the next step. The reason for this approach is to help you more easily identify what is causing the problem as soon as possible after it happens. For example, if things are working correctly, then you perform a task and then test what you did, and the task you performed fails, you can fairly assume that what you just did is directly or indirectly responsible for the problem, making problem identification easier. If you don't perform regular testing and don't notice a problem until after many tasks have been performed, then identifying the causes of problems is much more difficult. So, in essence, the best way to troubleshoot problems is by performing incremental testing. This also makes it much easier if you have a detailed installation plan that you can follow, helping you to ensure that you are performing all the necessary steps (including testing at appropriate places).

Do It Right the First Time

You can save a lot of troubleshooting problems by preventing them. Here's how.

❑ Be double sure that all of the hardware for your nodes and shared array are on Microsoft's cluster compatibility list.

❑ Be sure that you are using the latest hardware and software drivers and service packs.

❑ Create a detailed installation plan that you can use as your guide for the installation and for disaster recovery should the need arise.

❑ Learn as much as you can about clustering before you begin your installation. Many cluster problems are user-created because they person responsible guessed instead of knowing for sure what they were doing.

Gathering Information

To help identify the cause of a problem you often need lots of information. Unfortunately, the information you need may not exist, or it may be scattered about in many different locations, or it may be downright misleading. In any event, to troubleshoot problems, you have to find as much information as you can.

Here are some of the resources you can use to gather information to troubleshoot a cluster problem.

❑ Know what is supposed to happen. If you expect a specific result, and you are not getting it, be sure that you fully understand what is supposed to happen, and exactly what is happening. In other words, know the difference between the two.

❑ Know what happened directly before the problem occurred. This is much easier if you test often, as described earlier.

❑ Is the problem repeatable? Not all problems can be easily repeated, but if they can, this is useful information.

❑ When some problems occur, error messages appear on the screen. Be sure that you take screen snaps of any messages for references. Some DBAs have the habit of clicking OK after an error message without recording its exact content. Often, the exact content of a message is helpful if you need to search the Internet to learn more about it.

❑ There are a variety of logs you may be able to view, depending on how far along you are in the cluster setup process. These include the operating system logs (three of them); the cluster log (located at `c:\windows\cluster\cluster.log`); the SQL Server Setup log files (located at `%ProgramFiles%\Microsoft SQL Server\90\Setup Bootstrap\LOG\Summary.txt`); and the SQL Server 2005 log files.

❑ If the error messages you identify aren't obvious (are they ever?) search for them on the Internet, including newsgroups.

The more information you can gather about a problem, the better position you are to resolve the problem.

Resolving Problems

Sometimes a problem is obvious and the solution is obvious. If that's the case, you are lucky.

In many other cases, the problem you have may or may not be obvious, but the solution is not obvious. In these cases, we have found that instead of wasting a lot of time trying to identify and fix a problem, that the easier and quicker solution is to reinstall your cluster from scratch.

Many cluster problems are due to the complexity of the software involved, and we have discovered that it is often much faster to just rebuild the cluster from scratch, including the operating system. This is especially true if you have tried to install cluster services or SQL Server 2005 clustering and the setup process aborted during setup and did not uninstall itself cleanly.

When you are building a new cluster, rebuilding it to resolve problems is usually an option because time is not an issue. But what if you have a SQL Server 2005 cluster in production and it dies so bad that neither node works and you don't have time to rebuild it. Then what do you do? You bring in Microsoft.

Working with Microsoft

Operating a SQL Server 2005 cluster without having a Microsoft Technical Support contract is like operating a car without insurance. You can do it, but if you have any unexpected problems, you will be sorry you went without.

Generally, there are two main reasons you would need to call Microsoft Technical Support for clustering issues. First, it's a non-critical issue that you just can't figure out for yourself. In this case, you will be assigned an engineer, and over a period of several days, you will work with that engineer to resolve your problem. This often involves running an application provided by Microsoft to gather information about your cluster so the engineer can resolve it.

The second reason to call is because your production cluster is down and there are no obvious solutions to getting it back up quickly. Generally, in this case, we recommend you call Microsoft Technical Support as soon as you can to get the problem ticket started. In addition, you must emphasize to the technical call screener (the first person who answers the phone) and the engineer you are assigned to, that you are facing a production down situation and that you want to declare a critical situation (critsit). This tells Microsoft that your problem is top priority and you will get special service. When you declare a critsit, the other person on the phone may want to dissuade from doing so because it causes a chain of events to happen within Microsoft Technical Support they like to avoid. But if your production cluster is down, you need to emphasize the nature of your problem and tell them that you want to open the critsit. You may have to repeat this several times so that that the nature of your problem is fully understood. If it is, you will get immediate help with your problem until your cluster is back up and running.

Summary

Although this chapter is long, it is still only the tip of the iceberg when it comes to knowing everything the DBA should know about SQL Server 2005 clustering. In addition to reading this chapter, you should read all of the clustering articles in the SQL Server 2005 Books Online, and any additional information you can find on Microsoft's Web site and the Internet. As we said at the beginning of this chapter, clustering is an adventure, and after reading this chapter, we are sure you now agree.

Raymond James Lab Report

On October 10, 2005, Raymond James, Hewlett-Packard, and Microsoft went to the lab to evaluate the feasibility of upgrading the Raymond James data warehouse to SQL Server 2005. The evaluation took place in the HP labs on a Superdome and SAN environment similar to the one owned by Raymond James. One instance of SQL Server 2000 SP3 and one instance of SQL Server 2005 September CTP were installed and restored on a twelve-1.5GHz processor Superdome with 24GB of RAM and approximately 9TB of disk. The upgrade was performed by attaching and restoring the SQL 2000 SP3 databases to the 2005 instance. The objective of this test was for Raymond James to evaluate the amount of effort required to achieve benefits in areas of performance gains and reduction in maintenance time. The only preparation performed on the environment was that the statistics were updated on the SQL Server 2005 instance. Both of the instances shared the same resources, but only one of the instances at a time was active during the below tests. This ensured that only the versions of SQL Server were being evaluated as part of this test, since they were both running on the same hardware.

Please note that Raymond James and HP tracked resources consumes and time for each test. We obtained permission from Raymond James to share their findings along with their observations and executive summary.

> Raymond James Financial (NYSE-RJF) is a Florida-based diversified holding company providing financial services to individuals, corporations, and municipalities through its subsidiary companies. Its three wholly owned broker/dealers, Raymond James & Associates, Raymond James Financial Services, and Raymond James Ltd. have more than 4,800 financial advisors serving 1.2 million accounts in 2,200 locations throughout the United States, Canada, and overseas. In addition, total client assets are approximately $163 billion, of which approximately $30 billion are managed by the firm's asset management subsidiaries.

During the activity the Raymond James team set out and completed the following objectives:

- ❑ Migration of existing SQL2000 Data
- ❑ Installation Considerations

❑ Determination of the data transformation tools by comparing SQL Server Integration Services (SSIS) offering in SQL2005 versus Data Transformation Services (DTS)

❑ Extract Transact and Load (ETL) comparison of the database engines

❑ Speed of Relational Queries in SQL2005 versus SQL2000

❑ Database Maintenance timings

Raymond James made the following observations:

❑ Easy Migration

❑ Trouble-free Installation

❑ SSIS: The configuration options are much more intuitive and user-friendly when compared with DTS.

❑ ETL: Single day runs are equal, but 2005 runs faster with longer multi-day runs. However, there exist obvious differences in how SQL 2005 interprets SQL code within stored procedures when migrating stored procedures "as is." Some run faster as is, and some run longer as is. This indicates certain performance T-SQL enhancements that can probably be utilized to even further improve performance once stored procedures are migrated into 2005.

❑ Relational Queries: 2005 provided much faster query response times, with an average rate of four times faster without any T-SQL enhancements. Only one stored procedure ran slower, lending more weight to the notion that 2005 T-SQL enhancements can be utilized to further improve our KPI reports.

❑ Database Maintenance: Overall, no real difference.

Figures A-1 through A-7 show the results of the various tests.

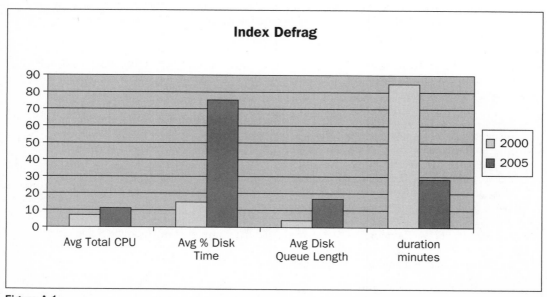

Figure A-1

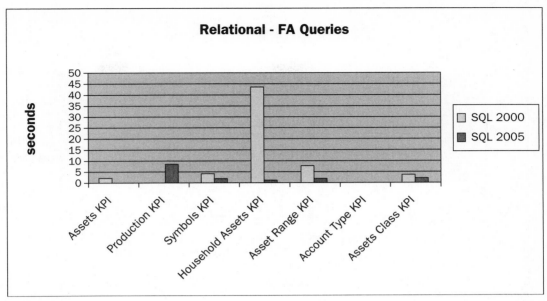

Figure A-2

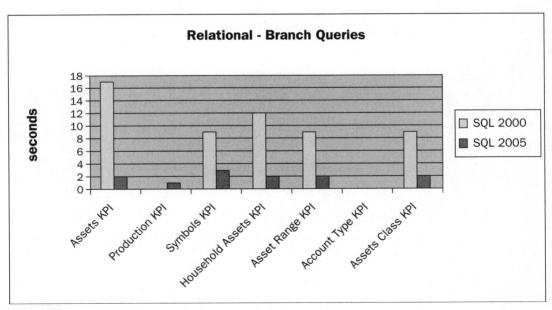

Figure A-3

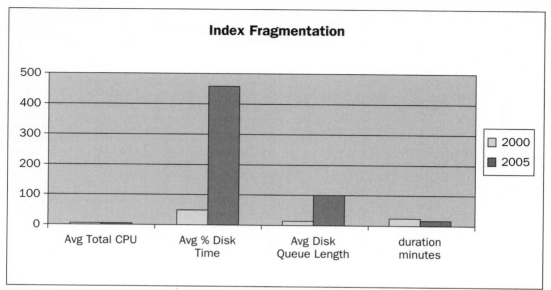

Figure A-4

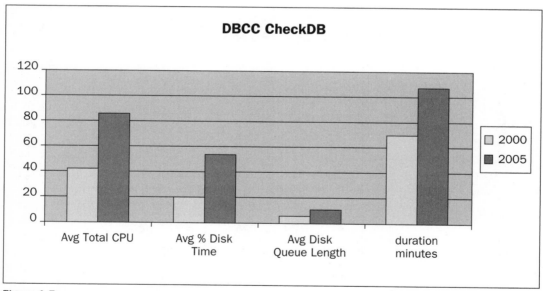

Figure A-5

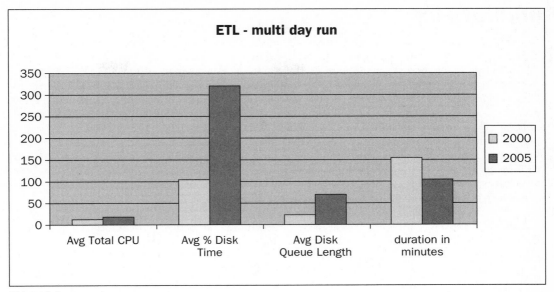

Figure A-6

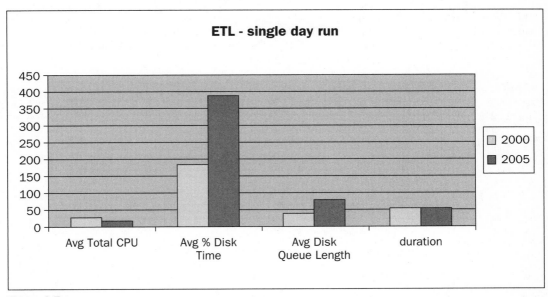

Figure A-7

Summary

Overall, the testing showed SQL Server 2005 is an improvement over SQL Server 2000 in ease of use and provides great performance gains with no additional tuning to existing code. The initial graphs show more disk activity and longer disk queues with shorter run times, which leads one to believe that 2005 has more parallelism and/or more asynchronous I/O—both good for throughput. These graphs also show more CPU utilization which, in light of the shorter run times, means more work is being completed per unit of time via parallelism/asynchronous I/O and/or improved execution efficiency (code tuning/compiler options, better memory utilization, or other means like improved locking). This is usually good overall because it means shorter batch run times. On the other hand, the increased CPU can also mean more pressure on storage, and in a mixed batch/online environment could require a re-tuning to throttle back batch CPU or storage utilization so online transactions can keep its original (SQL 2000) share of resources and original response times. It also looks like there are some areas where noticeably less CPU is used for a given task which is also a favorable indicator for batch and online.

Additionally, the data shows a few cases where the run times are longer with SQL2005, but that often happens with complex software where improvements in one area hurt another. However, SQL2005 relational queries showed much improved response times when compared to SQL2000. Perhaps as a result of query optimizer and tuning enhancements / overall better overall resource utilization by the relational engine.

Overall, these optimistic proof points demand more testing and investigation into SQL 2005 with a focus on the adoption of SQL 2005 T-SQL enhancements to induce performance gains in ETL processing similar to those seen with relational queries. OLAP and Analysis Server Cube generation seem to be the next logical functional steps. The testing provided Raymond James an invaluable gauge of the current state of SQL 2005 as well as a testimony of teaming of RJ, Microsoft, Intel, and HP. These initial results provide a clear roadmap and direction for further investigation.

Needless to say, with these results, Raymond James has put a plan in place to upgrade their enterprise to SQL Server 2005. We would like to acknowledge Bruce Phillipoom and Chad Miller of Raymond James Financial, Randy Baklini and the entire HP team for allowing us to share this great work with you.

Index